WITHDRAWN

THE CONSTITUTIONS OF THE COMMUNIST WORLD

A publication issued by the
Documentation Office for East European Law
University of Leyden

THE CONSTITUTIONS
OF
THE COMMUNIST
WORLD

Edited by

WILLIAM B. SIMONS

SIJTHOFF & NOORDHOFF   1980
Alphen aan den Rijn   The Netherlands
Germantown, Maryland   U.S.A.

Library of Congress Catalog Card Number: 80-65005

ISBN 90 286 0070 1

Copyright © 1980 Sijthoff & Noordhoff International Publishers B.V.,
Alphen aan den Rijn, The Netherlands

All rights reserved. No part of this publication may be reproduced, stored in a retrieval system, or transmitted, in any form or by any means, electronic, mechanical, photocopying, recording or otherwise, without the prior permission of the copyright owner.

Printed in The Netherlands.

TABLE OF CONTENTS

Preface	VII
Introduction	XI
List of contributors	XVII
Albania	1
Bulgaria	33
China	69
Cuba	93
Czechoslovakia	135
German Democratic Republic	159
Hungary	191
Kampuchea	215
Korea, Democratic People's Republic of	227
Mongolia	255
Poland	283
Romania	311
USSR	343
Viet-Nam	393
Yugoslavia	423
Appendix: Czechoslovakia	579
Systematic Index	625

PREFACE

The printed word: it can be immortal or out-of-date before the ink is dry. The constitutions (or fundamental laws, as they are often called) contained in this volume will certainly be subject to change, especially given the rôle that a constitution plays in the particular mixture of ideology and law that is common to those states comprising the communist world. But we nonetheless believe that students and scholars of political science, history, law, and communist affairs will find it useful to have a compilation in one volume of English translations of the constitutions of the communist world in force in 1979. Since most of the states listed in the table of contents have enacted new or revised constitutions in the last decade, the present collection will retain its usefulness for some time. We intend to keep the collection up-to-date by publishing any changes that may be made in these texts, or of entirely new constitutions that may be enacted, in the *Review of Socialist Law*, a quarterly publication of the Documentation Office for East European Law of the University of Leyden Faculty of Law.

In his volume *The Constitutions of the Communist-Party States* (Stanford, California 1968), Jan F. Triska presented the constitutions of the communist world that were then in force, as well as earlier texts that had been enacted in these states after the establishment of communist power. Most of these have since been superseded or substantially amended, and only the new or amended texts are presented in the present volume: it was not felt necessary to reproduce the old texts which are available for purposes of comparison and consultation in the Triska book.

What Triska has called the "communist-party states" I have chosen to refer to collectively as the "communist world", but this is merely a semantic difference, not one of substance, since those states whose constitutions appear in this book are—with one exception—the same as the fourteen states represented in Professor Triska's opus. We have decided to include the text of the 1975 Kampuchean Constitution of Pol Pot's Khmer Rouge government as the fifteenth member of the club, as it contains many of those fundamental principles which are common to the constitutions of the "group of fourteen". The 1960 Vietnamese Constitution has also been included, even though several sources have reported that a new draft constitution for the unified Socialist Republic of Viet-Nam was issued in April 1978; continued attempts on my part to obtain a copy of the draft text from either western or Vietnamese sources have proved to no avail. A similar fate has befallen my quest for information about a Laotian fundamental law. The appearance of a new Kampuchean Constitution also seems quite likely, given that one communist régime has been replaced by another.

A few words about the translations contained in this book. The majority of the constitutions published herein have been especially translated or revised for this project. Translating may not yet be a science, but it certainly is an art, and I believe that a translator is best able to perform his or her art when no burden of strict adherence to uniform style and usage is imposed. Of course, precision is important in translating, especially where legal texts are involved; perhaps the ultimate in precision could be obtained by having one person translate all fifteen constitutions appearing in this book. But since such a person to the best of my knowledge does not exist, I have chosen what I believe to be the best available alternative: each translator who has collaborated in this effort is a jurist (in one case, a jurist/linguist team) conversant not only with the language but also with the relevant legal institutions and concepts, both in the communist and western worlds.

A collection of translations is not a suitable vehicle for lengthy articles analyzing individual constitutions or discussing communist fundamental laws in a comparative context. But I did think that it would be of help to the user of this work if a brief introductory note preceded each translation; these notes have again all been prepared by jurists (in many cases, by the translator of the pertinent text), but again no standards were imposed upon the contributors. Each person was asked only to outline the constitution as he or she thought best.

This book began as an idea conceived by F.J.M. Feldbrugge, Professor of East European Law and Director of the Documentation Office for East European Law of the University of Leyden Faculty of Law. I am most grateful to Professor Feldbrugge for entrusting the realization of this project to me, and for his neverfailing help and guidance in bringing it to fruition. A word of thanks is also in order for Professor Zigurds L. Zile of the University of Wisconsin Law School, who started me out on the long road of the study of Soviet and socialist law, and for Professor Serge L. Levitsky, whose critical thoughts and comments are a continuing source of stimulation and inspiration. The fine work of those who have translated texts and/or prepared notes for this compilation speaks for itself; I am most appreciative of the cooperation and efforts of all the contributors. There are some other persons to whom I am also indebted for their behind-the-scenes help: Esselien M. 't Hart and Ania van der Meer for their excellent editorial and preparatory work; to my colleagues at the Documentation Office

Preface

for their continuing support and assistance; and to all those at Sijthoff & Noordhoff International Publishers who have helped to make this tome a reality.

Leyden, The Netherlands *William B. Simons*
September 1979

INTRODUCTION

A constitution—the legal definition of this term is basically the same in both communist and non-communist states: the fundamental law forming the basis of the body politic of both state and society. But here agreement would end, for the nature of a constitution and its rôle, function, and enactment, amendment, and application are viewed differently. In the West, a constitution is commonly held to be that cherished document, quoted and referred to as the legitimator of sovereign authority, the guarantor of the fundamental rights of citizens, the separator of powers; it is axiomatic in the West that a constitution provides for the rule of law and not of men. In the communist world, a constitution is not defined in the same way, but that does not necessarily mean that a constitution is therefore any less respected and cherished in communist countries than it is in western nations.

Communist constitutional theory has come a great distance since Marx and Engels first began putting their thoughts on paper in the last century. For them, the most important concept was the revolution rather than the constitution; they believed that if the proletariat followed only the rules of the constitutional game, they would never be able to free themselves from their chains of oppression. Eventually the revolution did occur, albeit in agrarian Russia and not in industrialized western Europe, as had been the original prognosis. And the new rulers of Soviet Russia wanted a constitution, for they felt it important to have a fundamental law to provide the basic framework for their new state structure, and a political document for both internal and external consumption. The first communist constitution of the Russian republic dealt briefly with communist ideology, and concentrated mainly on the state structure, the establishment and limitation of citizens' rights, and the economic basis of the new order.

The 1936 USSR Constitution (often called the "Stalin" Constitution) was subsequently adopted to take account of the changes that took place in the USSR following the establishment of communist power and the Soviet federation. Technically, the previous constitution could have been amended rather than totally replaced by a new document, but the whole procedure of drafting the new law, a nationwide discussion of its provisions, and its subsequent enactment provided the necessary pomp and circumstance commensurate with the advancement of the USSR from the establishment of the dictatorship of the proletariat phase to the construction of socialism, even though the text of the document was rather short on pure ideological content. But this, at the time and under the circumstances, was natural enough, since ideology was crowded out by the political and economic facts of the day—the USSR (along with its only fraternal communist state, Mongolia) was the proponent and practitioner of socialism in an otherwise hostile world of capitalist nations, and the continued strengthening of its internal political and economic system came first on the agenda.

After the end of World War II, the Stalin Constitution was used as the basic model for the fundamental laws of the people's democracies that were being established in Eastern Europe.[1] There were some national peculiarities of the new fraternal nations that had to be taken into account when drafting their new constitutions, but the general principles of the USSR Constitution came through loud and clear. The communist world had expanded and the constitutions increased in number.

The year 1957 was another significant date in the history of the constitutions of the communist world, for in October a declaration of the communist parties in power was made in Moscow to commemorate the 40th anniversary of the October 1917 Russian Revolution. The declaration enumerated principles and basic laws of socialism—guidance of the working masses by the Marxist-Leninist party, and the alliance of the working class with the peasantry and other working people; the abolition of capitalist ownership of the means of production and the socialization of agriculture; the planned development of the national economy; the carrying out of the socialist revolution in areas of ideology and culture; the abolition of national oppression and the establishment of friendship among the socialist nations; the defense of the achievements of socialism; and the promotion of proletarian internationalism.[2] This list was both reflective and prescriptive, since many of these principles were in the constitutions of the communist world, but other of these basic tenets were only obliquely referred to in the constitutions of that time. The 1957 declaration also made mention of the permissibility of some measure of national variation on socialist practices. And a good thing that it did since, although the existence of the declaration seemed to point toward the continued development of communist constitutions along a uniform line, as had hitherto been the case, the fact that one member of the communist commonwealth, Yugoslavia, did not sign the declaration indicated that perhaps the future road of communist constitutional development might not be so straight and narrow after all.

The new constitutions of the communist world of the 1960s and 1970s are still based upon the principles contained in the 1957 declaration, but there is a greater degree of national variation and diversity in the

Introduction

manner in which some of these principles are developed than was previously the case.

Communist constitutional theory has never recognized the western theories of either the separation of powers or the system of checks and balances,[3] although executive, legislative, and judicial branches of government are provided for in the constitutions of the communist world. But with regard to the executive branch, the Council of Ministers model is no longer the single pattern which it once was—taken from the 1936 USSR "Stalin" Constitution (as amended) and used in the countries of the people's democracies just after the Second World War. In examining the communist constitutions of the 1960s and 1970s, one can also find the Council of State type and the Presidential type of executive organization.[4] In the judicial sphere, some form of constitutional review (*e.g.* constitutional court, constitutional commission, supreme presidential body) has been established under the provisions of several communist constitutions.

The bills of rights in the new communist constitutions have in general been expanded in their scope, as compared with previous versions: new political, economic, and personal rights include those of housing, health care, family protection, scientific, technical and artistic creation, the right to submit proposals to state officials and agencies concerning the latter's activities, to the protection of one's honor and dignity, and of one's property. The duties of citizens have also been expanded: a duty to protect the environment and to preserve historical monuments, to respect the rights and interests of other citizens, for parents to raise their children properly and for children to aid their parents are some of the more important new additions that come to mind.[5]

Unlike their predecessors, most of the new constitutions contain a section on foreign policy, though there are noticeable differences in the manner in which this subject is treated; in part, these differences may be traced to the relationship that a particular communist state enjoys with either the USSR or the PRC, and a desire to maintain close contacts (*e.g.* GDR Art. 6(2)) or to stress national independence (*e.g.* Yugoslavia, Introduction IV).

The socio-political and ideological content of most of the new generation of constitutions has noticeably been altered. The 1974 Yugoslav Constitution provides perhaps the best example by containing an entire chapter of 65 articles devoted to the socio-political system, and there are numerous references made to politics and ideology in the new Preamble to the 1977 USSR Constitution, as well as the addition of a whole new chapter on social development. The leading rôle of the Marxist-Leninist party is now discussed in most of the recent constitutions in terms that more adequately reflect the position of influence and power exerted by the communist party in these societies, although some communist constitutions stress the party's rôle more strongly than do others. This new constitutional emphasis on, or realistic recognition of, the party's rôle has not however been to the total exclusion of other social organizations; in several of the communist countries (*e.g.* Bulgaria, Czechoslovakia, GDR, Hungary, Poland, and Viet-Nam), mention is made in the constitution of other political parties, and for the first time labor collectives are now listed as participants in the resolution of state affairs (*e.g.* Bulgaria, GDR, and USSR). There is also the entire system of the organizations of associated labor which are provided for throughout the Yugoslav Constitution. New provisions have also appeared which establish the participation of citizens in the administration of state and public affairs as constitutional principles (*e.g.* GDR and USSR), and the use of referenda for the resolution of important questions of state life (*e.g.* Bulgaria and USSR). Further in the ideological sphere, all of the states of the communist world (with the sole exception of Kampuchea) are now characterized as "socialist", and this too is in contrast to the previous versions of communist constitutions which stressed the dictatorship of the proletariat phase, but it is unclear exactly how the term "socialist" is used in the various fundamental laws in the sense of the Marxian progression to the ultimate goal: have these states arrived at socialism, are they building socialism, or rather is the term used in a less precise theoretical and looser propagandistic meaning?[6] It is clear however, that the USSR—which was proclaimed to be a socialist state in its 1936 constitution—has advanced to a new stage of political development along the road to the final construction of communism: the socialist "all-people's" state of a developed socialist society.

In viewing the communist constitutions as a whole, it is interesting to note the changed relationship between the USSR Constitution and the constitutions of those communist nations within the Soviet sphere of influence. The first generation of constitutions of the "people's democracies" were heavily influenced by, and to a great degree based upon, the then existing USSR Constitution of 1936. But some of the latest communist constitutions appear to have had a noticeable influence upon the new 1977 Soviet Constitution. Soviet President Brezhnev himself stated in his speech accompanying presentation of the draft 1977 USSR Constitution that "the experience of the constitutional development of the fraternal countries has been utilized in the preparation of the draft".[7]

Ideology, society and politics, and economics—the content of the constitutions of the communist world. But what of the functions of

Introduction

communist constitutions? We believe that they are two-fold: a fundamental law which lays down norms for state and society; and a political statement of what has been achieved and what remains to be carried out by state and society. As it were, both a legal and a propaganda function.[8] The normative function of communist constitutions is the subject of debate and discussion in communist legal literature.[9] In the early years of any communist state, when considerations of consolidation of power and the restructuring of the economic system are of primary importance, it is perhaps natural that the norms contained in a fundamental law are emphasized to a lesser degree than are the programmatic goals in the same law. But as the same communist state matures and its political and economic bases stabilize, the normative function of the fundamental law can be the subject of greater emphasis. One may argue that this seems to be the case in many of the countries of the present-day communist world—an interest in using law, and of course the fundamental law, as an instrument to achieve and promote societal programs and goals. One could point for example to the ambitious legislative program of the USSR which has been adopted on the basis of the new 1977 Soviet Constitution. However, the normative rôle of communist constitutions has not in the past excluded the propaganda function, nor is it likely to do so in the future. The constitutions of the communist world have always been used for internal as well as external consumption—to proclaim what has been achieved and to lay down the program of what is still to be accomplished.

There is much that one can derive from the study and comparison of the constitutions of the communist world—to see what type of norms and institutions are being provided for and to learn what lies ahead on the road to the ultimate goal of communism. But one must—in any society and under any legal system—not forget to look beyond the pure letter of the law, be it normative or programmatic, and examine the whole of society in an attempt to observe the degree and the manner in which the laws, fundamental and otherwise, are being implemented and the way in which they affect the people who make up the society. For perhaps it is rather academic to speak of the constitution of any society as the ultimate regulator of state and social affairs without taking into account that laws may rule, but that men create and carry out the laws, both in the non-communist and communist worlds.

NOTES

1. See John N. Hazard, "The Soviet Legal Pattern Spreads Abroad", *University of Illinois Law Forum* 1964 No. 1, 277–297.
2. A full text of the declaration of "the twelve", plus other related documents, and an overall introduction can be found in *The New Communist Manifesto and Related Documents*, (Dan N. Jacobs, ed.), 2nd ed., New York 1962, 176.
3. P.F. Martynenko, "Sotsialisticheskaia konstitutsiia — neposredstvenno deistvuiushchee pravo", *Problemy Pravovedeniia* 1979 No. 39, 6*ff*.
4. For an examination of these three forms of state power organization, see Georg Brunner, "The Functions of Communist Constitutions", 3 *Review of Socialist Law* 1977 No. 2, 130–137. See also Chris Osakwe, "The Common Law of Constitutions of the Communist-Party States", 3 *Review of Socialist Law* 1977 No. 2, 155–217.
5. However, the important question of the linkage (or absence thereof) of the rights and duties of citizens under communist constitutions remains still to be resolved.
6. The unresolved discussion in Soviet legal circles concerning the meaning and use of the term "socialist state" is referred to in the text and the notes of V.M. Korel'skii, "O prirode i tipicheskikh priznakakh sotsialisticheskogo gosudarstva", *Pravovedenie* 1979 No. 4, 12–17.
7. *Izvestiia*, 5 June 1977. English translation in *The Constitutions of the USSR and the Union Republics*, (F.J.M. Feldbrugge, ed.), Alphen aan den Rijn, The Netherlands 1979, 188–189. For a discussion of the influence of the constitutional development of the other communist states upon the USSR, see John N. Hazard, "A Constitution for 'Developed Socialism'", in *Soviet Law After Stalin, Part II, Social Engineering Through Law*, (D.D. Barry, G. Ginsburgs, P.B. Maggs, eds.), No. 20 (II) *Law in Eastern Europe*, (F.J.M. Feldbrugge, ed.), Alphen aan den Rijn, The Netherlands 1978, 24–27.
8. The propaganda value of communist constitutions is referred to in a positive way by N.A. Mikhaleva, "Poniatie i sistema printsipov sotsialisticheskoi konstitutsii", *Aktual'nye problemy gosudarstvenno-pravovoi nauki v razvitom sotsialisticheskom obshchestve*, Vol. 48 *Trudy VIuZI*, Moskva 1977, 51–52.
9. An analysis of the normative aspects of communist constitutions is contained in V.S. Osnovin, "Osobennosti konstitutsionnykh norm", *Sovetskoe Gosudarstvo i Pravo* 1979 No. 4, 12–19. See also Martynenko, *op. cit.*, note 2, 7*ff*.

CONTRIBUTORS TO THIS VOLUME

Max Azicri, Professor of Political Science, Edinboro State College, Edinboro, Pennsylvania

W.E. Butler, Professor of Comparative Law in the University of London

Catherine A. Crisham, Europa Institute, University of Leyden Faculty of Law

Joseph J. Darby, Professor of Law, University of San Diego, School of Law, San Diego, California

F.J.M. Feldbrugge, Professor of East European Law, Director of the Documentation Office for East European Law, University of Leyden Faculty of Law

William C. Jones, Professor of Law, Washington University, School of Law, St. Louis, Missouri

Youn-Soo Kim, Institute of Law, Politics, and Society of the Socialist States, University of Kiel, BRD

Simone-Marie Vrăbiescu Kleckner, Legal Librarian, United Nations, New York, New York

Marko Pavičić, Zagreb, Yugoslavia

William B. Simons, Documentation Office for East European Law, University of Leyden Faculty of Law

Ivan Sipkov, Assistant Chief, Law Library, European Law Division, The Library of Congress, Washington, DC

Smiljko Sokol, Assistant Professor, University of Zagreb Faculty of Law

William Sólyom-Fekete, Senior Legal Specialist, Law Library, European Law Division, The Library of Congress, Washington, DC

Hanna Szawlowski, Vancouver, BC, Canada

Richard Szawlowski, Professor of International Law, The Polish University, London

Th.J. Vondracek, Documentation Office for East European Law, University of Leyden Faculty of Law

ALBANIA

INTRODUCTION

William B. Simons

After centuries of rule by the Ottoman Empire, Albania became independent in 1912, and its first constitution, providing for a monarchy, was drawn up in 1914. Following World War I and occupation by foreign troops, another constitution was drafted in 1920, again providing for a monarchy, but in 1925, Albania was proclaimed a republic and a new constitution was promulgated. The President of Albania became King in 1928, and so yet another constitution was drafted. In 1939, Albania was occupied by Italian forces, and a new constitution established a monarchy under the House of Savoy. In 1943, after Italian capitulation, German troops occupied Albania until November 1944.

In November 1941, the Albanian Communist Party was formed and, in liberated areas, councils of national liberation were established. A civil war between pro- and anti-communist forces raged in 1943–1944, and on 24 May 1944, the I Anti-Fascist Congress of National Liberation was convened in the liberated town of Permet. The Congress elected an Anti-Fascist Council as its supreme legislative body. The Council, in turn, created an Anti-Fascist Committee which exercised the functions of a provisional revolutionary government. In October 1944, the II Anti-Fascist Congress was called, and at its sessions the Committee was proclaimed to be the Provisional Democratic Government of Albania. The II Congress approved basic laws concerning the organs of government and adopted a "Declaration of the Rights of Citizens" guaranteeing *inter alia*, freedom of conscience, expression, the press, assembly, the equality of sexes, and universal suffrage. On 29 November 1944, the whole of Albania was liberated. In August 1945, the Provisional Government confiscated large land holdings, nationalized the means of production, transportation, communication, and banks, and declared foreign trade to be a state monopoly. In December 1945, elections were held to elect a Constituent Assembly, which proclaimed Albania to be a People's Republic on 11 January 1946. The following month, a constitutional committee submitted a draft of a new constitution to a national discussion, and the fundamental law was confirmed on 14 March 1946.

The 1946 Constitution of the Albanian People's Republic in-

Introduction

corporated the August 1945 measures passed by the Provisional Government referred to above, and also provided for a system of an overall planned economy. However, nowhere in the new constitution was "socialism" mentioned. Private property and private initiative (later renamed "private enterprise in the economy") were provided for, if not used to the detriment of the public, and private inheritance was also guaranteed. Provisions were made for the expropriation of private property with compensation. The supreme state organs were the People's Assembly, elected for a four-year term with biannual sessions, and an 11-man Presidium elected by the People's Assembly (Arts. 53–56). Local organs of government were the people's councils. Universal suffrage was continued, and all elections were direct and secret, with the possibility of recalling elected representatives. The supreme executive and administrative organ was the Government composed of the Prime Minister, the Deputy Prime Minister, and other ministers. A bill of rights was also included in the 1946 law which provided for the equality of citizens—with a special guarantee of the equality of women and equal pay for equal work—and which repeated the rights provided for in the 1944 Declaration. New rights included the inviolability of the person, the home, and secrecy of correspondence. Freedom of scientific and artistic creation was also guaranteed, and author's rights were subject to protection. The right to petition state organs for the redress of wrongs was also granted to Albanian citizens, as was the right to complain against irregular or illegal decisions of administrative organs, or against officials for unjust acts in the fulfillment of their duties. Citizens were also allowed to seek compensation from the state or an official for damages resulting from illegal or unjust punishment. Minority rights were provided for, and the freedom to use minority languages and to develop minority cultures was also mentioned. The church was separated from the state, although citizens were expressly allowed under the 1946 Constitution to celebrate a religious marriage ceremony after the required state service. The duties of Albanian citizens were relatively few in number: the duty to work, to comply with the constitution and laws, to perform military service, and to pay income taxes.

The Albanian Constitution of 1946 was amended a number of times in the 1950s and 1960s. The most significant amendments were those of 4 July 1950 which gave the constitution a more noticeable socialist flavor which it lacked in its original version. The constitution now spoke of the "construction of the bases of socialism" and repeated the socialist principle "From each according to his capacity, to each according to his work". The provisions of the 1946 Constitution concerning agriculture mentioned only a state policy favoring small and middle peasants, but in the amendments of 1950, this section was preceded by mention of the state sponsorship of the socialist development of agriculture through state agricultural enterprises and cooperatives. The Communist Party (renamed the Albanian Workers' Party—AWP) was also referred to for the first time in the 1950 version of the Constitution in the article on the right of citizens to join together in organizations, and the AWP was characterized as the vanguard organization of the working class and the leading nucleus of all organizations of the working masses—both state and social. The bill of rights was also expanded through amendment: the right to rest, to a paid vacation, and to old age and disability pensions were listed, and the duty to protect and safeguard socialist property was also included. An additional paragraph was added to the Constitution stating that no sentences could be passed except on the basis of law. However, the right of citizens to claim compensation for unjust or illegal imprisonment was changed to compensation from the state or its officials for damages incurred through the illegal or incorrect fulfillment of their duties. In 1957, the formula for the number of deputies in the People's Assembly was changed from one deputy per 20,000 persons as it had been in the 1946 text, to one deputy per 8,000 persons. The Ministry of Justice was abolished in 1966, and in 1968 the original reference in the 1946 law to military and special courts was altered to read "other courts".

In 1971, the VI Congress of the Albanian Workers' Party adopted a decision on the necessity of preparing and adopting a new constitution. In January 1976, a draft text was submitted for public discussion and, following the VII AWP Congress, was adopted on 28 December. The second Albanian Constitution is longer than its predecessor (112 vs. 97 articles), and for the first time begins with a preamble. The preamble proclaims that Albania has entered the stage of the comprehensive construction of a socialist society, and also for the first time contains mention of the "state of the dictatorship of the proletariat" and "socialist democracy". The Albanian Workers' Party is prominently featured in the preamble, and under its banner and leadership, the Albanian people are to promote the construction of a socialist society and progress to the ultimate goal of a communist society. Lest there be any doubt about the importance of the role of the AWP, this formula is repeated in Articles 2 and 3. There are several new provisions in the 1976 Albanian Constitution: civil servants are to participate in direct productive work and are to be paid salaries in a fair ratio to those of workers, so as to prevent the formation of a privileged elite (Art. 9); state organizations are to involve the people in the government of the country and in the country's defense (Art. 13); material incentives are to be combined with moral ones to stimulate work (Art. 30); taxes on income have been abolished (Art. 31); and the protection of natural resources against pollution has been declared to be a duty of the state, of economic and state organizations, and of all citizens (Art. 20). A list of ministries, which was present in the 1946 text, has not been included in the 1976 law. A new section on "Education, Science, and Culture" has been added to the fundamental law, combining some principles found in the first Constitution but also introducing some new ones: the younger generation is to be educated in the spirit of socialism and communism, and education is to be built on the Marxist-Leninist world outlook. The bill of rights has also been expanded in the 1976 law. The rights of Albanian citizens are now explicitly inseparable from the fulfillment of their duties, and none of the rights granted to citizens may be exercised in opposition to the socialist order. Citizens continue to enjoy the right to unite in organizations, but for the first time membership in certain classes of organizations has been expressly forbidden. Parents have now been made responsible for the communist upbringing of their children, and the preservation and strengthening of the socialist order and the implementation of the rules of socialist community life have been included as duties for all Albanian citizens.

The portion of the Constitution dealing with the organs of state power have also been altered in the 1976 law. The competence of the People's Assembly is defined in greater detail, and the formula for representation has been changed from 8,000 citizens per deputy to a fixed number of 250 deputies for the national legislature. The supreme organ of state administration has been renamed the Council of Ministers, and a Presidium of the Council of Ministers has been formed. At the local levels, deputies to people's councils have been granted immunity from prosecution within the territory of the relevant council. The section of the Constitution dealing with the armed forces has been moved from its penultimate position in the 1946 law to a place of prominence following the 1976 provisions on the supreme organs of state administration, and the contents of the armed forces section have also been significantly altered. The armed forces are now led by the Albanian Workers' Party, and a Defense Council has been created; the post of supreme commander of the Albanian armed forces and of Chairman of the Defense Council has been assigned to the First Secretary of the AWP's Central Committee. A number of changes have also been made in the constitutional provisions on the courts and the attorney general's office. The separation of courts of justice from the administration, provided for in the first constitution, is missing from the 1976 text. The powers of the Attorney General have been expanded—he now has the right to object to unlawful acts and to demand their abrogation or amendment by the organ concerned, and he also has the task of informing the Presidium of the People's Assembly of any laws which are unconstitutional, and the Council of Ministers of any decisions which are not in accordance with the law.

Some significant provisions of the 1946 Albanian Constitution, which gave it a rather moderate approach to the building of socialism, do not appear in the 1976 law: private property and private enterprise in the economy have been abolished, and replaced by the more limited concept of private ownership; there is no longer any mention of state support to poor and middle peasants—rather, the emphasis is now on the transition of cooperative property into property of the entire people. And lastly, religion has been dealt a crushing blow: the preamble speaks of the destruction of the foundations of "religious obscurantism", Article 37 declares that the state recognizes no religion and carries out atheist propaganda, and there is no longer any constitutional mention of a religious marriage ceremony being allowed after the state one. The final and most serious change is contained in that portion of the 1976 text which forbids the creation of any sort of religious organization and the carrying out of any religious activities.

The 1976 Albanian Constitution bears the imprint of the father of socialist constitutions—the 1936 USSR Constitution; however, the Albanian text also in many respects displays its own independent development where it has gone even further than the Soviet model, *e.g. vis-à-vis* religion, and the influence of the Chinese Constitution can also be seen; the goal of the victory of the "socialist road over the capitalist road", and the Albanian opposition to all forms of hegemony. But the 1976 Albanian fundamental law also evidences a desire to remain ultimately independent even of their former allies the Chinese, with whom relations have cooled since the late 1960s, and to pursue their own road to the ultimate victory of communism. The text states that Albania will primarily rely on its own efforts to complete the construction of socialism; the stationing of foreign troops and bases on Albanian soil is not permitted; the acceptance or signing of capitulation or occupation is branded as treason; and it is prohibited to make any concessions to, accept any credits from, or even to create foreign or joint financial or economic institutions with capitalist, bourgeois, or revisionist monopolies or states.

CONSTITUTION OF THE PEOPLE'S SOCIALIST REPUBLIC OF ALBANIA OF 28 DECEMBER 1976

Preamble	8
The Social Order	10
The Political Order	10
The Economic Order	13
Education, Science, and Culture	16
The Fundamental Rights and Duties of Citizens	17
The Supreme Organs of State Power	21
The People's Assembly	21
The Presidium of the People's Assembly	23
The Supreme Organs of State Administration	25
The Country's Defense and the Armed Forces	26
The Local Organs of State Power and State Administration	27
The People's Courts	29
The Attorney General's Office	30
The Arms, the Flag, and the Capital	30
Final Provisions	31

CONSTITUTION OF THE PEOPLE'S SOCIALIST REPUBLIC OF ALBANIA*

Gazeta Zyrtare e Republikës Popullore të Shqipërisë 1976 No. 5

PREAMBLE

The Albanian people have blazed the path of history sword in hand. In the struggle with domestic and foreign enemies, they defended their existence as a people and as a nation and fought for national freedom and independence, for their native land and mother-tongue, for their livelihood and social justice. After centuries of bondage, they achieved a great victory with the creation of the independent national Albanian state on 28 November 1912.

The national, democratic, and revolutionary movement found a new impulse and a new content with the triumph of the Great Socialist October Revolution and the spread of communist ideas, which also marked a decisive turning-point for the destinies of the Albanian people.

Under the harsh conditions of the fascist and Nazi occupation, betrayed by the ruling classes, the Albanian people, under the leadership of the Communist Party of Albania (now the Albanian Workers' Party), rose up and, united in the National Liberation Front, threw themselves arms in hand into the greatest battle in their history for national and social liberation. From the flames of the battle for freedom, and on the ruins of the old state power, the new Albanian state of people's democracy emerged as a form of the dictatorship of the proletariat. On 29 November 1944 Albania won genuine independence, and the Albanian people took their destiny into their own hands. The People's Revolution triumphed and a new era dawned—the era of socialism.

In the conditions of the people's state power and under the leadership of the party of the working class, great socio-economic transformations took place, which were outlined in the first con-

---

* Text based on the official English and French draft constitution issued by the Albanian Government and on an English version of the new constitution. Text revised by Professor F.J.M. Feldbrugge and Catherine A. Crisham.

stitution of the socialist Albanian state. An end was put to the domination of foreign capital and to the plunder of the country's wealth. The capitalists and landowners saw their properties confiscated, and the principal means of production passed into the hands of the people. The way was open for the socialist industrialization of the country. Agrarian reform gave land to those who tilled it and the collectivization of agriculture set the peasants on the road of socialism.

Social ownership of the means of production and the unitary system of socialist economy replaced private ownership and the multi-form economy in the cities and in the countryside. The exploiting classes and the exploitation of man by man were liquidated. The entire social development proceeds consciously according to plan and in the interests of the people.

In socialist Albania, the working class is the leading class in the state and in society. New relations of mutual assistance and cooperation have been established between the two friendly classes of our society, the working class and the cooperative peasantry, as well as the stratum of the people's intelligentsia. The free labor of free people has become the decisive factor in the prosperity of the socialist fatherland and in raising the level of general and individual well-being. Albania has overcome its age-old backwardness and has been transformed into a country with advanced industry and agriculture.

The vital forces of the people were liberated and free rein was given to their inexhaustible creative energies. In the continuous process of the revolution, Albanian women gained equality in all fields, became a great social force, and are proceeding towards their complete emancipation. Education and culture have become the property of the broad masses of the people, and science and knowledge have been placed at the service of society. The foundations of religious obscurantism have been destroyed. The moral personality of the working man, his consciousness and world outlook, are formed on the basis of the proletarian ideology which has become the dominant ideology.

Socialism had demonstrated its absolute superiority over the old exploiting order.

Albania has entered the stage of the comprehensive construction of the socialist society. The great historic transformations have created new conditions for the continuous development of the socialist revolution.

The development of the class struggle in the cause of socialism; the continuous strengthening of the state of the dictatorship of the proletariat and the deepening of socialist democracy; the development of productive forces and the improvement of socialist production relations; the continuous improvement of the well-being of the working masses; the gradual narrowing of differences between industry and agriculture, the cities and the countryside and between mental and manual work; the affirmation of the personality of the individual within the framework of the socialist collectivity; the mastering of modern technology and science; and the continuous revolutionization of every aspect of the life of the country are the main lines along which the socialist society is advancing and growing stronger.

The Albanian people are determined to defend national independence, the people's state power, and their socialist achievements against any enemy. Socialist Albania remains an active factor in the struggle for national and social liberation, for peace, freedom, and the rights of all peoples against imperialism, reaction, and revisionism. In its foreign policy it is guided by the great ideals of socialism and communism, and it fights for their triumph throughout the world.

The Albanian people have found and continue to find constant inspiration in the great doctrine of Marxism-Leninism. Under its banner, and united around the Albanian Workers' Party and under its leadership, they are promoting the construction of socialist society in order to progress gradually, at a later stage, to communist society.

PART I

Chapter I. The Social Order

A. The Political Order

Article 1. Albania is a People's Socialist Republic.

Article 2. The People's Socialist Republic of Albania is a state of the dictatorship of the proletariat, which expresses and defends the interests of all the working people.

The People's Socialist Republic of Albania is based on the unity of the people around the Albanian Workers' Party and has as its foundation the alliance of the working class with the cooperative peasantry under the leadership of the working class.

Article 3. The Albanian Workers' Party, the vanguard of the working class, is the sole leading political force in the state and in society.

Marxism-Leninism is the dominant ideology in the People's Socialist Republic of Albania. The entire socialist social order evolves on the basis of its principles.

Article 4. The People's Socialist Republic of Albania constantly develops the revolution by adhering to the class struggle with the aim of attaining the ultimate victory of the socialist road over the capitalist road and the comprehensive construction of socialism and communism.

Article 5. All state power in the People's Socialist Republic of Albania emanates from the working people and belongs to them.

The working class, cooperative peasantry, and all other working people exercise state power through the representative organs as well as directly.

The representative organs are the People's Assembly and the people's councils.

Nobody, with the exception of the organs expressly defined in this Constitution, may exercise the people's sovereignty or any of its attributes in the name of the People's Socialist Republic of Albania.

Article 6. The representative organs direct and control the activity of all other state organs, which are responsible to the latter and render account to them.

Article 7. The representative organs and all other state organs rely in their work on the creative initiative of the working masses, involve them into the government of the country, and render account to them.

Article 8. The representative organs are elected by the people by universal, equal, direct, and secret ballot.

The electors have the right to recall their representative at any time if he has lost their political trust, if he fails to discharge the duties entrusted him, or when he acts in violation of the laws.

The organization and procedure of the elections are regulated by law.

Article 9. Civil servants serve the people and render account to them, participate also in direct productive work, and are paid salaries in fair ratio to those of the workers and cooperative peasants in order to prevent the creation of a privileged stratum. The ration of remuneration is fixed by law.

Article 10. The working class, as the leading class in society, the cooperative peasantry, and other working people, under the leadership of the Albanian Workers' Party, exercise direct and organized control over the activities of the state organs, economic and social organizations, and over their workers in order to defend the achievements of the revolution and to strengthen the socialist order.

Article 11. The organization of the state, state activities, and the entire political and economic life in the People's Socialist Republic of Albania, are based on the principle of democratic centralism and are carried out in accordance with it, combining centralized direction with the creative initiative of local organs and the working masses in the struggle against bureaucracy and liberalism.

Article 12. The precise and equal implementation of the Constitution and of the laws, which express the will of the working class and other working masses, is the duty of the state organs, of economic and social organizations, and officials, in all their activities.

Article 13. The state relies on the social organizations, cooperates with them, and creates the conditions for the furtherance of their activities.

The social organizations unite the masses and broad strata of the people, involve them in an organized fashion into the government of the country, socialist construction, and in the country's defense; they work for their communist education and concern themselves with solving their particular problems.

Article 14. In the construction of socialism, the People's Socialist Republic of Albania relies primarily on its own efforts.

Article 15. The People's Socialist Republic of Albania is guided in its foreign relations by the principles of Marxism-Leninism and proletarian internationalism, pursues a policy of friendship, collaboration, and mutual assistance with the socialist countries, supports the revolutionary movement of the working class and the struggle of the peoples for freedom, independence, social progress, and socialism, and relies on their solidarity.

The People's Socialist Republic of Albania is in favor of peace and good-neighborliness, and of relations with all states on the basis of equality, respect of sovereignty, noninterference in domestic affairs, and mutual benefit.

The People's Socialist Republic of Albania is opposed to all forms of aggression, colonial exploitation, tutelage, dictate and hegemony, national oppression, and racial discrimination. It adheres to the principle of the self-determination of peoples, the exercise of complete national sovereignty, and the equality of all countries in international relations.

B. The Economic Order

Article 16. The economy of the People's Socialist Republic of Albania is a socialist economy based on the socialist ownership of the means of production.

In the People's Socialist Republic of Albania there are no exploiting classes; private ownership and the exploitation of man have been abolished and are prohibited.

Article 17. Socialist property is the inviolable foundation of the socialist order, the source of the people's well-being and of the country's strength; it enjoys special protection of the state.

Socialist property consists of state property and cooperative property in agriculture.

Article 18. State property belongs to the entire people and is the highest form of socialist property.

The following are the exclusive property of the state: the land and underground resources; mines; forests; pastures; waters; natural energy resources; works and factories; machine and tractor stations; banks; roads and means of rail, water, and air transportation; post, telegraph, and telephone offices; radio and TV stations; cinematography.

All other assets created in the state sector or acquired by the state through law are also state property.

Article 19. Land is granted for social use to state enterprises and institutions, agricultural cooperatives, and social organizations, as well as to citizens for personal use. The use of land is granted free of charge.

Agricultural land can be used for other purposes only with the approval of the appropriate state organs.

Article 20. The protection of land, natural wealth, waters, and the atmosphere against deterioration and pollution is a duty of the state, of economic and social organizations, and of all citizens.

Article 21. Cooperative property belongs to groups of people working in agriculture, voluntarily united in agricultural cooperatives for the purpose of increasing production and well-being, and for the construction of socialism in rural areas and throughout the country.

The following are the property of agricultural cooperatives: buildings, machinery, equipment, means of transportation, tools, and implements; working and productive animals; fruit trees; agricultural and livestock produce; and all other assets needed for their activities.

Article 22. The state encourages the development and strengthening of agricultural cooperatives and their transformation into large modern units of large-scale socialist production.

Under certain conditions, the state supports the setting-up and development of cooperatives of a higher type in which it directly participates by means of investment, particularly with regard to the principal means of production.

The transition of cooperative property into property of the entire people takes place in conformity with objective conditions according to the free will of the cooperative peasants and with the approval of the state.

The state strives to reduce the disparities between town and country.

Article 23. The personal property of citizens is recognized and protected by the state.

The following are considered to be personal property: income from work and other lawful sources, dwelling houses, and other objects serving to satisfy the material and cultural needs of the family and the individual.

Objects belonging to the family [employed] in a cooperative, according to the statutes of the agricultural cooperatives, are also considered to be personal property.

Personal property cannot be used to the detriment of the social interest.

Article 24. Certain immovable assets of cooperative and personal property may be converted into state property, when this is required by the general interest. The criteria of conversion and the manner of compensation are fixed by law.

Article 25. The state organizes, directs, and develops the entire economic and social life according to a single general plan in order to satisfy the ever-growing material and cultural needs of society, strengthening the country's independence and defense while constantly increasing and improving socialist production on the basis of technical progress.

Article 26. In order to administer the assets of the entire people, the state creates enterprises which carry out their activities being guided by the general interests of society, as laid down in the state plan.

The manner of creating enterprises and the principles of their activities are determined by law.

Article 27. Foreign trade is a state monopoly.

Domestic trade is exercised primarily by the state which controls all activities in this field.

The selling price of the products of enterprises and the purchasing price of agricultural and livestock produce by the state are determined by the state.

Article 28. The granting of concessions to and the creation of other foreign or joint economic or financial institutions with capitalist, bourgeois, and revisionist monopolies and states, and the acceptance of credits from them, is prohibited in the People's Socialist Republic of Albania.

Article 29. Labor is the foundation of the entire socio-economic life of the country. Labor is the main source from which all citizens derive their livelihood.

The state strives to reduce the disparities between mental and physical work and between work in industry and agriculture.

The state cares about and adopts measures for labor safety and the qualifications of working people.

Article 30. The socialist principle "From each according to his ability, to each according to his work" is implemented in the People's Socialist Republic of Albania.

Equal pay is guaranteed for equal work.

The use of material incentives is correctly combined with moral incentives as a stimulus to work for the greatest possible results, giving priority to moral incentives.

The social consumption fund to meet the common needs of the citizens is continually increased in accordance with the possibilities created by the country's economic development.

The state exercises control over the amount of work and consumption.

Article 31. Citizens pay no levies or taxes whatsoever.

C. Education, Science, and Culture

Article 32. The state carries out broad ideological and cultural activities for the communist education of the working people and the formation of the new man.

The state devotes itself particularly to the all-round development and education of the younger generation in the spirit of socialism and communism.

Article 33. Education in the People's Socialist Republic of Albania is organized and directed by the state, is open to all, and is free of charge; it is built on the basis of the Marxist-Leninist world outlook and combines learning with production work and physical and military training.

Education follows the best traditions of the national and secular Albanian school.

Article 34. The state organizes and directs the development of science and technology in close connection with life and production, and in the service of the progress of society and the country's defense.

The state supports the dissemination of scientific knowledge among the masses and draws them widely into scientific research activities.

Article 35. The state protects the people's cultural heritage and devotes itself to the comprehensive development of the national socialist culture.

The state supports the development of socialist realist literature and art, which adhere to the ideals of socialism and communism and are permeated by the national and popular spirit.

Albania

Article 36. The state promotes the development of physical culture and sports on the basis of a massive movement to strengthen the health of the people, particularly of the younger generation, and to steel them for work and defense.

Article 37. The state recognizes no religion and supports and carries out atheist propaganda in order to implant a scientific materialist world outlook in people.

Chapter II. The Fundamental Rights and Duties of Citizens

Article 38. Citizens of the People's Socialist Republic of Albania are those who possess Albanian citizenship according to the law.

Article 39. The rights and duties of citizens are established on the basis of the reconciliation of the interests of the individual and those of the socialist society, with priority given to the general interest.

The rights of citizens are inseparable from the fulfillment of their duties and cannot be exercised in opposition to the socialist order.

The granting of more extensive and far-reaching rights to citizens is closely linked with the country's socialist development.

Article 40. All citizens are equal before the law.

No restriction or privilege in the rights and duties of citizens is recognized on account of sex, race, nationality, social position, or material situation.

Article 41. Liberated from political oppression and economic exploitation, women, as a great force of the revolution, participate actively in the socialist construction of the country and in the defense of the fatherland.

Women enjoy equal rights with men at work, in remuneration, in recreation, social security, education, socio-political activities, and in the family.

Article 42. National minorities are guaranteed protection and development of their culture and popular traditions, the use of their mother-tongue and its teaching in the schools, and equal development in all areas of social life.

Any national privileges or inequalities and any activities which violate the rights of national minorities are unconstitutional and punishable according to law.

Article 43. Citizens reaching the age of 18 have the right to vote and to be elected to all organs of state power.

Only those persons are excluded from the electoral right who have been deprived of this right by a court decision, as well as those who are mentally unfit and have been declared so by the courts.

Article 44. Citizens in the People's Socialist Republic of Albania enjoy the right to work, which is guaranteed by the state.

Work is both a duty and an honor for all able-bodied citizens.

Citizens have the right to choose and to exercise a profession according to their personal abilities and inclinations, and in compliance with the needs of society.

Article 45. Citizens enjoy the right to recreation after work. The working day and week and the paid annual vacation are regulated by law.

Vacation, cultural, and other such centers are created for the use of working people.

Article 46. Urban and rural workers are guaranteed the necessary livelihood in old age and in case of sickness or work disability.

The state takes under its special charge the invalids of the national liberation struggle, of the struggle to defend the country, and work invalids, and creates conditions for their rehabilitation.

Young children of those who have fallen in the defense of the country and in socialist construction are taken into the care of the state.

Article 47. The state guarantees citizens the necessary medical services and treatment in the medical centers of the country free of charge.

Article 48. Mothers and children enjoy special care and protection.

Mothers enjoy the right to paid leave prior to and after childbirth.

The state establishes maternity homes and child care centers and infant schools.

Article 49. Marriage and the family are under the care and protection of the state and of society.

Marriage is contracted before the competent state organs.

Parents are responsible for the upbringing and communist education of the children.

Children are duty-bound to care for parents who are disabled and without sufficient means of livelihood.

Children born out of wedlock enjoy the same rights and duties as those born within marriage.

Orphans without means of support are raised and educated by the state.

Article 50. Citizens enjoy the right to personal property.

The right of inheritance is regulated by law.

Article 51. The state guarantees the freedom of scientific work and literary and artistic creativity.

Authors' rights are protected by law.

Article 52. Citizens enjoy the right to education.

Eight-year education is universal and compulsory. The state aims at raising the level of compulsory education for everyone.

Article 53. Citizens enjoy the freedom of speech, press, organization, association, assembly, and public demonstration.

The state guarantees the realization of these freedoms, creates the necessary conditions to this end, and makes available the necessary material means.

Article 54. Citizens are guaranteed the right to unite in various organizations operating in the political, economic, cultural, and any other areas of the country's life.

Article 55. The creation of organizations of a fascist, anti-democratic, religious, or anti-socialist nature is prohibited.

Fascist, anti-democratic, religious, warmongering, and anti-socialist activities and propaganda are prohibited, as is the incitement of national and racial hatred.

Article 56. The state guarantees the inviolability of the person.

No one can be arrested without the decision of a court or the approval of a State Attorney. In special cases, stipulated by law, the competent organs may detain a person for up to three days.

No one can be convicted of a crime without the decision of a court or for an act which is not considered to be a crime by the law.

No one can be sentenced without being present at court, except in cases where it is proved that the defendant is legally missing.

No one can be interned or expelled, except in special cases determined by law.

Article 57. The home is inviolable. No one is permitted to enter another person's home without his consent, except the representatives of the competent state organs and under the conditions defined by law.

Article 58. The secrecy of correspondence and other means of communication may not be violated, except in the cases of criminal investigation, a state of emergency, or a state of war.

Article 59. Citizens enjoy the right to present petitions, complaints, remarks, and suggestions to the competent organs on personal, social, and state affairs.

In accordance with the conditions defined by law, citizens enjoy the right to claim compensation from the state or its officials for damage caused to them as a result of unlawful acts of state organs or officials in the exercise of their functions.

Article 60. Citizens are obliged to respect and observe the Constitution and other laws.

The preservation and strengthening of the socialist order and the implementation of the rules of socialist community life are the duty of all citizens.

Article 61. It is the duty of citizens to protect and strengthen socialist property.

Violation of socialist property constitutes a grave crime.

Article 62. The defense of the socialist fatherland is the noblest duty and highest honor for all citizens. Betrayal of the fatherland is the gravest of all crimes.

Article 63. Military service and constant training for the defense of the socialist fatherland are the duty of all citizens.

Article 64. Albanian citizens abroad enjoy the care and protection of the state.

Article 65. The right of asylum in the People's Socialist Republic of Albania is given to foreign citizens persecuted on account of their activities in the cause of the revolution and socialism, of democracy and national liberation, or in the cause of the progress of science and culture.

PART II

Chapter I. The Supreme Organs of State Power

A. The People's Assembly

Article 66. The People's Assembly is a supreme organ of state power, the bearer of the sovereignty of the people and of the state, and the sole legislative organ.

Article 67. The People's Assembly has the following main competences:

it defines, in accordance with the general line and directives of the Albanian Workers' Party, the main directions of the domestic and foreign policy of the state;

it approves and amends the Constitution and the laws, decides upon the conformity of the laws with the Constitution, and interprets laws;

it approves the plan for the country's economic and cultural development and the state budget;

it proclaims partial and general mobilization, the state of emergency, and the state of war in the event of armed agression against the People's Socialist Republic of Albania, or when this is necessary to fulfill obligations deriving from international treaties;

it ratifies and denounces international treaties of particular importance;

it grants amnesty;

it decides on national referenda;

it elects, appoints, and dismisses the Presidium of the People's Assembly, the Council of Ministers, the Supreme Court, the Attorney General and his deputies; these organs are responsible to the People's Assembly and render account to it;

it defines the administrative-territorial units;

it decides upon the creation or dissolution of ministries.

Article 68. The People's Assembly is composed of 250 deputies who are elected in constituencies with an equal number of inhabitants.

The People's Assembly is elected for a period of 4 years.

The People's Assembly is convened in its first session not later than two months from the day of its election.

Elections for the People's Assembly take place not later than three months from the day of the expiry of its mandate.

In the event of war or in other emergencies, the People's Assembly may prolong its activity beyond the term foreseen for as long as the state of emergency continues.

In certain special instances, the People's Assembly may decide on its dissolution before the expiry of the term for which it has been elected.

Article 69. The People's Assembly elects its presidency.

The activities of the People's Assembly are carried out in conformity with the rules approved by it.

Article 70. The People's Assembly convenes in ordinary sessions twice a year by decree of the Presidium of the People's Assembly.

The People's Assembly may be convened in extraordinary session by decree of the Presidium of the People's Assembly or at the request of one-third of the deputies.

The meetings of the People's Assembly open when the majority of deputies are present.

Article 71. The People's Assembly shall elect in its first session a commission to examine the credentials of the deputies. The People's Assembly confirms or annuls the credentials of the deputies on the recommendation of this commission.

It is the duty of the permanent commissions to examine the bills and decrees of the Presidium of the People's Assembly which are of a normative nature, to observe and control the activity of the state organs according to the different sectors, and to present the problems to the People's Assembly or the Presidium of the People's Assembly. *Ad hoc* commissions are established for special questions.

Article 72. It is the duty of the deputy to the People's Assembly to conscientiously and loyally serve the interests of the people and the cause of the fatherland and socialism, and to maintain close links with the electors and render account to them.

A deputy to the People's Assembly enjoys the right to demand explanation from all state organs and to intervene with them for the strict application of the Constitution and the laws.

The state organs are bound to consider the requests and proposals of deputies and to apply to them in accordance with the established rules.

Article 73. A deputy to the People's Assembly enjoys immunity.

A deputy may not be detained, arrested, or prosecuted without the approval of the People's Assembly or the Presidium of the People's Assembly, except in the case where he has clearly committed a serious crime.

Article 74. The right to initiate legislation belongs to the Presidium of the People's Assembly, the Council of Ministers, and deputies.

Laws and other acts of the People's Assembly are considered to have been approved when the majority of deputies present have voted for them.

Laws are promulgated not later than 15 days after their approval and enter into force 15 days after their publication in the official gazette, except in cases when the laws themselves provide otherwise.

B. The Presidium of the People's Assembly

Article 75. The Presidium of the People's Assembly is a supreme organ of state power and is in permanent session.

The Presidium of the People's Assembly is composed of the Chairman, three Deputy Chairmen, a Secretary, and 10 members.

Article 76. The Presidium of the People's Assembly is elected from the ranks of the People's Assembly in its first session and continues its activity until the election of the new Presidium.

The Presidium of the People's Assembly decides by majority vote when a majority of its members is present.

Article 77. The following are the main permanent competences of the Presidium of the People's Assembly:

it convenes the sessions of the People's Assembly;

it determines the date for the elections of the People's Assembly and the people's councils;

it awards decorations and honorary titles;

it grants or withdraws Albanian citizenship and accepts its renunciation;

it exercises the right of pardon;

it defines administrative-territorial divisions;

it concludes, ratifies, and denounces international treaties not examined by the People's Assembly itself;

it appoints and dismisses diplomatic representatives, acting on the recommendation of the Council of Ministers;

it accepts the credentials and letters of recall of the diplomatic representatives of foreign states;

it promulgates the laws and referenda decided upon by the People's Assembly.

Article 78. Between sessions of the People's Assembly, the Presidium of the People's Assembly exercises the following competences;

it controls the implementation of laws and decisions of the People's Assembly;

it controls the Council of Ministers, the Supreme Court, the Attorney General, and all other state organs, and summons them to report;

it appoints or dismisses the deputy chairmen of the Council of Ministers or individual ministers, acting on the recommendation of the chairman of the Council of Ministers; it appoints or dismisses individual members or Vice-Presidents of the Supreme Court and the deputies of the Attorney General; decrees for their appointment or dismissal must in all cases be submitted to the approval of the People's Assembly;

it issues decrees and decisions; decrees of a normative nature are submitted to the approval of the People's Assembly at its next session;

it proclaims, when it is impossible to convene the People's Assembly, partial and general mobilization, the state of emergency, and also the state of war in case of armed agression against the People's Socialist Republic of Albania or when this is necessary to fulfill obligations deriving from international treaties. In wartime, in the event that the convening of the People's Assembly is impossible, the Presidium of the People's Assembly exercises all the competences of the People's Assembly with the exception of amendments to the Constitution.

Article 79. The Presidium of the People's Assembly directs and controls the activities of the people's councils.

The Presidium of the People's Assembly may dissolve people's councils, appoint the provisional executive committees, and decide upon the election of a new people's council.

The Presidium of the People's Assembly abrogates the unlawful or irregular acts of the Council of Ministers, the people's councils, and the executive committees.

Chapter II. The Supreme Organs of State Administration

Article 80. The Council of Ministers is the supreme executive organ and issues orders.

The Council of Ministers is appointed at the first session of the People's Assembly.

The composition of the Council of Ministers is as follows: the Chairman, Deputy Chairman, and ministers.

The members of the Council of Ministers are appointed, as a rule, from among the ranks of the deputies of the People's Assembly.

The Council of Ministers decides by majority vote when a majority of its members are present.

Article 81. The following are the main competences of the Council of Ministers:

it directs the activities for the realization of the domestic and foreign policies of the state;

it issues decisions, ordinances, and instructions in accordance with and in pursuance of the Constitution and the laws;

it directs and controls the activities of the ministries, other central organs of the state administration, the executive committees of the people's councils, and determines their internal organization;

it draws up the draft plan for the country's economic and cultural development and the draft state budget; it organizes and controls the implementation of the plan and the budget, and it organizes and controls the state finances and the monetary and credit system;

it directs the activities necessary for the fulfillment of the duties with respect to the country's defense in conformity with the decisions of the Defense Council;

it adopts measures to secure, protect, and strengthen the socialist legal order and the rights of citizens;

it concludes and ratifies international agreements and denounces those not subject to ratification.

Article 82. The Council of Ministers abrogates unlawful or irregular acts of ministers or other central organs of the state administration, as well as of the executive committees of the people's councils.

The Council of Ministers suspends the application of unlawful or irregular decisions of people's councils and submits the question of their abrogation to a higher people's council or to the Presidium of the People's Assembly.

Article 83. The Chairman and Deputy Chairmen of the Council of Ministers constitute the Presidium of the Council of Ministers.

The Presidium of the Council of Ministers supervises, controls, and adopts decisions necessary for the accomplishment of the tasks determined by the Council of Ministers.

The Chairman of the Council of Ministers represents the Council of Ministers, presides over its meetings, and directs its activity.

Article 84. Ministries are central organs of state administration, specialized for particular branches of activity, and are directed by members of the Council of Ministers.

Article 85. Ministers are responsible for the activities of their respective ministries and those of the Council of Ministers, and direct and control the organs, enterprises, institutions, and economic organizations of their sector.

With respect to matters within their competence, ministers issue orders, regulations, and instructions in accordance with and in pursuance of the laws and the ordinances and decisions of the Council of Ministers.

Article 86. Ministers abrogate the unlawful or irregular orders and instructions of subordinate organs, enterprises, and institutions, and suspend the implementation of unlawful or irregular decisions of the executive committees of the people's councils which fall within their field of competence, presenting the question of their abrogation to the Council of Ministers.

Chapter III. The Country's Defense and the Armed Forces

Article 87. The state protects the achievements of the people's revolution and of socialist construction, and defends the freedom, national independence, and territorial integrity of the country.

The territory of the People's Socialist Republic of Albania is inalienable and its borders are inviolable.

Article 88. The defense of the country and of the achievements of socialism is guaranteed by the armed people, organized in the armed

Albania 27

forces which are comprised of the People's Army, the forces of the Ministry of Internal Affairs, and the voluntary forces of the people's self-defense.

The People's Army, as the main force for the country's defense, is an army of the people and serves the people.

The armed forces are led by the Albanian Workers' Party.

Article 89. The Defense Council is created to direct, organize, and mobilize all the forces and resources of the country in defense of the fatherland.

The First Secretary of the Central Committee of the Albanian Workers' Party is the Supreme Commander of the armed forces and Chairman of the Defense Council.

The Composition of the Defense Council is determined by the Presidium of the People's Assembly, acting on the recommendation of the Chairman of the Defense Council.

Article 90. No one has the right to sign or to accept, in the name of the People's Socialist Republic of Albania, the country's capitulation or occupation. Any such act is treason to the fatherland.

Article 91. The stationing of foreign bases and military forces on the territory of the People's Socialist Republic of Albania is not permitted.

Chapter IV. The Local Organs of State Power and State Administration

Article 92. The people's councils are the organs of state power which carry out the government of the country in their respective administrative-territorial units, with the broad participation of the working masses.

The people's councils direct all social life in political, economic, and socio-cultural fields, in the field of the country's defense, and [direct] the protection of the socialist legal order, reconciling local interests with general state interests.

The people's councils are elected for a term of three years.

Article 93. The people's council approves the plan and budget; elects and dismisses from its ranks persons in charge of the sections of the executive committee; directs and controls the activities of the people's councils at lower levels; and issues ordinances and decisions within the limits of its competences.

Article 94. The meetings of the people's council open when a majority of its members is present.

The people's council takes decisions by a majority vote of the members present.

Article 95. A higher people's council may dissolve a lower people's council, appoint a provisional executive committee, and order the election of a new people's council.

A higher people's council may dismiss the executive committee of a lower people's council and order a new election.

The people's council abrogates the unlawful or irregular acts of its own executive committee, of lower people's councils, and of the latter's executive committees.

Article 96. It is the duty of the members of the people's council to conscientiously and loyally serve the people, maintain close links with the electors, and render account to them; the members have the right to control state organs, enterprises, institutions, and agricultural cooperatives, and to demand from them strict observance of socialist legality.

The state organs concerned are obliged to examine the observations of the members of the people's councils and to adopt the necessary measures.

The members of the people's council enjoy immunity within the administrative-territorial unit of the people's council. They cannot be detained, arrested, or prosecuted without the approval of the people's council or of the executive committee, except in the case where they have clearly committed a serious crime.

Article 97. The executive committee is an executive organ of the people's council and it issues orders.

The executive committee continues its activity even after the expiry of the mandate of the people's council which elected it, until the first meeting of the new people's council.

Article 98. Between sessions of the people's council, the executive committee exercises the rights and duties of the people's council with the exception of those which, according to law, fall within the competence of the people's council alone.

The executive committee renders account for its activity to the people's council, submits to it its more important decisions for approval, and reports on the implementation of the decisions adopted by the people's council.

Article 99. The executive committee is subordinate to the people's council which elected it and to the next higher executive committee.

The executive committee of the higher people's council abrogates the unlawful or irregular acts of the lower executive committee and suspends those of the lower people's council, and submits the question of their abrogation to the competent people's council.

Article 100. The specialized organs created under the executive committees are subordinate to the people's council, its executive committee, and the higher organs of state administration; they render account to them and to the working masses.

Chapter V. The People's Court

Article 101. The people's courts are organs of the administration of justice.

The people's courts protect the socialist legal order, fight to prevent crime, and educate the working masses in the spirit of respect for and observance of socialist legality while relying on the active participation of the working masses.

The highest organ of justice is the Supreme Court which directs and controls the activity of the courts.

The Supreme Court is elected at the first session of the People's Assembly. The other people's courts are elected by the people in accordance with a procedure laid down by law.

The organization of the courts and trial procedure are laid down by law.

Article 102. The courts try criminal and civil matters, as well as other matters which fall within their competence according to law.

Trial takes place with the participation of assistant judges and is public, except in those cases where the law provides otherwise.

The Albanian language is used in court proceedings. Persons who do not speak Albanian may use their own language and make use of an interpreter.

The accused enjoys the right to defense.

Article 103. The court administers justice independently; it decides on the basis of the law alone and renders its judgment in the name of the people.

The verdict of the court may be annulled or amended by a competent court.

Chapter IV. The Attorney General's Office

Article 104. It is the duty of the Attorney General's Office to supervise the strict and equal observance of the law by the ministries and other central and local organs, the courts, the investigative organs, enterprises, institutions, organizations, officials, and citizens.

The Attorney General's Office has the right to object to any unlawful act and to demand its abrogation or amendment by the organs concerned. The Attorney General's request must be examined within the period fixed by law, otherwise the application of the act is suspended.

Article 105. The Attorney General submits to the People's Assembly and to the Presidium of the People's Assembly cases in which laws and decrees are not in conformity with the Constitution, and submits to the Council of Ministers cases in which decisions and ordinances are not in conformity with the laws.

Article 106. The Attorney General and his deputies are appointed in the first session of the People's Assembly.

State Attorneys are appointed by the Presidium of the People's Assembly.

PART III

Chapter I. The Arms, the Flag, and the Capital

Article 107. The Arms of the People's Socialist Republic of Albania bears a black double-headed eagle, encircled by two wheat sheaves, topped by a five-pointed red star, and tied at the bottom by a red ribbon bearing the inscription "24 May 1944".

Article 108. The state flag of the People's Socialist Republic of Albania has a red background with a black double-headed eagle in the center, topped by a five-pointed red star outlined in gold. The ratio between the width and length of the flag is 1:1.4.

Article 109. The capital of the People's Socialist Republic of Albania is Tirana.

Chapter II. Final Provisions

Article 110. The Constitution is the supreme law of the state.

All activities for the creation of legal rules are conducted on the basis of the Constitution and in complete conformity with it.

Article 111. Drafts for amendments to the Constitution may be presented by the Presidium of the People's Assembly, the Council of Ministers, or two-fifths of the deputies.

The approval of the Constitution and of amendments is made by a two-thirds majority of all deputies.

Article 112. This Constitution enters into force immediately. Tirana, 28 December 1976. No. 5506.

Haxhi Lleshi
Chairman of the Presidium of the People's Assembly of the People's Socialist Republic of Albania

Telo Mezini
Secretary of the Presidium of the People's Assembly of the People's Socialist Republic of Albania

BULGARIA

INTRODUCTION

Ivan Sipkov

Since the formation of the modern Bulgarian State in 1878, Bulgarian history has been distinguished, from the point of view of the law of state, by two major epochs: the period of the constitutional-parliamentary monarchy and the period of the people's republic. Accordingly, Bulgarian legal history ranges over two basic laws: (a) the Tirnovo Constitution of 16 April 1879, and (b) the Constitution of the People's Republic of 6 December 1947, with its variant of 18 May 1971.

During the time of transition, the Fatherland Front Government, which took power on 9 September 1944, declared in its Political Program[1] that the Tirnovo Constitution of 1879 should be restored, *i.e.* applied. However, the Law to Hold a Referendum of 2 August 1946,[2] is to be considered to a certain extent as an organic law having the significance and the task of a provisory and temporary constitution, for the Tirnovo Constitution had actually been in abeyance since 9 September 1944.

Formally, the second period began when the Constitution of the People's Republic was adopted by the (First Communist) Grand National Assembly on 4 December 1947.[3] This Assembly, elected on 27 October 1946, was considered a constituent one, according to Section 8 of the Law to Hold a Referendum and the law prescribing the manner in which the 1946 elections were to be carried out. The first Constitution of the Communist Government went into effect after publication in the *Dŭrzhaven Vestnik*. It was also known as the "Dimitrov Constitution" and was considered a close copy of the "Stalin Constitution" of 1936.

Only ten years later the Bulgarian Communist Party decided, at its VIIth Congress held in 1958,[4] to write a new constitution. The Third National Assembly, at its 3rd session of 14 March 1959,[5] appointed a Commission to prepare a draft for the amendment of the Constitution "to be introduced in the proper manner at one of the next sessions of the National Assembly." The Commission consisted of 33 members and a chairman, and it held its first meeting on 10 May 1959.[6] No deadline was given to the Commission and it submitted no draft; it only amended Articles 18, 19, and 47 of the Dimitrov Constitution.[7]

Introduction

The parliamentary groups of the Bulgarian Communist Party and the Bulgarian National Peasants' Union, at their meeting of 4 November 1961, decided to postpone discussion of the question of the "total amendment" (revision) of the Constitution to the Fourth National Assembly. At the VIIIth Congress of the BCP (November 1962), the Commission's chairman made a report on the work of this Commission. Indeed, several years later the Fourth National Assembly appointed, on 7 September 1964, another Constitutional Commission to prepare a draft of a new Constitution,[8] consisting of 60 members and a chairman, Todor Zhivkov, the present Prime Minister of the country. At the IXth BCP Congress, the decision was made that the Constitutional Commission should, among other things, legalize the role of the Communist Party. However, this body only amended Article 18, para. 2 of the basic law.[9]

A third commission to prepare a draft of a new constitution, consisting of 78 members under the chairmanship of Todor Zhivkov, was appointed by the Fifth National Assembly on 15 March 1968.[10] This Commission[11] presented on 30 March 1971, the new draft constitution to the National Assembly after being discussed in some 30,000 meetings, in which more than three million people participated. It retained the term "People's Republic", but defined Bulgaria as a "Socialist State", and included a provision for a State Council—a new constitutional organ with extensive powers. In his report to the 16th session of the National Assembly, held on 7 May 1971, the Chairman of the Constitutional Commission, Todor Zhivkov, stated that the new Constitution has the Program of the Bulgarian Communist Party as its theoretical basis and that the BCP is given constitutional recognition as a leading force in the state and society.[15]

Finally, in a decision of the National Assembly of 8 May 1971, published on the same day in *Dŭrzhaven Vestnik*, it was announced that the New Constitution of the Republic would be adopted "by an all-people referendum".[12] On the same day, a Law was published calling for the holding of a referendum on 16 May 1971.[13] The results were given on 18 May 1971, when the National Assembly declared its adoption; the new text was published in *Dŭrzhaven Vestnik* on 18 May 1971,[14] and it entered into force on this day.

As of 1 January 1979, no changes were made to the 1971 Constitution.

NOTES

1. *Rabotnichesko delo* (Sofia), daily newspaper, 18 September 1944.
2. Law to Hold a Referendum for the Abolition of the Monarchy and the Proclamation of the People's Republic and to Elect a Grand National Assembly, *Dŭrzhaven Vestnik* (official law gazette of Bulgaria, cited as *DV*), No. 174, 2 August 1946.
3. *DV* No. 284, 6 December 1947.
4. Seventh Congress of the Bulgarian Communist Party (hereinafter as BCP), Sofia, 1958, *Stenographic Minutes*, 928.
5. *Izvestiia na Prezidiuma na Narodnoto Sŭbranie* (official law gazette of Bulgaria during 1950–1961, cited as *IPNS*), No. 22, 17 March 1959, Appointment of a Commission for the Preparation of a Draft for the Revision of the Constitution.
6. *Rabotnichesko delo*, No. 162, 11 May 1959.
7. *IPNS* No. 89, 7 November 1961.
8. *DV* No. 73, 15 September 1964, Appointment of a Commission for the Preparation of a Draft of a New Constitution.
9. *DV* No. 97, 10 December 1965.
10. *DV* No. 22, 19 March 1968. Appointment of a Commission for the Preparation of a Constitution of the People's Republic of Bulgaria.
11. This Commission also submitted amendments to the Constitution (Sections 30, para. 2 and 48), *DV* No. 89, 19 November 1969.
12. *DV* No. 36, 8 May 1971.
13. *DV* No. 36, 8 May 1971. Law on Holding a Referendum for the Adoption of a New Constitution.
14. *DV* No. 39, 18 May 1971.
15. Todor Zhivkov, *Za Novata Konstitutsiia na N.R. Bŭlgariia* (On the New Constitution of the People's Republic of Bulgaria), Sofia 1971, 13.

CONSTITUTION OF THE PEOPLE'S REPUBLIC OF BULGARIA OF 18 MAY 1971

Preamble	38
Socio-Political Organization	39
Socio-Economic Organization	41
Basic Rights and Duties of the Citizens	45
National Assembly	50
State Council	55
Council of Ministers (Government)	58
People's Councils	61
Courts and Public Prosecutor's Office	63
Coat-of-Arms, Seal, Flag, Capital	66
Creation and Amendment of the Constitution	66
Transitional Provision	67

CONSTITUTION OF THE PEOPLE'S REPUBLIC OF BULGARIA*

Dŭrzhaven Vestnik 1971 No. 39.

We,
the citizens of the People's Republic of Bulgaria,
heirs to great revolutionary traditions, forged in age-long struggles for freedom and human rights, for people's power and a socialist reorganization of society,
whereas we base ourselves
on the historic victory of the Ninth of September Socialist Revolution of 1944, won under the leadership of the Bulgarian Communist Party and with the decisive help of the Soviet army—liberator of the working class, the toiling peasants, and the people's intelligentsia, united in the Fatherland Front;
on the successful development of our people's democratic state;
on the historically created unity of purpose and action between the Bulgarian Communist Party and the Bulgarian National Peasants' Union;
on the victory of socialism, which established complete supremacy of public property over the means of production and forever abolished the exploitation of man by man;
on the developed modern industry and developed cooperative rural economy, built with the heroic labor of a free people, which secure conditions for a constant increase of the people's well-being;
on the great successes, achieved in the field of education, science, and culture;
whereas we rely
on the cooperation and mutual assistance with the Union of Soviet Socialist Republics and the other countries of the socialist community;
on the support of the international communist and workers' movement and on all progressive forces in the world;
firmly resolved
to build under the leadership of the Bulgarian Communist Party and in fulfillment of its Program, a developed socialist society in our country, to increase by our labor the socialist property, the material and spiritual wealth of the people, to develop and delve socialist

* Translated by Ivan Sipkov.

democracy, to create ever more favorable conditions for the versatile blossoming of the free human personality;

to strengthen and expand the indissoluble alliance, friendship, and all-round cooperation with the Union of Soviet Socialist Republics and the other fraternal socialist countries;

to support the just struggle of the people for independence and social progress;

to cooperate for the consolidation of world peace, for understanding among all peoples of the earth;

whereas we point out the importance of the Constitution of the People's Republic of Bulgaria of 1947, and whereas we further develop its fundamental principles in view of the new stage in the building of a socialist society in our Homeland

have adopted
in an all-people voting
the present
Constitution.

Chapter I. Socio-Political Organization

Article 1. (1) The People's Republic of Bulgaria is a socialist state of the working people from town and village, headed by the working class.

(2) The leading force in society and the state is the Bulgarian Communist Party.

(3) The Bulgarian Communist Party shall direct the building up of a developed socialist society in the People's Republic of Bulgaria in close fraternal cooperation with the Bulgarian National Peasants' Union.

Article 2. (1) In the People's Republic of Bulgaria, all power emanates from the people and belongs to the people.

(2) The people shall exercise this power through freely elected representative organs—a National Assembly and people's councils—or directly.

Article 3. (1) The state shall serve the people by:

defending their interests and socialist achievements;

guiding in a planned manner the socio-economic development of the country;

creating conditions for a continuous improvement of the well-being, education, and public health of the people, as well as for the all-round development of science and culture;

securing man's free development, guaranteeing his rights and protecting his dignity;

organizing the defense of the nation's independence, and state sovereignty and territorial integrity of the country;

developing and consolidating friendship, cooperation, and mutual assistance with the Union of Soviet Socialist Republics and the other socialist countries;

pursuing a policy of peace and understanding with all countries and peoples.

(2) In carrying out its tasks, the state shall rely ever more widely on the public organizations.

Article 4. (1) The main directions in the development of the state in the building of a developed socialist society are:

constant broadening of democracy;

improvement of the organization and activities of the state apparatus;

strengthening of the people's control over the work of the state organs.

(2) The socialist state shall contribute in the development of the socialist society into a communist one.

Article 5. The fundamental principles on which the political system of society is built and functions are: national sovereignty, unity of power, democratic centralism, socialist democratism, legality, and socialist internationalism.

Article 6. (1) The representative organs shall be elected on the basis of universal, equal, and direct suffrage by secret ballot.

(2) The term of the mandate of the National Assembly shall be five years and of the people's councils, two and a half years.

(3) Eligible to vote and to be elected shall be all citizens of the People's Republic of Bulgaria who have completed eighteen years of age, irrespective of sex, ethnic origin, race, creed, education, occupation, official or social status, and property situation, with the exception of those placed under complete tutelage.

(4) The manner of electing the representative organs shall be determined by law.

Article 7. (1) The deputies and the councillors shall be responsible and accountable to their electors. They may be recalled even before the expiry of the term for which they are elected.

Bulgaria

(2) The recall of deputies shall take place by decision of the electors in the manner determined by the law.

Article 8. (1) The People's Republic of Bulgaria shall be governed strictly in accordance with the Constitution and the laws of the country.

(2) Strict observance of the Constitution and the laws shall be a basic duty of all state organs, officials, public organizations, and of the citizens.

(3) The consolidation of legality and the prevention of crimes and violations of the laws shall be the duty of the state, public organizations, and citizens.

Article 9. (1) The rights, freedoms, and duties provided in the Constitution shall be exercised and implemented on the basis of the latter, except when it stipulates that the conditions and manner for their realization shall be determined by the law.

(2) Rights and freedoms shall not be exercised to the detriment of public interests.

Article 10. (1) The public organizations shall unite and enlist the different strata of the population in socialist building, express and defend their specific interests, and work for raising their socialist consciousness.

(2) The public organizations shall ever more assist the state organs in the implementation of their tasks.

(3) The public organizations shall also perform state functions entrusted to them with their consent.

Article 11. The Fatherland Front is an embodiment of the alliance of the working class, the toiling peasants, and the people's intelligentsia. It is the social support of the people's power, a mass school for the patriotic and communist education of the population and the enlisting of the working people into the government of the country.

Article 12. The People's Republic of Bulgaria belongs to the world socialist community, which is one of the main conditions for its independence and all-round development.

Chapter II. Socio-Economic Organization

Article 13. (1) The economic system of the People's Republic of Bulgaria is socialist. It is based on the public ownership of the means of production, excludes the exploitation of man by man, and develops into a communist economy in a planned manner.

(2) The development of the socialist economy is basis for the all-round progress of society and of the free human personality, for the broadening of socialist democracy, for the people's well-being and the upswing of the Homeland.

(3) The economy of the People's Republic of Bulgaria develops as part of the world socialist economic system.

Article 14. The forms of ownership in the People's Republic of Bulgaria are: state (all-people's) ownership, cooperative ownership, ownership of the public organizations, and personal ownership.

Article 15. (1) State (all-people's) ownership is a higher form of socialist ownership and constitutes a unified fund. It determines the socialist character of the ownership of the cooperative and public organizations and enjoys special protection.

(2) The forms of public ownership gradually develop and draw closer together, eventually to evolve into a unified all-people's ownership.

Article 16. (1) Plants and factories, banks, underground resources, natural sources of power, nuclear energy, forests, pastures, waters, roads, railway, water and air transport, posts, telegraphs, telephones, radio and television are state (all-people's) ownership.

(2) In cases provided by the law, the cooperatives and public organizations may possess means of production and other property.

Article 17. (1) The state shall exercise its right of ownership by setting up economic and other organizations and participate in state-cooperative enterprises to which it grants property to be managed and administered, as well as through the activity of these organizations aimed at attainment of their granted or acquired rights.

(2) The state may grant to cooperative and public organizations and to citizens the right to use certain state property.

(3) The use of forests, pastures, waters, and quarries by cooperative organizations and citizens shall be regulated by law.

Article 18. The state economic organizations shall exercise their activity in accordance with the principles of self-support.

Article 19. (1) Cooperative ownership belongs to the collectives of working people, voluntarily united for the joint performance of economic activities, to cooperative unions, and to inter-cooperative organizations.

(2) The right of cooperative ownership shall be exercised in the interest of society and of the cooperators.

Article 20. (1) The ownership of the public organizations shall serve for the achievement of their tasks, including the implementation of the activities entrusted to them by state organs, as well as for the satisfaction of public interests.

(2) The public organizations may perform economic activities in accordance with their tasks in cases permitted by the law.

Article 21. (1) The citizens of the People's Republic of Bulgaria shall enjoy the right of personal ownership over property and objects for meeting their own needs and those of their families.

(2) Personal ownership are also the small means of production and the output of the households of cooperators and other working people from the land, placed at their disposal for personal use, as well as the small means of production used by the working people for the performance of other auxiliary activities and the output therefrom. The kind and number of the small means of production which may be possessed in an auxiliary economy shall be determined by law.

(3) For the purpose of satisfying the housing needs of the citizens, the state shall concede the right of construction on state lands and grant credits.

(4) The state shall protect personal ownership acquired by work and in any other lawful manner, including savings.

(5) The right of personal ownership may be entailed or restricted only by a law or with the consent of the owner.

(6) Citizens may not exercise their right of personal ownership and their other property rights to the detriment of the public interest.

Article 22. (1) The state shall direct the people's economy and the other sectors of public life on the basis of unified plans for socio-economic development with a view to meeting ever more fully the constantly growing material and cultural needs of the citizens.

(2) In its activity, the state shall rely on the initiative and the creative activities of the labor collectives, research institutes, and public organizations, and shall make use of moral stimuli and collective and individual material incentives.

(3) In elaborating and executing the plans for the socio-economic development, the state shall make effective use of the achievements of science and technology, the labor and material resources, and the advantages of the international socialist division of labor.

(4) The state budget shall be drawn up on the basis of the unified plan for socio-economic development.

Article 23. (1) The state shall encourage the cooperatives and their unions and support their activities.

(2) The state shall render all-round support to the labor-cooperative agricultural forms.

Article 24. The collectives of the working people shall participate directly and through organs elected by them in the management of the economic activity.

Article 25. The citizens may engage in farming, artisan, and other economic activities with their personal labor and with the labor of the members of their families, under conditions determined by the law. The law shall determine what means of production may be owned by these citizens.

Article 26. (1) Copyrights of works of science, literature, and art, as well as the rights of inventors and innovators shall be protected by the state.

(2) The state, cooperative, and public organizations shall create conditions conducive to the development of the creative activity and to using the works of authors, inventors, and innovators for the economic and cultural development of society.

(3) Authors, inventors, and innovators may not use their rights inconsistent with the public interests.

Article 27. The right of inheritance shall be recognized and guaranteed.

Article 28. The state may expropriate or restrict the right of ownership over the property of citizens, cooperatives, and public organizations for state and public needs against just compensation. The procedure of expropriation and the manner of compensation shall be determined by law.

Article 29. (1) The state may be granted by law the exclusive right to engage in certain kinds of economic activity.

(2) Foreign trade shall be an exclusive right of the state.

Article 30. (1) The land as a basic natural resource and means of production shall be protected and utilized in a manner most useful to society.
(2) The labor-cooperative agricultural farms shall use gratuitously the lands pooled by the cooperators, by other persons and organizations, or placed at their disposal by the state.
(3) The purpose of arable farm lands, pastures, and forests may be changed in the manner established by law.

Article 31. The protection and preservation of the nature and natural resources, the water, air, and soil, as well as the cultural monuments shall be an obligation of the state organs and enterprises, the cooperatives and public organizations, as well as a duty of every citizen.

Article 32. (1) Labor is a basic socio-economic factor.
(2) In the People's Republic of Bulgaria, the socialist principle "From each according to his abilities, to each according to his work" shall be applied. The public funds for satisfying the needs of the citizens shall be continuously increased.
(3) The state shall attend to the raising of the labor qualification and productive experience of the citizens. The protection of labor shall be regulated by law.

Article 33. (1) The state shall create the necessary conditions for the development of science and technology with a view to securing a scientific management of society, scientific and technical progress, and all-round economic and cultural growth.
(2) The state organs, the economic and other organizations, and all citizens shall be obliged to introduce the achievements of science and technology in all fields of public life.

Chapter III. Basic Rights and Duties of the Citizens

Article 34. Bulgarian citizenship shall be acquired and lost in the manner established by law.

Article 35. (1) All citizens of the People's Republic of Bulgaria shall be equal before the law.
(2) No privileges or limitations of rights based on ethnic belong-

ing, origin, creed, sex, race, education, social and material status shall be allowed.

(3) The state shall secure the equality of the citizens by creating conditions and opportunities for the exercise of their rights and the fulfillment of their duties.

(4) Every propagation of hatred or humiliation of man because of race, national or religious affiliation shall be forbidden and shall be punishable.

Article 36. Women and men shall have equal rights in the People's Republic of Bulgaria.

Article 37. Women-mothers shall enjoy protection and care on behalf of the state, the economic, and public organizations by securing a leave of absence before and after childbirth, by preserving her labor remuneration, free obstetric and medical care, maternity homes, alleviation in her work, and extension of the network of children's establishments, of the enterprises for communal and folk-life services, and of the public catering.

Article 38. (1) Marriage and family shall be under the protection of the state.

(2) Civil marriage solely shall be legal.

(3) The spouses shall have equal rights and obligations in marriage and in the family. Parents shall have the right and obligation to attend to the upbringing of their children and to their communist education.

(4) Children born out of wedlock shall enjoy equal rights with those born in wedlock.

Article 39. (1) The education of the young people in a communist spirit is a duty of the entire society.

(2) The family, the school, the state organs, and the public organizations shall devote special care to the intellectual, moral, aesthetic, cultural, and physical development of the young people, and to their labor training and polytechnical education.

(3) Youth shall enjoy special protection.

Article 40. (1) Citizens shall have the right to work.

(2) Every citizen shall have the right freely to choose his profession.

(3) The state shall guarantee the right to work by developing the socialist socio-economic system.

Article 41. (1) Work shall be remunerated in accordance with its quantity and quality.

(2) Working people shall have the right to safe and hygienic conditions of labor, which is secured by the introduction of the achievements of science and technology.

Article 42. (1) Citizens shall have the right to rest.

(2) This right shall be secured by reducing their working days without diminishing their labor remuneration or infringing upon other labor rights, by paid annual leave, and by a wide network of holiday houses, clubs, public libraries, houses of culture, and other places for leisure and culture.

Article 43. (1) Citizens shall have the right to insurance, pensioning, and assistance in case of incapacity for work due to sickness, accident, maternity, disability, old age, or death, and when bringing up a child, as well as to allowances in the cases established by law.

(2) This right shall be implemented by a unified system of social insurance and by setting aside the necessary funds from the national income for financing the insurances.

(3) The insured shall take part in the management of social insurance.

Article 44. Minor, underage, incapacitated, and old people, who have no relatives or have been deprived of the care of their relatives, shall enjoy the special protection of the state and of society.

Article 45. (1) Citizens shall have the right to free education in all types and grades of educational establishments under conditions determined by law.

(2) The educational establishments shall belong to the state.

(3) Education shall be based on the achievements of modern science and the Marxist-Leninist ideology.

(4) Primary education shall be compulsory.

(5) The state shall create conditions for the introduction of secondary education for all.

(6) The state shall further education, improve the general conditions for work at the educational establishments, grant scholarships, and encourage students who have displayed particular talents.

(7) Citizens of non-Bulgarian origin, in addition to the compulsory study of the Bulgarian language, shall have the right to study also their own language.

Article 46. (1) Creativeness in the field of science, art, and culture shall serve the people and develop in a communist spirit.

(2) The state shall devote special care to the development of science, art, and culture by setting up higher educational establishments, scientific-research institutes, publishing houses, libraries, museums, art galleries, theaters, cinemas, radio, and television.

Article 47. (1) The state shall devote all-round care to the people's health by organizing therapeutic, preventive, and other health establishments and services.

(2) The state and the public organizations shall disseminate health education and culture among the people and encourage physical culture and tourism.

(3) Every citizen shall have the right to free medical care.

(4) The state and the public organizations shall devote special care to the health of children and adolescents.

Article 48. (1) The freedom and inviolability of the person shall be guaranteed.

(2) No one can be detained for more than twenty-four hours without a decision of the court or the public prosecutor.

Article 49. The home shall be inviolable. Without the consent of the dweller no one can enter the dwelling or its premises, nor make a search there, except in the cases and under the conditions provided in the law.

Article 50. Every citizen shall have the right of defense against illegal interference in his personal or family life and infringement upon his honor and good name.

Article 51. The secrecy of correspondence, telephone conversations, and telecommunications shall be inviolable except in case of mobilization, state of war, or when authorized by the court or the public prosecutor.

Article 52. (1) Citizens may form organizations for political, professional, cultural, artistic, scientific, religious, sports, and other non-economic purposes.

(2) Citizens may unite in cooperatives for joint economic activity.

(3) Organizations directed against the socialist order of the People's Republic of Bulgaria and the rights of the citizens, which

propagate a fascist or other anti-democratic ideology, shall be prohibited.

(4) The public organizations and cooperatives may form unions or other associations.

Article 53. (1) The citizens shall be guaranteed freedom of conscience and of creed. They may perform religious rites and conduct anti-religious propaganda.

(2) The church shall be separated from the state.

(3) The legal status, the questions concerning the material support, and the right of internal organization and self-government of the different religious communities shall be regulated by law.

(4) The misuse of the church and religion for political purposes, as well as the setting up of political organizations on a religious basis, shall be prohibited.

(5) Religion shall be no justification for refusing to fulfill duties imposed by the Constitution or the laws.

Article 54. (1) Citizens shall enjoy freedom of speech, press, assembly, meetings, and demonstrations.

(2) These freedoms shall be guaranteed by placing the necessary material conditions for that purpose at the disposal of the citizens.

Article 55. Citizens shall have the right to make requests, complaints, and petitions. This right shall be implemented in the manner established by law.

Article 56. (1) The state shall be responsible for the damages caused by illegal acts or illegal official actions of its organs or officials.

(2) Every citizen shall have the right to initiate court proceedings against officials for crimes committed while performing their duties.

(3) Citizens shall have the right, in accordance with the conditions established by law, to compensation by officials for damages inflicted on them by the illegal performance of their duties.

Article 57. Bulgarian citizens abroad shall enjoy the protection of the People's Republic of Bulgaria and shall be obliged to fulfill their duties towards it.

Article 58. Citizens shall be obliged strictly and in good faith to observe and enforce the Constitution and the laws of the country.

Article 59. (1) Every able-bodied citizen shall be obliged to do socially useful work in accordance with his abilities and qualification.

(2) The fulfillment of the labor obligations shall be a matter of honor for every member of the socialist society.

Article 60. Citizens shall be obliged to guard and increase socialist property as an inviolable foundation of the socialist system, and to cooperate in strengthening the political, economic, and defensive might of the Homeland, the development of culture, and the prosperity of the people.

Article 61. (1) The defense of the Fatherland is a supreme duty and a matter of honor for every citizen.

(2) Treason and betrayal of the Fatherland are the gravest crimes against the people. They shall be punished with all the severity of the law.

Article 62. Military service shall be compulsory for all citizens in accordance with the law.

Article 63. (1) Every citizen shall be obliged to help preserve and consolidate peace.

(2) War incitement and propaganda shall be prohibited and punishable by law as grave crimes against peace and mankind.

Article 64. The tax duties of citizens shall be determined by law according to their income and property.

Article 65. The People's Republic of Bulgaria shall grant the right of asylum to foreigners persecuted for defending the interests of the working people, for participating in the national-liberation struggle, for progressive political, scientific, and artistic activity, for fighting racial discrimination or in defense of peace.

Chapter IV. National Assembly

Article 66. (1) The National Assembly is the supreme representative organ which expresses the will of the people and their sovereignty.

(2) The National Assembly is the supreme organ of state power.

Article 67. The National Assembly shall combine the legislative and executive activity of the state and exercise supreme control.

Article 68. The National Assembly shall consist of 400 deputies elected in constituencies with an equal number of inhabitants.

Article 69. (1) The mandate of the National Assembly shall end with the expiry of the term for which it was elected.

(2) The National Assembly may dissolve itself even before the expiry of the term of its mandate. In that case, it shall continue to perform its functions until the election of a new National Assembly.

(3) If the term of the mandate of the National Assembly expires during war time or in other exceptional circumstances, it may prolong it. It may also prolong the term of its mandate if a state of war is declared or if other exceptional circumstances set in during the time of elections. In those cases, elections for a new National Assembly shall be held within six months after the causes which necessitated the prolongation of its mandate have ceased to exist.

(4) The National Assembly may also prolong the term of its mandate up to one year for other important reasons.

Article 70. (1) Elections for the National Assembly shall be held two months after the expiry of its mandate at the latest.

(2) The newly-elected National Assembly shall be summoned for sessions one month after the elections at the latest.

Article 71. (1) The National Assembly shall be summoned for sessions by the State Council at least three times a year.

(2) The State Council shall also summon the National Assembly for session when over one-fifth of the deputies demand it.

Article 72. The first session of the newly-elected National Assembly shall be opened by the eldest deputy. Under his chairmanship, the deputies shall elect the President and the Deputy-Presidents of the National Assembly.

Article 73. (1) The President of the National Assembly shall:
 a) preside over the sessions of the National Assembly;
 b) submit a draft agenda of the sessions of the National Assembly;
 c) certify with his signature the text of the acts adopted by the National Assembly;
 d) organize the international relations of the National Assembly.

(2) The President of the National Assembly may entrust a Vice-President with the performance of these activities.

Article 74. (1) The National Assembly itself shall check the legality of the elections of the deputies. For that purpose, at its first session it shall elect from among its midst a Committee for Auditing the Elections, which at the second session after the election, at the latest, shall come forward with a conclusion before the National Assembly about their legality. The Committee shall do this also in case of partial elections of deputies.

(2) When the National Assembly finds that an election was held in violation of the law, it shall cancel it.

(3) The deputies shall take an oath before the National Assembly.

Article 75. The National Assembly itself shall establish its internal organization and the order of its work by a regulation.

Article 76. (1) The National Assembly shall elect from among its members standing and interim committees as its organs. It shall direct and control their activity.

(2) The committees shall be responsible for their activity and render an account to the National Assembly.

(3) The standing committees shall help the activity of the National Assembly, exercise on its behalf control over the ministries and the other departments and the local state organs, and assist in the enforcement of the laws and other acts adopted by the National Assembly.

(4) Interim committees shall be elected for issues which are not permanent in character, as well as for investigations and inquiries.

(5) All state organs, officials, public organizations, and citizens shall be obliged to present to the committees all the necessary information and documents related to their work.

Article 77. The National Assembly is the sole legislative organ of the People's Republic of Bulgaria and supreme organizer of the planned direction of social development.

Article 78. The National Assembly shall:
1. Implement the supreme direction of the state's domestic and foreign policy.
2. Adopt and amend the Constitution.
3. Determine which questions and in what order they are to be decided by referendum.
4. Adopt, amend, and repeal the laws.
5. Take measures for the enforcement of the laws and its other acts.

6. Adopt the unified plans for the socio-economic development of the country and the reports on their execution.

7. Adopt the state budget and the government report on the execution of the budget for the preceding year.

8. Establish taxes and fix their rates.

It may entrust the Council of Ministers with fixing the rates of taxes owed by state organizations.

9. Grant amnesty.

10. Decide the questions of the declaration of war and the conclusion of peace.

11. Appoint and remove from office the commander-in-chief of the Armed Forces.

12. Decide questions about changing the frontiers of the People's Republic.

13. Ratify and denounce international treaties.

14. Establish, close down, merge, and rename ministries and other departments of ministerial rank.

It may also create state and public organs of ministerial rank.

15. Determine the tasks and the organizations of the State Council, the Council of Ministers, the people's councils, the courts, and the Public Prosecutor's Office.

Within the system of the Council of Ministers, it may set up its own organs for direction and coordination in the administration of the state, and may determine the decisions as to which of them shall have the authority of government acts.

16. Elect and remove from office the State Council, the Council of Ministers, the Supreme Court, and the Chief Public Prosecutor of the People's Republic.

17. Exercise supreme control over the observance of the Constitution and the laws.

18. Exercise supreme control over the activity of the state organs.

19. It may entrust consenting public organizations with the performance of certain state functions.

Article 79. (1) The National Assembly shall adopt laws, decisions, declarations, and addresses.

(2) The laws and decisions of the National Assembly shall be binding for all state organs, public organizations, and individuals.

Article 80. (1) The right of legislative initiative shall be vested in the State Council, the Council of Ministers, the standing committees of the National Assembly, the deputies, the Supreme Court, and the Chief Public Prosecutor.

(2) The public organizations, in the person of the National Council of the Fatherland Front, the Central Council of Trade Unions, the Central Committee of the Dimitrov Young Communists League, and the Administrative Council of the Central Cooperative Union, shall also have the right of legislative initiative on questions pertaining to their activities.

Article 81. The National Assembly may be convened for a session if more than half of all deputies are present. Its decisions shall be taken by a simple majority of the deputies present, except when the Constitution requires another majority.

Article 82. The sittings of the National Assembly shall be public, except when it decides that important state interests require that some of the sittings be held behind closed doors.

Article 83. (1) Bills shall be adopted after two votings, which are to be carried out at different sittings. After being adopted at the first voting, the bill shall be sent to the respective committees for additional discussion before being put forward for a second voting.

(2) Upon decision of the National Assembly, the two votings of the bill may, as an exception, take place at one sitting and without additional discussion in the committees.

Article 84. (1) The laws, decisions, declarations, and addresses adopted by the National Assembly shall be published by the State Council in the State Gazette not later than 15 days after their adoption.

(2) The law shall enter into force three days after its publication, except when another term is specified in the law itself.

(3) The other acts of the National Assembly shall enter into force upon their adoption by the National Assembly.

Article 85. (1) The National Assembly shall see to it that the laws do not contradict the Constitution.

(2) It alone shall decide whether a law contradicts the Constitution and whether the conditions for its issuance required by the Constitution have been observed.

Article 86. The deputies shall be guided in their activity by the all-people interests and by the interests of their electors.

Article 87. (1) The deputies shall have the right to address interpellations to the Council of Ministers or to its individual members who shall be obliged to reply.

(2) Interpellations made at a session shall be answered at the same session or, upon decision of the National Assembly, at the following session.

(3) Interpellations made between sessions shall be answered at the following session.

(4) If the National Assembly so decides, discussions may take place on the interpellations and a decision may be taken.

Article 88. The deputies may not be detained and penal proceedings may not be initiated against them, except for grave offenses and this with the authorization of the National Assembly and if it is not in session, of the State Council. No authorization for detainment shall be required when a deputy is caught in the very act of a flagrant grave offense, in which case the National Assembly and, if it is not in session, the State Council shall be immediately informed.

Article 89. The deputies shall not be held criminally and disciplinarily responsible for the opinions expressed by them and for their voting in the National Assembly.

Chapter V. State Council

Article 90. (1) The State Council of the People's Republic of Bulgaria is the supreme continuously functioning organ of state power, which combines the taking of decisions with their execution.

(2) The State Council, as a supreme organ of the National Assembly, shall secure the unity of the legislative with the executive activity.

(3) It shall be responsible and give account to the National Assembly on its entire activity.

Article 91. Within the framework of the Constitution, the State Council shall organize and control the fulfillment of the basic tasks deriving from the laws and decisions of the National Assembly, exercise general direction and control over the work of the Council of Ministers and of the remaining state organs, take decisions, and implement executive and administrative activity on fundamental questions of the state government.

Article 92. (1) The State Council shall consist of a President, Deputy-Presidents, a Secretary, and members.

(2) The National Assembly shall elect the State Council from among the deputies at its first session with a majority of more than half of all deputies.

(3) The mandate of the State Council shall continue until the newly-elected National Assembly elects a State Council.

(4) The members of the State Council shall take an oath before the National Assembly.

Article 93. The State Council shall:

1. Call elections for a National Assembly and people's councils.

2. Determine the date for holding a referendum when there is a decision of the National Assembly on what question and in what order the referendum should be held.

3. Summon the National Assembly to sessions. Summon the National Assembly whose mandate has expired, in order to decide the question of prolonging the term of its mandate.

4. Exercise the right of legislative initiative.

5. Determine with regard to which bills, introduced into the National Assembly, a referendum should be held.

6. Publish the acts adopted by the National Assembly in the State Gazette.

7. Issue edicts and other legal acts on the basic questions deriving from the laws and decisions of the National Assembly.

8. Interpret the laws and normative edicts which are binding for all.

9. Implement the general direction of the defense and security of the country.

10. Appoint and remove from office the members of the State Defense Committee.

11. Appoint and remove from office the staff of the high command of the Armed Forces and award high military titles.

12. Represent the People's Republic of Bulgaria in its international relations.

13. Appoint, recall, and remove from office, on the proposal of the Council of Ministers, the diplomatic and consular representatives of the People's Republic of Bulgaria in other countries.

14. Ratify and denounce international treaties.

15. Establish diplomatic and consular ranks.

16. Set up and close down departments of non-ministerial rank, and appoint and remove from office their heads.

17. Exercise control over the activity of the Council of Ministers and the heads of the ministries and other departments.

18. Exercise control over the strict observance of the laws and

Bulgaria

other acts of the National Assembly, as well as over acts issued by itself.

19. Repeal the illegal or irregular acts of the Council of Ministers and the heads of the ministries or other departments.

20. Repeal the illegal or irregular acts of the people's councils and their executive and administrative organs.

21. Exercise the right of granting pardon.

22. Remit uncollectable debts to the state.

23. Establish orders and medals and award them.

24. Introduce honorary titles and bestow them.

25. Set up and close down administrative-territorial units. Change the boundaries of municipalities, town wards, and districts, and determine their administrative seats.

26. Grant, restore, and deprive of Bulgarian citizenship.

27. Grant the right of asylum.

Article 94. The State Council, in addition to the authorities under Article 93, during the period between sessions of the National Assembly, shall:

1. Implement the general direction of the domestic and foreign policy of the state.

2. In urgent cases, amend or supplement individual provisions of the laws by edicts.

Issue edicts on questions of a matter of principle, affecting the executive and administrative activity of the state.

The State Council shall submit the edicts issued under this paragraph to the National Assembly for approval at its following session.

3. Hear reports on the work of the Council of Ministers, or of any of its individual members, and take the appropriate decisions.

4. Upon recommendation of the President of the Council of Ministers, remove from office and appoint individual members of the Council of Ministers. The State Council is obliged to submit this decision to the National Assembly for approval at its next session.

5. Appoint and release from duty the Commander-in-Chief of the Armed Forces. This decision is submitted to the National Assembly for approval at its next session.

6. Implement the general direction and coordinate the work of the people's councils and the executive and administrative organs of the state.

7. Exercise general control over the activity of the Public Prosecutor's Office.

8. Proclaim general or partial mobilization, martial law, or any other state of emergency.

9. Take measures for collective defense jointly with other countries.

10. Proclaim a state of war in the case of an armed attack against the People's Republic of Bulgaria, or in the case where an international obligation for mutual defense has to be promptly carried out. The State Council shall summon the National Assembly to session to make a pronouncement on its own decisions.

Article 95. In case of war, if there is no possibility of convening the National Assembly, in addition to the mandate given to it, the State Council shall:

1. Issue edicts whereby laws may be repealed or amended, or legislatively unsettled matters may be settled. The State Council shall submit these edicts to the National Assembly for approval at its next session.

2. Adopt the unified plans for socio-economic development and the budget, as well as the reports on their execution.

3. Elect and remove from office the Council of Ministers, the Supreme Court, and the Chief Public Prosecutor.

Article 96. (1) The President of the State Council shall:

1. Organize and direct the work of the State Council.

2. Receive the credentials and recall letters of the foreign diplomatic representatives in the country.

(2) The State Council may entrust the President of the State Council with the implementation of some of its rights in the manner and in the cases determined by the law.

Article 97. (1) The State Council shall issue edicts and adopt decisions, addresses, and declarations.

(2) The normative edicts of the State Council shall enter into force three days after their publication in the State Gazette, except when another term is specified in the edict.

(3) The remaining enactments of the State Council shall enter into force from the day of their adoption, except when another term is specified in them.

Chapter VI. Council of Ministers (Government)

Article 98. The Council of Ministers (the Government) is the supreme executive and administrative organ of state power.

Article 99. (1) The Council of Ministers shall consist of a President of the Council of Ministers, Deputy-Presidents of the Council of Ministers, ministers, and heads of departments with the rank of ministries.

(2) The members of the Council of Ministers shall head a ministry or department, respectively. On decision of the National Assembly, individual members of the Council of Ministers may not be in direct charge of a ministry or department.

Article 100. The National Assembly shall determine the number, kind, and names of the ministries and of other departments with the rank of ministries.

Article 101. (1) The National Assembly shall elect the President of the Council of Ministers and on his proposal, the Deputy-Presidents, and the remaining members of the Council of Ministers.

(2) Members of the Council of Ministers may also be persons who are not deputies.

(3) The members of the Council of Ministers shall take an oath before the National Assembly.

Article 102. (1) The Council of Ministers shall implement its activity under the direction and control of the National Assembly, and, when it is not in session, under the direction and control of the State Council.

(2) The Council of Ministers shall be responsible for its entire activity to the National Assembly and shall be obliged to report to it annually.

(3) When the National Assembly shall not be in session, the Council of Ministers shall be responsible and report to the State Council.

Article 103. The Council of Ministers shall:
1. Organize the implementation of the domestic and foreign policy of the state.
2. Exercise the right of legislative initiative.
3. Draw up the drafts of the unified plans for socio-economic development of the country and submit them to the National Assembly.
4. Elaborate the draft of the annual state budget and submit it to the National Assembly.
5. Organize, direct, and control the fulfillment of the unified plans for socio-economic development of the country and of the state budget.

6. Ensure the conditions for the realization of the rights and freedoms of the citizens.

7. Maintain public order and security in the country.

8. Implement the general command of the Armed Forces.

9. Conclude international treaties.

10. Approve and denounce international treaties which are not subject to ratification.

11. Direct, coordinate, and exercise immediate control over the activity of the ministries and the other departments.

12. Implement direction and control over the executive committees of the people's councils.

13. Organize the execution of the acts of the National Assembly, the State Council, as well as of the acts issued by it.

14. Repeal the illegal or irregular acts and actions of ministers and heads of other departments.

15. Repeal the illegal or irregular acts and actions of the executive committees of the people's councils.

16. Suspend the execution of illegal or irregular acts and actions of the people's councils and refer the question of their repeal to the State Council.

Article 104. (1) The Council of Ministers shall adopt regulations, resolutions, and decisions.

(2) The normative acts of the Council of Ministers shall be published in the State Gazette and shall enter into force three days after their publication, except when another term is specified in them. All other acts of the Council of Ministers shall enter into force from the day of their adoption, except when another term is specified in them.

Article 105. The Council of Ministers may assume direct control of certain sectors of the administration by forming for this purpose commissions, councils, general directorates, and offices which do not have the rank of ministries.

Article 106. The members of the Council of Ministers shall direct the respective ministries or other departments on the basis of the acts of the National Assembly, the State Council, and the Council of Ministers.

Article 107. (1) The ministers and heads of departments with the rank of ministries shall have the right, within the limits of their competence, to issue orders and to repeal the illegal or irregular acts and actions of the respective special organs of the people's councils.

(2) Under the same conditions, they shall have the right to suspend the acts and actions of the executive committees of the people's councils. If the executive committee does not cancel the suspended act, the Council of Ministers shall decide over the dispute.

Article 108. (1) The ministers and heads of other departments shall issue regulations, directives, instructions, and orders.

(2) The regulations, directives, and instructions shall enter into force three days after the date of their publication in the State Gazette, except when another term has been set in them, and the orders from the date of their issuance except when another is specified.

Chapter VII. People's Councils

Article 109. (1) The territory of the People's Republic of Bulgaria shall be divided into municipalities and districts. Sofia shall be divided into administrative-territorial city districts.

(2) Other administrative-territorial units may be set up by law.

Article 110. Organs of the state power and people's self-government in the municipalities, the city districts, and the districts shall be the municipal, city district, and district people's councils.

Article 111. (1) The people's councils shall consist of councillors who in their activity shall be guided by the all-people interests, the interests of population in the districts and municipalities, as well as by the interests of the population in their electoral districts.

(2) The representation provisions for the election of councillors shall be determined by law.

Article 112. The people's councils shall implement the state policy within their territory. They shall engage in activities aimed at the implementation of all-people tasks and decide upon questions of local significance.

Article 113. The people's councils shall combine the work on taking decisions and their enforcement.

Article 114. (1) The people's councils, within the limits of their competence, shall direct the development of the economy, and the health-social, communal folk-life, and cultural-educational activities within their territory.

(2) They shall carry out their activities by a proper coordination of the all-state and local interests, of the branch and territorial planning for the complex development of the respective administrative-territorial unit.

(3) The people's councils shall work out and adopt their own plan for a socio-economic development and a budget in accordance with the unified plan for the socio-economic development and with the state budget, and organize and control their fulfillment.

(4) Within the limits of their competence they shall direct, coordinate, and control the activity of the economic organizations, as well as that of the departments located within their territory.

(5) Within the limits of their competence, the people's councils shall supervise the observance of public order, as well as legality and the protection of the citizens' rights, the protection of socialist property, and the strengthening of the country's defense capacity.

Article 115. The people's councils shall adopt decisions, ordinances, regulations, and instructions.

Article 116. The district people's councils shall be summoned to sessions not less than four times a year, and the municipal and city district councils—not less than six times.

Article 117. When deciding more important questions within their competence, affecting the interests of the population of the respective administrative-territorial unit and an individual inhabited area, the people's councils may take decisions on holding a plebiscite, including a referendum.

Article 118. (1) The people's councils shall elect and remove from office executive committees, and set up standing or interim committees and special organs.

(2) The executive committee shall be an executive and administrative organ of the people's council, elected from among the councillors.

(3) The members of the committees shall be elected and removed from office by the people's council.

Article 119. Executive and administrative organs in the districts and municipalities outside the system of the people's councils may be set up only by law.

Article 120. In their activity, the people's councils shall rely on the initiative and broad participation of the population, and shall work in close interaction with the political, trade union, and other public organizations.

Article 121. The people's councils shall render an account on their activity to the electors at least once a year, in the manner and order determined in the law.

Article 122. The people's councils shall direct and control the activities of their organs and repeal their illegal or irregular acts and actions.

Article 123. The hierarchically-superior people's councils shall direct and control the activity of the hierarchically-inferior people's councils.

Article 124. (1) The hierarchically-superior people's councils may repeal the illegal or irregular acts and actions of the hierarchically-inferior people's councils.

(2) The executive committees of the hierarchically-superior people's councils may suspend the enforcement of illegal or irregular acts and actions of the hierarchically-inferior people's councils, as well as repeal the illegal or irregular acts and actions of the executive committees of same people's councils.

(3) The organ which has suspended an illegal or irregular act or action of a people's council shall refer it for cancellation to the respective hierarchically-superior organ of state power.

(4) Disputes arising between ministries and heads of other departments, and executive committees of district people's councils shall be settled by the Council of Ministers.

Chapter VIII. Courts and Public Prosecutor's Office

Article 125. (1) The administration of justice in the People's Republic of Bulgaria shall be vested in the courts. They shall protect the social and state order established by the Constitution, the socialist property, the life, the freedom, the honor, the rights, and the legal interests of the citizens, as well as the rights and legal interests of the socialist organizations.

(2) The courts shall consolidate socialist legality and help the prevention of crimes and other law violations, and educate the

citizens in a spirit of loyalty to the Homeland and the socialist cause, of a conscious implementation of the laws, and of labor discipline.

(3) Within the limits of the law, the courts shall exercise judicial supervision over the acts of the administrative organs and the special jurisdictions.

Article 126. (1) In the People's Republic of Bulgaria, there shall be a Supreme Court, district courts, city district courts, and military courts.

(2) For certain kinds of cases, other organs administering justice may also be set up by law.

(3) No extraordinary courts shall be allowed.

Article 127. (1) Assessors shall take part in the administration of justice, except when otherwise provided in the law.

(2) In hearing the cases, the assessors shall have equal rights with the judges.

Article 128. Judges and assessors shall be elected. They may be recalled before the expiry of the term for which they were elected.

Article 129. (1) In implementing their functions, judges and assessors shall be independent and subject only to the law.

(2) Decisions and sentences shall be pronounced in the name of the people.

Article 130. The courts shall apply the laws strictly and equally with regard to all citizens and juridical persons.

Article 131. The organization of the courts, their subordination and jurisdiction, the order of determining the districts of the courts, the procedure of adjudicating the cases, the conditions, order, and term for the election, rendering an account, and recall of the judges and assessors shall be regulated by law.

Article 132. (1) The Supreme Court is the highest judicial organ and is elected for a period of five years. It shall exercise supreme judicial supervision over the activity of all courts and secure the strict and equal application of the laws by them.

(2) The Supreme Court shall also exercise judicial supervision over the activity of the special jurisdictions, unless otherwise provided in the law.

(3) The Supreme Court shall be responsible for and shall render an

account on its activity to the National Assembly and, between sessions, to the State Council.

Article 133. (1) Supervision over the strict and equal application of the laws by the ministries and other departments, the local state organs, economic and public organizations, officials, and citizens shall be implemented by the Chief Public Prosecutor.
(2) The Public Prosecutor's Office shall protect the rights and legal interests of the citizens. It shall organize and direct the struggle against crimes and other law violations by taking measures for their prevention and shall bring the perpetrators of the crimes to responsibility.
(3) The Public Prosecutor's Office shall be obliged to be particularly vigilant and to bring before the court and punish the perpetrators of crimes, which are detrimental to the independence and sovereignty of the People's Republic of Bulgaria, as well as to its political and economic interests.
(4) The public prosecutors shall take measures for the repealing of illegal acts and for the restoration of infringed rights.

Article 134. (1) The Chief Public Prosecutor shall be elected for a period of five years. He may be recalled even before the expiry of this period.
(2) All other public prosecutors shall be appointed and removed from office by the Chief Public Prosecutor and shall be subordinate to him.
(3) The Chief Public Prosecutor shall be responsible to the National Assembly and shall render an account on the activity of the public prosecutors to it, and between sessions, to the State Council.

Article 135. (1) When carrying out their official duties, the public prosecutors shall be independent and act only on the basis of the law.
(2) The organization of the Public Prosecutor's Office and the manner of the implementation of its activities shall be regulated by law.

Article 136. (1) Crimes and penalties shall be established only by law.
(2) No law establishing the punishability of an act or increasing the criminal responsibility shall have retroactive force.
(3) Penalties shall be personal and shall correspond to the crimes.
(4) Penalties for crimes may be imposed only by the established courts.

Article 137. (1) In the proceedings before the courts, the discovery of the objective truth shall be guaranteed.

(2) The hearing of the cases in all courts shall be public, except when the law provides otherwise.

Article 138. (1) In the realization of administration of justice, the citizens shall have the right of defense.

(2) The accused shall have the right to defense.

Chapter IX. Coat-of-Arms, Seal, Flag, Capital

Article 139. The coat-of-arms of the People's Republic of Bulgaria is round, with a lion rampant on a cog-wheel in the center of a sky-blue background. The background is flanked on both sides by wheat ears, enveloped in the middle in a national tricolor band; above the lion there is a red five-pointed star and below, where the wheat ears intertwine, the years of the foundation of the Bulgarian state and of the victory of the socialist revolution in Bulgaria are written in gold on a red band.

Article 140. The state coat-of-arms is depicted on a state seal. Around it there is an inscription "People's Republic of Bulgaria", and in the lower part "State Seal".

Article 141. The flag of the People's Republic of Bulgaria is tricolor—white, green, and red, placed horizontally. The state coat-of-arms is depicted in the left-hand upper corner of the white field.

Article 142. The capital of the People's Republic of Bulgaria is the city of Sofia.

Chapter X. Creation and Amendment of the Constitution

Article 143. (1) The adoption of a new Constitution and the amendment of the Constitution in force shall occur upon proposal of the State Council, the Government, or at least one-quarter of the deputies.

(2) The draft of a new Constitution and the bill for the amendment of the Constitution in force shall be placed on the agenda not earlier than one month and not later than three months after being submitted to the National Assembly.

(3) They shall be adopted when two-thirds of all deputies vote in their favor.

(4) The new Constitution and the law amending the Constitution in

force shall enter into force from the day of their publication in the State Gazette.

Transitional Provision

The Presidium of the Fifth National Assembly shall implement the rights of the State Council until the election of a State Council by the next National Assembly.

The present Constitution of the People's Republic of Bulgaria was adopted in all-people voting—referendum—on 16 May 1971, and was proclaimed on 18 May 1971, by the Fifth National Assembly at its 16th session in a solemn sitting.

G. Traikov
President of the Presidium of the
National Assembly

M. Minchev
Secretary of the Presidium of the
National Assembly

CHINA

INTRODUCTION

William C. Jones

The 1978 Constitution is the third formal constitution since the establishment of the People's Republic of China in 1949. In addition, there was a sort of provisional constitution—the Common Program—which was in force from 1949 until 1954. The structure of the governments purportedly established in all these constitutions—including the Common Program—is essentially the same. China is a unitary republic whose principal governing organ is an indirectly elected legislature. The constitutions all have provisions protecting political rights on the order of the American Bill of Rights, such as freedom of speech and religion, and freedom from arrest without a warrant. They also have provisions guaranteeing what one might call welfare or economic rights, such as the right to work, the right to medical care, and the right to an education. All provide for a court system headed by a Supreme Court. However, though many of the institutions referred to in the constitutions exist in a formal sense, they do not seem to be very active nor to have much power.

The Chinese organs that exercise real power are, of course, not those of government, but those of the Party. But even in the government, the institutions that matter are not the remnants of nineteenth century parliamentary democracy such as the Congress and the courts. Rather they are the Ministries—Agriculture, Planning, Public Security, and the like. These are scarcely mentioned in the constitutions. Moreover, the ministries are, in practice, grouped according to function, and the resulting "systems" might be said to be among the most important institutions in the Chinese polity. Thus ministries having to do with foreign affairs are part of the Foreign Affairs System. The courts, to the extent that they exist, are a part of the Political and Legal Affairs System—a system which is dominated by the Ministry of Public Security. Any description of the actuality of the Chinese polity would include the systems. They are not mentioned in the constitutions.

If they do not describe the actual government of the country, what significance do the constitutions have? For one thing, they seem to be regarded by the Chinese as important in legitimizing a change in government. The provisional constitution marked the establishment of the People's Republic. The first formal constitution (1954) indicated the completion of the task of acquiring effective political control throughout the country and the establishment of the basic institutions of socialism. The promulgation of the second constitution (1975) marked the completion of the reorganization of the country on the basis of the Cultural Revolution. The present constitution announces the establishment of the new government which has succeeded that of Mao and which has overturned the "Gang of Four" (and, some would say, repudiated the Cultural Revolution). If past practice continues in the post-Mao period, one can expect a significant change of government to produce a new constitution.

Perhaps, in a way, the style of the first constitutional document—the Common Program—is more descriptive of what Chinese constitutions are than the word "constitution". The constitutions indicate what the general thrust of the new government will be—what it believes the nature of the present situation is and where China should go.

On the other hand, all the constitutions contain the structure of a nineteenth century parliamentary democracy with a great many protections for civil rights. These obviously have some meaning for a significant number of Chinese intellectuals as evidenced by the recent (late 1978) wall posters and other expressions of opinion in Peking. The present government gives lip service to these notions. The existence of constitutions that purport to embody them may be one of the reasons that the notions exist. If so, and if a new government practicing these ideas should appear, one would then have a case of the new constitution creating or forming the government in fact. In the meantime, however, it seems safer to regard those parts of the constitution which establish policies and programs as the important ones. Which does not seem to be too inappropriate for a Marxist constitution after all.

If this is a correct interpretation of Chinese constitutions, the directions in which the new constitution differs most significantly from its immediate predecessor are set out in the preamble in the last part of the fourth paragraph. There it is stated that the general task is to "make China a great, powerful socialist country with modern agriculture, modern industry, modern national defense, and modern science and technology by the end of the century". In the comparable part of the 1975 constitution, after setting out the general task of carrying forward "the three great revolutionary movements", it is added that "we should build socialism independently and with the initiative in our own hands, through self-reliance, hard struggle, diligence, and thrift, and by going all out, aiming high, and achieving greater, faster, better, and more economical results...." The approach to economic development of the 1975–1976 government did emphasize national independence and mass-movements. The present government emphasizes modernization at all costs.

Along the same line, in the new constitution there is also particular emphasis on treating intellectuals well—presumably because they are necessary to quick modernization. Nothing at all was said about them in the previous document. The new one says (Preamble, sixth paragraph): "We should consolidate and expand the revolutionary united front which is led by the working class and based on the worker-peasant alliance and which unites the large numbers of intellectuals and other working people, patriotic democratic parties, patriotic personages, our compatriots in Taiwan, Hong Kong, and Macao, and our countrymen residing abroad." One speculates as to what this latter part indicates about the intention of the present government towards these areas. Initially, of course, it indicates a policy of accommodation towards all—Taiwan in particular. Just what is now taking place. But subsequently?

The final part of the same paragraph is also interesting, particularly for lawyers. It would seem to predict the current emphasis on the importance of "law" or control in dealing with some matters such as theft, and the need to relax control in other areas such as culture. It reads: "We should endeavor to create among the people of the whole country a political situation in which there are both centralism and democracy, both discipline and freedom, both unity of will and personal ease of mind and liveliness..." This may be related to Article 43—the reestablishment of the Procuracy whose effective abolition was recognized in Article 25 of the 1975 Constitution (it had taken place some years before). Judging from recent comments in the Chinese press on law and the Procuracy, there would seem to be a great deal of emphasis on adherence to rules and controlling discretion by means of the Procuracy. It is difficult to know what difference this has made in practice of course.

It is easy to point up the aspects of the constitution that seem to be significant now soon after its promulgation. One has only to look at the actions and statements of the government. It would, however, be a very rash man indeed who would attempt to predict what the next few years will bring to China. One of the biggest questions is the extent to which the tradition of Mao Tse-Tung will be carried on. At present, Mao is given a great deal of formal respect, but many of his substantive policies are being revised, and certain popular attacks on him are countenanced. The talk is all of modernization—and thus expertness—and order. Nevertheless, the methods that are being

Introduction

used to achieve these aims seem to be the mass-mobilization techniques associated with Mao. If the Chinese continue to promulgate new constitutions when significant changes in government take place, and if the significant changes in new constitutions appear to be primarily in the policy statements, then this would be some indication that the kind of government Mao presided over continues. On the other hand, if the institutions set up by the constitutions begin to assume real importance and function as the constitution indicates they should, this will show a radical change in the Chinese system. Of course, it is quite possible to have what appear to be significant changes in the system with no change in the constitution. This occurred several times in the period from the late 1950s to 1975. Chinese constitutions are, in other words, quite as puzzling as everything else in what we have, for some reason, ceased to call the Mysterious East.

CONSTITUTION OF THE PEOPLE'S REPUBLIC OF CHINA OF 5 MARCH 1978

Preamble	76
General Principles	78
The Structure of the State	82
The National People's Congress	82
The State Council	85
The Local People's Congresses and the Local Revolutionary Committees at Various Levels	86
The Organs of Self-Government of National Autonomous Areas	88
The People's Courts and the People's Procuracies	89
The Fundamental Rights and Duties of Citizens	90
The National Flag, the National Emblem, and the Capital	92

CONSTITUTION OF THE PEOPLE'S REPUBLIC OF CHINA*

Adopted on 5 March 1978 by the Fifth National People's Congress of the People's Republic of China at its first session.

PREAMBLE

After more than a century of heroic struggle the Chinese people, led by the Communist Party of China headed by our great leader and teacher Chairman Mao Tsetung, finally overthrew the reactionary rule of imperialism, feudalism, and bureaucrat-capitalism by means of people's revolutionary war, winning complete victory in the new-democratic revolution, and in 1949 founded the People's Republic of China.

The founding of the People's Republic of China marked the beginning of the historical period of socialism in our country. Since then, under the leadership of Chairman Mao and the Chinese Communist Party, the people of all our nationalities have carried out Chairman Mao's proletarian revolutionary line in the political, economic, cultural, and military fields, and in foreign affairs, and have won great victories in socialist revolution and socialist construction through repeated struggles against enemies, both at home and abroad, and through the great proletarian cultural revolution. The dictatorship of the proletariat in our country has been consolidated and strengthened, and China has become a socialist country with the beginnings of prosperity.

Chairman Mao Tsetung was the founder of the People's Republic of China. All our victories in revolution and construction have been won under the guidance of Marxism-Leninism-Mao Tsetung thought. The fundamental guarantee that the people of all our nationalities will struggle in unity and carry the proletarian revolution through to the end is always to hold high and staunchly to defend the great banner of Chairman Mao.

The triumphant conclusion of the first great proletarian cultural revolution has ushered in a new period of development in China's socialist revolution and socialist construction. In accordance with the

*Translation from Hsinhua News Agency, Peking PRC, 7 March 1978.

basic line of the Chinese Communist Party for the entire historical period of socialism, the general task for the people of the whole country in this new period is to persevere in continuing the revolution under the dictatorship of the proletariat, carry forward the three great revolutionary movements of class struggle, the struggle for production and scientific experiment, and make China a great, powerful socialist country with modern agriculture, modern industry, modern national defense, and modern science and technology by the end of the century.

We must persevere in the struggle of the proletariat against the bourgeoisie and in the struggle for the socialist road against the capitalist road. We must oppose revisionism and prevent the restoration of capitalism. We must be prepared to deal with subversion and aggression against our country by social-imperialism and imperialism.

We should consolidate and expand the revolutionary united front which is led by the working class and based on the worker-peasant alliance, and which unites the large numbers of intellectuals and other working people, patriotic democratic parties, patriotic personages, our compatriots in Taiwan, Hongkong, and Macao, and our countrymen residing abroad. We should enhance the great unity of all the nationalities in our country. We should correctly distinguish and handle the contradictions among the people and those between ourselves and the enemy. We should endeavor to create among the people of the whole country a political situation in which there are both centralism and democracy, both discipline and freedom, both unity of will and personal ease of mind and liveliness, so as to bring all positive factors into play, overcome all difficulties, better consolidate the proletarian dictatorship, and build up our country more rapidly.

Taiwan is China's sacred territory. We are determined to liberate Taiwan and accomplish the great cause of unifying our motherland.

In international affairs, we should establish and develop relations with other countries on the basis of the five principles of mutual respect for sovereignty and territorial integrity, mutual nonaggression, non-interference in each other's internal affairs, equality and mutual benefit, and peaceful coexistence. Our country will never seek hegemony, or strive to be a supervisor. We should uphold proletarian internationalism. In accordance with the theory of the three worlds, we should strengthen our unity with the proletariat and the oppressed people and nations throughout the world, the socialist countries, and the third world countries, and we should unite with all countries subjected to aggression, subversion, interference, control, and bullying by the social-imperialist and imperialist superpowers to form the broadest possible international united front against the hegemonism of the superpowers and against a new world war, and strive for the progress and emancipation of humanity.

Chapter I. General Principles

Article 1. The People's Republic of China is a socialist state of the dictatorship of the proletariat led by the working class and based on the alliance of workers and peasants.

Article 2. The Communist Party of China is the core of leadership of the whole Chinese people. The working class exercises leadership over the state through its vanguard, the Communist Party of China.

The guiding ideology of the People's Republic of China is Marxism-Leninism-Mao Tsetung thought.

Article 3. All power in the People's Republic of China belongs to the people.

The organs through which the people exercise state power are the National People's Congress and the local People's Congresses at various levels.

The National People's Congress, the local People's Congresses at various levels, and all other organs of state practice democratic centralism.

Article 4. The People's Republic of China is a unitary multinational state.

All the nationalities are equal. There should be unity and fraternal love among the nationalities and they should help and learn from each other. Discrimination against or oppression of any nationality, and acts which undermine the unity of the nationalities are prohibited. Big-nationality chauvinism and local-nationality chauvinism must be opposed.

All the nationalities have the freedom to use and develop their own spoken and written languages, and to preserve or reform their own customs and ways.

Regional autonomy applies in an area where a minority nationality lives in a compact community. All the national autonomous areas are inalienable parts of the People's Republic of China.

Article 5. There are mainly two kinds of ownership of the means of production in the People's Republic of China at the present stage: socialist ownership by the whole people, and socialist collective ownership by the working people.

The state allows nonagricultural individual laborers to engage in individual labor involving no exploitation of others, within the limits permitted by law and under unified arrangements and management by organizations at the basic level in cities and towns or in rural areas. At the same time, it guides these individual laborers step-by-step onto the road of socialist collectivization.

Article 6. The state sector of the economy, that is, the socialist sector owned by the whole people, is the leading force in the national economy.

Mineral resources, waters, and those forests, undeveloped lands and other marine and land resources owned by the state, are the property of the whole people.

The state may requisition by purchase, take over for use, or nationalize land under conditions prescribed by law.

Article 7. The rural people's commune sector of the economy is a socialist sector collectively owned by the masses of working people. At present, it generally takes the form of three-level ownership, that is, ownership by the commune, the production brigade, and the production team as the basic accounting unit. A production brigade may become the basic accounting unit when its conditions are ripe.

Provided that the absolute predominance of the collective economy of the people's commune is ensured, commune members may farm small plots of land for personal needs, engage in limited household side-line production, and in pastoral areas they may also keep a limited number of livestock for personal needs.

Article 8. Socialist public property shall be inviolable. The state ensures the consolidation and development of the socialist sector of the economy owned by the whole people, and of the socialist sector collectively owned by the masses of working people.

The state prohibits any person from using any means whatsoever to disrupt the economic order of the society, undermine the economic plans of the state, encroach upon or squander state and collective property, or injure the public interest.

Article 9. The state protects the right of citizens to own lawfully earned income, savings, houses, and other means of livelihood.

Article 10. The state applies the socialist principle: "He who does not work, neither shall he eat" and "From each according to his ability, to each according to his work".

Work is an honorable duty for every citizen able to work. The state promotes socialist labor emulation, and, putting proletarian politics in command, it applies the policy of combining moral encouragement with material reward, with the stress on the former, in order to heighten citizens' socialist enthusiasm and creativeness in work.

Article 11. The state adheres to the general line of going all out, aiming high, and achieving greater, faster, better, and more economical results in building socialism; it undertakes the planned, proportionate, and high-speed development of the national economy; and it continuously develops the productive forces, so as to consolidate the country's independence and security, and improve the people's material and cultural life step-by-step.

In developing the national economy, the state adheres to the principle of building our country independently, with the initiative in our own hands, and through self-reliance, hard struggle, diligence, and thrift; it adheres to the principle of taking agriculture as the foundation and industry as the leading factor; and it adheres to the principle of bringing the initiative of both the central and local authorities into full play under the unified leadership of the central authorities.

The state protects the environment and natural resources, and prevents and eliminates pollution and other hazards to the public.

Article 12. The state devotes major efforts to developing science, expands scientific research, promotes technical innovation and technical revolution, and adopts advanced techniques wherever possible in all departments of the national economy. In scientific and technological work, we must follow the practice of combining professional contingents with the masses, and combining learning from others with our own creative efforts.

Article 13. The state devotes major efforts to developing education in order to raise the cultural and scientific level of the whole nation. Education must serve proletarian politics and be combined with productive labor, and must enable everyone who receives an education to develop morally, intellectually, and physically, and become a worker with both socialist consciousness and culture.

Article 14. The state upholds the leading position of Marxism-Leninism-Mao Tsetung thought in all spheres of ideology and culture. All cultural undertakings must serve the workers, peasants, and soldiers, and serve socialism.

The state applies the principle of "letting a hundred flowers blossom and a hundred schools of thought contend" so as to promote the development of the arts and sciences and bring about a flourishing socialist culture.

Article 15. All organs of state must constantly maintain close contact with the masses of the people, rely on them, heed their opinions, be concerned for their weal and woe, streamline administration, practice economy, raise efficiency and combat bureaucracy.

The leading personnel of state organs at all levels must conform to the requirements for successors in the proletarian revolutionary cause and their composition must conform to the principle of the three-in-one combination of the old, the middle-aged, and the young.

Article 16. The personnel of state organs must earnestly study Marxism-Leninism-Mao Tsetung thought, wholeheartedly serve the people, endeavor to perfect their professional competence, take an active part in collective productive labor, accept supervision by the masses, be models in observing the Constitution and the law, correctly implement the policies of the state, seek the truth from facts, and must not have recourse to deception or exploit their position and power to seek personal gain.

Article 17. The state adheres to the principle of socialist democracy, and ensures to the people the right to participate in the management of state affairs and of all economic and cultural undertakings, and the right to supervise state organs and their personnel.

Article 18. The state safeguards the socialist system, suppresses all treasonable and counter-revolutionary activities, punishes all traitors and counter-revolutionaries, and punishes new-born bourgeois elements and other bad elements.

The state deprives of political rights, as prescribed by law, those landlords, rich peasants, and reactionary capitalists who have not yet been reformed, and at the same time it provides them with the opportunity to earn a living so that they may be reformed through labor and become law-abiding citizens supporting themselves by their own labor.

Article 19. The Chairman of the Central Committee of the Communist Party of China commands the armed forces of the People's Republic of China.

The Chinese People's Liberation Army is the workers' and peasants' own armed force led by the Communist Party of China; it is the pillar of the dictatorship of the proletariat. The state devotes major efforts to the revolutionization and modernization of the Chinese People's Liberation Army, strengthens the building of the militia, and adopts a system under which our armed forces are a combination of the field armies, the regional forces, and the militia.

The fundamental task of the armed forces of the People's Republic of China is: to safeguard the socialist revolution and socialist construction, to defend the sovereignty, territorial integrity, and security of the state, and to guard against subversion and aggression by social-imperialism, and their lackeys.

Chapter II. The Structure of the State

Part I. The National People's Congress

Article 20. The National People's Congress is the highest organ of state power.

Article 21. The National People's Congress is composed of deputies elected by the People's Congresses of the provinces, autonomous regions, and municipalities directly under the central government, and by the People's Liberation Army. The deputies should be elected by secret ballot after democratic consultation.

The National People's Congress is elected for a term of five years. Under special circumstances, its term of office may be extended or the succeeding National People's Congress may be convened before its due date.

The National People's Congress holds one session each year. When necessary, the session may be advanced or postponed.

Article 22. The National People's Congress exercises the following functions and powers:
   (1) to amend the Constitution;
   (2) to make laws;
   (3) to supervise the enforcement of the Constitution and the law;
   (4) to decide on the choice of the Premier of the State Council

upon the recommendation of the Central Committee of the Communist Party of China;

(5) to decide on the choice of other members of the State Council upon the recommendation of the Premier of the State Council;

(6) to elect the President of the Supreme People's Court and the Chief Procurator of the Supreme People's Procuracy;

(7) to examine and approve the national economic plan, the state budget, and the final state accounts;

(8) to confirm the following administrative divisions: provinces, autonomous regions, and municipalities directly under the central government;

(9) to decide on questions of war and peace; and

(10) to exercise such other functions and powers as the National People's Congress deems necessary.

Article 23. The National People's Congress has the power to remove from office the members of the State Council, the President of the Supreme People's Court, and the Chief Procurator of the Supreme People's Procuracy.

Article 24. The Standing Committee of the National People's Congress is the permanent organ of the National People's Congress. It is responsible and accountable to the National People's Congress.

The Standing Committee of the National People's Congress is composed of the following members:

the Chairman;
the Vice-Chairman;
the Secretary-General; and
other members.

The National People's Congress elects the Standing Committee of the National People's Congress and has the power to recall its members.

Article 25. The Standing Committee of the National People's Congress exercises the following functions and powers:

(1) conducts the election of deputies to the National People's Congress;

(2) convenes the sessions of the National People's Congress;

(3) interprets the Constitution and laws, and enacts decrees;

(4) supervises the work of the State Council, the Supreme People's Court, and the Supreme People's Procuracy;

(5) changes and annuls inappropriate decisions adopted by the

organs of state power of provinces, autonomous regions, and municipalities directly under the central government;

(6) decides on the appointment and removal of individual members of the State Council, upon the recommendation of the Premier of the State Council, when the National People's Congress is not in session;

(7) appoints and removes Vice-Presidents of the Supreme People's Court and Deputy Chief Procurators of the Supreme People's Procuracy;

(8) decides on the appointment and removal of plenipotentiary representatives abroad;

(9) decides on the ratification and abrogation of treaties concluded with foreign states;

(10) institutes titles of honor and decides on their conferment;

(11) decides on the granting of pardons;

(12) decides on the proclamation of a state of war in the event of armed attack on the country when the National People's Congress is not in session; and

(13) exercises such other functions and powers as are vested in it by the National People's Congress.

Article 26. The Chairman of the Standing Committee of the National People's Congress presides over the work of the Standing Committee; receives foreign diplomatic envoys; and in accordance with the decisions of the National People's Congress or its Standing Committee promulgates laws and decrees, dispatches and recalls plenipotentiary representatives abroad, ratifies treaties concluded with foreign states, and confers state titles of honor.

The Vice-Chairmen of the Standing Committee of the National People's Congress assist the Chairman in his work and may exercise part of the Chairman's functions and powers on his behalf.

Article 27. The National People's Congress and its Standing Committee may establish special committees as deemed necessary.

Article 28. Deputies to the National People's Congress have the right to address inquiries to the State Council, the Supreme People's Court, the Supreme People's Procuracy, and the ministries and commissions of the State Council, which are all under obligation to answer.

Article 29. Deputies to the National People's Congress are subject to supervision by the units which elect them. These electoral units have the power to replace at any time the deputies they elect, as prescribed by law.

Part II. The State Council

Article 30. The State Council is the central People's Government and the executive organ of the highest organ of state power; it is the highest organ of state administration.

The State Council is responsible and accountable to the National People's Congress, or, when the National Congress is not in session, to its Standing Committee.

Article 31. The State Council is composed of the following members:
the Premier;
the Vice-Premiers;
the Ministers; and
the Ministers heading the commissions.

The Premier presides over the work of the State Council, and the Vice-Premiers assist the Premier in his work.

Article 32. The State Council exercises the following functions and powers:

(1) formulates administrative measures, issues decisions and orders, and verifies their execution in accordance with the Constitution, laws, and decrees;

(2) submits proposals on laws and other matters to the National People's Congress or its Standing Committee.

(3) exercises unified leadership over the work of the ministries and commissions, and other organizations under it;

(4) exercises unified leadership over the work of local organs of state administration at various levels throughout the country;

(5) draws up and puts into effect the national economic plan and the state budget;

(6) protects the interests of the state, maintains public order, and safeguards the rights of citizens;

(7) confirms the following administrative divisions: autonomous prefectures, counties, autonomous counties, and cities;

(8) appoints and removes administrative personnel according to the provisions of the law; and

(9) exercises such other functions and powers as are vested in it by the National People's Congress or its Standing Committee.

Part III. The Local People's Congresses and the Local Revolutionary Committees at Various Levels

Article 33. The administrative division of the People's Republic of China is as follows:

(1) the country is divided into provinces, autonomous regions, and municipalities directly under the central government;

(2) provinces and autonomous regions are divided into autonomous prefectures, counties, autonomous counties, and cities; and

(3) counties and autonomous counties are divided into people's communes and towns.

Municipalities directly under the central government and other large cities are divided into districts and counties. Autonomous prefectures are divided into counties and cities.

Autonomous regions, autonomous prefectures, and autonomous counties are all national autonomous areas.

Article 34. People's Congresses and Revolutionary Committees are established in provinces, municipalities directly under the central government, counties, cities, municipal districts, people's communes, and towns.

People's Congresses and Revolutionary Committees of the people's communes are organizations of political power at the grassroots level, and are also leading organs of collective economy.

Revolutionary Committees at the provincial level may establish administrative offices as their agencies in prefectures.

Organs of self-government are established in autonomous regions, autonomous prefectures, and autonomous counties.

Article 35. Local People's Congresses at various levels are local organs of state power.

Deputies to the People's Congresses of provinces, municipalities directly under the central government, counties, and cities divided into districts are elected by People's Congresses at the next lower level by secret ballot after democratic consultation; deputies to the People's Congresses of cities not divided into districts, and of municipal districts, people's communes, and towns are directly elected by the voters by secret ballot after democratic consultation.

The People's Congresses of provinces and municipalities directly under the central government are elected for a term of five years. The People's Congresses of counties, cities, and municipal districts are elected for a term of three years. The People's Congresses of people's communes and towns are elected for a term of two years.

Local People's Congresses at various levels hold at least one session each year, which is to be convened by Revolutionary Committees at the corresponding levels.

The units and electorates which elect the deputies to the local People's Congresses at various levels have the power to supervise, remove, and replace their deputies at any time according to the provisions of the law.

Article 36. Local People's Congresses at various levels, in their respective administrative areas, ensure the observance and enforcement of the Constitution, laws, and decrees; ensure the implementation of the state plan; make plans for local economic and cultural development, and for public utilities; examine and approve local economic plans, budgets, and final accounts; protect public property; maintain public order; safeguard the rights of citizens and the equal rights of minority nationalities; and promote the development of socialist revolution and socialist construction.

Local People's Congresses may adopt and issue decisions within the limits of their authority as prescribed by law.

Local People's Congresses elect and have the power to recall members of Revolutionary Committees at the corresponding levels. People's Congresses, at the county level and above, elect and have the power to recall the presidents of the people's courts and the chief procurators of the people's procuracies at the corresponding levels.

Deputies to local People's Congresses at various levels have the right to address inquiries to the Revolutionary Committees, people's courts, people's procuracies, and organs under the Revolutionary Committees at the corresponding levels, which are all under obligation to answer.

Article 37. Local Revolutionary Committees at various levels, that is, local people's governments, are the executive organs of local People's Congresses at the corresponding levels, and they are also local organs of state administration.

A local Revolutionary Committee is composed of a chairman, vice-chairman, and other members.

Local Revolutionary Committees carry out the decisions of People's Congresses at the corresponding levels, as well as the decisions and orders of the organs of state administration at higher levels, direct the administrative work of their respective areas, and issue decisions and orders within the limits of their authority as prescribed by law. Revolutionary Committees, at county level and above, appoint or remove the personnel of organs of state according to the provisions of the law.

Local Revolutionary Committees are responsible and accountable to People's Congresses at the corresponding levels, and to the organs of state administration at the next higher level, and work under the unified leadership of the state council.

Part IV. The Organs of Self-Government of National Autonomous Areas

Article 38. The organs of self-government of autonomous regions, autonomous prefectures, and autonomous counties are People's Congresses and Revolutionary Committees.

The election of the People's Congresses and Revolutionary Committees of national autonomous areas, their terms of office, their functions and powers, and also the establishment of their agencies should conform to the basic principles governing the organization of local organs of state as specified in Chapter Two, Part III of the Constitution.

In autonomous areas where a number of nationalities live together, each nationality is entitled to appropriate representation in the organs of self-government.

Article 39. The organs of self-government of national autonomous areas exercise autonomy within the limits of their authority as prescribed by law, in addition to exercising the functions and powers of local organs of state as specified by the Constitution.

The organs of self-government of national autonomous areas may, in the light of the political, economic, and cultural characteristics of the nationality or nationalities in a given area, make regulations and submit them to the Standing Committee of the National People's Congress for approval.

In performing their functions, the organs of self-government of national autonomous areas employ the spoken and written language or languages commonly used by the nationality or nationalities in the locality.

Article 40. The higher organs of state fully safeguard the exercise of autonomy by the organs of self-government of national autonomous areas, take into full consideration the characteristics and needs of the various minority nationalities, make a major effort to train cadres of the minority nationalities, and actively support

China

and assist all the minority nationalities in their socialist revolution and construction, and thus advance their socialist economic and cultural development.

Part V. The People's Courts and the People's Procuracies

Article 41. The Supreme People's Court, local people's courts at various levels, and special people's courts exercise judicial authority. The people's courts are formed as prescribed by law.

In accordance with law, the people's courts apply the system whereby representatives of the masses participate as assessors in administering justice. With regard to major counter-revolutionary or criminal cases, the masses should be drawn in for discussion and suggestions.

All cases in the people's courts are heard in public, except those involving special circumstances as prescribed by law. The accused has the right to defense.

Article 42. The Supreme People's Court is the highest judicial organ.

The Supreme People's Court supervises the administration of justice by local people's courts at various levels and by special people's courts; people's courts at the higher levels supervise the administration of justice by people's courts at the lower levels.

The Supreme People's Court is responsible and accountable to the National People's Congress and its Standing Committee. Local people's courts at various levels are responsible and accountable to local People's Congresses at the corresponding levels.

Article 43. The Supreme People's Procuracy exercises procuratorial authority to ensure observance of the Constitution and the law by all the departments under the State Council, the local organs of state at various levels, the personnel of organs of state, and the citizens. Local people's procuracies and special people's procuracies exercise procuratorial authority within the limits prescribed by law. The people's procuracies are formed as prescribed by law.

The Supreme People's Procuracy supervises the work of local people's procuracies at various levels and of special people's procuracies. People's procuracies at the higher levels supervise the work of those at the lower levels.

The Supreme People's Procuracy is responsible and accountable to the National People's Congress and its Standing Committee. Local people's procuracies at various levels are responsible and accountable to People's Congresses at the corresponding levels.

Chapter III. The Fundamental Rights and Duties of Citizens

Article 44. All citizens who have reached the age of eighteen have the right to vote and to stand for election, with the exception of persons deprived of these rights by law.

Article 45. Citizens enjoy freedom of speech, correspondence, the press, assembly, association, procession, demonstration, and the freedom to strike, and have the right to "speak out freely, air their views fully, hold great debates, and write big-character posters".

Article 46. Citizens enjoy freedom to believe in religion and freedom not to believe in religion, and to propagate atheism.

Article 47. The citizens' freedom of person and their homes are inviolable.

No citizens may be arrested except by decision of a people's court or with the sanction of a people's procuracy, and the arrest must be made by a public security organ.

Article 48. Citizens have the right to work. To ensure that citizens enjoy this right, the state provides employment in accordance with the principle of over-all consideration, and, on the basis of increased production, the state gradually increases payment for labor, improves working conditions, strengthens labor protection, and expands collective welfare.

Article 49. Working people have the right to rest. To ensure that working people enjoy this right, the state prescribes working hours and systems of vacations, and gradually expands material facilities for the working people to rest and recuperate.

Article 50. Working people have the right to material assistance in old age, and in case of illness or disability. To ensure that working people enjoy this right, the state gradually expands social insurance, social assistance, public health services, cooperative medical services, and other services.

The state cares for and ensures the livelihood of disabled revolutionary armymen and the families of revolutionary martyrs.

Article 51. Citizens have the right to education. To ensure that citizens enjoy this right, the state gradually increases the number of schools of various types and of other cultural and educational institutions, and popularizes education.

The state pays special attention to the healthy development of young people and children.

Article 52. Citizens have the freedom to engage in scientific research, literary and artistic creation, and other cultural activities. The state encourages and assists the creative endeavors of citizens engaged in science, public health, sports, and other cultural work.

Article 53. Women enjoy equal rights with men in all spheres of political, economic, cultural, social, and family life. Men and women enjoy equal pay for equal work.

Men and women shall marry of their own free will. The state protects marriage, the family, and mother and child.

The state advocates and encourages family planning.

Article 54. The state protects the just rights and interests of overseas Chinese and their relatives.

Article 55. Citizens have the right to lodge complaints with organs of state at any level against any person working in an organ of state, enterprise, or institution for the transgression of law or neglect of duty. Citizens have the right to appeal to organs of state at any level against any infringement of their rights. No one shall suppress such complaints and appeals, or retaliate against persons making them.

Article 56. Citizens must support the leadership of the Communist Party of China, support the socialist system, safeguard the unification of the motherland and the unity of all nationalities in our country, and abide by the Constitution and the law.

Article 57. Citizens must take care of and protect public property, observe labor discipline, observe public order, respect social ethics, and safeguard state secrets.

Article 58. It is the lofty duty of every citizen to defend the motherland and resist aggression.

It is the honorable obligation of citizens to perform military service and to join the militia according to the law.

Article 59. The People's Republic of China grants the right of residence to any foreign national persecuted for supporting a just cause, for taking part in revolutionary movements, or for engaging in scientific work.

Chapter IV. The National Flag, the National Emblem, and the Capital

Article 60. The national flag of the People's Republic has five stars on a field of red.

The national emblem of the People's Republic of China is: *tien an men* in the center, illuminated by five stars, and encircled by ears of grain and a cogwheel.

The Capital of the People's Republic of China is Peking.

CUBA

INTRODUCTION

Max Azicri

The 1976 Cuban Constitution is the first of its kind in the Western Hemisphere. Although social reformism has been a significant influence in Latin American constitutionalism—demonstrated, among others, by such landmarks as the 1917 Mexican and 1940 Cuban Constitutions—it was, however, with this last Cuban Constitution that socialist jurisprudence, for the first time, would play a central philosophical and legal role characterizing a state constitution in the Americas.

Nevertheless, for Cuba its new Constitution meant much more than just an innovative political charter in the history of hemispheric legal traditions. From the standpoint of the ongoing process of revolutionary state-building (*i.e.* establishing the administrative structures needed for development as well as differentiating new social and political roles), Cuba's socialist Constitution was promulgated at a time when the regime wanted to put an end to the provisional era represented by its executive and law-making ministerial Cabinet which had lasted for sixteen years. By then the government was seeking purposely the actual institutionalization of the revolution. Thus, new political institutions were created; the functions of governmental administrative structures were further defined, becoming directly related to such political institutions as the Organs of People's Power—the new deliberative and legislative assemblies set up at the municipal, provincial and national levels (Arts. 73, 88, 96, 97, and 102).

Furthermore, the Cuban Communist Party was recognized as the leading and central political institution in the system (Art. 5), as it was already established by the First Party Congress held in December 1975. Meanwhile, the Party was also extricated from any possible interference in administrative (governmental) functions, as it happened so often in the past. The existent mass organizations were recognized for their social and political functions as an integral part of the newly institutionalized revolutionary polity (Art. 7).

In short, the 1976 Constitution embraced within its legal framework the politico-institutional growth experienced in Cuba in the 1970s. The many social, economic, and political changes brought about by two decades of revolutionary government were also integrated and harmonized within this constitutional structure which includes, (1) the reaffirmation of Marxism-Leninism as the official revolutionary ideology (Preamble of the Constitution); (2) the establishment of a single (Communist) party system (Art. 5); (3) the effective implementation of democratic centralism which is built as an operational and institutionalized principle defining the nature of relations among the organs of the state (Art. 66); (4) the recognition that political power is wielded by the working people in a dictatorship of the proletariat fashion, and exercised "directly or through the assemblies of People's Power and other organs of the state" in alliance with the "peasants and the remaining strata of urban and rural workers" (Art. 4); (5) the administration and institutionalization of a socialist economic system with public ownership of the means of production which would abolish "the exploitation of man by man", although there are still instances in which private property is allowed (*i.e.* the "right of small farmers to own their lands", individual ownership of earnings and savings, and "personal or family work tools") (Arts. 14–27); (6) the implementation of a reward system according to a socialist stage of development, "from each according to his ability, to each according to his work" (Art. 19); and (7) the application of proletarian internationalism as a central political value guiding the country's international relations with other socialist states, progressive countries opposing imperialism, and national liberation movements (Art. 12).

In some instances, the organizational arrangements of Cuba's present political system have departed from other socialist experiences, particularly in the case of a single person heading both the state and the government—who would become President of the Council of State (political organ) and of the Council of Ministers (governmental/administrative body) (Arts. 72, 91). Although this kind of organization is more in line with Latin American practice of favoring a strong executive, it is a departure, however, of earlier revolutionary political modalities when there were a President and a Prime Minister, representing respectively the state and the government.

Participation by the people in state organs, directly or through their representatives, is guaranteed by the combined principles of "socialist democracy, unity of power and democratic centralism", which have been integrated into the operational rules of these political structures (Art. 66). Hence, the pyramid represented by the Organs of People's Power is based on municipal delegates elected directly by the people at the grassroots level, followed by provincial and national layers occupied by provincial delegates and national deputies, respectively, who are (indirectly) elected by the municipal assemblies (Arts. 67–99, 100–120).

The National Assembly of People's Power stands as "the supreme organ of the state", and is the only one invested with "constituent [constitutional reform power] and legislative authority" (Arts. 67, 68). However, in addition to this body, legislation can also be proposed by the Council of State, the Council of Ministers, the National Committee of Cuban Trade Unions, the People's Supreme Court, the Attorney General of the Republic, and by interested citizens (a legislative proposal by the latter would need to carry at least 10,000 signatures from citizens eligible to vote) (Art. 86). The deputies of the National Assembly elect from their own ranks the members of the Council of State. This collegial body represents the National Assembly, functioning within its sessions (the National Assembly meets for a period of two or three days twice a year, in July and December; in a significant way, its legislative functions are made possible by the work performed all year round by its Standing Committees).

The highest executive and administrative organ of government is the Council of Ministers. From this body, an Executive Committee is organized with special control and organizing powers. This powerful committee is constituted by the President, First Vice-President and the Vice-Presidents of the Council of Ministers (thus, the head of state and government presides also over the Executive Committee) (Arts. 93, 94).

Other significant features of the 1976 Cuban Constitution are: (1) the defense of the family rendered by the state, the principle of equality that applies to both husband and wife in the exercise of their marital life, and the lack of distinction that exists regarding children who are born in or out of wedlock (Arts. 34–37); (2) the social obligation of providing free education to all citizens, while promoting "the communist education of the new generations" (Arts. 38–39); (3) the protection of equal rights for all citizens regardless of their "race, color, sex or national origin" (women's rights are explicitly expressed as equal to men's) (Arts. 40–43); (4) the state guarantee that all citizens would enjoy rights (and duties) such as, remunerated work; social security; health protection and care; education, sports, and recreation; freedom of speech and of the press ("in keeping with the objectives of socialist society"); to assembly, demonstration and association; freedom to practice and to profess any religious belief (although the state educates the people in "the scientific materialist concept of the universe"); and the inviolability of the home, mail, and persons (penal laws would only

Introduction

be retroactive when they benefit the accused or the person who has been sentenced). On the other hand, citizens' duties include work discipline, caring for public and social property, respecting the rights of others, and the defense of the socialist homeland (Arts. 44–65).

All in all, Cuba's socialist Constitution is representative of the country's present domestic and international reality, of its historical and cultural heritage, as well as of the changes that occurred under the revolution. Also, it blends nicely in its twelve chapters and 141 articles Marxist-Leninist ideology with political pragmatism, and some previous constitutional experience with the influence of other socialist constitutions.

CONSTITUTION OF THE REPUBLIC OF CUBA OF 24 FEBRUARY 1976 (AS AMENDED)

Preamble	100
Political, Social, and Economic Principles of the State	101
Citizenship	108
The Family	109
Education and Culture	110
Equality	111
Fundamental Rights, Duties, and Guarantees	112
Principles of the Organization and Operation of State Organs	116
Supreme Organs of People's Power	117
Local Organs of People's Power	126
The Courts and the Attorney General	131
The Electoral System	133
Constitutional Reforms	134

CONSTITUTION OF THE REPUBLIC OF CUBA*

Gaceta Oficial de la República de Cuba, 24 February 1976
(as amended by Law on Constitutional Reform, 28 June 1978).

PREAMBLE

We, Cuban citizens,
  heirs and continuators of the creative work and the traditions of combativeness, firmness, heroism, and sacrifice fostered by our ancestors:
— by the Indians who preferred extermination to submission;
— by the slaves who rebelled against their masters;
— by those who awoke the national consciousness and the ardent Cuban desire for an independent homeland and liberty;
— by the patriots who, in 1868, launched the wars of independence against Spanish colonialism and those who, in the last drive of 1895, brought them to the victory of 1898, victory usurped by the military intervention and occupation of Yankee imperialism;
— by the workers, peasants, students, and intellectuals who struggled for over fifty years against imperialist domination, political corruption, the absence of people's rights and liberties, unemployment, and exploitation by capitalists and landowners;
— by those who promoted, joined, and developed the first organizations of workers and peasants, spread socialist ideas, and founded the first Marxist and Marxist-Leninist movements;
— by the members of the vanguard of the generation of the centenary of the birth of Martí who, imbued with his teachings, led us to the people's revolutionary victory of January;
— by those who defended the Revolution at the cost of their lives, thus contributing to its definitive consolidation;
guided
  by the victorious doctrine of Marxism-Leninism;
basing ourselves
  on proletarian internationalism, on the fraternal friendship, help, and cooperation of the Soviet Union and other socialist countries, and on the solidarity of the workers and the peoples of Latin America and of the world;

*An English translation of the 1976 Cuban Constitution was published in 11 *Granma* (Official Organ of the Central Committee of the Communist Party of Cuba), 7 March 1976 No. 10, 2–11. Text revised by William B. Simons.

and having decided

to carry forward the triumphant Revolution of the Moncada and of the Granma, of the Sierra and of Girón under the leadership of Fidel Castro, which, sustained by the closest unity of all revolutionary forces and of the people, won full national independence, established the revolutionary power, carried out democratic changes, started the construction of socialism, and, under the direction of the Communist Party, continues said construction with the objective of building a communist society;

aware

that all regimes of the exploitation of man by man cause the humiliation of the exploited and the degradation of the human nature of the exploiters;

that only under socialism and communism, when man has been freed from all forms of exploitation—slavery, servitude, and capitalism—can full dignity of the human being be attained; and

that our Revolution uplifted the dignity of the country and of Cubans;

we declare

our will that the law of laws of the Republic be guided by the following strong desire of José Martí, at last achieved:

> "I want the fundamental law of our republic to be the tribute of Cubans to the full dignity of man";

and adopt

by means of our free vote in a referendum, the following:

Chapter I. Political, Social, and Economic Principles of the State

Article 1. The Republic of Cuba is a socialist state of workers and peasants, and all other manual and intellectual workers.

Article 2. The national symbols are those which have presided for over one hundred years in the Cuban struggles for independence, the rights of the people, and social progress:
 the flag of the lone star;
 the anthem of Bayamo;
 the coat of arms of the royal palm.

Article 3. The Capital of the Republic is the city of Havana.

Article 4. In the Republic of Cuba, all the power belongs to the working people who exercise it either directly or through the

Assemblies of People's Power and other organs of the state which derive their authority from these Assemblies.

The power of the working people is sustained by the firm alliance of the working class with the peasants and the remaining strata of urban and rural workers, under the direction of the working class.

Article 5. The Communist Party of Cuba, the organized Marxist-Leninist vanguard of the working class, is the highest leading force of society and of the state, which organizes and guides the common effort toward the goals of the construction of socialism and progress toward a communist society.

Article 6. The Young Communist League, the organization of the progressive youth, under the direction of the Party, works to prepare its members as future members of the Party and contributes to the education of the new generations along the ideals of communism by means of their participation in a program of studies, and in patriotic, labor, military, scientific, and cultural activities.

Article 7. The Cuban socialist state recognizes, protects, and stimulates social and mass organizations, such as the Central Organization of Cuban Trade Unions, which is made up of the key class in our society, the Committees for the Defense of the Revolution, the Federation of Cuban Women, the National Association of Small Farmers, the Federation of University Students, the Federation of Secondary Education Students, the Union of Pioneers of Cuba, and others which, having risen from the historic process of the struggles of our people, gather in their midst the various sectors of the population, represent specific interests of the same, and incorporate them to the tasks of the edification, consolidation, and defense of the socialist society.

In its activities, the state relies on the social and mass organizations which, in addition, directly fulfill the state functions that are intended to be assumed by the same, in accordance with the Constitution and the law.

Article 8. The socialist state:
  a) carries out the will of the working people and
— channels the efforts of the nation in the construction of socialism;
— maintains and defends the integrity and the sovereignty of the country;
— guarantees the liberty and the full dignity of man, the enjoyment

of his rights, the exercise and fulfillment of his duties, and the integral development of his personality;
— consolidates the ideology and the rules of communal life and of conduct proper for a society free from the exploitation of man by man;
— protects the constructive work of the people, and the property and riches of the socialist nation;
— directs in a planned way the national economy;
— assures the educational, scientific, technical, and cultural progress of the country;
 b) as the power of the people and for the people, guarantees
— that every man or woman, who is able to work, has the opportunity to have a job with which to contribute to the good of society and to the satisfaction of individual needs;
— that no disabled person be left without adequate means of subsistence;
— that no sick person be left without medical care;
— that no child be left without schooling, food, and clothing;
— that no young person be left without the opportunity to study;
— that no one be left without access to studies, culture, and sports;
 c) works to achieve that no family be left without a comfortable place to live.

Article 9. The Constitution and the laws of the socialist state are the juridical expression of the socialist production relationships and of the interests and will of the working people.

All state organs, their leaders, officials, and employees function within the limits of their respective competency and are under the obligation to strictly observe socialist legality and to look after the same within the whole context of society.

Article 10. The Cuban socialist state exercises its sovereignty:
 a) over the entire national territory, which consists of the island of Cuba, Youth Island, and all other adjacent islands and keys, internal waters, territorial waters to the limit as determined by law, and over the air space which corresponds to the above;
 b) over the natural resources, flora, and fauna on and under the ocean floor and those in waters adjacent to our territorial waters, to the limit as determined by law and in accordance with international practice.

The Republic of Cuba rejects and considers illegal and null all treaties, pacts, and concessions which were signed in conditions of inequality, or which disregard or diminish its sovereignty over any part of the national territory.

Article 11. The Republic of Cuba is part of the world socialist community, which constitutes one of the fundamental premises for its full independence and development.

Article 12. The Republic of Cuba espouses the principles of proletarian internationalism and the combative solidarity of peoples, and

a) condemns imperialism, the promoter and supporter of all fascist, colonialist, neocolonialist, and racist manifestations, as the main force of aggression and war, and the worst enemy of the people;

b) condemns imperialist intervention, whether direct or indirect, in the internal and external affairs of any state, and, therefore, armed aggression and economic blockade, as well as any other form of economic coercion and of interference with or threat to the integrity of states and to the political, economic, and cultural elements of nations;

c) considers wars of aggression and conquest to be international crimes, recognizes the legitimacy of wars of national liberation, as well as of armed resistance to aggression and conquest, and considers that its help to those under attack and to the peoples who struggle for their liberation constitutes its internationalist right and duty;

d) recognizes the right of the people to repel imperialist and reactionary violence with revolutionary violence and to struggle by all means within their reach for the right to determine freely their own destiny and the economic and social system in which they choose to live;

e) works for an honorable and lasting peace, based on respect for the independence and sovereignty of peoples and on their right to self-determination;

f) establishes its international relations on the principles of equality of rights, sovereignty, and independence of states and on mutual interest;

g) bases its relations with the Union of Soviet Socialist Republics and with other socialist countries on socialist internationalism, and on the common objectives of the construction of a new society, fraternal friendship, cooperation, and mutual assistance;

h) aspires to establish along with the countries of Latin America and of the Caribbean—freed from foreign domination and internal oppression—one large community of nations joined by the fraternal ties of historical tradition and the common struggle against colonialism, neocolonialism, and imperialism, in the same desire to foster national and social progress;

i) develops fraternal relations and relations of collaboration with the countries that uphold anti-imperialist and progressive positions;

j) maintains friendly relations with those countries which—although having a different political, social, and economic system—respect its sovereignty, observe the rules of coexistence among states and the principles of mutual conveniences, and adopt an attitude of reciprocity with our country;

k) determines its affiliation with international agencies and its participation in international conferences and meetings, bearing in mind the interests of peace and socialism, the liberation of people, the progress of science, technology, and culture, international exchange, and the respect for our country's own national rights.

Article 13. The Republic of Cuba grants asylum to those who are persecuted because of the struggle for the democratic rights of the majorities; for national liberation; against imperialism, fascism, colonialism, and neocolonialism; for the abolition of racial discrimination; for the rights of workers, peasants, and students, and the redress of their grievances; for their progressive political, scientific, artistic, and literary activities; for socialism and peace.

Article 14. In the Republic of Cuba, the socialist system of economy, based on the people's socialist ownership of the means of production and on the abolition of the exploitation of man by man, rules.

Article 15. Socialist state property, which is the property of the entire people, is irreversibly established over the lands that do not belong to small farmers or to cooperatives formed by the same; over the subsoil, mines, natural resources, and flora and fauna in the marine area, over which it has jurisdiction, woods, waters, means of communication; over the sugar mills, factories, basic means of transportation; and over all those enterprises, banks, installations, and properties that have been nationalized and expropriated from the imperialists, landholders, and the bourgeoisie; as well as over people's farms, factories, enterprises, and economic, social, cultural, and sports facilities built, fostered, or purchased by the state and those which will be built, fostered, or purchased by the state in the future.

Article 16. The state organizes, directs, and controls the economic life of the nation in accordance with the Central Plan of Socio-

Economic Development in whose elaboration and execution the workers of all the branches of the economy and of other spheres of social life take an active and conscious part.

The development of the economy serves the purpose of strengthening the socialist system; of increasingly satisfying the material and cultural needs of society and of the citizens; of promoting the flowering of the human personality and its dignity; and serves the progress and security of the country, and the national capacity to fulfill the internationalist duties of our people.

Article 17. The state organizes enterprises and other economic entities for the administration of the socialist property of the entire people.

The structure, powers, and functions of the state enterprises and economic entities of production and service, and the system of their relations are regulated by law.

Article 18. Foreign trade is the exclusive function of the state. The law determines the state institutions and officials authorized to establish foreign trade enterprises and to standardize and regulate export and import transactions, and those vested with legal power to sign commercial agreements.

Article 19. In the Republic of Cuba, the socialist principle "From each according to his ability, to each according to his work", rules.

The law establishes the regulations which guarantee the effective fulfillment of this principle.

Article 20. The state recognizes the ownership of small farmers of their lands, and other means and implements of production, in accordance with that established by law.

Small farmers have the right to group themselves in the manner and following the requirements established by law, both for the purpose of agricultural production and for obtaining state loans and services.

The establishment of agricultural cooperatives, in these instances and in the manner established by law, is authorized. Ownership of the cooperatives constitutes a form of collective ownership on the part of the peasants in those cooperatives.

The state supports the cooperative production of small farmers, as well as individual production which contributes to the growth of the national economy.

The state fosters the participation of small farmers, freely and voluntarily, in state projects and units of agricultural production.

Article 21. Small farmers have the right to sell their land with the previous authorization of the state agencies, as determined by law. In all cases, the state has preferential right to the purchase of the land while paying a fair price.

Land leases, share cropping, mortgages, and all other forms which entail a lien on the land or partial cession to private individuals of the rights and title to the land, which is the property of the small farmers, are all prohibited.

Article 22. The state guarantees personal ownership of earnings and savings derived from one's own work, of the dwelling to which one has legal title, and of the other possessions and objects which serve to satisfy one's material and cultural needs.

Likewise, the state guarantees ownership of citizens of their personal or family work tools, as long as these tools are not employed in exploiting the work of others.

Article 23. The state recognizes the ownership of political, social, and mass organizations of the goods intended for the fulfillment of their goals.

Article 24. The law regulates the right to inherit legal title to a place of residence and to other goods in personal ownership.

The land of a small farmer may only be inherited by the heirs who are personally involved in its cultivation, save for the exceptions established by law.

With regard to goods which are part of cooperatives, the law determines the conditions under which said goods may be inherited.

Article 25. The expropriation of property for reasons of public benefit or social interest, and with due compensation is authorized.

The law establishes the method for the expropriation and the bases on which the need for and usefulness of this action are to be determined, as well as the form of compensation, taking into account the interests and economic and social needs of the person whose property has been expropriated.

Article 26. Anybody who suffers damages or injuries, unjustly caused by a state official or employee while in the performance of his public functions, has the right to claim and obtain the corresponding damages or indemnification in the manner established by law.

Article 27. To ensure the well-being of citizens, the state and society are the protectors of the environment. It is incumbent upon the competent agencies and upon each and every citizen to watch over the cleanliness of the waters and of the air, and to protect the soil, flora, and fauna.

Chapter II. Citizenship

Article 28. Cuban citizenship is acquired by birth or through naturalization.

Article 29. Cuban citizens by birth are:
  a) those born in our territory, with the exception of the children of foreign persons on the service of their government or international organizations;
  b) those born abroad, at least one of whose parents is Cuban and on an official mission;
  c) those born abroad, at least one of whose parents is Cuban, who have complied with the formalities stipulated by law;
  d) those born outside our territory, at least one of whose parents is Cuban, and who have lost their citizenship, provided they apply for Cuban citizenship according to the procedures stated by law;
  e) foreigners who, by virtue of their exceptional merits won in the struggles for Cuba's liberation, were considered Cuban citizens by birth.

Article 30. Cuban citizens by naturalization are:
  a) those foreigners who acquire Cuban citizenship in accordance with the regulations established by law;
  b) those who contributed to the armed struggle against the tyranny overthrown on 1 January 1959, provided they show proof of this in the legally established form and;
  c) those who, having been arbitrarily deprived of their citizenship of origin, obtain Cuban citizenship by virtue of an express agreement of the Council of State.

Article 31. Neither marriage nor its dissolution affect the citizenship status of either of the spouses or their children.

Article 32. Cuban citizenship is lost by:

a) those who become citizens of another country;

b) those who, without the Government's permission, serve another nation in military functions or in posts entailing authority or jurisdiction;

c) those who, on foreign territory, conspire or act in any way against the people of Cuba and their socialist and revolutionary institutions;

d) naturalized Cubans residing in the country where they were born, unless they express their desire to maintain Cuban citizenship to the corresponding consular authority every three years;

e) naturalized citizens who accept double citizenship.

The law may determine crimes and causes of unbecoming behavior that may lead to the loss of citizenship by naturalization through a nonappealable judgment by a court.

The formalization of the loss of citizenship for the reasons stated in clauses (b) and (c) is made effective by a decree issued by the Council of State.

Article 33. Cuban citizenship may be regained in those instances and in the manner prescribed by law.

Chapter III. The Family

Article 34. The state protects the family, motherhood, and matrimony.

Article 35. Marriage is a voluntarily established union between a man and a woman, who are legally fit to marry, in order to live together. It is based on the full equality of rights and duties for the partners, who must see to the support of the home and the all-round education of their children through a joint effort compatible with the social activities of both.

The law regulates the formalization, recognition, and dissolution of marriage, and the rights and obligations deriving from such acts.

Article 36. All children have the same rights, regardless of being born in or out of wedlock.

Any qualification concerning the nature of the relationship is abolished.

No statement shall be made either with regard to the difference in birth or the civil status of the parents in the registration of the children's birth or in any other documents that mention parenthood.

The state guarantees, through adequate legal means, the determination and recognition of paternity.

Article 37. The parents have the duty to provide nourishment for their children; to help them to defend their legitimate interests and to realize their just aspirations; and to contribute actively to their education and all-round development as useful well-prepared citizens for life in a socialist society.

It is the children's duty, in turn, to respect and help their parents.

Chapter IV. Education and Culture

Article 38. The state develops, fosters, and promotes education, culture, and science in all their manifestations.

Its educational and cultural policy is based on the following principles:

a) the state bases its educational and cultural policy on the scientific world view, established and developed by Marxism-Leninism;

b) education is a function of the state. Consequently, educational institutions belong to the state. The fulfillment of the educational function constitutes a task in which all society participates and which is based on the conclusions and contributions made by science and on the closest relationship between study and life, work and production;

c) the state must promote the communist education of the new generations and the training of children, young people, and adults for social life. In order to make this principle a reality, general education and specialized scientific, technical, or artistic education are combined with work, research and development, physical education, sports, participation in political and social activities, and military training;

d) education is provided free of charge. The state maintains a broad scholarship system for students and provides the workers with multiple opportunities to study, with a view to the universalization of education. The law establishes the integration and structure of the national system of education and the extent of compulsory education, and defines the minimum level of general education that every citizen must acquire;

e) artistic creativity is free as long as its content is not contrary to the Revolution. Forms of expression of art are free;

f) in order to raise the level of culture of the people, the state promotes and develops artistic education, the vocation for creation, and the cultivation and appreciation of art;

g) creation and research in science are free. The state encourages and facilitates research and gives priority to that which is aimed at solving problems related to the interests of society and the well-being of the people;

h) the state makes it possible for the workers to engage in scientific work and to contribute to the development of science;

i) the state develops, fosters, and promotes all forms of physical education and sports as a means of education and of contribution to the all-round development of the citizens;

j) the state sees to the conservation of the nation's cultural heritage and artistic and historic wealth. The state protects national monuments and places known for their natural beauty or their artistic or historic value;

k) the state promotes the participation of the citizens, through the country's social and mass organizations, in the development of its educational and cultural policy.

Article 39. The education of children and young people in the spirit of communism is the duty of all of society.

The state and society give special protection to children and young people.

It is the duty of the family, the schools, state agencies, and social and mass organizations to pay special attention to the all-round development of children and young people.

Chapter V. Equality

Article 40. All citizens have equal rights and are subject to equal duties.

Article 41. Discrimination because of race, color, sex, or national origin is forbidden and will be punished by law.

The institutions of the state educate everyone, from the earliest possible age, in the principle of equality among human beings.

Article 42. The state consecrates the right achieved by the Revolution that all citizens, regardless of race, color, or national origin:

— have access, in keeping with their merits and abilities, to all

positions and jobs of the state, public administration, and of production and services;
— can reach any rank of the Revolutionary Armed Forces and of Security and internal order, in keeping with their merits and abilities;
— be given equal pay for equal work;
— have the right to education at all national educational institutions, ranging from elementary schools to universities, which are the same for all; be given medical care in all medical institutions;
— live in any sector, zone, or area, and stay in any hotel;
— be served at all restaurants and other public service establishments;
— use, without any separation, all means of transportation by sea, land, and air;
— enjoy the same resorts, beaches, parks, social centers, and other centers of culture, sports, recreation, and rest.

Article 43. Women have the same rights as men in the economic, political, and social fields, as well as in the family.

In order to assure the exercise of these rights and especially the incorporation of women into socially organized work, the state sees to it that they are given jobs in keeping with their physical makeup; they are given paid maternity leave before and after giving birth; the state organizes such institutions as children's day-care centers, semiboarding schools and boarding schools; and it strives to create all the conditions which help to make real the principle of equality.

Chapter VI. Fundamental Rights, Duties, and Guarantees

Article 44. Work in a socialist society is a right and duty and a source of pride for every citizen.

Work is remunerated according to its quality and quantity; when it is so provided, the needs of the economy and of society, the choice of the worker, and his skill and ability are taken into account; this is ensured by the socialist economic system, which facilitates social and economic development without crises, and has thus eliminated unemployment and the "dead season".

Nonpaid, voluntary work carried out for the benefit of all society in industrial, agricultural, technical, artistic, and service activities is recognized as playing an important role in the formation of our people's communist awareness.

Cuba

Every worker has the duty to faithfully carry out tasks corresponding to him at his job.

Article 45. All those who work have the right to rest, which is ensured by the eight-hour work day, a weekly rest period, and annual paid vacations.

The state contributes to the development of vacation plans and facilities.

Article 46. By means of the Social Security System, the state ensures adequate protection to every worker who is unable to work because of age, illness, or disability.

If the worker dies, this protection will be extended to his family.

Article 47. The state protects, by means of social aid, senior citizens lacking financial resources or anyone to take them in or care for them, and anyone who is unable to work and has no relatives who can help him.

Article 48. The state ensures the right to protection, safety, and hygiene on the job by means of the adoption of adequate measures for the prevention of accidents at work and occupational diseases.

Anyone who suffers an accident on the job or is affected by an occupational disease has the right to medical care and to compensation or retirement in those cases in which temporary or permanent work disability ensues.

Article 49. Everyone has the right to health protection and care. The state ensures this right:
— by providing free medical and hospital care through the facilities of the rural medical service network, polyclinics, hospitals, preventive and specialized treatment centers;
— by providing free dental care;
— by promoting the health publicity campaigns, health education, regular medical examinations, general vaccinations, and other measures to prevent the outbreak of disease. All the population cooperates in these activities and plans through the social and mass organizations.

Article 50. Everyone has the right to an education. This right is ensured by the free and widespread system of schools, semiboarding, and boarding schools, and by scholarships for all kinds and all levels of education, and because of the fact that all education material is provided free of charge, which gives all children and young people, regardless of their family's economic position, the opportunity to study in keeping with their ability, social demands, and the needs of socio-economic development.

Adults are also ensured this right, education for them being free of charge with the specific facilities regulated by law, by means of the adult education, technical and vocational education, training courses in state agencies and enterprises, and by advanced courses for workers.

Article 51. Everyone has the right to physical education, sports, and recreation.

Enjoyment of this right is ensured by including the teaching and practice of physical education and sports in the curricula of the national educational system; and by the broad nature of the instruction and resources placed at the service of the people, which makes possible the practice of sports and recreation on a mass basis.

Article 52. Citizens have freedom of speech and of the press in keeping with the goals of the socialist society. Material conditions for the exercise of that right are provided by the fact that the press, radio, television, movies, and other organs of the mass media are state or social property and can never be private property. This assures their use at the exclusive service of the working people and in the interests of society.

The law regulates the exercise of these freedoms.

Article 53. The rights to assembly, demonstration, and association are exercised by workers, both manual and intellectual, peasants, women, students, and other sectors of the working people, and they have the necessary means for this. The social and mass organizations have all the facilities they need to carry out those activities in which their members have full freedom of speech and opinion based on the unlimited right of initiative and criticism.

Article 54. The socialist state, which bases its activity on and educates the people in the scientific materialist concept of the universe, recognizes and ensures freedom of conscience and the right of everyone to profess any religious belief and to practice, within the framework of respect for the law, the belief of his preference.

The law regulates the activities of religious institutions.

It is illegal and punishable by law to oppose one's faith or religious belief to the Revolution, education or to the fulfillment of the duty to work, to the defense of the homeland with arms, to the show of reverence for its symbols, and to other duties established by the Constitution.

Article 55. The home is inviolable. Nobody can enter the home of another against his will, except in those cases provided for by law.

Article 56. Correspondence is inviolable. It can only be seized, opened, and examined in those instances provided for by law. Secrecy is maintained on matters other than those which led to the examination.

The same principle is to be applied with respect to cable, telegraph, and telephone communications.

Article 57. Freedom and the inviolability of the person is ensured to all those who live in the country.

Nobody can be arrested, except in those cases, in the manner, and with the guarantees prescribed by law.

The person who has been arrested or the prisoner is inviolable in his personal integrity.

Article 58. Nobody can be tried or sentenced, except by a competent tribunal by virtue of laws which existed prior to the crime and with the formalities and guarantees which the laws establish.

Every accused person has the right to defense.

No violence or pressure of any kind can be used against people to force them to testify.

All statements obtained in violation of the above precept are null and void, and those responsible for the violation will incur those sanctions which are determined.

Article 59. Confiscation of property is only applied as a punishment by the authorities in the cases and under the procedures determined by law.

Article 60. Penal laws are retroactive when they benefit the accused or person who has been sentenced. Other laws are not retroactive, unless the contrary is decided for reasons of social interest or because it is useful for public purposes.

Article 61. None of the freedoms which are recognized for citizens can be exercised contrary to what is established in the Constitution and the laws, or contrary to the existence and goals of the socialist state, or contrary to the decision of the Cuban people to build socialism and communism. Violations of this principle are punishable.

Article 62. Every citizen has the right to file complaints with and send petitions to the authorities and to be given the pertinent response or attention within a reasonable length of time, in accordance with the law.

Article 63. It is the duty of every citizen to care for public and social property, to accept work discipline, to respect the rights of others, to observe the standards of socialist living, and to fulfill civic and social duties.

Article 64. Defense of the socialist Fatherland is the greatest honor and the supreme duty of every Cuban.

The law regulates the military service which Cubans must perform.

Treason to the Fatherland is the most serious of crimes; those who commit it are subject to the most severe penalties.

Article 65. Strict fulfillment of the Constitution and the laws is the strict duty of all.

Chapter VII. Principles of the Organization and Operation of State Organs

Article 66. State organs are set up, operate, and carry out their activities based on the principles of socialist democracy, unity of power, and democratic centralism, which are manifest in the following forms:

a) all organs of state power, their executive organs, and all the courts are elected and subject to reelection at regular intervals;

b) the masses control the activity of the state agencies, their deputies, delegates, and officials;

c) those elected must render an account of their work to their electors, and the latter have the right to recall the former when they are not worthy of the trust placed in them;

d) every state organ develops, in a far-reaching manner within its jurisdiction, initiatives aimed at taking advantage of the resources and possibilities which exist on a local level and the inclusion of the social and mass organizations in their work;

e) decisions of higher-level state organs are compulsory for lower-level ones;

f) lower-level state organs are responsible to higher-level ones and must render account of their work;

g) in the activities of local administrative and executive organs, there is a system of dual subordination: subordination to the corresponding organ of People's Power, and subordination to the higher-level organ responsible for administrative matters, which are also under the jurisdiction of the local organ;

h) freedom of discussion, criticism, and self-criticism, and subordination of the minority to the majority prevail in all collegiate state organs.

Chapter VIII. Supreme Organs of People's Power

Article 67. The National Assembly of People's Power is the supreme organ of state power and represents and expresses the sovereign will of all the working people.

Article 68. The National Assembly of People's Power is the only organ in the Republic vested with constituent and legislative authority.

Article 69. The National Assembly of People's Power is composed of deputies elected by the municipal Assemblies of People's Power according to the manner and in the proportion determined by law.

Article 70. The National Assembly of People's Power is elected for a period of five years.

This period can only be extended by virtue of a resolution of the Assembly itself in the event of war, or in the case of other exceptional circumstances which may impede the normal conduct of elections and while such circumstances exist.

Article 71. Thirty days after all the deputies to the National Assembly of People's Power are elected, the Assembly meets on its own right under the presidency of the oldest deputy assisted by the two youngest deputies acting as secretaries.

The session includes the verification of the validity of the election of the deputies, the swearing in of the deputies, and the election by the deputies of the President, the Vice-President, and the Secretary of the National Assembly of People's Power, who proceed to assume their posts immediately.

Next, the Assembly proceeds to elect the Council of State.

Article 72. The National Assembly of People's Power elects, from among its deputies, the Council of State, which consists of one President, one First Vice-President, five Vice-Presidents, one Secretary, and 23 other members.

The President of the Council of State is, at the same time, the Head of State and the Head of Government.

The Council of State is accountable for its action to the National Assembly of People's Power, to which it must render account of all its activities.

Article 73. The National Assembly of People's Power is vested with the following powers:

a) deciding on reforms to the Constitution, in accordance with Article 141;

b) approving, modifying, and annulling laws after consulting with the people when it is considered necessary in view of the nature of the law in question;

c) deciding on the constitutionality of laws, decree-laws, decrees, and all other general provisions;

d) annulling in total or in part the decree-laws issued by the Council of State;

e) discussing and approving the national plans for economic and social development;

f) discussing and approving the state budget;

g) approving the principles of the system for planning and management of the national economy;

h) approving the monetary and credit system;

i) approving the general outlines of foreign and domestic policy;

j) declaring a state of war in the event of military aggression, and approving peace treaties;

k) establishing and modifying the politico-administrative division of the country, in accordance with Article 100;

l) electing the President, Vice-President, and Secretary of the National Assembly;

m) electing the President, the First Vice-President, the Vice-Presidents, the Secretary, and the other members of the Council of State;

n) appointing, at the initiative of the President of the Council of

State, the First Vice-President, the Vice-President, and other members of the Council of Ministers;

o) electing the President, Vice-President, and other judges of the People's Supreme Court;

p) electing the Attorney General and the deputy attorneys general of the Republic;

q) appointing permanent and temporary commissions;

r) revoking the election or appointment of those persons elected or appointed by it;

s) exercising supreme supervision over the organs of state and government;

t) keeping informed on, evaluating, and adopting pertinent decisions on the reports on the rendering of accounts submitted by the Council of State, the Council of Ministers, the People's Supreme Court, the Office of the Attorney General of the Republic, and the Provincial Assemblies of People's Power;

u) annulling those provisions or decree-laws of the Council of State, and the decrees or resolutions of the Council of Ministers which are contrary to the Constitution or the laws;

v) annulling or modifying those resolutions or provisions of the local organs of People's Power which violate the Constitution, the laws, the decree-laws, the decrees, and other provisions issued by a higher-level organ, or those which are detrimental to the interests of other localities or the general interests of the nation;

w) granting amnesty;

x) calling for the holding of a referendum in those instances provided for by the Constitution, and in others which the Assembly considers pertinent;

y) establishing its rules and regulations; and

z) all other powers vested by this Constitution.

Article 74. All laws and resolutions of the National Assembly of People's Power, with the exception of those relating to reforms in the Constitution, are adopted by a simple majority vote.

Article 75. All laws approved by the National Assembly of People's Power go into effect on the date determined by those laws in each case.

Laws, decree-laws, decrees and resolutions, regulations, and other general provisions of the national organs of the state are published in the Official Gazette of the Republic.

Article 76. The National Assembly of People's Power holds two regular sessions a year and a special session when requested by one-third of the membership or when convened by the Council of State.

Article 77. More than half of the total number of deputies must be present for a session of the National Assembly of People's Power to be held.

Article 78. All sessions of the National Assembly of People's Power are public, except when the Assembly resolves to hold a closed-door session on the grounds of state interests.

Article 79. The President of the National Assembly of People's Power is vested with the power to:

    a) preside over the sessions of the National Assembly and see that its regulations are put into effect;

    b) convene the regular sessions of the National Assembly;

    c) propose the draft agenda for the sessions of the National Assembly;

    d) sign and order the publication in the Official Gazette of the Republic of the laws and resolutions adopted by the National Assembly;

    e) organize the international relations of the National Assembly;

    f) conduct and organize the work of the permanent and temporary commissions appointed by the National Assembly;

    g) attend the meetings of the Council of State; and

    h) with all other powers assigned to him by this Constitution or by the Assembly.

Article 80. The status of deputy does not entail personal privileges or economic benefits of any kind.

The deputies to the National Assembly of People's Power combine their activities as such with their duties and their regular everyday tasks.

To the extent that their work as deputies demands, they are given leave without pay and receive a daily allowance equivalent to their salary and whatever additional expenses they may incur in the exercise of their duties.

Article 81. No deputy to the National Assembly of People's Power may be arrested or placed on trial without the authorization of the Assembly—or the Council of State, if the Assembly is not in session—except in the cases of flagrant offenses.

Article 82. It is the duty of the deputies to the National Assembly of People's Power to exercise their duties for the benefit of the people's interests, stay in contact with their electors, listen to their grievances, suggestions, and criticism, explain the policy of the state to them, and periodically render account to them of the results of their activities.

Likewise, it is the deputies' duty to render account of their activities to the Assembly any time the Assembly deems it necessary.

Article 83. The deputies to the National Assembly of People's Power may be recalled by their electors at any time in the manner and procedure established by law.

Article 84. The deputies to the National Assembly of People's Power have the right to address inquiries to the Council of State, the Council of Ministers, or the members of either, and to have these inquiries answered during the course of the same session or at the next session.

Article 85. It is the duty of all state organs and enterprises to render all necessary cooperation to the deputies in the discharge of their duties.

Article 86. The proposal of laws is the responsibility of:
 a) the deputies to the National Assembly of People's Power;
 b) the Council of State;
 c) the Council of Ministers;
 d) the commissions of the National Assembly of People's Power;
 e) the Central Organizations of Cuban Trade Unions, and the national offices of the other social and mass organizations;
 f) the People's Supreme Court, in matters related to the administration of justice;
 g) the Office of the Attorney General of the Republic, in matters within its jurisdiction;
 h) the citizens. In this case, it is a necessary prerequisite that the proposal be made by at least 10,000 citizens who are eligible to vote.

Article 87. The Council of State is the organ of the National Assembly of People's Power that represents it in the period between sessions, puts its resolutions into effect, and complies with all the other duties assigned by the Constitution.

It is collegiate, and for national and international purposes it is the supreme representative of the Cuban state.

Article 88. The Council of State is vested with the power to:

a) summon special sessions of the National Assembly of People's Power;

b) set the date for the elections for the periodic reelection of the National Assembly of People's Power;

c) issue decree-laws in the period between sessions of the National Assembly of People's Power;

d) give existing laws a general and binding interpretation whenever necessary;

e) exercise legislative initiative;

f) make all the necessary arrangements for the holding of referenda called for by the National Assembly of People's Power;

g) decree general mobilization whenever the defense of the country makes it necessary, and assume the authority to declare war in the event of aggression or to approve peace treaties—duties which the Constitution assigns to the National Assembly of People's Power—when the Assembly is in recess and cannot be called to session with the necessary security and urgency;

h) replace, at the initiative of its President, the members of the Council of Ministers in the period between sessions of the National Assembly of People's Power;

i) issue general instructions to the courts through the Governing Council of the People's Supreme Court;

j) issue instructions to the Office of the Attorney General of the Republic;

k) appoint and remove, at the initiative of its President, the diplomatic representatives of Cuba in other states;

l) grant decorations and honorary titles;

m) name commissions;

n) grant pardons;

o) ratify or denounce international treaties;

p) grant or refuse recognition to diplomatic representatives of other states;

q) suspend those provisions of the Council of Ministers and the resolutions and provisions of the local Assemblies of People's Power which do not conform to the Constitution or the laws, or when they are detrimental to the interests of other localities or to the general interests of the country, reporting on this action to the National Assembly of People's Power in the first session held following the suspension agreed upon;

r) annul those resolutions and provisions of the executive committees of the local organs of People's Power which contravene the

Constitution, the laws, the decree-laws, the decrees, and other provisions issued by a higher-level organ, or when they are detrimental to the interests of other localities or to the general interests of the country;

s) approve its rules and regulations;

t) it is also vested with the other powers conferred by the Constitution and laws, or granted by the National Assembly of People's Power.

Article 89. All the decisions of the Council of State are adopted by a simple majority vote of its members.

Article 90. The mandate entrusted to the Council of State by the National Assembly of People's Power expires at the time of the establishment of a new Assembly by virtue of the periodic reelections of the Assembly.

Article 91. The President of the Council of State is the Head of Government and is vested with the power to:

a) represent the state and the government, and conduct their general policy;

b) organize, conduct the activities of, call for the holding of, and preside over the sessions of the Council of State and the Council of Ministers;

c) control and supervise the development of the activities of the ministries and other central agencies of administration;

d) assume the leadership of any ministry or central agency of administration;

e) propose to the National Assembly of People's Power, once elected by the latter, the members of the Council of Ministers;

f) accept the resignation of the members of the Council of Ministers or propose either to the National Assembly of People's Power or to the Council of State the replacement of any of those members and, in both cases, to propose the corresponding replacements;

g) receive the credentials of the heads of foreign diplomatic missions. This responsibility may be delegated to any of the Vice-Presidents of the Council of State;

h) assume the supreme command of the Revolutionary Armed Forces;

i) sign the decree-laws and other resolutions of the Council of State, and arrange for their publication in the Official Gazette of the Republic; and

j) assume all other duties assigned by the Constitution or the Assembly.

Article 92. In case of the absence, illness, or death of the President of the Council of State, the First Vice-President assumes the President's duties.

Article 93. The Council of Ministers is the highest-ranking executive and administrative organ, and constitutes the Government of the Republic.

The number, denomination, and functions of the ministries and central agencies making up the Council of Ministers are determined by law.

Article 94. The Council of Ministers is composed of the Head of State and Government, as its President, the First Vice-President, the Vice-Presidents, the President of the Central Planning Board, the Ministers, the Secretary, and the other members as determined by law.

Article 95. The President, the First Vice-President, and the Vice-Presidents of the Council of Ministers constitute its Executive Committee.

The members of the Executive Committee control and coordinate the work of the ministries and central organizations by sectors.

In emergency cases, the Executive Committee may rule on matters normally under the jurisdiction of the Council of Ministers.

Article 96. The Council of Ministers is vested with the power to:

a) organize and conduct the political, economic, cultural, scientific, social, and defense activities outlined by the National Assembly of People's Power;

b) propose the projects for the general plans for the socio-economic development of the state, and, after these are approved by the National Assembly of People's Power, organize, conduct, and supervise their implementation;

c) conduct the foreign policy of the Republic and relations with other governments;

d) approve international treaties and submit them to ratification by the Council of State;

e) direct and control foreign trade;

f) draw up the draft for the state budget and, once it is approved

Cuba

by the National Assembly of People's Power, to see to its implementation;

g) adopt measures aimed at strengthening the monetary and credit system;

h) draw up bills and submit them for consideration to the National Assembly of People's Power or the Council of State, accordingly;

i) see to national defense, the maintenance of domestic order and security, the protection of citizens' rights, and the protection of lives and property in the event of natural disasters;

j) conduct the administration of the state unifying, coordinating, and supervising the activities of the ministries and other central agencies of the administration;

k) implement the laws and resolutions of the National Assembly of People's Power and the decree-laws and provisions issued by the Council of State and, if necessary, dictate the corresponding regulations;

l) issue decrees and provisions on the basis of and pursuant to the existing laws, and supervise their implementation;

m) grant territorial asylum;

n) determine the general organization of the Revolutionary Armed Forces;

o) assume the direction and the methodological and technical supervision over the administrative functions of local organs of People's Power through the corresponding ministries and other central agencies;

p) revoke or annul those provisions issued by ministers, heads of central agencies, and the administrative bodies of local organs of People's Power which are contrary to the instructions issued from a higher level and whose implementation is obligatory;

q) propose to the National Assembly of People's Power the annulment of, or to the Council of State the suspension of, those resolutions and provisions issued by the Assemblies of the local organs of People's Power which contravene existing laws and other provisions, or which are detrimental to the interests of other communities or the general interests of the country;

r) name the commissions it deems necessary to facilitate the implementation of the tasks assigned to it;

s) appoint and remove officials in keeping with the powers vested in it by the law; and

t) assume any duty assigned by the National Assembly of People's Power or the Council of State.

Article 97. The Council of Ministers is accountable to and periodically renders account of its activities to the National Assembly of People's Power.

Article 98. The members of the Council of Ministers are vested with the power to:

a) conduct the affairs and tasks of the ministry or agency under their care, issuing the necessary resolutions and provisions to that effect;

b) dictate, in the event it is not the specific duty of another state organ, the necessary regulations for the implementation and application of those laws and decree-laws which concern them;

c) attend the sessions of the Council of Ministers, with the authority to speak and vote, and submit for the consideration of the Council whatever bill, decree-law, decree, resolution, or any other proposal they consider advisable;

d) appoint, in accordance with law, the officials of their agency;

e) it is also vested with any other power assigned by the Constitution and laws.

Article 99. The General Secretary of the Central Organization of Cuban Trade Unions has the right to participate in the sessions of the Council of Ministers and of its Executive Committee.

Chapter IX. Local Organs of People's Power

Article 100. For political-administrative purposes, the country is divided into provinces and municipalities; their number, boundaries, and names are established by law.

The law can also establish other divisions.

Article 101. The Assemblies of Delegates of People's Power, established in the political and administrative divisions into which the country is divided by law, are the superior local organs of state power.

Article 102. The local Assemblies of Delegates of People's Power are vested with the highest authority for the exercise of their state functions in the area under their jurisdiction. To this effect, they govern in all that concerns them, and, by means of the organs which they establish, direct economic, production, and service units which are directly subordinate to them and carry out the activities required in order to meet the needs for welfare, economic, cultural, educational, and recreational services of the collective in the territory under the jurisdiction of each.

They also aid in the development of activities and the fulfillment of plans of those units in their territory which are not subordinated to them.

Article 103. For the exercise of their functions, the local Assemblies of People's Power are backed up by the initiative and the broad participation of the population, and they act in close coordination with social and mass organizations.

Article 104. The local organs of People's Power, to the corresponding extent and in accordance with the law, participate in the preparation, subsequent implementation, and control of the Uniform Socio-Economic Plan adopted by the state.

Article 105. Within the limits of their jurisdiction, the provincial and municipal Assemblies of People's Power:

a) obey and help to enforce the general laws and regulations which come from higher-level state organs;

b) adopt agreements and enact measures;

c) annul, suspend, or modify, as the case may be, the resolutions and measures of the organs subordinate to them which violate the Constitution or the laws, decree-laws, decrees, regulations, or resolutions enacted by the higher-level organs of state power, or those which are detrimental to the interests of other communities or the general interests of the country;

d) elect their executive committee and determine its organization, functioning, and tasks, in accordance with the law;

e) revoke the mandate of the members of the respective executive committees;

f) determine the organization, operation, and tasks of the administrative leadership in the different branches of socio-economic activity;

g) appoint, replace, or dismiss the heads of their administrative departments;

h) set up and dissolve work commissions;

i) elect and recall, in accordance with the provisions of the law, the judges of the people's courts in the area under their respective jurisdictions;

j) study and evaluate the rendering of account reports presented by their executive committees, judicial organs, and assemblies which are their immediate subordinates, and adopt the pertinent decisions regarding those reports;

k) protect and defend the rights of citizens and socialist property;

l) work to strengthen socialist legality, uphold internal order, and strengthen the country's defense capacity;

m) carry out the other functions assigned by the Constitution and the laws.

Article 106. On the second Sunday following the election of all the delegates to the municipal Assembly of People's Power, it meets by right under the presidency of the oldest delegate in order to confirm the validity of the election of the delegates and, once this has been done, it will elect the executive committee and the delegates to the provincial Assemblies. The two youngest delegates act as secretaries.

The other local Assemblies are set up in the same manner where indicated by law.

Article 107. The regular and extraordinary sessions of the local Assemblies of People's Power are public. Only when state secrets or the dignity of persons are involved will this not be the case.

Article 108. In order for sessions of the Assemblies of People's Power to be valid, more than half the total number of members must be present. Agreements are adopted by simple majority.

Article 109. The administrative departments are subordinate to their respective Assemblies, its executive committee, and the higher-level organ of the corresponding administrative branch.

Article 110. The permanent work commissions organized by branches of production and services, or by field of work, aid the Assemblies and their executive committees in their respective activities and in controlling administrative leadership and local enterprises.

Temporary commissions fulfill specific tasks assigned within the time limits indicated.

Article 111. The Assemblies are reelected every two and a half years, which is the term of a delegate.

This term can only be extended by decision of the National Assembly of People's Power, in those instances indicated in Article 70.

Article 112. The mandate of the delegates can only be revoked by their electors, who can do so at any time, by the procedure established by law. The law also establishes the instances and the manner for replacing delegates when they are impaired from performing their duties.

Article 113. The delegates carry out the mandate of their electors in the interests of the entire community, and they must:

a) make the opinions, needs, and problems expressed by their electors known to the Assembly;

b) report to their electors on the policy of the Assembly and the measures adopted for solving the problems posed by the population or outline the reasons why they have not been solved;

c) render account of their work on a regular basis to their electors and to the Assembly to which they belong.

Article 114. The executive committee is the collegiate organ elected by the provincial and municipal Assemblies of People's Power to carry out the functions assigned by the Constitution and by the laws, as well as the tasks given it by the Assembly.

The executive committee is made up of the number of members determined by law and they elect, with the ratification of the Assembly, a President, a Vice-President, and a Secretary, who also hold those posts in the Assembly.

Article 115. The election of the members of the executive committees of the municipal and provincial Assemblies takes place from among the ranks of Assembly delegates.

In all cases, the election takes place by virtue of candidacies proposed in the manner established by law.

The President of every municipal executive committee is also, by right, a delegate to the provincial Assembly of People's Power.

Article 116. The executive committee has the authority to:

a) convene regular and special sessions of the Assembly;

b) publish and implement the agreements adopted by the Assembly;

c) suspend the implementation of any measure enacted by the immediate subordinate local Assemblies of People's Power, when it violates the Constitution, the laws, or other measures enacted by the higher-level organs of state power, or when it is detrimental to the interests of other communities or the general interests of the country;

d) annul, in the instances referred to in clause c), the provisions, agreements, and resolutions of the executive committees of the immediate subordinate local Assemblies of People's Power in those periods in which the Assembly, to which they pertain, is not in session;

e) study, evaluate, and adopt the pertinent decisions regarding the rendering of account reports presented by the immediate subordinate executive committee;

f) direct and control administrative leadership and local enterprises;

g) appoint and replace officials of administrative leadership and of local enterprises;

h) adopt pertinent measures to aid in the development of the activities and the fulfillment of the plans of the units established in the territory of the respective Assemblies which are not subordinate to it;

i) suspend and temporarily replace the heads of administrative departments and local enterprises, giving an account of the Assembly, which may ratify or modify the decision.

Article 117. In the periods between Assembly sessions, the executive committee assumes its functions which are indicated in clauses a), b), h), k), and l) of Article 105.

The agreements and general measures adopted by the executive committee in the exercise of those powers must be ratified, modified, or annulled by the Assembly in the first meeting it holds afterward.

Article 118. The executive committee periodically renders an account of its work in the Assembly and to the immediate higher-level executive committee.

Article 119. The mandate given to the executive committees ceases when new provincial and municipal Assemblies of People's Power, respectively, are set up.

Article 120. The President of the executive committee has the power to:

a) convene and preside over the sessions of the Assembly;

b) see to it that the Regulations of the Assemblies are enforced;

c) convene and preside over the meetings of the executive committee;

d) organize the activities of the executive committee.

The President may delegate some of these functions to the Vice-President.

Chapter X. The Courts and the Attorney General

Article 121. The function of administering justice flows from the people and is carried out on their behalf by the People's Supreme Court and the other tribunals which are set up by law.

The jurisdiction and competence of the courts on their different levels will be adjusted to the political-administrative division of the country and the needs of the judicial process.

The law regulates the organization of the courts; the authority and the form of exercising it; the standards that judges must meet; the manner in which they must be elected; the period of time they are to serve in their respective positions, and the method for recalling them.

Article 122. The courts constitute a system of state organs which are set up with functional independence from all other systems, and they are only subordinate to the National Assembly of People's Power and the Council of State.

Article 123. The main objectives of the activities of the court are:

a) to maintain and strengthen socialist legality;

b) to safeguard the economic, social, and political regime established in this Constitution;

c) to protect socialist property and the personal property of citizens and others, which this Constitution recognizes;

d) to safeguard the rights and legitimate interests of state agencies and those of economic and social institutions and the masses;

e) to protect the life, freedom, dignity, honor, property, family relations, and other legitimate rights and interests of citizens;

f) to prevent violations of the law and anti-social conduct, restrain and reeducate those who are guilty of such violations or conduct, and reestablish the rule of legal standards when demands are made in protest against their violation;

g) to increase awareness as to the need for strictly observing the law, making timely comments in their decisions aimed at educating citizens in the conscious and voluntary fulfillment of their duty of loyalty to the Fatherland, the cause of socialism, and the norms of socialist living.

Article 124. The People's Supreme Court is the ultimate judicial authority and its decisions in this field are final.

Through its Governing Council, it can propose laws and issue regulations; make decisions and enact norms whose implementation is obligatory for all people's courts and, based on their experience, it issues instructions which are also obligatory in order to establish uniform judicial practice in the interpretation and application of the law.

Article 125. The judges, in their function of administering justice, are independent and only owe obedience to the law.

Article 126. The sentences and other decisions of the courts, pronounced or enacted within the limits of their jurisdiction, must be obeyed and implemented by state agencies, economic and social institutions, and citizens, by those directly affected and by those who do not have a direct interest in their implementation but have the duty to participate in it.

Article 127. All courts function in a collegiate form.

Professional and lay judges participate in the administration of justice with equal duties and rights.

Priority should be given to the judicial functions assigned to the lay judge in view of their social importance.

Article 128. Courts render an account of their work to the Assembly that elected them at least once a year.

Article 129. A judge can only be recalled by the organ which elected him.

Article 130. It falls within the jurisdiction of the Office of the Attorney General of the Republic, as its main objective, to control socialist legality by seeing to it that the law and other legal regulations are obeyed by state agencies, economic and social institutions, and citizens.

The law determines the manner, duration, and occasion in which the Attorney General exercises those powers.

Article 131. The Office of the Attorney General of the Republic constitutes an organic unit which is only subordinate to the National Assembly of People's Power and the Council of State.

The Attorney General of the Republic receives instructions directly by the Council of State.

The Attorney General of the Republic will handle the direction and control of all the work done by his office all over the country.

The Attorney General of the Republic is a member of the Governing Council of the People's Supreme Court.

The organs of the Office of the Attorney General are organized in a vertical manner all over the country. They are subordinate only to the Attorney General of the Republic and are independent of all local organs.

Article 132. The Attorney General of the Republic and the assistant attorneys general are elected and subject to recall by the National Assembly of People's Power. The law establishes their term of office.

Article 133. The Attorney General of the Republic renders an account of his work to the National Assembly of People's Power at least once a year.

Chapter XI. The Electoral System

Article 134. In all elections and referenda, voting is free, equal, and secret. Each voter has only one vote.

Article 135. All Cubans over 16 years of age, men and women alike, have the right to vote except those who:
 a) are mentally disabled and have been declared so by court;
 b) those who have committed a crime and because of this have lost the right to vote.

Article 136. All Cuban citizens, men and women alike, who have full political rights can be elected.

If the election is for deputies to the National Assemblies of People's Power, they must be more than 18 years old.

Article 137. Members of the Revolutionary Armed Forces and other military institutions of the nation have the right to elect and be elected, just like any other citizen.

Article 138. The law determines the number of delegates that make up each of the Assemblies in proportion to the number of people who live in each of the political-administrative regions into which the country is divided; it also regulates the procedure and manner of the election.

The delegates to the municipal Assemblies are elected from previously determined electoral districts.

Article 139. The municipal Assemblies elect, by means of a secret ballot, the delegates to the provincial Assemblies of People's Power.

Article 140. In order for a delegate to be considered elected, he must get more than half the number of votes cast in the district.

If this does not happen, the law regulates the manner in which new elections will be held in order to decide who is elected from among those with the most votes.

Chapter XII. Constitutional Reforms

Article 141. This Constitution can only be totally or partially modified by the National Assembly of People's Power by means of resolutions adopted by roll-call vote by a majority of no less than two-thirds of the total number of members.

If the modification is total or has to do with the integration and authority of the National Assembly of People's Power, or its Council of State, or the rights and duties contained in the Constitution, the approval of the majority of citizens with the right to vote is required through a referendum organized for this purpose by the Assembly.

CZECHOSLOVAKIA

INTRODUCTION

Th. J. Vondracek

Shortly after the proclamation of an independent Czechoslovak Republic on 28 October 1918, with Thomas G. Masaryk as its first President, a provisional Constitution was adopted on 13 November 1918. This Constitution was later on replaced by the definitive and comprehensive Constitution of 29 February 1920.

The 1920 Constitution was mainly shaped in accordance with the constitutional patterns of the West European democracies and, as a matter of principle, adhered to the doctrine of separation of powers as conceived by Montesquieu.

Following the change of government on 25 February 1948—in the West generally seen as a *coup d'état*, in the East as a result of a legally thwarted attempt of reactionaries to restore full capitalism—Czechoslovakia adopted its first socialist Constitution, proclaiming the country to be a people's democracy. This Constitution, of 9 May 1948, published as Law No. 150/1948 *Sbírka zákonů*, (Collection of Laws) rejected the doctrine of separation of powers and replaced it, according to the constitutional system of the Soviet Union, with the doctrine of unity of state power. Nevertheless, the 1948 Constitution retained, mainly in its phraseology, clear vestiges of the former doctrine. State power was apportioned among the following organs:
— the unicameral National Assembly as the supreme body of legislative power;
— the Government as the body vested with governmental and executive power;
— the Judiciary in which judicial power was vested;
— the President as chief of state chosen by the National Assembly for the same term of seven years as under the previous Constitution; he could not be called to account for the exercise of his functions, but every governmental or executive act of the President needed the countersignature of the competent member of the Government—a construction very reminiscent of the 1920 Constitution.

The 1948 Constitution contained in its first Chapter no less than 38 articles relating to fundamental rights and freedoms. Slovakia was granted only a limited degree of autonomy. There was no mention in the Constitution of the Communist Party of Czechoslovakia and its dominant role.

Introduction

On 11 July 1960, Czechoslovakia adopted its second socialist Constitution, promulgated as Law No. 100/1960 *Sbírka zákonů*. By it, the country's status as people's democracy was upswung to that of a socialist state, and its name was changed from Czechoslovak Republic (ČSR) into Czechoslovak Socialist Republic (ČSSR), indicating that it had attained the same level of historic development as the Soviet Union. The state was said to be founded on a union of workers, peasants, and the intelligentsia, headed by the class of workers. The Communist Party was now explicitly proclaimed to be the leading force in the state and society.

Although the country had achieved the rank of a socialist state, the dictatorship of the proletariat was fully maintained, as President and Party leader Gustáv Husák repeatedly declared. The qualification "socialist" also referred to the fact that the private production sector had shrunk to an almost negligible extent, whereas, in the former phase, the private and capitalist sector still comprised 39% and the socialist sector 61% of the total.

In addition, the above-mentioned vestiges of Montesquieu's doctrine were erased. Apart from that, the 1960 Constitution did not change much with respect to the organization of the state. To be sure, the organs of local power, called National Committees, gained more elbowroom. They were, to take an example, empowered to establish comrades' courts in conformity with the Soviet model. However, during the Dubček-period these quasi-courts were sharply criticized and subsequently abolished. They were never restored.

The most important change which affected the constitutional system was introduced by Constitutional Law No. 143/1968 (several times since amended), converting the unitary state into a federation of two constituent republics: the Czech Socialist Republic (ČSR) and the Slovak Socialist Republic (SSR). The Federation as a whole (ČSSR) being sovereign, each of the constituent republics was likewise proclaimed to be sovereign. Contrary to the Soviet approach, the constituent republics of Bohemia-Moravia and Slovakia have not been granted the formal right to secession.

As a consequence of the federalization, there operate in the country three legislatures, three governments, and three supreme courts. The federal legislature, named the Federal Assembly, consists of two houses—the House of the People and the House of the Nations. In the latter House, the Czech and Slovak nations are each represented by the equal number of 75 deputies. The distribution of the state powers between the federation and the constituent republics is quite similar to that of the Soviet Union: the most important powers (such as foreign affairs, defense, and the monetary system) are allocated to the federation; others are assigned to the federation and the republics concurrently; and some are conferred upon each republic only. The 1968 Constitutional Law provides for the setting up of a Constitutional Court in order to insure the constitutionality of all laws and other enactments. Moreover, private citizens are said to enjoy the right to appeal to the Court whenever fundamental rights and freedoms are infringed. The Court, however, has never been set up.

The 1960 Constitution has been amended in substance by the following six Constitutional Laws: Nos. 143/1968, 144/1968, 57/1969, 155/1969, 43/1971, and 62/1978 *Sbírka zákonů*. Law No. 144/1968, for example, governs the legal position of the most important minorities, *i.e.* the Hungarian, German, Polish, and Ukrainian (Ruthenian) citizens of Czechoslovakia. The law ensures that these nationalities exercise their own political rights and pursue their own cultural development. In addition to these Constitutional Laws, a number of other Constitutional Laws have been passed which do not change the text proper of the 1960 Constitution, but nevertheless supplement the constitutional system. For example, Law No. 10/1969 provides for the establishment of a Council for the Defense of the State, whose meetings can be presided over by the President of the Republic. That Council is thus to be considered a constitutional body, although the Constitution does not mention it.

The most significant impact on the 1960 Constitution was produced by Constitutional Law 1968 No. 143, which remodeled the country into a federation as mentioned above. Constitutional Law 1970 No. 125, amending the 1968 Law on federalization, enlarged the federal powers and, accordingly, shrunk the powers of both constituent republics (especially in the domain of the economy), so marking a wary step backwards. The text of the 1968 Constitutional Law on the Czechoslovak Federation, as amended, is attached to the present volume in a separate appendix.

CONSTITUTION OF THE CZECHOSLOVAK SOCIALIST REPUBLIC OF 11 JULY 1960 (AS AMENDED)

Preamble	140
The Social Order	142
Rights and Duties of Citizens	146
The National Committees	150
The Courts and the Procuracy	153
General and Concluding Provisions	157

CONSTITUTION OF THE CZECHOSLOVAK SOCIALIST REPUBLIC*

Sbírka zákonů Československá socialistiká republika 1960 No. 100, as amended 1968 Nos. 143, 144; 1969 Nos. 57, 155; 1971 No. 43; 1978 No. 62

The National Assembly has decided to establish the following Constitutional Law:

PREAMBLE

I.

We, the working people of Czechoslovakia, solemnly declare:

The social order for which whole generations of our workers and the other working people have fought, and which they had in view as a model since the victory of the Great Socialist October Revolution, has also become reality with us, under the leadership of the Communist Party of Czechoslovakia.

Socialism has prevailed in our Fatherland!

We have entered a new era of our history, and we are determined to go forward to new, still higher goals. In bringing the socialist construction to a conclusion, we are moving towards the building of a mature socialist society and are gathering strength for the transition to communism.

We shall continue along this road hand in hand with our great ally, the fraternal Union of Soviet Socialist Republics, and with all the other friendly countries of the world system of socialism, of which our Republic constitutes a solid link.

We desire to live in peace and friendship with all nations of the world and to contribute to peaceful coexistence and good relations between states with different social systems. Through a consistent, peaceful policy, and through the all-round development of our country, we shall help to convince all nations of the advantages of socialism, which alone leads to the welfare of all mankind.

*Translated by Th. J. Vondracek.

II.

Fifteen years ago, in the year 1945, our working people, liberated by the heroic Soviet Army from the chains of fascist occupation, have decided, after the experience with the bourgeois Republic, to build up their liberated country as a People's Democracy whose mission was to ensure the peaceful development towards socialism. The Communist Party of Czechoslovakia, the tried vanguard of the working class, steeled in the struggle under the bourgeois Republic and during the occupation, took its stand at the head of the Republic. The last full-dressed attempt of international and domestic reaction to reverse this development was repelled by the determined action of the working people in February 1948.

Our working people thus first freed themselves from foreign domination and then also from capitalistic exploitation, and became rulers in their own country. In those fifteen years they have achieved, by their work and purposeful efforts, such successes in all domains of human endeavor that were inconceivable under capitalism. The advantages of the socialist order have also become absolutely clear and convincing to us.

The appearance of our country has undergone a fundamental transformation. Our national economy is developing and gaining strength as never before. Production is increasing from year to year, and the living standard of all working people is continuously rising. There are no longer any exploitative classes with us, and exploitation of man by man has forever been put to an end. There are no longer economic crises nor unemployment. Education and culture are becoming the common asset of all the working people.

Both nations, the Czechs and the Slovaks, which have created the Czechoslovak Republic, live in fraternal concord. Slovakia soon overcame its former backwardness and rose to an advanced level of industry as well as agriculture.

The Czechoslovak state, into which the working people, headed by the working class, organized themselves, has become a people's organization in the truest sense of the word—a socialist state.

In our country, all the fundamental tasks of the transition from a capitalistic to a socialist society have already been resolved. Liberated human labor has become the basic factor in our entire society. It is today not merely a duty but also a matter of honor for every citizen. The basic principle of socialism has already taken shape: "From each according to his abilities, to each according to his work."

The People's Democracy, as a road to socialism, has fully tried itself: it has led us to the victory of socialism.

III.

All our endeavors are now directed towards the creation of the material and spiritual conditions for the transition of our society to communism.

While developing socialist statehood, we shall furthermore perfect our socialist democracy by extending participation of the working people in the administration of the state and in the management of the economy, strengthening the political and moral unity of our society, safeguarding the defense of our country, guarding the revolutionary achievements of the people, and creating conditions for the development of all their creative abilities.

At a later stage of development in which labor becomes the primary necessity of life, we desire to achieve an expansion of the forces of production and a multiplication of the wealth of society to such a degree that it will be possible to satisfy all the growing needs of society and the all-round development of each of its members. It will then be possible to realize the highest principle of distribution—the principle of communism: "From each according to his abilities, to each according to his needs."

In order to consolidate all the results achieved so far by the strife and labor of our people, and at the same time to show our unbreakable will to achieve still higher goals, we enact today the present socialist Constitution of our Republic.

Chapter I. The Social Order

Article 1. (1) The Czechoslovak Socialist Republic is a socialist state founded on the firm union of the workers, peasants, and the intelligentsia, with the working class at its head.

(2) (Repealed by Constitutional Law No. 143, *Sbírka zákonů ČSSR* 1968.)

(3) The Czechoslovak Socialist Republic is a part of the world system of socialism; it strives for friendly relations with all nations and for the ensurance of lasting peace throughout the world.

Article 2. (1) All power in the Czechoslovak Socialist Republic belongs to the working people.

(2) The working people exercise state power through representative bodies which are elected by them, controlled by them, and accountable to them.

(3) Representative bodies of the working people in the Czechoslovak Socialist Republic are: the Federal Assembly, the Czech National Council, the Slovak National Council, and the National Committees. The powers of the other state organs are derived from them.

(4) Representative bodies and all the other state organs rely in their activities on the creative initiative and direct participation of the working people and their organizations.

Article 3. (1) The right to elect all representative bodies is universal, equal, direct, and by secret ballot. Every citizen who has reached the age of 18 years has the right to vote. Every citizen who has reached the age of 21 years has the right to be elected.

(2) Members of representative bodies, that is deputies, must maintain continuous contacts with their constituents, heed their initiatives, render an account of their activity, and report to them on the activities of the body of which they are members.

(3) A member of any representative body may be recalled at any time by a decision of his constituents.

Article 4. The leading force of society and the state is the vanguard of the working class, the Communist Party of Czechoslovakia, a voluntary combative union of the most active and conscious citizens from the ranks of the workers, peasants, and the intelligentsia.

Article 5. For the development of common activities, for an all-round and active participation in the life of society and the state, and for the exercise of their rights, the working people unite themselves into voluntary social organizations, in particular the Revolutionary Trade Union Movement, and cooperative, youth, cultural, physical training, and other organizations; some of the tasks of the state organs are gradually transferred to the social organizations.

Article 6. The National Front of Czechs and Slovaks, in which the social organizations are included, is the political expression of the union of the working people of the towns and countryside, led by the Communist Party of Czechoslovakia.

Article 7. (1) The economic basis of the Czechoslovak Socialist Republic is the socialist economic system, which excludes any form of exploitation of man by man.

(2) The socialist economic system, in which the means of produc-

tion are socialized and the entire national economy is directed by plan, ensures, with the conscious cooperation of all citizens, the rapid development of production and an unremitting rise of the living standard of the working people.

(3) Labor in a socialist society is labor for the benefit of the society as a whole, and at the same time for the benefit of the worker himself.

Article 8. (1) Socialist social ownership has two basic forms: state ownership, which is ownership of all people (national property), and cooperative ownership (property of people's cooperatives).

(2) National property is in particular: the mineral wealth and the basic sources of energy; the basic forestry fund, streams of water, natural medicinal springs; means of industrial production, public transport, and communications; banking and insurance institutions; the broadcasting, television, and motion-picture industry; and furthermore, also the most important social institutions, such as health institutions, schools, and scientific institutes.

(3) Land united for the purpose of joint cooperative cultivation is in social use by unitary agricultural cooperatives.

Article 9. Within the limits of the socialist economic system, small private business, based on personal labor and excluding exploitation of other people's labor, is allowed.

Article 10. (1) The citizen's personal ownership of consumer goods, in particular personal and domestic utensils, family houses, as well as savings acquired by labor, is inviolable.

(2) Inheritance of personal property is guaranteed.

Article 11. (1) The state establishes economic organizations, in particular national enterprises, which, as independent juridical persons, are entrusted with the administration of part of the national property.

(2) Unitary agricultural cooperatives are voluntary associations of working peasants for joint socialist agricultural production. The state supports their development in every aspect and effectively assists the cooperative peasants in developing large-scale socialist agricultural production, thereby making use of advanced science and technology. The state likewise supports the development of other people's cooperatives in accordance with the interests of society.

(3) All economic activities of state and other socialist economic

organizations are carried out in mutual harmony and are directed according to the principles of democratic centralism. At the same time, the participation and creative initiative of the working people and their social organizations, in particular the Revolutionary Trade Union Movement, are systematically applied to the widest extent at all levels of management.

Article 12. (Repealed by the Constitutional Law No. 143, *Sbírka zákonů ČSSR* 1968.)

Article 13. (1) All organizations and all citizens, upon whom any task is devolved which is connected with the implementation of the State Plan for the Development of the National Economy, are bound to exert every effort and to employ the utmost initiative to bring the task to the best possible end.

(2) All economic organizations are bound to systematically create the material, technical, and organizational conditions for their activities, in accordance with the long-term plans for the development of the national economy, in such a way that their planned tasks can be implemented.

Article 14. (1) The state directs its entire policy, in particular its economic policy, so that the all-round development of production on the basis of the continuous progress of science and technology and the increase of labor productivity will ensure the full development of socialist society and create the conditions for a gradual transition to communism, including in particular the overcoming of substantial differences between physical and mental labor and between town and countryside.

(2) The realization of those goals is made possible by the comradely cooperation of the Czechoslovak Socialist Republic with the Union of Soviet Socialist Republics and with the other countries of the world system of socialism. The Czechoslovak Socialist Republic systematically develops and strengthens that cooperation, which is based on mutual comradely assistance and the international socialist division of labor.

Article 15. (1) The state conducts an economic, health, social, and cultural policy which enables the physical and mental abilities of all the people to develop continuously, in concurrence with the growth of production, the rise of the living standard of the population and the gradual reduction of working time.

(2) The state takes care of the improvement and all-round pro-

tection of nature and the preservation of the beauties of the landscape of the Fatherland so as to create an increasingly rich source of prosperity for the people and appropriate surroundings for the working people which would benefit their health and make their recreation possible.

Article 16. (1) The entire cultural policy in Czechoslovakia and the development of civilization, education, and teaching are carried out in the spirit of the scientific world-view of Marxism-Leninism, and in close connection with the life and work of the people.

(2) The state, in common with the social organizations, gives all possible assistance to creative activity in science and the arts, endeavors to achieve a steadily higher and broader civilization of the working people and their active participation in scientific and artistic creation, and ensures that the results of this activity serve the entire people.

(3) The state and social organizations systematically endeavor to free the consciousness of the people from the remnants of an exploiter's society.

Article 17. (1) All citizens and all state and social organizations adjust all their behavior to the legal order of the socialist state, and ensure the full observance of socialist legality in the life of society.

(2) Social organizations, in fulfilling their mission, guide citizens to observe the laws, maintain labor discipline and comply with the rules of socialist community life, and endeavor to forestall and prevent infringements thereof.

Article 18. (1) The central direction of society and the state, in accordance with the principle of democratic centralism, is effectively combined with the broad powers and responsibility of the lower organs, drawing on the active participation of the working people and using their creative initiative.

(2) In accordance with the scientific world-view, the results of scientific research are fully applied in the society of the working people for the direction of the society and the planning of its further development.

Chapter II. Rights and Duties of Citizens

Article 19. (1) In a society of working people, in which exploitation of man by man is abolished, the development and interests of each of its members are in accordance with the development and interests of the whole of society. The rights, freedoms, and duties of citizens thus serve both the free and all-round development and expression of the personality of the citizens and, at the same time, the strengthening and development of the socialist society; they are broadened and deepened with its development.

(2) In a society of working people, the individual can achieve full development of his abilities and assert his justified interests only by actively participating in the development of the whole society, first and foremost by assuming an appropriate share of social labor. Therefore, labor in the interests of the whole is the primary duty, and the right to labor the primary right of every citizen.

Article 20. (1) All citizens have equal rights and equal duties.

(2) The equality of all citizens before the law is guaranteed, regardless of nationality and race.

(3) Men and women have an equal position in the family, at work, and in public activities.

(4) The society of working people ensures the equality of the citizens before the law by creating equal possibilities and equal opportunities in all areas of social life.

Article 21. (1) All citizens have the right to work and to remuneration for work performed according to its quantity, quality, and social significance.

(2) The right to work and to remuneration for work performed is ensured by the entire socialist economic system, which does not know economic crises or unemployment, and which guarantees a continuous rise in the real value of remuneration for work.

(3) The state directs its policy so that, as production develops and productivity increases, a gradual reduction of working time without a reduction in wages can be achieved.

Article 22. (1) All working people have the right to leisure after work.

(2) This right is ensured by the legal regulation of working time and paid holidays, as well as by the care of the state and social organizations to effectuate the fullest utilization of free time of the working people for their recreation and cultural life.

Article 23. (1) All working people have the right to the protection of their health and to medical care, as well as the right to material security in old age and in case of disability.

(2) State and social organizations ensure those rights by the prevention of diseases, the whole public health system, the network of medical and social institutions, by the continuous expansion of free medical care, as well as by organized care for safety at work, by health insurance, and by pension security.

Article 24. (1) All citizens have the right to education.

(2) The right to education is ensured free of charge by a system of basic, secondary, and university-level schools. School attendance of all youth is compulsory for a period established by a Law passed by the Federal Assembly. The organization of studies for employed persons, free vocational training in industrial enterprises and unitary agricultural cooperatives, and cultural and educational activities undertaken by the state and the social organizations serve to further advance the level of education.

(3) All education and teaching are based on the scientific worldview and on a close relationship between school and the life and work of the people.

Article 25. (Repealed by Constitutional Law No. 144, *Sbírka zákonů ČSSR* 1968.)

Article 26. (1) Motherhood, marriage, and the family are protected by the state.

(2) The state and society ensure that the family is a sound foundation for the development of young people. The state affords special relief and support to large families.

(3) Society secures for all children and young people every opportunity for the all-round development of their physical and mental abilities. This development is ensured through the care provided by the family, the state, and the social organizations, as well as by the special adjustment of labor conditions for young people.

Article 27. The equal position before the law of women in the family, at work, and in public life is ensured by the special adjustment of labor conditions and special health care during pregnancy and motherhood, as well as by the development of institutions and services which enable women to participate fully in the life of society.

Article 28. (1) In accordance with the interests of the working people, freedom of expression in all fields of public life, including in particular freedom of speech and of the press, is guaranteed to all citizens. Citizens exercise those freedoms both in the interests of developing their personality and creative efforts, and of actively participating in the administration of the state and in the economic and cultural development of the country. For the same purpose, the freedom of assembly and the freedom of street marches and demonstrations are guaranteed.

(2) These freedoms are ensured by making available publishing houses and printing enterprises, public buildings, halls, and free space, as well as broadcasting, television, and other facilities to working people and their organizations.

Article 29. Citizens and organizations have the right to submit proposals, suggestions, and complaints to representative bodies and other state organs; state organs are obliged to deal with them responsibly and promptly.

Article 30. (1) The inviolability of the person is guaranteed. No one may be prosecuted except in cases established by law and by due process of law. No one may be taken into custody except in cases established by law and on the basis of a decision made by the court or the Procurator.

(2) Punishment may be imposed only by virtue of law.

Article 31. The inviolability of the home, the secrecy of letters, and the secrecy of other means of communication, as well as freedom of movement are guaranteed.

Article 32. (1) Freedom of confession is guaranteed. Everyone may profess any religious faith or be without religious conviction, and may perform religious acts insofar as this does not contravene the law.

(2) Religious faith or conviction cannot constitute a ground for anyone to refuse to perform civil duties imposed on him by law.

Article 33. The Czechoslovak Socialist Republic grants the right of asylum to citizens of a foreign state, persecuted for defending the interests of working people, for participating in national liberation movements, for scientific or artistic creations, or for actions in defense of peace.

Article 34. Citizens are bound to observe the Constitution and other laws, and in all their actions to pay heed to the interests of the socialist state and society of the working people.

Article 35. Citizens are bound to protect and strengthen socialist ownership as the inviolable foundation of the socialist order and the source of prosperity of the working people, and the wealth and strength of the Fatherland.

Article 36. Citizens are bound conscientiously and honorably to perform public functions to which they are called by the working people, and to consider their fulfillment for the benefit of society as a matter of honor.

Article 37. (1) The defense of the Fatherland and its socialist order is the supreme duty and a matter of honor for every citizen.

(2) Citizens are bound to serve in the Armed Forces in accordance with law.

Article 38. An integral part of the duty of every citizen is to respect the rights of his fellow citizens and to conscientiously observe the rules of socialist community life.

[Chapter III: Articles 39–60, Chapter IV: Articles 61–65, Chapter V: Articles 66–72, and Chapter VI: Articles 73–85. (Repealed by Constitutional Law No. 143, *Sbírka zákonů ČSSR* 1968.) See the Appendix to this volume at 579*ff.*]

Chapter VII. The National Committees

Article 86. (1) The National Committees are organs of state power and administration in territorial areas which are determined by Laws of the National Councils.

(2) The National Committees consist of deputies, elected by the people, who are accountable to the people and who may be recalled by the people.

(3) The National Committees are elected for a term of office of five years.

(4) Conditions for the exercise of the right to elect and to be elected to the National Committees, and the manner in which the election and the recall of deputies are performed, are established by law.

Article 87. (1) The National Committees rely in all their activities on the constant and active participation of the working people of their territory. In this way they engage, to the widest extent, the working people in the administration of the state, make use of their experience, and learn from it.

(2) The National Committees cooperate closely with the other organizations of the people; they rely on their collaboration and assist them in accomplishing their tasks.

Article 88. (1) The National Committees and their deputies are accountable to their constituents for their activities.

(2) A deputy of a National Committee is bound to work in his constituency, maintain constant contact with his constituents, confer with them, heed their initiatives, render account to them for his activity, and report to them on the activities of the National Committee.

(3) A deputy of a National Committee is bound to take part in the work of the National Committee, to carry out initiatives, and to work in some of its commissions.

(4) A deputy of a National Committee makes the following vow at the first meeting of the National Committee he attends:

> "I promise upon my honor and conscience to be faithful to the Czechoslovak Socialist Republic and to the cause of socialism. I shall respect the will and the interests of the people, observe the Constitution and other laws of the Republic, and work for their implementation."

Article 89. The National Committees, with the broad participation of the citizens,
— direct, organize, and ensure in a planned manner the development of their territory with respect to the economy, culture, and health and social services; their primary tasks include the satisfaction of the material and cultural needs of the working people to an ever wider extent; to this end they set up economic institutions and cultural, health, and social institutions, and direct their activities;
— ensure the protection of socialist ownership and all the achievements of the working people, the maintenance of the socialist order in society, the observance of the rules of socialist community life, and strengthen the defense capability of the Republic;
— safeguard the implementation of laws and see to their observance, and ensure the protection and realization of the rights and the assertion of the justified interests of the working people and socialist organizations.

Article 90. (1) The National Committees are guided in their activities by the State Plan for the Development of the National Economy. They take part in its drafting and implementation. They draft the plan for the development of their territory in accordance with and on the basis of the State Plan.

(2) They possess the necessary material and financial resources to ensure the implementation of the planned tasks and make use of them as responsible managers.

(3) The basis of the financial management of the National Committees are their budgets, which they draft themselves, and which constitute a part of the State Budget.

Article 91. The levels and types of National Committees, as well as their status, jurisdiction, and organization are determined, within the limits of the Constitutional Laws of the Czechoslovak Socialist Republic, by Laws of the National Councils.

Article 92. The jurisdiction and the accountability of the National Committees at the respective levels are laid down so that they may, with a broad participation of the working people, most effectively ensure economic and cultural development and satisfy the needs of the citizens of their territories.

Article 93. (1) In their work, the National Committees combine the accomplishment of state-wide tasks with the satisfaction of the special needs of their territories and the interests of the citizens.

(2) The National Committees are guided by the principle that the interests of all the people of the Czechoslovak Socialist Republic are superior to provincial and local interests, and in all their activities they educate citizens to a conscious and voluntary performance of their duties towards society and the state.

Article 94. For the implementation of their tasks, the National Committees may issue generally binding orders for their territories.

Article 95. (1) The National Committees establish within their jurisduction a council, commissions, and other organs, and direct their work.

(2) The council, under the guidance of the National Committee, directs and unites the work of the other organs of the National Committee and its organizations and institutions. The council is elected by the National Committee from among its members for the whole term of office. The council and its members are accountable for their activities to the National Committee, which may recall the council and its members at any time.

(3) The commissions are the initiatory, supervisory, and executive

organs of the National Committee for individual fields or branches of its activities. They possess those powers necessary for these goals. The commissions, to which a National Committee elects its members and other citizens, systematically widen the participation of the working people in the activities of the National Committee. The commissions are accountable to the National Committee and its council.

Article 96. (1) Higher-level National Committees guide and direct the activities of lower-level National Committees. In doing so, they fully respect the latter's jurisdiction and responsibility. They rely on their initiative and experience, and implement their tasks in constant cooperation with them.

(2) National Committees are guided in their activities by the Laws and the orders and decisions of the Government, as well as by the decisions and directives of higher state organs; decisions of National Committees of a lower level, which are in defiance thereof, may be set aside by a National Committee of a higher level or by the Government.

Chapter VIII. The Courts and the Procuracy

Article 97. (1) The courts and the Procuracy protect the socialist state, its social order, and the rights and justified interests of citizens and organizations of the working people.

(2) The courts and the Procuracy in all their activities educate citizens to be loyal to their Fatherland and to the cause of socialism, to observe the laws and rules of socialist community life, and to honorably perform their duties towards state and society.

The Courts

Article 98. (1) Justice in the Czechoslovak Socialist Republic is administered by elected and independent courts.

(2) The courts are: the Supreme Court of the Czechoslovak Socialist Republic, the Supreme Court of the Czech Socialist Republic, the Supreme Court of the Slovak Socialist Republic, regional and district courts, and military courts.

(3) The provisions relating to regional and district courts also apply to courts with similar jurisdiction but otherwise designated.

(4) The jurisdiction of the courts in reviewing the legality of decisions made by administrative organs is established by a Law of the Federal Assembly.

Article 99. (1) The highest judicial organ in the Czechoslovak Socialist Republic is the Supreme Court of the Czechoslovak Socialist Republic, which oversees the decision-making of the Supreme Courts of the constituent republics, supervises the legality of the decision-making of all courts, and ensures its uniformity by:

a) deciding on ordinary remedies concerning decisions made by military courts in cases established by law,

b) deciding on complaints for violations of law challenging decisions made by the Supreme Courts of the constituent republics and all military courts,

c) issuing opinions to ensure the uniform interpretation of the laws.

(2) The Supreme Court of the Czechoslovak Socialist Republic furthermore decides on the recognition of decisions of foreign courts on the territory of the Czechoslovak Socialist Republic; in cases established by the laws on judicial and notarial proceedings, it determines the jurisdiction of the courts and state notary offices, and settles disputes regarding their jurisdiction, and in cases established by law it reviews the legality of decisions made by the federal organs of state administration. The Supreme Court of the Czechoslovak Socialist Republic reviews the legality of final judgments which impose capital punishment; exceptions may be laid down by a Law of the Federal Assembly only with respect to martial law proceedings or to judicial proceedings in time of military emergency.

(3) The highest judicial organ in the Czech Socialist Republic is the Supreme Court of the Czech Socialist Republic, and the highest judicial organ in the Slovak Socialist Republic is the Supreme Court of the Slovak Socialist Republic. The Supreme Court of a constituent republic supervises the legality of decision-making of all other courts in that republic.

Article 100. (1) In judicial proceedings, decisions are made by a panel or by a single judge. Laws regulating judicial proceedings determine in which panels and in which cases people's judges participate in the decision-making, and in which cases decisions are made by a single judge; only a professional judge may decide as a single judge.

(2) Professional and people's judges are equal in making decisions.

(3) The court of first instance is, as a rule, the district court.

Article 101. (1) Judges of the Supreme Court of the Czechoslovak Socialist Republic and professional judges of military courts are elected by the Federal Assembly; it elects the judges of the Supreme Court of the Czechoslovak Socialist Republic, as a rule, from among the same number of citizens of the Czech Socialist Republic and the Slovak Socialist Republic. Judges of the Supreme Courts of the constituent republics and professional judges of regional and district courts are elected by the National Council of the respective republic.

(2) The Chairman and Deputy Chairman of the Supreme Court of the Czechoslovak Socialist Republic are elected by the Federal Assembly from among the judges of that court. If it elects a citizen of the Czech Socialist Republic as the Chairman of the Supreme Court of the Czechoslovak Socialist Republic, it elects as the Deputy Chairman a citizen of the Slovak Socialist Republic, or *vice versa.*

(3) People's judges of regional and district courts are elected by National Committees; the election of people's judges of military courts is regulated by law.

(4) Professional judges are elected for a term of office of ten years; people's judges are elected for a term of office of four years.

(5) Judges may be recalled by the organ which elected them. The conditions for recalling a judge, as well as the conditions for other forms of termination of a judicial function prior to the expiration of the electoral term, are established by the laws regulating the election of judges.

Article 102. Judges are independent in the exercise of their functions and are bound solely by the legal order of the socialist state. They are obliged to follow the laws and other legal regulations, and to interpret them in accordance with socialist legal consciousness.

(2) (Repealed by Constitutional Law No. 155, *Sbírka zákonů ČSSR* 1969.)

Article 103. (1) The courts proceed so that the real circumstances of the case are ascertained, and they base their decisions on these findings.

(2) All court proceedings are, in principle, oral and public. The public may be excluded only in cases established by law.

(3) The accused is guaranteed the right to defense.

(4) Decisions are pronounced in the name of the Republic and, without exception, in public.

The Procuracy

Article 104. (1) Supervision of the consistent execution and observance of the laws and other legal regulations by the ministries and other organs of state administration, National Committees, courts, economic and other organizations, and by citizens is vested in the Procuracy, headed by the Procurator General of the Czechoslovak Socialist Republic.

(2) The Procuracy consists of the Procuracy General of the Czechoslovak Socialist Republic, the Procuracy General of the Czech Socialist Republic, the Procuracy General of the Slovak Socialist Republic, and of lower offices as established by a Law of the Federal Assembly. The Procuracies General of a constituent republic are headed by the Procurator General of that republic.

Article 105. (1) The Procurator General of the Czechoslovak Socialist Republic is appointed and recalled by the President of the Czechoslovak Socialist Republic. If the Procurator General of the Czechoslovak Socialist Republic is a citizen of the Czech Socialist Republic, a citizen of the Slovak Socialist Republic is appointed his First Deputy, or *vice versa*.

(2) The Procurator General of a constituent republic is appointed and recalled by the Presidium of the National Council of that republic. The proposal to appoint the Procurator General of a constituent republic is made by the Procurator General of the Czechoslovak Socialist Republic, who may also propose to the Presidium of the National Council of the respective republic to recall the Procurator General of that republic.

(3) The Procurator General of the Czechoslovak Socialist Republic is accountable to the Federal Assembly, which may propose to the President of the Czechoslovak Socialist Republic to recall him.

(4) The Procurator General of a constituent republic is, to the full extent of his competence, accountable to the National Council of that republic.

Article 106. (1) The organs of the Procuracy exercise their powers independently of local organs. In all their activities, they draw on the initiative of the working people and their organizations.

(2) The organs of the Procuracy General of the Czechoslovak Socialist Republic and of military procuracies are subordinate to the Procurator General of the Czechoslovak Socialist Republic. The Procurators General of the constituent republics are subordinate to him in exercising supervision over the uniform execution and observance of the laws and other legal regulations issued by organs of the Czechoslovak Socialist Republic.

(3) The organs of the Procuracy in the Czech and the Slovak Socialist Republics are subordinate to the Procurator General of the respective republic. They are subordinate to the Procurator General

of the Czechoslovak Socialist Republic only by way of exception in cases established by law.

Article 106a. Reports on the state of socialist legality.

(1) The Federal Assembly considers reports of the Supreme Court of the Czechoslovak Socialist Republic and the Procurator General of the Czechoslovak Socialist Republic on the state of socialist legality.

(2) The National Council of a constituent republic considers reports of the Supreme Court of that republic and the Procurator General of that republic on the state of socialist legality.

[Constitutional Law No. 155, *Sbírka zákonů ČSSR* 1969, which amended and supplemented Chapter Eight of the Constitution, contains furthermore the following provisions:
Section 2. Decisions made by courts, Procuracies, and state notary offices are valid and enforceable throughout the Czechoslovak Socialist Republic.
Section 3. (1) The Federal Assembly regulates by law the organization and the functions of the courts, the legal position of judges and judicial expectants, the organization and the functions of the Procuracies, and the legal position of Procurators, investigating officers, and legal expectants of the Procuracies, the organization and the functions of state notary offices, notarial proceedings, and the legal position of state notaries.

(2) The election and recall of people's judges of regional and district courts are regulated by laws of the National Councils; the election of the other judges, including judges of military courts, their appointment to judicial offices, and their recall are regulated by law.

(3) A Law of the Federal Assembly may entrust the regulation of the matters specified by paragraph 1 to the legislatures of the constituent republics. Unless the Federal Assembly regulates the matters specified by paragraph 1 to their full extent, the National Councils may regulate them by their own legislation.]

Chapter IX. General and Concluding Provisions

Articles 107, 108, and 109. (Repealed by Constitutional Law No. 143, *Sbírka zákonů ČSSR* 1968.)

Article 110. (1) The state emblem of the Czechoslovak Socialist Republic consists of a red escutcheon in the shape of a Hussite shield, charged with a five-pointed star in the main upper part and a double-tailed white lion bearing a red inescutcheon on its chest showing a blue silhouette of the Kriváň Mountain and a gold-tinctured bonfire. The emblem is edged in gold.

(2) The state flag of the Czechoslovak Socialist Republic consists of a lower red stripe and an upper white stripe, with a blue wedge between them running from the staff to the middle of the flag.

(3) Particulars of the state emblem and the state flag, as well as their proper display, are established by law.

Article 111. (Repealed by Constitutional Law No. 143, *Sbírka zákonů ČSSR* 1968.)

Article 112. (1) The Constitution comes into force on the day of its approval by the National Assembly.

(2) As of that day, the previous Constitution and all other Constitutional Laws which amended and supplemented it cease to have effect.

GERMAN DEMOCRATIC REPUBLIC

INTRODUCTION

Joseph J. Darby

The year 1968 is a notable one in German history because of two events which then took place. In that year troops of the German Democratic Republic, together with military units of certain other member states of the Warsaw Pact, invaded Czechoslovakia and put an end to that country's short-lived attempt to humanize Communism. Irresistible and consistently colder political winds blowing from Moscow had an immediate chilling effect on the exercise of personal liberties in Czechoslovakia, and the promise of the "Prague Spring" was gradually abandoned to the realities of Soviet foreign policy. In the same year, the German Democratic Republic adopted its second constitution. This 1968 Constitution has been well analyzed elsewhere,[1] and the later version, reflecting amendments adopted in 1974 and being the subject of the translation which follows, contains few surprises for the Western reader.

To be sure, one who is aware of the eight-year prison sentence recently imposed by a court of the German Democratic Republic on Rudolf Bahro for publishing a book[2] critical of the régime would be puzzled at the wording of Article 27, which guarantees to every citizen of the German Democratic Republic the right to freely and publicly express his opinion, and which provides that "nobody may be placed at a disadvantage for exercising this right". On the other hand, those familiar with the existence and purpose of the Berlin wall and the mined, fenced, and militarily patrolled rural boundaries of the German Democratic Republic will not be surprised to find that the Constitution provides no right to emigrate. Article 32 guarantees citizens the right to move freely within the country, but the text is silent on the right of expatriation.

As is well known, the subject of human rights is a dismal one at best in Communist countries. The catalogue of guarantees placed in the text of this constitution must doubtlessly please its draftsmen, who learned well from Stalin that paper will stand up to anything that is printed on it. The Western observer will wince, however, when he reads such things as "...the individual is the main concern of the efforts of socialist society and its state" (Art. 2), "...all power serves.... the free development of the individual" (Art. 4), and "... the German Democratic Republic is pursuing a foreign policy which promotes peace" (Art. 6).

Not all of the constitution is propaganda, however. The drafters lapsed into lucid intervals when they underscored the totalitarian nature of the régime by stating that "the German Democratic Republic is... under the leadership of the... Marxist-Leninist party" (Art. 1), is inviolably founded on "the socialist ownership of the means of production" (Art. 2), and "has entered into a perpetual and irrevocable alliance with the Union of Soviet Socialist Republics" (Art. 6). Consistent with the essence of the Brezhnev Doctrine, Article 6 also states that "the German Democratic Republic is an inseparable part of the socialist community of states". This phrase, which did not appear in the 1968 Constitution, was clearly inspired by the Warsaw Pact's invasion of Czechoslovakia and represents a successful attempt to write into the corpus of East German constitutional law an important goal of Soviet foreign policy.

Despite these examples of unexpected candor, the Constitution retains much that Western observers have come to anticipate in Communist public law documents. The strident ideological character of the language, the emphasis on the elimination of former problems through Communist rule—these are all familiar hallmarks of Communist legal theory. Still, even if one concedes that ideological self-adulation belongs in a Communist constitution, one might still question whether a constitution, even one which expresses a philosophical world-outlook that is entirely inconsistent with individual and corporate freedom as we know it in the West, is the proper place to insult your enemies. Article 18, after informing the reader that socialist culture in the German Democratic Republic "serves peace, humanism, and the development of socialist society", goes on to explain that in doing so, "it it is struggling against the imperialist anticulture, which serves psychological warfare and the degradation of man".

In the evaluation of any legal document, it is necessary to look past the printed text and to attempt to know the spirit of the way with which it is applied or ignored. The reader of the document which follows is therefore well advised to heed the counsel of Thomas à Kempis: "O, how good... not to give full credence till the truth be tried".[3]

NOTES

1. Michael Bothe, "The 1968 Constitution of East Germany", 17 *American Journal of Comparative Law*, 1969, 268. An English language translation appears in Peaslee, *Constitutions of Nations*, Vol. III, The Hague 1968, 331.
2. Rudolf Bahro, *Die Alternative: Zur Kritik der real existierenden Sozialismus*, Köln 1977.
3. *The Imitation of Christ*, Book 3.

CONSTITUTION OF THE GERMAN DEMOCRATIC REPUBLIC OF 9 APRIL 1968 (AS AMENDED)

Preamble	164
Foundations of Socialist Social and State Order	164
Political Foundations	164
Economic Foundations, Science, Education, and Culture	167
Citizens and Organizations in Socialist Society	170
Fundamental Rights and Duties of Citizens	170
Enterprises, Cities, and Local Communities in Socialist Society	175
Labor Unions and their Rights	176
Socialist Production Cooperatives and their Rights	177
Structure and System of State Management	178
The People's Chamber	178
The Council of State	181
The Council of Ministers	183
Local Popular Representative Bodies and their Organs	185
Socialist Legality and the Administration of Justice	186
Concluding Provisions	189

CONSTITUTION OF THE GERMAN DEMOCRATIC REPUBLIC*

Gesetzblatt der Deutschen Demokratischen Republik 1968, Teil I No. 8 (as amended). Consolidated text in *Gesetzblatt der DDR* 1974, Teil I No. 47.

PREAMBLE

Continuing the revolutionary tradition of the German working class and resting upon the liberation from fascism, the people of the German Democratic Republic, in conformity with the processes of historical development of our time, are achieving their right to social-economic, state, and national self-determination, and are shaping a developed socialist society.

Filled with the determination to freely chart its own course of unwaveringly continuing along the road of socialism, communism, peace, democracy, and friendship among peoples, the people of the German Democratic Republic have given themselves this constitution.

PART I. FOUNDATIONS OF SOCIALIST SOCIAL AND STATE ORDER

Chapter I. Political Foundations

Article 1. The German Democratic Republic is a socialist state of workers and peasants. It is the political organization of the urban and rural working population under the leadership of the working class and its Marxist-Leninist party.

The capital of the German Democratic Republic is Berlin.

The state flag of the German Democratic Republic consists of the colors black-red-gold and bears in the center on both sides the state insignia of the German Democratic Republic.

The state insignia of the German Democratic Republic consist of a hammer and sickle surrounded by a wreath of ears of grain around the lower part of which a black-red-gold band is wound.

*Translated by Joseph J. Darby.

Article 2. (1) All political power in the German Democratic Republic is exercised by the urban and rural working population. The individual is the main concern of all efforts of socialist society and its state. The continued improvement of the material and cultural standard of living of the people on the basis of the rapid rate of growth of socialist production, of improved efficiency, of scientific-technical progress, and of the growth of labor productivity—this is the decisive task of a developed socialist society.

(2) The inviolable foundations of a socialist social order are formed by the firm alliance of the working class with the class of cooperative peasants, the intelligentsia, and other sectors of the population, by the socialist ownership of the means of production, and by the management and planning of social development in accordance with the most advanced scientific knowledge.

(3) The exploitation of man by man has been abolished forever. What the people produce belongs to the people. The socialist principle "from each according to his abilities, to each according to what he has produced" is being put into practice.

Article 3. (1) The alliance of all sections of the population is expressed organizationally in the National Front of the German Democratic Republic.

(2) The parties and mass organizations of all sections of the population unite in the National Front of the German Democratic Republic to take common action to develop a socialist society. In this way, all citizens are learning to live together in socialist society in accordance with the principle that each individual is responsible for the whole.

Article 4. All power serves the welfare of the people. It ensures a peaceful life, protects socialist society, and guarantees the socialist way of life of citizens, the free development of the individual, defends his dignity, and guarantees the rights established in this constitution.

Article 5. (1) The citizens of the German Democratic Republic exercise their political power through democratically-elected popular representative bodies.

(2) The popular representative bodies are the foundation of the system of state organs. Their activities are based on the active participation of all citizens in the preparation, execution, and control of their decisions.

(3) At no time and under no circumstances may state power be

exercised by anyone other than the constitutionally-prescribed organs.

Article 6. (1) Faithful to the interests of the people and to its international obligations, the German Democratic Republic has eliminated militarism and National Socialism in its territory. It is pursuing a foreign policy which promotes socialism, peace, understanding among peoples, and security.

(2) The German Democratic Republic has entered into a perpetual and irrevocable alliance with the Union of Soviet Socialist Republic. This close and fraternal alliance guarantees to the people of the German Democratic Republic further progress on the road to socialism and peace.

The German Democratic Republic is an inseparable part of the socialist community of states. Faithful to the principles of socialist internationalism, it contributes to its strengthening, maintains and develops friendships, universal cooperation, and mutual assistance to all states of the socialist community.

(3) The German Democratic Republic supports the states and the peoples who are struggling against imperialism and colonialism and for freedom and independence in their efforts to achieve social progress. The German Democratic Republic is committed to the realization of the principles of the peaceful coexistence of states of differing social structures and, on the basis of equality and mutual respect, actively cooperates with all states.

(4) The German Democratic Republic is dedicated to peace and cooperation in Europe, a stable peaceful order throughout the world, and to universal disarmament.

(5) Militaristic and revenge-seeking propaganda of any type, incitement to war, and the dissemination of religious, racial, or national hatred will be punished as crimes.

Article 7. (1) The state authorities guarantee the territorial integrity of the German Democratic Republic and the inviolability of its state borders, including its air space and territorial waters, as well as the protection and exploitation of its continental shelf.

(2) The German Democratic Republic provides for the national defense, as well as for the protection of the socialist order and the peaceful life of its citizens. The National People's Army and the other national defense components protect the socialist achievements of the people against all attacks from outside. In the interest of safeguarding the peace and security of the socialist state, the National People's Army maintains a close and fraternal military

relationship with the armies of the Soviet Union and other socialist states.

Article 8. (1) The generally recognized rules of international law which serve to promote peace and peaceful cooperation among peoples are binding on the state and its citizens.

(2) The German Democratic Republic will never wage a war of conquest or deploy its armed forces for the purpose of suppressing the freedom of another nation.

Chapter II. Economic Foundations, Science, Education, and Culture

Article 9. (1) The national economy of the German Democratic Republic is based on the socialist ownership of the means of production. It develops in accordance with the economic laws of socialism on the basis of socialist production relationships and the conscientious achievement of socialist economic integration.

(2) The national economy of the German Democratic Republic serves to strengthen the socialist order and to enable its citizens to ever more effectively satisfy their material and cultural needs, and to develop their personalities and their socialist social relationships.

(3) The basic principle of the management and planning of the national economy, as well as of all other social activities has been established in the German Democratic Republic. The national economy of the German Democratic Republic is a socialist planned economy. The central state management and planning of the basic policy relating to social development is linked up with the separate responsibility of local state authorities and enterprises, as well as with the initiative of the working population.

(4) The establishment of the monetary and financial system falls within the competence of the socialist state. Duties and taxes are levied by statute.

(5) Foreign economic relations, including foreign trade and regulation of the value of currencies, is a state monopoly.

Article 10. (1) Socialist property consists of:
— property owned by the state;
— property owned by collectives;
— property owned by social organizations of citizens.

(2) To protect and to augment socialist property is the duty of the socialist state and its citizens.

Article 11. (1) The personal property of the citizens and the right to inheritance are guaranteed.

Personal property serves to satisfy the material and cultural needs of the citizens.

(2) The rights of authors and inventors are protected by the socialist state.

(3) Property rights, as well as the rights of authors and inventors, may not be exercised contrary to the interests of society.

Article 12. (1) Mineral resources, mines, power stations, dams and large bodies of water, the natural resources of the continental shelf, industrial enterprises, banks and insurance companies, state farms, traffic arteries, the means of transportation of the railroads, ocean shipping and civil aviation, the post and telecommunications system are state property. Private ownership thereof is not permitted.

(2) The socialist state guarantees that state property shall be used for the purpose of achieving the greatest advantage for society. In doing so, the state is assisted by a socialist planned economy and a socialist economic law. State property is basically used and managed by the state enterprises and state institutions. The state can transfer by contract the use and management of its property to cooperative or social organizations and associations. Any such transfer must serve to promote the interests of the general public and to augment the social wealth.

Article 13. The implements, machines, equipment, and buildings of agricultural, craftmen's and other socialist cooperatives, as well as the livestock of agricultural production cooperatives, and the yield gained from the cooperative use of the soil and cooperative production are cooperative property.

Article 14. (1) Private economic associations for the establishment of economic power are not permitted.

(2) Small handicraft and other commercial organizations which are maintained largely by personal labor may operate legally. The state assists them to observe their obligations to a socialist society.

Article 15. (1) The land of the German Democratic Republic is one of its most valuable natural resources. It must be protected and utilized rationally. Land used for agriculture and forestry may be removed from such use only with the permission of the responsible state authorities.

(2) In the interest of the citizens' welfare, both the state and society are entrusted with the protection of nature. Keeping the air and waters clean, as well as protecting plant and animal life and the scenic beauty of the homeland are duties performed by the appropriate authorities and, moreover, are the concern of every citizen.

Article 16. Expropriations are permitted only for a public purpose, on the basis of law, and in exchange for appropriate compensation. They may only take place when the desired public purpose cannot be achieved in any other way.

Article 17. (1) The German Democratic Republic promotes science, research, and education for the purpose of protecting and enriching society and the life of the citizenry. In doing so, it is assisted by the combination of the scientific-technical revolution and the advantages of socialism.

(2) The German Democratic Republic assures all citizens a high standard of education corresponding to the constantly expanding social requirements through the integrated socialist educational system. It enables the citizens to shape socialist society and to participate creatively in the development of socialist democracy.

(3) Any misuse of science directed against peace, international understanding, or against the life and the dignity of the individual is prohibited.

Article 18. (1) Socialist national culture is one of the foundations of socialist society. The German Democratic Republic promotes and protects socialist culture, which serves peace, humanism, and the development of socialist society. It is struggling against the imperialist anti-culture, which serves psychological warfare and the degradation of man. Socialist society promotes the cultural life of the working population, cultivates all the humanistic values of the national cultural heritage and of world culture, and develops socialist national culture as an affair of all the people.

(2) The promotion of the arts, of the artistic interests and abilities of the whole working population, and the dissemination of artistic works and productions is an obligation of the state and of all social forces. Artistic work is based upon a close contact between the artist and the life of the people.

(3) Physical culture, sports, and tourism, as elements of socialist culture, serve the all-round physical and intellectual development of the citizens.

PART II. CITIZENS AND ORGANIZATIONS IN SOCIALIST SOCIETY

Chapter I. Fundamental Rights and Duties of Citizens

Article 19. (1) The German Democratic Republic guarantees to all citizens the exercise of their rights and their participation in the conduct of social development. It guarantees socialist legality and the security of the law.

(2) All state authorities, all social forces, and each individual citizen are required to respect and protect the dignity and freedom of the individual.

(3) Free from exploitation, oppression, and economic dependence, every citizen has equal rights and abundant opportunity to develop his abilities to the fullest extent and to freely decide to develop his talents for the good of society and for his own benefit in a socialist society. In this way he realizes the freedom and dignity of his own personality. Relations between citizens are characterized by mutual respect and assistance, as well as by the principles of socialist morality.

(4) The conditions for the acquisition and loss of citizenship of the German Democratic Republic are determined by law.

Article 20. (1) Irrespective of his nationality, his race, his philosophical or religious beliefs, his social origin and position, every citizen of the German Democratic Republic has the same rights and duties. Freedom of conscience and freedom of belief are guaranteed. All citizens are equal before the law.

(2) Men and women have equal rights and have the same legal status in all branches of social, state, and personal life. The advancement of women, especially with regard to vocational qualifications, is a task of society and the state.

(3) Young people are provided with special assistance in their social and vocational development. They have every opportunity to participate responsibly in the development of the socialist social order.

Article 21. (1) Every citizen of the German Democratic Republic has the right to fully participate in the shaping of the political, economic, social, and cultural life of socialist society and of the socialist state. The principle "participate in working, in planning and in governing" applies.

(2) The right of codetermination and participation is guaranteed by the fact that citizens:
— democratically elect all authoritative bodies, and participate in their activities and in the conduct, planning, and shaping of social life;
— may demand an accounting from their popular representative bodies, their deputies, and the leaders of state and economic bodies concerning their activities;
— express their will and their demands with the authority of their social organizations;
— may submit their petitions and proposals to the social, state, and economic bodies and institutions;
— express their will through plebiscites.

(3) The exercise of the right of codetermination and participation is a serious moral obligation for every citizen.

The exercise of social or state functions is recognized and supported by society and by the state.

Article 22. (1) Every citizen of the German Democratic Republic who is eighteen years of age on election day is entitled to vote.

(2) Every citizen who is eighteen years of age on election day may be elected to the People's Chamber or to the local popular representative bodies.

(3) The management of the elections by democratically formed electoral commissions, popular discussion of basic policy questions, and the nomination and examination of candidates by the voters are inalienable socialist electoral principles.

Article 23. (1) The defense of peace and of the socialist fatherland and its achievements is the right and honorable duty of citizens of the German Democratic Republic. Every citizen has an obligation to serve and to make a contribution to the defense of the German Democratic Republic in accordance with the laws.

(2) No citizen may participate in warlike activities which serve to oppress a people.

(3) The German Democratic Republic can grant asylum to citizens of other states or to stateless persons if they are being persecuted for political, scientific, or cultural activity in the defense of peace, democracy, the interests of the working people, or because of their participation in a social or national struggle for liberation.

Article 24. (1) Every citizen of the German Democratic Republic has the right to work. He has the right to a job and to choose it freely in accordance with social needs and his personal qualifications. He has the right to be paid in accordance with the quality and quantity of his work. Men and women, young people, and adults have the right to equal pay for equal work output.

(2) Socially useful activity is an honorable duty of every citizen able to work. The right to work and the duty to work form a unity.

(3) The right to work is guaranteed:
— by socialist ownership of the means of production;
— by socialist management and planning of the social reproduction process;
— by the steady and planned growth of the socialist productive forces and the productivity of labor;
— by the consistent carrying out of the scientific-technical revolution; and
— by the constant training and continuing education of the citizens and by a uniform socialist labor law.

Article 25. (1) Every citizen of the German Democratic Republic has the same right to education. The educational institutions are open to everyone. A uniform socialist educational system guarantees to every citizen a continuous socialist upbringing, training, and continuing education.

(2) The German Democratic Republic ensures the steady progress of its people toward a socialist community of universally educated and harmoniously developed people imbued with the spirit of socialist patriotism and internationalism, and possessing an advanced general and specific education.

(3) All citizens have the right to participate in cultural life. This becomes increasingly significant in conditions characterized by a scientific-technical revolution and ever more exacting intellectual demands. State and society encourage the participation of citizens in cultural life, physical culture and sports, for the complete expression of the socialist personality and for the growing fulfillment of cultural interests and needs.

(4) In the German Democratic Republic, compulsory education extends through the tenth grade. Ten years of attendance at a general polytechnic secondary school will satisfy this requirement. In certain cases, secondary school education may be completed within the framework of vocational training or adult education programs for the working population. All young people have the right and the duty to learn a vocation.

(5) Special school and training institutions exist for mentally and physically handicapped children and adults.

(6) The state and all social forces join together in providing these educational and training services.

Article 26. (1) The state ensures the possibility of promotion to the next level of education, up to the highest educational institutions, the universities and colleges, in accordance with the performance principle, social needs, and the social structure of the population.

(2) There are no tuition fees. Training allowances and free study materials are provided according to social criteria.

Article 27. (1) Every citizen of the German Democratic Republic has the right, in accordance with the principles of this constitution, to freely and publicly express his opinion. This right is not restricted by any service or employment relationship. Nobody may be placed at a disadvantage for exercising this right.

(2) Freedom of the press, radio, and television are also guaranteed.

Article 28. (1) Within the framework of the principles and goals of this constitution, all citizens have the right of peaceful assembly.

(2) The use of the material prerequisites for the unhindered exercise of this right, of assembly buildings, streets and places of demonstration, printing presses and means of communication, is guaranteed.

Article 29. Consistent with the principles and goals of this constitution, citizens of the German Democratic Republic have the right of association in order to pursue their interests through common action in political parties, social organizations, associations, and collectives.

Article 30. (1) The person and liberty of every citizen of the German Democratic Republic are inviolable.

(2) Restrictions are permissible only in connection with criminal prosecutions or civil commitments and must be sanctioned by law. In this respect, the rights of such citizens may be restricted only to the extent that it is legally permissible and unavoidable.

(3) Every citizen has the right to request assistance from state and social bodies in an attempt to protect his liberty and the inviolability of his person.

Article 31. (1) Postal and telecommunication secrecy is inviolable.

(2) It may be restricted only in accordance with the law if the

security of the socialist state or a criminal prosecution necessitate it.

Article 32. Within the framework of the law, every citizen of the German Democratic Republic has the right to move freely within the state territory of the German Democratic Republic.

Article 33. (1) Every citizen of the German Democratic Republic has the right to request legal protection from the authorities of the German Democratic Republic when abroad.

(2) No citizen of the German Democratic Republic may be extradited to a foreign power.

Article 34. (1) Every citizen of the German Democratic Republic has the right to leisure time and recreation.

(2) The right to leisure time and recreation is guaranteed by:
— legal limitations on the number of daily and weekly working hours;
— an annual vacation with full pay; and
— the planned expansion of a system of state and other social recreation and vacation centers.

Article 35. (1) Every citizen of the German Democratic Republic has the right to the protection of his health and his working capacity.

(2) This right is guaranteed by the planned improvement of working and living conditions, public health, a comprehensive social policy, the promotion of physical culture, school and state sport activity, and tourism.

(3) A social insurance system provides material security, medical aid, medication, and other types of medical benefits free of charge in the event of illness or accident.

Article 36. (1) Every citizen of the German Democratic Republic has the right to social care in old age or invalidity.

(2) This right is guaranteed by an expanding material, social, and cultural welfare system and the care of elderly and disabled citizens.

Article 37. (1) Every citizen of the German Democratic Republic has the right to dwelling space for himself and his family in accordance with economic possibilities and local conditions. The state is obligated to implement this right by promoting the construction of housing, the maintenance of existing housing, and public control over the equitable distribution of dwelling space.

(2) There is legal protection in eviction cases.

(3) The home of every citizen is inviolable.

Article 38. (1) Marriage, family, and motherhood are under the special protection of the state.

Every citizen of the German Democratic Republic has the right to respect for, and protection and promotion of, his marriage and family.

(2) This right is guaranteed by the equality of man and wife in marriage and family, and by social and state assistance to citizens in strengthening and developing their marriage and family. Large families, and fathers and mothers living alone receive the care and support of the socialist state through special provisions.

(3) Mother and child enjoy the special protection of the socialist state. Maternity leave, special medical care, material and financial support during childbirth, and state subsidies to support children are provided.

(4) It is the right and the highest duty of parents to bring up their children to become healthy, happy, competent, all-round, and patriotic citizens. Parents have the right to a close and trusting working relationship with the social and state educational institutions.

Article 39. (1) Every citizen of the German Democratic Republic has the right to profess religious faith and to carry out religious activities.

(2) The churches and other religious communities conduct their affairs and carry out their activities in conformity with the Constitution and statutory provisions of the German Democratic Republic. Details may be worked out through agreements.

Article 40. Citizens of the German Democratic Republic of Sorb nationality have the right to maintain their native language and culture. The exercise of this right is encouraged by the state.

Chapter II. Enterprises, Cities, and Local Communities in Socialist Society

Article 41. The socialist enterprises, cities, local communities, and associations of local communities are, within the framework of central state management and planning, self-responsible communities in which citizens work and shape their social relationships. They safeguard the basic rights of citizens, the effective linking of individual and social interests, as well as a many sided social-political and cultural-intellectual life. Interference with their rights is possible only on the basis of law.

Article 42. (1) In the enterprises, the activities of which provide the basis for the creation and increase of social wealth, the working population cooperates directly and with the assistance of their elected representatives in management. Details are regulated by statute or charter.

(2) In order to increase social productivity, it is possible for the state authorities, enterprises, and cooperatives to form associations and companies, as well as to develop other types of cooperative arrangements.

Article 43. (1) The cities, local communities, and associations of local communities of the German Democratic Republic provide the conditions necessary to ever more satisfactorily fulfill the material, social, cultural, and other common needs of the citizens. In the fulfillment of these tasks, they work together with the enterprises and cooperatives of their area. All citizens participate in this by exercising their political rights.

(2) The popular representative bodies elected by citizens are responsible for the accomplishment of the social functions of the cities and local communities. They decide their affairs on their own responsibility on the basis of law. They are responsible for the rational utilization of all assets of state property at their disposal.

Chapter III. Labor Unions and Their Rights

Article 44. (1) The free labor unions, united in the Confederation of Free German Trade Unions, represent the most comprehensive class organizations of the working class. They safeguard the interests of the workers, employees, and intelligentsia through comprehensive co-determination in the state, economy, and society.

(2) The labor unions are independent. No one may restrict or hinder them in their activities.

(3) Through the activity of their organizations and organs, their representatives in the elected bodies of state power, and their proposals to state and economic bodies, the labor unions play a decisive role:
— in shaping socialist society;
— in managing and planning the national economy;
— in accomplishing the scientific-technical revolution;

— in developing working and living conditions, health protection and labor safety, a cultural working environment, and the cultural and athletic activities of the working population. The labor unions cooperate in the enterprises and institutions in drafting plans. They manage the permanent production councils.

Article 45. (1) The labor unions have the right to conclude agreements with state organs, with enterprise management, and with other leading economic bodies on all questions concerning the working and living conditions of the working population.

(2) The labor unions take an active part in the shaping of the socialist legal system. They have the right to initiate legislation and to exercise social control in safeguarding the legally guaranteed rights of the working population.

(3) The labor unions administer the social insurance system of the workers and employees on the basis of the self-administration of the insured. They participate in the comprehensive material and financial assistance and care of citizens in case of sickness, accidents at work, invalidity, and old age.

(4) All state bodies and economic managers are obligated to ensure a close and trusting cooperation with the labor unions.

Chapter IV. Socialist Production Cooperatives and Their Rights

Article 46. (1) The agricultural production cooperatives are voluntary associations of peasants for the purpose of common socialist production, for the ever more complete satisfaction of their material and cultural needs, and for supplies to the people and to the national economy. They are themselves responsible, on the basis of law, for shaping their working and living conditions.

(2) Through their organizations and their representatives in the state organs, the agricultural production cooperatives take an active part in the state management and planning of social development.

(3) The state helps the agricultural production cooperatives to develop socialist large-scale production on the basis of advanced science and technology.

(4) The same principles apply to the socialist production cooperatives of fishermen, gardeners, and craftsmen.

PART III. STRUCTURE AND SYSTEM OF STATE MANAGEMENT

Article 47. (1) The structure and activities of the state organs are determined by the aims and tasks of state power as set forth in this constitution.

(2) The sovereignty of the working people, which is realized on the basis of democratic centralism, is the fundamental principle of state structure.

Chapter I. The People's Chamber

Article 48. (1) The People's Chamber is the supreme organ of state power of the German Democratic Republic. It decides in its plenary sessions the basic questions of state policy.

(2) The People's Chamber is the sole constitutional and legislative organ in the German Democratic Republic. No one can limit its rights.

The People's Chamber implements in its activities the principle of the unity of decision and enforcement.

Article 49. (1) The People's Chamber, by means of statutes and resolutions which are final and binding on all, sets the developmental goals of the German Democratic Republic.

(2) The People's Chamber determines the main rules for the cooperation of citizens, organizations, and state organs, as well as their tasks in implementing the state plans for social development.

(3) The People's Chamber guarantees the implementation of its statutes and resolutions. It lays down the principles governing the activities of the Council of State, the Council of Ministers, the National Defense Council, the Supreme Court, and the Procurator General.

Article 50. The People's Chamber elects the Chairman and members of the Council of State, the Chairman and members of the Council of Ministers, the Chairman of the National Defense Council, the President and judges of the Supreme Court, and the Procurator General. They can be recalled at any time by the People's Chamber.

Article 51. The People's Chamber approves state treaties of the German Democratic Republic and other international legal agreements whenever they have the effect of changing statutes

German Democratic Republic

enacted by the People's Chamber. It decides on the termination of these treaties.

Article 52. The People's Chamber decides on the state of defense of the German Democratic Republic. In emergency situations, the Council of State is authorized to decide on the state of defense. The Chairman of the Council of State proclaims the state of defense.

Article 53. The People's Chamber can decide to hold plebiscites.

Article 54. The People's Chamber is composed of 500 deputies who are elected by the people for 5 years in free, general, equal, and secret elections.

Article 55. (1) The People's Chamber elects a Presidium for the electoral term.

The Presidium is composed of the President of the People's Chamber, a Vice-President, and other members.

(2) The Presidium directs the work of the People's Chamber in accordance with its agenda.

Article 56. (1) The deputies of the People's Chamber fulfill their responsibilities in the interest and welfare of the whole population.

(2) The deputies encourage the cooperation of citizens in the drafting and enforcement of laws in cooperation with the committees of the National Front of the German Democratic Republic, the social organizations, and the state organs.

(3) The deputies maintain close contact with their electors. They are obligated to listen to their proposals, suggestions, and criticism, and to treat them carefully and conscientiously.

(4) The deputies explain the policies of the socialist state to the citizens.

Article 57. (1) The deputies of the People's Chamber are obligated to hold regular visiting hours and discussions, and to report to the electors on their activities.

(2) A deputy who grossly violates his duties can be recalled by the electors in accordance with statutorily established procedures.

Article 58. The deputies of the People's Chamber have the right to participate in the meetings of the local popular representative bodies in an advisory capacity.

Article 59. Every deputy has the right to put questions to the Council of Ministers and to each of its members.

Article 60. (1) All state and economic organs are obligated to assist the deputies in fulfilling their tasks.

(2) The deputies of the People's Chamber enjoy the right of immunity. Restrictions on their personal liberty, searches of their houses, confiscations, or criminal prosecutions are permissible only with the consent of the People's Chamber or, at times when it is not in session, of the Council of State. The decision of the Council of State requires confirmation by the People's Chamber.

The deputies of the People's Chamber are entitled to refuse to testify against persons who have confided facts to them in the course of their duties as deputies, or to whom they have confided facts in the course of their duties as deputies, as well as about these facts themselves.

(3) Deputies shall incur no professional or other type of personal disadvantage because of their activities as deputies. They are released from their occupational duties to the extent that this is necessary in order to enable them to serve as deputies. They shall continue to receive their salaries and wages.

Article 61. (1) The People's Chamber forms committees from its members. In close cooperation with the voters, these committees discuss draft legislation and exercise a continuous control over the enforcement of the law.

(2) The committees may demand the presence of competent ministers and heads of other state bodies in their deliberations in order to obtain information. All state bodies are obligated to provide the committees with the information required.

(3) The committees have the right to call upon experts for continuing or temporary cooperation.

Article 62. (1) The People's Chamber is convened not later than the 30th day after its election. The first session is convened by the Council of State.

(2) Further sessions of the People's Chamber are convened by the Presidium of the People's Chamber.

(3) The Presidium of the People's Chamber is obligated to convene the People's Chamber when the latter has so resolved, or when at least one-third of the deputies have demanded it.

(4) The sessions of the People's Chamber are public. At the

request of at least two-thirds of the deputies present, the public may be excluded.

Article 63. (1) The People's Chamber has a quorum if more than half of the deputies are present.

(2) The People's Chamber reaches its decisions by a majority vote. Amendments to the Constitution require the votes of at least two-thirds of the elected deputies.

Article 64. (1) The People's Chamber can be dissolved before the expiration of its electoral term only through its own resolution.

(2) Such a resolution needs the affirmative votes of at least two-thirds of the elected deputies.

(3) New elections must be held at the latest on the 60th day after the expiration of the electoral term or on the 45th day after the dissolution of the People's Chamber.

Article 65. (1) The deputies of the political parties and mass organizations represented in the People's Chamber, the committees of the People's Chamber, the Council of State, the Council of Ministers, and the Confederation of Free German Labor Unions all have the right to introduce draft legislation.

(2) The committees of the People's Chamber discuss the draft legislation and present their versions of it to the plenary session of the People's Chamber.

(3) Drafts of basic laws are, prior to their enactment, submitted to the population for discussion. The results of these popular discussions are evaluated in the final drafting.

(4) Laws enacted by the People's Chamber are promulgated in the Legal Gazette by the Chairman of the Council of State within one month.

(5) Laws come into force on the 14th day after their promulgation, if not otherwise specified.

Chapter II. The Council of State

Article 66. (1) As the organ of the People's Chamber, the Council of State fulfills the tasks which have been assigned to it by the constitution, as well as by the laws and resolutions of the People's Chamber. It is responsible to the People's Chamber for its activities. It passes resolutions in order to carry out its assigned tasks.

(2) The Council of State represents the German Democratic Republic in international law. It ratifies and promulgates state trea-

ties and other types of international agreements requiring ratification.

Article 67. (1) The Council of State consists of the Chairman, the Vice-Chairman, the members, and the Secretary.

(2) The Chairman, the Vice-Chairman, the members, and the Secretary of the Council of State are elected by the People's Chamber at its first session after the new election for a term of 5 years.

(3) The strongest faction of the People's Chamber shall submit the nomination for the post of Chairman of the Council of State.

(4) After the electoral term of the People's Chamber has expired, the Council of State continues its activities until a new Council of State has been elected by the People's Chamber.

Article 68. At the commencement of their term in office, the Chairman, the Vice-Chairman, the members, and the Secretary of the Council of State take the following oath:

> "I swear to devote my efforts to the welfare of the people of the German Democratic Republic, to safeguard its Constitution and laws, to fulfill my duties conscientiously, and to do justice to all."

Article 69. The Chairman directs the work of the Council of State. In the event he is unable to do so, his duties will be performed by the Vice-Chairman.

Article 70. On behalf of the People's Chamber, the Council of State assists the local popular representative bodies as organs of the unitary socialist state power, encourages their democratic activity in shaping the developed socialist society, and exercises an influence in safeguarding and constantly strengthening socialist legality in the activities of the local popular representative bodies.

Article 71. (1) The Chairman of the Council of State appoints and recalls the plenipotentiaries of the German Democratic Republic in foreign states. He accepts the credentials and recall documents of diplomatic representatives of foreign states who are accredited to him.

(2) The Council of State determines military ranks, diplomatic ranks, and other special titles.

Article 72. The Council of State issues the writ for elections to the People's Chamber and the other popular representative bodies.

Article 73. (1) The Council of State passes fundamental resolutions on matters involving the defense and security of the country. It also organizes national defense with the help of the National Defense Council.

(2) The Council of State appoints the members of the National Defense Council. The National Defense Council is responsible to the People's Chamber and the Council of State for its activities.

Article 74. (1) On behalf of the People's Chamber, the Council of State exercises a continuous control over the constitutionality and legality of the activities of the Supreme Court and the Procurator General.

(2) The Council of State exercises the right of amnesty and pardon.

Article 75. The Council of State establishes state orders, distinctions, and honorary titles which are awarded by its Chairman.

Chapter III. The Council of Ministers

Article 76. (1) As an organ of the People's Chamber, the Council of Ministers is the Government of the German Democratic Republic. On behalf of the People's Chamber, it directs the uniform execution of state policies and organizes the fulfillment of political, economic, cultural, social, and defense tasks assigned to it. It is responsible and accountable to the People's Chamber for its activities.

(2) The Council of Ministers manages the national economy and the other social sectors. It ensures the planned proportionate development of the national economy, the harmoniously blended formation of social sectors and territories, and the implementation of the socialist economic integration.

(3) The Council of Ministers directs the execution of the foreign policy of the German Democratic Republic in accordance with the principles of this constitution. It expands the extensive cooperation with the Union of Soviet Socialist Republics and with other socialist states, and ensures an active contribution by the German Democratic Republic to the consolidation of the socialist community of states.

(4) The Council of Ministers, in accordance with its competence, decides upon the conclusion and termination of international treaties. It prepares state treaties.

Article 77. The Council of Ministers addresses itself to unresolved tasks of state domestic and foreign policy, and submits drafts of legislation and resolutions to the People's Chamber.

Article 78. (1) The Council of Ministers directs, coordinates, and controls the activities of the ministers, the other central state organs, and the district councils. It encourages the application of scientific methods of management and the inclusion of the working population in the implementation of the policies of the socialist state. It ensures that the state organs subordinate to it, the leading economic organs, combines, enterprises, and institutions carry out their activities on the basis of statute and other legal provisions.

(2) The Council of Ministers, within the framework of the statutes and resolutions of the People's Chamber, issues regulations and passes resolutions.

Article 79. (1) The Council of Ministers is composed of the Chairman of the Council of Ministers, the Vice-Chairman, and the members.

(2) The Chairman of the Council of Ministers is nominated by the strongest faction of the People's Chamber and is charged by the People's Chamber with forming the Council of Ministers.

(3) The Chairman and the members of the Council of Ministers are elected by the People's Chamber after new elections for a term of five years.

(4) The Chairman and the members of the Council of Ministers are sworn in on the constitution by the Chairman of the Council of State.

Article 80. (1) The Council of Ministers is a collective working organ. All members of the Council of Ministers bear responsibility for its activities. Each minister is responsible for the particular field assigned to him.

(2) The Council of Ministers forms the Presidium of the Council of Ministers from its ranks.

(3) The Chairman of the Council of Ministers heads the Council of Ministers and the Presidium.

(4) After the expiration of the electoral term of the People's Chamber, the Council of Ministers continues its activities until the new Council of Ministers has been elected by the People's Chamber.

Chapter IV. Local Popular Representative Bodies and Their Organs

Article 81. (1) The local popular representative bodies, elected by citizens having the right to vote, are the organs of state power in the districts, regions, cities, municipal districts, local communities, and associations of local communities.

(2) The local popular representative bodies decide, on the basis of law and on their own responsibility, on all matters which concern their area and its citizens. They organize citizen participation in the shaping of political, economic, cultural, and social life, and cooperate with the social organizations of the working population.

(3) The activities of the local popular representative bodies are directed toward:

the expansion and protection of socialist property; the continuing improvement of the working and living conditions of the citizens; the promotion of the social and cultural life of the citizens and their communities; the raising of the level of the social state and legal consciousness of the citizens, and the preservation of public order; the strengthening of socialist legality, and the safeguarding of the rights of the citizens.

Article 82. (1) The local popular representative bodies pass resolutions which are binding on their organs and institutions, as well as on the popular representative bodies, communities, and citizens of their area. These resolutions shall be published.

(2) The local popular representative bodies have their own income and exercise control over the spending of it.

Article 83. (1) To meet its responsibilities, every local popular representative body elects its council and committees. Whenever possible, the council members should also already be deputies. Persons who are not deputies may be appointed to serve on the committees.

(2) The council ensures the development of the activities of the local popular representative body and organizes the management of its social development within its field of responsibility. It is responsible to the popular representative body for all its actions and is accountable to its superior council. The council works collectively.

(3) The committees organize the expert participation of the citizens in the preparation and implementation of the resolutions of the popular representative body. They control the enforcement of the statutes and other legal provisions, as well as of the resolutions

passed by the popular representative body through the council and its specialized bodies.

Article 84. In order to jointly accomplish their tasks, the local popular representative bodies may form associations.

Article 85. The tasks and powers of the local popular representative bodies, their deputies, committees, and their councils in the districts, regions, cities, municipal districts, local communities, and associations of local communities are defined by statute.

PART IV. SOCIALIST LEGALITY AND THE ADMINISTRATION OF JUSTICE

Article 86. Socialist society, the political power of the working people, and their state and legal system are the basic guarantees for the observance and enforcement of the Constitution in the spirit of justice, equality, fraternity, and humanity.

Article 87. Society and state guarantee legality by involving the citizens and their organizations in the administration of justice and in the social and state control over the observance of socialist law.

Article 88. The responsibility of all state and economic leaders to the citizens is guaranteed by a system of compulsory accountability.

Article 89. (1) Statutes and other generally-binding legal regulations of the German Democratic Republic are published in the Legal Gazette and elsewhere.

(2) Legal regulations of the local popular representative bodies and their organs are published in an appropriate manner.

(3) Legal regulations may not contradict the constitution. The People's Chamber decides in case of doubt on the constitutionality of legal regulations.

Article 90. (1) The administration of justice serves to implement socialist legality, and to protect and develop the German Democratic Republic and its state and social order. It protects freedom, a peaceful life, and the right and dignity of man.

(2) It is the joint concern of socialist society, its state, and all citizens to combat and prevent crime and other violations of law.

(3) Participation by citizens in the administration of justice is guaranteed. Details are provided by statute.

Article 91. The generally accepted norms of international law relating to the punishment of crimes against peace and humanity and of war crimes are directly valid law. Crimes of this kind are not subject to the statute of limitations.

Article 92. Jurisdiction in the German Democratic Republic is exercised by the Supreme Court, the District Courts, the Regional Courts, and the social courts within the framework of the tasks assigned to them by statute. In military matters, jurisdiction is exercised by the Supreme Court, military tribunals, and military courts.

Article 93. (1) The Supreme Court is the highest court of jurisdiction.

(2) The Supreme Court directs the judicial activity of the courts on the basis of the constitution, statutes, and other legal regulations of the German Democratic Republic. It ensures a uniform application of the law by all courts.

(3) The Supreme Court is responsible to the People's Chamber and, between its sessions, to the Council of State.

Article 94. (1) Only persons who are loyally devoted to the people and their socialist state, and who possess extensive knowledge and experience, maturity, and character may be judges.

(2) The democratic election of all judges, lay judges, and members of social courts guarantees that justice will be administered by men and women from all classes and sections of the people.

Article 95. All judges, lay judges, and members of social courts are elected either by popular representative bodies or directly by the citizens. They report to their electors concerning their work. They may be recalled by their electors if they violate the constitution or the statutes or, in any other manner, seriously breach their duties.

Article 96. (1) The judges, lay judges, and members of social courts are independent in their administration of justice. They are bound only by the constitution, statutes, and other legal regulations of the German Democratic Republic.

(2) Lay judges exercise their judicial function to the full extent and have the same voting rights as professional judges.

Article 97. In order to safeguard the socialist social and state order and the rights of citizens, the Public Procurator's Office supervises the strict adherence to socialist legality on the basis of the statutes and other legal regulations of the German Democratic Republic. It protects the citizens from violations of the law. The Public Procurator's Office directs the struggle against crime, and ensures that persons who have committed crimes and other legal offenses are called to account before the court.

Article 98. (1) The Public Procurator's Office is directed by the Procurator General.

(2) The public procurators of the districts and regions, as well as the military procurators, are subordinate to the Procurator General.

(3) The procurators are appointed and recalled by the Procurator General and are responsible to him and bound by his instructions.

(4) The Procurator General is responsible to the People's Chamber and, between its sessions, to the Council of State.

Article 99. (1) Criminal liability is determined by the statutes of the German Democratic Republic.

(2) An act is criminally punishable only if it was defined by statute at the time of its commission, if the perpetrator acted in a blameworthy fashion, and if his guilt is proved beyond doubt. Penal statutes have no retroactive effect.

(3) Criminal prosecution must be in accordance with the penal law.

(4) The rights of citizens may be restricted in connection with a criminal proceeding only to the extent that it is statutorily allowed and unavoidable.

Article 100. (1) Only a judge may decide that a person be placed in preventive detention. Persons under arrest must be brought before a judge not later than one day after their arrest.

(2) Within the framework of their responsibilities, the judge or the public procurator has to determine whether, at any time, the prerequisites justifying preventive detention are still present.

(3) The public procurator must inform the next of kin of the arrested person within 24 hours after the first judicial interrogation. Exceptions to this rule are permissible only if such notification would jeopardize the purpose of the investigation. In such cases, notification is made after the reasons for the jeopardy have ceased to exist.

Article 101. (1) No one shall be deprived of his lawful judge.
(2) Special courts are inadmissible.

Article 102. (1) Every citizen has the right to be heard in court.
(2) The right of defense is guaranteed throughout the entire criminal proceeding.

Article 103. (1) Every citizen may submit petitions (suggestions, proposals, applications, or complaints) to the popular representative bodies, their deputies, or to the state and economic organs. This right is also available to social organizations and communities. They may not be placed at a disadvantage as a result of exercising this right.
(2) Organs responsible for making decisions are obligated to consider the petitions of citizens or communities within the legally prescribed period of time and to notify the petitioners of the results.

Article 104. (1) State organs are civilly liable for personal injury or property damage which their employees, acting illegally, cause to citizens.
(2) The prerequisites and procedures relating to state liability are set forth in statutes.

PART V. CONCLUDING PROVISIONS

Article 105. The constitution is directly valid law.

Article 106. The constitution may be amended only by the People's Chamber of the German Democratic Republic by a statute which expressly amends or supplements the text of the constitution.

HUNGARY

INTRODUCTION

William Sólyom-Fekete

Hungary did not have a written constitution until the end of the Second World War. The Hungarian constitution, like that of England, was formed from several different laws and not from a single piece of formal legislation. It may be said that the description of the English constitution by Sidney Low, the well-known British constitutionalist, applies equally well to the constitution of Hungary:

> "Other constitutions have been built, that of England has been allowed to grow, and so the organism has gradually adapted itself to its environment. Its development has been biological rather than technical and for this reason it is still instinct with vitality, while some of its imitators show the signs of stiffness and desiccation."[1]

The situation changed fundamentally in 1946 when the National Assembly enacted Law No. I of 1946 on the Form of Government of Hungary.[2] This law included the basic elements of a modern constitution, although formally it was not regarded as such.

The first constitution, both in form and substance, was enacted by the Hungarian Parliament on 20 August 1949, as Law No. XX of 1949 on the Constitution of the Hungarian People's Republic.[3]

The 1949 Constitution was a slavish imitation of the Soviet-type constitutions, with some variations resulting from the historical and political differences between the Soviet Union and Hungary. According to this Constitution, Hungary became a people's republic which "is the state of the workers and working peasants".[4]

On the 10th anniversary of its promulgation, István Dobi, then Chairman of the Presidium of the People's Republic, proudly wrote that the essence of the Hungarian Constitution "is the creation of a governmental organization that lays the foundation of the power of the social class which became the ruling class, and assures the accomplishments of its political aims".[5]

The Constitution of 1949 soon required major and minor amendments to make it conform with the ever-changing methods and aims of the Communist Party. Between 1949 and 1957, 11 amendments were enacted.[6] In 1956, the Presidium of the People's Republic issued its Edict No. 33 of 1956 on the Amalgamation and Termination of Certain Ministries, which also amended the Con-

Introduction

stitution, in spite of the fact that Article 20(4) of the then valid version (Art. 30(5) of the present version) expressly provided that the Presidium had no power to amend the Constitution.

These numerous amendments, as well as the changing economic and political situation, made it desirable to create a new constitution more in line with the new economic management policy introduced in 1968. The political changes carried out in the late 1960s, and early 1970s, especially in the fields of electoral laws, administrative reorganization, and jurisdiction of the local councils, also called for a new constitutional basis.

Several East European countries enacted new constitutions during those years: Bulgaria (1971), Czechoslovakia (1960), Romania (1965), and Yugoslavia (1974). Albania and Poland also adopted new constitutions in 1975 and 1976 respectively, after having enacted basic amendments a few years earlier. The German Democratic Republic enacted a new constitution in 1968, and extensively amended the same in 1974. The Hungarian People's Republic chose the form of extensive amendments to the 1949 Constitution because "the situation was not ripe enough" to create a new constitution, according to Gyula Kállai, the Chairman of the Committee Preparing the Constitutional Amendments. He justified this decision before the Parliament by saying that:

> "The Constitution of 1949 properly expresses even today the characteristics of [state] power, social order, and aims of the development; therefore, in spite of the achievement of immense progress, only the amendment of the Constitution became appropriate."[7]

However, the fact is that the amendments proposed by this Committee and enacted by Parliament on 19 April 1972, after a debate lasting less than one day, basically changed the 1949 Constitution in substance as well as in form. Starting with the preamble, the entire text of the much amended Constitution has been revised, and even the organization of its provisions is completely different. It may be said that the 1972 version of the 1949 Constitution remained the same only in name and in its basic principles expressing the Communist ideology prevailing at a given time.

Only the wish to stress the continuity of the present regime could have fostered the fiction that the 1949 Constitution is still in force in an amended form. This seemed to be necessary at a time when certain forces inside and outside the country tried to attach the stigma of "revisionism" to the ruling party and government leaders.

This wholesale revision was the reason why the regular amendment procedure was abandoned. In previous amendments, the section of the Constitution in question was repealed and the proposed new provision substituted. Since the regular amendment procedure was inapplicable in this case, the amending law simply stated that Parliament amends the 1949 Constitution and "establishes the text of the Constitution of the Hungarian People's Republic in force".

The government and party leaders of Hungary decided in 1975 to extend the elective terms of Parliament, the local councils, the President of the Supreme Court, and of the Chief Prosecutor of the Hungarian People's Republic. To accomplish these changes, four sections of the prevailing text had to be amended. The present translation encompasses the amended version of the sections affected. It should be noted that the amendments entered into force on the day of their promulgation, 12 April 1975, with the exception of the amendment of Article 42(2) pertaining to the term of the local councils, which will be made effective by a special statute.

NOTES

1. Sidney Low, *The Governance of England*, London 1915, 6.
2. *Országos Törvénytár*, 31 January 1946, 1–2.
3. *Magyar Közlöny*, 20 August 1949, 1355–1362.
4. *Id.*, Sec. 2.
5. A *Magyar Népköztársaság Alkotmánya*, Budapest 1959, 4.
6. The following amendments have been promulgated in *Magyar Közlöny*: Law No. IV of 1950 (10 December 1950); Law No. I of 1952 (6 June 1952); Law No. IV of 1953 (24 March 1953); Law No. VI of 1953 (7 July 1953); Law No. III of 1954 (24 Janury 1954); Law No. VII of 1954 (29 June 1954); Law No. VIII of 1954 (25 September 1954); Law No. II of 1955 (1 May 1955); Law No. IV of 1955 (19 November 1955); Edict No. 33 of 1956 (29 December 1956); Law No. II of 1957 (23 May 1957).
7. *Népszabadság*, 20 April 1972, 1.

CONSTITUTION OF THE HUNGARIAN PEOPLE'S REPUBLIC OF 20 AUGUST 1949 (AS AMENDED)

Preamble	196
The Social Order of the Hungarian People's Republic	197
The Parliament of the Hungarian People's Republic and the Presidium of the Hungarian People's Republic	200
The Council of Ministers of the Hungarian People's Republic	204
The Councils	206
The Judicial Organization	207
The Public Prosecutors	208
Basic Rights and Duties of Citizens	209
The Basic Principles of Elections	211
The Coat-of-Arms, the Flag, and the Capital of the Hungarian People's Republic	212
Final Provisions	212

CONSTITUTION OF THE HUNGARIAN PEOPLE'S REPUBLIC*

Magyar Közlöny 1949, pp. 1355–1362 (as amended).
Consolidated text in *Magyar Közlöny* 1972 No. 32, and subsequent amendment in *Magyar Közlöny* 1975 No. 23.

Hungary was preserved and supported for more than a millennium by the work and sacrifice of her people and their strength in molding society. State power, at the same time, was the tool of the ruling classes in suppressing and exploiting people deprived of their rights. Our nation pursued a difficult struggle for social progress and national independence; it defended and preserved our national existence amidst countless tribulations.

A new era of our history commenced when the Soviet Union, in the course of its victory in World War II, liberated our country from fascist oppression and opened the way toward democratic development for the Hungarian people. The working people, with the friendly assistance of the Soviet Union, reconstructed the war-torn country which was lying in ruins. The Hungarian workers' class—in alliance with the working peasantry and in cooperation with the progressive intellectuals—achieved and strengthened the power of the working people in the fight against the lords and protectors of the old regime.

With the leadership of the working class hardened in the revolutionary struggles, enriched with the experiences of the Soviet Republic of 1919, and supported by the community of socialist countries, our nation laid the foundations of socialism. The socialist conditions of production became predominant in our country. In place of the old, a new country was born in which state power serves the interests of the people and the unfolding of the productive forces and the welfare of the citizens. The Hungarian people, in close national unity, are working on completing the building of socialism.

The Constitution of the Hungarian People's Republic is the expression of the basic changes carried out in the life of our country, of the historic results of the struggle for social progress, and of the efforts to build a new country.

*Translated by William Sólyom-Fekete.

The Constitution, as the basic law of the Hungarian People's Republic, guarantees our achievements and further progress toward socialism.

Chapter I. The Social Order of the Hungarian People's Republic

Article 1. Hungary is a People's Republic.

Article 2. (1) The Hungarian People's Republic is a socialist state.

(2) All power in the Hungarian People's Republic belongs to the working people.

(3) The leading class of society in the Hungarian People's Republic is the working class, which exercises its power in alliance with the peasantry united in the cooperatives and with the intellectuals and other working strata of society.

(4) The workers of the cities and the country exercise their power through their elected representatives, who are responsible to the people.

(5) The citizens participate directly in the administration of public affairs at their place of work and residence.

Article 3. The leading force of society is the Marxist-Leninist party of the working class.

Article 4. (1) The Hungarian People's Republic shall assure the participation of social organizations in the constructive work of socialism.

(2) The Patriotic People's Front shall organize the forces of society to complete the building of socialism and to solve political, economic, and cultural problems; it shall cooperate in the election and work of the representative organs of the state.

(3) The trade unions shall protect and strengthen the power of the people and shall protect and represent the interests of the workers.

Article 5. (1) The Hungarian People's Republic shall protect the freedom and power of the working people and the independence of the country, shall fight against any form of exploitation of the people by the people, and shall organize the forces of society to complete the building of socialism.

(2) The Hungarian People's Republic, as a part of the socialist world organization, shall develop and strengthen its friendship with

the socialist countries; it shall strive to cooperate with all nations and countries of the world in the interests of peace and human progress.

Article 6. (1) With the elimination of the exploiting classes, the socialist conditions of production became preponderant in the Hungarian People's Republic. The basis of the economic order is the social ownership of the means of production.

(2) The Hungarian People's Republic shall support and protect all forms of social ownership.

Article 7. The national economic plan shall determine the economic life of the Hungarian People's Republic. The state shall direct and supervise the people's economy supported by enterprises, cooperatives, and institutions in social ownership, in the interest of the development of productive forces, the increase of socialist property, the systematic raising of the economic and cultural standards of the citizens, and the increase of the defensive strength of the country.

Article 8. (1) State property forms the assets of the entire nation.

(2) The following shall be, above all, in state ownership: the deposits within the bowels of the earth, the land holdings of the state, natural resources, significant plants and mines, railroads, public roads, waterways and airways, banks, the post, telegraph, telephone, radio, and television.

(3) A special law shall determine the scope of state ownership, as well as the scope of the exclusive economic activities of the state.

Article 9. Government enterprises and economic agencies shall independently manage the assets entrusted to them in the manner and under the responsibility established by law in the service of the general interests of society.

Article 10. (1) Cooperatives shall be a part of the socialist order of society; they shall serve the interests of their membership in concurrence with the social and economic goals of the socialist state.

(2) The state shall support the cooperative movement of the workers based on voluntary association, the development of socialist cooperative ownership; it shall assure the independence of cooperatives, and it shall exercise supervision of their activities in the interest of implementing socialist cooperative principles.

(3) The Hungarian People's Republic shall take special care of the agricultural production cooperatives of the peasantry. It shall protect and support the socialist cooperative ownership of the land.

Article 11. The Hungarian People's Republic shall recognize and protect personal property.

Article 12. The state shall recognize the economic activities of small-scale producers of commodities which are useful to society. Private ownership and private initiative, however, may not violate public interests.

Article 13. The Constitution shall guarantee the right of inheritance.

Article 14. (1) Labor shall be the foundation of the social order of the Hungarian People's Republic.

(2) It shall be the right and duty of every able-bodied citizen to work according to his ability.

(3) Citizens shall serve the cause of socialist construction by their labor, their participation in socialist competition, by increasing labor discipline, and improving working methods.

(4) The Hungarian People's Republic shall strive for the consistent realization of the socialist principle: "From each according to his ability, to each according to his work."

Article 15. The Hungarian People's Republic shall protect the institutions of marriage and the family.

Article 16. The Hungarian People's Republic shall take special care of the development and socialist education of the youth; it shall protect the interests of youth.

Article 17. The Hungarian People's Republic shall protect the life, physical safety, and health of citizens, and shall assist them in the event of sickness, disability, or old age.

Article 18. The Hungarian People's Republic shall organize and support scientific work that promotes the development of society, assist the arts serving progress, and assure the steady increase of citizens' education and culture.

Chapter II. The Parliament of the Hungarian People's Republic and the Presidium of the Hungarian People's Republic

The Parliament

Article 19. (1) Parliament shall be the highest representative organ of state power in the Hungarian People's Republic.

(2) Parliament shall exercise all the rights deriving from the sovereignty of the people, shall assure the constitutional order of society, and shall determine the organization, direction, and conditions of government.

(3) Parliament within this jurisdiction shall:

a) write the Constitution of the Hungarian People's Republic;

b) enact laws;

c) establish the national economic plan;

d) determine the state budget and approve its implementation;

e) discuss and approve the program of the government;

f) ratify international agreements in the name of the Hungarian People's Republic;

g) decide on the problems of declaring a state of war and a conclusion of peace;

h) elect the Presidium of the Hungarian People's Republic;

i) elect the Council of Ministers of the Hungarian People's Republic;

j) create ministries;

k) elect the President of the Supreme Court of the Hungarian People's Republic and the Chief Prosecutor of the Hungarian People's Republic;

l) supervise compliance with the Constitution; annul any actions of government agencies which are in conflict with the Constitution, or violate the interests of society.

Article 20. (1) Parliament shall be elected for a term of five years.

(2) Members of Parliament shall carry out their activities in the interest of their constituents, the public.

(3) Members of Parliament shall regularly give an account of their activities to their constituents.

(4) Members of Parliament shall not be arrested, nor may criminal proceedings be instituted against them without the consent of Parliament, unless they were apprehended in the act of committing a crime.

(5) All political, economic, or other activities and conduct that are

Hungary

detrimental to the interests of society shall be incompatible with the mandate of a Member of Parliament.

Article 21. (1) Parliament shall elect a speaker, deputy speakers, and recorders from among its members.
(2) Parliament shall create standing committees from among its members and may appoint a committee to investigate any matter.
(3) It shall be the duty of administrative authorities, offices, and institutions, as well as of the citizens of the country, to furnish any data requested by parliamentary committees or to testify before committees.

Article 22. (1) Parliament shall convene in regular session at least twice a year.
(2) Parliament shall be convoked by virtue of a resolution of the Presidium of the Hungarian People's Republic or upon the written request of one-third of its members.
(3) The Presidium shall take care of the convocation of Parliament.

Article 23. Sessions of Parliament, as a rule, shall be open to the public. In exceptional cases, Parliament may decide to sit in closed session.

Article 24. (1) The presence of at least one-half of the members shall be required for a quorum of Parliament.
(2) Parliament shall pass on resolutions by a simple majority of votes.
(3) The vote of two-thirds of all the Members of Parliament shall be required to amend the Constitution.
(4) Parliament shall establish the rules for its activity and the course of debate in the Rules of Order.

Article 25. (1) The Presidium of the Hungarian People's Republic, the Council of Ministers, every committee of Parliament, or any Member of Parliament shall have the right to introduce bills.
(2) The legislative power shall be vested in Parliament.

Article 26. A law adopted by Parliament shall be signed by the Chairman and the Secretary of the Presidium of the Hungarian People's Republic. The Chairman of the Presidium shall be in charge of the promulgation of a law. A law shall be promulgated in the official gazette.

Article 27. Members of Parliament may ask questions of the Presidium of the Hungarian People's Republic, as well as of the Council of Ministers, or any member thereof, the secretaries of state, the President of the Supreme Court, and the Chief Prosecutor in regard to matters within their respective jurisdictions. Whoever is asked a question shall give his answer in Parliament.

Article 28. (1) Parliament may resolve its dissolution even before the expiration of its term.

(2) Parliament, in case of war or other extraordinary circumstances, may resolve the prolongation of its term for a definite period of time.

(3) In the event of war or other extraordinary circumstances, an already dissolved Parliament may be recalled by the Presidium of the Hungarian People's Republic. Parliament recalled in such a manner shall itself decide upon the prolongation of its mandate.

(4) A new Parliament shall be elected within three months after the expiration of the term, or the dissolution of Parliament.

(5) The Presidium shall convoke the newly-elected Parliament within one month after its election.

The Presidium

Article 29. (1) During its first session, Parliament shall elect from among its own members the Presidium of the Hungarian People's Republic, [consisting of] the Chairman of the Presidium, two Deputy Chairmen, the Secretary, and 17 members.

(2) The Chairman, Deputy Chairmen, and members of the Council of Ministers, as well as the secretaries of state as the leading officials of the state's administrative agencies—shall not be elected to the Presidium.

Article 30. (1) The Presidium of the Hungarian People's Republic shall:

a) schedule the parliamentary elections;

b) convoke Parliament;

c) introduce bills;

d) have the right to call for a referendum in questions of national significance;

e) conclude and ratify international agreements in the name of the Hungarian People's Republic;

f) appoint and receive ambassadors and envoys;

g) elect professional judges;

h) appoint secretaries of state and government employees for important assignments as determined by law, as well as higher ranking officers of the armed forces;

i) establish and award the orders and titles of the Hungarian People's Republic and approve the acceptance of foreign orders and titles;

j) exercise the right to grant amnesty.

(2) The Presidium shall supervise the implementation of the Constitution. Within this jurisdiction, it shall annul or amend all such statutory provisions, administrative resolutions, or actions which are in conflict with the Constitution.

(3) The Presidium shall exercise constitutional supervision over the local councils; it shall

a) schedule the general elections of the councils;

b) take care of the protection of the rights of the councils;

c) dissolve a council any activity of which violates the Constitution or seriously jeopardizes the interests of the people.

(4) The Presidium shall decide on all matters that are referred to its jurisdiction by a special law.

(5) The Presidium shall exercise the jurisdiction of Parliament if Parliament is not in session; however, it may not amend the Constitution.

(6) Statutory provisions enacted by the Presidium are edicts. These shall be presented to Parliament at the next session thereof.

Article 31. (1) The Presidium of the Hungarian People's Republic, in the event of war or danger which seriously jeopardizes the security of the state, may create a defense council empowered with extraordinary jurisdiction.

(2) The danger that seriously jeopardizes the security of the state, and the termination thereof, shall be established and promulgated by the Presidium.

Article 32. (1) The mandate of the Presidium of the Hungarian People's Republic shall expire when Parliament elects a new Presidium.

(2) The Presidium shall be responsible to Parliament and shall tender a report of its activities to Parliament.

(3) Parliament shall have the right to recall the Presidium or any member thereof.

(4) In addition to the Chairman and the Secretary, the presence of at least nine members shall constitute a quorum of the Presidium.

(5) The Chairman and the Secretary shall sign any resolution or measure of the Presidium. Its edicts shall be promulgated in the official gazette.

(6) If the Chairman or the Secretary of the Presidium is prevented [from acting], the Deputy Chairman or a member designated by the Presidium shall act respectively.

(7) The Presidium itself shall establish its own standing orders.

Chapter III. The Council of Ministers of the Hungarian People's Republic

Article 33. (1) The Council of Ministers [government] shall consist of:
   a) the Chairman of the Council of Ministers;
   b) the Deputy Chairmen;
   c) the Ministers of State;
   d) the ministers in charge of the different ministries and the Chairman of the National Planning Board.

(2) Parliament, upon the recommendation of the Presidium of the Hungarian People's Republic, shall elect or relieve the Council of Ministers, the Chairman, and the members of the Council of Ministers.

(3) Members of the Council of Ministers shall have the right to participate and to a voice in the sessions of Parliament.

Article 34. The list of the ministries of the Hungarian People's Republic shall be determined by a special law.

Article 35. (1) The Council of Ministers shall:
   a) protect and ensure the public and social order and the rights of citizens;
   b) assure the implementation of the laws and edicts;
   c) direct the work of the ministries and other agencies directly subordinated to it, and coordinate their activities;
   d) direct the councils and supervise of the legality of their activities;
   e) assure the preparation of the national economic plan, and ensure the implementation thereof;
   f) determine the direction of scientific and cultural development, [and] assure the personal and material conditions necessary thereto;
   g) determine the system of social and health services, and assure the financial funding thereof;

h) conclude and approve international agreements;

i) perform all the duties referred to its jurisdiction by statutory provisions.

(2) The Council of Ministers shall issue decrees and pass resolutions in the discharge of its duties. These shall be signed by the Chairman of the Council of Ministers. A decree or resolution of the Council of Ministers shall not conflict with any law or edict. Decrees of the Council of Ministers shall be promulgated in the official gazette.

(3) The Council of Ministers shall annul or amend all statutory provisions, resolutions, or dispositions issued by subordinate agencies that are in conflict with a law or violate the public interests.

(4) The Council of Ministers shall annul such ordinances or resolutions of the councils as violate the interests of society.

Article 36. The Council of Ministers, in the discharge of its duty, shall cooperate with the social organizations concerned.

Article 37. (1) The Chairman of the Council of Ministers shall preside over the meetings of the Council of Ministers and provide for the implementation of the decrees and resolutions of the Council of Ministers.

(2) The ministers shall, in accordance with the statutory provisions and the resolutions of the Council of Ministers, manage the branches of state administration within their jurisdiction and direct the subordinate agencies.

(3) The Chairman, Deputy Chairmen, and members of the Council of Ministers in the discharge of their duties may issue decrees. These, however, shall not conflict with any law, edict, and decree or resolution of the Council of Ministers. The decrees shall be promulgated in the official gazette.

Article 38. A Secretary of State assigned to direct an agency with nationwide jurisdiction, in the discharge of his duty as determined by the Council of Ministers, may issue dispositions which shall be binding upon government agencies, enterprises, cooperatives, and other economic institutions. These shall be promulgated in the official gazette. Such dispositions shall not conflict with any law, edict, decree, or resolution of the Council of Ministers, or with the decrees of the ministers.

Article 39. (1) The Council of Ministers shall be responsible for its activities to Parliament. It shall render reports regularly about its work to Parliament.

(2) Members of the Council of Ministers and the secretaries of state shall be responsible to the Council of Ministers and to Parliament; they shall render reports on their activities to the Council of Ministers and to the Parliament. Their legal status and the manner of impeachment shall be regulated by a special law.

Article 40. (1) The Council of Ministers may create governmental commissions to perform certain duties.

(2) The Council of Ministers may act directly, or through a member thereof, in any matter pertaining to state administration.

(3) The Council of Ministers shall have the right to place any branch of the state administration under its direct supervision and to create separate agencies for this purpose.

Chapter IV. The Councils

Article 41. (1) The territory of the Hungarian People's Republic shall be divided into the Capital, counties, cities, and townships.

(2) Counties may be divided into districts; the Capital and the major cities into boroughs.

Article 42. (1) Councils shall be formed in the Capital, in counties, in the boroughs of the Capital, and in cities and townships. A joint council may be formed by more than one township.

(2) Members of the councils shall be elected for a term of five years.

(3) The council shall discharge its duties with the active participation of the population; in its work, it shall seek the support of social organizations and shall cooperate with agencies not under the council.

(4) Members of councils shall regularly give an account of the work of the council and their own activities to their constituents.

Article 43. (1) The council shall:

a) represent the interests of the population and accomplish within its territorial venue the self-government of the working people;

b) assure the attainment of the central state and local goals, the independent discharge of duties referred to its jurisdiction, the implementation of statutory provisions;

c) determine on the basis of the national economic plan and the state budget its own plan and budget, direct and supervise the implementation of the plans and the use of the budget, and independently manage its own financial means;

d) assure territorial and settlement development, organize the fulfillment of the needs of the population;

e) participate in guaranteeing the public and social order and the protection of socialist property.

(2) The council, within its scope of activity shall issue ordinances or pass resolutions which, however, shall not conflict with any law, edict, decree, or resolution of the Council of Ministers, ministerial decrees, dispositions of a secretary of state, or with an ordinance of a higher-ranking council. Council ordinances shall be promulgated in the usual local manner.

Article 44. (1) The council shall elect an executive committee, form committees, and create specialized agencies, and it may establish enterprises or institutions.

(2) Detailed rules pertaining to councils shall be established by law.

Chapter V. The Judicial Organization

Article 45. (1) The administration of justice in the Hungarian People's Republic shall be vested in the Supreme Court of the Hungarian People's Republic, in county courts, and in district courts.

(2) Special courts may be established by law to handle certain types of cases.

Article 46. Courts shall sit in panels consisting of professional judges and lay assessors. Exceptions to this rule may be established by law.

Article 47. The Supreme Court of the Hungarian People's Republic shall exercise policy-making supervision over the judicial activities and practice of all courts. Directives of principle and decisions of principle rendered by the Supreme Court shall be binding upon all courts.

Article 48. (1) Judicial positions in the Hungarian People's Republic shall be filled through elections; the elected judges may be recalled for reasons determined by law.

(2) The President of the Supreme Court shall be elected by

Parliament at its first session for a term lasting until the first session of the next Parliament.

(3) Professional judges shall be elected by the Presidium of the Hungarian People's Republic in a manner established by law.

Article 49. (1) Trials before the courts shall be open to the public, unless exceptions are established by law.

(2) Persons under criminal proceedings shall be entitled to the right of defense in every phase of the proceedings.

Article 50. (1) The courts of the Hungarian People's Republic shall protect and assure the state, economic, and social order, [and] the rights and lawful interests of citizens, and punish perpetrators of criminal acts.

(2) Judges shall be independent and subject only to the law.

(3) Rules pertaining to the courts shall be established by law.

Chapter VI. The Public Prosecutors

Article 51. (1) The Chief Prosecutor of the Hungarian People's Republic and the organization of public prosecution shall ensure the consistent prosecution of every act violating or jeopardizing the legal order of society or the security and independence of the state, as well as the protection of the rights of the citizens.

(2) Public prosecutors shall exercise supervision over the legality of the investigation and represent the state in criminal court proceedings.

(3) Public prosecutors shall cooperate to assure that state, social, and cooperative agencies, as well as citizens, comply with the laws and shall make others comply as well. In case of any violation of the law, they shall take steps to defend legality.

Article 52. (1) The Chief Prosecutor of the Hungarian People's Republic shall be elected by Parliament at its first session for a term lasting until the first session of the next Parliament.

(2) The Chief Prosecutor shall be responsible to Parliament and shall render a report on his activities.

Article 53. (1) The Chief Prosecutor of the Hungarian People's Republic shall appoint the public prosecutors.

(2) The Chief Prosecutor shall manage and direct the organization of public prosecution.

(3) Rules pertaining to public prosecutors shall be established by law.

Chapter VII. Basic Rights and Duties of Citizens

Article 54. (1) The Hungarian People's Republic shall respect human rights.

(2) The rights of citizens in the Hungarian People's Republic shall be exercised in accordance with the interests of socialist society; the exercise of rights shall be inseparable from the fulfillment of the duties of citizens.

(3) Rules pertaining to the basic rights and duties of citizens in the Hungarian People's Republic shall be established by law.

Article 55. (1) The Hungarian People's Republic shall assure for its citizens the right to work, as well as remuneration commensurate with the quantity and quality of the work performed.

(2) The Hungarian People's Republic shall implement this right through the planned development of the productive forces of the people's economy and by the manpower management based on the national economic plan.

Article 56. (1) The Hungarian People's Republic shall assure for its citizens the right to rest.

(2) The Hungarian People's Republic shall implement this right through the legal determination of working time, the assurance of a paid vacation, and assistance to organized recreation.

Article 57. (1) The citizens of the Hungarian People's Republic shall have the right to protection of life, physical safety, and health.

(2) The Hungarian People's Republic shall implement this right through organizing labor safety, health institutions, and medical care, as well as protecting the human environment.

Article 58. (1) The citizens of the Hungarian People's Republic shall be entitled to financial support in the event of old age, illness, or disability.

(2) The Hungarian People's Republic shall implement the right to financial support within the framework of social insurance and the system of social institutions.

Article 59. (1) The Hungarian People's Republic shall assure the right to education of the citizens.

(2) The Hungarian People's Republic shall implement this right through extending public education to all in free and compulsory general schools, as well as through secondary and higher education, extension training of adults, and through giving financial assistance to persons who receive an education.

Article 60. The Hungarian People's Republic shall assure the freedom of scientific work and artistic production.

Article 61. (1) The citizens of the Hungarian People's Republic shall be equal before the law and shall enjoy equal rights.

(2) The law shall severely punish every kind of discrimination against citizens on the grounds of sex, religious denomination, or nationality.

(3) The Hungarian People's Republic shall guarantee equal rights to all nationalities living within its territory, the use of and education in their native language, and the preservation and promotion of their own culture.

Article 62. (1) Men and women in the Hungarian People's Republic shall enjoy equal rights.

(2) Equal rights for women shall be implemented by: the assurance of an opportunity for proper employment and working conditions; paid maternity leave in the event of pregnancy and childbirth; increased legal protection of mothers and children, as well as the system of maternity and child care institutions.

Article 63. (1) The Hungarian People's Republic shall guarantee the freedom of conscience of citizens and the right to the free practice of religion.

(2) The Hungarian People's Republic, in the interest of assuring freedom of conscience, shall separate the church from the state.

Article 64. The Hungarian People's Republic, consistent with the interests of socialism and the people, shall guarantee freedom of speech, freedom of the press, and freedom of assembly.

Article 65. (1) The Hungarian People's Republic shall guarantee the right of association. A special law shall regulate the right of association.

(2) Workers may form mass organizations and mass movements to protect the order and achievements of socialism, to promote increased participation in the socialist work of construction and public

life, to expand culture and educational work, to ensure the rights and duties of the people, and to promote international solidarity.

Article 66. The Hungarian People's Republic shall guarantee the personal freedom and inviolability of citizens, the respect of the secrecy of correspondence, and the privacy of the home.

Article 67. Whoever is prosecuted for his democratic attitude or for his activities in the interests of social progress, liberation of the people, and protection of the peace shall be entitled to the right of asylum in the Hungarian People's Republic.

Article 68. (1) All citizens shall have the right to participate in the administration of public affairs; it shall be their obligation to meticulously discharge [the duties of] their public offices.

(2) Citizens may offer suggestions in the public interest to the state or social organizations. These shall be judged on their merit.

Article 69. It shall be the fundamental duty of the citizens of the Hungarian People's Republic to protect the assets of the nation, to strengthen socialist property, to increase the economic power of the Hungarian People's Republic, to enrich its culture, to protect the country's natural and cultural treasures, and to strengthen the order of society.

Article 70. (1) The defense of the country shall be the duty of every citizen of the Hungarian People's Republic.

(2) Citizens shall perform military service on the basis of the universal system of the draft.

(3) The betrayal of the causes of the country and the people, violation of the military oath, desertion to the enemy, espionage, and any act detrimental to the military power of the state shall be severely punished by law.

Chapter VIII. The Basic Principles of Elections

Article 71. (1) Citizens shall elect the members of Parliament, as well as the members of township, city, or Capital borough councils on the basis of universal, equal, and direct suffrage by secret ballot.

(2) Members of the Council of the Capital shall be elected by the borough councils and the members of county councils by the city and township councils by secret ballot.

(3) Members of Parliament or members of councils may be recalled by their constituents.

Article 72. (1) All citizens of the Hungarian People's Republic who are of age shall have the right to vote.

(2) Every citizen entitled to vote shall have one vote in elections. Every vote shall be equal.

(3) The law shall establish the cases for exclusion from the suffrage.

Article 73. (1) Whoever has the right to vote may be elected as a member of Parliament or a member of a council.

(2) A special law shall regulate the election and recall of members of Parliament and members of councils.

Chapter IX. The Coat-of-Arms, The Flag, and the Capital of the Hungarian People's Republic

Article 74. The coat-of-arms of the Hungarian People's Republic is as follows: a red-white-green escutcheon with arched sides in a light blue field surrounded by a wreath of wheat. The wreath shall be entwined on the left with a red, white, and green ribbon, and on the right with a red ribbon. Above the escutcheon a five-pointed red star, placed in the middle, shall cast golden rays on the field.

Article 75. The flag of the Hungarian People's Republic shall be red, white, and green.

Article 76. The Capital of the Hungarian People's Republic is Budapest.

Chapter X. Final Provisions

Article 77. (1) The Constitution shall be the fundamental law of the Hungarian People's Republic.

(2) The Constitution, as well as all constitutional statutory provisions, shall be equally binding on all agencies of the state and all citizens.

(3) It shall be the duty of all agencies of the state and all citizens to comply with the Constitution and the constitutional statutory pro-

visions, and in the discharge of their duties, to make others comply with the same.

Article 78. (1) The Constitution of the Hungarian People's Republic shall enter into force on the day of its promulgation; the Council of Ministers shall ensure the implementation thereof.

(2) The Council of Ministers shall introduce in Parliament the bills required for the implementation of the Constitution.

Pál Losonczi
Chairman of the Presidium of the People's Republic

Lajos Cseterki
Secretary of the Presidium of the People's Republic

KAMPUCHEA

INTRODUCTION

William B. Simons

For much of the period between the 17th and early 19th centuries, Cambodia was under Vietnamese (and Thai) suzerainty, and thereafter became a French protectorate and later a colony in the French-created Indochinese Union together with Laos and the three provinces of Viet-Nam. The French—who had continued to administer Indochina through most of World War II and Japanese occupation—were overthrown by the Japanese in early 1945, but managed to reassert their control over Cambodia until 1953 when, on 9 November, King Norodom Sihanouk proclaimed the country to be independent. In 1955, Sihanouk put his father on the throne and established a mass political movement—the People's Socialist Community—as a result of which Sihanouk became Cambodian Prime Minister and later chief of state when his father died in 1960 and no successor to the throne was named. Sihanouk sought to remain neutral in the struggle on his doorstep between the government of South Viet-Nam and communist-led insurgents, and for a time he was successful until 1965 when North Vietnamese and guerrilla troops began using Cambodian soil in their struggle against the South Vietnamese regime. Unhappy with this situation, a Cambodian Army General, Lon Nol, called for the removal of North Vietnamese and communist guerrilla forces from Cambodian territory, and overthrew Sihanouk's government of 18 March 1970; a republic under Lon Nol's leadership was established on 9 November 1970. Sihanouk then travelled to Peking where he formed a government-in-exile of national unity based on the "United National Front of Kampuchea" and proclaimed an alliance with the People's Republic of China, North Viet-Nam, and North Korea. Although United States and South Vietnamese forces entered Cambodia temporarily to help Lon Nol purge the country of communist rebels, the new Cambodian republic remained subject throughout its existence to continuing insurgent pressure.

The struggle for ultimate control of Cambodia was waged between Lon Nol's troops and those of the Khmer Rouge, a communist-based group which had been opposed by Sihanouk when the latter was still in power. The Lon Nol-inspired republic collapsed in early 1975, as the Khmer Rouge occupied the capital, Phnom Penh, on 17 April

Introduction

1975. A new Democratic Kampuchea was proclaimed in late April, and Sihanouk was named as chief of state. However, Sihanouk and his cabinet subsequently submitted their resignation to the National Assembly, which met in January 1976. On 5 January 1976, the Constitution of Democratic Kampuchea was promulgated, and Pol Pot, Secretary General of the Communist Party, became Premier.

The Constitution—a mere 21 articles plus a preamble—describes the Kampuchean state as a neutral and democratic state of "industrial workers, peasants, and other workers" (Art. 1). All important means of production have been nationalized, and the Constitution mentions that the "collective principle" applies to both management and work. Legislative power under the fundamental law has been placed in a 250-member Assembly of People's Representatives elected by a secret and direct ballot for a five-year term; the executive organ of state is the Government, which is appointed by the Assembly. A three-man Presidium of State, chosen by the Assembly for a five-year term, is charged by the Kampuchean Constitution of 1976 with representing the state inside and outside the country (Art. 11). A bill of rights proclaims that citizens have the right to work and, indeed, that there is no unemployment in Democratic Kampuchea. The compliment of the constitutional "full employment" proclamation can be found in the duty of Kampuchean citizens under Article 14 to defend and build the country. The Revolutionary Army of Kampuchea also has its duties spelled out in the Constitution—to defend Kampuchean territorial integrity and to take part in the country's construction. All citizens are equal under the provisions of the Constitution—with special mention of the equality of the sexes—and both polygamy and polyandry are outlawed. Citizens are guaranteed freedom of religion under Article 20, but an important caveat prohibits "any reactionary religion". Brief mention is made of the judicial system of popular courts, which are selected and designated at all levels by the National Assembly. Article 10 broadly states that "systematically hostile or destructive activities that endanger the people's state" are punished with the most severe penalty (presumably some type of death penalty), and that all other cases are to be dealt with by means of "reeducation".

Many constitutions of communist states close with a section on the symbols of state authority—the flag, emblem, and perhaps the anthem—and usually a procedure for constitutional amendment or change; the Kampuchean Constitution makes no provision for amending or changing the fundamental law and its chapters on the state symbols are in the middle of the text. The concluding section of the Constitution is on foreign policy. This section amiably proclaims a determination to maintain friendly relations with all countries on the basis of mutual respect for sovereignty and territorial integrity, but militantly continues its nonalignment by prohibiting the establishment of foreign military bases on its territory and foreign interference in its internal affairs.

Constitutional proscriptions notwithstanding, foreign states ultimately played a role in the fate of Democratic Kampuchea. Guerrillas continued to oppose the Pol Pot regime, and on 2 December 1978, a Front of National Union for the Salvation of Kampuchea (FNUSK) was formed with aid from the Socialist Republic of VietNam to pursue the struggle against the incumbent Cambodian regime until the latter was forced to retreat from the capital in January of 1979 and to wage its own guerrilla compaign against FNUSK. As of mid-1979, western and communist sources still had no information as to whether and when the new FNUSK government in Cambodia might draft a new constitution. But in December 1978 FNUSK did issue an 11-point declaration of its policies:[1] in addition to listing its intent to "overthrow the dictatorial regime" of Pol Pot, it proclaimed an independant economic policy leading toward "authentic socialism", and announced the abolition of all forms of arbitrariness and forced labor; respect for the family was also listed as a goal of FNUSK. In addition, the declaration mentioned peaceful coexistence, respect for territorial integrity and sovereignty, and the mutual non-interference in the affairs of other countries, as well as the desire to reestablish friendly relations with the neighboring countries of Southeast Asia. The declaration, however, repeated the prohibition of the Pol Pot Constitution against the establishment of foreign military bases on Cambodian soil.

One communist country, Romania, by the summer of 1979 had still refused to recognize the FNUSK government in Phnom Penh.

NOTE

1. "Cambodge: De la chute de Pol Pot au nouveau régime", *Sudestasie Information*, Paris 1979.

CONSTITUTION OF DEMOCRATIC KAMPUCHEA OF 5 JANUARY 1976

Preamble	220
The State Regime	221
The Economic Regime	221
The Culture	221
The Principle of Management and Work	221
The Legislative Power	221
The Executive Organ	222
The Judiciary	222
The Presidium of State	223
The Rights and Duties of Every Citizen of Kampuchea	223
The Capital	224
The National Flag	224
The National Emblem	224
The National Anthem	224
The Revolutionary Army of Kampuchea	224
Faiths and Religions	225
Foreign Policy	225

CONSTITUTION OF DEMOCRATIC KAMPUCHEA*

Fundamental and Sacred Aspirations of the Industrial Workers, Peasants, and other Workers, and the Soldiers and Officers of the Revolutionary Army of Kampuchea.

Having regard to:
the leading role played by the people, especially by industrial workers, small and middle peasants, and by other strata of workers, in the countryside and in the cities, who compose more than 95 percent of the whole nation of Kampuchea and who have borne the heaviest load of the war of popular and national liberation, consenting unceasingly to the greatest sacrifices in terms of lives, property, and feelings for the sake of service at the front, and sending unhesitatingly their children and their husbands to fight by tens and hundreds of thousands on the battlefield,

Having regard to:
the tremendous sacrifices willingly made by the three categories of the Revolutionary Army of Kampuchea who, in the blaze of the war of popular and national liberation, valiantly fought, night and day, in any season, dry or rainy, suffering all kinds of hardships and privations, when lacking everything: food, medicine, clothes, ammunition...,

Having regard to:
the aspirations of the whole people of Kampuchea and of the Revolutionary Army of Kampuchea, which wish to create an independent, united, peaceful, neutral, nonaligned Kampuchea sovereign in its territorial integrity, in a society where happiness, equality, justice, and genuine democracy reign, where there are neither rich nor poor people, neither oppressive nor oppressed classes, a society in which the whole people lives in harmony, in a framework of national unity, and join their efforts in productive labor, to build and defend the country together,

Having regard to:
the Resolution of the Special National Congress held on 25, 26, and 27 April 1975, which solemnly proclaimed its recognition and

*Text based on an official French translation issued by the government of Democratic Kampuchea. Text revised by Catherine A. Crisham.

respect of the above-mentioned aspirations of the whole people and of the Revolutionary Army of Kampuchea,

The Constitution of Kampuchea stipulates the following:

Chapter I. The State Regime

Article 1. The State of Kampuchea is in its territorial integrity, an independent, united, peaceful, neutral, non-aligned, sovereign, and democratic state.

The State of Kampuchea is a state of industrial workers, peasants, and other workers of Kampuchea.

The official name of the state of Kampuchea is: "Democratic Kampuchea".

Chapter II. The Economic Regime

Article 2. All important means of production are the collective property of the people's state and of the people in common.

Articles of everyday life remain in individual ownership.

Chapter III. The Culture

Article 3. The culture of Democratic Kampuchea has a national, popular, progressive, and wholesome character, serving the tasks of defending and building a country continuously growing in prosperity.

The new culture resolutely fights against the depraved and reactionary culture of the oppressive classes and of the forces of colonialism and imperialism in Kampuchea.

Chapter IV. The Principle of Management and Work

Article 4. Democratic Kampuchea applies the collective principle, both in relation to management and to work.

Chapter V. The Legislative Power

Article 5. The legislative power lies with the Assembly of representatives of industrial workers, peasants, and other workers.

The official name of this Assembly is: "Assembly of the People's Representatives of Kampuchea".

The Assembly of the People's Representatives of Kampuchea has 250 members representing industrial workers, peasants, other workers and the Revolutionary Army of Kampuchea, distributed as follows:

Representatives of peasants	150
Representatives of industrial workers and other workers	50
Representatives of the Revolutionary Army	50

Article 6. Members of the Assembly of the People's Representatives of Kampuchea are chosen every 5 years by the people in general elections by secret and direct ballot.

Article 7. The Assembly of the People's Representatives of Kampuchea adopts legislation and defines the various internal and external policies of Democratic Kampuchea.

Chapter VI. The Executive Organ

Article 8. The Government is an organ charged with the execution of laws and the implementation of all the policies defined by the Assembly of the People's Representatives of Kampuchea.

The Government is designated by the Assembly of the People's Representatives of Kampuchea. It is responsible to this Assembly for all its activities both inside and outside the country.

Chapter VII. The Judiciary

Article 9. Justice is exercised by the people. The popular courts of justice administer and defend the people's justice, defend the people's democratic liberties, and punish any act directed against the people's state or transgressing its laws.

All instances of courts of justice are selected and designated by the Assembly of the People's Representatives.

Article 10. The following acts transgress the laws of the people's State:
— any systematically hostile or destructive activities that endanger the people's state shall be punished with the most severe penalty;

— cases other than those mentioned above shall be dealt with by means of reeducation within the framework of state organs or people's organizations.

Chapter VIII. The Presidium of State

Article 11. Democratic Kampuchea has a Presidium of State chosen and nominated every 5 years by the Assembly of the People's Representatives of Kampuchea. The Presidium of State is charged with the representation of the state of Kampuchea inside and outside the country within the limits of the Constitution of Democratic Kampuchea and in conformity with the laws and policies defined by the Assembly of the People's Representatives of Kampuchea.

The Presidium of State is composed of:
— a President,
— a first Vice-President,
— a second Vice-President.

Chapter IX. The Rights and Duties of Every Citizen of Kampuchea

Article 12. Every citizen of Kampuchea has the full right to enjoy material, moral, and cultural life, the conditions of which are constantly improving. Every citizen of Kampuchea is fully assured of the means of existence.

Every industrial worker is the master of his factory.
Every peasant is the master of his ricefields and lands.
All other workers have the right to work.
There is absolutely no unemployment in Democratic Kampuchea.

Article 13. A full equality among all citizens of Kampuchea should prevail in a society based on equality, justice, democracy, harmony, happiness, in a framework of national unity in order to defend and build the country together.

Men and women are equal in every sphere of life.
Polygamy and polyandry are prohibited.

Article 14. Every citizen has the duty to defend and build the country in accordance with his means and his capacities.

Chapter X. The Capital

Article 15. The capital of Democratic Kampuchea is Phnom Penh.

Chapter XI. The National Flag

Article 16. The Kampuchea National Flag has the following form and significance:

The field is red with a yellow, three-towered monument in the center.

The red field symbolizes the revolutionary movement, the resolute and valiant struggle of the people of Kampuchea for national liberation, defense, and construction.

The yellow monument symbolizes the national tradition and the people of Kampuchea engaged in defending and building a country which is ever more glorious.

Chapter XII. The National Emblem

Article 17. The National Emblem is made up of a system of dikes and irrigation canals symbolizing modern agriculture, and a factory symbolizing industry, enclosed within two arc-shaped sheaves of paddy and bearing the inscription "Democratic Kampuchea".

Chapter XIII. The National Anthem

Article 18. The National Anthem of Democratic Kampuchea is "The Glorious 17th of April".

Chapter XIV. The Revolutionary Army of Kampuchea

Article 19. The Revolutionary Army of Kampuchea with its three categories—regular, regional, and guerrilla fighters—is the Army of the People, of which the men and women soldiers and officers are the sons and daughters of industrial workers, peasants, and other categories of workers. It defends the power of the people of Kampuchea, and defends in its territorial integrity the independent, united, peaceful, neutral, nonaligned, sovereign state of Democratic Kampuchea; at the same time, it takes part in the construction of a country which is ever more glorious and in the constant improvement of the well-being of the people which enjoy ever greater prosperity.

Chapter XV. Faiths and Religions

Article 20. Every citizen of Kampuchea has the right to hold any faith or religion, and has also the right to hold no faith or religion.

Any reactionary religion which threatens the interests of Kampuchea and its people is strictly prohibited.

Chapter XVI. Foreign Policy

Article 21. Democratic Kampuchea is guided by good will and is firmly determined to maintain close and friendly relations with all countries having common borders with it and with all countries throughout the world, near or far, on the strict basis of mutual respect of sovereignty and territorial integrity.

Democratic Kampuchea abides by a policy of independence, peace, neutrality, and nonalignment. No foreign country whatever is permitted to establish military bases on its territory; it resolutely opposes foreign interference in its internal affairs and resolutely combats subversive and aggressive acts from outside, whether of military, political, cultural, economical, social, diplomatic, or of so-called humanitarian character.

Democratic Kampuchea does not interfere in any way in the internal affairs of any country. It scrupulously abides by the principle that every country is sovereign and has the right to determine and decide by itself its internal affairs without external interference.

Democratic Kampuchea resolutely establishes itself as a member of the great family of nonaligned countries.

Democratic Kampuchea will do its utmost to develop solidarity with the peoples of the Third World in Asia, Africa, and Latin America, and with all peace and justice-loving peoples in the world, and to foster active mutual aid and support in the struggle against imperialism, colonialism, and neo-colonialism, in the cause of independence, peace, friendship, democracy, justice, and progress in the world.

KOREA

INTRODUCTION

Youn-Soo Kim

The Korean Democratic People's Republic (*Chosōn-Minchu-Chuih-Inmin-Kong-Hwakuk*, hereafter referred to as the KDPR) adopted a new Socialist Constitution on 27 December 1972. This Constitution—the second Constitution of the KDPR—is composed of 11 chapters and 149 articles, and according to the President of the KDPR, Kim Il-Sung, "correctly reflects the achievements made in the socialist revolution and the building of socialism in the KDPR".

The Workers' Party of Korea (*Chosōn-Rodong-Dang*, WPK) decided in October 1972 to establish a commission to draft a new constitution for the KDPR. The draft constitution was made public through the report on the Fifth Plenary Meeting of the Fifth Central Committee of the WPK held from 23–26 October 1972. The Supreme People's Assembly (*Ch'eko-Inmin-Hoeui*, SPA) ratified the new socialist constitution at their first session on 27 December 1972.

The Socialist Constitution of the KDPR has two principal characteristics: (1) the expression of Korean nationalism; and (2) the creation of a strong Presidency.

According to Article 4 of the 1972 Constitution, the central principle of the policy of the KDPR is the *Chuch'e* idea of the WPK. *Chuch'e* means that Korea must struggle to attain political independence, economic self-reliance, and national self-defense. This policy developed as the result of the Sino-Soviet dispute, which resulted, subsequent to 1959, in Soviet economic pressure and Chinese military intervention against the KDPR. Since the KDPR could not take any retaliatory action against either the USSR or China because of possible intervention similar to that in Prague in 1968, Kim Il-Sung adopted "active neutrality" in the Sino-Soviet conflict and turned to *Chuch'e*. This policy has continued, and the KDPR is making every possible effort today to build a *Chuch'e*-state, including emphasis on nationalism in its foreign policy. For example, Article 16 of the Constitution provides that: "The KDPR is completely equal and independent in its relations with foreign countries".

Such an expression of nationalism by the KDPR is not restricted to its foreign policy but is actively pursued in its economic policy as well. For example, the KDPR adopted Kim Il-Sung's policy of the so-called *Chōngsanri* spirit and the *Chōngsanri* method in order to "achieve the complete victory of socialism in the northern half of Korea" (Arts. 5, 12). The *Chōngsanri* method is to "make the masses of the people the masters of state management and [to] give a full and concrete expression to the principle and method of mass leadership which renders it possible to mobilize all the strength and wisdom of the masses of the people in the revolution and construction".

The *Chollima* movement in the KDPR is a "general line in the building of socialism" (Art. 13). Its objective is to "achieve the complete victory of socialism" through the *Chōngsanri* spirit and by *Chōngsanri* methods as rapidly as a "flying horse" (*Chollima*). This flying horse is a white horse in Korean mythology which could travel more than 1,000 miles in a day.

The second principal characteristic of the 1972 KDPR Constitution is the creation of a strong presidential system. According to the new Constitution of 1972, the President of the KDPR is both the head of state (Art. 89) as well as the supreme commander of all the armed forces (Art. 93). However, the President of the KDPR has not only a symbolic function as in other socialist countries, but also politically absolute powers. The President of the KDPR "directly guides the Central People's Committee", *i.e.* the policy-making organ of the KDPR (Arts. 91, 100), and "convenes and presides over meetings of the Administration Council", *i.e.* the policy-executing organ of the KDPR (Arts. 92, 107).

The President of the KDPR thus has absolute leadership of all state organs, except the SPA. The President of the KDPR is "elected by the SPA and the term of office is four years" (Art. 90). The President of the KDPR "is accountable to the SPA for his activities" (Art. 98). In practice, however, the leading power in the communist countries, as in the KDPR, is the Politburo of the Communist Party. Since Kim Il-Sung is the General Secretary of the WPK and because the Government and the SPA are "guided in their activity by the *Chuch'e* idea of the WPK" (Art. 4), the political power of the President of the KDPR is thus in fact absolute.

Important is the fact that the KDPR has adopted a non-Soviet and non-Chinese Constitution; *i.e.* it has written an original Korean Constitution as a jurisprudential demonstration of its *Chuch'e*.

The 1948 Constitution of the KDPR was an imitation of the

so-called 1936 Stalin Constitution of the USSR. However, the 1972 Constitution of the KDPR departed from many points of the Stalinist model. At the same time, it also differs substantively from the Chinese Constitution. Accordingly, it can be defined as "a synthesis of the constitutional models of the socialist countries". Essential points are:

> (1) The KDPR departs from the Sino-Soviet state structure. The KDPR has set up an independent policy-making organ, the Central People's Committee (Arts. 100–106) and an independent policy-executing organ, the Administration Council (Arts. 107–114). The most important factor in the new government of the KDPR is "the triangular relationship established between the three key institutions of the KDPR: The Politburo of the WPK, the Central People's Committee, and the Administration Council";
> (2) The KDPR created a "western-style" presidency (Arts. 89–99);
> (3) As a completely original provision, the KDPR no longer has a system of income taxation, because this is seen as a "holdover of the old society" (Art. 33); and,
> (4) There is to be cooperative ownership of land (Art. 20). By contrast, the Soviet system places all land ownership in the state, although it allots state land to cooperatives for permanent use.

Although the KDPR is a divided nation, it is according to the Constitution to strive to reunify the country peacefully on a democratic basis (Art. 5). Significant is that Article 103 of the 1948 Constitution provided that the capital city of the KDPR is Seoul, *i.e.* the current capital of the ROK. The 1972 Socialist Constitution corrected this "constitutional inconsistency" and it makes clear that the capital of the KDPR is Pyongyang (Art. 149). The Socialist Constitution is valid only in the northern half of the Korean peninsula. When Korea under the leadership of the KDPR is reunified, the validity of the Socialist Constitution of the KDPR is to extend to all areas of the Korean peninsula, and the KDPR is to "represent the interests of all the Korean people" (Art. 1). Hence, the peaceful reunification of the country is one of the political aims of the KDPR which is anchored in its constitution.

SOCIALIST CONSTITUTION OF THE DEMOCRATIC PEOPLE'S REPUBLIC OF KOREA OF 27 DECEMBER 1972

Politics	232
The Economy	234
Culture	237
Fundamental Rights and Duties of Citizens	239
The Supreme People's Assembly	242
The President of the Democratic People's Republic of Korea	245
The Central People's Committee	246
The Administration Council	247
The Local People's Assembly, People's Committee, and Administrative Committee	249
The Courts and the Procurator's Office	252
Emblem, Flag, and Capital	254

SOCIALIST CONSTITUTION OF THE DEMOCRATIC PEOPLE'S REPUBLIC OF KOREA*

Adopted on 27 December 1972 by the Fifth Supreme People's Assembly of the Democratic People's Republic of Korea at its first session.

Chapter I. Politics

Article 1. The Democratic People's Republic of Korea is an independent socialist state representing the interests of all the Korean people.

Article 2. The Democratic People's Republic of Korea rests on the politico-ideological unity of the entire people, based on the worker-peasant alliance led by the working class, on the socialist relations of production, and the foundation of an independent national economy.

Article 3. The Democratic People's Republic of Korea is a revolutionary state power which has inherited the brilliant traditions formed during the glorious revolutionary struggle against the imperialist aggressors and for the liberation of the homeland and for the freedom and well-being of the people.

Article 4. The Democratic People's Republic of Korea is guided in its activity by the *Chuch'e* idea of the Workers' Party of Korea, a creative application of Marxism-Leninism to the conditions of our country.

Article 5. The Democratic People's Republic of Korea strives to achieve the complete victory of socialism in the northern half, drive out foreign forces on a national scale, reunify the country peacefully on a democratic basis, and attain complete national independence.

Article 6. In the Democratic People's Republic of Korea, class

*Translation published by the Foreign Languages Publishing House, Pyongyang DPRK 1972.

antagonisms and all forms of exploitation and oppression of man by man have been eliminated for ever.

The state defends and protects the interests of the workers, peasants, soldiers, and working intellectuals freed from exploitation and oppression.

Article 7. The sovereignty of the Democratic People's Republic of Korea rests with the workers, peasants, soldiers, and working intellectuals.

The working people exercise power through their representative organs—the Supreme People's Assembly and local People's Assemblies at all levels.

Article 8. The organs of state power at all levels from the county People's Assembly to the Supreme People's Assembly are elected on the principle of universal, equal, and direct suffrage by secret ballot.

Deputies to the organs of state power at all levels are accountable to the electors for their activities.

Article 9. All state organs in the Democratic People's Republic of Korea are formed and run in accordance with the principle of democratic centralism.

Article 10. The Democratic People's Republic of Korea exercises the dictatorship of the proletariat and pursues class and mass lines.

Article 11. The state defends the socialist system against the subversive activities of hostile elements at home and abroad and revolutionizes and working-classizes the whole of society by intensifying the ideological revolution.

Article 12. The state thoroughly applies in all its work the great *Chŏngsan ri* spirit and *Chŏngsan ri* method to guarantee that the higher bodies help the lower, the masses' opinions are respected, and their conscious enthusiasm is roused by giving priority to political work, work with people.

Article 13. The *Chollima* Movement in the Democratic People's Republic of Korea is the general line in the building of socialism.

The state accelerates socialist construction to the maximum by constantly developing the *Chollima* Movement in depth and breadth.

Article 14. The Democratic People's Republic of Korea is based on the all-people, nationwide system of defense, and carries through a self-defensive military line.

It is the mission of the Armed Forces of the Democratic People's Republic of Korea to protect the interests of the workers, peasants, and other working people, to defend the socialist system and revolutionary gains, and to safeguard the freedom and independence of the country and peace.

Article 15. The Democratic People's Republic of Korea protects the democratic, national rights of Koreans overseas and their legitimate rights under international law.

Article 16. The Democratic People's Republic of Korea is completely equal and independent in its relations with foreign countries.

The state establishes diplomatic as well as political, economic, and cultural relations with all friendly countries, on the principles of complete equality, independence, mutual respect, noninterference in each other's internal affairs, and mutual benefit.

The state, in accordance with the principles of Marxism-Leninism and proletarian internationalism, unites with the socialist countries, unites with all peoples of the world opposed to imperialism, and actively supports and encourages their national-liberation and revolutionary struggles.

Article 17. The law of the Democratic People's Republic of Korea reflects the will and interests of the workers, peasants, and other working people, and it is consciously observed by all state organs, enterprises, social cooperative organizations, and citizens.

Chapter II. The Economy

Article 18. In the Democratic People's Republic of Korea, the means of production are owned by the state and cooperative organizations.

Article 19. The property of the state belongs to the whole people.

The state may own property without limit.

All natural resources of the country, major factories and enterprises, ports, banks, transport and communication establishments are owned solely by the state.

State property plays a leading role in the economic development of the Democratic People's Republic of Korea.

Article 20. The property of cooperative organizations is collectively owned by the working people involved in the cooperative economy.

Land, draught animals, farm implements, fishing boats, buildings, as well as small and medium factories and enterprises may be owned by cooperative organizations.

The state protects the property of cooperative organizations by law.

Article 21. The state strengthens and develops the socialist cooperative economic system and gradually transforms the property of cooperative organizations into the property of all the people on the basis of the voluntary will of the entire membership.

Article 22. Personal property is property for the personal use of the working people.

The personal property of the working people is derived from socialist distribution according to work done and from additional benefits granted by the state and society.

The products from the inhabitants' supplementary husbandry, including those from the small plots of cooperative farmers, are also personal property.

The state protects the working people's personal property by law and guarantees their right to inherit it.

Article 23. The state regards it as the supreme principle of its activities to steadily improve the material and cultural standards of the people.

The constantly increasing material wealth of society in the Democratic People's Republic of Korea is used entirely to promote the well-being of the working people.

Article 24. The foundation of an independent national economy in the Democratic People's Republic of Korea is the material guarantee of the prosperity and development of the country, and the improvement of the people's well-being.

In the Democratic People's Republic of Korea, the historic task of industrialization has been accomplished successfully.

The state strives to consolidate and develop the successes in industrialization and to further strengthen the material and technical foundations of socialism.

Article 25. The state accelerates the technical revolution to eliminate the distinctions between heavy and light labor and between agricultural and industrial labor, to free the working people from arduous labor, and to gradually narrow the difference between physical and mental labor.

Article 26. The state enhances the role of the country and strengthens its guidance and assistance to the countryside in order to eliminate the difference between town and country and class distinction between workers and peasants.

The state undertakes at its own expense the building of production facilities for the cooperative farms and modern houses in the countryside.

Article 27. The working masses are the makers of history. Socialism and communism are built by the creative labor of millions of working people.

All the working people of the country take part in labor, and work for the country and the people and for their own benefit by displaying conscious enthusiasm and creativity.

The state correctly applies the socialist principle of distribution according to the quantity and quality of work done, while constantly raising the political and ideological consciousness of the working people.

Article 28. The working day is eight hours. The state reduces the length of the working day for arduous trades and other special categories of work.

The state guarantees that working hours are fully utilized through the proper organization of labor and the strengthening of labor discipline.

Article 29. In the Democratic People's Republic of Korea, the minimum age for starting work is 16 years.

The state prohibits the employment of children under working age.

Article 30. The state directs and manages the nation's economy through the *Taean* work system, an advanced socialist form of economic management whereby the economy is operated and managed scientifically and rationally on the basis of the collective strength of the producer masses, and through the new system of agricultural guidance whereby agricultural management is done by industrial methods.

Article 31. The national economy of the Democratic People's Republic of Korea is a planned economy.

In accordance with the laws of economic development of socialism, the state draws up and carries out the plans for the development of the national economy so that the balance of accumulation and consumption can be maintained correctly, economic construction accelerated, the people's living standards steadily raised, and the nation's defense potential strengthened.

The state ensures a high rate of growth in production and a proportionate development of the national economy by implementing a policy of unified and detailed planning.

Article 32. The Democratic People's Republic of Korea compiles and implements the state budget according to the national economic development plan.

The state systematically increases its accumulation and expands and develops socialist property by intensifying the struggle for increased production and economy, and by exercising strict financial control in all fields.

Article 33. The state abolishes taxation, a holdover of the old society.

Article 34. In the Democratic People's Republic of Korea, foreign trade is conducted by the state or under its supervision.

The state develops foreign trade on the principles of complete equality and mutual benefit.

The state pursues a tariff policy in order to protect the independent national economy.

Chapter III. Culture

Article 35. In the Democratic People's Republic of Korea, all people study and a socialist national culture flourishes and develops fully.

Article 36. The Democratic People's Republic of Korea, by thoroughly carrying out the cultural revolution, trains all the working people to be builders of socialism and communism who are equipped with a profound knowledge of nature and society, and a high level of culture and technology.

Article 37. The Democratic People's Republic of Korea builds a true people's revolutionary culture which serves the socialist working people.

In building a socialist national culture, the state opposes the cultural infiltration of imperialism and the tendency to return to the past, and protects the heritage of national culture and takes over and develops it in keeping with socialist reality.

Article 38. The state eliminates the way of life left over from the old society and introduces the new socialist way of life in all fields.

Article 39. The state carries into effect the principles of socialist pedagogy and brings up the rising generation to be steadfast revolutionaries who fight for society and the people, to be men of a new communist mould who are knowledgeable, virtuous, and healthy.

Article 40. The state gives top priority to public education and the training of cadres for the nation, and blends general education with technological education, and education with productive labor.

Article 41. The state introduces universal compulsory ten-year senior middle school education for all young people under working age.

The state grants to all pupils and students education free of charge.

Article 42. The state trains competent technicians and experts by developing the general educational system, as well as different forms of part-time education for those at work.

Students of higher educational institutions and higher specialized schools are granted scholarships.

Article 43. The state gives all children a compulsory one-year preschool education.

The state brings up all children of preschool age in crèches and kindergartens at state and public expense.

Article 44. The state accelerates the nation's scientific and technological progress by thoroughly establishing *Chuch'e* in scientific research and strengthening creative cooperation between scientists and producers.

Article 45. The state develops a *Chuch'e*-oriented, revolutionary literature and art, national in form and socialist in content.

The state encourages the creative activities of writers and artists, and draws the broad masses of workers, farmers, and other working people into literary and artistic activities.

Article 46. The state safeguards our language from the policy of the imperialists and their stooges aimed at destroying it, and develops it to meet present-day needs.

Article 47. The state steadily improves the physical fitness of the working people.

The state fully prepares the entire people for work and national defense by popularizing physical culture and sports and developing physical training for national defense.

Article 48. The state consolidates and develops the system of universal free medical service and pursues a policy of preventive medical care so as to protect people's lives and promote the health of the working people.

Chapter IV. Fundamental Rights and Duties of Citizens

Article 49. In the Democratic People's Republic of Korea, the rights and duties of citizens are based on the collectivist principle of "One for all and all for one".

Article 50. The state effectively guarantees genuine democratic rights and liberties, as well as the material and cultural well-being of all citizens.

In the Democratic People's Republic of Korea, the rights and freedoms of citizens increase with the consolidation and development of the socialist system.

Article 51. Citizens all enjoy equal rights in the political, economic, and cultural and all other spheres of state and public activity.

Article 52. All citizens who have reached the age of 17 have the right to elect and to be elected, irrespective of sex, race, occupation, length of residence, property status, education, party affiliation, political views, and religion.

Citizens serving in the Armed Forces also have the right to elect and to be elected.

Those who are deprived by a court decision of the right to vote and insane persons are denied the right to elect and to be elected.

Article 53. Citizens have freedom of speech, the press, assembly, association, and of demonstration.

The state guarantees conditions for the free activities of democratic political parties and social organizations.

Article 54. Citizens have freedom of religious belief and freedom of anti-religious propaganda.

Article 55. Citizens are entitled to make complaints and submit petitions.

Article 56. Citizens have the right to work.

All able-bodied citizens can choose occupations according to their desire and skills, and are provided with stable jobs and working conditions.

Citizens work according to their ability and receive remuneration according to the quantity and quality of work done.

Article 57. Citizens have the right to rest. This right is ensured by the eight-hour working day, paid leave, accommodation at health resorts and holiday homes at state expense, and by an ever-expanding network of cultural facilities.

Article 58. Citizens are entitled to free medical care, and persons who have lost the ability to work because of old age, sickness, or deformity, old people, and children without supporters have the right to material assistance. This right is ensured by free medical care, a growing network of hospitals, sanatoria, and other medical institutions, and the state social insurance and security system.

Article 59. Citizens have the right to education. This right is ensured by an advanced educational system, free compulsory education, and other state educational measures for the people.

Article 60. Citizens have freedom of scientific, literary, and artistic pursuits.

The state grants benefits to innovators and inventors.

Copyright and patent rights are protected by law.

Article 61. Revolutionary fighters, the families of revolutionary and patriotic martyrs, the families of People's Armymen, and disabled soldiers enjoy the special protection of the state and society.

Article 62. Women are accorded equal social status and rights with men.

The state affords special protection to mothers and children through maternity leave, shortened working hours for mothers of large families, a wide network of maternity hospitals, creches, and kindergartens, and other measures.

The state frees women from the heavy burden of household chores and provides every condition for them to participate in public life.

Article 63. Marriage and the family are protected by the state.

The state pays great attention to consolidating the family, the cell of society.

Article 64. Citizens are guaranteed inviolability of the person and the home, and privacy of correspondence.

No citizen can be placed under arrest except by law.

Article 65. All Korean citizens in foreign lands are legally protected by the Democratic People's Republic of Korea.

Article 66. The Democratic People's Republic of Korea extends the right of asylum to foreign citizens persecuted for fighting for peace and democracy, national independence and socialism, or for the freedom of scientific and cultural pursuits.

Article 67. Citizens must strictly observe the laws of the state and the socialist norms of life and the socialist rules of conduct.

Article 68. Citizens must display a high degree of collectivist spirit.

Citizens must cherish their collective and organization, and develop the revolutionary trait of working devotedly for the good of society and the people and for the interests of the homeland and the revolution.

Article 69. It is the sacred duty and honor of citizens to work.

Citizens must voluntarily and honestly participate in work and strictly observe labor discipline and working hours.

Article 70. Citizens must take good care of state and communal property, combat all forms of misappropriation and wastage, and run the nation's economy assiduously with the attitude of masters.

The property of the state and social cooperative organizations is inviolable.

Article 71. Citizens must heighten their revolutionary vigilance against the maneuvres of the imperialists and all hostile elements opposed to our country's socialist system, and must strictly preserve state secrets.

Article 72. National defense is a supreme duty and honor for citizens.

Citizens must defend the country and serve in the army, as stipulated by law.

Treason against the country and the people is the most heinous of crimes.

Those who betray the country and the people are punished with all the severity of the law.

Chapter V. The Supreme People's Assembly

Article 73. The Supreme People's Assembly is the highest organ of state power in the Democratic People's Republic of Korea.

Legislative power is exercised exclusively by the Supreme People's Assembly.

Article 74. The Supreme People's Assembly is composed of deputies elected on the principle of universal, equal, and direct suffrage by secret ballot.

Article 75. The Supreme People's Assembly is elected for a term of four years.

A new Supreme People's Assembly is elected according to the decision of the Standing Committee of the Supreme People's Assembly prior to the expiry of its term of office. When unavoidable circumstances render the election impossible, the term of office is prolonged until the election.

Article 76. The Supreme People's Assembly has the authority to:
(1) adopt or amend the Constitution, laws, and ordinances;

(2) establish the basic principles of domestic and foreign policies of the state;

(3) elect the President of the Democratic People's Republic of Korea;

(4) elect or recall the Vice-Presidents of the Democratic People's Republic of Korea, and the Secretary and members of the Central People's Committee on the recommendation of the President of the Democratic People's Republic of Korea;

(5) elect or recall members of the Standing Committee of the Supreme People's Assembly;

(6) elect or recall the Premier of the Administration Council on the recommendation of the President of the Democratic People's Republic of Korea;

(7) elect or recall the Vice-Chairmen of the National Defense Commission on the recommendation of the President of the Democratic People's Republic of Korea;

(8) elect or recall the President of the Central Court, and appoint or remove the Procurator General of the Central Procurator's Office;

(9) approve the state plan for the development of the national economy;

(10) approve the state budget;

(11) decide on questions of war and peace.

Article 77. The Supreme People's Assembly holds regular and extraordinary sessions.

The regular session is convened once or twice a year by the Standing Committee of the Supreme People's Assembly.

The extraordinary session is convened when the Standing Committee of the Supreme People's Assembly deems it necessary, or at the request of a minimum of one-third of the total number of deputies.

Article 78. The Supreme People's Assembly needs more than half the total number of deputies to meet.

Article 79. The Supreme People's Assembly elects its Chairman and Vice-Chairmen.

The Chairman presides over the session.

Article 80. Items to be considered at the Supreme People's Assembly are submitted by the President of the Democratic People's Republic of Korea, the Central People's Committee, the Standing

Committee of the Supreme People's Assembly, and the Administration Council. Items can also be presented by deputies.

Article 81. The first session of the Supreme People's Assembly elects a Credentials Committee and on hearing the Committee's report, adopts a decision confirming the credentials of deputies.

Article 82. The laws, ordinances, and decisions of the Supreme People's Assembly are adopted when more than half of the deputies present give approval by a show of hands.

The Constitution is adopted or amended with the approval of more than two-thirds of the total number of deputies to the Supreme People's Assembly.

Article 83. The Supreme People's Assembly can appoint a Budget Committee, a Bills Committee, and other necessary Committees.

The Committees of the Supreme People's Assembly assist in the work of the Supreme People's Assembly.

Article 84. Deputies to the Supreme People's Assembly are guaranteed inviolability as such.

No deputy to the Supreme People's Assembly can be arrested without the consent of the Supreme People's Assembly or, when it is not in session, without the consent of its Standing Committee.

Article 85. The Standing Committee of the Supreme People's Assembly is a permanent body of the Supreme People's Assembly.

Article 86. The Standing Committee of the Supreme People's Assembly consists of the Chairman, Vice-Chairmen, Secretary, and members.

The Chairman and Vice-Chairmen of the Supreme People's Assembly are concurrently the Chairman and Vice-Chairmen of its Standing Committee.

Article 87. The Standing Committee of the Supreme People's Assembly has the duties and authority to:

(1) examine and decide on bills in the intervals between sessions of the Supreme People's Assembly and obtain the approval of the next session of the Supreme People's Assembly;

(2) amend current laws and ordinances when the Supreme People's Assembly is not in session and obtain the approval of the next session of the Supreme People's Assembly;

(3) interpret current laws and ordinances;

(4) convene the session of the Supreme People's Assembly;

(5) conduct the election of deputies to the Supreme People's Assembly;

(6) work with the deputies to the Supreme People's Assembly;

(7) work with the Committees of the Supreme People's Assembly in the intervals between sessions of the Supreme People's Assembly;

(8) organize the elections of deputies to the local People's Assemblies;

(9) elect or recall the judges and people's assessors of the Central Court.

Article 88. The Standing Committee of the Supreme People's Assembly adopts decisions.

Chapter VI. The President of the Democratic People's Republic of Korea

Article 89. The President of the Democratic People's Republic of Korea is the Head of State and represents state power in the Democratic People's Republic of Korea.

Article 90. The President of the Democratic People's Republic of Korea is elected by the Supreme People's Assembly.

The term of office of the President of the Democratic People's Republic of Korea is four years.

Article 91. The President of the Democratic People's Republic of Korea directly guides the Central People's Committee.

Article 92. The President of the Democratic People's Republic of Korea, when necessary, convenes and presides over meetings of the Administration Council.

Article 93. The President of the Democratic People's Republic of Korea is the supreme commander of all the Armed Forces of the Democratic People's Republic of Korea and the Chairman of the National Defense Commission, and commands all the Armed Forces of the state.

Article 94. The President of the Democratic People's Republic of Korea promulgates the laws and ordinances of the Supreme People's

Assembly, the decrees of the Central People's Committee, and the decisions of the Standing Committee of the Supreme People's Assembly.

The President of the Democratic People's Republic of Korea issues edicts.

Article 95. The President of the Democratic People's Republic of Korea exercises the right of granting special pardon.

Article 96. The President of the Democratic People's Republic of Korea ratifies or abrogates treaties concluded with other countries.

Article 97. The President of the Democratic People's Republic of Korea receives the letters of credence and recall of diplomatic representatives accredited by foreign states.

Article 98. The President of the Democratic People's Republic of Korea is accountable to the Supreme People's Assembly for his activities.

Article 99. The Vice-Presidents of the Democratic People's Republic of Korea assist the President in his work.

Chapter VII. The Central People's Committee

Article 100. The Central People's Committee is the highest leadership organ of state power in the Democratic People's Republic of Korea.

Article 101. The Central People's Committee is headed by the President of the Democratic People's Republic of Korea.

Article 102. The Central People's Committee consists of the President and Vice-Presidents of the Democratic People's Republic of Korea and the Secretary and members of the Central People's Committee.

The term of office of the Central People's Committee is four years.

Article 103. The Central People's Committee has the duties and authority to:

(1) draw up the domestic and foreign policies of the state;

(2) direct the work of the Administration Council and the local People's Assemblies and People's Committees;

(3) direct the work of judicial and procuratorial organs;

(4) guide the work of national defense and state political security;

(5) ensure the observance of the Constitution, the laws and ordinances of the Supreme People's Assembly, the edicts of the President of the Democratic People's Republic of Korea, and the decrees, decisions, and directives of the Central People's Committee, and annul the decisions and directives of state organs which contravene them;

(6) establish or abolish ministries, respective executive bodies of the Administration Council;

(7) appoint or remove Vice-Premiers, Ministers, and other members of the Administration Council on the recommendation of the Premier of the Administration Council;

(8) appoint or recall ambassadors and ministers;

(9) appoint or remove high-ranking officers and confer military titles of generals;

(10) institute decorations, titles of honor, military titles, and diplomatic ranks, and confer decorations and titles of honor;

(11) grant general amnesties;

(12) institute or change administrative districts;

(13) proclaim a state of war and issue orders for mobilization in case of emergency.

Article 104. The Central People's Committee adopts decrees and decisions and issues directives.

Article 105. The Central People's Committee establishes a Domestic Policy Commission, a Foreign Policy Commission, a National Defense Commission, a Justice and Security Commission, and other respective Commissions to assist it in its work.

The members of the Commissions of the Central People's Committee are appointed or removed by the Central People's Committee.

Article 106. The Central People's Committee is accountable to the Supreme People's Assembly for its activities.

Chapter VIII. The Administration Council

Article 107. The Administration Council is the administrative and executive body of the highest organ of state power.

The Administration Council works under the guidance of the President of the Democratic People's Republic of Korea and the Central People's Committee.

Article 108. The Administration Council consists of the Premier, Vice-Premiers, Ministers, and other necessary members.

Article 109. The Administration Council has the duties and authority to:

(1) direct the work of ministries, organs directly under its authority, and local administrative committees;

(2) establish or abolish organs directly under its authority;

(3) draft the state plan for the development of the national economy and adopt measures to put it into effect;

(4) compile the state budget and adopt measures to implement it;

(5) organize and execute the work of industry, agriculture, domestic and foreign trade, construction, transport, communications, land administration, municipal administration, science, education, culture, health services, etc.;

(6) adopt measures to strengthen the monetary and banking system;

(7) conclude treaties with foreign countries and conduct external affairs;

(8) build up the people's Armed Forces;

(9) adopt measures to maintain public order, to protect the interests of the state, and to safeguard the rights of citizens;

(10) annul the decisions and directives of the state administrative organs which run counter to the decisions and directives of the Administration Council.

Article 110. The Administration Council convenes the Plenary Meeting and the Permanent Commission.

The Plenary Meeting consists of all members of the Administration Council. The Permanent Commission consists of the Premier, Vice-Premiers, and other members of the Administration Council appointed by the Premier.

Article 111. The Plenary Meeting of the Administration Council discusses and decides on new, important problems arising in state administration.

The Permanent Commission of the Administration Council discusses and decides on matters entrusted to it by the Plenary Meeting of the Administration Council.

Article 112. The Administration Council adopts decisions and issues directives.

Article 113. The Administration Council is accountable for its activities to the Supreme People's Assembly, the President of the Democratic People's Republic of Korea, and the Central People's Committee.

Article 114. A ministry is a departmental executive body of the Administration Council.
 A ministry issues directives.

Chapter IX. The Local People's Assembly, People's Committee, and Administrative Committee

Article 115. The People's Assembly of the province (or municipality directly under central authority), city (or district), and county is the local organ of state power.

Article 116. The local People's Assembly consists of deputies elected on the principle of universal, equal, and direct suffrage by secret ballot.

Article 117. The term of office of the People's Assembly of the province (or municipality directly under central authority) is four years, and that of the People's Assembly of the city (or district) and county is two years.

Article 118. The local People's Assembly has the duties and authority to:
 (1) approve the local plan for the development of the national economy;
 (2) approve the local budget;
 (3) elect or recall the Chairman, Vice-Chairmen, Secretary, and members of the People's Committee at the corresponding level;
 (4) elect or recall the Chairman of the Administrative Committee at the corresponding level;
 (5) elect or recall the judges and people's assessors of the court at the corresponding level;
 (6) annul inappropriate decisions and directives of the People's Committee at the corresponding level and the People's Assemblies and People's Committees at the lower levels.

Article 119. The local People's Assembly convenes regular and extraordinary sessions.

The regular session is convened once or twice a year by the People's Committee at the corresponding level.

The extraordinary session is convened when the People's Committee at the corresponding level deems it necessary, or at the request of a minimum of one-third of the total number of deputies.

Article 120. The local People's Assembly needs more than half the total number of deputies to meet.

Article 121. The local People's Assembly elects its Chairman.

The Chairman presides over the session.

Article 122. The local People's Assembly adopts decisions.

The decision of the local People's Assembly is announced by the Chairman of the People's Committee at the corresponding level.

Article 123. The People's Committee of the province (or municipality directly under central authority), city (or district), and county exercises the function of the local organ of state power when the People's Assembly at the corresponding level is not in session.

Article 124. The local People's Committee consists of the Chairman, Vice-Chairmen, Secretary, and members.

The term of office of the local People's Committee is the same as that of the corresponding People's Assembly.

Article 125. The local People's Committee has the duties and authority to:

(1) convene the session of the People's Assembly;

(2) organize work for the election of deputies to the People's Assembly;

(3) work with the deputies to the People's Assembly;

(4) adopt measures to implement the decisions of the corresponding People's Assembly and the People's Committees at higher levels;

(5) direct the work of the Administrative Committee at the corresponding level;

(6) direct the work of the People's Committees at lower levels;

(7) direct the work of the state institutions, enterprises, and social cooperative organizations within the given area;

(8) annul inappropriate decisions and directives of the Administrative Committee at the corresponding level and the People's

Committees and Administrative Committees at lower levels, and suspend the implementation of inappropriate decisions of the People's Assemblies at lower levels;

(9) appoint or remove the Vice-Chairmen, Secretary, and members of the Administrative Committee at the corresponding level.

Article 126. The local People's Committee adopts decisions and issues directives.

Article 127. The local People's Committee is accountable for its activities to the corresponding People's Assembly and to the People's Committees at higher levels.

Article 128. The Administrative Committee of the province (or municipality directly under central authority), city (or district), and county is the administrative and executive body of the local organ of state power.

Article 129. The local Administrative Committee consists of the Chairman, Vice-Chairmen, Secretary, and members.

Article 130. The local Administrative Committee has the duties and authority to:

(1) organize and carry out all administrative affairs in the given area;

(2) carry out the decisions and directives of the People's Assembly and People's Committee at the corresponding level, and of the organs at higher levels;

(3) draft the local plan for the development of the national economy, and adopt measures to implement it;

(4) compile the local budget, and adopt measures for its implementation;

(5) adopt measures to maintain public order, to protect the interests of the state, and to safeguard the rights of citizens in the given area;

(6) guide the work of the Administrative Committees at lower levels;

(7) annul inappropriate decisions and directives of the Administrative Committees at lower levels.

Article 131. The local Administrative Committee adopts decisions and issues directives.

Article 132. The local Administrative Committee is accountable for its activities to the People's Assembly and People's Committee at the corresponding level.

The local Administrative Committee is subordinate to the higher Administrative Committees and to the Administration Council.

Chapter X. The Courts and the Procurator's Office

Article 133. Justice is administered by the Central Court, the Court of the province (or municipality directly under central authority), the People's Courts, and the Special Court.

Judgment is rendered in the name of the Democratic People's Republic of Korea.

Article 134. The judges and people's assessors of the Central Court are elected by the Standing Committee of the Supreme People's Assembly.

The judges and people's assessors of the Court of the province (or municipality directly under central authority) and the People's Court are elected by the People's Assembly at the corresponding level.

The term of office of judges and people's assessors is the same as that of the People's Assembly at the corresponding level.

Article 135. The Chairman and judges of the Special Court are appointed or removed by the Central Court.

The people's assessors of the Special Court are elected by servicemen and employees at their respective meetings.

Article 136. The functions of the Court are to:

(1) protect through judicial activities the power of the workers and peasants and the socialist system established in the Democratic People's Republic of Korea, the property of the state and social cooperative organizations, personal rights as guaranteed by the Constitution, and the lives and property of citizens against all infringements;

(2) ensure that all state institutions, enterprises, social cooperative organizations, and citizens strictly observe state laws and actively struggle against class enemies and all law-breakers;

(3) give judgments and findings with regard to property and conduct notarial work.

Article 137. Justice is administered by the court consisting of one judge and two people's assessors. In special cases, there may be three judges.

Article 138. Court cases are heard in public and the accused is guaranteed the right of defense.
Hearings may be closed to the public as stipulated by law.

Article 139. Judicial proceedings are conducted in the Korean language.
Foreign citizens may use their own language during court proceedings.

Article 140. In administering justice, the court is independent, and judicial proceedings are carried out in strict accordance with the law.

Article 141. The Central Court is the highest judicial organ of the Democratic People's Republic of Korea.
The Central Court supervises the judicial activities of all the courts.

Article 142. The Central Court is accountable for its activities to the Supreme People's Assembly, the President of the Democratic People's Republic of Korea, and the Central People's Committee.
The Court of the province (or municipality directly under central authority) and the People's Court are accountable for their activities to their respective People's Assembly.

Article 143. Investigation and prosecution are conducted by the Central Procurator's Office, the Procurator's Offices of the province (or municipality directly under central authority), city (or district) and county and Special Procurator's Office.

Article 144. The functions of the Procurator's Office are to:
(1) ensure the strict observance of state laws by state institutions, enterprises, social cooperative organizations, and by citizens;
(2) ensure that decisions and directives of state organs conform with the Constitution, the laws and ordinances of the Supreme People's Assembly, the edicts of the President of the Democratic People's Republic of Korea, the decrees, decisions, and directives of the Central People's Committee, the decisions of the Standing Committee of the Supreme People's Assembly, and with the decisions and directives of the Administration Council;
(3) expose and institute legal proceedings against criminals and

offenders so as to safeguard the power of the workers and peasants and the socialist system from all forms of encroachment, and protect the property of the state and social cooperative organizations and personal rights as guaranteed by the Constitution, and the lives and property of citizens.

Article 145. Investigation and prosecution are conducted under the coordinated leadership of the Central Procurator's Office, and all Procurator's Offices are subordinate to their higher offices and to the Central Procurator's Office.

Procurators are appointed or removed by the Central Procurator's Office.

Article 146. The Central Procurator's Office is accountable for its activities to the Supreme People's Assembly, the President of the Democratic People's Republic of Korea, and the Central People's Committee.

Chapter XI. The Emblem, Flag, and Capital

Article 147. The national emblem of the Democratic People's Republic of Korea is adorned with the design of a grand hydroelectric power plant under the beaming light of a five-pointed red star, ovally framed with ears of rice bound with a red band bearing the inscription "The Democratic People's Republic of Korea".

Article 148. The national flag of the Democratic People's Republic of Korea has a red panel across the middle, bordered above and below in sequence by a thin white stripe and a broad blue stripe. On the red panel near the staff is depicted a five-pointed red star within a white circle.

The ratio of width to length is 1:2.

Article 149. The capital of the Democratic People's Republic of Korea is Pyongyang.

MONGOLIA

INTRODUCTION*

W.E. Butler

In 1911 Mongolia proclaimed its independence from China and in the course of the next decade achieved a measure of international recognition, notwithstanding a brief period of relapse into the state structure of the Republic of China. A people's revolution in 1921 established a kind of constitutional monarchy under which the Bogdo-khan retained principal authority over religious affairs and a nominal veto power over secular matters, principal responsibility for the latter passing to the Mongolian People's Party, whose first Party Congress was held in early March 1921. The Bogdo-khan died in May 1924, and within less than a month Mongolia proclaimed itself to be a "people's republic". In August 1924, the Mongolian People's Party renamed itself the Mongolian People's Revolutionary Party at the Third Party Congress, an appellation it has retained to the present.

1924 Constitution. The first proper Constitution in Mongolian history was adopted by the Great Khural on 26 November 1924.[1] Observers at the time were impressed by the close affinities between the Mongolian Constitution and that of the RSFSR and to some extent of the USSR. Vaksberg noted that the "external similarity" between the Mongolian and RSFSR provisions on the rights of the working people was "complete" and found the following articles of the Mongolian Constitution wholly received or adapted from the RSFSR:[2]

	Mongolian Constitution	*RSFSR Constitution*
Articles	3	3, 13, 14, 16, 17, 22, 23
	9, 10	27, 28
	27	37, 34
	35	64, 65
	37, 43, 41	80, 81, 83
	5	49

*I am grateful to The British Academy and to the Mongolian State University for making it possible to visit Mongolia in September 1979 to gather materials on the Mongolian legal system.

Engel'feld spoke of the 1924 Constitution as "... one of the most valuable historical documents of our epoch..." but nevertheless concluded—with some exaggeration—that it represented "... a copy of the Soviet and earlier RSFSR [constitutions] and reflects only very slightly the ways and mores of Outer Mongolia itself...".[3] To Mongolian eyes, the 1924 Constitution summed up the achievements of the Mongolian Revolution and gave them concrete organizational expression. In state structure it was perhaps closest to the constitutions of Bukhara and Khorezm, which later became autonomous entities within the RSFSR. The Constitution represented legislative consolidation of state power, abandonment of a monarchical theocracy, a basic statement of socio-economic and political rights and freedoms, and a commitment to other fundamental social transformations in the direction of socialism.[4]

1940 Constitution. In his report to the VIII Great People's Khural in 1940, the Mongolian Prime Minister Choibalsan declared: "We are guided in our activity by the experience of the great country of socialism, the experience of the Soviet Union. Consequently, only the Constitution of the Soviet Union may be a model for us in drafting our new Constitution".[5] In its original redaction of 30 June 1940 the MPR Constitution did indeed follow the model of the 1936 USSR Constitution, although the original version was significantly amended to bring it even closer in 1944, 1949, 1952, 1957, and 1959.[6] Political rights, including the right of suffrage, were restored to former lamas and feudal elements by constitutional amendments introduced in 1949; direct elections of agencies of state power (instead of lower bodies electing higher ones) were instituted, electoral districts were reorganized, secret balloting (instead of voting by hands at open meetings) was introduced, terminological distinctions were drawn among enactments of the Great People's Khural, its Presidium, and other governmental acts, and the "Little Khural" was abolished, its functions being transferred to the Great People's Khural.[7] The amendments of 1952, 1957, and 1959 dealt principally with electoral matters and reorganization of local government.

The 1940 Constitution formally committed Mongolia to a "non-capitalist path of development," a course of societal development unique among socialist legal systems. A commitment to state planning was expressed in Article 4, the private ownership of cattle, agricultural implements, raw materials, manufactured products, household articles, dwellings, and the like was guaranteed, and the state undertook to assist the development of the arats and their voluntary and cooperative associations. Mongolia was a society in transition from "Feudalism" to socialism, by-passing capitalism.[8]

1960 Constitution. The changes introduced by the 1960 Constitution have been extensively analyzed.[9] The external format was substantially reworked in comparison with the 1940 Constitution; an extensive preamble placed socio-economic and political developments in Mongolia squarely within the context of developments in the Soviet Union, recounted past achievements and a renewed commitment to completing the construction of socialism, enunciated a declaration of basic foreign policy aims, and proclaimed the Mongolian People's Revolutionary Party to be the guiding and directing force of society. Democratic centralism as a principle of state administration was awarded constitutional recognition. The socialist system of economy and socialist ownership (now divided into state and cooperative ownership) were declared to be the economic basis of society; private ownership of the instruments and means of production was abolished and personal ownership of citizens in their labor incomes and savings, housing, subsidiary husbandry, personal articles, and inheritance was protected. The essential structure of the state in the 1960 Constitution follows that of the 1940 Constitution as amended to 1959. The fundamental rights of citizens are treated in a separate chapter and considerably expanded and reworked. Of particular interest is the concluding article, unique among socialist constitutions, providing for the repeal of constitutional provisions as the various functions of the state die away under communism.

Amendments to the 1960 Constitution. The 1960 MPR Constitution has been amended several times, and it is a sad reflection on Mongolian legal scholarship that complete and precise data on the dates and decree numbers of the amending enactments is not readily available. Indeed, Mongolian jurists in October 1979 did not themselves have available a text of the Constitution in Mongolian which incorporated the 1978 amendments.

The English text of the 1960 MPR Constitution as amended to 1 October 1979, reproduced below, I have translated from a Russian text published at Ulan Bator ca. 1960–1961. I have compared my version with a later English version undated (ca. 1971) issued at Ulan Bator and incorporated all amendments reflected therein. These have been double-checked against the Mongolian text of the MPR Constitution as amended to 20 April 1973. Amendments introduced after 1973 have been supplied to me orally by Mr. E. Avermid, of the law department in the Faculty of Social Sciences, Mongolian State University, who is a specialist in the Mongolian theory of state and law.

The amendments consist principally of the following:

(1) an expansion of the right of legislative initiative to include the Central Council of Mongolian Trade Unions and the Revolutionary Youth League (Article 19, para. two);

(2) an increase in the term of powers or office for certain bodies or officials: the Great People's Khural from three to four years (Article 22); the MPR Supreme Court from three to four years (Article 66); city and people's courts from two to three years (Articles 67, 68); the Procurator of the MPR from three to four years (Article 73).

(3) the introduction of deputy chairmen in place of the deputy chairman in the Presidium of the Great People's Khural and the abolition of a specific number of Presidium members (Article 29);

(4) the introduction of district (*raion*) as an administrative-territorial subdivision of cities and population centers (Articles 46, 47, 49, 50, 52, 55, and 68).

TEXTS OF MONGOLIAN CONSTITUTIONS

1924 Constitution. The 1924 Constitution was promulgated in the old Mongolian script. The first Russian text appeared in the local Russian newspaper *Izvestiia Ulan-Bator-Khoto* 1924 Nos. 138 ff. Durdenevskii and Lundshuveit reproduced this text in *Konstitutsii vostoka*, (V.N. Durdenevskii, ed.), Leningrad 1926, which in turn was translated into German in I.J. Korostovetz and E. Hauer, *Von Cinggis Khan zur Sowjetrepublik*, Berlin 1926; and the German version was translated into English and published in *Constitutions of the Communist Party States*, (J.F. Triska, ed.), Stanford 1968. There are two superior Russian versions, one by M.A. Vaksberg, *Konstitutsiia revoliutsionnoi Mongolii*, Irkutsk 1925, and another by Gurside and Gombo Badmazhapov in *Mongol'skoe zakonodatel'stvo*, (P. Vsesviatskii, intro.), Ulan Bator 1928. A Russian text also appears in *Revoliutsionnye meropriiatiia narodnogo pravitel'stva Mongolii v 1921–1924 gg.; dokumenty*, (Ts. Puntsagnorov, ed.), Moskva 1960. Another English version was published for some years in *The China Year Book* for 1928 and thereafter.

The 1940 Constitution is available in Russian in *Sovetskoe gosudarstvo i pravo* 1947 No. 8, 36–49; English versions appear in 3 *Soviet Press Translations* 1948 No. 1, 3–14; 23 *Washington Law Review* 1948, 181–204; and J.F. Triska, *op. cit.* As amended to 1949, Russian texts are published in *Konstitutsiia (osnovnoi zakon) Mongol'skoi Narodnoi Respubliki*, Moskva 1950, *ibid.* Moskva 1952. As amended to 1952, for Russian texts see *Konstitutsiia i osnovnye zakonodatel'nye akty Mon-*

gol'skoi Narodnoi Respubliki, (S.S. Demidov, ed.), Moskva 1952; *Mongol'skaia narodnaia respublika; sbornik statei*, (I. Ia. Zlatkin, ed.), Moskva 1952; in German, *Die Verfassung der asiatischen Länder der Volksdemokratie*, (H. Engelhart, intro.), Berlin 1955; in English, A.J. Peaslee, *Constitutions of Nations*, 2d ed., Vol. II, The Hague 1956, 720–736. For the 1957 redaction in Russian, see *Konstitutsii stran narodnoi demokratii*, (V.N. Durdenevskii, ed.), Moskva 1958.

For the 1960 Constitution in Russian, see *Osteuropa Recht* 1960 No. 4, 251–263; *40 let Narodnoi Mongolii*, Moskva 1961; *Konstitutsiia Mongol'skoi narodnoi respubliki*, Ulan Bator 1961; in English: *Constitutions of the Countries of the World*, (A.P. Blaustein and G.H. Flanz, eds.), New York 1971-; Secretariat of the Asian-African Legal Consultative Committee, *Constitutions of Asian Countries*, New Delhi 1968. French and English texts undated, but ca. 1961 and 1971, also have been issued in Ulan Bator, and see Triska, *op. cit.*

NOTES

1. It has been suggested that in a sense the Solemn Treaty [*Kliatvennyi dogovor*] of 1921 between the Bodgo-khan and the People's Government, which distributed power between them respectively, was the first Constitution. See P. Vsesviatskii, in *Mongol'skoe zakonodatel'stvo*, Ulan Bator 1928.

2. M.A. Vaksberg, *Konstitutsiia revoliutsionnoi Mongolii*, Irkutsk 1925, 21.

3. V.V. Engel'feld, *Kitaiskii parlament i parlamentarism. Politicheskaia organizatsiia sovremennoi Mongolii*, Kharbin 1926, 169.

4. B. Shirendyb, *Istoriia mongol'skoi narodnoi revoliutsii 1921 goda*, Moskva 1971.

5. Quoted from *Sovremennaia Mongoliia* 1940 No. 3, 4; also see J.N. Hazard, "The Constitution of the Mongol People's Republic and Soviet Influence", 21 *Pacific Affairs* 1948, 162–170.

6. Electoral rights were conferred upon persons previously deprived of those rights under Article 71 of the 1940 Constitution by a decree of the Presidium of the Little Khural adopted 28 September 1944, which decree was to be submitted for confirmation to the next regular session of the Little Khural and thence to the Great People's Khural. It is unclear whether this was done; Triska, who does not produce the 1940 Constitution as amended, includes the text of the 1944 decree as a separate item. The 1949 amendments, which entailed extensive renumbering of the articles of the Constitution, incorporated in any event the substance of the 1944 decree.

7. See Tsedenbal's speech on constitutional reform, reproduced in Iu. Tsedenbal, *Istoricheskii put' razvitiia sotsialisticheskoi monopolii*, Ulan Bator 1976, 62–92.

8. Shirendyb, *By-Passing Capitalism*, Ulan Bator 1968.

9. G. Ginsburgs, "Mongolia's 'Socialist' Constitution", 34 *Pacific Affairs* 1961, 141–156.

CONSTITUTION OF THE MONGOLIAN PEOPLE'S REPUBLIC OF 6 JULY 1960 (AS AMENDED)

Preamble	262
The Essence and General Principles of State Organization	263
Basic Economic Principles and Functions of the State	264
Highest Agencies of State Power	266
Highest and Central Agencies of State Administration	270
The Local Agencies of State Power and State Administration	272
Court and Procuracy	275
Basic Rights and Freedoms of Citizens and Guarantees of Ensuring Them	276
Basic Duties of Citizens	279
Arms, Flag, Capital	280
On Changing and Repealing the MPR Constitution	281

CONSTITUTION OF THE MONGOLIAN PEOPLE'S REPUBLIC*

Adopted on 6 July 1960 by the Fourth Convocation of the Great People's Khural of the Mongolian People's Republic at its first session (as amended to 1 October 1979).

PREAMBLE

The Great October Socialist Revolution, which laid the basis for the transition of mankind from capitalism to communism, was a turning point in the history of the age-old liberation struggle of the Mongolian people which opened for them the opportunity to create their own sovereign, independent people's democratic state.

The Mongolian People's Republic arose and was confirmed as a result of the victory of the 1921 people's revolution, the liquidation by the Mongolian people of the domination of imperialist colonizers, the overthrow of the power of feudal lords, and the abolition of serfdom.

The Mongolian People's Republic grew and gained strength with the fraternal socialist assistance of the Soviet Union, as a result of consolidating its political and economic independence in the stubborn struggle against imperialist aggression and internal reaction, as a result of overcoming grave consequences of the previously existing system of national and social oppression of the people, as well as the liquidation of the class of feudal lords and the creation of a socialist national economy and culture.

In the course of the transition made by the Mongolian People's Republic from feudalism to socialism, bypassing the capitalist stage of development in accordance with the teachings of V.I. Lenin, fundamental revolutionary socio-economic transformations were effectuated, a new socialist economy was created, the victory of socialist production relations throughout the entire national economy of the country was maintained, and enormous historical successes in raising the material and cultural level of the people were attained.

The Mongolian People's Republic sets before it the goal of com-

*Translation Copyright © 1979 by W.E. Butler.

pleting socialist construction and of thereafter building a communist society.

The Mongolian People's Republic conducts a peace-loving foreign policy directed toward ensuring a durable peace, friendship and cooperation with all peoples on the basis of the principles of peaceful coexistence, strengthening in every possible way the fraternal relations of indestructible friendship, close cooperation and mutual assistance established and developing among peoples of the countries of the world system of socialism on the basis of the unshakeable principle of proletarian internationalism.

The highest duty of the MPR, the most important condition of its all-round prosperity and the further strengthening of its independence, is a constant concern for every possible strengthening of the unity and solidarity of the peoples of the socialist countries on the basis of the principles of Marxism-Leninism.

The guiding and directing force of society and the state in the MPR is the Mongolian People's Revolutionary Party, which is guided in its activity by the all-triumphant Marxist-Leninist theory.

I. SOCIO-ECONOMIC STRUCTURE OF THE MONGOLIAN PEOPLE'S REPUBLIC

Chapter I. The Essence and General Principles of State Organization

Article 1. The MPR is a socialist state of workers, *arats* (herdsmen and cultivators) organized in cooperatives, and the laboring intelligentsia, based on an alliance of the working class with the *arats* organized in cooperatives.

Article 2. The Mongolian People's Republic is a socialist state which exists and is developing in the form of a people's democracy.

Article 3. All power in the Mongolian People's Republic shall belong to the working people. The working people shall exercise state power through state representative agencies—the khurals of people's deputies.

Article 4. Khurals of people's deputies shall be elected by citizens of the MPR on the basis of universal, equal, and direct suffrage by secret ballot.

The procedure for holding elections for agencies of state power shall be established by a special statute.

Article 5. Democratic centralism shall be the basic principle for the organization and the activity of all state agencies.

All state agencies shall be obliged to rely upon the working masses and constantly strengthen their links with them.

Article 6. All khurals of people's deputies shall be accountable and responsible to the electors.

Each deputy shall be obliged to report to the electors on his work and the work of khurals of people's deputies and may be recalled at any time by the electors in the procedure established by law.

Article 7. All state agencies shall be obliged to observe precisely the Constitution and laws of the MPR.

Chapter II. Basic Economic Principles and Functions of the State

Article 8. The economic basis of the MPR shall comprise the socialist system of economy and socialist ownership of the means of production created as a result of the prolonged and arduous struggle of the working people of the MPR and confirmed as a result of the abolition of private ownership of the means of production and the elimination of the exploitation of man by man.

Article 9. Socialist ownership in the MPR shall have two forms: state ownership (the wealth of the whole people) and cooperative ownership (ownership of agricultural associations and other types of cooperatives).

Article 10. The land and its minerals, forest, water and its wealth, state factories, plants, mines, electric power stations, railway, motor vehicle, water, and air transport, highways, means of communication, banks, state agricultural enterprises and the basic housing fund in cities and other population centers, raw materials, materials and products of state enterprises, state trade and procurement enterprises, scientific and cultural institutions, and also the property of all state organizations and institutions shall be state ownership, that is, the wealth of the whole people.

Article 11. Social enterprises in agricultural associations and other cooperative organizations with all their equipment and inventory, the products they produce, social structures, tractors, combines and other agricultural machines and implements, means of transport, social livestock and other social property shall comprise the social socialist ownership of these associations and cooperative organizations.

Every household of an agricultural association shall receive its basic income from the personal participation of each household member in the social production of the association and have a personal subsidiary husbandry, the size of which shall be established by the charter of the agricultural association.

Article 12. Land occupied by an agricultural association shall be allocated to it for permanent use free of charge.

Article 13. The right of personal ownership of citizens in their labor incomes and savings, housing and subsidiary husbandry, articles of personal consumption and household implements, and equally the right to inherit personal ownership of citizens, shall be protected by law. It shall be prohibited to use the right of personal ownership to the detriment of state and social interests.

Article 14. The socialist state shall protect and strengthen social socialist ownership, ensure the active participation of members of society in economic and cultural construction, strengthen socialist labor discipline in every possible way, and organize the defense of the country against imperialist aggression.

Article 15. The economic life of the Mongolian People's Republic shall be determined and directed by a single state national economic plan in the interests of the constant growth and development of productive forces of the country, the interests of the uninterrupted ensuring of expanded socialist reproduction and steady use of material well-being and cultural level of the working people.

The economic policy of the state shall be so directed that the requirements of the economic laws of socialism are properly reflected in the national economic plan.

The national economic plan of the MPR confirmed by the Great People's Khural shall acquire the force of a law.

The direction of the national economy on the part of the state should invariably be accompanied by the extensive introduction of the strictest records and control over production and distribution and over the measure of labor and the measure of consumption.

Article 16. The finance and credit policy of the MPR shall be directed toward the constant growth of the economic might of the country, the development and strengthening of socialist ownership, the development of socialist culture, and an increase in the well-being of the working people.

In accordance with the plan for the development of the national economy, the state annually shall draw up its financial plan in the form of a state budget confirmed and published in the form of a law.

Incomes and accumulations of the socialist economy shall be the principal source of revenues of the MPR state budget.

Article 17. The purpose of socialist production in the MPR, its moving force, shall be the creation in ever growing amounts of the social product for the accumulation of national income necessary for the maximal satisfaction of the constantly growing personal and collective requirements of members of a socialist society.

The entire national income in the MPR, after deducting the social fund going for the expansion of socialist production, the creation of reserves, the development of education and public health, the maintenance of the aged and disabled, as well as the satisfaction of other collective requirements of members of society, shall be distributed among them in accordance with the quality and quantity of labor expended on the basis of the principle of socialism: "From each according to his ability, to each according to his labor".

Labor in the MPR shall be a necessary condition and basis for the realization of expanded socialist reproduction and a source for the creation of material and spiritual benefits for the constant increase in the well-being of the working people.

II. STATE STRUCTURE OF THE MONGOLIAN PEOPLE'S REPUBLIC

Chapter III. Highest Agencies of State Power

A. The MPR Great People's Khural

Article 18. The Great People's Khural shall be the highest agency of state power of the Mongolian People's Republic.

Article 19. Legislative power of the MPR shall be effectuated exclusively by the Great People's Khural. The Presidium of the MPR

Great People's Khural, the MPR Council of Ministers, the deputies of the MPR Great People's Khural, permanent commissions of the MPR Great People's Khural, the MPR Supreme Court, and the Procuracy of the MPR shall have the right of legislative initiative.

The right of legislative initiative shall appertain to the Mongolian trade unions through its Central Council and to the Mongolian Revsomol through its Committee.

Article 20. The MPR Great People's Khural shall exercise full power in the state. In particular, there shall be subject to the jurisdiction of the Great People's Khural:

a) confirmation and change of the MPR Constitution;

b) adoption of laws;

c) establishment of basic principles and measures in the domain of internal and foreign policy;

d) election of the Presidium of the Great People's Khural;

e) formation of the Council of Ministers;

f) confirmation of newly-organized, abolished, or reorganized ministries and other central agencies of state administration comprising the MPR Council of Ministers;

g) consideration and confirmation of the national economic plan of the republic;

h) consideration and confirmation of the state budget and the report on its execution;

i) confirmation of edicts adopted by the Presidium of the Great People's Khural in the interval between Sessions of the Great People's Khural and subject to confirmation by the Great People's Khural;

j) promulgation of acts on amnesty;

k) deciding questions of peace and defense of the socialist motherland.

Article 21. The Great People's Khural shall be elected by citizens of the Mongolian People's Republic by electoral districts according to the norm of one deputy per four thousand persons of the populace.

Article 22. The Great People's Khural shall be elected for a term of four years.

Article 23. Elections of a new MPR Great People's Khural shall be designated by the Presidium of the Great People's Khural two months before the expiry of the powers of the Great People's Khural.

Article 24. The newly-elected Great People's Khural shall be convoked by the Presidium of the outgoing Great People's Khural not later than two months from the election date.

Article 25. Regular Sessions of the Great People's Khural shall be convoked once a year.

Extraordinary Sessions of the Great People's Khural may be convoked either at the initiative of the Presidium of the Great People's Khural or at the request of not less than one-third of the deputies.

Article 26. The Great People's Khural shall elect the chairman of the Great People's Khural and four of his deputies. The chairman shall direct sessions of the Great People's Khural and conduct its internal proceedings.

Article 27. The Great People's Khural shall elect a credentials commission which shall verify the powers of deputies of the MPR Great People's Khural.

Article 28. The Great People's Khural shall create permanent commissions: budget-economic, legislative proposals, foreign affairs, and nationality affairs.

If necessary, the Great People's Khural also shall create other commissions. The work procedure of the commissions shall be determined by the Great People's Khural.

Article 29. The Great People's Khural shall elect the Presidium of the Great People's Khural composed of the Chairman, Deputy Chairmen, Secretary, and members of the Presidium of the Great People's Khural.

Article 30. A law shall be considered to be confirmed if it is adopted by the MPR Great People's Khural by a simple majority of votes.

Laws and decrees adopted by the MPR Great People's Khural shall be published over the signatures of the Chairman and Secretary of the Presidium of the MPR Great People's Khural except for decrees concerning the election of the Presidium of the Great People's Khural, which shall be published over the signature of the Chairman of the Great People's Khural.

Article 31. Deputies of the Great People's Khural, and also deputies of local khurals, shall have the right to question members of the respective agencies of state administration on matters within their competence. The respective agency of administration must give an answer to the question of a deputy.

Article 32. A deputy of the MPR Great People's Khural may not be arrested or brought to criminal responsibility without the consent of the Great People's Khural, and in the interval between Sessions of the Great People's Khural, without the consent of its Presidium.

B. Presidium of the Great People's Khural

Article 33. The Presidium of the Great People's Khural shall, in the interval between Sessions of the Great People's Khural, be the highest agency of state power.

Article 34. The Presidium of the Great People's Khural shall:
 a) exercise control over the implementation of the Constitution and laws of the MPR;
 b) designate elections to the Great People's Khural;
 c) convoke Sessions of the Great People's Khural;
 d) give an interpretation of prevailing laws;
 e) promulgate edicts;
 f) conduct an all-people's poll (referendum);
 g) repeal decrees and regulations of the MPR Council of Ministers and local khurals of people's deputies if they fail to conform to a law;
 h) form new, abolish, or reorganize existing ministries and other central agencies of state administration with subsequent submission for confirmation of the Great People's Khural;
 i) appoint to or relieve from office ministers and other members of the government upon the recommendation of the Chairman of the Council of Ministers, with subsequent submission for confirmation of a Session of the Great People's Khural;
 j) exercise the right of pardon;
 k) establish orders and medals of the MPR, and also honorary, military, and other titles of the MPR;
 l) award orders and medals of the MPR and confer honorary titles of the MPR upon the recommendation of the MPR Council of Ministers;
 m) appoint and recall MPR diplomatic representatives to foreign states;
 n) accept credentials and letters of recall from diplomatic representatives of foreign states accredited to it;

o) give powers to the Council of Ministers to conclude treaties and agreements with other states;

p) ratify and denounce treaties and agreements with other states;

q) in the interval between Sessions of the Great People's Khural declare a state of war in the event of a military attack on the MPR, and also, if necessary, fulfill international treaty obligations for mutual defense from attack;

r) declare a general or partial mobilization;

s) admit to MPR citizenship and authorize withdrawal from MPR citizenship;

t) confirm upon the recommendation of the Council of Ministers the formation or abolition of *aimags* (or cities), *somons* (or *khorons*), and also the administrative division of *aimags* (or cities), *somons* (or *khorons*).

Article 35. Upon the expiry of the powers of the MPR Great People's Khural, the Presidium of the Great People's Khural shall retain their powers until the formation by the newly-elected Great People's Khural of a Presidium of the MPR Great People's Khural.

Article 36. The Presidium of the Great People's Khural shall be responsible and accountable to the Great People's Khural in all its activity.

Chapter IV. Highest and Central Agencies of State Administration

Article 37. The MPR Council of Ministers shall be the highest executive and administrative agency of state administration of the Mongolian People's Republic.

Article 38. The MPR Council of Ministers shall be responsible and accountable in its activity to the Great People's Khural and, in the interval between Sessions of the latter, to the Presidium of the Great People's Khural.

Article 39. The MPR Council of Ministers shall promulgate decrees and regulations on the basis of or in execution of prevailing laws and shall verify their execution.

Article 40. Decrees and regulations of the MPR Council of Ministers shall be binding for execution on the entire territory of the MPR.

Article 41. The Council of Ministers of the Mongolian People's Republic shall:

a) unify and direct the activity of MPR ministries and other institutions within its jurisdiction with regard to the direction of state economic and cultural construction;

b) exercise direction over planning the national economy, take measures to carry out the national economic plan and the state and local budgets, and direct the realization of financial and credit policy;

c) exercise general direction in the domain of relations with foreign states and exercise a monopoly of foreign trade;

d) exercise general direction in matters of the defense and construction of the armed forces of the country, and also determine the quota of citizens to be called for active military service;

e) take measures for the defense of the interests of the state and the protection and all possible strengthening of socialist ownership as the economic basis of the socialist state;

f) take measures to ensure social order and protect the personal and property rights of citizens;

g) direct and orient directly the work of *aimag* (or city) executive administrations of khurals of people's deputies;

h) change or repeal, when necessary, the orders and instructions of ministries and departments subordinate to the Council of Ministers and other agencies of administration;

i) form, when necessary, departments and institutions attached to the Council of Ministers for matters of economic and cultural construction;

j) confirm models and issue authorization for the manufacture of the State Arms for agencies and institutions of state administration.

Article 42. The MPR Council of Ministers shall be formed by the Great People's Khural composed of the Chairman of the MPR Council of Ministers, the Deputy Chairman of the MPR Council of Ministers, and Ministers of the MPR.

Article 43. Ministries and departments shall be central MPR agencies of state administration. Ministers and directors of departments of the MPR shall direct the respective branch of state administration and bear full responsibility for the state and activity thereof to the Council of Ministers. The work of MPR ministries and departments shall be organized on the basis of the consistent implementation of the principles of one-man-leadership and collegiality in discussing questions on the basis of constantly raising the personal responsibility of each worker.

Article 44. The competence of each ministry and department shall be determined by a Statute on it worked out on the basis of laws and confirmed by the MPR Council of Ministers.

Article 45. Ministers of the MPR and directors of departments shall, within the limits of their competence, promulgate orders and instructions and also verify their execution. These orders and instructions shall be promulgated on the basis of and in execution of prevailing MPR laws, as well as decrees and regulations of the Council of Ministers of the Mongolian People's Republic.

Chapter V. Local Agencies of State Power and State Administration

Article 46. The territory of the MPR shall be divided administratively into *aimags* and cities. *Aimags* in turn shall be divided into *somons*, and cities and population centers, into districts and *khorons*.

Article 47. Khurals of people's deputies elected by the populace of the respective localities for a term of two years shall be the agencies of state power in *aimags*, cities, *somons*, districts, and *khorons*.

Article 48. Norms of representation for local khurals of people's deputies shall be determined by the Presidium of the MPR Great People's Khural.

Article 49. Regular Sessions of *aimag* and city khurals of people's deputies shall be convoked by their executive administrations at least twice a year.

Extraordinary Sessions of local khurals of people's deputies shall be convoked at the request of at least half of the deputies of the khural or upon the initiative of the executive administration, and also upon the instruction of the Presidium of the Great People's Khural.

The executive administration of a local khural of people's deputies shall inform the populace in good time about the period and agenda for a regular khural Session and ensure the participation of representatives of the working people in the work of the khural Session.

Article 50. *Aimag*, city, *somon*, district, and *khoron* khurals of people's deputies shall elect a Chairman and Secretary during the Session in order to conduct sessions of the Session.

Article 51. For current work, *aimag* and city khurals of people's deputies shall elect, as their executive and administrative agency, executive administrations comprising 7 to 11 persons: Chairman, Deputy Chairman, Executive Secretary, and members.

Article 52. The executive administrations, elected in numbers of 5 to 9 persons and comprising the Chairman, Deputy Chairman, Secretary, and members, shall be the executive and administrative organizations of *somon*, district, and *khoron* khurals of people's deputies.

Article 53. The chairmen of executive administrations shall direct all the work of these administrations, convoke sessions of the executive administrations, and preside at them.

Article 54. Upon the expiry of the powers of *aimag* and city, *somon* and *khoron* khurals of people's deputies, their executive administrations shall retain these powers until the formation of the new executive and administrative agencies by the newly-elected khurals.

Article 55. *Aimag*, city, *somon*, district, and *khoron* khurals of people's deputies and their executive administrations shall:
 a) direct economic and cultural-political construction on its territory;
 b) direct and control the work of economic and cooperative organizations;
 c) confirm the economic plan and local budget; take measures to fulfill them;
 d) direct the activity of agencies of administration subordinate to them;
 e) ensure observance of the rules of socialist community life, protect the rights and interests of state enterprises and institutions, agricultural associations, and other cooperatives and also protect the rights of citizens;

f) ensure the precise observance of laws, and also the strict fulfillment of decisions of superior agencies;

g) ensure the extensive and active participation of the working people in all domains of state, economic, and cultural construction.

Article 56. Local khurals of people's deputies shall adopt decrees within the limits of rights granted them by law.

Article 57. Superior khurals of people's deputies shall have the right to change or repeal decrees of inferior khurals of people's deputies, as well as decrees and regulations of executive administrations.

Article 58. Superior executive administrations of khurals of people's deputies shall have the right to change or repeal decrees and regulations of inferior executive administrations and to suspend decrees of inferior khurals of people's deputies.

Article 59. An executive administration of a local khural of people's deputies shall be directly accountable both to the khural of people's deputies which elected it and to the executive agency of the superior khural of people's deputies.

Article 60. Local khurals of people's deputies shall create permanent commissions for individual branches of its activity and involve in their work a broad *aktiv* from among the working people.

Article 61. Sections and administrations shall be organized in *aimag* and city executive administrations in order to direct individual branches of work. They shall be subordinate in their activity, respectively, both to the executive administration of the *aimag* or city khural of people's deputies and to the respective MPR ministry or department.

Article 62. The deputies of local khurals of the MPR may not be arrested or brought to criminal responsibility without the consent of the respective khural, and in the interval between Sessions of the khural, without the consent of the respective executive administration.

Chapter VI. Court and Procuracy

A. The Court

Article 63. Justice in the MPR shall be effectuated in accordance with laws by the Supreme Court of the republic, *aimag* and city courts, special courts of the MPR, and also precinct people's courts.

Article 64. Cases shall be considered in all courts by permanent judges with the participation of people's assessors, except for instances specially provided for by law.

Article 65. The MPR Supreme Court shall be the highest judicial agency. The Supreme Court shall direct all MPR judicial agencies, and also establish supervision over their judicial activity.

Article 66. The MPR Supreme Court shall be elected by the Great People's Khural for a term of four years. The MPR Supreme Court shall be responsible and accountable to the MPR Great People's Khural and its Presidium.

Article 67. A city or *aimag* court shall be elected by city or *aimag* khurals of people's deputies for a term of three years.

Article 68. Precinct people's courts shall be elected by citizens of the respective *aimag, somon,* city, district, or *khoron* on the basis of universal, direct, and equal suffrage by secret ballot for a term of three years. Citizens who have attained 23 years of age and have not been convicted may be elected judges and people's assessors.

Article 69. Court proceedings shall be conducted in the Mongolian language, while ensuring for persons who do not have a command of this language full familiarization with the materials of the case through an interpreter, as well as the right to speak in court in their native language.

Article 70. Cases shall be examined in all courts openly, the accused being ensured the right to defense. Closed judicial sessions shall be permitted in instances specially provided for by law.

Article 71. When considering a case, judges shall be independent and subordinate only to law.

B. The Procuracy

Article 72. Supreme supervision over the precise observance of laws by all ministries and other central agencies of administration, institutions and organizations within their jurisdiction, local state agencies, and also all social and cooperative organizations, as well as both officials and citizens of the MPR, shall be effectuated by the Procurator of the Republic.

Article 73. The MPR Procurator shall be appointed by the Great People's Khural for a term of four years. The MPR Procurator shall be responsible and accountable to the MPR Great People's Khural and to its Presidium.

Article 74. Procuracy supervision in localities shall be effectuated by *aimag*, city and precinct procurators appointed by the MPR Procurator for a term of three years.

Article 75. Procurators in localities shall exercise their functions, being subordinate only to the superior procurator.

III. BASIC RIGHTS AND DUTIES OF CITIZENS OF THE MONGOLIAN PEOPLE'S REPUBLIC

Chapter VII. Basic Rights and Freedoms of Citizens and Guarantees of Ensuring Them

Article 76. Citizens of the MPR shall have equal rights irrespective of sex, racial or national affiliation, confession of faith, or social origin and status.

Article 77. Citizens of the MPR shall have the right to labor and to payment for labor in accordance with its quantity and quality.

This right shall be ensured by all the advantages confirmed in the MPR by the socialist system of economy, giving each MPR citizen every opportunity to apply his knowledge and labor without obstruction in any branch of the economy and culture and to receive guaranteed remuneration in accordance with labor expended.

Article 78. Citizens of the MPR shall have the right to leisure.

This right shall be ensured by the establishment of a maximum working day of eight hours, the reduction of the working day for a number of special professions, the establishment of a weekly day off, annual leaves for workers and employees while retaining earnings, and granting the working people sanatoriums, rest homes, theaters, clubs, and other institutions to service the working people.

The policy of the MPR shall be directed toward increasing thereafter, as the productive forces of the country develop, the free time of the working people at the expense of reducing the working time and improving and bringing closer to the working people various services so that they can use their free time not only for leisure but also for their physical and spiritual growth and to improve their knowledge.

Article 79. Citizens of the MPR shall have the right to material assistance in old-age, in the event of loss of capacity to work, illness or loss of breadwinner.

This right shall be ensured by rendering assistance to the working people through a system of social insurance, state pensions, special funds of cooperative organizations, and also the extensive development of a network of medical institutions, resorts, free medical care for the working people, and the development of a system of labor protection.

Article 80. Citizens of the MPR shall have the right to education. This right shall be ensured by study free of charge, an extensive network of schools of general education, secondary specialized educational institutions, institutions of higher education, and also the development of a system for raising the qualifications, and a system of state stipends for students of secondary specialized educational institutions, and institutions of higher education.

Article 81. Citizens of the MPR shall have the right to participate freely in the administration of state and society and also in the direction of economic life of this country, both through their representative agencies and directly. This right shall be ensured by granting all citizens the real possibility of extensive participation in all domains of state, political, economic, and cultural construction of the country, in particular, participation in elections, referendums, organizations of various democratic societies, and so forth.

The right to elect and be elected to all agencies of state power shall be granted to all citizens of the MPR who have attained 18 years of age, except for persons deemed mentally ill.

Article 82. Citizens of the MPR shall have the right to unite in social organizations: trade unions, cooperative associations, youth, sport, and other organizations; cultural and scientific societies, and also societies for strengthening peace and friendship between peoples, and so forth.

The most active and conscious citizens from the ranks of workers, *arats* organized in cooperatives, and the laboring intelligentsia shall unite in the Mongolian People's Democratic Party, which is the vanguard and leader of all state and other mass organizations of the working people.

Article 83. Citizens of the MPR shall, irrespective of their nationality, have equal rights in all domains of state, economic, cultural, and socio-political life of the country.

Any direct or indirect limitation of the rights of citizens for reasons of racial or national affiliation and the advocacy of ideas of chauvinism or nationalism shall be prohibited by law. The MPR shall ensure the representatives of all nationalities residing on the territory of the republic the opportunity to develop national culture and to study and conduct correspondence in their native language.

The MPR shall grant the right of asylum to foreign citizens persecuted for defending the interests of the working people, for national liberation struggle, for activity to strengthen peace, or for scientific activity.

Article 84. Women in the MPR shall be granted rights equal with men in all domains of economic, state, cultural, and socio-political life. The exercise of these rights shall be ensured by granting women labor conditions equal with men, leisure, social insurance, education, state protection of the interests of mother and child, state assistance to mothers with many children, granting women paid maternity and postnatal leave, and expanding the network of maternity homes, kindergartens, and nurseries.

The obstruction in any form whatever of the equality of women shall be prohibited by law.

Article 85. Every citizen of the Mongolian People's Republic shall have the right to have recourse to and to submit written and oral complaints and applications against illegal actions of state agencies or individual officials, or facts of manifestations of bureaucratism and red-tape at any agencies of state power and administration. State agencies and officials shall be obliged to consider immediately the applications and complaints submitted, to take measures to eliminate the violation of laws and procedures, and to reply to the applicant regarding the substance of the application or complaint.

Article 86. In the MPR religion shall be separated from the state and school. The freedoms of belief and anti-religious propaganda shall be granted to the citizens of the MPR.

Article 87. In accordance with the interests of the working people and with a view to developing and strengthening the state system of the MPR, citizens of the MPR shall be guaranteed by law:
1. freedom of speech;
2. freedom of press;
3. freedom of assembly and meetings;
4. freedom of demonstrations and processions.

These rights and freedoms shall be ensured by granting the working people and their organizations the necessary material conditions for their effectuation.

Article 88. Citizens of the Mongolian People's Republic shall be ensured inviolability of the person, inviolability of their dwellings, and secrecy of correspondence. No one may be subjected to arrest other than by decree of a court or with the sanction of a procurator.

Chapter VIII. Basic Duties of Citizens

Article 89. Every citizen of the MPR shall be obliged to:
a) devote all his efforts and knowledge to the cause of the construction of communism, remembering that honest and conscientious labor for the benefit of society is a source of the growth of wealth and might of the socialist state and raising the well-being of the working people;
b) strictly observe the Constitution of the MPR, precisely execute laws, and observe labor discipline, observe the rules of socialist community life, and actively struggle against all anti-social phenomena;
c) ensure the unity of personal and social interests and place the interests of society and the state first;
d) care for, as the apple of his eye, the sacred and inviolable basis of the socialist system: social socialist ownership, and strengthen and increase it in every possible way;
e) consider the strengthening of the internationalist friendship of peoples as an objective necessity and in his area promote by his

practical activities the cause of strengthening the friendship and solidarity of the working people and the unity and solidarity of the peoples of the socialist camp headed by the Soviet Union, and resolutely struggle against any kind of phenomena capable of harming this sacred friendship and unity;

f) nurture the rising generation in a spirit of love for labor, discipline and organization, collectivism, and respect for the interests of society, in the spirit of a communist attitude toward labor and socialist ownership, unlimited loyalty to the socialist motherland, the ideas of communism and the principles of proletarian internationalism, and in a spirit of respect for all working people regardless of their nationality;

g) actively promote the strengthening of the people's democratic system, strictly preserve the state secrecy, and be vigilant with respect to enemies;

h) sacredly defend the socialist motherland from the enemies of socialism. Military service in the People's Army of the MPR shall be an honorable duty of MPR citizens;

i) precisely fulfill all his civic duties and require the same from other citizens.

IV. MISCELLANEOUS PROVISIONS

Chapter IX. Arms, Flag, Capital

Article 90. The State Arms of the Mongolian People's Republic shall reflect the essence of the state and the idea of friendship of peoples and shall show the national and economic peculiarities of the country.

The arms of the MPR shall consist of a circle framed by ears of grain whose stalks are fastened to a cog-wheel. They all shall be tied together by a red and blue ribbon with the inscription *"MHP"*.

In the center of the circle shall be the symbolic figure of a working man on horseback galloping upward toward the sun—communism—against a background of a relief typical for the MPR (mountains, forest-steppe, and desert).

In the center of the upper portion of the circle where the tips of the ears of grain meet shall be depicted a five-pointed star with the sign *"soëmbo"* within it.

Article 91. The state flag of the Mongolian People's Republic shall proceed from the state arms and shall consist of a red and blue

Mongolia

cloth, wherein a sky-blue strip occupies one-third of the middle of the flag, and the two other parts located on both sides are red.

In the upper portion of the red cloth affixed at the staff shall be a gold five-pointed star under which is the mark "*soëmbo*", also gold. The proportion of the width to length shall be 1:2.

Article 92. The city of Ulan-Bator shall be the capital of the Mongolian People's Republic.

Chapter X. On Changing and Repealing the MPR Constitution

Article 93. Changes in the Constitution of the Mongolian People's Republic shall be made only by decision of the Great People's Khural adopted by a majority of not less than two-thirds of the votes.

Article 94. As individual functions of the state gradually die out under communism, the constitutional provisions concerning them also shall be repealed.

The Constitution of the MPR will be repealed when the need for the existence of the state, which is the principal instrument for building socialism and communism, disappears, when it will be replaced by a communist association of working people.

POLAND

INTRODUCTION

Richard Szawlowski

Poland, with her statehood dating back to the Xth century, has a long constitutional tradition. The pertinent development in the pre-partition period (until the end of the XVIIIth century) climaxed in the May 1791 Constitution, a very progressive document for its time, placed, chronologically, between the Constitution of the United States of America of 1787 and the French Constitution of September 1791. After independence was regained after World War I, the genuinely democratic Constitution of March 1921 was adopted (*Dziennik Ustaw* 1921 No. 44 item 267). It was amended in 1926, after Piłsudski's *coup d'état*, and replaced by a new Constitution in April 1935 (*Dziennik Ustaw* 1935 No. 30 item 227), reflecting certain authoritarian trends represented by the new ruling circles.

The Communist régime imposed on Poland at the turn of 1944–1945 proclaimed in its "July [1944] Manifesto" (published as an Annex to *Dziennik Ustaw*, No. 1, which started to come out in Lublin) that the 1935 Constitution was illegal, and declared that the new authorities were acting on the basis of the 1921 Constitution and that the "fundamental principles" of that Constitution were going to remain in force until the election of a Constitutional Seym. In reality, irrespective of what may have been meant by "fundamental principles", it would be difficult to detect, during the years that followed, anything still kept of the democratic 1921 Constitution.

After the falsified general elections of January 1947, the "Constitutional Seym", in February of that year, adopted what was popularly called the "Little Constitution" (*Mała Konstytucja*, official title: "Constitutional Act on the Structure and the Scope of Activities of the Highest Organs of the Polish Republic"—*Dziennik Ustaw* 1947 No. 18 item 71). Once again reference was made to the "fundamental principles" of the 1921 Constitution.

The first fully-fledged Constitution of what was started to be called "Polish People's Republic" came in July 1952 (*Dziennik Ustaw* 1952 No. 32 item 232). It was a strongly Soviet-inspired document. The later liberal political events of the "Polish October" of 1956 did

Introduction 285

not find any expression in the Constitution, except in the introduction of a new Chapter 3a in December 1957, reestablishing the Supreme Board of Control (abolished in December 1952) and making it an organ of the Seym.

Fairly far-reaching amendments of the 1952 Constitution took place only in February 1976 (*Dziennik Ustaw* 1976 No. 5 item 29; consolidated text in *Dziennik Ustaw* 1976 No. 7 item 36). The most important innovations then introduced to the Constitution were the declaration that the Polish People's Republic was "a socialist state" (Art. 1); the introduction of the Polish United Workers' Party into the Constitution as "the leading political force of society in the building of socialism" (Art. 3, para. 1); the introduction of the passage on "strengthening friendship and cooperation with the Union of Soviet Socialist Republics and other socialist states" (Art. 6, point 2); and the replacement of Chapter 3a by Chapter 4, by virtue of which the Supreme Board of Control ceased to be an organ of the Seym and was placed under the supervision of the President of the Council of Ministers (retreat from the 1957 reform).

Concerning the background to the 1976 constitutional reform, it was first mentioned when the Party decided at its VIth Congress in December 1971 that a new Constitution should be prepared (see *Nowe Drogi* 1972 No. 1, p. 164). But the matter was put forward in a concrete form only after the VIIth Congress of the Party in December 1975, and this time the aim was not a new basic law but just amendments to the 1952 one. What is worth mentioning is that the 1976 constitutional reform met with widespread political protests on certain points by intellectuals, students, etc. This struggle, launched in a situation when the full text of the proposed amendments was never published (*sic*), was a unique phenomenon by Communist standards, all the more so as it achieved limited success. The best known was the elimination of the proposed linking of the enjoyment of civil and political rights with the fulfillment of duties (which one finds in the later Constitutions of Albania of December 1976—Art. 39, and of the USSR of October 1977—Art. 59). There was also a certain tuning down of the provision on the links with the USSR (which, as originally proposed, had been more or less equivalent to Art. 6, para. 2 of the East German Constitution of 1968, as amended in 1974). For English translations of some memoranda and letters produced in connection with the proposed constitutional amendments (and also demanding the introduction of new rights, etc.) by oppositional circles, see *Dissent in Poland. Reports and Documents in Translation, December 1975–July 1977*, published by the Association of Polish Students and Graduates in Exile, London 1977, pp. 11–24. See also the chapter on "The Legitimization of the Totalitarian System and Public Opposition to it" in Peter Raina, *Political Opposition in Poland, 1954–1977*, London 1978.

CONSTITUTION OF THE POLISH PEOPLE'S REPUBLIC OF 22 JULY 1952 (AS AMENDED)

Preamble	288
The Political Structure	289
Social and Economic Structure	291
The Supreme Organs of State Power	293
The Supreme Board of Control	296
The Supreme Organs of State Administration	297
Local Organs of State Power and Administration	299
The Courts and the Public Prosecutor's Office	301
Fundamental Rights and Duties of Citizens	303
Principles of Electoral Law	308
The Coat-of-Arms, Colors, National Anthem, and Capital of the Polish People's Republic	309
Amendment of the Constitution	310

CONSTITUTION OF THE POLISH PEOPLE'S REPUBLIC*

Dziennik Ustaw 1952 No. 32 item 232 (as amended).
Consolidated text in *Dziennik Ustaw* 1976 No. 7 item 36.

The Polish People's Republic is a republic of the working people.

The Polish People's Republic recurs to the loftiest progressive traditions of the Polish nation and realizes the ideals of liberation of the Polish working masses.

The Polish working people, under the leadership of the heroic working class and relying upon the alliance of workers and peasants, fought for decades for liberation from national bondage imposed by the Prussian, Austrian, and Russian partitioners and colonizers, just as they fought for the abolition of exploitation by Polish capitalists and landowners.

During the occupation, the Polish nation waged an unyielding heroic battle against the bloody hitlerite invasion. The historic victory of the Union of Soviet Socialist Republics over fascism liberated the Polish territories, enabled the Polish working people to take over power, and created conditions for the national rebirth of Poland within new, just boundaries. The Recovered Territories reverted to Poland forever.

By embodying in action the historic precepts of the Manifesto of the Polish Committee of National Liberation of 22 July 1944, and developing its programmatic principles, people's power—thanks to the selfless and creative efforts of the Polish working people in their struggle against the furious resistance of the remnants of the old capitalist-landowner régime—has achieved great social changes. As a result of revolutionary struggles and transformations, the power of the capitalists and landowners has been overthrown, a state of people's democracy has been consolidated, and a new social system, answering to the interests and aspirations of the wide masses, is taking shape and growing in strength.

The legal principles of this system are established by the Constitution of the Polish People's Republic.

The basis of the people's power in Poland today lies in the alliance

*Translated by Hanna and Richard Szawlowski.

of the working class with the working peasantry. The foremost role in this alliance belongs to the working class, as the leading class of the people, which rests upon the revolutionary achievements of the Polish and international workers movement, and on the historic experience of the victorious construction of socialism in the Union of Soviet Socialist Republics, the first state of workers and peasants.

Carrying out the will of the Polish Nation, and in accordance with its call, the Constitutional Seym of the Republic of Poland solemnly adopts the present Constitution as the basic law by which the Polish Nation and all the organs of power of the Polish working people shall be guided, with the aim of:

— strengthening the People's State as the fundamental authority ensuring the fullest flourishing of the Polish Nation, its independence and sovereignty;

— speeding up the political, economic, and cultural development of the Motherland and the growth of its strength;

— deepening the patriotic feelings, unity, and cohesion of the Polish Nation in its struggle for further improvement of social conditions, for complete elimination of exploitation of man by man, and for the realization of the great ideals of socialism;

— tightening the bonds of friendship and cooperation between nations, based on the alliance and brotherhood which today link the Polish Nation with the peace-loving nations of the world in their pursuit of a common aim: the prevention of aggression and the consolidation of world peace.

Chapter I. The Political Structure

Article 1. (1) The Polish People's Republic is a socialist state.

(2) In the Polish People's Republic, power is vested in the working people of town and country.

Article 2. (1) The working people exercise state authority through their representatives elected to the Seym of the Polish People's Republic and to the national councils in universal, equal, and direct elections by secret vote.

(2) Representatives of the people in the Seym of the Polish People's Republic and in the national councils are accountable to their electorate and may be recalled by them.

Article 3. (1) The leading political force of society in the building of socialism is the Polish United Workers' Party.

(2) Cooperation between the Polish United Workers' Party, the United Peasant Party, and the Democratic Party forms the basis of the National Unity Front.

(3) The National Unity Front provides a common framework for the activities of social organizations of the working people and the patriotic integration of all citizens—members of the party [Polish United Workers' Party], [of the other] political parties, and non-party members, irrespective of their relationship with religion, around the vital interests of the Polish People's Republic.

Article 4. In the Polish People's Republic, the basic aim of the activity of the state is the universal development of a socialist society, the development of the creative forces of the nation and of every human being, and increasingly improved satisfaction of the needs of the citizens.

Article 5. The Polish People's Republic:

(1) protects and develops the socialist accomplishments of the Polish working people of town and country, their power and freedom;

(2) ensures citizens' participation in government and promotes the development of various forms of self-government of the working people;

(3) develops the productive forces and the economy of the country by planned exploitation and enrichment of its material resources, rational organization of labor, and continuous progress in science and technology;

(4) strengthens social property as the main foundation of the country's economic strength and the welfare of the nation;

(5) turns into reality the principles of social justice, eliminates the exploitation of man by man, and counteracts violations of the principles of social intercourse;

(6) creates conditions for the continuous growth of prosperity and the gradual obliteration of the distinctions between town and country, and between manual and mental work;

(7) in its concern for the development of the nation, it cares for the family, maternity, and the raising of the younger generation;

(8) looks after the health of the population;

(9) develops education and makes it available to all;

(10) safeguards the all-round development of science and of the national culture.

Article 6. In its policy, the Polish People's Republic:

(1) guides itself by the interests of the Polish nation, its sovereignty, independence, and security, and the will for peace and cooperation between nations;

(2) aligns itself with the lofty traditions of solidarity with the forces of freedom and progress, and strengthens friendship and cooperation with the Union of Soviet Socialist Republics and other socialist states;

(3) bases relations with states of differing social structures upon principles of peaceful coexistence and cooperation.

Article 7. The Polish People's Republic realizes and develops a socialist democracy.

Article 8. (1) The laws of the Polish People's Republic express the interests and will of the working people.

(2) Strict adherence to the laws of the Polish People's Republic is the basic duty of every state organ and every citizen.

(3) All organs of state power and administration act on the basis of legal provisions.

Article 9. All organs of state power and administration lean in their activities on the conscious, active participation of the widest masses of the people, and it is their duty to:

(1) give an account to the nation of their activities;

(2) examine carefully, and take into consideration, in accordance with laws in force, just proposals, complaints, and wishes of the citizens;

(3) clarify to the working masses the basic aims and guiding principles of the policy of the people's authorities in the individual fields of state, economic, and cultural activities.

Article 10. The armed forces of the Polish People's Republic stand guard over the sovereignty and independence of the Polish nation, and its security and peace.

Chapter II. Social and Economic Structure

Article 11. (1) The socialist economic system, based on the socialized means of production and socialist relations of production, is the foundation of the social and economic system of the Polish People's Republic.

(2) The Polish People's Republic develops the economic and cul-

tural life of the country on the basis of a national social-economic plan.

(3) The fundamental aim of the social-economic policy of the Polish People's Republic is the systematic amelioration of the living, social, and cultural standards of society, the continuous development of the productive forces of the country, and the strengthening of the power, defensive capacity, and independence of the Motherland.

(4) The state has a monopoly of foreign trade.

Article 12. (1) The property of the whole nation, in particular: mineral deposits, the basic sources of energy, state lands, water, state forests, mines, state industrial, agricultural, and trade enterprises, state communal facilities, banks, state housing reserves, roads, state means of communication, transport, telegraphs and telephones, radio, television and film, state social, educational, scientific and cultural institutions, are subject to the special care and protection of the state and all its citizens.

(2) The Polish People's Republic ensures the protection and rational management of the natural environment, which is the wealth of the whole nation.

Article 13. State enterprises, managing rationally the part of the property of the whole nation entrusted to them, realize economic and social tasks in a planned manner. The personnel of the enterprises take part in managing the enterprises.

Article 14. (1) The Polish People's Republic strengthens, in a planned manner, the economic bond between town and country on the basis of brotherly cooperation between workers and peasants.

(2) With this aim, the Polish People's Republic ensures a continuous increase of the production of the state industries, serving the satisfaction of the comprehensive productive and consumption needs of the rural population, while at the same time exerting an influence in a planned way on the constant growth of agricultural commodity production which supplies industry with raw materials and the urban population with foodstuffs.

Article 15. The Polish People's Republic, in its concern with provision of food for the nation:

(1) creates conditions for agriculture which ensure a constant rise in agricultural production, conducive to socialist transformation of the countryside and to the raising of the prosperity of the farmer;

(2) takes care of the proper utilization of the land as the wealth of the whole nation;

(3) looks after individual farms of working peasants, lends them assistance in increasing production and raising the technical-agricultural level, supports the development of agricultural self-management, especially agricultural circles and their cooperatives, supports the development of cooperation and the specialization of production, and widens the links between individual farms and the state socialist economy;

(4) lends support and assistance to collective farms being set up on the voluntary principle, and especially to agricultural cooperative farms;

(5) develops and strengthens state farms, which constitute a highly productive form of socialist economy in agriculture, inculcating technical agricultural progress and exerting a good influence on the development of the whole of agriculture.

Article 16. The Polish People's Republic supports the development of various forms of the cooperative movement in town and country, lends it comprehensive assistance in the fulfillment of its tasks, and guarantees special care and protection to cooperative property as social property.

Article 17. The Polish People's Republic recognizes and protects, on the basis of laws in force, individual property and the right to inherit land, buildings, and other means of production belonging to peasants, craftsmen, and home workers.

Article 18. The Polish People's Republic guarantees full protection of personal property of citizens and the right to inherit such property.

Article 19. (1) Work is the right, duty, and point of honor of every citizen. By their work, by the observance of work discipline, competition in work, and perfecting of its methods, the working people of town and country enhance the strength and power of the Motherland, raise the level of prosperity of the nation, and speed up the full realization of the socialist system.

(2) Leaders in work and work veterans are respected by all the nation.

(3) The Polish People's Republic increasingly brings into effect the principle: "From each according to his ability, to each according to his work".

Chapter III. The Supreme Organs of State Power

Article 20. (1) The supreme organ of state power is the Seym of the Polish People's Republic.

(2) The Seym, as the highest exponent of the will of the working people of town and country, realizes the sovereign rights of the nation.

(3) The Seym enacts laws, passes resolutions determining the fundamental directions of activity of the state, and exercises control over the activity of other organs of state power and administration.

Article 21. (1) The Seym is composed of 460 deputies.

(2) The validity of the election of a deputy is confirmed by the Seym.

(3) A deputy may not be prosecuted or arrested without the consent of the Seym, and in the period when the Seym is not in session, without the consent of the State Council.

Article 22. (1) The Seym deliberates in sessions. The sessions of the Seym are convened by the State Council at least twice a year. The State Council is also under an obligation to convene a session upon the written motion of one-third of the total number of deputies.

(2) The first session of a newly-elected Seym should be convened within a month from the date of the election.

Article 23. (1) The Seym elects from among its members a Speaker, deputy speakers, and committees.

(2) The Speaker, or, in his stead, a deputy speaker, presides over debates and keeps a watch on the course of the work of the Seym.

(3) The debates of the Seym are open. The Seym may resolve that debates be closed if the welfare of the state demands this.

(4) The work agenda of the Seym and the nature and number of committees are determined by standing orders adopted by the Seym.

Article 24. (1) The Seym adopts national social-economic plans for several-year periods.

(2) The Seym adopts the state budget every year.

(3) The Seym approves the report of the government on the execution of the budget and the national social-economic plan for the previous year.

Article 25. (1) The right to initiate legislation is vested in the State Council, the Government, and the deputies.

(2) Laws enacted by the Seym are signed by the Chairman of the State Council and its Secretary. Publication of a law in the Journal of Laws [*Dziennik Ustaw*] is by order of the Chairman of the State Council.

Article 26. The Seym may appoint a committee to examine a specific matter. The terms of reference and the procedure of conducting business of the committee are determined by the Seym.

Article 27. The President of the Council of Ministers or individual ministers are under an obligation to give an answer to an interpellation by a deputy within the period and according to procedure determined by the Seym.

Article 28. (1) The Seym is elected for a term of four years.

(2) Elections to the Seym are ordered by the State Council not later than a month before the expiry of the term of office of the Seym, the date of the elections being set on a work-free day falling within two months after the expiry of the term of office of the Seym.

Article 29. (1) At its first sitting, the Seym elects, from among its members, the State Council composed of:
— the Chairman of the State Council;
— four Deputy Chairmen;
— the Secretary of the State Council;
— eleven members.

(2) The Speaker of the Seym and the deputy speakers may be elected to the State Council as Deputy Chairmen or as members.

(3) After the expiry of the term of office of the Seym, the State Council acts until the election of a State Council by a newly-elected Seym.

Article 30. (1) The State Council:
1. orders elections to the Seym;
2. convenes sessions of the Seym;
3. watches over the compatibility of the law and the Constitution;
4. determines a universally binding interpretation of laws;
5. issues decrees having the force of law;
6. appoints and recalls plenipotentiary representatives of the Polish People's Republic in other states;
7. receives letters of credence and of recall of diplomatic

representatives of other states accredited to the State Council;
8. ratifies and denounces international treaties;
9. fills civilian and military posts specified by the law;
10. confers orders, distinctions, and honorary titles;
11. exercises the right of pardon;
12. performs other functions vested in the State Council by the Constitution or conferred upon it by law.

(2) The State Council is accountable in all its activities to the Seym.

(3) The State Council acts as a collective body.

(4) The State Council is represented by the Chairman or his deputy.

Article 31. (1) In periods between sessions of the Seym, the State Council issues decrees which have the force of law. The State Council submits the decrees to the Seym for approval at the closest session.

(2) Decrees issued by the State Council are signed by the Chairman of the State Council and its Secretary. Publication of a decree in the Journal of Laws is by order of the Chairman of the State Council.

Article 32. The State Council exercises supreme supervision over the national councils. Specific powers of the State Council in this field are determined by law.

Article 33. (1) A decision regarding a state of war may be made only in the event of an armed attack being made on the Polish People's Republic, or if the necessity for joint defense against aggression should result from international treaties. Such a decision is adopted by the Seym, and when the Seym is not in session, by the State Council.

(2) The State Council may proclaim martial law on part or on the whole of the territory of the Polish People's Republic, if this is necessitated by considerations of the defense or security of the state. For the same reasons, the State Council may proclaim partial or general mobilization.

Chapter IV. The Supreme Board of Control

Article 34. (1) The Supreme Board of Control is called upon to supervise the economic, financial, and organizational-administrative activities of the supreme and local organs of the state administration,

Poland

the social and cooperative organizations and units subordinate to them, from the point of view of the performance of the tasks of the social-economic plan, legality, good management, expediency, and integrity.

(2) The Supreme Board of Control also carries out supervision over units of the non-socialized economy in connection with the performance of tasks assigned to them by state organs or organizations belonging to the socialized economy, and also examines the compatibility between the activities of these units with the law in force and with the interests of the community.

Article 35. (1) The activities of the Supreme Board of Control serve the Seym, the State Council, and the Council of Ministers in the fulfillment of their functions.

(2) The President of the Council of Ministers exercises supervision over the Supreme Board of Control.

(3) The Supreme Board of Control performs examinations assigned by the Seym and the State Council, gives information on the results of these examinations, and presents periodic reports to the State Council.

Article 36. (1) The President of the Supreme Board of Control is appointed and recalled by the Seym on the motion of the President of the Council of Ministers made in agreement with the Chairman of the State Council.

(2) The organization and mode of functioning of the Supreme Board of Control are determined by law.

Chapter V. The Supreme Organs of State Administration

Article 37. (1) The Seym appoints and recalls the Government of the Polish People's Republic – the Council of Ministers – or its individual members.

(2) During the periods between sessions of the Seym, the State Council appoints and recalls members of the Council of Ministers on the motion of the President of the Council of Ministers. The State Council submits its decision to the Seym for approval at the closest session.

Article 38. (1) The Council of Ministers is the supreme executive and administrative organ of state power.

(2) The Council of Ministers is responsible and accountable to the

Seym for its activities, and when the Seym is not in session, to the State Council.

Article 39. (1) The Council of Ministers is composed of:
— the President of the Council of Ministers as its chairman;
— the Deputy Presidents of the Council of Ministers;
— the President of the Supreme Board of Control;
— the ministers;
— the chairmen of committees and commissions specified by law which fulfill the functions of the supreme organs of state administration.

(2) The President and Deputy Presidents of the Council of Ministers make up the Government Presidium. The Council of Ministers may appoint other members from among its membership to the composition of the Government Presidium.

Article 40. (1) The President of the Council of Ministers directs the work of the Council of Ministers and the Government Presidium.

(2) The President of the Council of Ministers issues ordinances and orders on the basis of laws and with the purpose of their implementation.

Article 41. The Council of Ministers:
(1) coordinates the activities of ministries and other organs subordinate to it and gives direction to their work;
(2) adopts every year and submits to the Seym the draft state budget, adopts and submits to the Seym the draft national social-economic plan for a several-year period;
(3) adopts the annual national social-economic plans;
(4) ensures the implementation of laws;
(5) watches over the execution of the national social-economic plan and the state budget;
(6) submits a report to the Seym every year on the execution of the state budget;
(7) ensures the protection of public order, of the interests of the state, and of the rights of citizens;
(8) on the basis of laws and with the aim of their implementation, issues ordinances, adopts resolutions, and watches over their execution;
(9) exercises general guidance in the field of relations with other states;
(10) exercises general guidance in the field of the defense capacity of the country and the organization of the armed forces of the

Polish People's Republic, and establishes every year the contingent of citizens to be called up for active military service;

(11) directs the work of local administrative organs.

Article 42. (1) Ministers direct specified branches of state administration. The office of a minister is created by means of a law.

(2) Ministers issue ordinances and orders on the basis of laws and with the aim of their implementation.

(3) The Council of Ministers may rescind an ordinance or an order issued by a minister.

Chapter VI. Local Organs of State Power and Administration

Article 43. (1) The local organs of state power and the fundamental organs of community self-government of the town and country working people in communes, towns, districts of larger cities, and voivodeships are the national councils.

(2) A joint national council may serve as an organ of state power and community self-government in two different units of territorial division of the same level.

(3) The terms of office of the national councils of individual levels are established by law.

Article 44. The national councils express the will of the working people and develop their creative initiative and activities with the aim of increasing the strength, prosperity, and culture of the nation.

Article 45. The national councils strengthen the link between the state authorities and the working people of town and country, drawing increasing numbers of the working people into participating in governing the state, and cooperate with the self-government of the inhabitants.

Article 46. The national councils direct all-round social-economic and cultural development, and exert an influence on all administrative and economic units in their area, inspire and coordinate their activities, and exert control over them. The national councils link the needs of the area with general state aims and tasks.

Article 47. The national councils are constantly concerned about the everyday needs and interests of the people, combat all manifestations of an arbitrary and bureaucratic attitude towards the citizen, and exercise and develop social supervision over the activities of [state] offices, enterprises, establishments, and institutions.

Article 48. The national councils take care of the maintenance of public order and watch over the observance of the people's law and order, protect social property, safeguard the rights of citizens, and cooperate in strengthening the defense capacity and security of the state.

Article 49. (1) The national councils exploit all the resources and possibilities of an area for its comprehensive economic and cultural development, for better and better satisfaction of the needs of the population in the field of supplies and services, and for the expansion of communal, educational, cultural, sanitary, and sport institutions and facilities.

(2) The national councils adopt social-economic plans and budgets of voivodeships, towns, districts [of larger cities], and communes on the motion of local administrative organs.

Article 50. (1) The national councils deliberate in sessions.

(2) The national councils elect presidia from among their membership to direct the preparation of sessions, conduct deliberations, coordinate the work of committees, and give help to councillors in the execution of their mandate.

Article 51. (1) The voivodes, presidents or heads of towns, district heads, and heads of communes are the local organs of state administration and the executive and administrative organs of the national councils.

(2) A local organ of the state administration is subordinate to a higher level organ of state administration, and in the sphere of the fulfillment of tasks established by the national council, to the proper national council.

Article 52. (1) The voivodes, presidents or heads of towns, district heads, and heads of communes exercise state administration on the basis of legal provisions and in accordance with directions established by higher organs.

(2) The voivodes and presidents of towns of the level of voivodeships are the representatives of the Government in their area.

Article 53. The national councils appoint committees for individual spheres of their activities. The committees of the national councils maintain constant and close links with the population, mobilize it for cooperation in the realization of the tasks of the council, carry out social supervision on behalf of the council, and take the initiative in their relations with the council and its organs.

Article 54. The national council rescinds a decision of a national council of a lower-level if the decision is counter to the law or at variance with the basic line of the policy of the state.

Article 55. The detailed composition and the terms of reference and rules of procedure of the national councils and their organs are established by law.

Chapter VII. The Courts and the Public Prosecutor's Office

Article 56. (1) The administration of justice in the Polish People's Republic is carried out by the Supreme Court, the voivodeship courts, regional courts, and special courts.
(2) In cases of infringements, judgment is made by collegia for infringement cases.
(3) The organization, jurisdiction, and procedure of the courts and collegia for cases of infringements are established by laws.

Article 57. The courts pronounce judgment in the name of the Polish People's Republic.

Article 58. The courts stand guard over the régime of the Polish People's Republic, protect the achievements of the Polish working people, safeguard the people's law and order, social property, and the rights of citizens, and punish offenders.

Article 59. (1) The hearing of cases and the passing of judgment in courts takes place with the participation of people's assessors, with the exception of cases specified by law.
(2) During the passing of judgment in courts, the people's assessors have equal rights with the judges.
(3) The people's assessors are elected by the national councils.
(4) The procedure of election of assessors of the voivodeship, regional, and special courts, and their term of office are established by law.

Article 60. (1) Judges are appointed and recalled by the State Council.

(2) The procedure for the appointment and recall of judges is established by law.

Article 61. (1) The Supreme Court is the highest judicial organ and supervises the activities of all other courts in the sphere of passing of judgment.

(2) The procedure of carrying out supervision by the Supreme Court is established by law.

(3) The Supreme Court is appointed by the State Council for a term of five years.

(4) The State Council appoints from among the judges of the Supreme Court the First President and the Presidents of the Supreme Court, and recalls them from these positions.

Article 62. Judges are independent and subject only to the law.

Article 63. (1) The hearing of cases in all courts of the Polish People's Republic is held in public. The law may specify exceptions to this principle.

(2) The accused is granted the right to legal defense. The accused may have a defense counsel either of his own choice or appointed by the court.

Article 64. (1) The Prosecutor General of the Polish People's Republic safeguards the people's law and order, watches over the protection of social property, and ensures respect for the rights of citizens.

(2) The Prosecutor General watches particularly over the prosecution of offenses against the régime, the safety and independence of the Polish People's Republic.

(3) The terms of reference and the modes of activity of the Prosecutor General are established by law.

Article 65. (1) The Prosecutor General of the Polish People's Republic is appointed and recalled by the State Council.

(2) The mode of appointing and recalling of prosecutors subordinate to the Prosecutor General, as well as the principles of the organization and procedure of the organs of the prosecutor's office, are established by law.

(3) The Prosecutor General is accountable to the State Council for the activities of the Prosecutor's office.

Article 66. The organs of the prosecutor's office are subject to the Prosecutor General of the Polish People's Republic and are independent of the local organs in the exercise of their functions.

Chapter VIII. Fundamental Rights and Duties of Citizens

Article 67. (1) The Polish People's Republic, in consolidating and multiplying the gains of the working people, strengthens and extends the rights and freedoms of the citizens.

(2) Citizens of the Polish People's Republic have equal rights regardless of sex, birth, education, profession, nationality, race, religion and social origin, and position.

(3) Citizens of the Polish People's Republic should fulfill their obligations towards the Motherland honestly, and contribute to its development.

Article 68. (1) Citizens of the Polish People's Republic have the right to work, that is, the right to employment paid in accordance with the quantity and quality of work done.

(2) The right to work is assured by the socialist economic system, the planned development of the means of production, the rational exploitation of all elements of production, the constant inculcation of scientific-technical progress in the national economy, and the system of education, and raising of professional qualifications. The proper realization of the right to work is ensured by socialist labor legislation.

Article 69. (1) Citizens of the Polish People's Republic have the right to rest.

(2) The right to rest is ensured to the workers by legislated reduction of working hours by means of the application of the eight hour working-day and a shorter work time in cases specified by law, days off work established by the law, and annual paid holidays.

(3) The organizing of employees' holidays, the development of tourism, health resorts, sports facilities, houses of culture, clubs, recreation rooms, parks, and other leisure facilities create possibilities for healthy and cultural rest for increasingly large numbers of working people in town and country.

Article 70. (1) Citizens of the Polish People's Republic have the right to health protection and to assistance in the event of sickness or incapacity for work.

(2) This right is increasingly being brought into effect by means of:

1. the development of social insurance in the event of sickness, old age, and incapacity for work, and the development of various forms of social assistance;

2. the development of state-organized health protection and raising of the health standards of the population, unpaid medical assistance for all working people and their families, and constant improvement of safety conditions, protection and hygiene of work, widely developed prevention of diseases and their combatting, and care for invalids;

3. the development of hospitals, sanatoria, medical aid clinics, health centers, and sanitary facilities.

Article 71. Citizens of the Polish People's Republic have the right to take advantage of the benefits of the natural environment and the duty to preserve it.

Article 72. (1) Citizens of the Polish People's Republic have the right to an education.
(2) The right to an education is assured to an increasing degree by:
1. unpaid schooling;
2. universal compulsory primary schools;
3. the universalization of secondary schooling;
4. the development of higher education;
5. assistance from the state in raising the qualifications of citizens employed in industrial establishments and other centers of employment in town and country;
6. a system of state scholarships, the development of live-in schools, boarding schools, and academic dormitories, and other forms of material assistance for the children of workers, working peasants, and the intelligentsia.

Article 73. (1) Citizens of the Polish People's Republic have the right to benefit from cultural achievements and to creative participation in the development of the national culture.
(2) This right is increasingly ensured by the development and giving of access to the working people of town and country of libraries, books, the press, radio, cinemas, theaters, museums and exhibitions, houses of culture, clubs, and recreation rooms, and the comprehensive promotion and encouragement of the cultural creativity of the masses of the people and the development of their creative talents.

Article 74. The Polish People's Republic fosters the comprehensive development of learning based upon the achievements of the most advanced thought of mankind and of Polish progressive thought—learning in the service of the nation.

Article 75. The Polish People's Republic concerns itself with the development of literature and art which express the needs and aspirations of the nation and which are in accord with the best progressive traditions of Polish creativity.

Article 76. The Polish People's Republic ensures comprehensive care for veterans of the struggles for national and social liberation.

Article 77. The Polish People's Republic accords special protection to the creative intelligentsia—those working in science, education, literature, and art, and pioneers of technical progress, rationalizers, and inventors.

Article 78. (1) Women in the Polish People's Republic have equal rights with men in all spheres of state, political, economic, social, and cultural life.
(2) The equality of women is guaranteed by:
1. an equal right with men to work and pay according to the principle "equal pay for equal work", the right to rest, to social insurance, to education, to honors and distinctions, and to the holding of public office;
2. care for mother and child, protection of expectant mothers, paid holiday during the period before and after confinement, the development of a network of maternity homes, creches, and nursery schools, and the extension of a network of service establishments and communal eating places.
(3) The Polish People's Republic strengthens the position of women in society, especially of mothers and women who work professionally.

Article 79. (1) Marriage, motherhood, and the family are under the care and protection of the Polish People's Republic. The state gives particular care to families with many children.
(2) It is the duty of parents to bring up children as honest citizens of the Polish People's Republic, conscious of their responsibilities.
(3) The Polish People's Republic ensures the realization of rights and responsibilities as regards alimony.

(4) Children born out of wedlock have the same rights as children born in wedlock.

(5) In its concern for the welfare of the family, the Polish People's Republic aims at an amelioration of the housing situation, develops and supports, with the participation of the citizens, various forms of residential construction, especially of cooperative construction, and cares for the rational management of housing resources.

Article 80. The Polish People's Republic gives particularly careful attention to the upbringing of youth, ensures them the widest possibilities of development, and creates conditions for active participation of the young generation in social, political, economic, and cultural life, forming a feeling of co-responsibility on the part of youth for the development of the Motherland.

Article 81. (1) Citizens of the Polish People's Republic enjoy, irrespective of nationality, race, and religion, equal rights in all fields of state, political, economic, social, and cultural life. Infringements of this principle by any direct or indirect granting of privilege, or restriction of rights on account of nationality, race, or religion, is subject to punishment.

(2) The spreading of hatred or contempt, and the provocation of strife or humiliation of a human being on account of differences of nationality, race, or religion are forbidden.

Article 82. (1) The Polish People's Republic ensures freedom of conscience and religion to citizens. The church and other religious associations may freely exercise their religious functions. It is forbidden to force citizens not to take part in religious activities or rites. It is also forbidden to force anyone to participate in religious activities or rites.

(2) The church is separated from the state. The principles of the relationship between church and state, and the legal and patrimonial position of religious associations are established by laws.

Article 83. (1) The Polish People's Republic guarantees its citizens freedom of speech, of the press, of assembly and gatherings, processions, and demonstrations.

(2) Making printing shops, supplies of paper, public buildings and halls, means of communication, the radio, and other essential material means available for the use of the working people and its organizations serves to realize this freedom.

Article 84. (1) With the aim of development of political, social, economic, and cultural activities of the working people of town and country, the Polish People's Republic guarantees to citizens the right of association.

(2) Political organizations, trade unions, associations of working peasants, cooperative associations, youth, women's, sports, and defense organizations, cultural, technical, and scientific associations, as well as other social organizations of the working people, unite the citizens for active participation in political, social, economic, and cultural life.

(3) The creation of associations and participation in associations whose aim or activities are directed against the political and social system or against the legal order of the Polish People's Republic are forbidden.

Article 85. A distinguished social role is played in the Polish People's Republic by trade unions, which are the universal organization which participates in the formulation and realization of tasks connected with the social-economic development of the country; the trade unions represent the interests and rights of the working people, and are schools of citizen activities and involvement in the building of a socialist society.

Article 86. (1) Citizens of the Polish People's Republic participate in exercising social supervision, and in consultations and discussions on the key problems relating to the development of the country, and submit proposals.

(2) Citizens enjoy the right to approach all state organs with complaints and grievances.

(3) Appeals, complaints, and grievances of citizens should be examined and settled quickly and justly. Those guilty of protraction or manifesting a soulless and bureaucratic attitude to appeals, complaints, and grievances of citizens will be held responsible.

Article 87. (1) The Polish People's Republic guarantees to citizens inviolability of the person. Deprivation of a citizen's freedom may only take place in cases specified by the law. The detained person must be set free if he has not been served an arrest warrant issued by the court or the prosecutor within 48 hours from the time of arrest.

(2) The law protects the inviolability of the home and the privacy of correspondence. The carrying out of a house search is allowable only in cases specified by the law.

(3) Loss of property may occur only in cases provided for by law, on the basis of a final judgment.

Article 88. The Polish People's Republic grants asylum to citizens of foreign countries persecuted for defending the interests of the working masses, struggling for social progress, activity in defense of peace, fighting for national liberation, or for scientific activity.

Article 89. Polish citizens abroad enjoy the protection of the Polish People's Republic.

Article 90. A citizen of the Polish People's Republic is bound by duty to abide by the provisions of the Constitution and the laws and socialist work discipline, to respect the principles of social intercourse, and to fulfill his responsibilities towards the state conscientiously.

Article 91. Every citizen of the Polish People's Republic is bound by duty to safeguard social property and to strengthen it as the unshakable foundation of the development of the state and the source of the wealth and strength of the Motherland.

Article 92. (1) Defense of the Motherland is the most sacred duty of every citizen.

(2) Military service is an honorable patriotic duty of citizens of the Polish People's Republic.

Article 93. (1) Vigilance against enemies of the state and the diligent guarding of state secrets is the duty of every citizen of the Polish People's Republic.

(2) Treason against the Motherland: spying, weakening of the armed forces, desertion to the enemy—are punishable with all the severity of the law as the gravest crime.

Chapter IX. Principles of Electoral Law

Article 94. Elections to the Seym and to the national councils are universal, equal, and direct, and are carried out by secret vote.

Article 95. Every citizen who has attained the age of 18, irrespective of sex, nationality and race, religion, education, length of residence, social origin, profession, and amount of property, enjoys the right to vote.

Article 96. Every citizen may be elected to a national council after attaining the age of 18, and to the Seym after attaining the age of 21.

Article 97. Women enjoy all electoral rights on an equal basis with men.

Article 98. Members of the armed forces enjoy all electoral rights on an equal basis with civilians.

Article 99. Electoral rights are not accorded to mentally-ill persons and persons who are deprived by court decision of public rights.

Article 100. Candidates for deputies to the Seym and for membership of the national councils are nominated by the political and social organizations in town and country.

Article 101. A deputy and member of a national council must give an account to the electors of their work and of the activities of the organ to which they were elected.

Article 102. The mode of nomination of candidates and conducting of elections and the procedure for the recall of deputies and members of national councils are established by law.

Chapter X. The Coat-of-Arms, Colors, National Anthem, and Capital of the Polish People's Republic

Article 103. (1) The coat-of-arms of the Polish People's Republic is the image of a white eagle on a red field.
(2) The colors of the Polish People's Republic are white and red.
(3) The national anthem of the Polish People's Republic is the "Dąbrowski Mazurka".
(4) Details are determined by law.

Article 104. The coat-of-arms, colors, and national anthem of the Polish People's Republic are treated with honor and are subject to special protection.

Article 105. The capital of the Polish People's Republic is the city of heroic traditions of the Polish nation—Warsaw.

Chapter XI. Amendment of the Constitution

Article 106. Amendment of the Constitution may be made only by means of an act passed by the Seym of the Polish People's Republic by a majority of at least two-thirds of votes, at least half the total number of deputies being present.

ROMANIA

INTRODUCTION

Simone-Marie Vrăbiescu Kleckner

The People's Republic of Romania[1] was proclaimed on 30 December 1947, and its Constitution promulgated on 13 April 1948.[2] This Constitution derived its pattern from the Constitutions of the Soviet Union, but preserved some neo-latin features, and thus resulted in a mixture of liberal and socialist elements.

The need for a new Constitution came about in the early 1950s, reflecting the many economic changes that took place since 1947, *i.e.* nationalization, collectivization, monetary reform, etc. This second Constitution was adopted by the Grand National Assembly of 24 September 1952.[3] It was nearly a reproduction of the 1936 Soviet Constitution where the political foundation of the country rests on the worker-peasant alliance and on the leading force of the Communist Party. The independence and sovereignty of Romania were ensured by the USSR.

Stalin's death marked a new era, bringing about a new trend of national communism in the early 1960s, which continues to this day. This phase is reflected in the third Constitution, which replaces that of 1952, adopted by the Grand National Assembly on 21 August 1965.[4]

The framework of the 1965 Constitution remains essentially that of the 1952 document, but all references to the Soviet Union are deleted. The Romanian State is described as a socialist sovereign, independent, and unitary Republic (Art. 1).

This Constitution is the one in force today, although it underwent eight amendments since 1965.[5]

The ideological, political, and economic provisions are the same—the sovereign power belongs to the people based on the worker-peasant alliance, and the leading political power is the Communist Party (Arts. 2, 3), which through mass and public organization achieves an organized link with the working class (Art. 27). The planned economy is described as such.

The rights and duties of citizens are based on the principle of equality regardless of nationality, race, sex, or religion (Art. 17). Emphasis is placed on the following rights: the right to work, to rest, to material security, to education, free use of the national language,

Introduction

equal rights of women (Arts. 17–24), the right of association, freedom of speech, press, assembly, if not used against the socialist system, freedom of conscience, inviolability of the person and domicile, secrecy of correspondence, right to petition, to personal property, inheritance, and asylum (Arts. 27–28). The duties concern observance of the Constitution, mandatory military service, and defense of the Homeland (Arts. 39–41).

The supreme bodies of state power are: the Grand National Assembly, the State Council, and the President of the Socialist Republic of Romania.

The Grand National Assembly is the supreme body of state power representing the people as a whole, having legislative power (Arts. 42 and 56) and the exclusive right to promulgate the Constitution (Art. 43, para. 1). In addition, it passes the state budget and economic plans (Art. 43, para. 3), except in case of emergency when the state Council exercises these powers as well (Art. 64, para. 1). Among other functions, it elects and recalls the other bodies of state power and other state organs, directs and controls the activity of all state bodies, regulates the electoral system, ratifies and terminates international treaties, establishes guidelines of foreign policy, and declares a state of emergency or of war (Art. 43). It meets in ordinary sessions, by State Council decree, twice a year (Art. 54), and consists of 349 deputies (Art. 44). The right to nominate candidates is vested in the Front of Socialist Unity (Art. 25). The election of deputies, from among the FSU candidates, is done by universal, equal, direct, and secret vote (Art. 25), for a five-year legislative term (Art. 44). Deputies are given immunity (Art. 61). The Grand National Assembly elects standing committees (Art. 52) and exercises its control over the constitutionality of the laws through the Constitutional and Judicial Committees (Art. 53).

The State Council is the supreme body of state power with permanent activity (Art. 62), is elected by the Grand National Assembly from among its members (Art. 65), and is responsible to it (Art. 70). In 1974, a part of its functions were conferred on the President of the Socialist Republic who is also the President of the State Council (Art. 66). On a permanent basis, among others, the State Council convenes the Grand National Assembly, organizes the Ministries and other state bodies, and ratifies those treaties which do not imply amendment of laws (Art. 63). On a temporary basis between the sessions of the Grand National Assembly, it has the power of appointment, grants amnesty, and declares partial or total mobilization in case of emergency (Art. 64).

The President of the Socialist Republic of Romania is the chief of state (Art. 71), Commander-in-Chief of the Armed Forces (Art. 74), and represents state power in domestic affairs and international relations. He is elected by the Grand National Assembly (Art. 72) and is responsible for his entire activity to it (Art. 76). He has the power of appointment, grants honors, pardons, citizenship, and asylum, proclaims a state of emergency, concludes international treaties, and issues decrees and decisions (Art. 75).

The central and local bodies of state administration represent the Government.

The Council of Ministers is the supreme body of state administration elected by the Grand National Assembly and responsible to it (Arts. 77–85).

The People's Councils are local bodies representing state power in territorial-administrative units, and are aimed at the decentralization of administration (Arts. 86–100).

The judicial organs' main characteristic is to protect the social system (Art. 102). Justice is rendered by the Supreme Court, county and local courts, and the military courts (Art. 101). The Supreme Court is appointed by the Grand National Assembly (Art. 105) and is responsible to it (Art. 106). Judges are governed by law (Art. 108).

The public prosecutor's office is headed by an Attorney General, appointed by the Grand National Assembly (Art. 114), responsible to it, and, between its sessions, to the State Council (Art. 115).

NOTES

1. After the two principalities of Wallachia and Moldavia united under the name of Romania in 1861, the first Romanian Constitution was promulgated in July 1866. After World War I, when the kingdom of Romania recovered its territories, a second Constitution was promulgated on 23 March 1923. A third Constitution was adopted on 20 February 1938, but was suspended in 1940 when the 1923 Constitution was reinstated on 12 September 1944.

2. *Official Monitor* No. 47 bis, (April 1948?).

3. *Buletinul Oficial al Republicii Socialiste România* No. 1, 27 September 1952.

4. *Buletinul Oficial al Republicii Socialiste România*, Partea I, No. 1, 21 August 1965.

5. —Law No. 1, 1968 (*Bul. Ofic.* No. 16, 16 February 1968) amended the provisions regarding the territorial-administrative units and the organization of the central and local bodies of state power.

— Law No. 56, 1968 (*Bul. Ofic.* No. 168, 26 December 1968) increased the autonomy of the People's Councils while preserving a close collaboration with the central bodies on problems of general interest.

— Law No. 1, 1969 (*Bul. Ofic.* No. 31, 13 March 1969) increased the attributions of the standing committees of the Grand National Assembly and enlarged the composition of the State Council.

— Law No. 26, 1971 (*Bul. Ofic.* No. 157, 17 December 1971) enlarged the composition of the Permanent Bureau of the Council of Ministers.

— Law No. 1, 1972 (*Bul. Ofic.* No. 41, 24 April 1972) increased the duration of the Grand National Assembly legislature and the term of the People's Councils from 4 to 5 years.

— Law No. 1, 1972 (*Bul. Ofic.* No. 41, 24 April 1972) increased the Constitution by creating a new body of state power: the President of the Socialist Republic of Romania.

— Law No. 66, 1974 (*Bul. Ofic.* No. 161, 23 December 1974) included the creation of a new permanent and representative body of all mass and public organizations: the Front of Socialist Unity; it changed the composition of the State Council, Council of Ministers and People's Councils.

— Law No. 2, 1975 (*Bul. Ofic.* No. 30, 21 March 1975) changed the Constitutional Committee of the Grand National Assembly into the Constitutional and Judicial Committee, increasing its power of control over the constitutionality of the laws. It analyses among other institutions, the activity of the Ministry of Justice, the Supreme Court and the Public Prosecutor's Office.

CONSTITUTION OF THE SOCIALIST REPUBLIC OF ROMANIA OF 21 AUGUST 1965 (AS AMENDED)

The Socialist Republic of Romania	318
The Fundamental Rights and Duties of Citizens	321
The Supreme Bodies of State Power	325
The Grand National Assembly	325
The State Council	330
The President of the Socialist Republic of Romania	332
Central Bodies of State Administration	334
The Local Bodies of State Power and Local Bodies of State Administration	336
Judicial Organs	339
Organs of the Public Prosecutor's Office	340
Insignia of the Socialist Republic of Romania	341
Final Provisions	342

CONSTITUTION OF THE SOCIALIST REPUBLIC OF ROMANIA*

Buletinul Oficial al Republicii Socialiste România,
Partea I, No. 1, 21 August 1965 (as amended).
Consolidated text in *Buletinul Oficial*, No. 167, 27 December 1974,
and subsequent amendment in
Buletinul Oficial, No. 30, 21 March 1975.

Chapter I. The Socialist Republic of Romania

Article 1. Romania is a socialist republic. The Socialist Republic of Romania is a sovereign, independent, and unitary state of the working people from cities and villages. Its territory is inalienable and indivisible.

Article 2. In the Socialist Republic of Romania, the entire power belongs to the people, free and master of its fate.

The people's power is based upon the worker-peasant alliance. Closely united, the working class—the society's leading class, the peasantry, the intellectuals, and the other categories of working people regardless of nationality, are building the socialist system and creating the conditions for the transition to communism.

Article 3. In the Socialist Republic of Romania, the leading political power of the society as a whole is the Romanian Communist Party.

Article 4. The people, the sovereign holder of power, exercise it through the Grand National Assembly and the People's Councils, bodies elected by universal, equal, direct, and secret vote.

The Grand National Assembly and the People's Councils constitute the basis for the entire system of state bodies.

The Grand National Assembly is the supreme body of state power, under whose direction and control all the other state bodies conduct their activities.

Article 5. The Romanian national economy is a socialist economy based on socialist ownership over the means of production.

*Translated by Simone-Marie Vrăbiescu Kleckner.

In the Socialist Republic of Romania, exploitation of man by man is abolished forever, and the socialist principle of distribution is carried out in accordance with the quantity and quality of work.

Work is a duty of honor for every citizen of the country.

Article 6. Socialist ownership over the means of production is either state ownership—over goods owned by the people as a whole, or cooperative ownership—over goods owned by each cooperative organization.

Article 7. The wealth of the subsoil whatever its nature, the mines, the state-landed properties, the forests, the waters, the natural energy sources, the factories and plants, the banks, the state farms, the stations for agricultural mechanization, the means of communication, the state means of transportation and communication, the state buildings and dwellings, and the property of the sociocultural state institutions belong to the people as a whole and are state property.

Article 8. Foreign trade is a state monopoly.

Article 9. The land, livestock, tools, installations, and constructions owned by the agricultural cooperatives of production are cooperative property.

The plot of land used by the households of cooperative farmers is cooperative property according to the Rules of the Agricultural Cooperatives of Production.

The dwelling and annex buildings, the land on which they stand, as well as the productive livestock and the small agricultural inventory are the personal property of the cooperative farmers according to the Rules of the Agricultural Cooperatives.

The tools, machines, installations, and constructions of the handicraft cooperatives and of the consumers' cooperatives are cooperative property.

Article 10. The agricultural cooperatives of production, being a socialist system of agricultural organization, ensure the conditions for intensive farming and the application of advanced science, and contribute to the development of the national economy by increasing output, and to the continuous improvement of the standard of living of the peasantry and of the people as a whole.

The state assists the agricultural cooperatives of production and protects their property. Likewise, the state assists the other cooperative organizations and protects their property.

Article 11. In the system of cooperative agriculture, the state guarantees the peasants who cannot associate themselves with agricultural cooperatives of production, the ownership over the land they farm themselves with their families, over the tools used for these purposes, as well as over productive and labor animals.

Likewise, craftsmen are guaranteed ownership over their own workshops.

Article 12. Land and buildings may only be expropriated for works of public interest and for an adequate amount of compensation.

Article 13. In the Socialist Republic of Romania, all state activity is aimed at the development of the system and the prosperity of the socialist nation, the continual rise of material and cultural well-being, the assurance of liberty and human dignity, and the multilateral assertion of the human personality.

For these purposes, the Romanian Socialist State:

organizes, plans, and directs the national economy;

protects socialist property;

guarantees in full the exercise of human rights, ensures socialist legality, and protects the rule of law;

expands education at all levels, ensures conditions for the promotion of science, the arts, and culture, and carries out the protection of public health;

ensures the country's defense and organizes its armed forces;

organizes relations with other countries.

Article 14. The Socialist Republic of Romania maintains and promotes friendly relations and fraternal collaboration with socialist states in the spirit of socialist internationalism, promotes relations of collaboration with countries having other socio-political systems, and is active in international organizations in order to promote peace and understanding among people.

The foreign relations of the Socialist Republic of Romania are based on the principles of respect for sovereignty and national independence, equal rights and mutual advantage, and noninterference in internal affairs.

Article 15. The territory of the Socialist Republic of Romania is organized in territorial-administrative units: counties, cities, and communes.

The capital of the Socialist Republic of Romania is the Municipality of Bucharest, which is organized in districts.

The main cities may be organized as municipalities.

Article 16. Romanian citizenship shall be acquired and forfeited as prescribed by law.

Chapter II. The Fundamental Rights and Duties of Citizens

Article 17. The citizens of the Socialist Republic of Romania, regardless of nationality, race, sex, or religion, have equal rights in all fields of economic, political, judicial, social, and cultural life.

The state guarantees the equality of rights to citizens. No restriction of these rights and no difference in their exercise is permitted on the grounds of nationality, race, sex, or religion.

Any attempt aiming to establish such restrictions, any nationalist-chauvinist propaganda, and the fomentation of racial or national hatred are punished by law.

Article 18. In the Socialist Republic of Romania, the citizens have the right to work. Each citizen is given the possibility to exercise an activity in the economic, administrative, social, or cultural field according to his training, and to be remunerated in accordance with its quantity and quality. For equal work there is equal pay.

Measures for the protection and security of labor, as well as special measures for the protection of the working women and youth are established by law.

Article 19. The citizens of the Socialist Republic of Romania have the right to rest.

The right to rest is guaranteed to those who work by establishing the maximum duration of a working day at eight hours, a weekly rest, and annual paid vacations.

In the areas of hard work or very hard work, the working day is reduced to less than eight hours without any reduction in pay.

Article 20. The citizens of the Socialist Republic of Romania have the right to be insured for old age, illness, or disability.

The right to insurance is provided for workers and public employees through pensions and illness compensation paid by the state social insurance system, and for members of cooperative organizations or other public organizations through the insurance established by these organizations. The state provides medical assistance through its health units.

Paid maternity leave is guaranteed.

Article 21. The citizens of the Socialist Republic of Romania have the right to education.

The right to education is ensured through general compulsory education, through free education at all levels, as well as through the system of state scholarships.

Education in the Socialist Republic of Romania is state education.

Article 22. In the Socialist Republic of Romania, the co-inhabiting nationalities are ensured the free use of their native language, as well as books, newspapers, magazines, theaters, and education at all levels in their own language. In the territorial-administrative units also inhabited by population other than Romanian, all bodies and institutions shall also use, orally or in writing, the language of the respective nationality and shall appoint public employees from among them or other citizens who know the language and the way of life of the local population.

Article 23. In the Socialist Republic of Romania, women have equal rights with men.

The state protects marriage and the family, and defends the interests of mother and child.

Article 24. The Socialist Republic of Romania ensures to youth the necessary conditions for the development of their intellectual and physical aptitudes.

Articles 25. The citizens of the Socialist Republic of Romania have the right to vote and to be elected to the Grand National Assembly and the People's councils.

Voting is universal, equal, direct, and secret. All citizens having reached eighteen years of age have the right to vote.

Citizens with voting rights who reach twenty-three years of age may be elected deputies to the Grand National Assembly and to the People's Councils.

The right to nominate candidates is vested in the Front of Socialist Unity, the largest permanent political body, which, having a representative character, is revolutionary and democratic, and constitutes the framework of organized unity under the leadership of the Romanian Communist Party of the political and social forces of our socialist nation, and of all the mass and public organizations for the participation of the people as a whole in the implementation of the Party and state domestic and foreign policy, and for the conduct of all fields of activity.

The electors have the right to recall anytime their deputy in accordance with the procedure prescribed by law.

The mentally handicapped or deficient people, as well as persons deprived of rights for the period of time established by the sentence of a court decision, do not have the right to vote or to be elected.

Article 26. The most advanced and conscientious citizens from among workers, peasants, intellectuals, and other categories of working people join in the Romanian Communist Party, the highest form of organization of the working class, its vanguard detachment.

The Romanian Communist Party expresses and faithfully serves the aspirations and vital interests of the people, performs the role of leader in all fields in the construction of socialism, and directs the activity of mass and public organizations, as well as that of the state bodies.

Article 27. The citizens of the Socialist Republic of Romania have the right to associate themselves in trade unions, cooperatives, youth, women's, and socio-cultural organizations, and in creative unions, scientific, technical, and sports associations, as well as in other public organizations.

The state assists the activity of mass and public organizations, and creates conditions for the development of the material basis of those organizations and protects their property.

The mass and public organizations ensure broad participation of the popular masses in the political, economic, social, and cultural life of the Socialist Republic of Romania, and in the exercise of public control—an expression of democratic spirit of the socialist system. Through the mass and public organizations, the Romanian Communist Party creates an organized link with the working class, the peasantry, the intellectuals, and other categories of working people by mobilizing them in the struggle for the accomplishment of the building of socialism.

Article 28. The citizens of the Socialist Republic of Romania are guaranteed the freedom of speech, of the press, of reunion, of meeting, and of demonstration.

Article 29. The freedom of speech, of the press, of reunion, of meeting, and of demonstration cannot be used for purposes against the socialist system and the interest of the workers.

Any association of a fascist or anti-democratic character is prohibited. Participation in such associations and propaganda of a fascist or anti-democratic character are punished by law.

Article 30. The freedom of belief is guaranteed to all citizens of the Socialist Republic of Romania.

Anybody is free to share or not to share a religious belief. The freedom to practice a religious cult is guaranteed. Religious cults shall freely organize and function. Religious cults' means of organization and management are regulated by law.

The school is separate from the church. No religious confession, congregation, or community can open or maintain any other teaching institution than the special schools for the training of the servants of the church.

Article 31. The citizens of the Socialist Republic of Romania are guaranteed the inviolability of the person.

No person can be detained or arrested if there is no evidence or real indication that he or she has committed an act proscribed and punished by law. The investigating organs may decide on the retention of a person for a maximum period of twenty-four hours. No one can be arrested, except on the basis of a warrant of arrest issued by the court or public prosecutor.

The right of defense is guaranteed throughout the trial.

Article 32. The domicile is inviolable. No one can enter the home of a person without consent, except in the cases and in the conditions specially provided for by law.

Article 33. The secrecy of correspondence and telephone conversations is guaranteed.

Article 34. The right to petition is guaranteed. The state bodies have the obligation to resolve citizens' petitions regarding their personal or public rights and interests.

Article 35. Persons injured in one of his or her rights by an illegal act of a state organ may ask the competent bodies for the annulment of the act and reparation for the damage caused in accordance with the conditions prescribed by law.

Article 36. The right to possess personal property is protected by law.

Objects of personal property consist of the income and savings derived from work, the dwelling house, the out-buildings, and the land on which they are built, as well as goods of personal use and comfort.

Article 37. The right to inheritance is protected by law.

Article 38. The Socialist Republic of Romania grants the right of asylum to foreign citizens persecuted for their activity in the defense of the interests of workers, for their participation in the struggle for national self-determination or in defense of peace.

Article 39. Every citizen of the Socialist Republic of Romania is bound to observe the Constitution and the laws, to defend the socialist property, and to contribute to the strengthening and development of the socialist system.

Article 40. Military service within the ranks of the Armed Forces of the Socialist Republic of Romania is mandatory and constitutes a duty of honor for the citizens of the Socialist Republic of Romania.

Article 41. To defend the homeland is the sacred duty of each citizen of the Socialist Republic of Romania. Violation of the military oath, treason of the homeland, desertion to the enemy, and injury caused to the state's capacity of defense constitute capital offenses against the people and are punished with utmost severity by law.

Chapter III. The Supreme Bodies of State Power

The Grand National Assembly

Article 42. The Grand National Assembly, the supreme body of state power, is the sole legislative body of the Socialist Republic of Romania.

Article 43. The Grand National Assembly has the following main functions:

(1) adopts and amends the Constitution of the Socialist Republic of Romania;

(2) regulates the electoral system;

(3) adopts the single national plan of economic and social development, the state budget, and the general final account of the budgetary period;

(4) organizes the Council of Ministers; establishes the general norms of organization and functioning of the ministries and the other central state bodies;

(5) regulates the administration of justice and the Public Prosecutor's Office;

(6) establishes the norms of organization and functioning of the People's Councils;

(7) establishes the administrative organization of the territory;

(8) grants amnesty;

(9) ratifies and terminates international treaties that imply amendment of laws;

(10) elects and dismisses the President of the Socialist Republic of Romania;

(11) elects and recalls the State Council;

(12) elects and recalls the Council of Ministers;

(13) elects and recalls the Supreme Court and the Prosecutor General;

(14) exercises general control over the implementation of the Constitution. The Grand National Assembly solely controls the constitutionality of the laws;

(15) controls the activity of the President of the Socialist Republic of Romania and of the State Council;

(16) controls the activity of the Council of Ministers, of the ministries, and of the other central bodies of state administration;

(17) hears reports concerning the Supreme Court's activity and controls its directives;

(18) controls the activity of the Public Prosecutor's Office;

(19) exercises general control over the activity of the People's Councils;

(20) establishes the general guideline of foreign policy;

(21) proclaims a state of emergency in the interest of the country's defense, public order, or security of the state in some localities or throughout the entire territory of the country;

(22) declares partial or general mobilization;

(23) declares a state of war. A state of war can only be declared in the case of armed aggression directed against the Socialist Republic of Romania or against another state towards which the Socialist Republic of Romania has mutual defense obligations arising from international treaties, if the situation for which the obligation to declare the state of war has occurred as stipulated.

Article 44. The deputies of the Grand National Assembly are elected by constituencies having the same number of inhabitants. The establishment of the constituencies is determined by a State Council decree.

Each constituency elects one deputy.

The Grand National Assembly consists of three hundred and forty-nine deputies.

Article 45. The Grand General Assembly is elected for a five-year legislative term.

The Grand National Assembly's mandate cannot be discontinued prior to the adjournment of the legislative term for which it has been elected. The mandate expires on the date when the election for a new Grand National Assembly is being held.

In case circumstances arise to prevent elections, the Grand National Assembly may decide to extend its mandate throughout the duration of those circumstances.

Article 46. The elections for the Grand National Assembly are held on one of the non-working days of the month of March of the year in which the prior legislative term expired. In the case provided for in paragraph three of Article 45, elections are held within the following two months from the expiration of the legislative term for which the mandate of the Grand National Assembly has been extended.

The newly-elected Grand National Assembly is convened during the following three months after the mandate of the prior Grand National Assembly has expired.

Article 47. The Grand National Assembly verifies the legality of each deputy's election, deciding upon validation or annulment.

In the case of annulment of an election, the deputy's rights and duties cease from the moment of annulment.

Article 48. The Grand National Assembly adopts its rules of procedure.

Article 49. The Grand National Assembly establishes its annual budget, which is included in the state budget.

Article 50. The Grand National Assembly elects for the duration of its legislative term the Bureau of the Grand National Assembly, consisting of the President of the Grand National Assembly and four Vice-Presidents.

Article 51. The President of the Grand National Assembly conducts the proceedings of the Grand National Assembly's sessions.

The President of the Grand National Assembly may designate any of the Vice-Presidents to fulfill some of his functions.

Article 52. The Grand National Assembly elects standing committees from among the deputies.

The standing committees examine or debate bills, decrees, decisions, or any other legal instruments to be adopted, as well as any other matters at the request of the Grand National Assembly or of the State Council.

Likewise, at the request of the Grand National Assembly or of the State Council, the standing committees, each in accordance with its competence, hear periodically or by topics the reports submitted by the heads of any bodies of state administration, of the Supreme Court and Public Prosecutor's Office on the activities of these bodies, as well as the reports of the presidents of the executive committees or executive bureaus of the People's Councils on the activities of these councils, and analyze the way in which the above-mentioned bodies carry out the Romanian Communist Party's policy and ensure the enforcement of the law.

The committees submit reports, opinions, or proposals in connection with all the matters mentioned in paragraphs two and three to the Grand National Assembly or to the State Council.

The Grand National Assembly may elect temporary committees for any matter or activity, establishing the authority and nature of activity for each of these committees.

All state bodies and employees have the duty to submit the requested information or documentation to the committees of the Grand National Assembly.

Article 53. The Grand National Assembly elects a Constitutional and Judicial Committee for the duration of its legislative term to exercise control over the constitutionality of the laws, as well as over the preparation for the adoption of laws.

Experts who are not deputies can be elected to the Constitutional and Judicial Committee, although not exceeding one-third of the total membership of the Committee.

The Constitutional and Judicial Committee submits reports or opinions regarding the constitutionality of the laws to the Grand National Assembly. Likewise, it controls the constitutionality of the decrees, which include provisions having the force of law, and the decisions of the Council of Ministers in accordance with the Rules of Procedure of the Grand National Assembly.

The provisions of Article 52 apply equally to the Constitutional and Judicial Committee.

Article 54. The Grand National Assembly conducts business in sessions.

The Grand National Assembly's regular sessions are convened at the proposal of the Bureau of the Grand National Assembly twice a year.

The Grand National Assembly is, whenever necessary, convened in special sessions at the initiative of the State Council, the Bureau of the Grand National Assembly, or of at least one-third of the total number of deputies.

The sessions of the Grand National Assembly are convened by State Council decree.

Article 55. The Grand National Assembly operates if at least one-half plus one of the total number of deputies is present.

Article 56. The Grand National Assembly adopts laws and decisions.

The laws and decisions take effect if adopted by a majority vote of the Grand National Assembly's deputies.

The Constitution is adopted and amended by the vote of at least two-thirds of the total number of the Grand National Assembly's deputies.

The Grand National Assembly's laws and decisions are signed by the President or Vice-President of the Grand National Assembly who conducts the meeting.

Article 57. After their adoption by the Grand National Assembly, the laws are signed by the President of the Socialist Republic of Romania and published in the Official Bulletin of the Socialist Republic of Romania within a maximum of ten days.

Article 58. Each deputy of the Grand National Assembly has the right to question and address interpellations to the Council of Ministers or to any of its members.

Within the framework of the control exercised by the Grand National Assembly, a deputy may question and address interpellations to the President of the Supreme Court and the Attorney General.

The person receiving a question or an interpellation has the obligation to reply orally or in written form within a maximum of three days, and in any event during the same session.

Article 59. In view of the preparation for the debates in the Grand National Assembly or of the interpellations, the deputy has the right to ask necessary information from any state body through the Bureau of the Grand National Assembly.

Article 60. Each deputy has the obligation to periodically submit to his electors reports of his activity and that of the Grand National Assembly.

Article 61. No deputy of the Grand National Assembly can be detained, arrested, or tried for a criminal matter without prior consent of either the Grand National Assembly during a session, or of the State Council between sessions.

A deputy may be detained without consent only in the case of a flagrant offense.

The State Council

Article 62. The State Council of the Socialist Republic of Romania is the supreme body of state power with a permanent activity and is subordinate to the Grand National Assembly.

Article 63. The State Council permanently exercises the following main functions:
  (1) establishes the election date for the Grand National Assembly and the People's Councils;
  (2) organizes the ministries and the other central state bodies;
  (3) ratifies and terminates international treaties, with the exception of those whose ratification is incumbent on the Grand National Assembly;
  (4) establishes military ranks;
  (5) institutes decorations and honorary titles.

Article 64. The State Council exercises, between the Grand National Assembly's sessions, the following main functions:
  (1) establishes norms having the force of law without, however,

being able to amend the Constitution. The norms having the force of law are submitted for debate in the next session of the Grand National Assembly in accordance with the rules of procedure for the enactments of laws. The State Council can adopt the sole national plan of economic and social development, the state budget, as well as the general final account for the budgetary period only when the Grand National Assembly cannot convene due to exceptional circumstances;

(2) appoints and dismisses the Prime Minister;

(3) appoints and recalls the Council of Ministers and the Supreme Court when the Grand National Assembly cannot convene due to exceptional circumstances;

(4) interprets in a general mandatory way the laws in force;

(5) grants amnesty;

(6) controls the enforcement of laws and decisions of the Grand National Assembly, the activity of the Council of Ministers, and of the ministries and other central bodies of state administration, as well as the activity of the Public Prosecutor's Office; hears the reports of the Supreme Court and controls its directives; controls the decisions of the People's Councils;

(7) declares partial or total mobilization in case of emergency;

(8) declares a state of war in case of emergency;

A state of war can only be declared in case of armed aggression against the Socialist Republic of Romania or against another state towards which the Socialist Republic of Romania has mutual defense obligations arising from international treaties, if the situation for which the obligation to declare the state of war has occurred as stipulated.

The functions provided for in this Article can be exercised by the State Council when the Grand National Assembly is in session, but is not convened at a plenary level, and economic and social activities call for an immediate adoption of measures; the adopted norms having force of law are submitted to the Grand National Assembly for debate in accordance with the rules of procedure for the enactment of laws upon the resumption of the activities at a plenary level.

Article 65. The State Council is elected by the Grand National Assembly from among its members during the first session of the legislative term. The State Council functions until the new State Council is elected during the following legislative term.

Article 66. The President of the Socialist Republic of Romania is the President of the State Council.

Article 67. The State Council consists of a President, Vice-Presidents, and members.

Article 68. The State Council functions according to the principle of collective leadership.

Article 69. The State Council issues decrees and adopts decisions.

The decrees and decisions are signed by the President of the Socialist Republic of Romania. The normative decrees are published in the Official Bulletin of the Socialist Republic of Romania.

Article 70. The State Council submits to the Grand National Assembly reports on the exercise of its functions, as well as on the observance and enforcement of laws and decisions adopted by the Grand National Assembly for the entire state activity.

The State Council as a whole and each of its members are responsible to the Grand National Assembly for the entire activity of the State Council.

The President of the Socialist Republic of Romania

Article 71. The President of the Socialist Republic of Romania is the Chief of State and represents state power in domestic and international relations of the Socialist Republic of Romania.

Article 72. The President of the Socialist Republic of Romania is elected by the Grand National Assembly for the duration of its legislative term in its first session and remains in office until the election of the President in the next legislative term.

Article 73. Upon this election, the President of the Socialist Republic of Romania takes the following oath of office before the Grand National Assembly:

> "I swear to faithfully serve the Homeland, to act firmly to defend the independence, sovereignty, and integrity of the country, for the well-being and happiness of the people as a whole, and for building socialism and communism in the Socialist Republic of Romania.
>
> I swear to abide by and defend the Constitution and the laws of the country, and to do my utmost for the consistent implementation of the principles of socialist democracy, and for asserting the standards of socialist ethics and equity in the society's life.
>
> I swear to continuously promote the foreign policy of friendship and alliance with all socialist states, of collaboration based on total equal rights with all nations

of the world regardless of their social system, of solidarity with progressive revolutionary forces throughout the world, and of peace and friendship among nations.

I swear to always perform my duty with honor and devotion for the glory and greatness of our socialist nation, the Socialist Republic of Romania."

Article 74. The President of the Socialist Republic of Romania is the Commander-in-Chief of the Armed Forces and President of the Defense Council of the Socialist Republic of Romania.

Article 75. The President of the Socialist Republic of Romania performs, in conformity with the Constitution and the laws, the following main functions:

(1) presides over the State Council;

(2) presides over the meetings of the Council of Ministers when necessary;

(3) appoints and dismisses, at the proposal of the Prime Minister, the Deputy Prime Ministers and the ministers and chiefs of other central bodies of state administration who are part of the Council of Ministers; appoints and dismisses the chiefs of central state bodies who are not members of the Council of Ministers; appoints and dismisses the members of the Supreme Court;

(4) appoints and dismisses the President of the Supreme Court and the Attorney General, when the Grand National Assembly is not convened at a plenary level;

(5) confers the ranks of general, admiral, and marshal;

(6) awards decorations and titles of honor; authorizes the wearing of decorations conferred by other countries;

(7) grants pardon;

(8) grants citizenship, and approves the waiver and the withdrawal of Romanian citizenship; approves the establishment of domicile in Romania of citizens of other states;

(9) grants the right of asylum;

(10) determines the ranks for diplomatic missions, and accredits and recalls the diplomatic representatives of the Socialist Republic of Romania;

(11) receives the credentials or notifications of departure of foreign diplomatic representatives;

(12) concludes international treaties on behalf of the Socialist Republic of Romania; for this purpose, he may delegate his power to the Prime Minister, or to members of the Council of Ministers, or to some diplomatic representatives;

(13) proclaims, in case of urgency, a state of emergency in some localities or throughout the entire territory of the country, in order

to defend the Socialist Republic of Romania, and to ensure public order or the security of the state.

The President of the Socialist Republic of Romania, in exercising his duties, issues presidential decrees or decisions.

Article 76. The President of the Socialist Republic of Romania is responsible for his entire activity to the Grand National Assembly.

The President of the Socialist Republic of Romania periodically submits reports regarding the exercise of his duties and the development of the state to the Grand National Assembly.

Chapter IV. Central Bodies of State Administration

Article 77. The Council of Ministers is the supreme body of state administration.

The Council of Ministers generally directs executive activity for the entire territory of the state and has the following main functions:

(1) establishes general measures for the achievement of domestic and foreign policy;

(2) decides upon the necessary measures to organize and ensure the enforcement of laws:

(3) directs, coordinates, and controls the activity of the ministries and the other central bodies of state administration;

(4) elaborates on the draft of the single national plan of economic and social development, on the state budget, as well as any other bills; elaborates on draft decrees;

(5) establishes measures for the achievement of the single plan of economic and social development and of the state budget; draws up the general report regarding the achievement of the single national plan of economic and social development, and the general final account of the budgetary period;

(6) establishes economic organizations, enterprises, and state institutions of national interest;

(7) takes measures to ensure the public order, to defend the interest of the state, and to protect human rights;

(8) takes measures for the general organization of the Armed Forces and the establishment of the annual enrollments of citizens due to perform their military service in accordance with the decisions of the Defense Council;

(9) exerts general leadership in the area of international relations, and takes measures for the conclusion of international agreements;

(10) supports the activity of mass and public organizations;

(11) exerts its leadership and control over the activity of the executive committees and executive bureaus of the People's Councils in accordance with provisions provided for by law.

Article 78. The Council of Ministers is elected by the Grand National Assembly, in its first session, for the duration of the legislative term. The Council of Ministers functions until the election of the new Council of Ministers in the next legislative term.

Article 79. In exercising its functions, the Council of Ministers adopts decisions on the basis and for the purpose of enforcement of the laws.

Decisions having a normative character are published in the Official Bulletin of the Socialist Republic of Romania.

Article 80. The Council of Ministers consists of: the Prime Minister, Vice Prime Ministers, ministers, ministers state-secretaries, and chiefs of other central bodies of state administration as provided for by law.

Likewise, the President of the Central Council of the General Confederation of Trade Unions, the President of the National Union of the Cooperatives of Agricultural Production, the President of the Women's National Council, and the First Secretary of the Central Committee of the Union of Communist Youth are part of the Council of Ministers as members.

Article 81. The Council of Ministers functions according to the principle of collective leadership, thereby ensuring the unity of the political and administrative activity of the ministries and of other central bodies of state administration.

Article 82. The Council of Ministers as a whole and each of its members is responsible to the Grand National Assembly, except during the period between sessions when it is responsible to the State Council. Each member of the Council of Ministers is responsible for his own activity, as well as for the entire activity of the Council.

Article 83. The ministries and the other central bodies of state administration implement state policy in the branches or fields of activity for which they have been established.

They direct, guide, and control the enterprises, economic organizations and state institutions subordinate to them.

Article 84. The ministers and chiefs of the other central bodies of state administration issue instructions and orders, as well as other acts as provided for by law, on the basis of the laws and decisions of the Council of Ministers with a view towards their enforcement; their acts, having a normative character, shall be published in the Official Bulletin of the Socialist Republic of Romania.

Article 85. The ministers and chiefs of other central bodies of state administration are responsible for the activity of the bodies they direct to the Council of Ministers.

Chapter V. The Local Bodies of State Power and Local Bodies of State Administration

Article 86. The People's Councils are the local bodies of state power within the territorial administrative units in which they have been elected.

The People's Councils direct local activity by ensuring the economic, socio-cultural, and administrative-urbanistic development, the defense of socialist ownership, the protection of human rights, socialist legality and the maintenance of public order of the territorial units in which they have been elected.

The People's Councils organize the participation of the citizens in the process of solving state and public affairs on a local level.

Article 87. The People's Council performs the following main functions:

(1) adopts the local budget and economic plan, approves the final account of the budgetary period;

(2) appoints or recalls the executive committee or bureau, as the case may be;

(3) establishes local economic organizations, state enterprises, and institutions;

(4) directs, guides, and controls the activity of the executive committee or bureau, as the case may be, of the specialized local bodies of state administration, and of economic organizations, enterprizes, and institutions under its subordination;

(5) controls the decisions of the People's Councils which are hierarchically subordinate;

(6) appoints and dismisses the judges, the people's assessors, and the county's Chief Prosecutor or the Chief Prosecutor for the Municipality of Bucharest in accordance with the law.

Article 88. The People's Councils consist of deputies elected by constituencies, one deputy elected for each constituency.

The People's Councils' constituencies, formed for the election of deputies, have the same number of inhabitants.

The term of the People's Councils for counties and for the Municipality of Bucharest is a five-year period, but for municipalities such as the districts of the Municipality of Bucharest, cities, and communes, the duration is for a two-year period.

The election date of the People's Councils shall be established by law.

Article 89. The People's Councils elect from among deputies standing committees, which assist them in the completion of their duties.

Article 90. The People's Councils work in sessions; the sessions are convened by the executive committee or bureau, as the case may be.

The People's Councils are, whenever necessary, convened in special sessions at the initiative of the executive committee or bureau, as the case may be, or of at least one-third of the total number of deputies.

Article 91. The People's Councils operate when at least one-half plus one of the total number of deputies are present.

Article 92. Each deputy has the obligation to periodically report to his electors on his activity and on that of the People's Council within his constituency.

Article 93. People's Councils adopt decisions.

A decision takes effect if adopted by a majority vote of the People's Council deputies.

Decisions having a normative character shall be communicated to the citizens as provided for by law.

Article 94. The executive committee or executive bureau of the People's Council are local bodies of state administration having general jurisdiction within the territorial-administrative unit in which the People's Council has been elected.

Article 95. The executive committee and executive bureau of the People's Council have the following main functions:

(1) enforce the laws, decrees, as well as decisions of the Council of Ministers and other acts issued by superior bodies;

(2) enforce the decisions of the People's Councils which have elected them;

(3) elaborate on the draft of the economic plan and local budget;

(4) carry out the economic plan and local budget, draw up a report regarding the achievement of the local economic plan and give the final account of the budgetary period;

(5) direct, guide, and control the activity of the specialized local bodies of state administration;

(6) direct, guide, coordinate, and control the activity of economic organizations, enterprises, and institutions under their subordination;

(7) direct, guide, and control the activity of the People's Councils' executive committee or bureau, as the case may be, hierarchically subordinate to the People's Councils which elected them.

Between the sessions of the People's Council, the executive committee or bureau, as the case may be, also carries out the functions of the Council, with the exceptions of those provided for in Article 87, paragraphs 1, 2, 4, 5, and 6, and submits the adopted decisions for ratification to the People's Council at its first session.

Article 96. The People's Councils of counties and the Municipality of Bucharest and its districts, as well as those of municipalities, elect executive committees, whereas the People's Councils of cities and communes elect executive bureaus.

The executive committee or executive bureau is elected from among the deputies of the People's Council for the duration of the term of that Council at the first session after its election.

After the expiration of the term of the People's Council, the executive committee or bureau, as the case may be, continues to function until the election of the new executive committee or bureau.

Article 97. The executive committee or bureau, as the case may be, of the People's Council consists of a President, one or more Vice-Presidents, and other members as prescribed by law.

Article 98. In exercising its functions, the executive committee or executive bureau issues decisions on the basis of the law for the purpose of its enforcement.

Decisions having a normative character shall be communicated to the citizens as provided for by law.

Article 99. The executive committee or executive bureau conducts its activity in accordance with the principle of collective leadership.

The executive committee or bureau, each as a whole, and each of its members are responsible to the People's Council by which they were elected, as well as to the executive committee or executive bureau of the People's Council hierarchically superior, and to the Council of Ministers.

Each member of the executive committee or executive bureau is responsible for his own activity, as well as for the entire activity of the body whose member he is.

Article 100. Besides the executive committees or bureaus, as the case may be, the People's Councils organize as prescribed by law, specialized local bodies of state administration. The local specialized bodies of state administration are subordinate both to the People's Council and the executive committee or bureau, as the case may be, as well as to the central and local bodies of state administration which are hierarchically superior.

Chapter VI. Judicial Organs

Article 101. In the Socialist Republic of Romania justice is, according to law, rendered by the Supreme Court, county courts, local courts, and military courts.

Article 102. Through adjudication, the courts protect the socialist system and human rights, educating the citizens in the spirit of respect for the law.

The courts, in imposing penal sanctions, pursue the improvement and reeducation of the offenders, as well as the prevention of the commission of new offenses.

Article 103. The courts adjudicate under their jurisdiction civil, criminal, and any other cases.

In cases specified by law, the courts exercise their control over the decisions of administrative or public bodies having jurisdictional authority.

The courts adjudicate the injured persons' claims of their damaged rights by administrative acts being able, according to the law, to rule over the legality of those acts.

Article 104. The Supreme Court exercises general control over the judicial activity of all the courts. The manner of exercising this control is established by law.

In view of a uniform application of the laws throughout the judicial activity, the Supreme Court at the plenary level issues directives.

Article 105. The Supreme Court is appointed by the Grand General Assembly for the duration of the legislative term at its first session.

The Supreme Court functions until the appointment of the new Supreme Court in the following legislative term.

Article 106. The Supreme Court is responsible for its activity to the Grand National Assembly and, between sessions, to the State Council.

Article 107. The court's administration, its jurisdiction, and rules of procedure are established by law.

The adjudication of cases in the lower courts and in military courts is achieved with the participation of the people's assessors, unless otherwise provided for by law.

Article 108. The judges and the people's assessors are appointed in accordance with the procedure established by law.

Article 109. In the Socialist Republic of Romania, the judicial proceedings are conducted in the Romanian language, ensuring the use of the national language in the territorial-administrative units also inhabited by population other than Romanian.

The parties who do not speak the language in which the judicial proceedings are conducted are given the possibility to be informed about the facts of the case through a translator, as well as the right to speak in court and to draw final conclusions in their own language.

Article 110. The adjudication is deliberated in public sessions, unless otherwise prescribed by law.

Article 111. In their judicial activity, the judges and the people's assessors are independent and only subjected to the law.

Chapter VII. Organs of the Public Prosecutor's Office

Article 112. The Public Prosecutor's Office of the Socialist Republic of Romania supervises the activity of the organs of the prosecution and of the organs enforcing the execution of the penalties, and watches, as prescribed by law, the observance of the law, the protection of the socialist system, and the rights and lawful interests of socialist organizations and of other judicial persons, as well as of the citizens.

Article 113. The chief of the Public Prosecutor's Office is the Prosecutor General. The organs of the Public Prosecutor's Office are the Prosecutor General's Office, the county and local public prosecutor's offices, and the judge advocate offices of the military courts.

The organs of the Public Prosecutor's Office are hierarchically subordinate.

Article 114. The Prosecutor General is appointed by the Grand National Assembly for the duration of the legislative term at its first session, and functions until the appointment of the new Prosecutor General in the first session of the next legislative term.

Public prosecutors are appointed as prescribed by law, with the exception of those provided for in paragraph 6 of Article 87.

Article 115. The Prosecutor General is responsible for the activity of the Public Prosecutor's Office to the Grand National Assembly and, between sessions, to the State Council.

Chapter VIII. Insignia of the Socialist Republic of Romania

Article 116. The emblem of the Socialist Republic of Romania represents wooded mountains above which the sun is rising. At the emblem's left side there is an oil derrick. The emblem is surrounded by a wreath of sheaves of wheat. At the top of the emblem there is a five-pointed star. At the bottom of the emblem, the sheaves are wrapped into a tricolor ribbon bearing the words "*Republica Socialista România*".

Article 117. The state seal bears the state emblem surrounded by the words "*Republica Socialista România*".

Article 118. The flag of the Socialist Republic of Romania bears red, yellow, and blue colors arranged vertically with a blue stripe next to the staff. The emblem of the Socialist Republic of Romania is placed in the center.

Article 119. The Grand National Assembly approves the National Anthem of the Socialist Republic of Romania.

Chapter IX. Final Provisions

Article 120. The present Constitution enters into force on the date of its adoption.

Article 121. The Constitution of 24 September 1952, as well as any legal provisions, decrees, and other normative acts contrary to the provisions of the present Constitution, are abrogated on the same date.

USSR

INTRODUCTION

William B. Simons

Provisions for the first Soviet Constitution were made in January 1918 when the third All-Russian Congress of Soviets instructed its executive committee to prepare for submission to the next congress a draft constitution of the Russian Federal Republic. Although several drafts were formulated, nothing was prepared when the fourth congress met in April 1918. The congress decided, therefore, to appoint a constitutional commission, which produced a draft constitution in early July of the same year for presentation to the fifth congress. After a few minor changes, the draft text was confirmed on 10 July 1918 by the fifth congress and entered into force on 19 July 1918. This 90-article document proclaimed the establishment of the dictatorship of the proletariat to be its fundamental task and that all central and local power in the new federal Russian Republic belonged to the Soviets of Workers', Soldiers', and Peasants' Deputies. Its first four chapters repeated the text of the Declaration of Rights of the Toiling and Exploited People, adopted at the III All-Russian Congress of Soviets in January 1918, and laid down the basic economic foundation for the establishment of socialism by, *inter alia*, nationalizing land and proclaiming the intention to transfer the means of production to state ownership. Local government under the 1918 Constitution was made up of local Soviets—whose existence in many areas preceded the adoption of the first constitution—directly elected for a term of three months (the term was extended to two years in 1921) to decide local matters; each local Soviet then elected an executive committee to deal with routine administrative matters. The central organs of state government consisted of: the All-Russian Congress of Soviets elected indirectly by provincial and large city Soviets whose competence extended to matters of the federation and questions of national importance; the Central Executive Committee (CEC) elected by the Congress of Soviets to formulate policy; and the Council of People's Commissars formed by the CEC to carry out ministerial duties. The 1918 RSFSR Constitution contained a bill of rights, which enumerated several freedoms, such as speech, press, and assembly, but denied these freedoms to those persons who used them to the detriment of the socialist revolution. A separate chapter on elections also denied class enemies of the new Soviet state the right to vote for and be elected to Soviets, and an additional chapter made provisions for recall by the electorate of their deputies. There was, however, no specific provision made in the constitution for the courts or the procuracy (attorney general).

In December 1922, Belorussia, the Ukraine, and the Transcaucasian Federation (Azerbaidzhan, Georgia, and Armenia) joined together with the RSFSR to form the Union of Soviet Socialist Republics; the first USSR Constitution became provisionally effective on 6 July 1923 and was ratified by the USSR CEC on 31 January 1924. The Constitution began with a Declaration of the Union which, though stressing the need to create a "common front of the Soviet Republics against the surrounding capitalist world", still characterized the new union as a decisive step toward the union of the toilers of all countries into a World Soviet Socialist Republic. The powers and authority of the newly-created federal state and of the constituent republics were outlined in the new Constitution, but the same basic state organization was carried over from the 1918 RSFSR fundamental law. There was no bill of rights in the 1923 text since those contained in the constitutions of the republics remained in force. The constituent republics in the USSR were also granted the right to withdraw freely from the union—a right which no republic has ever exercised but which remained a constitutional rule in the 1936 and 1977 USSR Constitutions.

In 1935, a drafting committee was formed to prepare amendments to the 1923/1924 USSR Constitution. But under Stalin's chairmanship, the committee instead produced a completely new draft Constitition which was accepted by the CEC on 11 June 1936. After a series of mass meetings where changes and amendments to the draft were proposed, the 146-article Stalin Constitution was adopted by the Congress of Soviets on 5 December 1936. One of the main reasons given for enacting a new document rather than amending the old one was the achievement of socialism in the Soviet Union and the disappearance of antagonistic classes. Socialist ownership of the means of production was no longer a constitutionally-proclaimed goal, but rather a fact reflected in the first chapter of the 1936 Constitution. A manifesto-type preamble—present in the 1918 RSFSR and 1924 USSR Constitutions—was not made part of the 1936 document. However, a bill of rights was now included in the federal constitution, retaining the provision from the earlier RSFSR text that these fundamental rights were to be exercised in the interests of the workers and to strengthen the socialist system. The Central

Executive Committee and the Congress of Soviets were replaced by a bicameral Supreme Soviet, and the state administrative structure was described in greater detail in the 1936 constitution than it had been in earlier texts. The constituent republics were renamed "union republics" and their number was increased to eleven: the Central Asian republics of Khorezm and Bokhara, which had adopted Soviet-style constitutions in 1922, joined the USSR as the Uzbek and Turkmen Republics in 1924, and the Uzbek Republic was divided in 1929 allowing its Tadzhik populace to join the USSR as the Tadzhik Republic. The 1936 Constitution provided for the splitting up of the Transcaucasian Federation into its three component parts, each becoming a separate republic in the federation, and two ethnic minority areas in Central Asia were also added to the USSR as the Kazakh and Kirgiz Republics. For the first time, the Communist Party of the Soviet Union (CPSU) was mentioned in the fundamental law, although only in two places—in Article 126 on the right of citizens to unite in public organizations, and in Article 141 on the right of organizations and societies of workers to nominate candidates for election. A separate chapter was also introduced on the courts and the procuracy. Subsequently, the 1936 Constitution was amended on several occasions, *inter alia*, to allow the constituent republics the right to conduct foreign relations and to establish military forces, and to alter the minimum age requirement for election to the Supreme Soviet (18 years in the original 1936 version, amended to 23 years in 1945). In addition, the number of union republics was increased in 1940 with the addition, to the USSR, of the three Baltic states of Latvia, Lithuania, and Estonia, plus Moldavia and Karelo-Finland (the latter lost its republican status and was made a part of the RSFSR in 1956).

In 1961, the CPSU held its XXIII Congress and adopted a revised Program. This Program was certain to have an influence upon the future development of the constitution since it stated that the dictatorship of the proletariat—"having brought about the victory of socialism and the transition of society to the full-scale construction of communism"—had served its function and was no longer necessary. The state would now become a state of the whole people—an all-people's state. The Party would continue to play a predominant role in the building of communism in the all-people's state, but at the same time public organizations, as well as the populace, would play a greater part in the administration of state and social affairs. Khrushchev had suggested amending the USSR Constitution in the late 1950s, but after fostering the theory of the all-people's state, and thus changing the political basis upon which the Soviet state was constituted, he announced the formation of a drafting committee in 1962, under his chairmanship, to prepare a new text of the fundamental law.

After Khrushchev's "retirement" in 1964, Leonid Brezhnev assumed chairmanship of the drafting committee, and in the 1960s and 1970s much speculation centered around when the new draft constitution would appear. Without much advance warning, a draft text was published on 4 June 1977, and was subject to official nationwide discussion and consideration, and an "unofficial" discussion through the medium of *samizdat* and Russian emigré publications. This discussion resulted in a reported 400,000 proposals for amendments and changes, and thereafter the Constitutional Commission recommended changes in 110 articles plus the addition of one new article. The final version of the new USSR Constitution, as reproduced in the present volume, was enacted by the USSR Supreme Soviet on 7 October 1977 and went into effect on the same day.

The 1977 Brezhnev Constitution does not break in any way with past Soviet constitutional history; indeed, the preamble, which is as notable by its presence in 1977 as it was by its absence in 1936, speaks of the preservation of the ideas and principles of the 1918 RSFSR Constitution and the 1924 and 1936 USSR Constitutions.

There is, to be sure, much that is new, or altered, or refined in the 1977 Constitution as compared with its 1936 predecessor. To begin with, the new text is longer (174 vs. 146 articles) and in general more detailed than the 1936 version. The dictatorship of the proletariat has now given way to the "socialist all-people's state", and the doctrinal purgatory of a "developed socialist society" along the road to full communism—a notion introduced into the body of Marxism-Leninism and the 1961 CPSU Program by Khrushchev—is now enshrined in the fundamental law. As a result of this progress made towards the final goal, the Soviets of Working People's Deputies have now been renamed simply Soviets of People's Deputies. The 1936 Constitution was based on the "state law" model, *i.e.* the theory that a constitution is to be reflective of the state structure prevailing at a given period. However, the 1977 Constitution appears to mark the victory of the competing "constitutional law" school, which holds that a constitution is both reflective of what has already been achieved and, at the same time, programmatic of what remains to be done, and is not limited to describing the state structure alone, but also concerns social policy and relationships. In this regard, the place of the Communist Party in the constitution has finally come to reflect its predominant role in the Soviet state and social life. The preamble tells of the CPSU's leading role in contemporary society, and both in the preamble and in the first chapter. it is referred to as the leading and guiding force in society and as the nucleus of all political and social organizations.

The nature of the Soviet political system, whose basic direction is now characterized as the "further unfolding of socialist democracy", is defined in greater detail in the 1977 Constitution: labor collectives—as participants in the discussion and resolution of state and public affairs—are mentioned for the first time, as is worker participation in certain areas of economic management through the medium of the labor collectives; another new provision lists trade unions, the Komsomol (Communist Youth League), and cooperative and other social organizations as participants in the administration of state and public affairs and in the resolution of political, economic, and socio-cultural problems; nationwide polls (referenda), formerly a prerogative of the USSR Supreme Soviet under the 1936 text, have been given a place of greater importance in the new constitution, where in Article 5 it is stated that the "most important questions of life of the state...are put to a nationwide vote (referendum)". The 1977 Constitution also mentions the drawing together of collective-farm/cooperative ownership with state ownership—a policy publicized at previous Party congresses but not found in the 1936 law. New sections have been added to the 1977 Constitution—there are now separate chapters on the political and economic systems, as well as for foreign policy and the defense of the socialist fatherland. Several provisions of the 1977 Constitution reflect the interest and involvement of the Soviet Union in contemporary world affairs: Article 29 enshrines the fundamental principles of the 1975 Helsinki Agreement, and the prohibition of war propaganda set forth in Article 28 can be directly traced to the UN Human Rights Covenants. New articles in the 1977 text speak of the right to health care, housing, and the achievements of culture, the right to participate in the administration of state and public affairs, the freedom of scientific, technical, and artistic creation (together with specific mention of protection afforded to the rights of authors, inventors, and rationalizers), and state protection of the family. In addition, citizens are now given the right to bring legal action against acts violating the law or exceeding official authority, and can also claim compensation for damages inflicted through unlawful acts of state and social organizations and officials. Judicial protection against attacks on citizens' honor and dignity, and their lives, health, and personal freedom and property is also for the first time raised to the level of a constitutional provision.

Introduction 349

Two additional changes, which might at first glance seem to be of only superficial significance, can be seen as complementing the primary position of the CPSU in the new text. Firstly, the term of office of the USSR Supreme Soviet has been extended from the previous four years to five years, and this may result in the eventual integrating of the Supreme Soviet term with that of the CPSU congresses, which are required by the Party rules to be held every five years. Secondly, the post of First Deputy Chairman of the Presidium of the USSR Supreme Soviet has been created, thereby allowing Party Secretary Brezhnev to also assume the post of Presidium President.

On the other hand, there are many principles from the 1936 Constitution which have been carried over into the 1977 law—in general, the basic political, economic, and social structure of the Soviet state remains unchanged. Although ownership of trade unions and other social organizations has been added as a third form of socialist ownership, the basic form of ownership continues to be state ownership, and remuneration for labor continues to be based on the principle of the quantity and quality of the work performed. The fundamental freedoms of speech, the press, assembly, meetings, street marches and demonstrations continue to be guaranteed insofar as they are "in accord with the interests of the people and the strengthening and development of socialist society". Similarly, although there have been minor changes in the new constitution as regards the state and federal structure of the USSR, *e.g.* the republican armed forces are no longer mentioned, and the long list of various ministries is likewise absent, the basic structure of the state apparatus and the federation remains unchanged.

SELECTED BIBLIOGRAPHY

1. *The Constitutions of the USSR and the Union Republics: Analysis, Texts, Reports* (F.J.M. Feldbrugge, ed.), Alphen aan den Rijn 1979. This work contains a parallel translation of the 1936 and 1977 USSR Constitutions, plus those portions of the 1977 draft text which were not included in the final version. It also contains a detailed analysis of the ideological, political, and legal issues in the new constitution, and translations of Brezhnev's two main speeches on the new Constitution, as well as translations of the new 1978 union republic constitutions.

2. *Encyclopedia of Soviet Law* (F.J.M. Feldbrugge, ed.), Leyden 1973.

3. "Die neue Verfassung der UdSSR", 24 *Osteuropa Recht* 1978 Nos. 1–2.

4. *Konstitutsiia razvitogo sotsializma*, Moskva 1978.

5. John N. Hazard, "A Constitution for Developed Socialism", in *Soviet Law After Stalin, Part II, Social Engineering Through Law* (D. Barry, G. Ginsburgs, P. Maggs, eds.), published as No. 22 (II) *Law in Eastern Europe* (F.J.M. Feldbrugge, ed.), Alphen aan den Rijn, The Netherlands 1978, 1–33.

6. Ivo Lapenna, "Marxism and the Soviet Constitutions", *Conflict Studies* April 1979 No. 106.

7. Pierre et Marie Lavigne, *Regards sur la Constitution soviétique de 1977*, Paris 1979.

8. P. Biscaretti di Ruffia, G. Crespi Reghizzi, *La costituzione sovietica del 1977. Un sessantennio di evoluzione costituzionale nell'URSS*, Milano 1979.

9. Robert Sharlet, *The New Soviet Constitution of 1977. Analysis and Text*, Brunswick, Ohio 1978.

10. Andrew Sorokowski, "The 1977 USSR Constitution: A Document of Social, National and International Consolidation", 1 *Hastings International and Comparative Law Review* 1978 No. 2, 325–366.

CONSTITUTION OF THE USSR OF 7 OCTOBER 1977

Preamble	352
The Political System	354
The Economic System	356
Social Development and Culture	358
Foreign Policy	360
Defense of the Socialist Fatherland	360
USSR Citizenship. The Equality of Citizens	361
The Basic Rights, Freedoms, and Obligations of Citizens of the USSR	362
The USSR—A Federal State	368
The Soviet Socialist Union Republic	370
The Autonomous Soviet Socialist Republic	371
The Autonomous Province and the Autonomous Area	372
The System and Principles of Operation of the Soviets of People's Deputies	373
The Electoral System	374
The People's Deputy	375
The Supreme Soviet of the USSR	376
The Council of Ministers of the USSR	382
The Supreme Organs of State Power and Administration of a Union Republic	385
The Supreme Organs of State Power and Administration of an Autonomous Republic	386
Local Organs of State Power and Administration	387
Courts and Arbitration	388
The Procuracy	390
The Arms, Flag, Anthem, and Capital of the USSR	391
The Operation of the Constitution of the USSR and the Procedure for its Amendment	391

CONSTITUTION (FUNDAMENTAL LAW) OF THE UNION OF SOVIET SOCIALIST REPUBLICS*

Vedomosti SSSR 1977 No. 41 item 617.

PREAMBLE

The Great Socialist October Revolution, carried out by the workers and peasants of Russia under the leadership of the Communist Party, headed by V.I. Lenin, overturned the power of the capitalists and landowners, broke the chains of oppression, established the dictatorship of the proletariat, and created the Soviet state—a state of a new type, the basic instrument to defend the revolutionary achievements and to build socialism and communism. The world-wide historical turning-point of mankind from capitalism to socialism began.

Having emerged victorious in the civil war and having repulsed imperialist intervention, Soviet power has wrought the most profound socio-economic transformations, forever put an end to the exploitation of man by man and to class antagonisms and national hostility. The association of Soviet Republics in the Union of Soviet Socialist Republics enhanced the forces and possibilities of the people of the country for the building of socialism. Public ownership of the means of production and genuine democracy for the working masses were consolidated. For the first time in the history of mankind, a socialist society was created.

The unfading feat of the Soviet people and its Armed Forces in winning an historic victory in the Great Patriotic War has become a shining manifestation of the strength of socialism. This victory strengthened the authority and the international position of the USSR and opened new favorable opportunities for the growth of the forces of socialism, national liberation, democracy, and peace throughout the world.

Continuing their creative activity, the working people of the Soviet Union have ensured the rapid and all-round development of the country and the perfection of the socialist system. The union be-

*Translated by F.J.M. Feldbrugge and William B. Simons.

tween the working class, the collective farm peasantry, and the people's intelligentsia, and the friendship between the nations and nationalities of the USSR have been consolidated. The socio-political and ideological unity of Soviet society, the leading force of which is the working class, has taken shape. Having fulfilled the tasks of the dictatorship of the proletariat, the Soviet state has become an all-people's state. The leading role of the Communist Party, the vanguard of the whole people, has grown to maturity.

A developed socialist society has been built in the USSR. At this stage, as socialism is developing on its own basis, the creative forces of the new system and the advantages of the socialist way of life are becoming more and more manifest, and the working people enjoy more and more the fruits of the great revolutionary achievements:

— a society in which powerful productive forces and a progressive science and culture have been created, and in which the well-being of the people is constantly growing and ever more and more favorable conditions for the all-round development of the individual are taking shape;

— a society of mature socialist social relationships in which, on the basis of the rapprochement of all classes and social strata, of the legal and factual equality of all nations and nationalities, and of their fraternal cooperation, a new historical community of people—the Soviet people—has taken shape;

— a society of working people—patriots and internationalists—who are to a high degree organized, ideologically committed, and conscious;

— a society in which the law of life is the concern of all for the welfare of each and the concern of each for the welfare of all;

— a society of genuine democracy, the political system of which ensures the effective administration of all public affairs, the ever more active participation of the working people in the life of the state, and the combination of genuine rights and freedoms of citizens with their obligations and responsibility towards society.

A developed socialist society is a necessary stage on the road to communism.

The highest goal of the Soviet state is the building of a classless communist society in which social communist self-government will be developed. The main tasks of the socialist all-people's state are: to create the material and technical basis of communism; to perfect socialist social relationships and their transformation into communist relationships; to rear members of a communist society; to raise the material and cultural level of the life of the working people; to ensure the security of the country; and to promote the strengthening of peace and the development of international cooperation.

The Soviet people,

guided by the ideas of scientific communism and remaining true to their revolutionary traditions,

supported by the great socio-economic and political achievements of socialism, striving towards the further development of socialist democracy,

taking into account the international position of the USSR as a component part of the world system of socialism and recognizing their international responsibility,

preserving the continuity of the ideas and principles of the first Soviet Constitution of 1918, the Constitution of the USSR of 1924, and the Constitution of the USSR of 1936,

affirm the foundations of the social system and the policies of the USSR, establish the rights, freedoms, and obligations of citizens, and the principles of organization and the aims of the socialist all-people's state, and proclaim them in this Constitution.

I. THE FOUNDATIONS OF THE SOCIAL SYSTEM AND THE POLICIES OF THE USSR

Chapter I. The Political System

Article 1. The Union of Soviet Socialist Republics is a socialist all-people's state expressing the will and the interests of the workers, the peasants, and the intelligentsia, and of the working people of all the nations and nationalities of the country.

Article 2. All power in the USSR belongs to the people.

The people exercise state power through the Soviets of People's Deputies, which constitute the political foundation of the USSR.

All other state organs are under the control of and accountable to the Soviets of People's Deputies.

Article 3. The Soviet state is organized and functions in accordance with the principle of democratic centralism: all organs of state power are elected from the lowest to the highest, they are accountable to the people, and the decisions of higher organs are binding for lower organs. Democratic centralism combines unified leadership with local initiative and creative activity and with the responsibility of every state organ and official for the tasks entrusted to them.

Article 4. The Soviet state and all its organs function on the basis of socialist legality and ensure the protection of the legal order, the interests of society, and the rights and freedoms of citizens.

State and social organizations and officials are bound to observe the Constitution of the USSR and Soviet laws.

Article 5. The most important questions of the life of the state are submitted for nationwide discussion and are also put to a nationwide vote (referendum).

Article 6. The Communist Party of the Soviet Union is the leading and guiding force of Soviet society and the nucleus of its political system and of state and social organizations. The CPSU exists for the people and serves the people.

Armed with Marxist-Leninist doctrine, the Communist Party determines the general perspective of the development of society and the course of the domestic and foreign policy of the USSR, directs the great creative activity of the Soviet people, and imparts a planned and scientifically-sound character to their struggle for the victory of communism.

All party organizations function within the framework of the Constitution of the USSR.

Article 7. In accordance with their statutory functions, trade unions, the All-Union Leninist Communist Youth League, cooperative and other social organizations participate in the administration of state and public affairs and in the resolution of political, economic, and socio-cultural problems.

Article 8. Labor collectives participate in the discussion and resolution of state and public affairs; in the planning of production and social development; in the training and placement of personnel; in the discussion and resolution of questions of the administration of enterprises and institutions, of the improvement of the conditions of labor and everyday life, and of the utilization of resources allocated for the development of production as well as for socio-cultural measures and material incentives.

Labor collectives develop socialist competition; promote the dissemination of progressive work-methods, and the strengthening of labor discipline; educate their members in the spirit of communist morality; and concern themselves with raising their political awareness, culture, and professional qualifications.

Article 9. The basic direction of the development of the political system of Soviet society is the further unfolding of socialist democracy: the ever-widening participation of citizens in the administration of the affairs of the state and of society, the perfection of the state apparatus, the growth of the activity of social organizations, the strengthening of people's control, the reinforcement of the legal basis of the life of the state and of society, the extension of publicity, and permanent consideration of public opinion.

Chapter II. The Economic System

Article 10. The foundation of the economic system of the USSR is socialist ownership of the means of production in the form of state (all-people's) and collective-farm/cooperative ownership.

Property of trade unions and other social organizations, necessary for the realization of their statutory functions, is also socialist property.

The state protects socialist ownership and creates conditions for its increase.

No one has the right to use socialist property for purposes of personal gain and other selfish purposes.

Article 11. State ownership, the common heritage of the entire Soviet people, is the basic form of socialist ownership.

The land, its mineral wealth, the waters, and the forests are within the exclusive ownership of the state. The state owns the basic means of production in industry, construction, and agriculture, the means of transportation and communication, the banks, the property of commercial, municipal, and other enterprises organized by the state, the basic municipal housing fund, as well as other property necessary for the realization of the functions of the state.

Article 12. The property of collective farms and other cooperative organizations and their associations consists of the means of production and other property necessary for the realization of their statutory functions.

The land occupied by collective farms is allocated to them for their free use and for an unlimited time.

The state promotes the development of collective-farm/cooperative ownership and its drawing together with state ownership.

Collective farms, as well as other land users, are bound to utilize land efficiently, to treat it with care, and to increase its productiveness.

Article 13. Earned income constitutes the basis of personal property of citizens of the USSR. Articles of everyday use, of personal consumption and comfort, and of the subsidiary household, a dwelling, and savings from labor may be held in personal ownership. Personal ownership of citizens and the right to its inheritance are protected by the state.

Citizens may have the use of plots of land, made available in the manner provided by law, in order to run a subsidiary household (including the keeping of livestock and fowl), to engage in fruit and vegetable gardening, and also for individual housing construction. Citizens are bound to rationally utilize the plots of land made available to them. The state and the collective farm render aid to citizens in running the subsidiary household.

Property in the personal ownership or use of citizens must not serve for the derivation of unearned income or be used to the detriment of the interests of society.

Article 14. The labor of Soviet people, free from exploitation, is the source of the growth of public wealth and of the well-being of the people and of every Soviet citizen.

In accordance with the principle of socialism: "From each according to his abilities, to each according to his work", the state supervises performance and consumption. It determines the rate of tax on income subject to taxation.

Socially useful labor and its results determine the position of man in society. The state, combining material and moral incentives, and encouraging inventiveness and a creative attitude to work, furthers the transformation of labor into the prime necessity of life of every Soviet man and woman.

Article 15. The highest goal of social production under socialism is the fullest possible satisfaction of the growing material and spiritual needs of the people.

Relying on the creative activity of working people and socialist competition, and on the achievements of scientific-technical progress, and perfecting the forms and methods of economic management, the state ensures the growth of labor productivity, the increased efficiency of production and quality of work, and a dynamic, planned, and balanced development of the national economy.

Article 16. The economic system of the USSR constitutes a single economic complex embracing all units of social production, distribution, and exchange within the territory of the country.

The economic system is managed on the basis of state plans of economic and social development, taking into account the branch and territorial principles, and combining centralized leadership with the economic independence and initiative of enterprises, associations, and other organizations. At the same time, economic accountability, profit, production costs, and other economic levers and stimuli are actively utilized.

Article 17. Individual labor activity in the sphere of trades and crafts, agriculture, serving the everyday needs of the population, as well as other forms of activity based exclusively on the individual labor of citizens and the members of their families, are permitted in the USSR in accordance with the law. The state regulates individual labor activity, ensuring its utilization in the interests of society.

Article 18. In the interests of present and future generations, the necessary measures are taken in the USSR for the protection and the scientifically-sound and rational utilization of the land and its mineral wealth, water resources, the plant and animal world, for the preservation of the purity of air and water, for safeguarding the reproduction of natural resources, and for the improvement of the human environment.

Chapter III. Social Development and Culture

Article 19. The indestructible union of workers, peasants, and the intelligentsia constitutes the social foundation of the USSR.

The state promotes the strengthening of the social homogeneousness of society, the effacement of class differences and of the essential differences between town and country and between mental and physical labor, and the all-round development and rapprochement of the nations and nationalities of the USSR.

Article 20. In accordance with the communist ideal: "The free development of each is the condition for the free development of all", the state has as its goal the expansion of the actual possibilities for citizens to apply their creative forces, abilities, and talents, and for the all-round development of the individual.

Article 21. The state concerns itself with the improvement of working conditions and labor safety and the scientific organization of labor, and with the reduction and, ultimately, with the complete elimination of heavy physical labor on the basis of the comprehensive mechanization and automation of production processes in all branches of the national economy.

Article 22. A program of transforming agricultural labor into a variety of industrial labor; of widening in rural areas the network of institutions for public education, culture, health care, trade and public catering, services for everyday needs, and public utilities; and of transforming villages into well-appointed settlements is consistently implemented in the USSR.

Article 23. On the basis of the growth of labor productivity, the state follows an unswerving course for raising the level of wages and the real income of working people.

Public funds for consumption are created in order to more fully satisfy the needs of Soviet people. The state, with the broad participation of social organizations and labor collectives, ensures the growth and the equitable distribution of these funds.

Article 24. State systems of health care, social insurance, trade and public catering, services for everyday needs, and public utilities are operated and expanded in the USSR.

The state encourages the activity of cooperative and other social organizations in all spheres of services to the population. The state promotes the development of mass physical culture and sport.

Article 25. In the USSR there exists and is continually perfected a single system of national education which ensures the general educational and professional training of citizens, serves the communist upbringing and the spiritual and physical development of young people, and prepares them for work and social activity.

Article 26. In accordance with the needs of society, the state ensures the planned development of science and the training of scientific personnel, and organizes the implementation of the results of scientific research in the national economy and in other spheres of life.

Article 27. The state concerns itself with the protection, multiplication, and broad utilization of spiritual values for the purpose of the moral and aesthetic upbringing of Soviet people and the raising of their cultural level.

The development of professional art and popular artistic creativeness receives every encouragement in the USSR.

Chapter IV. Foreign Policy

Article 28. The USSR unswervingly conducts a Leninist peace policy and stands for consolidation of the security of peoples and broad international cooperation.

The foreign policy of the USSR is directed at ensuring favorable international conditions for the building of communism in the USSR, defending the state interests of the Soviet Union, strengthening the positions of world socialism, supporting the struggle of peoples for national liberation and social progress, at preventing aggressive wars, bringing about universal and complete disarmament, and consistently implementing the principle of peaceful coexistence of states with different social systems.

In the USSR, war propaganda is forbidden.

Article 29. Relations between the USSR and other states are shaped on the basis of the observance of the principles of sovereign equality; of mutual renunciation of the use of force or the threat of force; of the inviolability of borders; of the territorial integrity of states; of the peaceful settlement of disputes; of noninterference in internal affairs; of respect for human rights and fundamental freedoms; of the equality of peoples and the right of peoples to decide their own destiny; of cooperation between states; and of the conscientious fulfillment of obligations arising from generally recognized principles and norms of international law and from treaties concluded by the USSR.

Article 30. The USSR, as a component part of the world system of socialism and the socialist commonwealth, develops and strengthens friendship, cooperation, and mutual comradely assistance with the countries of socialism on the basis of the principle of socialist internationalism, and actively participates in economic integration and in the international socialist division of labor.

Chapter V. Defense of the Socialist Fatherland

Article 31. Defense of the socialist Fatherland is one of the most important functions of the state and is a concern of the whole people.

In order to defend the socialist achievements, the peaceful labor of the Soviet people, and the sovereignty and territorial integrity of the state, the Armed Forces of the USSR have been created and universal military service has been established.

The duty of the Armed Forces of the USSR to the people is reliably to defend the socialist Fatherland and to remain in constant combat readiness, guaranteeing an instant rebuff to any aggressor.

Article 32. The state ensures the security and defense capability of the country and equips the Armed Forces of the USSR with everything they require.

The duties of state organs, social organizations, officials, and citizens in ensuring the security of the country and the strengthening of its defense capability are defined by legislation of the USSR.

II. THE STATE AND THE INDIVIDUAL

Chapter VI. USSR Citizenship. The Equality of Citizens

Article 33. A single union citizenship has been established in the USSR. Every citizen of a union republic is a citizen of the USSR.

The grounds and the procedure for acquiring and losing Soviet citizenship are defined by the Law on Citizenship of the USSR.

Citizens of the USSR abroad enjoy the defense and protection of the Soviet state.

Article 34. Citizens of the USSR are equal before the law regardless of origin, social and property status, race or nationality, sex, education, language, attitude towards religion, type and character of occupation, place of residence, and of other circumstances.

The equality of citizens of the USSR is ensured in all fields of economic, political, social and cultural life.

Article 35. Women and men in the USSR have equal rights.

The exercise of these rights is ensured by according women equal opportunities with men in receiving education and professional training, in labor, remuneration, and professional advancement, in socio-political and cultural activity, as well as by special measures for the protection of women's labor and health; by creating conditions allowing women to combine work with motherhood; by the legal protection of and by material and moral support for mother and child, including the granting of paid leave and other benefits to pregnant women and mothers; and by a gradual reduction of working time for women with young children.

Article 36. Citizens of the USSR of different races and nationalities have equal rights.

The exercise of these rights is ensured by a policy of comprehensive development and rapprochement of all nations and nationalities of the USSR, by educating citizens in the spirit of Soviet patriotism and socialist internationalism, and by the possibility to use one's native language and the languages of other peoples of the USSR.

Any direct or indirect restriction of rights whatsoever, the establishment of direct or indirect privileges for citizens on grounds of race or nationality, as well as any preaching of racial or national exclusiveness, hostility, or contempt are punished by law.

Article 37. Foreign citizens and stateless persons in the USSR are guaranteed the rights and freedoms provided for by law, including the right to apply to a court and other state organs for the protection of the personal, property, family, and other rights which belong to them.

Foreign citizens and stateless persons within the territory of the USSR are bound to respect the Constitution of the USSR and to observe Soviet laws.

Article 38. The USSR grants the right of asylum to foreigners, persecuted for defending the interests of the working people and the cause of peace, for participating in revolutionary or national liberation movements, or for progressive socio-political, scientific, or other creative activities.

Chapter VII. The Basic Rights, Freedoms, and Obligations of Citizens of the USSR

Article 39. Citizens of the USSR enjoy the full range of the socio-economic, political, and personal rights and freedoms proclaimed and guaranteed by the Constitution of the USSR and Soviet laws. The socialist system ensures the widening of rights and freedoms and the continuous improvement of the living conditions of citizens in accordance with the fulfillment of the programs of socio-economic and cultural development.

In exercising their rights and freedoms, citizens may not injure the interests of society and the state or the rights of other citizens.

Article 40. Citizens of the USSR have the right to work, that is, to guaranteed employment with remuneration in accordance with the quantity and quality of the work, and not lower than the minimum rate established by the state, including the right to choose a profession, occupation, and work in accordance with their vocation, ability, professional training, and education, taking into account the needs of society.

This right is ensured by the socialist economic system, the continuous growth of the productive forces, free professional training, the improvement of work skills, training in new fields, and the development of the systems of professional guidance and job placement.

Article 41. Citizens of the USSR have the right to rest.

This right is ensured by establishing a workweek not exceeding 41 hours for workers and employees, and a reduced workday for a number of professions and types of work, and by reduced working hours at night; by granting annual paid leave and weekly rest days, as well as by an expansion of the network of cultural-educational and health institutions and the development of mass sports, physical culture, and tourism; by the creation of favorable possibilities for rest in one's place of residence and of other conditions for a rational use of free time.

The length of working time and rest for collective farmers is regulated by the collective farms.

Article 42. Citizens of the USSR have the right to health care.

This right is ensured by free professional medical assistance provided by state health institutions; by expanding the network of institutions for medical treatment and improvement of the health of citizens; by the development and perfection of safety technology and industrial sanitation; by taking extensive preventive measures; by measures to improve the environment; by special care for the health of the younger generation, including the prohibition of child labor not connected with training and labor education; and by furthering scientific research aimed at the prevention of disease and the reduction of its incidence and at ensuring a long and active life for citizens.

Article 43. Citizens of the USSR have the right to material security in old age, in case of illness, complete or partial loss of the ability to work, as well as of loss of the breadwinner.

This right is guaranteed by the social insurance of workers, employees, and collective farmers; by allowances for temporary disability; by the payment of old-age and disability pensions, and pensions for the loss of the breadwinner at the expense of the state and of collective farms; by the employment of citizens who have partially lost the ability to work; by care for elderly citizens and invalids; and by other forms of social insurance.

Article 44. Citizens of the USSR have the right to housing.

This right is ensured by the development and protection of the state and social housing fund, by assistance to cooperative and individual housing construction, by a fair distribution, under social supervision, of living space made available in accordance with the realization of the program for the construction of well-built housing, and also by moderate payments for rent and municipal services. Citizens of the USSR are bound to treat carefully the housing made available to them.

Article 45. Citizens of the USSR have the right to education.

This right is ensured by free education at all levels, the implementation of universal compulsory secondary education of young people, and the extensive development of professional-technical, specialized secondary, and higher education on the basis of connecting learning with life and production; by the development of correspondence and evening education; by granting state stipends and other benefits to pupils and students; by the free issue of school textbooks; by the possibility for instruction in school in one's native language; and by the creation of conditions for self-education.

Article 46. Citizens of the USSR have the right to use the achievements of culture.

This right is ensured by the general accessibility of the treasures of national and world culture in state and public collections; by the development and balanced distribution of cultural-educational institutions within the territory of the country; by the development of television and radio, of book publishing and the periodic press, and of the network of free libraries; and by expanding cultural exchanges with foreign states.

Article 47. Citizens of the USSR, in accordance with the goals of communist construction, are guaranteed freedom of scientific, technical, and artistic creation. This freedom is ensured by extensively furthering scientific research and the activities of inventors and rationalizers, and by the development of literature and the arts. The state creates the necessary material conditions for these developments and provides support to voluntary societies and creative unions, and organizes the introduction of inventions and rationalization proposals in the national economy and other spheres of life.

The rights of authors, inventors, and rationalizers are protected by the state.

Article 48. Citizens of the USSR have the right to participate in the administration of state and public affairs, and in the discussion and adoption of laws and decisions of general state and local significance.

This right is ensured by the possibility to participate in elections for and to be elected to Soviets of People's Deputies and other elective state organs, and to take part in nationwide discussions and votes, in people's control, in the work of state organs, social organizations, and organs of social initiative, and in meetings of labor and residential collectives.

Article 49. Every citizen of the USSR has the right to submit proposals to state organs and social organizations concerning the improvement of their activity and to criticize shortcomings in their work.

Officials are bound to consider, within the established time-limits, the proposals and applications of citizens, to reply to these, and to take the measures necessary.

Persecution on account of criticism is prohibited. Persons engaging in persecution for criticism are held responsible.

Article 50. In accordance with the interests of the people and in order to strengthen and develop the socialist system, citizens of the USSR are guaranteed freedom of speech, of the press, of assembly, of meetings and of street marches, and demonstrations.

The exercise of these political freedoms is ensured by making available public buildings, streets, and squares to the working people and their organizations, by the wide dissemination of information, and by the opportunity to make use of press, television, and radio.

Article 51. In accordance with the goals of communist construction, citizens of the USSR have the right to unite in social organizations, which promote the development of political activity and initiative and the satisfaction of their diverse interests.

Social organizations are guaranteed the conditions for the successful fulfillment of their statutory functions.

Article 52. Citizens of the USSR are guaranteed freedom of conscience, that is, the right to profess any religion or to profess no religion at all, and to perform religious rites, or to conduct atheist propaganda. The incitement of hostility and hatred in connection with religious beliefs is prohibited.

The church in the USSR is separated from the state, and the school from the church.

Article 53. The family is under the protection of the state.

Marriage is based on the voluntary consent of the woman and the man; spouses are completely equal in family relationships.

The state shows concern for the family by creating and developing an extensive network of children's institutions and organizations, by organizing and perfecting everyday services and public catering, by paying childbirth allowances, and by granting allowances and benefits to large families, as well as other forms of allowances and aid to the family.

Article 54. Citizens of the USSR are guaranteed inviolability of the person. No one may be arrested unless on the basis of a court order or with the sanction of the procurator.

Article 55. Citizens of the USSR are guaranteed inviolability of the home. No one has the right, without lawful grounds, to enter a home against the will of the persons residing therein.

Article 56. The private life of citizens and the secrecy of correspondence, telephone conversations, and telegraph messages are protected by law.

Article 57. It is the duty of all state organs, social organizations, and officials to respect the person and to protect the rights and freedoms of citizens.

Citizens of the USSR have the right to judicial protection against attacks on their honor and dignity, their lives and health, and their personal freedom and property.

Article 58. Citizens of the USSR have the right to address complaints against actions of officials and of state and social organs. Complaints must be considered in the manner and within the time-limits established by law.

Complaints may be brought to a court, in the manner established by law, against actions which violate the law or exceed the authority of officials and which infringe the rights of citizens.

Citizens of the USSR have the right to compensation for damages inflicted by unlawful actions of state and social organizations, as well as of officials, in the course of the performance of their official duties.

Article 59. The exercise of rights and freedoms is inseparable from the performance by the citizen of his duties.

The citizen of the USSR is bound to observe the Constitution of the USSR and Soviet laws, to respect the rules of socialist community life, and to bear with dignity the high calling of citizen of the USSR.

Article 60. Conscientious labor in one's chosen field of socially useful activity and observance of labor discipline is the duty and a matter of honor for every Soviet citizen who is able to work. Avoiding socially useful work is incompatible with the principles of a socialist society.

Article 61. The citizen of the USSR is bound to safeguard and strengthen socialist property. It is the duty of the citizen of the USSR to fight theft and waste of state and social property, and to treat the wealth of the people with care.

Persons infringing upon socialist property are punished according to law.

Article 62. The citizen of the USSR is bound to safeguard the interests of the Soviet state and to promote the growth of its power and authority.

The defense of the socialist Fatherland is the sacred duty of every citizen of the USSR.

Treason to the Motherland is the gravest crime against the people.

Article 63. Military service in the ranks of the Armed Forces of the USSR is the honorable duty of Soviet citizens.

Article 64. It is the duty of every citizen of the USSR to respect the national dignity of other citizens and to strengthen the friendship of the nations and nationalities of the multinational Soviet state.

Article 65. The citizen of the USSR is bound to respect the rights and lawful interests of other persons, to be intolerant of anti-social behavior, and to promote in every way the protection of public order.

Article 66. Citizens of the USSR are bound to show concern for the upbringing of children, to prepare them for socially useful labor, and to raise worthy members of a socialist society. Children are bound to show concern for their parents and render them aid.

Article 67. Citizens of the USSR are bound to protect nature and safeguard its riches.

Article 68. Concern for the preservation of historical monuments and other cultural treasures is the duty and obligation of citizens of the USSR.

Article 69. It is the international duty of citizens of the USSR to promote the development of friendship and cooperation with peoples of other countries and the maintenance and strengthening of world peace.

III. THE NATIONAL AND STATE STRUCTURE OF THE USSR

Chapter VIII. The USSR—A Federal State

Article 70. The Union of Soviet Socialist Republics is a unitary, federal, multinational state, formed on the basis of the principle of socialist federalism, and as the result of the free self-determination of nations, and the voluntary association of equal Soviet Socialist Republics.

The USSR embodies the state unity of the Soviet people and brings together all the nations and nationalities for the purpose of jointly building communism.

Article 71. In the Union of Soviet Socialist Republics are united:
 the Russian Soviet Federative Socialist Republic,
 the Ukrainian Soviet Socialist Republic,
 the Belorussian Soviet Socialist Republic,
 the Uzbek Soviet Socialist Republic,
 the Kazakh Soviet Socialist Republic,
 the Georgian Soviet Socialist Republic,
 the Azerbaidzhan Soviet Socialist Republic,

the Lithuanian Soviet Socialist Republic,
the Moldavian Soviet Socialist Republic,
the Latvian Soviet Socialist Republic,
the Kirgiz Soviet Socialist Republic,
the Tadzhik Soviet Socialist Republic,
the Armenian Soviet Socialist Republic,
the Turkmen Soviet Socialist Republic,
the Estonian Soviet Socialist Republic.

Article 72. Each union republic retains the right freely to secede from the USSR.

Article 73. The jurisdiction of the Union of Soviet Socialist Republics, through its highest organs of state power and administration, encompasses:

(1) admitting new republics into the USSR; confirming the formation of new autonomous republics and autonomous provinces within the union republics;

(2) determining the state border of the USSR and confirming changes of boundaries between union republics;

(3) establishing general principles for the organization and functioning of republic and local organs of state power and administration;

(4) ensuring the unity of legislative regulation within the entire territory of the USSR and establishing principles of legislation of the USSR and the union republics;

(5) conducting a unified socio-economic policy and directing the economic system of the country; determining the basic directions of scientific-technical progress and the general measures for a rational utilization and protection of natural resources; formulating and confirming the state plans of economic and social development of the USSR and confirming reports on their fulfillment;

(6) formulating and confirming the integrated state budget of the USSR and confirming the report on its fulfillment; directing the uniform monetary and credit system; establishing the taxes and revenues which go to form the state budget of the USSR; determining a prices and wages policy;

(7) directing the branches of the national economy and the associations and enterprises of union subordination; the over-all direction of the branches of union republic subordination;

(8) questions of peace and war, the defense of the sovereignty and the protection of the state borders and territory of the USSR, organizing defense, and directing the Armed Forces of the USSR;

(9) ensuring state security;

(10) representing the USSR in international relations; the contacts of the USSR with foreign states and international organizations; establishing a general procedure for and coordination of the relations of union republics with foreign states and international organizations; foreign trade and other forms of foreign economic activities on the basis of the monopoly of the state;

(11) supervising the observance of the Constitution of the USSR and ensuring the conformity of the Constitutions of the union republics with the Constitution of the USSR;

(12) resolving other questions of all-union importance.

Article 74. The laws of the USSR have equal force within the territory of all the union republics. In the event of a discrepancy between the law of a union republic and all-union law, the law of the USSR prevails.

Article 75. The territory of the Union of Soviet Socialist Republics is one and includes the territories of the union republics.

The sovereignty of the USSR extends to its entire territory.

Chapter IX. The Soviet Socialist Union Republic

Article 76. A union republic is a sovereign Soviet socialist state which has united itself with other Soviet republics in the Union of Soviet Socialist Republics.

Outside the limits indicated in Article 73 of the Constitution of the USSR, a union republic independently exercises state power within its territory.

A union republic has its own Constitution, which conforms to the Constitution of the USSR and takes account of the special character of the republic.

Article 77. A union republic participates in the resolution of questions within the jurisdiction of the USSR in the Supreme Soviet of the USSR, in the Presidium of the Supreme Soviet of the USSR, in the Government of the USSR, and in other organs of the USSR.

A union republic ensures integrated economic and social development within its territory, facilitates the exercise of the authority of the USSR within its territory, and implements the decisions of the supreme organs of state power and administration of the USSR.

With regard to questions within its jurisdiction, a union republic coordinates and supervises the activities of enterprises, institutions, and organizations of union subordination.

Article 78. The territory of a union republic may not be altered without its consent. The boundaries between union republics may be altered by mutual agreement of the union republics concerned, subject to confirmation by the USSR.

Article 79. A union republic determines its division into territories, provinces, areas, and districts, and resolves other questions of administrative-territorial organization.

Article 80. A union republic has the right to enter into relations with foreign states, to conclude treaties with them and to exchange diplomatic and consular representatives, and to participate in the activities of international organizations.

Article 81. The sovereign rights of the union republics are protected by the USSR.

Chapter X. The Autonomous Soviet Socialist Republic

Article 82. An autonomous republic is part of a union republic.

Outside the limits of the rights of the USSR and the union republic, an autonomous republic independently resolves questions within its jurisdiction.

An autonomous republic has its own Constitution, which conforms to the Constitution of the USSR and the Constitution of the union republic, and which takes into account the special character of the autonomous republic.

Article 83. An autonomous republic participates in the resolution of questions within the jurisdiction of the USSR and the union republic through the supreme organs of state power and administration of the USSR and the union republic respectively.

The autonomous republic ensures integrated economic and social development within its territory, facilitates the exercise within its territory of the authority of the USSR and the union republic, and implements the decisions of the supreme organs of state power and administration of the USSR and the union republic.

With regard to questions within its jurisdiction, an autonomous republic coordinates and supervises the activities of enterprises, institutions, and organizations of union and republic (union republic) subordination.

Article 84. The territory of the autonomous republic may not be altered without its consent.

Article 85. The Russian Soviet Federative Socialist Republic contains the Bashkir, Buriat, Dagestan, Kabardino-Balkar, Kalmyk, Karelian, Komi, Mari, Mordvinian, North Ossetian, Tatar, Tuva, Udmurt, Chechen-Ingush, Chuvash, and Iakut Autonomous Soviet Socialist Republics.

The Uzbek Soviet Socialist Republic contains the Kara-Kalpak Autonomous Soviet Socialist Republic.

The Georgian Soviet Socialist Republic contains the Abkhaz and Adzhar Autonomous Soviet Socialist Republics.

The Azerbaidzhan Soviet Socialist Republic contains the Nakhichevan' Autonomous Soviet Socialist Republic.

Chapter XI. The Autonomous Province and the Autonomous Area

Article 86. An autonomous province is part of a union republic or a territory. A law on an autonomous province is adopted by the Supreme Soviet of a union republic on the recommendation of the Soviet of People's Deputies of an autonomous province.

Article 87. The Russian Soviet Federative Socialist Republic contains the Adyge, Gorno-Altai, Jewish, Karachai-Cherkess, and Khakass autonomous provinces.

The Georgian Soviet Socialist Republic contains the South Ossetian autonomous province.

The Azerbaidzhan Soviet Socialist Republic contains the Nagorno-Karabakh autonomous province.

The Tadzhik Soviet Socialist Republic contains the Gorno-Badakhshan autonomous province.

Article 88. An autonomous area is part of a territory or a province. A Law on Autonomous Areas is adopted by the Supreme Soviet of a union republic.

IV. SOVIETS OF PEOPLE'S DEPUTIES AND THE PROCEDURE FOR THEIR ELECTION

Chapter XII. The System and Principles of Operation of the Soviets of People's Deputies

Article 89. The Soviets of People's Deputies: the Supreme Soviet of the USSR; the Supreme Soviets of the union republics; the Supreme Soviets of the autonomous republics; the territorial and provincial Soviets of People's Deputies; the Soviets of People's Deputies of autonomous provinces and autonomous areas; district, city, city-district, settlement, and village Soviets of People's Deputies—constitute an integrated system of organs of state power.

Article 90. The term of office of the Supreme Soviet of the USSR, the Supreme Soviets of the union republics, and the Supreme Soviets of autonomous republics is five years.

The term of office of local Soviets of People's Deputies is two and a half years.

Elections for Soviets of People's Deputies are called not later than two months before the expiration of the term of office of the Soviets concerned.

Article 91. The most important questions within the jurisdiction of the respective Soviets of People's Deputies are considered and resolved at their sessions.

The Soviets of People's Deputies elect standing commissions and create executive and administrative, as well as other organs accountable to them.

Article 92. The Soviets of People's Deputies set up organs of people's control, combining state supervision with social supervision by working people in enterprises, collective farms, institutions, and organizations.

The organs of people's control supervise the fulfillment of state plans and assignments, combat violations of state discipline, manifestations of localism, a departmental approach to business, mismanagement and wastefulness, red tape and bureaucracy, and they assist in perfecting the work of the state apparatus.

Article 93. The Soviets of People's Deputies, directly and through organs created by them, direct all branches of state, economic, and socio-cultural construction, adopt decisions, ensure their execution, and supervise their implementation.

Article 94. The activities of the Soviets of People's Deputies are based on the collective, free, and businesslike discussion and resolution of questions, on openness, on the regular accounting of executive and administrative organs, and other organs created by the Soviets, to the Soviets and to the population, and on the widespread enlistment of citizens to participate in the work of the Soviets.

The Soviets of People's Deputies and the organs created by them systematically inform the population about their work and the decisions taken.

Chapter XIII. The Electoral System

Article 95. Elections of deputies to all Soviets of People's Deputies are held on the basis of universal, equal, and direct suffrage by secret ballot.

Article 96. Elections of deputies are universal: all citizens of the USSR who have reached the age of 18 years have the right to vote and to be elected, with the exception of persons who have, in the manner established by law, been declared insane.

A citizen of the USSR who has reached the age of 21 years may be elected as a deputy to the Supreme Soviet.

Article 97. Elections of deputies are equal: each voter has one vote; all voters participate in elections on an equal basis.

Article 98. Elections of deputies are direct: the deputies of all Soviets of People's Deputies are elected directly by the citizens.

Article 99. The voting in elections of deputies is secret: checking on the expression of the will of the voter is not allowed.

Article 100. The right to nominate candidates for election as deputies belongs to organizations of the Communist Party of the Soviet Union, of trade unions, and of the All-Union Leninist Communist League of Youth, to cooperative and other social organizations, to labor collectives, as well as to assemblies of servicemen according to military units.

Citizens of the USSR and social organizations are guaranteed the free and all-round discussion of the political, professional, and personal qualities of the candidates for election as deputies, as well as the right to campaign at meetings, in the press, and on television and radio.

Expenses connected with conducting elections for Soviets of People's Deputies are borne by the state.

Article 101. Elections of deputies to Soviets of People's Deputies are held on the basis of electoral districts.

A citizen of the USSR may not, as a rule, be elected to more than two Soviets of People's Deputies.

Elections of deputies to Soviets of People's Deputies are conducted by electoral commissions, composed of representatives of social organizations, labor collectives, and assemblies of servicemen according to military units.

The procedure for conducting elections to the Soviets of People's Deputies is defined by laws of the USSR, the union republics, and the autonomous republics.

Article 102. The voters give mandates to their deputies.

The appropriate Soviets of People's Deputies consider the mandates of the voters, take account of them while formulating the plans of economic and social development and drawing up of the budget, organize the implementation of mandates, and inform the citizens about their realization.

Chapter XIV. The People's Deputy

Article 103. Deputies are plenipotentiary representatives of the people in the Soviets of People's Deputies.

By participating in the work of the Soviets, the deputies resolve questions of state, economic, and socio-cultural construction, organize the implementation of the decisions of the Soviets, and supervise the work of state organs, enterprises, institutions, and organizations.

In his activity, a deputy is guided by the general interests of the state, takes into account the demands of the population of his constituency, and seeks to implement the mandates of his constituents.

Article 104. A deputy exercises his powers without interrupting his work in production or service.

During the sessions of the Soviet, as well as in order to exercise the powers of a deputy in other instances provided for by law, the deputy is relieved from performing his duties in production or service, while retaining his average earnings at his place of permanent employment.

Article 105. A deputy has the right to address inquiries to the appropriate state organs and officials, who are obliged to answer the inquiries at the session of the Soviet.

A deputy has the right to address himself to all state and social organs, enterprises, institutions, and organizations concerning questions within the scope of his activity as a deputy, and to participate in the consideration of the questions raised by him. The heads of the state and social organs, enterprises, institutions, and organizations concerned are obliged to receive the deputy without delay and to consider his proposals within the established time-limit.

Article 106. A deputy is ensured the conditions for the unhindered and effective exercise of his rights and execution of his duties.

The immunity of deputies, as well as other guarantees of a deputy's activities, are established by the Law on the Status of Deputies and by other legislative acts of the USSR and the union and autonomous republics.

Article 107. A deputy is obliged to report on his work and the work of the Soviet to his constituents, as well as to the collectives and social organizations which nominated him as a candidate for election.

A deputy, who has not justified the trust of his constituents, may at any time be recalled by a decision of a majority of his constituents in the manner established by law.

V. THE SUPREME ORGANS OF STATE POWER AND ADMINISTRATION OF THE USSR

Chapter XV. The Supreme Soviet of the USSR

Article 108. The supreme organ of state power of the USSR is the Supreme Soviet of the USSR.

The Supreme Soviet of the USSR is empowered to decide all questions assigned to the jurisdiction of the USSR by the present Constitution.

The adoption of the Constitution of the USSR and of amendments therein; the admission of new republics to the USSR and the confirmation of the formation of new autonomous republics and autonomous provinces; the confirmation of state plans of economic and social development of the USSR, and of the state budget of the USSR and the reports on their fulfillment; and the formation of USSR organs accountable to the Supreme Soviet—are within the exclusive competence of the Supreme Soviet of the USSR.

Laws of the USSR are adopted by the Supreme Soviet of the USSR, or by a nationwide vote (referendum) conducted on the basis of a decision of the Supreme Soviet of the USSR.

Article 109. The Supreme Soviet of the USSR consists of two chambers: the Soviet of the Union and the Soviet of Nationalities.

The chambers of the Supreme Soviet have equal rights.

Article 110. The Soviet of the Union and the Soviet of Nationalities consist of an equal number of deputies.

The Soviet of the Union is elected on the basis of electoral districts with an equal number of inhabitants.

The Soviet of Nationalities is elected according to the following formula: 32 deputies from each union republic, 11 deputies from each autonomous republic, 5 deputies from each autonomous province, and one deputy from each autonomous area.

On the recommendation of the mandates commission elected by them, the Soviet of the Union and the Soviet of Nationalities decide on the recognition of the credentials of the deputies and, in the event of a violation of electoral legislation, on finding the election of individual deputies null and void.

Article 111. Each chamber of the Supreme Soviet of the USSR elects a Chairman of the chamber and four Deputy Chairmen.

The Chairmen of the Soviet of the Union and the Soviet of Nationalities preside over the meetings of the respective chambers and are in charge of their proceedings.

The Chairmen of the Soviet of the Union and the Soviet of Nationalities alternately conduct the joint meetings of the chambers of the Supreme Soviet of the USSR.

Article 112. Sessions of the Supreme Soviet of the USSR are convened twice a year.

Extraordinary sessions are convened by the Presidium of the Supreme Soviet of the USSR at its own initiative, as well as on the proposal of one of the union republics or of not less than one-third of the deputies of one of the chambers.

A session of the Supreme Soviet of the USSR consists of separate and joint meetings of the chambers, as well as of meetings of standing commissions of the chambers or commissions of the Supreme Soviet of the USSR held between sessions. A session is opened and closed at separate or joint meetings of the chambers.

Article 113. The right of legislative initiative in the Supreme Soviet of the USSR belongs to the Soviet of the Union, the Soviet of Nationalities, the Presidium of the Supreme Soviet of the USSR, the Council of Ministers of the USSR, the union republics through their supreme organs of state power, commissions of the Supreme Soviet of the USSR and standing commissions of its chambers, deputies of the Supreme Soviet of the USSR, the Supreme Court of the USSR, and the Procurator General of the USSR.

Social organizations, through their all-union organs, also enjoy the right of legislative initiative.

Article 114. Draft bills and other questions, referred for consideration to the Supreme Soviet of the USSR, are discussed by the chambers at their separate or joint meetings. When necessary, the draft bill or, as the case may be, the question may be referred for preliminary or additional consideration to one or several commissions.

A law of the USSR is considered adopted if, in each of the chambers of the Supreme Soviet of the USSR, a majority of the total number of deputies voted in favor of it. Decrees and other acts of the Supreme Soviet of the USSR are adopted by a majority of the total number of deputies of the Supreme Soviet of the USSR.

Draft bills and other highly important questions of the life of the state may be submitted to a nationwide discussion by a decision of the Supreme Soviet of the USSR or of the Presidium of the Supreme Soviet of the USSR, adopted at their own initiative, or on the proposal of a union republic.

Article 115. In the event of disagreement between the Soviet of the Union and the Soviet of Nationalities, the question is referred for settlement to a conciliation commission, formed by the chambers on a parity basis, after which the question is considered a second time by the Soviet of the Union and the Soviet of Nationalities at a joint meeting. If even in such a case no agreement is reached, the question is carried over for consideration at the next session of the

Supreme Soviet of the USSR or is submitted by the latter to a nationwide vote (referendum).

Article 116. Laws of the USSR, decrees, and other acts of the Supreme Soviet of the USSR are published in the languages of the union republics over the signatures of the Chairman and Secretary of the Presidium of the Supreme Soviet of the USSR.

Article 117. A deputy to the Supreme Soviet of the USSR has the right to address inquiries to the Council of Ministers of the USSR, and to ministers and heads of other organs formed by the Supreme Soviet of the USSR. The Council of Ministers of the USSR or the official to whom an inquiry has been addressed is obliged to give an oral or written reply at the given session of the Supreme Soviet of the USSR within a period of three days.

Article 118. A deputy to the Supreme Soviet of the USSR may not be prosecuted, arrested, or subjected to judicially imposed administrative penalties without the consent of the Supreme Soviet of the USSR, and, during the time between its sessions, without the consent of the Presidium of the Supreme Soviet of the USSR.

Article 119. At a joint meeting of the chambers, the Supreme Soviet of the USSR elects the Presidium of the Supreme Soviet of the USSR, the permanently functioning organ of the Supreme Soviet of the USSR, accountable to the latter in all its activities and exercising, within the limits provided for by the Constitution, the functions of the supreme organ of state power of the USSR during the time between sessions of the Supreme Soviet of the USSR.

Article 120. The Presidium of the Supreme Soviet of the USSR is elected from among the deputies and consists of the Chairman of the Presidium of the Supreme Soviet, the First Deputy Chairman, fifteen Deputy Chairmen—one from each union republic, the Secretary of the Presidium, and twenty-one members of the Presidium of the Supreme Soviet of the USSR.

Article 121. The Presidium of the Supreme Soviet of the USSR:
    (1) calls elections to the Supreme Soviet of the USSR;
    (2) convenes the sessions of the Supreme Soviet of the USSR;
    (3) coordinates the activities of the standing commissions of the chambers of the Supreme Soviet of the USSR;
    (4) supervises the observance of the Constitution of the USSR and

ensures that the Constitutions and laws of the union republics conform to the Constitution and laws of the USSR;

(5) interprets the laws of the USSR;

(6) ratifies and denounces treaties to which the USSR is a party;

(7) annuls decrees and resolutions of the Council of Ministers of the USSR and of Councils of Ministers of union republics where they do not conform to the law;

(8) establishes military and diplomatic ranks and other special ranks; confers military and diplomatic ranks and other special ranks;

(9) institutes orders and medals of the USSR; establishes honorary titles of the USSR; awards orders and medals of the USSR; confers honorary titles of the USSR;

(10) admits persons to citizenship of the USSR and decides questions of the renunciation and deprivation of citizenship of the USSR and of granting asylum;

(11) issues all-union acts of amnesty and grants pardon;

(12) appoints and recalls diplomatic representatives of the USSR to foreign states and at international organizations;

(13) accepts credentials and letters of recall of diplomatic representatives of foreign states accredited to it;

(14) forms the Council of Defense of the USSR and confirms its composition, appoints and replaces the high command of the Armed Forces of the USSR;

(15) proclaims, in the interests of the defense of the USSR, martial law in specific localities or for the whole country;

(16) proclaims general or partial mobilization;

(17) during the time between the sessions of the Supreme Soviet of the USSR, proclaims a state of war in the event of a military attack on the USSR or when necessary to fulfill treaty obligations concerning mutual defense against aggression;

(18) exercises other powers established by the Constitution and laws of the USSR.

Article 122. The Presidium of the Supreme Soviet of the USSR, during the time between the sessions of the Supreme Soviet, and with subsequent submission for confirmation at the next session of the Supreme Soviet:

(1) amends, when necessary, legislative acts of the USSR in force;

(2) confirms boundary changes between union republics;

(3) forms and abolishes ministries of the USSR and state committees of the USSR on the proposal of the Council of Ministers of the USSR;

(4) dismisses and appoints individual persons as members of the

Council of Ministers of the USSR on the recommendation of the Chairman of the Council of Ministers of the USSR.

Article 123. The Presidium of the Supreme Soviet of the USSR issues edicts and adopts resolutions.

Article 124. Upon expiration of the term of office of the Supreme Soviet of the USSR, the Presidium of the Supreme Soviet of the USSR retains its powers until the formation of a new Presidium by the newly-elected Supreme Soviet of the USSR.

The newly-elected Supreme Soviet of the USSR is convened by the Presidium of the outgoing Supreme Soviet of the USSR not later than two months after the elections.

Article 125. The Soviet of the Union and the Soviet of Nationalities elect from among the deputies standing commissions for the preliminary consideration and preparation of questions within the jurisdiction of the Supreme Soviet of the USSR, as well as for promoting the implementation of laws of the USSR and other decisions of the Supreme Soviet of the USSR and its Presidium and the supervision of the activities of state organs and organizations. The chambers of the Supreme Soviet of the USSR may also create joint commissions on a parity basis.

The Supreme Soviet of the USSR creates, when it considers it necessary, investigative, revision, and other commissions on any question.

All state and social organs, organizations, and officials are bound to comply with the requests of the commissions of the Supreme Soviet of the USSR and of the commissions of its chambers, and to submit to them the necessary materials and documents.

The recommendations of the commissions must be considered by the state and social organs, institutions, and organizations. The commissions must be informed within the established time-limit about the results of the consideration or of the measures taken.

Article 126. The Supreme Soviet of the USSR supervises the activities of all state organs accountable to it.

The Supreme Soviet of the USSR sets up a Committee of People's Control of the USSR which heads the system of organs of people's control.

The organization and manner of operation of the organs of people's control are defined by the Law on People's Control in the USSR.

Article 127. The manner of operation of the Supreme Soviet of the USSR and its organs is defined by the Regulations of the Supreme Soviet of the USSR and by other laws of the USSR issued on the basis of the Constitution of the USSR.

Chapter XVI. The Council of Ministers of the USSR

Article 128. The Council of Ministers of the USSR—the Government of the USSR—is the supreme executive and administrative organ of state power of the USSR.

Article 129. The Council of Ministers of the USSR is set up by the Supreme Soviet of the USSR at a joint meeting of the Soviet of the Union and the Soviet of Nationalities and is composed of: the Chairman of the Council of Ministers of the USSR, First Deputy Chairmen and Deputy Chairmen, the ministers of the USSR, and chairmen of state committees of the USSR.

The chairmen of the Councils of Ministers of the union republics are members of the Council of Ministers of the USSR by virtue of their office.

On the recommendation of the Chairman of the Council of Ministers of the USSR, the Supreme Soviet of the USSR may include the heads of other organs and organizations of the USSR as members of the Government of the USSR.

The Council of Ministers of the USSR lays down its powers before the newly-elected Supreme Soviet of the USSR at the first session of the latter.

Article 130. The Council of Ministers of the USSR is responsible and accountable to the Supreme Soviet of the USSR and, during the time between the sessions of the Supreme Soviet of the USSR, to the Presidium of the Supreme Soviet of the USSR, to whom it is accountable.

The Council of Ministers of the USSR regularly reports on its work to the Supreme Soviet of the USSR.

Article 131. The Council of Ministers of the USSR is empowered to resolve all questions of state administration within the jurisdiction of the USSR insofar as they do not, according to the Constitution, come within the competence of the Supreme Soviet of the USSR and the Presidium of the Supreme Soviet of the USSR.

Within the limits of its authority, the Council of Ministers of the USSR:

(1) ensures the management of the national economy and socio-cultural construction; formulates and takes measures to ensure the growth of the well-being and culture of the people, to develop science and technology, to rationally utilize and protect natural resources, to strengthen the monetary and credit system, to implement a uniform policy of prices, wages, social welfare, and state insurance organization, and a uniform system of accounting and statistics; organizes the administration of industrial, construction, and agricultural enterprises and associations, transport and communications enterprises, banks, as well as other organizations and institutions of union subordination;

(2) formulates and submits to the Supreme Soviet of the USSR current and long-range state plans of the economic and social development of the USSR and the state budget of the USSR; takes measures to implement state plans and the budget; submits reports on the fulfillment of the plans and the budget to the Supreme Soviet of the USSR;

(3) takes measures to defend the interests of the state, to protect socialist property and public order, and to safeguard and defend the rights and freedoms of citizens;

(4) takes measures to ensure state security;

(5) exercises general leadership over the organization of the Armed Forces of the USSR and determines the annual contingents of citizens subject to be called up for active military service;

(6) exercises general leadership in the field of relations with foreign states, foreign trade, and economic, scientific-technical, and cultural cooperation of the USSR with foreign countries; takes measures to ensure the fulfillment of treaties of the USSR; confirms and denounces intergovernmental treaties;

(7) sets up, when necessary, committees, chief administrations, and other departments attached to the Council of Ministers of the USSR for matters of economic, socio-cultural, and defense organization.

Article 132. The Presidium of the Council of Ministers of the USSR, consisting of the Chairman of the Council of Ministers of the USSR, the First Deputy Chairmen and the Deputy Chairmen, functions as a permanent organ of the Council of Ministers of the USSR for the resolution of questions connected with ensuring the management of the national economy and other questions of state administration.

Article 133. The Council of Ministers of the USSR, on the basis and in pursuance of laws of the USSR and other decisions of the Supreme Soviet of the USSR and its Presidium, issues decrees and resolutions and verifies their execution. The execution of decrees and resolutions of the Council of Ministers of the USSR is obligatory throughout the territory of the USSR.

Article 134. The Council of Ministers of the USSR, in questions within the jurisdiction of the USSR, has the right to suspend the execution of decrees and resolutions of the Councils of Ministers of the union republics, as well as to annul acts of ministries of the USSR, state committees of the USSR, and other organs subordinate to it.

Article 135. The Council of Ministers of the USSR coordinates and directs the work of all-union and union republic ministries and state committees of the USSR, and other organs subordinate to it.

All-union ministries and state committees of the USSR direct the branches of administration entrusted to them or exercise inter-branch control, throughout the territory of the USSR, either directly or through organs created by them.

Union republic ministries and state committees of the USSR direct the branches of administration entrusted to them or exercise inter-branch control, as a rule, through the corresponding ministries, state committees, and other organs of the union republics, and administer directly the individual enterprises and associations of union subordination. The manner of transferring enterprises and associations of republic or local subordination to union subordination is determined by the Presidium of the Supreme Soviet of the USSR.

Ministries and state committees of the USSR are responsible for the state and the development of the spheres of administration entrusted to them; they issue acts within the limits of their competence and on the basis and in pursuance of the laws of the USSR, other decisions of the Supreme Soviet of the USSR and its Presidium, and decrees and resolutions of the Council of Ministers of the USSR; and they organize and verify their execution.

Article 136. The competence of the Council of Ministers of the USSR and its Presidium, the procedure of their activity, the relations of the Council of Ministers with other state organs, as well as the list of all-union and union republic ministries and state committees of the USSR are defined, on the basis of the Constitution, by the Law on the Council of Ministers of the USSR.

VI. PRINCIPLES OF THE STRUCTURE OF THE ORGANS OF STATE POWER AND ADMINISTRATION IN THE UNION REPUBLICS

Chapter XVII. The Supreme Organs of State Power and Administration of a Union Republic

Article 137. The supreme organ of state power of a union republic is the Supreme Soviet of the union republic.

The Supreme Soviet of a union republic is empowered to resolve all questions assigned to the jurisdiction of the union republic by the Constitution of the USSR and the Constitution of the union republic.

The adoption of the Constitution of a union republic and of amendments therein, the confirmation of state plans of economic and social development, of the state budget of the union republic and reports on their fulfillment; the formation of organs accountable to the Supreme Soviet of the union republic—belong to the exclusive competence of the union republic.

Laws of a union republic are adopted by the Supreme Soviet of the union republic or by a national vote (referendum) conducted on the basis of a decision of the Supreme Soviet of the union republics.

Article 138. The Supreme Soviet of a union republic elects the Presidium of the Supreme Soviet, the permanently functioning organ of the Supreme Soviet of the union republic, accountable to the latter in all its activities. The composition and powers of the Presidium of the Supreme Soviet of a union republic are defined by the Constitution of the union republic.

Article 139. The Supreme Soviet of a union republic sets up the Council of Ministers of the union republic—the Government of the union republic—the supreme excutive and administrative organ of state power of the union republic.

The Council of Ministers of a union republic is responsible and accountable to the Supreme Soviet of the union republic and, during the time between the sessions of the Supreme Soviet, to the Presidium of the Supreme Soviet of the union republic, to whom it is accountable.

Article 140. The Council of Ministers of a union republic issues decrees and resolutions on the basis and in pursuance of legislative acts of the USSR and the union republic, and of decrees and resolutions of the Council of Ministers of the USSR, and organizes and verifies their execution.

Article 141. The Council of Ministers of a union republic has the right to suspend the execution of decrees and resolutions of the Councils of Ministers of autonomous republics and to annul decisions and resolutions of executive committees of territorial, provincial, and city (in cities of republican subordination) Soviets of People's Deputies, of Soviets of People's Deputies of autonomous provinces, and in union republics not divided into provinces, of executive committees of district and corresponding city Soviets of People's Deputies.

Article 142. The Council of Ministers of a union republic coordinates and directs the work of union republic and republic ministries and state committees of the union republic, and other organs subordinate to it.

Union republic ministries and state committees of a union republic direct the branches of administration entrusted to them or exercise inter-branch control, being subordinate to the Council of Ministers of the union republic, as well as to the corresponding union republic ministry of the USSR or state committee of the USSR.

Republic ministries and state committees direct the branches of administration entrusted to them or exercise inter-branch control, being subordinate to the Council of Ministers of the union republic.

Chapter XVIII. The Supreme Organs of State Power and Administration of an Autonomous Republic

Article 143. The supreme organ of state power of an autonomous republic is the Supreme Soviet of the autonomous republic.

The adoption of the Constitution of an autonomous republic and of amendments therein; the confirmation of state plans of economic and social development, as well as of the state budget of the autonomous republic; the formation of organs accountable to the Supreme Soviet of the autonomous republic—belong to the exclusive competence of the Supreme Soviet of the autonomous republic.

Laws of an autonomous republic are adopted by the Supreme Soviet of the autonomous republic.

Article 144. The Supreme Soviet of an autonomous republic elects the Presidium of the Supreme Soviet of the autonomous republic and sets up the Council of Ministers of the autonomous republic—the Government of the autonomous republic.

Chapter XIX. Local Organs of State Power and Administration

Article 145. The organs of state power in the territories, provinces, autonomous provinces, autonomous areas, districts, cities, city-districts, settlements, and rural settlements are the corresponding Soviets of People's Deputies.

Article 146. Local Soviets of People's Deputies resolve all questions of local importance, keeping in mind general state interests and the interests of the citizens living in the territory of the Soviet, implement the decisions of higher state organs, direct the activity of lower-level Soviets of People's Deputies, and also participate in the discussion of questions of republic and all-union importance, and submit proposals concerning these questions.

Within their territory, local Soviets of People's Deputies direct state, economic, and socio-cultural organization; confirm plans of economic and social development and the local budget; exercise leadership over the activities of state organs, enterprises, institutions, and organizations, subordinate to them; ensure observance of laws, the protection of state and public order and of the rights of citizens; and promote the strengthening of the defense capability of the country.

Article 147. Within the limits of their authority, local Soviets of People's Deputies ensure integrated economic and social development within their territory; supervise the observance of legislation by enterprises, institutions, and organizations subordinate to higher bodies and located on this territory; coordinate and supervise their activities in the fields of land use, protection of nature, construction, utilization of labor resources, production of consumer goods, and socio-cultural services, services for everyday needs, and other services for the population.

Article 148. Local Soviets of People's Deputies adopt decisions within the limits of the authority granted to them by the legislation of the USSR, the union republic, and the autonomous republic. The execution of decisions of local Soviets is obligatory for all enterprises, institutions, and organizations located on the territory of the Soviet, as well as for officials and citizens.

Article 149. The executive committees elected by the local Soviets from among their deputies are the executive and administrative organs of the local Soviets of People's Deputies.

Executive committees report at least once a year to the Soviets which have elected them, as well as at meetings of labor collectives and at citizens' places of residence.

Article 150. Executive committees of local Soviets of People's Deputies are directly accountable to the Soviet which has elected them, as well as to the higher executive administrative organ.

VII. THE ADMINISTRATION OF JUSTICE, ARBITRATION, AND PROCURATORIAL SUPERVISION

Chapter XX. Courts and Arbitration

Article 151. Justice in the USSR is administered only by the courts.

In the USSR function the Supreme Court of the USSR; Supreme Courts of union republics; Supreme Courts of autonomous republics; territorial, provincial, and city courts; courts of autonomous provinces; courts of autonomous areas; district (city) people's courts; as well as military tribunals in the Armed Forces.

Article 152. All courts in the USSR are formed on the principle that judges and people's assessors are elected.

People's judges of district (city) people's courts are elected for a term of five years by secret ballot by the citizens of the district (city) on the basis of universal, equal, and direct suffrage. People's assessors of district (city) people's courts are elected for a term of two and a half years by open ballot at meetings of citizens at their place of work or residence.

Higher courts are elected for a term of five years by the corresponding Soviets of People's Deputies.

Judges of military tribunals are elected for a term of five years by the Presidium of the Supreme Soviet of the USSR, and people's assessors for a term of two and a half years by meetings of servicemen.

Judges and people's assessors are responsible to their constituents or to the organs which have elected them, report to them, and may be recalled by them in the manner established by law.

Article 153. The Supreme Court of the USSR is the supreme judicial organ of the USSR and supervises the judicial activities of the courts of the USSR, as well as of the courts of the union republics within the limits established by law.

The Supreme Court of the USSR is elected by the Supreme Soviet of the USSR and consists of the chairman, his deputies, members, and people's assessors. The chairmen of the Supreme Courts of the union republics are members of the Supreme Court of the USSR by virtue of their office.

The organization and manner of operation of the Supreme Court of the USSR are defined by the Law on the Supreme Court of the USSR.

Article 154. In all courts, civil and criminal cases are considered by a panel; in the court of first instance—with the participation of people's assessors. In the administration of justice, people's assessors enjoy all the rights of a judge.

Article 155. Judges and people's assessors are independent and subject only to law.

Article 156. Justice is administered in the USSR on the principle of the equality of citizens before the law and the court.

Article 157. The examination of cases in all courts is open. The hearing of cases in a closed session of the court is permitted only in cases established by law and with the observance of all the rules of court procedure.

Article 158. The accused is ensured the right to defense.

Article 159. Judicial proceedings are conducted in the language of the union republic or autonomous republic, of the autonomous province, the autonomous area, or in the language of the majority of the population of the given locality. The right fully to familiarize oneself with the materials of the case, participation in court proceedings through an interpreter, and the right to address the court in one's native language are ensured to persons who take part in a case and do not master the language in which the proceedings are conducted.

Article 160. No one may be convicted of the commission of a crime, as well as be subjected to criminal punishment other than by a judgment of the court and in accordance with the law.

Article 161. There are colleges of advocates to render legal assistance to citizens and organizations. In cases provided for by legislation, citizens receive legal assistance free of charge.

The organization and manner of operation of the Bar are defined by legislation of the USSR and union republics.

Article 162. The participation of representatives of social organizations and labor collectives is permitted in judicial proceedings in civil and criminal cases.

Article 163. Economic disputes between enterprises, institutions, and organizations are resolved by the organs of state arbitration within the limits of their competence.

The organization and manner of operation of the organs of state arbitration are defined by the Law on State Arbitration of the USSR.

Chapter XXI. The Procuracy

Article 164. The Procurator General of the USSR and his subordinate procurators are charged with the supreme supervision over the exact and uniform execution of the law by all ministries, state committees and departments, enterprises, institutions, and organizations, executive and administrative organs of local Soviets of People's Deputies, collective farms, cooperative and other social organizations, officials, as well as citizens.

Article 165. The Procurator General of the USSR is appointed by the Supreme Soviet of the USSR, is responsible and accountable to it, and during the time between the sessions of the Supreme Soviet, to the Presidium of the Supreme Soviet of the USSR, to whom he is accountable.

Article 166. The procurators of the union republics, autonomous republics, territories, provinces, and autonomous provinces are appointed by the Procurator General of the USSR. The procurators of autonomous areas and district and city procurators are appointed by the procurators of the union republics and confirmed by the Procurator General of the USSR.

Article 167. The term of office of the Procurator General of the USSR and all procurators of lower rank is five years.

Article 168. The organs of the Procuracy exercise their powers independently from any local organs whatsoever and are subordinate only to the Procurator General of the USSR.

The organization and manner of operation of the organs of the Procuracy are defined by the Law on the Procuracy of the USSR.

VIII. THE ARMS, FLAG, ANTHEM, AND CAPITAL OF THE USSR

Article 169. The state arms of the Union of Soviet Socialist Republics consists of a representation of a sickle and hammer against the background of a globe, in the rays of the sun and framed by ears of grain, with an inscription in the languages of the union republics: "Proletarians of All Countries, Unite!". There is a five-pointed star in the upper part of the arms.

Article 170. The state flag of the Union of Soviet Socialist Republics consists of a rectangular red cloth with a representation in its upper corner, near the staff, of a golden sickle and hammer, and over them a red five-pointed star, edged in gold. The ratio of the width of the flag to its length is 1:2.

Article 171. The state anthem of the Union of Soviet Socialist Republics is confirmed by the Presidium of the Supreme Soviet of the USSR.

Article 172. The capital of the Union of Soviet Socialist Republics is the city of Moscow.

IX. THE OPERATION OF THE CONSTITUTION OF THE USSR AND THE PROCEDURE FOR ITS AMENDMENT

Article 173. The Constitution of the USSR has supreme legal force. All laws and other acts of state organs are issued on the basis of and in accordance with the Constitution of the USSR.

Article 174. The Constitution of the USSR is amended by a decision of the Supreme Soviet of the USSR, adopted by a majority of not less than two-thirds of the total number of deputies of each of its chambers.

VIET-NAM

INTRODUCTION

William B. Simons

French colonial control over Indochina began in 1858 with the occupation of Tourane (Da Nang) and of Saigon in the following year. The entire southern delta region of Cochinchina (a name used by some westerners to refer to all of Viet-Nam but by the French to refer only to the southern region) was conquered by the French in the mid-1860s, and the central coastal region of Annam and the northern area around Hanoi known as Tongking became French protectorates in 1883. The French set up an Indochinese Union to administer their colonial possessions, and by 1893 this came to consist of the three areas of Viet-Nam, plus Laos and Cambodia. During World War II, Indochina remained under nominal French administration but the real power lay in the hands of the Japanese Army of Occupation, who, fearing French uprisings as Japanese power waned in the last stages of the Pacific campaign, ousted the French in early 1945 and granted "independence" to the last French-appointed Vietnamese Emperor Bao-Dai. The French, seeking to reestablish their position in Indochina after the war, were confronted with uprisings in the three Vietnamese areas organized by the Revolutionary League for the Independence of Viet-Nam (Viet Minh). Forces loyal to the communist leader Ho Chi Minh entered Hanoi in August 1945 and quickly took control of the area before the French were able to react to the Japanese surrender. In the southern portion of Viet-Nam, Bao-Dai abdicated to a Provisional Executive Committee—installed in Saigon and under the domination of the Viet Minh—which placed itself under the Hanoi government on 25 August 1945. A Provisional Government of the Democratic Republic of Viet-Nam (DRVN) was formed by the Viet Minh on 29 August, and the DRVN was proclaimed to be independent on 2 September. The French, not willing to lose completely their control of and influence in Indochina, attempted to come to a *modus vivendi* with Ho Chi Minh, but were unsuccessful. The DRVN approved its own 70-article constitution on 8 November 1946, and what had been sporadic armed conflicts between the Viet Minh and French forces turned into a total Indochinese War in December of 1946.

Introduction

The first Indochinese War officially ended on 21 July 1954 with the signing of the Geneva cease-fire accord, which established temporary northern and southern zones at the 17th parallel—the former under the control of the Viet Minh-backed government of Ho Chi Minh, and the south (the Republic of Viet-Nam) under the control of Bao-Dai.

Although provision was made in the Geneva accord for elections to be held in the south and the north for the eventual reunification of the country, the goal of reunification came to be overshadowed by the efforts of the South Vietnamese rulers and their allies, the United States—which had replaced France in Indochina after 1954— to resist the "communist aggression" of the North and of local insurgent forces and to keep the dominoes from falling.

In 1956, against the background of the conflict of the South Vietnamese government and communist guerilla, the North Vietnamese decided to form a constitutional committee to amend their 1946 DRVN Constitution. In 1958, the committee's goal became the drafting of an entire new constitution, and the public was invited to send suggestions to the committee; a reported 1,700 such suggestions were received. The draft of the new constitution was published on 1 April 1959, adopted on 31 December 1959, and promulgated on 1 January 1960.

The 112-article 1960 DRVN Constitution begins with a rather long preamble which narrates the history of Viet-Nam and prominently mentions both its President Ho Chi Minh and the Communist Party, as well as the desire of the Vietnamese people to strengthen the unity of the socialist camp headed by the USSR. The preamble also looks to the reunification of North and South, as it describes Viet-Nam as "a single entity". The DRVN is characterized in the Constitution as a people's democracy advancing to socialism. In furtherance of this goal, all economic activities are led by the state according to a unified economic plan. Although the mineral resources, water, forests, and undeveloped lands have been nationalized, and state ownership of the means of production is listed as the first (and most important) type of ownership in the transition to socialism, provision in the fundamental law is also made for ownership of certain means of production by cooperatives, individual working people and handicraftsmen, and national capitalists (Art. 11); the right of individual peasants to own land and means of production is also provided for by the 1960 law. The state does have the right, however, to nationalize means of production with appropriate compensation. The inheritance of private property is also guaranteed in the constitution.

A bill of rights provides for the equality of citizens, with emphasis on equal rights—and equal pay for equal work—for women. The fundamental freedoms of speech, press, assembly, association, and religious belief are mentioned in the Constitution, as are inviolability of the person, the home, and mail. A right of citizens to freedom of movement and residence in the DRVN law parallels a similar right in other communist constitutions. However, all the freedoms granted under the Constitution are prohibited from being used to the detriment of the state or people. Vietnamese citizens may lodge complaints against illegal acts of state officials, and may also claim compensation for damages caused by infringement of their rights by state officials. The right of Vietnamese citizens to work is matched by their duty to work, and to observe labor discipline; the payment of taxes is also mentioned as a specific duty in the Constitution. In addition, military service is required of citizens.

The system of government under the Constitution consists of a National Assembly, elected for a four-year term and convened twice a year; a list of the Assembly's functions is set forth in Article 50. A Standing Committee is elected by the Assembly to act as its executive committee, and the competences of the Committee are found in Article 53. All deputies to the Assembly are granted immunity from prosecution under the provisions of the Constitution. A President of the DRVN is elected for a four-year term by the National Assembly, as is a Vice-President. *Inter alia*, the President is Supreme Commander of the Armed Forces and the National Defense Council; he also appoints or removes the Prime Ministers, Vice-Premiers, and other members of the Council of Ministers, and has the prerogative to attend and preside over meetings of the Council of Ministers. The latter is the supreme administrative organ of the DRVN, and the functions of the Council of Ministers are laid down in Article 74. Provision is also made in the 1960 DRVN Constitution for a newly-created Special Political Conference—convened and presided over by the President and consisting of the President, Vice-President, the Chairman of the National Assembly's Standing Committee, and "other persons concerned"—to examine major problems of the country. The opinions of the Conferences are to be made known to the National Assembly and its Standing Committee, as well as to the Council of Ministers and other bodies (Art. 67). At the local level, People's Councils are the elective organs of state authority. All elections to the National Assembly, as well as to the People's Councils, are characterized in the Vietnamese fundamental law as direct, universal, equal, and secret (Art. 5), and deputies at all levels may be

Introduction

recalled by the electorate. A separate chapter on courts and people's organs of control (a Soviet-style procuracy) provides for people's courts and military courts, as well as for the establishment of special courts. Judges of the lower-level people's courts are elected, and proceedings are conducted with the participation of people's assessors. A right of defense is guaranteed in the Constitution (Art. 101), as is the right of the national minorities in Viet-Nam to use their own languages in court proceedings. A Supreme People's Court functions under the Constitution as the supreme judicial organ; the President of the Court is appointed by the National Assembly, and the Vice-Presidents and judges by the Standing Committee of the Assembly. The independence of people's courts is provided for under the fundamental law (Art. 100), but a condition of that independence appears to be the "responsibility" of people's courts to corresponding People's Councils, and the right of the latter to elect and remove the presidents of the former. Likewise, the Supreme People's Court is responsible to the National Assembly and its Standing Committee (Art. 104). The Supreme People's Organ of Control has the task of insuring the observance of all laws of the DRVN, and its competence to do so extends to the Council of Ministers, local organs of state and officials thereof, and to citizens, but not to the National Assembly, its Standing Committee, or to the President. The Procurator General is appointed by the National Assembly, and his deputies and local procurators by the Assembly's Standing Committee.

In the 1960s, the communist insurgency against the South Vietnamese government led to the second Indochinese War which eventually saw United States troops committed in direct action against local guerillas and regular forces from North Viet-Nam. The US withdrew its forces from the conflict under the provisions of the 1973 Paris Accord, but the hostilities continued until reunification of all of Viet-Nam became a reality in April of 1975 when communist forces entered Saigon and South Viet-Nam ceased to exist.

On 25 July 1976, the National Assembly of a reunified Viet-Nam met to hear Party First Secretary Lê Duan's report on the tasks of the revolution in its new stage—the transition to socialism. The Assembly adopted a new name for reunified Viet-Nam—the Socialist Republic of Viet-Nam—on 2 July 1976, and also instructed the constitutional committee to prepare a new fundamental law for the SRVN. The Assembly declared that the 1960 Constitution would remain in force for the entire country until the adoption of a new text. It had been reported that a draft of the new law was first circulated to Party and government officials for comments in April 1978, but unfortunately efforts to obtain a copy of the draft from both western and Vietnamese sources have proved to no avail.

SELECTED BIBLIOGRAPHY

Demokraticheskaia Respublika V'etnam. Konstitutsiia, zakonodatel'nye akty, dokumenty (The Democratic Republic of Viet-Nam. Constitution, Normative Acts, Documents), Moskva 1955, contains a Russian-language translation of the November 1946 Constitution of the DRVN.

Bernard B. Fall, *The Two Viet-Nams. A Political and Military Analysis*, 2nd rev. ed., New York 1967.

———, "Die neue Verfassung der Demokratischen Republik Vietnam", 6 *Osteuropa Recht* 1960 Nos. 2/3, 145–153.

George Ginsburgs, "The Genesis of the People's Procuracy in the Democratic Republic of Vietnam", 5 *Review of Socialist Law* 1979 No. 2, 187–201, for a detailed analysis of the Procuracy in Viet-Nam, which was not even mentioned in the 1946 DRVN Constitution.

CONSTITUTION OF THE DEMOCRATIC REPUBLIC OF VIET-NAM OF 1 JANUARY 1960

Preamble	400
The Democratic Republic of Viet-Nam	403
Economic and Social System	404
Fundamental Rights and Duties of Citizens	406
The National Assembly	409
The President of the Democratic Republic of Viet-Nam	413
The Council of Ministers	414
The Local People's Councils and the Local Administrative Committees at All Levels	416
The People's Councils and Administrative Committees in Autonomous Zones	419
The People's Courts and the People's Organs of Control	419
The National Flag, the National Emblem, and the Capital	421
Amendment of the Constitution	421

CONSTITUTION OF THE DEMOCRATIC REPUBLIC OF VIET-NAM*

Adopted on 31 December 1959 by the Ninth Session of the National Assembly of the Democratic Republic of Viet-Nam at its first convocation.

PREAMBLE

Viet-Nam is a single entity from Lang-son to Camau.

The Vietnamese people, throughout their thousands of years of history, have been an industrious working people who have struggled unremittingly and heroically to build their country and to defend the independence of their Fatherland.

Throughout more than eighty years of French colonial rule and five years of occupation by the Japanese fascists, the Vietnamese people consistently united and struggled against domination by the foreign aggressors in order to liberate their country.

From 1930 onwards, under the leadership of the Indochinese Communist Party—now the Viet-Nam Lao-Dong Party—the Vietnamese revolution advanced into a new stage. The persistent struggle, full of hardship and heroic sacrifice, of our people against imperialist and feudal domination won great success: the August Revolution was victorious, the Democratic Republic of Viet-Nam was founded, and, on 2 September 1945, President Ho Chi Minh proclaimed Viet-Nam's independence to the people and the world. For the first time in their history, the Vietnamese people had founded an independent and democratic Viet-Nam.

On 6 January 1946, the entire Vietnamese people, from North to South, enthusiastically took part in the first general elections to the National Assembly. The National Assembly adopted the first Constitution, which clearly recorded the great successes of our people and highlighted the determination of the entire nation to safeguard the independence and unity of the Fatherland and to defend the freedom and democratic rights of the people.

However, the French imperialists, assisted by the US imperialists, again provoked an aggressive war in an attempt to seize our country

*Published in English by the Foreign Languages Publishing House, Hanoi 1960.

and once more enslave our people. Under the leadership of the Vietnamese working-class party and the government of the Democratic Republic of Viet-Nam, our entire people, united as one, rose to fight the aggressors and save their country. At the same time, our people carried out land rent reduction and land reform with the aim of overthrowing the landlord class, and restoring the land to those who till it. The long, hard and extremely heroic war of resistance of the Vietnamese people, which enjoyed the sympathy and support of the socialist countries, of the oppressed peoples and of friends of peace throughout the world, won glorious victory. With the Dien Bien Phu victory, the Vietnamese people defeated the French imperialists and the US interventionists. The 1954 Geneva Agreements were concluded: peace was restored in Indochina on the basis of recognition of the independence, sovereignty, unity, and territorial integrity of our country.

This major success of the Vietnamese people was also a common success of the liberation movement of the oppressed peoples, of the world front of peace, and of the socialist camp.

Since the restoration of peace, in completely liberated north Viet-Nam, our people have carried through the national people's democratic revolution. But the South is still under the rule of the imperialists and feudalists; our country is still temporarily divided into two zones.

The Vietnamese revolution has moved into a new position. Our people must endeavor to consolidate the North, taking it towards socialism; and to carry on the struggle for peaceful reunification of the country and completion of the tasks of the national people's democratic revolution throughout the country.

In the last few years, our people in the North have achieved many big successes in economic rehabilitation and cultural development. At present, socialist transformation and construction are being successfully carried out.

Meanwhile, in the South, the US imperialists and their henchmen have been savagely repressing the patriotic movement of our people. They have been strengthening military forces, and carrying out their scheme of turning the southern part of our country into a colony and military base for their war preparations. They have resorted to all possible means to sabotage the Geneva Agreements and undermine the cause of Viet-Nam's reunification. But our southern compatriots have constantly struggled heroically and refused to submit to them. The people throughout the country, united as one, are holding aloft the banner of peace, national unity, independence, and democracy, resolved to march forward and win final victory. The cause of the peaceful reunification of the Fatherland will certainly be victorious.

In the new stage of the revolution, our National Assembly must amend the 1946 Constitution in order to adapt it to the new situation and tasks.

The new Constitution clearly records the great revolutionary gains in the recent past, and clearly indicates the goal of struggle of our people in the new stage.

Our state is a people's democratic state based on the alliance between the workers and peasants and led by the working class. The new Constitution defines the political, economic, and social system of our country, the relations of equality and mutual assistance among the various nationalities in our country, and provides for the taking of the North towards socialism, the constant improvement of the material and cultural life of the people, and the building of a stable and strong North Viet-Nam as a basis for the struggle for the peaceful reunification of the country.

The new Constitution defines the responsibilities and powers of the state organs and the rights and duties of citizens, with a view to developing the great creative potentialities of our people in national construction and in the reunification and defense of the Fatherland.

The new Constitution is a genuinely democratic Constitution. It is a force inspiring the people throughout our country to march forward enthusiastically and win new successes. Our people are resolved to develop further their patriotism, their tradition of solidarity, their determination to struggle, and their ardor in work. Our people are resolved to strengthen further solidarity and unity of mind with the brother countries in the socialist camp headed by the great Soviet Union, and to strengthen solidarity with the peoples of Asia and Africa and peace-loving people all over the world.

Under the clearsighted leadership of the Viet-Nam Lao-Dong Party, the Government of the Democratic Republic of Viet-Nam and President Ho Chi Minh, our entire people, broadly united within the National United Front, will surely win glorious success in the building of socialism in North Viet-Nam and the struggle for national reunification. Our people will surely be successful in building a peaceful, unified, independent, democratic, prosperous, and strong Viet-Nam, making a worthy contribution to the safeguarding of peace in Southeast Asia and the world.

Chapter I. The Democratic Republic of Viet-Nam

Article 1. The territory of Viet-Nam is a single, indivisible whole from North to South.

Article 2. The Democratic Republic of Viet-Nam, established and consolidated as a result of victories won by the Vietnamese people in the glorious August Revolution and the heroic Resistance, is a people's democratic state.

Article 3. The Democratic Republic of Viet-Nam is a single multinational state.

All the nationalities living on Vietnamese territory are equal in rights and duties. The state has the duty to maintain and develop the solidarity between the various nationalities. All acts of discrimination against, or oppression of any nationality, all actions which undermine the unity of the nationalities, are strictly prohibited.

All nationalities have the right to preserve or reform their own customs and habits, to use their spoken and written languages, and to develop their own national culture.

Autonomous zones may be established in areas where people of national minorities live in compact communities. Such autonomous zones are inalienable parts of the Democratic Republic of Viet-Nam.

The state strives to help the national minorities to make rapid progress and to keep pace with the general economic and cultural advance.

Article 4. All power in the Democratic Republic of Viet-Nam belongs to the people. The people exercise power through the National Assembly and the People's Councils at all levels elected by the people and responsible to the people.

The National Assembly, the People's Councils at all levels, and the other organs of state practice democratic centralism.

Article 5. Election of deputies to the National Assembly and the People's Councils at all levels proceeds on the principle of universal, equal, direct, and secret suffrage.

Deputies to the National Assembly and People's Councils at all levels may be recalled by their constituents before their term of office expires if they show themselves to be unworthy of the confidence of the people.

Article 6. All organs of state must rely on the people, maintain close contact with them, heed their opinions, and accept their supervision.

All personnel of organs of state must be loyal to the people's democratic system, observe the Constitution and the law, and wholeheartedly serve the people.

Article 7. The state strictly prohibits and punishes all acts of treason, opposition to the people's democratic system, or opposition to the reunification of the Fatherland.

Article 8. The armed forces of the Democratic Republic of Viet-Nam belong to the people; their duty is to safeguard the gains of the revolution, and defend the independence, sovereignty, territorial integrity, and security of the Fatherland, and the freedom, happiness, and peaceful labor of the people.

Chapter II. Economic and Social System

Article 9. The Democratic Republic of Viet-Nam is advancing step-by-step from people's democracy to socialism by developing and transforming the national economy along socialist lines, transforming its backward economy into a socialist economy with modern industry and agriculture, and an advanced science and technology.

The fundamental aim of the economic policy of the Democratic Republic of Viet-Nam is continuously to develop the productive forces with the aim of raising the material and cultural standards of the people.

Article 10. The state leads all economic activities according to a unified plan.

The state relies on the organs of state, trade union organizations, cooperatives, and other organizations of the working people to elaborate and carry out its economic plans.

Article 11. In the Democratic Republic of Viet-Nam during the present period of transition to socialism, the main forms of ownership of means of production are: state ownership, that is, ownership by the whole people; cooperative ownership, that is, collective ownership by the working masses; ownership by individual working people; and ownership by the national capitalists.

Article 12. The state sector of the economy, which is a form of ownership by the whole people, plays the leading role in the national economy. The state ensures priority for its development.

All mineral resources and waters, and all forests, undeveloped land, and other resources defined by law as belonging to the state are the property of the whole people.

Article 13. The cooperative sector of the economy is a form of collective ownership by the working masses.

The state especially encourages, guides, and helps the development of the cooperative sector of the economy.

Article 14. The state by law protects the right of peasants to own land and other means of production.

The state actively guides and helps the peasants to improve farming methods and increase production, and encourages them to organize producers', supply and marketing, and credit cooperatives, in accordance with the principle of voluntariness.

Article 15. The state by law protects the right of handicraftsmen and other individual working people to own means of production.

The state actively guides and helps handicraftsmen and other individual working people to improve their enterprises, and encourages them to organize producers' and supply and marketing cooperatives in accordance with the principle of voluntariness.

Article 16. The state by law protects the right of national capitalists to own means of production and other capital.

The state actively guides the national capitalists in carrying out activities beneficial to national welfare and the people's livelihood, contributing to the development of the national economy, in accordance with the economic plan of the state. The state encourages and guides the national capitalists in following the path of socialist transformation through the form of joint state-private enterprises and other forms of transformation.

Article 17. The state strictly prohibits the use of private property to disrupt the economic life of society or to undermine the economic plan of the state.

Article 18. The state protects the right of citizens to possess lawfully-earned incomes, savings, houses, and other private means of life.

Article 19. The state by law protects the right of citizens to inherit private property.

Article 20. Only when such action is necessary in the public interest, does the state repurchase, requisition, or nationalize with appropriate compensation means of production in city or countryside, within the limits and in the conditions defined by law.

Article 21. Labor is the basis on which the people develop the national economy and raise their material and cultural standards.

Labor is a duty and a matter of honor for every citizen.

The state encourages the creativeness and the enthusiasm in labor of workers by hand and brain.

Chapter III. Fundamental Rights and Duties of Citizens

Article 22. Citizens of the Democratic Republic of Viet-Nam are equal before the law.

Article 23. Citizens of the Democratic Republic of Viet-Nam who have reached the age of eighteen have the right to vote, and those who have reached the age of twenty-one have the right to stand for election, whatever their nationality, race, sex, social origin, religion, belief, property status, education, occupation, or length of residence, except insane persons and persons deprived by a court or by law of the right to vote and stand for election.

Citizens serving in the army have the right to vote and stand for election.

Article 24. Women in the Democratic Republic of Viet-Nam enjoy equal rights with men in all spheres of political, economic, cultural, social, and domestic life.

For equal work, women enjoy equal pay with men. The state ensures that women workers and office employees have fully-paid periods of leave before and after child-birth.

The state protects the mother and child and ensures the development of maternity hospitals, crèches, and kindergartens.

The state protects marriage and the family.

Article 25. Citizens of the Democratic Republic of Viet-Nam enjoy freedom of speech, freedom of the press, freedom of assembly, freedom of association and freedom of demonstration. The state guarantees all necessary material conditions for citizens to enjoy these freedoms.

Article 26. Citizens of the Democratic Republic of Viet–Nam enjoy freedom of religious belief; they may practice or not practice a religion.

Article 27. Freedom of the person of citizens of the Democratic Republic of Viet-Nam is guaranteed. No citizen may be arrested except by decision of a people's court or with the sanction of a People's Organ of Control.

Article 28. The law guarantees the inviolability of the homes of the citizens of the Democratic Republic of Viet-Nam and inviolability of mail.

Citizens of the Democratic Republic of Viet-Nam enjoy freedom of residence and movement.

Article 29. Citizens of the Democratic Republic of Viet-Nam have the right to complain of and denounce to any organ of state any servant of the state for transgression of law. These complaints and denunciations must be investigated and dealt with rapidly. People suffering loss owing to infringement by servants of the state of their rights as citizens are entitled to compensation.

Article 30. Citizens of the Democratic Republic of Viet-Nam have the right to work. To guarantee to citizens enjoyment of this right, the state, by planned development of the national economy, gradually creates more employment and better working conditions and wages.

Article 31. Working people have the right to rest. To guarantee to working people enjoyment of this right, the state prescribes working hours and holidays for workers and office employees, and gradually expands material facilities to enable working people to rest and build up their health.

Article 32. Working people have the right to material assistance in old age, and in case of illness or disability. To guarantee to working people enjoyment of this right, the state gradually expands social insurance, social assistance, and public health service.

Article 33. Citizens of the Democratic Republic of Viet-Nam have the right to education. To guarantee to citizens enjoyment of this right, the state enforces step-by-step the system of compulsory education, gradually extends the various types of schools and other cultural institutions, extends the various forms of supplementary cultural, technical, and professional education in public services and factories, and in other organizations in town and countryside.

Article 34. Citizens of the Democratic Republic of Viet-Nam enjoy freedom to engage in scientific research, literary and artistic creation, and other cultural pursuits. The state encourages and assists creative work in science, literature, art, and other cultural pursuits.

Article 35. The state pays special attention to the moral, intellectual, and physical education of youth.

Article 36. The state protects the proper rights and interests of Vietnamese resident abroad.

Article 37. The Democratic Republic of Viet-Nam grants the right of asylum to any foreign national persecuted for demanding freedom, for supporting a just cause, for taking part in the peace movement, or for engaging in scientific activity.

Article 38. The state forbids any person to use democratic freedoms to the detriment of the interests of the state and of the people.

Article 39. Citizens of the Democratic Republic of Viet-Nam must abide by the Constitution and the law, uphold discipline at work, keep public order, and respect social ethics.

Article 40. The public property of the Democratic Republic of Viet-Nam is sacred and inviolable. It is the duty of every citizen to respect and protect public property.

Article 41. Citizens of the Democratic Republic of Viet-Nam have the duty to pay taxes according to law.

Article 42. To defend the Fatherland is the most sacred and noble duty of citizens of the Democratic Republic of Viet-Nam.

It is the duty of citizens to perform military service in order to defend the Fatherland.

Chapter IV. The National Assembly

Article 43. The National Assembly is the highest organ of state authority in the Democratic Republic of Viet-Nam.

Article 44. The National Assembly is the only legislative authority of the Democratic Republic of Viet-Nam.

Article 45. The term of office of the National Assembly is four years.

A new National Assembly must be elected two months before the term of office of the sitting National Assembly expires.

The electoral procedure and the number of deputies are prescribed by law.

In the event of war or other exceptional circumstances, the National Assembly may decide to prolong its term of office and take necessary measures to ensure its activities and those of deputies.

Article 46. The National Assembly meets twice a year, convened by its Standing Committee. The Standing Committee of the National Assembly may convene extraordinary sessions of the National Assembly according to its decisions, or at the request of the Council of Ministers, or of a minimum of one-third of the total number of deputies.

The Standing Committee of the National Assembly must convene the new National Assembly not later than two months after the elections.

Article 47. When the National Assembly meets, it elects a presidium to conduct its sittings.

Article 48. Laws and other decisions of the National Assembly require a simple majority vote of all deputies to the National Assembly, except for the case specified in Article 112 of the Constitution.

Article 49. Laws must be promulgated not later than fifteen days after their adoption by the National Assembly.

Article 50. The National Assembly exercises the following functions:
   (1) to enact and amend the Constitution;
   (2) to enact laws;

(3) to supervise the enforcement of the Constitution;

(4) to elect the President and Vice-President of the Democratic Republic of Viet-Nam;

(5) to choose the Prime Minister of the Government upon the recommendation of the President of the Democratic Republic of Viet-Nam and the Vice-Premiers and the other component members of the Council of Ministers upon the recommendation of the Prime Minister;

(6) to choose the Vice-President and the other component members of the National Defense Council upon the recommendation of the President of the Democratic Republic of Viet-Nam;

(7) to elect the President of the Supreme People's Court;

(8) to elect the Procurator General of the Supreme People's Organ of Control;

(9) to remove the President and Vice-President of the Democratic Republic of Viet-Nam, the Prime Minister, the Vice-Premiers, and the other component members of the National Defense Council, the President of the Supreme People's Court, and the Procurator General of the Supreme People's Organ of Control;

(10) to decide upon national economic plans;

(11) to examine and approve the state budget and the financial report;

(12) to fix taxes;

(13) to decide the establishment and abolition of ministries and of organs having a status equal to that of a ministry;

(14) to ratify the boundaries of provinces, autonomous regions, and municipalities directly under the central authority;

(15) to decide on general amnesties;

(16) to decide on questions of war and peace; and

(17) to exercise other necessary functions as defined by the National Assembly.

Article 51. The Standing Committee of the National Assembly is a permanent executive body of the National Assembly and is elected by it. The Standing Committee is composed of:
— the Chairman;
— the Vice-Chairmen;
— the Secretary General; and
— other members.

Article 52. The Standing Committee of the National Assembly is responsible to the National Assembly and reports to it.

The National Assembly has power to remove any member of the Standing Committee.

Article 53. The Standing Committee of the National Assembly exercises the following functions.

(1) to proclaim and conduct the election of deputies to the National Assembly;

(2) to convene the National Assembly;

(3) to interpret the laws;

(4) to enact decrees;

(5) to decide on referenda;

(6) to supervise the work of the Council of Ministers, the Supreme People's Court, and the Supreme People's Organ of Control;

(7) to revise or annul decisions, orders, and directives of the Council of Ministers which contravene the Constitution, laws, and decrees; to revise or annul inappropriate decisions issued by the People's Councils of provinces, autonomous regions, and municipalities, directly under the central authority; and to dissolve the above-mentioned People's Councils if they do serious harm to the people's interests;

(8) to decide on the appointment or removal of the Vice-Premiers and the other component members of the Council of Ministers when the National Assembly is not in session;

(9) to appoint or remove the Vice-Presidents and judges of the Supreme People's Court;

(10) to appoint or remove the Deputy Procurators General and procurators of the Supreme People's Organ of Control;

(11) to decide on the appointment or removal of plenipotentiary diplomatic representatives of the Democratic Republic of Viet-Nam to foreign states;

(12) to decide on the ratification or abrogation of treaties concluded with foreign states, except when the Standing Committee considers it necessary to refer such ratification or abrogation to the National Assembly for decision;

(13) to decide on military, diplomatic, and other grades and ranks;

(14) to decide on the granting of pardons;

(15) to institute and decide on the award of state orders, medals, and titles of honor;

(16) to decide, when the National Assembly is not in session, on the proclamation of a state of war in the event of armed attack on the country;

(17) to decide on general or partial mobilization;

(18) to decide on the enforcement of martial law throughout the country or in certain areas.

Apart from these functions, the National Assembly may, when necessary, invest the Standing Committee with other functions.

Article 54. The decisions of the Standing Committee of the National Assembly must be approved by a simple majority vote of its members.

Article 55. The Standing Committee of the National Assembly exercises its functions until a new Standing Committee is elected by the succeeding National Assembly.

Article 56. The National Assembly elects a commission for examination of the qualifications of deputies to the National Assembly. The National Assembly will base itself on the reports of this commission in deciding on the recognition of the qualifications of deputies.

Article 57. The National Assembly establishes a Law Drafting Committee, a Planning Board and Budget Commission, and other committees which the National Assembly deems necessary to assist the National Assembly and its Standing Committee.

Article 58. The National Assembly, or its Standing Committee when the National Assembly is not in session, may, if necessary, appoint commissions of inquiry to investigate specific questions.

All organs of state, people's organizations, and citizens concerned are required to supply all information necessary to these commissions when they conduct investigations.

Article 59. Deputies to the National Assembly have the right to address questions to the Council of Ministers and to organs under the authority of the Council of Ministers.

The organs to which questions are put are obliged to answer within a period of five days. In the event of investigations having to be carried out, the answer must be given within one month.

Article 60. No deputy to the National Assembly may be arrested or tried without the consent of the National Assembly or, when the National Assembly is not in session, of its Standing Committee.

Chapter V. The President of the Democratic Republic of Viet-Nam

Article 61. The President of the Democratic Republic of Viet-Nam is the representative of the Democratic Republic of Viet-Nam in internal affairs as well as in foreign relations.

Article 62. The President of the Democratic Republic of Viet-Nam is elected by the National Assembly of the Democratic Republic of Viet-Nam. Any citizen of the Democratic Republic of Viet-Nam who has reached the age of thirty-five is eligible to stand for election as President of the Democratic Republic of Viet-Nam.

The term of office of the President of the Democratic Republic of Viet-Nam corresponds to that of the National Assembly.

Article 63. The President of the Democratic Republic of Viet-Nam, in pursuance of decisions of the National Assembly or its Standing Committee, promulgates laws and decrees; appoints or removes the Prime Minister, the Vice-Premiers, and the other component members of the Council of Ministers; appoints or removes the Vice-President and the other component members of the National Defense Council; promulgates general amnesties and grants pardons; confers orders, medals, and titles of honor of the state; proclaims a state of war; orders general or partial mobilization; and proclaims martial law.

Article 64. The President of the Democratic Republic of Viet-Nam receives plenipotentiary representatives of foreign states; and, in pursuance of decisions of the National Assembly or its Standing Committee, ratifies treaties concludes with foreign states, appoints or recalls plenipotentiary representatives of the Democratic Republic of Viet-Nam to foreign states.

Article 65. The President of the Democratic Republic of Viet-Nam is the Supreme Commander of the Armed Forces of the country, and is President of the National Defense Council.

Article 66. The President of the Democratic Republic of Viet-Nam has power, when necessary, to attend and preside over the meetings of the Council of Ministers.

Article 67. The President of the Democratic Republic of Viet-Nam, when necessary, convenes and presides over the Special Political Conference.

The Special Political Conference is composed of the President and Vice-President of the Democratic Republic of Viet-Nam, the Chairman of the Standing Committee of the National Assembly, the Prime Minister, and other persons concerned.

The Special Political Conference examines major problems of the country. The President of the Democratic Republic of Viet-Nam submits the view of this conference to the National Assembly, the Standing Committee of the National Assembly, the Council of Ministers, or other bodies concerned, for their consideration and decision.

Article 68. The Vice-President of the Democratic Republic of Viet-Nam assists the President in his duties. The Vice-President may exercise such part of the functions of the President as the President may entrust to him.

The provisions governing the election and term of office of the President apply also to the election and term of office of the Vice-President.

Article 69. The President and Vice-President of the Democratic Republic of Viet-Nam exercise their functions until the new President and Vice-President take office.

Article 70. Should the President of the Democratic Republic of Viet-Nam be incapacitated for a prolonged period by reason of ill health, the functions of President shall be exercised by the Vice-President.

Should the office of President of the Democratic Republic of Viet-Nam fall vacant, the Vice-President shall fulfill functions of President until the election of a new President.

Chapter VI. The Council of Ministers

Article 71. The Council of Ministers is the executive organ of the highest organ of state authority; it is the highest administrative organ of the Democratic Republic of Viet-Nam.

The Council of Ministers is responsible to the National Assembly and reports to it, or, when the National Assembly is not in session, to the Standing Committee of the National Assembly.

Article 72. The Council of Ministers is composed of:
— the Prime Minister;

Viet-Nam

— the Vice-Premiers;
— the ministers;
— the heads of State Commissions; and
— the Director-General of the National Bank.

The organization of the Council of Ministers is determined by law.

Article 73. Basing itself on the Constitution, laws, and decrees, the Council of Ministers formulates administrative measures, issues decisions, and orders and verifies their execution.

Article 74. The Council of Ministers exercises the following functions:

(1) to submit draft laws, draft decrees, and other drafts to the National Assembly and the Standing Committee of the National Assembly;

(2) to centralize the leadership of the ministries and organs of state under the authority of the Council of Ministers;

(3) to centralize the leadership of the administrative committees at all levels;

(4) to revise or annul inappropriate decisions of the ministries, and organs of state under the authority of the Council of Ministers; to revise or annul inappropriate decisions of administrative organs at all levels;

(5) to suspend the execution of inappropriate decisions of the People's Councils of provinces, autonomous zones, and municipalities directly under the central authority, and recommend to the Standing Committee of the National Assembly revision or annulment of these decisions;

(6) to put into effect the national economic plans and the provisions of the state budget;

(7) to control domestic and foreign trade;

(8) to direct cultural and social work;

(9) to safeguard the interests of the state, to maintain public order, and to protect the rights and interests of citizens;

(10) to lead the building of the armed forces of the state;

(11) to direct the conduct of foreign relations;

(12) to administer affairs concerning the nationalities;

(13) to ratify territorial boundaries of administrative areas below the provincial level;

(14) to carry out the order of mobilization, martial law, and all other necessary measures to defend the country;

(15) to appoint and remove personnel of organs of state, according to provisions of law.

Besides these functions, the National Assembly or its Standing Committee may invest the Council of Ministers with other functions.

Article 75. The Prime Minister presides over the meetings of the Council of Ministers and leads its work. The Vice-Premiers assist the Prime Minister in his work and may replace him in the event of his absence.

Article 76. The Ministers and heads of organs of state under the authority of the Council of Ministers lead the work of their respective departments under the unified leadership of the Council of Ministers.

Within the jurisdiction of their respective departments, in accordance with and in pursuance of laws and decrees, decisions, orders, and directives of the Council of Ministers, they may issue orders and directives and supervise their execution.

Article 77. In the discharge of their functions, members of the Council of Ministers bear responsibility before the law for such acts as contravene the Constitution and the law and do harm to the state or the people.

Chapter VII. The Local People's Councils and the Local Administrative Committees at All Levels

Article 78. The administrative division of the Democratic Republic of Viet-Nam is as follows:

The country is divided into provinces, autonomous zones, and municipalities directly under the central authority.

Provinces are divided into districts, cities, and towns.

Districts are divided into villages and townlets.

Administrative units in autonomous zones will be determined by law.

Article 79. People's Councils and administrative committees are established in all the above-mentioned administrative units.

Cities may be divided into wards with a ward People's Council and administrative committee, according to decision of the Council of Ministers.

Article 80. Local People's Councils at all levels are the organs of state authority in their respective areas.

People's Councils at all levels are elected by the local people and are responsible to them.

Article 81. The term of office of the People's Councils of provinces, autonomous zones, and municipalities directly under the central authority is three years.

The term of office of the People's Councils of districts, cities, towns, villages, townlets, and wards is two years.

The term of office of the People's Councils at all levels in autonomous zones is fixed by law.

The electoral procedure and the number of representatives to People's Councils at all levels are determined by law.

Article 82. The People's Councils ensure observance and execution of state laws in their respective areas; draw up plans for local economic and cultural development and public works; examine and approve local budgets and financial reports; maintain public order and security in their areas; protect public property, protect the rights of citizens, and safeguard the equal rights of the nationalities.

Article 83. The local People's Councils issue decisions for execution in their areas on the basis of state law and of decisions taken at higher levels.

Article 84. The People's Councils elect administrative committees and have power to recall members of administrative committees.

The People's Councils elect, and have power to recall, the presidents of the People's Courts at corresponding levels.

Article 85. The People's Councils have power to revise or annul inappropriate decisions issued by administrative committees at corresponding levels, as well as inappropriate decisions issued by People's Councils and administrative committees at the next lower level.

Article 86. The People's Councils at all levels have power to dissolve People's Councils at the next lower level when the latter do serious harm to the people's interests. Such a decision must be ratified by the People's Council at the next higher level prior to its application. A decision of dissolution issued by the People's Councils of provinces, autonomous zones, and municipalities directly under the central authority is subject to endorsement by the Standing Committee of the National Assembly prior to its application.

Article 87. The administrative committees at all levels are the executive organs of the local People's Councils at corresponding levels, and are the administrative organs of state in their respective areas.

Article 88. The administrative committee is composed of a President, one or several Vice-Presidents, a secretary, and a number of committee members.

The term of office of an administrative committee is the same as that of the People's Council which elected it.

On the expiration of the term of office of the People's Council or in the event of its dissolution, the administrative committee continues to exercise the above functions until a new People's Council has elected a new administrative committee.

The organization of administrative committees at all levels is determined by law.

Article 89. The administrative committees at all levels direct the administrative work in their respective areas, carry out the decisions issued by People's Councils at corresponding levels and the decisions and orders issued by organs of state at higher levels.

The administrative committees at all levels, within the limits of the authority prescribed by law, issue decisions and orders and verify their execution.

Article 90. The administrative committees at all levels direct the work of their subordinate departments and the work of administrative committees at lower levels.

The administrative committees at all levels have power to revise or annul inappropriate decisions of their subordinate departments and of administrative committees at lower levels.

The administrative committees at all levels have power to suspend the carrying out of inappropriate decisions of People's Councils at the next lower level, and to propose to People's Councils at corresponding levels the revision or annulment of such decisions.

Article 91. The administrative committees at all levels are responsible to the People's Councils at corresponding levels and to the administrative organs of state at the next higher level and shall report to these bodies.

The administrative committees at all levels are placed under the leadership of the administrative committees at the next higher level, and under the unified leadership of the Council of Ministers.

The People's Councils and Administrative Committees in Autonomous Zones

Article 92. The organization of the People's Councils and administrative committees in autonomous zones are based on the basic principles governing the organization of the People's Councils and administrative committees at all levels, as defined above.

Article 93. In the autonomous zones where a number of nationalities live together, they are entitled to appropriate representation on the People's Councils.

Article 94. The People's Councils and the administrative committees in autonomous zones work out plans for economic and cultural development suited to the local conditions, administer their local finances, and organize their local self-defense and public security forces, within the limits of autonomy prescribed by law.

Article 95. The People's Councils in autonomous zones may, within the limits of autonomy, and basing themselves on the political, economic, and cultural characteristics of the nationalities in their respective areas, draw up statutes governing the exercise of autonomy and regulations concerning particular problems, to be put into effect in their areas, after endorsement by the Standing Committee of the National Assembly.

Article 96. The higher organs of state must ensure that the People's Councils and administrative committees in the autonomous zones exercise their right to autonomy, and assist the minority peoples in the full promotion of their political, economic, and cultural development.

Chapter VIII. The People's Courts and the People's Organs of Control

The People's Courts

Article 97. The Supreme People's Court of the Democratic Republic of Viet-Nam, the local people's courts, and the military courts are judicial organs of the Democratic Republic of Viet-Nam.

Special courts may be set up by the National Assembly in certain cases.

Article 98. The system of elected judges according to the procedure prescribed by law applies to the people's courts.

The term of office of the President of the Supreme People's Court is five years.

The organization of the people's courts is determined by law.

Article 99. Judicial proceedings in the people's courts must be carried out with the participation of people's assessors according to law. In administering justice, people's assessors enjoy the same powers as judges.

Article 100. In administering justice, the people's courts are independent and subject only to law.

Article 101. Cases in the people's courts are heard in public, unless otherwise provided for by law.

The right to defense is guaranteed the accused.

Article 102. The people's courts ensure that all citizens of the Democratic Republic of Viet-Nam belonging to national minorities may use their own spoken and written languages in court proceedings.

Article 103. The Supreme People's Court is the highest judicial organ of the Democratic Republic of Viet-Nam.

The Supreme People's Court supervises the judicial work of local peoples' courts, military courts, and special courts.

Article 104. The Supreme People's Court is responsible to the National Assembly and reports to it, or when the National Assembly is not in session, to its Standing Committee. The local people's courts are responsible to the local People's Councils at corresponding levels and report to them.

The People's Organs of Control

Article 105. The Supreme People's Organ of Control of the Democratic Republic of Viet-Nam controls the observance of the law by all departments of the Council of Ministers, all local organs of state, persons working in organs of state, and all citizens.

Local organs of the People's Organ of Control and military organs of control exercise control authority within the limits prescribed by law.

Article 106. The term of office of the Procurator General of the Supreme People's Organ of Control is five years.

The organization of the People's Organs of Control is determined by law.

Article 107. The People's Organs of Control at all levels work only under the leadership of their higher control organs and the unified leadership of the Supreme People's Organ of Control.

Article 108. The Supreme People's Organ of Control is responsible to the National Assembly and reports to it, or when the National Assembly is not in session, to its Standing Committee.

Chapter IX. The National Flag, the National Emblem and the Capital

Article 109. The national flag of the Democratic Republic of Viet-Nam is a red flag, with a five-pointed gold star in the middle.

Article 110. The national emblem of the Democratic Republic of Viet-Nam is round in shape, has a red ground with ears of rice framing a five-pointed gold star in the middle and with a cogwheel and the words "Democratic Republic of Viet-Nam" at the base.

Article 111. The capital of the Democratic Republic of Viet-Nam is Hanoi.

Chapter X. Amendment of the Constitution

Article 112. Only the National Assembly has power to revise the Constitution. Amendments to the Constitution require a two-thirds majority vote of all deputies to the National Assembly.

YUGOSLAVIA

INTRODUCTION

Smiljko Sokol

The Yugoslav Constitution enacted in 1974 was preceded by several constitutions and constitution-related acts. The first of these, the 1946 Constitution (passed on 31 January 1946; *Službeni list FNRJ* [Official Gazette], 1946 No. 10), provided legal and political foundations for the continuation of the socialist revolution after the working class had seized political power during the National Liberation Struggle (1941–1945). It introduced the administrative model of management in the economy and other spheres of social labor.

The Fundamental Law of 1953 (passed on 13 January 1953; *Službeni list FNRJ* 1953 No. 3) sanctioned the system of workers' self-management which had been introduced by the Workers' Councils Act in 1950. It brought the organization of the Federation into accord with progress made in the development of self-management, decentralization of decision-making, and the strengthening of the principle of socialist legality.

The expansion of the self-management rights of working people in economic organizations, the introduction of self-management in social activities (education, culture, science, health and social welfare services), and its increasing application on a territorial basis, especially through the communal system, created conditions for enacting the Constitution of 1963 (7 April 1963; *Službeni list SFRJ* 1963 No. 14). This sanctioned social self-management as the basic form of social decision-making in Yugoslavia and at the same time, through a set of programmatic norms, provided conditions for accelerating its application in all spheres of social activity.

The 1963 Constitution, like the 1974 Constitution, regulated not only the organization of government and the rights, freedoms, and duties of citizens, as was the case with the previous constitutions, but it also comprehensively defined the fundamental characteristics of all basic socio-economic and socio-political relations and institutions in Yugoslav society. It was, therefore, not only a state constitution but also the country's basic social charter. In addition, the makers of the 1963 Constitution were faced with the task of determining the political forms of the organization of a society which was increasingly based on self-management, but in which state power was still to a

Introduction

considerable extent socially necessary in objective terms. This problem of duality in Yugoslav socialist society, *i.e.* the fact that it was organized both on a self-management and a state basis, was not always most appropriately solved by the institutional forms introduced by the 1963 Constitution, even though in principle it successfully expressed their dialectical interrelationship. This was the basic reason why the 1963 Constitution was soon revised, although its fundamental conceptions were fully confirmed in social practice and were therefore endorsed by the 1974 Constitution.

The 1963 Constitution was revised three times by sets of constitutional amendments. Six amendments were passed on 18 April 1967 (*Službeni list SFRJ* 1967 No. 18), thirteen on 26 December 1968 (*Službeni list SFRJ* 1968 No. 55) and twenty-three on 30 June 1971 (*Službeni list SFRJ* 1971 No. 29).

The SFRY Constitution now in force was promulgated on 21 February 1974 (*Službeni list SFRJ* 1974 No. 9). While endorsing the basic principles and conceptions of the 1963 Constitution, the new Constitution introduced considerable changes in many of its provisions pertaining to the organization of the socio-economic and political system.

Three basic groups of changes were introduced by the Constitution of 1974 relative to the 1963 Constitution. First of all, significant changes were made in the system of the pooling of labor and regarding the realization of workers' self-management rights. According to the 1974 Constitution, basic organizations of associated labor are the smallest work units in which workers are able by pooling labor and resources directly to decide (by referenda and at workers' assemblies) on the use of the income they generate through their labor, and on relations among themselves. From basic organizations of associated labor develop other, broader forms of the pooling of labor and resources (work organizations, composite organizations of associated labor), and the so-called free exchange of labor through which (within self-managing communities of interest) education, science, culture, health and welfare services are financed directly by users of the respective services, without the intermediary of government organs.

Furthermore, a delegate system was introduced under which working people in basic organizations of associated labor, in local communities, and in socio-political organizations (the Socialist Alliance, the Confederation of Trade Unions, the League of Communists) elect delegates to the assemblies of socio-political communities and thus exercise permanent control over the latter's work. As a result, political power stems from and is linked to the self-management organization of society, both organizationally and functionally. The delegate system and its institutions have also brought about significant changes in the assembly system, both with respect to the composition of the assemblies of socio-political communities and their relations with executive and administrative agencies.

The third group of changes relate to the federal system, which has been brought into accord with the level attained in the development of self-management and in social decentralization of decision-making. Relative to the 1963 Constitution, the 1974 Constitution has to a considerable extent narrowed the powers of the Federation in favor of the socialist republics and autonomous provinces and has, in addition, extended and reinforced the various forms of participation by the republics and autonomous provinces in the exercise of federal functions. Thus, the Federal Constitution may only be amended with the agreement of all republics and autonomous provinces, whose consent is also required for the adoption of all enactments concerning the Federation's economic functions (economic plans, budget, tariffs, etc.).

Yugoslavia's constitutional order and her entire socio-economic and political system differ significantly from those in other European socialist states. By having introduced social self-management as the basic and general model of social decision-making as early as 1950, Yugoslavia has gradually but consistently been moving away from the administrative, statist, and centralist system, and has, through a whole array of original constitutional, economic, and political institutions, built a specific form of socialist democracy of her own.

CONSTITUTION OF THE SOCIALIST FEDERAL REPUBLIC OF YUGOSLAVIA OF 21 FEBRUARY 1974

Introductory Part	428
The Socialist Federal Republic of Yugoslavia	444
The Social System	446
The Socio-Economic System	446
The Foundations of the Socio-Political System	475
The Freedoms, Rights, and Duties of Man and the Citizen	498
Constitutionality and Legality	509
Courts and Office of the Public Prosecutor	511
National Defense	515
Relations in the Federation and the Rights and Duties of the Federation	517
Relations in the Federation	517
The Rights and Duties of the Federation	531
Organization of the Federation	537
The Assembly of the Socialist Federal Republic of Yugoslavia	537
The Presidency of the Socialist Federal Republic of Yugoslavia	549
The President of the Republic	555
The Federal Executive Council	558
Federal Administrative Agencies	563
The Federal Court, the Office of the Federal Public Prosecutor, and the Office of the Social Attorney of Self-Management	565
The Constitutional Court of Yugoslavia	567
The Formal Declaration	574
Amending the Constitution of the Socialist Federal Republic of Yugoslavia	575
Transitional and Concluding Provisions	576

CONSTITUTION OF THE SOCIALIST FEDERAL REPUBLIC OF YUGOSLAVIA*

Službeni list SFRJ 1974 No. 18.

INTRODUCTORY PART

Basic Principles

I.

The nations of Yugoslavia, proceeding from the right of every nation to self-determination, including the right to secession, on the basis of their will freely expressed in the common struggle of all nations and nationalities in the National Liberation War and Socialist Revolution, and in conformity with their historic aspirations, aware that further consolidation of their brotherhood and unity is in the common interest, have, together with the nationalities with which they live, united in a federal republic of free and equal nations and nationalities and founded a socialist federal community of working people—the Socialist Federal Republic of Yugoslavia, in which, in the interests of each nation and nationality separately and of all of them together, they shall realize and ensure:
— socialist social relations based on self-management by working people and the protection of the socialist self-management system;
— national freedom and independence;
— brotherhood and unity of the nations and nationalities;
— uniform interests of the working class, and solidarity among workers and all working people;
— possibilities and freedoms for the all-round development of the human personality and for the rapprochement of the nations and nationalities, in conformity with their interests and aspirations on the road to the creation of an ever-richer culture and civilization in socialist society;
— unification and adjustment of efforts to develop the economic

*Translated by Marko Pavičić.

foundations of a socialist society and the prosperity of the people;
— a system of socio-economic relations and uniform foundations for a political system which will ensure the common interests of the working class and all working people, and the equality of the nations and nationalities;
— linking of Yugoslavia's aspirations with the progressive strivings of mankind.

Working people and the nations and nationalities shall exercise their sovereign rights in the Socialist Republics, and in the Socialist Autonomous Provinces in conformity with their constitutional rights, and shall exercise these rights in the Socialist Federal Republic of Yugoslavia when in their common interests it is so specified by the present Constitution.

Working people and the nations and nationalities shall make decisions in the Federation according to the principles of agreement among the Republics and Autonomous Provinces, solidarity and reciprocity, equal participation by the Republics and Autonomous Provinces in federal organs, in line with the present Constitution, and according to the principle of responsibility of the Republics and Autonomous Provinces for their own development and for the development of the socialist community as a whole.

II.

The socialist social system of the Socialist Federal Republic of Yugoslavia is based on the power of the working class and all working people, and on relations among people as free and equal producers and creators whose labor serves exclusively for the satisfaction of their personal and common needs.

These relationships are based on the socio-economic status of the working man which ensures him that, by working with socially-owned resources and by deciding directly and on an equal footing with other working people in associated labor on all matters concerning social reproduction under conditions and relations of mutual interdependence, responsibility, and solidarity, he shall realize his personal material and moral interests and the right to benefit from the results of his current and past labor, and from the achievements of general material and social progress, and that on this basis he shall satisfy his personal and social needs and develop his working and other creative abilities.

In conformity with this, man's inviolable status and role shall be based on:

— social ownership of the means of production which precludes the return of any kind of system of exploitation of man, and which, by ending the alienation of the working class and working people from the means of production and other conditions of labor, ensures self-management by working people in production, in the distribution of the product of labor, and in guidance of the development of society on self-management foundations;

— emancipation of labor as a means of transcending the historically conditioned socio-economic inequalities and dependence of people in labor, which shall be ensured through the elimination of antagonism between labor and capital and of any form of wage-labor relationships, all-round development of productive forces, a rise in labor productivity, a reduction in working hours, development and application of science and technical achievements, increasing provision of higher education for all, and a rise in the culture of the working people;

— right to self-management on the basis of which every working man shall decide on an equal footing with other working people on his own labor and on the conditions and results of labor, on his own and common interests, and on the guidance of social development, and shall exercise power and manage other social affairs;

— right of the working man to enjoy the fruits of his labor and of the economic progress of the social community in keeping with the principle: "From each according to his abilities—to each according to his labor", provided he ensures the development of the economic foundations of his own and social labor, and contributes to the satisfaction of other social needs;

— man's economic, social, and personal security;

— solidarity and reciprocity by everyone towards all and by all towards everyone, based on the awareness of working people that they can realize their lasting interests only on the basis of these principles;

— free initiative in the development of production and other social and personal activities for the benefit of man and the social community;

— democratic political relations which make it possible for man to realize his interests, the right to self-management and other rights, to develop his personality through direct activity in social life, and especially in bodies of self-management, socio-political organizations and other social organizations and associations, which he himself sets up and through which he exercises an influence on the development of social consciousness and on the expansion of conditions for his

own activity and for the attainment of his interests and rights;
— equality of rights, duties, and responsibilities of people, in conformity with constitutionality and legality.

The socio-economic and political system stems from this position of man, and it shall serve him and his role in society.

Any form of the management of production and of other social activities, and any form of distribution that distorts social relationships based on the above defined position of man—be it through bureaucratic arbitrariness, technocratic usurpation, or privileges based on the monopoly of management of the means of production, or the appropriation of social resources on a group-property basis, or any other mode of privatization of such resources, or in the form of private-property or particularist selfishness, or through any form restricting the working class in playing its historic role in socio-economic and political relations and in organizing power for itself and for all working people, shall be contrary to the socio-economic and political system laid down by the present Constitution.

III.

Social ownership, as an expression of socialist socio-economic relationships among people, shall be the basis of free associated labor and of the ruling position of the working class in production and in social reproduction as a whole; it shall also be the basis of personal property acquired through one's own labor and serving for the satisfaction of man's needs and interests.

Socially-owned means of production, being the common, inalienable basis of social labor and social reproduction, shall exclusively serve as a basis for the performance of work aimed at the satisfaction of the personal and common needs and interests of working people, and at the development of the economic foundations of socialist society and socialist relations of self-management. Socially-owned means of production, including the means for expanded reproduction, shall be managed directly by associated workers working with such means, in their own interests and in the interests of the working class and socialist society. In performing these social functions, associated workers shall be responsible to one another and to the socialist community as a whole.

Social ownership of the means of production and other resources shall ensure that everyone becomes integrated, under equal conditions, into associated labor working with social resources, and that, by realizing his right to work with social resources, and on the basis of his own labor, he earns income for the satisfaction of his personal and common needs.

Since no one has the right of ownership over the social means of production, nobody—not socio-political communities, nor organizations of associated labor, nor groups of citizens, nor individuals—may appropriate on any legal-property grounds the product of social labor or manage and dispose of the social means of production and labor, or arbitrarily determine conditions for distribution.

Man's labor shall be the only basis for the appropriation of the product of social labor and for the management of social resources.

The distribution of income between the part which serves for the expansion of the economic foundations of social labor and the part which serves for the satisfaction of the personal and common needs of working people, in conformity with the principle of distribution according to work performed, shall be decided upon by the working people who generate this income, in compliance with mutual responsibility and solidarity and with socially-determined fundamentals of and criteria for the acquisition and distribution of income.

Resources earmarked for the replacement and expansion of the economic foundations of social labor shall be the common basis for the maintenance and development of society, *i.e.* for social reproduction realized on the basis of self-management by the working people through all forms of the pooling of labor and resources and through mutual cooperation among organizations of associated labor.

Basic organizations of associated labor, which are the fundamental form of associated labor in which workers exercise their inalienable right by working with social resources to manage their own labor and conditions of labor and to decide on the results of their labor, shall be the basis of all forms of the pooling of labor and resources and of self-management integration.

By realizing the results of their joint labor in terms of value on the market under conditions of socialist commodity production, workers shall, through direct linkage, self-management agreements and social compacts concluded by their organizations of associated labor and other self-managing organizations and communities, and by planning work and development, integrate social labor, promote the entire system of socialist socio-economic relations, and control the blind forces of the market.

The monetary and credit system shall be a constituent part of relations in social reproduction based on self-management by workers in associated labor working with social resources, and the entire income realized in such relations shall be an inalienable part of the income of basic organizations of associated labor.

Proceeding from the interdependence of the producing, trading, and financial spheres of associated labor, as parts of the unified system of social reproduction, workers in organizations of associated labor shall regulate their mutual relations in social reproduction and shall cooperate in such a way as will ensure workers in production the right to decide on the results of their own current and past labor in the entirety of these relations.

Working people shall ensure the satisfaction of their personal and common needs and interests in the field of education, science, culture, health, and other social activities, which are part of the unified process of social labor, by freely exchanging and pooling their labor and the labor of workers in organizations of associated labor operating in the above fields. Working people shall achieve such free exchange of labor directly, through organizations of associated labor and within the framework of or through self-managing communities of interest. Such relations shall ensure working people in these activities the same socio-economic status as that enjoyed by workers in other organizations of associated labor.

To achieve a fuller, more rational, and organized satisfaction of their personal and common needs and interests in social activities and in certain activities in material production, working people shall together with workers in organizations of associated labor in such activities, set up communities of interest in which they shall freely exchange labor and directly regulate relations of common interest. Workers and working people shall also form self-managing communities of interest by pooling resources on the basis of the principles of reciprocity and solidarity.

Working people who independently carry out activities with their own personal labor and resources in citizens' ownership shall, on the basis of their own labor, have, in principle, the same socio-economic status and basically the same rights and obligations as workers in organizations of associated labor.

Enjoying the right of ownership of arable land, as spelled out in the present Constitution, farmers shall have the right and obligation to exploit this land for the purposes of promoting agricultural production in their own interest and in the interest of the socialist community. The socialist community shall give full support to farmers in raising the productivity of their labor and in freely associating in cooperatives and other forms of association in order to promote the conditions of their work and life.

In order to achieve organized integration of farmers in socialist self-management socio-economic relations and to foster agricultural production, conditions shall be ensured for the development of agriculture on the basis of social resources and social labor, and so shall conditions for the association of farmers in, and their cooperation with, organizations of associated labor according to the principles of free choice and equality.

In order to provide economic foundations for the equality of the nations and nationalities of Yugoslavia, to equalize the economic conditions of the social life and work of working people, and to achieve the most harmonious possible development of the economy as a whole, in the Socialist Federal Republic of Yugoslavia special attention shall, in the common interest, be paid to the faster development of productive forces in economically underdeveloped Republics and Autonomous Provinces, and to this end the necessary resources shall be ensured and other measures taken.

In order to promote the conditions of life and work, create foundations for their stability and the fullest utilization of possibilities for the development of society's productive forces and for raising the productivity of their own and total social labor, to develop socialist relations of self-management on this basis, and to control the blind forces of the market, workers in basic and other organizations of associated labor and working people in self-managing communities of interest and other self-managing organizations and communities, and also in socio-political communities, shall, by relying on science and the assessment of development possibilities based thereon, and by planning their work and development, adjust relations in social reproduction and direct the development of social production and other social activities to serve their common interests and aims determined on a self-management basis.

IV.

In the Socialist Federal Republic of Yugoslavia, all power shall be vested in the working class in alliance with all working people in towns and villages.

In order to create a society of free producers, the working class and all working people shall develop socialist self-management democracy as a special form of the dictatorship of the proletariat; they shall ensure this through:

— revolutionary abolition of and constitutional ban on any form of socio-economic and political relations and organization based on class exploitation and property monopoly, or on any kind of political action aimed at the establishment of such relations;

— realization of self-management in organizations of associated labor, local communities, self-managing communities of interest and other self-managing organizations and communities, and also in socio-political communities and society as a whole, and through the mutual linkage of and cooperation among such organizations and communities;
— free and equal self-management regulation of mutual relations and adjustment of the common and general interests of working people and their self-managing organizations and communities by self-management agreements and social compacts;
— decision-making by working people in the realization of power and in the management of other social affairs in basic organizations of associated labor and other basic self-managing organizations and communities, through delegations and delegates in the managing bodies of self-managing organizations and communities, and also through delegations and delegates to the assemblies of socio-political communities and other bodies of self-management;
— keeping the working people informed of all questions significant for the realization of their socio-economic status and for the fullest and most competent possible decision-making in the performance of functions of power and management of other social affairs;
— public character of work of all organs of power and self-management, and of holders of self-management, public, and other social functions;
— personal responsibility of holders of self-management, public, and other social functions, responsibility of organs of power and self-management, recallability of holders of self-management, public, and other social functions, and restriction of their re-election and re-appointment to specific functions;
— realization of supervision by workers and other working people and of social control in general over the work of holders of self-management, public, and other social functions in self-managing organizations and communities and in socio-political communities;
— realization and protection of constitutionality and legality;
— socio-political activity by socialist forces organized in socio-political organizations;
— free and all-round activity by people.

Self-management by working people in basic organizations of associated labor, local communities, self-managing communities of interest, and other basic self-managing organizations and communities shall be the basis of a uniform system of self-management by and power of the working class and all working people.

In order to ensure conditions for their life and work and for social development and the creation of the socialist community, working people in the Communes, as self-managing and basic socio-political communities, shall realize their common interests, exercise power, and manage other social affairs by linking their organizations of associated labor and other self-managing organizations and communities through the activity of socio-political organizations, and through self-management agreements, social compacts, and the functioning of assemblies as the common bodies of all working people and their organizations and communities.

The constitutionally-established functions of power and management of social affairs in socio-political communities shall be conducted by the assemblies of socio-political communities, as elected and recallable delegations of working people in self-managing organizations and communities and socio-political organizations, and by other agencies responsible to the assemblies.

In order to ensure the fullest possible participation of working people and all organized socialist forces in the realization of power and management of other social affairs, and in order to adjust their common and general social interests, organs of socio-political communities shall consider initiatives, opinions, and proposals of socio-political organizations, take stands thereon, and cooperate with socio-political organizations.

The working class and all working people shall, through state power by means of generally-binding rules, secure socialist social relations, the development of society and management of social affairs on a self-management basis, protect the freedoms of man and the citizen, socialist self-management relations and the self-management rights of working people, and shall settle social conflicts and protect the constitutionally-established order.

The self-management status and rights of the working man in basic and other organizations of associated labor, local communities, self-managing communities of interest, and in other self-managing organizations and communities, the self-management status of working people in the Communes, free association on the basis of self-management, activities and creative endeavor by working people, the equality of the nations and nationalities, and the freedom, rights, and duties of man and the citizen, as laid down by the present Constitution, shall be the basis, limit, and direction for the realization of the rights and duties of socio-political communities in exercising the functions of power.

Social self-protection, as a function of a society based on self-management, shall be achieved through activities by working people, citizens, organizations of associated labor and other self-managing organizations and communities, socio-political and other organizations, and socio-political communities, with a view to safeguarding the constitutional order, the self-management rights of working people, and other rights and freedoms of man and the citizen, protecting social property, ensuring the personal and property security of working people and citizens, and achieving free social development.

In order to realize and adjust their interests and self-managing rights in line with the general interests of socialist society, and in order to conduct certain social affairs and develop various activities, working people and citizens shall freely combine in socio-political and other social organizations and citizens' associations, as constituent parts of the socialist system based on self-management.

Socio-political organizations, as a form of free socialist political organization of working people based on class socialist foundations, shall be constituent parts of and active factors in the development and protection of socialist society based on self-management.

V.

The freedoms, rights, and duties of man and the citizen, as spelled out by the present Constitution, are an inseparable part and expression of democratic socialist self-management relations in which man is becoming liberated from any form of exploitation and arbitrariness and, with his labor, is creating conditions for the all-round and free expression and protection of his personality and respect for human dignity. The freedoms and rights of man and the citizen shall only be restricted by the equal freedoms and rights of others and by the interests of socialist society. Socialist society shall ensure conditions for the fullest possible realization and protection of the freedoms and rights laid down by the present Constitution. Any activity infringing the freedom and rights of man and the citizen shall be contrary to the interests of socialist society.

Proceeding from the fact that education, science, and culture are essential factors in the development of socialist society, the rise in labor productivity, the development of people's creative forces and the all-round development of the human personality, the humanization of socialist relations of self-management and society's general progress, the socialist community shall ensure freedom of creative endeavor and create conditions for the development and promotion of education and scientific, cultural and artistic creativity, so that they may contribute as successfully as possible to the rise in the creative abilities of the working people, the promotion of socialist social relations, and the all-round development of a free and humanized personality.

The system of upbringing and education shall be based on the achievements of modern science, especially of Marxism as the foundation of scientific socialism, and shall be instrumental in training young people for work and self-management, and in educating them in the spirit of achievements of the Socialist Revolution, the socialist code of ethics, self-management democracy, socialist patriotism, brotherhood and unity, equality of the nations and nationalities, and socialist internationalism.

Working people in organizations of associated labor and other self-managing organizations and communities shall, on the basis of solidarity, reciprocity, and socialist humanism, ensure their economic and social security, and shall create increasingly favorable conditions for their life and work, and for the development of an all-round personality in the working man. These aims of welfare policy shall be attained through constant improvement and equalization of the conditions of life and work, transcendence, on the basis of solidarity and reciprocity, of differences stemming from economic undevelopment and other unequal conditions of life and work, equalization of possibilities for education and work, and through the prevention and elimination of social differences which are not based on the application of the principle of distribution according to work performed.

The socialist social community shall ensure financial and other conditions for the realization of the rights of veterans, disabled veterans, and dependents of veterans killed in war, which guarantee their social security.

In order to conserve and improve the human environment, working people and citizens, organizations of associated labor, other self-managing organizations and communities, and socialist society shall ensure conditions to preserve and improve natural and other values of the human environment conducive to a healthy, safe, and active life and work for the present and future generations.

VI.

The working people and citizens, nations and nationalities of Yugoslavia are determined to direct their forces towards peaceful creative work and the construction of their self-management socialist community, and consistently to pursue a policy of peace and against aggression, war, and aggressive pressure of any kind. In order to secure their peaceful development and socialist construction, they are determined with all available forces and resources, through armed struggle and other forms of total national defense, to protect and defend their freedom, independence, sovereignty, territorial integrity, and the socialist self-management order of the Socialist Federal Republic of Yugoslavia. For this purpose, the working people and citizens and the nations and nationalities of Yugoslavia shall organize and build up a system of total national defense, as an inseparable part of the socialist self-management social system, aware that the defensive ability of society and the defensive preparedness of the country are the greater and possibility for aggression the smaller, the more developed total national defense is as a form and substance of the defensive organization of the social community. The strengthening of the defensive ability of the country shall be a component part of the policy of peace and international cooperation based on terms of equality.

Total national defense in the Socialist Federal Republic of Yugoslavia is an integrated system covering the organization, preparation, and participation of the Federation, Republics, Autonomous Provinces, Communes, organizations of associated labor, local communities, self-managing communities of interest and other self-managing organizations and communities, socio-political and social organizations, working people, and citizens in armed struggle and in all other forms of resistance, and in the performance of other duties concerning the defense of the country. In total national defense, armed struggle shall be the decisive form of resisting aggression. The Armed Forces of the Socialist Federal Republic of Yugoslavia shall be the principle factor in armed struggle and shall be a unified whole. The supreme administration and command of the Armed Forces shall ensure the unity and indivisibility of armed struggle.

VII.

Proceeding from the conviction that peaceful coexistence and active cooperation among states and peoples, irrespective of differences in their social systems, are indispensable conditions for peace and social progress in the world, the Socialist Federal Republic of Yugoslavia shall base its international relations on the principles of respect for national sovereignty and equality, non-interference in the internal affairs of other countries, socialist internationalism, and settlement of international disputes by peaceful means. In its international relations, the Socialist Federal Republic of Yugoslavia shall adhere to the principles of the United Nations Charter, fulfill its international commitments, and take an active part in the activities of the international organizations to which it is affiliated.

In order to carry these principles into effect, the Socialist Federal Republic of Yugoslavia shall strive:

— for the establishment and development of all forms of international cooperation conducive to the consolidation of peace, the strengthening of mutual respect, equality, and friendship among nations and states and their rapprochement; for the broadest and freest possible exchange of material and intellectual goods, for the freedom of mutual exchange of information, and for the development of other relations contributory to the realization of common economic, cultural, and other interests of states, nations, and people, especially to the development of democratic and socialist relations in international cooperation, and to socialist progress in general, to the overcoming of the bloc divisions of the world, to the renunciation of the use of force or threat of force in international relations, and to the attainment of general and complete disarmament;

— for the right of every nation freely to determine and build up its own social and political system by ways and means of its own free choice;

— for the right of nations to self-determination and national independence, and for their right to wage a liberation war to attain these aims;

— for respect for the rights of national minorities, including the rights of members of Yugoslav nations living in other countries as national minorities;

— for international support for peoples waging a just struggle for their national independence and liberation from imperialism, colonialism, and all other forms of national oppression and subjugation;

— for the development of such international cooperation as will ensure equality in economic relations in the world, sovereign exploitation of national natural resources, and the creation of conditions conducive to the accelerated development of underdeveloped countries;

— for respect for generally accepted rules of international law.

In pressing for all-round political, economic, and cultural cooperation with other nations and states, the Socialist Federal Republic of Yugoslavia, as a socialist community of nations, holds the view that this cooperation should contribute to the creation of those democratic forms of linkage among states, nations and people which suit the interests of nations and social progress, and is in this respect an open community.

All organs, organizations, and individuals shall be bound in international economic, political, cultural, and other relations, and in their relations with organs and organizations abroad, to abide by these principles of the foreign policy and international activity of the Socialist Federal Republic of Yugoslavia, and to strive for their realization.

VIII.

The League of Communists of Yugoslavia, as the initiator and organizer of the National Liberation War and Socialist Revolution, and as the conscious champion of the aspirations and interests of the working class, has become, by the laws of historical development, the leading organized ideological and political force of the working class and of all working people in the creation of socialism and in the realization of solidarity among working people, and of brotherhood and unity among the nations and nationalities of Yugoslavia.

Under conditions of socialist democracy and social self-management, the League of Communists of Yugoslavia, with its guiding ideological and political action, shall be the prime mover and exponent of political activity aimed at safeguarding and further developing the socialist revolution and socialist social relations of self-management, and especially at the strengthening of socialist social and democratic consciousness, and shall be responsible therefor.

The Socialist Alliance of the Working People of Yugoslavia, created during the National Liberation War and Socialist Revolution as a voluntary and democratic front of working people and citizens and all organized socialist forces, headed by the Communist Party, and further developed under conditions of a socialist society based on self-management, shall be the broadest base for socio-political activity in the socialist system of self-management.

In the Socialist Alliance of the Working People of Yugoslavia, working people and citizens, the League of Communists of Yugoslavia, as the leading ideological and political force, and other socio-political organizations, and all organized socialist forces shall realize the political unity and unity of action of socialist forces, and shall guide social development on the foundations of the power of and self-management by the working class and all working people, and for this purpose they shall:

— discuss social questions and take political initiative in all fields of social life, adjust views, lay down political stands regarding the solution of such questions, the guidance of social development, the realization of the rights and interests of working people and citizens, the realization of the equality of the nations and nationalities, and the promotion of socialist self-management democratic relations, submit proposals for the solution of social questions, and issue guidelines to their delegates to the assemblies of socio-political communities;

— draw up joint programs for social activity and lay down common criteria for the election of delegations in basic organizations of associated labor, local communities, and other self-managing organizations and communities, and for the election of delegates to the assemblies of socio-political communities; ensure democratic nomination and determination of candidates for members of delegations in self-managing organizations and communities, and candidates for delegates to the assemblies of socio-political communities, and candidates for the performance of self-management, public, and other social functions in socio-political communities; consider general issues of cadre policy and the build-up of cadres, and lay down criteria for the selection of cadres;

— monitor the work of the organs of power and of the managing bodies of self-managing organizations and communities, and of the holders of self-management, public, and other social functions, express their opinions and pass judgments and exercise social supervision and criticism of their work, especially with regard to ensuring the publicity of and responsibility for their work;

— create conditions for the all-round participation of young people and their organizations in social and political life;

— make sure that working people and citizens are kept informed, and ensure their influence on the social system of information and the realization of the role of the press and other media of public information and communication;

— fight for humane relationships among people, for the development of socialist democratic consciousness and norms of socialist life, and to prevent practices which check the development of socialist self-management democratic social relations or are in any way harmful to them.

Within the framework of their rights and duties, the socio-political communities shall be obliged to secure material and other conditions for the realization of the constitutionally-defined functions of the Socialist Alliance of the Working People of Yugoslavia.

Workers organized on a voluntary basis in trade unions, as the broadest organizations of the working class, shall strive to: realize the constitutionally-defined status of the working class; achieve socialist self-management relations and the decisive role of workers in the management of social reproduction; realize the interests and self-management and other rights of workers in all fields of work and life, ensure equality among workers in the pooling of labor and resources, the acquisition and distribution of income, and the determination of common scales for distribution according to the results of labor; ensure self-management linkage and integration of various fields of social labor; further the development of the productive forces of society and the raising of labor productivity; guide self-management adjustment of individual, common, and general social interests; take care of the education of workers and their training for the performance of self-management and other social functions; ensure democratic nomination and determination of candidates for delegates to managing bodies in organizations of associated labor and other self-managing organizations and communities, and of candidates for delegations in such organizations and communities, and for delegates to the assemblies of socio-political communities; ensure the broadest possible participation of workers in the exercise of the functions of power and management of other social affairs; realize the interests of the working class in cadre policy; protect workers' rights; ensure workers' social security, the development of their standard of living, and the development and strengthening of solidarity and the raising of the class consciousness and responsibility among self-managers.

Trade unions shall initiate self-management agreements and social compacts and take direct part in their negotiation; they shall submit proposals to the managing bodies of self-managing organizations and communities, the assemblies of socio-political communities, and other state and social organs concerning the solution of questions relating to the economic and social position of the working class.

IX.

The socio-economic and political system and other relations laid down by the present Constitution are aimed at broadening conditions for the further development of socialist society, overcoming its contradictions, and achieving such social progress as will, on the basis of the all-round development of productive forces, high labor productivity, affluence of products, and all-round development of man as an emancipated personality, make possible the development of those social relations in which the Communist principle: "From each according to his abilities; to each according to his needs", shall be realized.

To this end bodies of self-management, state organs, self-managing organizations and communities, socio-political and other organizations, working people and citizens directly—are called upon through the entirety of their activities:

— to expand and strengthen the economic foundations of society and of the life of individuals by developing productive forces, raising the productivity of labor, and continually promoting socialist self-management relations;

— to create conditions under which socio-economic differences between intellectual and physical labor will gradually be transcended, and under which human labor will tend to become an ever fuller expression of creative endeavor and of the human personality;

— to expand and develop all forms of self-management and socialist self-management democracy, especially in those fields where the functions of political power predominate; to curb coercion and create conditions for its elimination; and to build up relations among people based on an awareness of common interests, on the socialist code of ethics, and man's free creative endeavor;

— to contribute to the realization of human freedoms and rights, the humanization of the social environment and the human personality, the strengthening of solidarity and humaneness among people, and respect for human dignity;

— to develop all-round cooperation and rapprochement with all nations, in keeping with the progressive aspirations of mankind for the creation of a free community of all nations of the world.

X.

By expressing the basic principles of a socialist society based on self-management and its progress, this section of the present Constitution shall be both the basis of and a directive for the interpretation of the Constitution and laws, and for the action of all and everyone.

PART I. THE SOCIALIST FEDERAL REPUBLIC OF YUGOSLAVIA

Article 1. The Socialist Federal Republic of Yugoslavia is a federal state having the form of a state community of voluntarily united nations and their Socialist Republics, and of the Socialist Autonomous Provinces of Vojvodina and Kosovo, which are constituent parts of the Socialist Republic of Serbia, based on the power of and self-management by the working class and all working people; it is at the same time a socialist self-management democratic community of working people and citizens, and of nations and nationalities having equal rights.

Article 2. The Socialist Federal Republic of Yugoslavia consists of the Socialist Republic of Bosnia-Herzegovina, the Socialist Republic of Croatia, the Socialist Republic of Macedonia, the Socialist Republic of Montenegro, the Socialist Republic of Serbia, the Socialist Autonomous Province of Vojvodina and the Socialist Autonomous Province of Kosovo, which are constituent parts of the Socialist Republic of Serbia, and the Socialist Republic of Slovenia.

Article 3. The Socialist Republics are states based on the sovereignty of the people and the power of and self-management by the working class and all working people, and are socialist, self-managing democratic communities of working people and citizens, and of nations and nationalities having equal rights.

Article 4. The Socialist Autonomous Provinces are autonomous socialist self-managing democratic socio-political communities based on the power of and self-management by the working class and all working people, in which working people, nations, and nationalities realize their sovereign rights, and when so specified by the Constitution of the Socialist Republic of Serbia in the common interests of the working people, nations, and nationalities of that Republic as a whole, they do so also within the Republic.

Article 5. The territory of the Socialist Federal Republic of Yugoslavia is a single unified whole and consists of the territories of the Socialist Republics.

The territory of a Republic may not be altered without the consent of that Republic, and the territory of an Autonomous Province—without the consent of that Autonomous Province.

The frontiers of the Socialist Federal Republic of Yugoslavia may not be altered without the consent of all Republics and Autonomous Provinces.

Boundaries between the Republics may only be altered on the basis of mutual agreement, and if the boundary of an Autonomous Province is involved—also on the basis of the latter's agreement.

Article 6. The coat-of-arms of the Socialist Federal Republic of Yugoslavia is a field encircled by ears of wheat tied at the base by a blue band bearing the date 29 XI 1943. Between the tips of the ears is a five-pointed star. In the center of the field are six torches set obliquely whose flames fuse into a single flame.

Article 7. The flag of the Socialist Federal Republic of Yugoslavia consists of three colors: blue, white, and red, with a five-pointed red star in the center. The ratio of the width to the length of the flag is one to two. The colors of the flag are set horizontally, in the following order from above: blue, white, and red. Each color occupies one-third of the width of the flag. The star has a regular five-pointed form and a golden (yellow) border. The central point of the star coincides with the point in which the diagonals of the flag intersect. The top point of the star extends as far as the center of the blue band of the flag, the lower points of the star assuming their respective places in the red band.

Article 8. The Socialist Federal Republic of Yugoslavia has an anthem.

Article 9. The capital of the Socialist Federal Republic of Yugoslavia is Belgrade.

PART II. THE SOCIAL SYSTEM

Chapter I. The Socio-Economic System

1. The Status of Man in Associated Labor, and Social Property

Article 10. The socialist socio-economic system of the Socialist Federal Republic of Yugoslavia shall be based on freely associated labor and socially-owned means of production, and on self-management by the working people in production and in the distribution of the social product in basic and other organizations of associated labor, and in social reproduction as a whole.

Article 11. Man's economic and social status shall be determined by labor and the results of labor, on the basis of equal rights and responsibilities.

No one may gain any material or other benefits, directly or indirectly, by exploiting the labor of others.

No one may in any way make it impossible for a worker to decide, or restrict him in deciding, on an equal footing with other workers, on his labor and the conditions and results of his labor.

Article 12. The means of production and other means of associated labor, products generated by associated labor and income realized through associated labor, resources for the satisfaction of common and general social needs, natural resources, and goods in public use shall be social property.

No one may acquire the right of ownership of the social resources which are conditions of labor in basic and other organizations of associated labor, or are the economic foundations for the realization of the functions of self-managing communities of interest and of other self-managing organizations and communities, and of socio-political communities.

Social resources may not be used for the appropriation of the surplus-labor of others, nor for creating conditions for such appropriation.

Article 13. Workers in associated labor working with socially-owned resources shall have the inalienable right to work with such resources to satisfy their personal and social needs, and to manage, freely and on an equal footing with other workers in associated labor, their labor and the conditions and results thereof.

The rights, obligations, and responsibilities concerning the disposal, utilization, and management of social resources shall be regulated by the Constitution and statute in line with the nature and purpose of such resources.

Article 14. Exercising their right to work with socially-owned resources, all workers in associated labor working with socially-owned resources shall be guaranteed the right in the basic organizations of associated labor in which they work and in any other forms of pooling of labor and resources, together and on equal footing with other workers, to manage the work and business of the organizations of associated labor and affairs and resources concerning the totality of relations in social reproduction, to regulate mutual relations in labor, to decide on income realized through various forms of the pooling of labor and resources, and to earn personal income.

Basic organizations of associated labor are the basic forms of associated labor in which workers, directly and on terms of equality, realize their socio-economic and other self-management rights, and decide on other questions concerning their socio-economic status.

Any act or conduct that violates these rights of workers shall be unconstitutional.

Article 15. In exercising the right to work with social resources, workers in associated labor shall in their common and general social interest be mutually responsible for using such resources in a socially and economically opportune manner, for constantly renewing, expanding, and improving them, as the economic foundations of their own and of total social labor, and for fulfilling their working obligations conscientiously.

In the exercise of their right to work with social resources, workers in associated labor may not acquire material benefits or other advantages that are not based on their labor.

Article 16. Workers in organizations of associated labor operating in the fields of education, science, culture, health, social welfare, and other social activities shall earn income through a free exchange of their labor for the labor of the working people whose needs and interests in these fields they satisfy.

Workers in such organizations of associated labor shall carry out such free exchange of labor directly with the working people whose needs and interests they satisfy or through their organizations of associated labor and self-managing communities of interest, or within the framework of self-managing communities of interest.

Through a free exchange of labor, workers in organizations of associated labor in social activities shall have the same socio-economic status as workers in organizations of associated labor in other activities.

The principles of free exchange of labor shall also apply to the earning of income by workers in organizations of associated labor in other activities in which the action of market laws cannot be a basis for the adjustment of work and needs, nor a basis for assessing the value of the results of labor.

Article 17. Total income resulting from the joint labor of workers in a basic organization of associated labor and from total social labor, earned through various forms of the pooling of labor and resources on the basis of the action of market laws and of the conditions of income earning, socially-determined on a self-management basis, shall be decided upon by workers in basic organizations of associated labor in conformity with their constitutional rights and responsibilities towards other workers in associated labor and towards the social community as a whole.

Basic organizations of associated labor shall distribute among themselves the entire income jointly realized through the pooling of labor and resources according to their contribution to the realization of such income, on the basis of criteria spelled out by them in self-management agreements.

Income realized in a basic organization of associated labor shall provide the economic foundations for the right of workers to decide on the conditions of their labor and the distribution of income, and to earn personal incomes.

Article 18. The part of income which is the result of work performed under exceptionally favorable natural conditions or which is the result of exceptional privileges on the market, or of any other exceptional privileges in income earning, shall be used, in line with self-management agreements and statute, for the development of the organization of associated labor in which such income has been realized, or for the development of the economic foundations of associated labor in the Commune, Republic, or Autonomous Province concerned.

The administration of the part of income used for the development of the economic foundations of associated labor in the Commune, Republic, or the Autonomous Province shall be based on the principles of self-management.

Article 19. Workers in a basic organization of associated labor shall allocate income for their personal and collective consumption, the expansion of the economic foundations of associated labor, and to the reserve fund.

Workers shall allocate for their total personal and collective consumption a part of income which is proportionate to their contribution to the realization of this income made through their labor and the investment of social resources stemming from their past labor.

Article 20. In line with the principle of distribution according to work performed and the rise in productivity of his own and total social labor, and in line with the principle of solidarity of workers in associated labor, every worker shall be entitled, from the income of his basic organization of associated labor, to a personal income for the satisfaction of his personal, common, and general social needs, according to the results of his labor and his personal contribution made to the increase in the income of the basic organization with his current and past labor.

Article 21. Workers in a basic organization of associated labor shall, together with workers in other organizations of associated labor, determine the common fundamentals of and scales for the distribution of income and the allocation of resources for personal income.

Should the distribution of income or the allocation of resources for personal incomes infringe relations corresponding to the principle of distribution according to work performed or upset the course of social reproduction, measures may be introduced by statute to ensure the equality of workers in the application of the principle of distribution according to work performed, or to prevent or eliminate disruptions in social reproduction.

Article 22. Every worker in associated labor working with social resources shall be guaranteed the right to a personal income and other rights stemming from labor, to an amount or extent which ensures his economic and social security.

The amount of his guaranteed personal income and the extent of other guaranteed rights, and the manner of their realization, shall be determined by self-management agreements, social compacts, and statute, depending on the general level of productivity of total social labor and on the general conditions prevailing in the environment in which the worker lives.

Article 23. A temporary restriction on the use by workers in basic organizations of associated labor of a part of the means of social reproduction, or an obligation to pool part of such means to finance certain indispensable needs of social reproduction, may be introduced by statute under conditions specified by the constitution. The obligatory pooling of part of the means of social reproduction may not lastingly deprive workers in basic organizations of associated labor of their rights concerning such means.

Article 24. Organizations of associated labor and/or other social legal entities shall be liable for their obligations to the extent of the social resources they manage.

Article 25. The rights of organizations of associated labor and other social legal entities regarding real property, individual movables, and other rights in social ownership may, against compensation and by a procedure specified by statute, be expropriated or restricted if this is required by statutorily-defined needs of land development planning or the construction of projects of social significance, or by some other general interest specified by statute.

As regards the rights concerning the land or other natural resources thus expropriated, the organization of associated labor or other social legal entity involved shall only be entitled to compensation for the labor and resources invested in such land or other natural resources. If the land or other natural resources concerned are conditions of labor, the organization of associated labor or other social legal entity shall be entitled to compensation which will ensure that these conditions do not deteriorate.

Article 26. Workers in a basic organization of associated labor which in its activity makes use of the resources of other organizations of associated labor, which are on that account entitled to a share in jointly earned income, must, within the framework of income thus earned, be ensured resources for their personal and collective consumption in line with the common fundamentals and scales in force in the organizations of associated labor, and also to resources for the expansion of the economic foundations of labor according to their contribution to the jointly earned income.

Criteria for determining the contribution to the jointly earned income shall be laid down by self-management agreement, in line with the uniform principles concerning the pooling of resources, as spelled out by federal statute.

Organizations of associated labor which pool resources may not, on this ground, acquire any lasting right to a share in the income of the organization of associated labor which, in its operations, makes use of these resources.

The right to a share in jointly earned income on account of the pooling of resources shall cease when, in addition to an adequate share in the jointly earned income, the organization of associated labor has also been returned the resources through the pooling of which this right was acquired or, when in conformity with the self-management agreement, the right to the restitution of resources has ceased to exist.

Article 27. Organizations of associated labor may, under conditions and within the limits laid down by federal statute, use resources of foreign persons for the conduct of their business.

Workers in organizations of associated labor which make use of resources invested by foreign persons shall have the same socio-economic and other self-management rights as workers in the organizations of associated labor which, in their operations, use resources of other domestic organizations of associated labor.

A foreign person who has invested resources in an organization of associated labor in the Socialist Federal Republic of Yugoslavia may share in the income of this organization only within the limits and under conditions prescribed for mutual relations among domestic organizations of associated labor.

The rights of foreign persons to resources invested in an organization of associated labor in the Socialist Federal Republic of Yugoslavia may not be restricted by statute or another enactment after the contract from which these rights stem has become legally valid.

Article 28. In order to expand the economic foundations of labor, organizations of associated labor may collect financial resources from citizens and ensure them, in addition to the repayment of these resources, compensation for investment in the form of interest or other benefits determined by statute.

Article 29. Workers who in an organization of associated labor perform administrative-professional, auxiliary, and similar activities of common interest to several organizations operating within it, and workers who perform such activities in an agricultural or other kind of cooperative, and also workers in an organization of a business association, bank, or insurance community, shall form a work community. Workers in such a work community may organize themselves into an organization of associated labor under conditions specified by statute.

Workers who, in an organization of associated labor perform other activities of common interest to several organizations operating within it, and workers who perform such activities on behalf of an agricultural or other kind of cooperative, shall form a work community if there are no constitutionally-determined conditions for them to organize themselves into a basic organization of associated labor.

Workers in such work communities shall be entitled to resources for their personal and collective consumption in line with the principle of distribution according to work performed and in line with the fundamentals and scales applicable in organizations of associated labor, and also to other self-management rights of workers in organizations of associated labor, in line with the nature of activities they perform and with the common interests for the purpose of which these work communities have been formed.

The mutual rights, obligations, and responsibilities of workers in such work communities and of the users of their services shall be regulated by self-management agreements, and mutual relations among workers in such work communities shall be regulated by their self-management enactments in conformity with self-management agreements.

Article 30. Workers in work communities which perform activities on behalf of self-managing communities of interest and of other self-managing organizations and communities, and their associations, socio-political organizations, and other social organizations, associations of citizens, and organs of socio-political communities, shall be entitled to resources for personal and collective consumption in line with the principle of distribution according to work performed and with socially-determined fundamentals and scales applicable to organizations of associated labor. They shall also have other self-management rights in conformity with the nature of activities they perform and the social and political responsibility of the organizations, communities, and organs on whose behalf they perform such activities—for the purpose of realization of their functions and tasks.

The mutual rights, duties, and responsibilities of workers in such work communities, and the organizations, communities, and organs on whose behalf they perform activities, shall be regulated by self-management agreement or by contract, in conformity with statute.

The rights, powers, and responsibilities of organizations, communities, and organs may not be transferred to the work communities which perform activities on their behalf.

The rights, obligations, and responsibilities of workers in work communities of the organs of socio-economic communities shall be regulated by statute, and when this is allowed by the nature of activity of the organ concerned—also by self-management agreement or contract entered into between the work communities and these organs and by self-management enactments of the work communities.

Active military personnel and civil persons serving in the Armed Forces of the Socialist Federal Republic of Yugoslavia shall realize corresponding rights in conformity with federal statute, in line with the nature of activities and character of the Armed Forces.

Article 31. Working people who with their personal labor independently perform as their occupation an artistic or other cultural activity, or a legal or other professional activity shall, in principle, have the same socio-economic status and basically the same rights and obligations as workers in organizations of associated labor.

Working people performing some of these activities may pool their labor and form temporary or lasting work communities, which shall basically have the same status as organizations of associated labor and in which the working people shall basically have the same rights and duties as workers in organizations of associated labor.

Conditions under which such working people and their work communities realize their rights and perform their obligations, and conditions under which in performing such activities they may make use of and manage social resources, shall be specified by statute. The way in which such working people will cooperate with organizations of associated labor, and the manner of their participation in the creation of conditions for work in these organizations and in the use of the results of their labor expressed as jointly realized income, shall also be specified by statute.

Article 32. Workers in organizations of associated labor shall, in line with the principles of reciprocity and solidarity, jointly and on an equal footing ensure continuous improvement in the living conditions of workers by allocating and pooling resources for this purpose, and in other ways.

Organizations of associated labor and socio-political communities shall be bound, in conformity with the principles of reciprocity and solidarity, to provide economic and other kinds of assistance to organizations of associated labor which have run into exceptional economic difficulties, and to take measures for their financial rehabilitation, if this is in the common interest of organizations of associated labor, or in the social interest.

An organization of associated labor, alone or in agreement with other organizations of associated labor, shall, in keeping with the principles of reciprocity and solidarity, ensure resources for the employment, retraining, and the realization of the acquired rights of workers, if their work is no longer needed in their organization of associated labor, or if an organization operating within it has ceased to operate.

Until he has been ensured an appropriate job which corresponds to his abilities and qualifications, no worker may lose the status of worker in a basic organization of associated labor if, due to technological or other kinds of innovation which contribute to the rise in labor productivity or to a greater success of the organization, his work is no longer needed in this organization.

An obligation to pool resources for these purposes and for

employment in general may be introduced by statute, and conditions for using such resources regulated by it.

Article 33. Workers in associated labor shall contribute to the satisfaction of constitutionally-determined general social needs in socio-political communities by paying taxes and other dues to these communities on the income of their basic organizations of associated labor and on their personal incomes, in line with the purpose or aims served by the resources collected through such taxes and dues.

The obligation to pay taxes and other dues to socio-political communities shall be determined in accordance with the ability of the economy to ensure, in line with the level of productivity of social labor as a whole, and in conformity with the requirements of material and social development which correspond to the economy's possibilities and to the long-term interests of the development of the productive forces of society, the satisfaction of the personal and common needs of workers and the requirements of expanded reproduction. These obligations shall be spelled out in accordance with the ability of organizations of associated labor to secure, in line with the general obligations of the economy, the results of their labor and the business success achieved by them, the satisfaction of these needs.

These principles shall also apply if a socio-political community with its enactments imposes some temporary restriction on the use of resources managed by workers in organizations of associated labor, or introduces an obligation to pool such resources.

2. Pooling of Labor and Means of Social Reproduction

Article 34. Workers in basic organizations of associated labor shall freely pool their labor and means of social reproduction in work organizations and in other forms of the pooling of labor and resources.

Mutual rights, obligations, and responsibilities stemming from the various forms of the pooling of labor and resources shall be regulated by workers in basic organizations of associated labor through self-management agreements in conformity with statute, ensuring within the totality of these relations the constitutionally-guaranteed rights of the workers.

Article 35. A work organization is an independent self-managing organization of workers linked in labor by common interests and organized in the basic organizations of associated labor which make up the work organization, or of workers directly linked together through the unity of the labor process.

A work organization may be founded by organizations of associated labor, self-managing communities of interest, local communities, socio-political communities, and other social legal entities.

A work organization may, under conditions and in the way specified by statute, be founded by working people with a view to realizing their right to work or to satisfying their needs with the goods and services of the organization they are founding. A work organization may, in conformity with statute, also be founded by civil legal entities.

Working people and/or civil legal entities which have invested their resources in an organization of associated labor founded by them, may with respect to this organization have, on account of such resources, only those rights which citizens have with respect to organizations of associated labor which collect resources from them for the purposes of expanding the economic foundations of labor.

It may be laid down by statute that working people and civil legal entities may not found work organizations in charge of the performance of specific activities.

Work organizations shall have the same status and workers in them the same socio-economic and other self-managing rights and responsibilities, regardless of who has founded the work organizations.

Article 36. Workers in a unit of a work organization which makes up a working whole in which the results of their joint labor can be expressed in terms of value within the work organization or on the market, and in which the workers can realize their socio-economic and other self-management rights, shall have the right and duty to organize such a unit of the work organization as a basic organization of associated labor.

Workers in a work organization which does not have conditions for its individual units to be organized as basic organizations of associated labor, shall have in their work organization the same rights as those vested in workers in basic organizations of associated labor.

Socio-economic and other self-management relations in a basic organization of associated labor shall be regulated by its by-laws and other self-management enactments, in line with the constitution and statute.

If a dispute has arisen in connection with the establishment of a basic organization of associated labor, the rights, obligations, and responsibilities of the workers who have decided to establish a separate basic organization of associated labor may not be altered against their will pending the settlement of the dispute.

Article 37. Workers in a basic organization of associated labor shall have the right to separate their basic organization from the work organization of which it is a part.

A basic organization of associated labor thus separated shall be bound, in agreement with other basic organizations of associated labor and the work organization as a whole, to regulate the way and terms of fulfillment of its obligations towards them undertaken prior to separation, and to make good any losses caused by the separation.

Workers may not separate their basic organization of associated labor from the work organization of which it is a part if this should, contrary to the general interest, lead to a major hindrance or prevention of work in other basic organizations making part of the work organization or in the work organization as a whole.

Article 38. Work organizations may associate in various forms of composite organizations of associated labor, and basic organizations of associated labor and work organizations may combine into communities and other forms of integration of organizations of associated labor to pursue specific common interests.

Obligatory integration of certain kinds of organizations of associated labor in communities aimed at ensuring, in the general interest, the unity of the system of work in appropriate spheres may, under conditions specified by the constitution, be introduced by statute or by a decision of the assembly of a socio-political community based on statutory authority.

Article 39. Organizations of associated labor, self-managing communities of interest, and other social legal entities may by self-management agreement found a bank as a special organization in charge of the conduct of credit and other bank activities, and pool in it, together with other persons, resources with a view to pursuing common interests regarding provision of funds for the performance, expansion, and promotion of the activities of the organizations of associated labor and other self-managing organizations and communities, and with a view to pursuing other common interests.

Social legal entities with whose resources such a bank operates shall manage the bank's business. The income realized by the bank shall, after operating costs have been covered and allocations to the work community made, be distributed among these social legal entities.

Social legal entities shall have the right to manage specified affairs of such a bank in the bank's unit which operates with their resources.

No socio-political community may found a bank, nor manage the affairs of one.

Mutual relations among social legal entities whose resources are used by a bank in its operations, the management of the bank, and its business shall be regulated by the self-management agreement on the founding of the bank, its by-laws, and statute.

Article 40. Business activities of financial organizations founded to operate savings accounts, the management of such organizations, and the management of bank operations in connection with savings accounts shall be regulated by statute in line with the uniform principles of the credit system.

The rights of citizens to take part, on account of their savings accounts, in the management of operations of such financial organizations, and to enjoy, in addition to stipulated interest, other benefits, shall be regulated by statute.

Article 41. Organizations of associated labor, self-managing communities of interest, and other social legal entities shall in organizations of associated labor which, besides other activities, engage in banking and similar business, have, in principle, the same rights in respect of this business as social legal entities have in a bank which operates with their resources.

If internal banking or similar operations are organized in an organization of associated labor, such operations shall be governed by the principles applying to banking operations.

Article 42. Organizations of associated labor, self-managing communities of interest, socio-political communities, and other social legal entities may by self-management agreement found a community of life and property insurance for the same, related, or different risks or losses, or for several different kinds of risk or loss, and may pool in it, together with other persons, on principles of reciprocity and solidarity, resources for life and property insurance and for the purposes of eliminating or lessening the unfavorable effects of such losses.

In an insurance community in which resources have been pooled for the purposes of life and property insurance against various kinds of risk or loss, insurees who pool resources to insure themselves against the same or related kinds of risk or loss shall form separate risk communities and shall pool resources in separate insurance funds for such losses. Insurees in a risk community shall, in agreement with other insurees in the same insurance community, lay down under what conditions the assets of the funds earmarked for the settlement of damages for one kind of loss may be used for the settlement of damages for another kind of loss.

Social legal entities which pool resources in an insurance community or a risk community shall manage the business of such a community.

Mutual relations among social legal entities which pool resources in an insurance community, the management of such a community, and its operations shall be regulated by the self-management agreement on the founding of the community, its by-laws or other self-management enactments, and by statute.

Citizens and civil legal entities—insurees shall participate in the management of their respective insurance communities or risk communities, and shall have other rights in them in conformity with their by-laws and statute.

Article 43. Relations between organizations of associated labor engaged in the sale of goods and services, and producing and other organizations with which they do business, shall be based on the principles of cooperation and self-management pooling of labor and resources within the framework of this cooperation. Such organizations shall, on a basis of equality, exercise a mutual influence on business and development policies, bear joint risks and joint responsibility for the expansion of the economic foundations of labor and the rise in labor productivity in production and trade, and shall share in the income earned through such cooperation according to their contribution to the realization of this income.

Organizations of associated labor which engage in the export and import trade, and operate on the principle of obligatory cooperation with producing and other organizations of associated labor on behalf of which they carry out export and import operations, and which within the framework of such cooperation formulate a joint policy of production and/or other activities, and export-import policy, shall distribute income earned through such cooperation as their joint income, and shall jointly share the risk of their business and responsibility for promoting production and trade, in conformity with self-managing agreement or contract on this cooperation.

It shall be regulated by federal statute in what cases and under what conditions organizations of associated labor engaging in the export-import, wholesale and retail trade, and in other statutorily-defined trading activities, shall be bound to pool their labor and resources with producing and other organizations of associated labor with which they do business. The manner and form of pooling labor and resources, the way of deciding on joint business operations, joint risk bearing, and the determination of principles of distribution of jointly earned income shall be regulated by federal statute.

Organizations of associated labor which engage in the sale of consumer goods and services shall be bound, in the way specified by statute, to cooperate and conclude agreements with self-managing communities of interest, local communities and other communities, and consumer organizations regarding affairs of common concern.

Article 44. Organizations of associated labor may carry out their activities and invest the means of social reproduction abroad, under conditions and within the limits laid down by federal statute.

Rights and resources acquired abroad on any ground by an organization of associated labor shall become a component part of the social resources managed by the workers of this organization.

Workers in an organization of associated labor operating abroad shall have the same rights, obligations, and responsibilities as the workers of this organization working in Yugoslavia.

Article 45. Basic and other organizations of associated labor, their communities, and other forms of association of organizations of associated labor, banks, communities of life and property insurance, and other financial organizations shall be legal entities vested with rights, obligations, and responsibilities, as spelled out by the constitution, statute, self-management agreements on association, or the enactments on their founding.

Such organizations, communities, and associations and their rights, obligations, and responsibilities shall be inscribed in a register.

Article 46. Against organizations of associated labor, their communities, or other associations of such organizations in which the realization of workers' self-management rights has been substantially infringed, or which do not fulfill their statutory obligations or have caused serious damage to social interests, temporary measures specified by statute may be taken under conditions and by a procedure provided for by statute. If this is necessary in order to prevent such practices, the realization of individual self-management rights of the workers, organizations, or associations, and their organs may be temporarily restricted by such measures.

Article 47. If a dispute arises in an organization of associated labor between workers in individual units of the organization, or between the workers and organs of the organization, or the workers of the organization and an organ of a socio-political community, which it has not been possible to settle by regular proceedings, the workers shall have the right and duty to present their demands in connection with the dispute through their trade union organization.

The competent trade union organization shall have the right and duty, on the request of workers, or on its own initiative, to institute proceedings for the settlement of the dispute, and in such proceedings, together with the appropriate managing bodies of the organization of associated labor concerned, or with organs of the socio-political community concerned, to lay down the basic principles and criteria for the solution of the question that has caused the dispute.

Article 48. Organizations of associated labor and organizations of business associations which engage in economic activities may, under conditions and by a procedure laid down by federal statute, be dissolved if they do not fulfill statutory conditions for the performance of their activities, if for a prolonged time they have not been able to renew the social resources with which they operate and to ensure the realization of the constitutionally-guaranteed rights of workers concerning their economic and social security, or if they are not in a position to fulfill other statutory or contractual obligations.

Organizations of associated labor which perform social activities may be dissolved, under conditions and by a procedure specified by statute, if they do not meet the conditions spelled out by statute or if the conditions for the performance of their activities do not exist.

Article 49. It may be laid down by statute or a decision of the assembly of a socio-political community made on statutory authority that specific activities or affairs of organizations of associated labor which perform social activities shall be treated as being of special social interest; the mode of realization of such special social interest and the realization of workers' self-management rights in line with such interest may, at the same time, be regulated by this statute or decision.

If so required by a special social interest, the mode of realization of such interest in the activity of organizations of associated labor which carry out economic activities may be regulated by statute or a decision of the assembly of a socio-political community made on statutory authority, when such activities are an irreplaceable condition of the life and work of citizens or of the work of other organizations in a specific field.

Article 50. Organizations of associated labor which carry out economic activities and their business associations shall associate in chambers of economy or other general associations with a view jointly to promoting work and business, adjusting special, common, and general social interests, reaching agreement on working and development plans and programs, and on the self-management regulation of socio-economic relations, initiating self-management agreements and social compacts, adopting legislation and formulating economic policy, and with a view to considering and resolving other questions of common concern.

In order to realize these aims, organizations of associated labor performing social activities may also form associations for individual activities or for individual spheres of work, as well as other general associations.

3. Self-Managing Communities of Interest

Article 51. Self-managing communities of interest shall be formed by working people, directly or through their self-managing organizations and communities, to satisfy their personal and common needs and interests and to adjust work in the spheres for which communities of interest are being created to these needs and interests.

The rights, obligations, and responsibilities in mutual relations in a self-managing community of interest shall be regulated by its founding self-management agreement, by its by-laws, and by other self-management enactments.

To satify their needs and interests in self-managing communities of interest, working people shall pay contributions to these communities from their personal incomes and from the income of basic organizations of associated labor, in line with the purpose or aims for which these resources are to be used.

Article 52. Workers and other working people who in the fields of education, science, culture, health, and social welfare realize, on the principles of reciprocity and solidarity, their personal and common needs and interests, and workers in organizations of associated labor which carry out activities in these fields, shall form self-managing communities of interest in which they shall freely exchange labor, pool labor and resources, and shall jointly and on equal terms decide on the performance of these activites in line with common interests, shape the policy concerning the development and promotion of these activities, and realize other common interests.

Mutual relations in such self-managing communities of interest shall be regulated so as to ensure the rights of the workers and other working people who have pooled resources in them to decide on these resources, and also the rights of the workers in organizations of associated labor which perform activities in the field for which a particular community of interest has been formed, to realize through free exchange of labor the same socio-economic status as workers in other organizations of associated labor.

Self-managing communities of interest may also be formed on such foundations in other fields of social activity.

Article 53. In order to ensure their social security, working people shall form self-managing communities of interest in the fields of pension and disability insurance, and other forms of social security, in which they will pool resources for the purpose and determine, on the principles of reciprocity and solidarity, and past labor, their common and individual obligations towards these communities and the common and individual rights they will realize in them.

Self-managing communities of interest may also be formed on such foundations in other fields, in which, through the pooling of resources into joint funds, specific common interests will be realized on the principles of reciprocity and solidarity.

Article 54. Working people, directly or through their organizations of associated labor and other self-managing organizations and communities, shall form self-managing communities of interest in the housing sector, in which such organizations and communities shall pool resources for housing construction, formulate housing construction policy and programs, and together with tenants manage residential buildings and dwellings in social ownership, and shall realize other common interests.

Federal legislation may provide for the formation of special communities of interest for housing construction and management of dwellings for the needs of active military personnel and civilian persons serving in the Armed Forces of the Socialist Federal Republic of Yugoslavia, and also for the needs of workers and officials of federal agencies.

Article 55. In the fields of communal activities, power production, water management, transport and other activities in the sphere of material production, if the permanent performance of such activities is indispensable for the satisfaction of the needs of specific beneficiaries, self-managing communities of interest of organizations of associated labor in these fields and of users of their products and services may be formed in which they will realize common interests specified by self-management agreement.

Article 56. In order to ensure the most direct possible realization of their self-management rights and interests, workers and other working people and their organizations of associated labor and other self-managing organizations and communities—members of a self-managing community of interest, shall have the right, within this community of interest, under conditions specified by the self-management agreement on the formation of the self-managing community of interest or by its by-laws, to organize themselves into a basic community or unit for a specific sphere or for the realization of specific common interests, and to realize in such basic community or unit their specific self-management rights and interests.

Self-managing communities of interest may combine into broader communities of interest and form federations and other associations of communities of interest, and also set up other forms of mutual cooperation.

When a self-managing community of interest is being formed for an area wider than the territory of a Commune, communities may be set up for the territories of individual Communes as parts of this self-managing community of interest.

Article 57. Self-managing communities of interests and basic communities and units making part of them, and also associations of self-managing communities of interest, shall be legal entities with the rights, obligations, and responsibilities vested in them under the constitution, statute, self-management agreement on the formation of the community of interest and/or association of communities of interest, and under their by-laws.

Article 58. Formation of a self-managing community of interest may be made compulsory by statute or by a decision of the Commune assembly based on statutory authority, or such a community may be so formed when the specific activities or affairs covered by such a community are of special social interest. In the same way, principles may be laid down concerning its organization and mutual relations in it, and it may be made obligatory to pay a contribution to a community so formed.

Self-managing communities of interest must perform activities or affairs which, according to the relevant statute or decision of the assembly of the socio-political community based on statutory authority, are defined as being of special social interest in the way laid down in this statute or decision of the assembly of the socio-political community.

Article 59. If a self-managing community of interest which performs activities or affairs of special social interest does not take a decision on which the work of the community of interest essentially depends, the assembly of the socio-political community may, under conditions and by a procedure specified by statute, issue a ruling providing for a temporary solution of this question.

Temporary measures provided by statute may be taken against a self-managing community of interest in the same cases and under the same conditions as such measures may be taken against organizations of associated labor.

4. Resources of Socio-Political Organizations and of Other Social Organizations

Article 60. Socio-political organizations and other statutorily-defined social organizations may acquire resources and/or specific rights to resources and use such resources, as social, in the pursuit of their aims and dispose of them in conformity with the by-laws of such organizations and statute. Such organizations may, under conditions spelled out by statute, organize an economic or other activity in line with their aims, and may share in income realized through such an activity for the pursuance of these aims.

5. The Socio-Economic Status and Association of Farmers

Article 61. Farmers and members of their households engaged in farming and working with resources subject to the right of ownership shall be guaranteed the right to realize the constitutionally-defined self-management status in socialist socio-economic relationships, to make use of the results achieved through their labor, to satisfy their personal and social needs and, on the basis of their contributions, to enjoy social security benefits in accordance with the principles of reciprocity and solidarity.

On the basis of their personal labor, farmers shall, in principle, have the same status and basically the same rights as workers in associated labor working with social resources. Farmers shall also have corresponding rights and obligations with regard to the pooling of labor and resources, and also in trade relations on the market and in credit relations.

Article 62. Farmers may pool their labor and resources in agricultural cooperatives and in other forms of farmers' association, or pool them with organizations of associated labor.

Agricultural cooperatives shall, in principle, have the same status, rights, obligations, and responsibilities as organizations of associated labor.

With respect to resources which they pool in agricultural cooperatives, farmers may retain the right of ownership or may establish the right to the restitution of the value of such resources and other rights on the ground of their pooling in conformity with the pooling contract and the by-laws of the cooperatives concerned.

Farmers who have pooled their labor and resources in an agricultural cooperative shall be entitled to part of the income earned by the cooperative, proportionately to how much they have contributed to the realization of this income with their own labor and the pooling of resources and/or through their joint work with the cooperative. The part of income which the cooperative has realized in excess of this amount shall, as social property, be allocated to the funds of the agricultural cooperative and shall be used for the expansion and promotion of its activities.

Article 63. By pooling their labor and means of labor freely and on terms of equality with workers in associated labor working with social resources, farmers shall expand the economic foundations of their labor and shall make use of the results of general economic and social development and on this basis more fully satisfy their personal and social needs and develop their working and other abilities.

Farmers who pool their labor and means of labor, directly or through agricultural cooperatives or other forms of association of farmers, with an organization of associated labor and lastingly cooperate with it, shall manage on an equal footing with the workers of this organization common affairs and jointly decide on jointly earned income, and shall share in its distribution according to their contribution to the realization of this income, in conformity with the self-management agreement.

6. Independent Personal Labor with Resources in Citizens' Ownership

Article 64. Freedom of independent personal labor with means of labor in citizens' ownership shall be guaranteed, provided the performance of activities with personal labor corresponds to the mode, economic basis, and possibilities of personal labor, and provided it is not contrary to the principle of income earning according to work performed or to other foundations of the socialist social system.

Conditions for performing activities with independent personal labor with means of labor in citizens' ownership, and property rights to such means of labor and to business premises used for the performance of activities with independent personal labor, shall be regulated by statute.

If so required by the social interest, it may be specified by statute which activities may not be performed by independent personal labor with means of labor in citizens' ownership.

Article 65. Working people who independently perform activities with their own personal labor and with resources in citizens' ownership may form a cooperative and in it, in accordance with the principles of equality, pool their labor and means of labor, and jointly dispose of the income earned by the cooperative.

Cooperatives formed by working people who independently perform activities with personal labor and with resources in citizens' ownership, shall have the status, rights, obligations, and responsibilities of an agricultural cooperative, and its members shall have the same status, rights, obligations, and responsibilities as members of an agricultural cooperative.

Article 66. Working people who independently perform activities with their own personal labor with resources in citizens' ownership may, in conformity with contracts and statute, pool their labor and means of labor with organizations of associated labor in various forms of cooperation and other forms of business collaboration. Within the framework of this cooperation, such working people shall share in the management of joint affairs, jointly decide on jointly earned income, and shall share in its distribution proportionately to their contribution to the realization of such income.

Article 67. A working man who independently performs activities with his personal labor using resources in citizens' ownership may, on a self-management basis, pool his labor and means of labor with the labor of other persons, within the framework of an organization of associated labor founded under contract.

A working man who has pooled his labor and resources with the labor of other people in such a contractual organization of associated labor shall have the right to conduct, as manager, the business of the contractual organization and, together with other workers, to decide on its operation and development.

The manager and workers in a contractual organization of associated labor shall, on the basis of their labor, be entitled to resources for the satisfaction of their personal and common needs; the manager shall, on account of the resources which he has pooled, also be entitled to part of the income accruing to him in conformity with the principles applying to the pooling of labor and social resources in organizations of associated labor.

The part of income realized in a contractual organization of associated labor which is left after the allocation of resources for the satisfaction of the personal and common needs of the manager and workers, and of the part of income accruing to the manager on account of the resource he has pooled in the organization, shall become social property. The workers, together with the manager, shall on the basis of their labor manage this part of income as social resources.

The terms and the mode of formation and operation of a contractual organization of associated labor, and its rights, obligations, and responsibilities, shall be regulated by statute, and the mutual rights, obligations, and responsibilities of the manager and workers shall be regulated by contract in conformity with statute. The mode and terms of the pooling of resources, and the mode and terms of their withdrawal or the restitution of the resources invested by the manager in the contractual organization, shall also be regulated by contract.

The manager of a contractual organization of associated labor shall retain the right of ownership over, and other contractual rights regarding, the resources he has pooled in this organization. With the withdrawal or repayment of these resources, the rights the manager enjoys in the contractual organization in his capacity of manager shall be extinguished.

Article 68. It shall be regulated by statute in which activities, in line with their nature and social needs, and under what conditions a working man who independently performs activities with his personal labor and resources in citizens' ownership may, exceptionally and to a limited extent, without forming a contractual organization of associated labor, make use of the additional labor of other persons by employing them.

A working man and the workers he wishes to employ shall enter into an employment contract in conformity with the collective contract entered into between the relevant trade union and the appropriate chamber of economy or another association representing working people who independently perform activities with their personal labor and resources in citizens' ownership. Such collective contracts shall ensure such workers, in accordance with the rights of workers in associated labor, the right to resources for the satisfaction of personal and common needs, and other rights which ensure their material and social security.

It may be regulated by statute that the part of income which is the result of the surplus-labor of workers employed by a working man who independently performs an activity with his personal labor and resources in citizens' ownership, shall become social property and shall be used for development needs.

7. Social Planning

Article 69. Workers in basic and other organizations of associated labor and working people in self-managing communities of interest, local communities, and other self-managing organizations and communities in which they manage the affairs and means of social reproduction, shall have the right and duty, by relying on scientific achievements and the appraisal of development possibilities based thereon, and by taking into account economic laws, independently to adopt working and development plans and programs for their organizations and communities, to adjust such plans and programs both mutually and to the social plans of the socio-political communities, and on this basis to ensure adjustment of relations in the totality of social reproduction and the guidance of material and social development as a whole, in line with common interests and aims laid down on a self-management basis.

Article 70. Working and development plans and programs of basic organizations of associated labor and of the organizations of associated labor of which they are part shall be adopted and implemented in relations of cooperation and mutual interdependence stemming from the pooling of labor and resources in such organizations in conformity with self-management agreements, provided that workers in the basic organizations of associated labor are ensured the right to decide on the adoption of such plans and programs.

Basic and other organizations of associated labor integrated in self-managing communities of interest, or other self-managing organizations and communities, shall pass and implement their working and development plans and programs in conformity with common interests and aims and/or in conformity with the joint plans and programs laid down by mutual agreement within the framework of such self-managing organizations and communities.

Organizations of associated labor, self-managing communities of interest, and other self-managing organizations and communities shall adjust their working and development plans and programs to the plans and programs of other self-managing organizations and communities with which they have specific common interests and aims which stem from their cooperation and mutual interdependence in social reproduction and which they determine on the basis of self-management agreements.

Mutual obligations laid down by mutual agreement by basic and other organizations of associated labor and other self-managing organizations and communities with a view to realizing a joint plan, may not be rescinded or changed during the period of time for which the plan has been adopted.

Article 71. Social plans of socio-political communities shall be adopted on the basis of agreements on the common interests and aims of economic and social development in the Communes, municipal or regional communities, Autonomous Provinces, Republics, and the Federation, and on the basis of the working and development plans and programs of organizations of associated labor, self-managing communities of interest, and other self-managing organizations and communities, and on the basis of jointly appraised development possibilities and conditions.

Social plans of socio-political communities shall lay down a common development policy and guidelines and frameworks for the adoption of measures of economic policy and of administrative and organizational measures which ensure conditions for the fulfillment of such plans.

Article 72. Working and development plans of organizations of associated labor and other self-managing organizations and communities, and social plans of socio-political communities may provide for investment or other aims and tasks, or steps may be taken to begin their implementation only on condition that financial and other necessary conditions for their fulfillment have been ensured in the way regulated by statute.

The fulfillment of special tasks aimed at attaining the targets spelled out by social plans may be laid down as obligatory for certain organizations of associated labor or other self-managing organizations and communities only in agreement with the organization or community concerned. If the fulfillment of such tasks has been laid down as a joint obligation for several organizations or communities, or as an obligation for an organ of a socio-political community, such organizations and/or communities and organs shall, by mutual agreement, lay down their mutual rights and obligations and their joint and individual responsibility for the fulfillment of such obligation.

If the social plan lays down, on the basis of jointly determined interests and aims of development, that the fulfillment of specific tasks is indispensable for social reproduction, and if organizations of associated labor or other self-managing organizations and communities have not been able to ensure by agreement resources and other necessary conditions for their fulfillment, an obligation to pool resources for the purpose can be introduced by legislation, in conformity with the constitution, and other measures may be prescribed for the purpose of fulfillment of such tasks.

Article 73. Statutes and other regulations and enactments which lay down obligations for the budgets and funds of socio-political communities, may not be passed before the organ which wants to pass the relevant statute, regulation, or enactment has established that resources for the fulfillment of such obligations have been secured.

Article 74. Workers in organizations of associated labor and working people in other self-managing organizations and communities, and their bodies, shall be responsible for the fulfillment of the working and development plans of their organizations and communities, and of general aims and tasks laid down by the social plans of socio-political communities, and shall be bound to take the necessary measures and action to achieve them.

Organs of socio-political communities shall be obliged by the regulations they pass and the measures they take for the fulfillment of social plans to ensure general conditions for as harmonious and stable development as possible, and by means of such regulations and measures to adjust as much as possible the special interests and independent operation of organizations of associated labor and other self-managing organizations and communities to the common development interests and targets laid down by social plans.

8. Social System of Information, Social Accountancy, Record-Keeping, and Statistics

Article 75. The social system of information shall ensure congruous recording, collection, processing, and presentation of data and facts significant for recording, planning, and guiding social development, and shall ensure accessibility of information on such data and facts.

Activities relating to the social system of information shall be of special social concern.

Article 76. Workers in organizations of associated labor and working people in other self-managing organizations and communities, bodies of such organizations and communities, and organs of socio-political communities, shall be obliged to organize bookkeeping and record-keeping of facts important for the work and decision-making in such organizations and communities.

Organizations of associated labor and other self-managing organizations and communities, and socio-political communities shall be bound to supply organizations in charge of bookkeeping, record-keeping, and statistics with data of importance for the adjustment of relations in social reproduction and the guidance of development, and for the realization of the rights of working people in other self-managing organizations and communities to be kept informed of facts and relations of common and general concern.

Article 77. Record-keeping and informative-analytical affairs concerning the use of social resources, supervision of the accuracy of data concerning the use of such resources, supervision of the legality of their use, and supervision of the fulfillment of obligations of organizations of associated labor, and other self-managing organizations and communities, and of socio-political communities, and other statutorily-defined activities of social accountancy, shall be carried out by the Social Accountancy Service. This service shall also be in charge of affairs concerning money transfers in the country.

The Social Accountancy Service shall supply organizations of associated labor and other social legal entities with data on the basis of which working people and bodies of self-management workers' supervision will be able to have an insight into the economic situation and financial and economic operations of their own and other organizations and communities.

Yugoslavia

The Social Accountancy Service shall be independent in its work.

The Social Accountancy Service shall operate in conformity with statute and other rules and shall, within the framework of its rights and duties, be responsible for their implementation.

9. Law of Property Relations

Article 78. Citizens shall be guaranteed the right of ownership of movable property used for personal consumption or for the satisfaction of their cultural and other personal needs.

Citizens may own residential houses and dwellings for their personal and family needs. Residential houses and dwellings and movables, which serve personal needs and which are subject to the right of ownership, may be used as a means of earning income only in the way and under conditions spelled out by statute.

Article 79. The limits and conditions under which associations of citizens and other civil legal entities may have the right of ownership of real property and of movables, which serve for the satisfaction of the common interests of their members and for the fulfillment of the aims for which they have been founded, and conditions under which they can use them, shall be regulated by statute.

Article 80. Farmers shall be guaranteed the right of ownership of arable agricultural land up to a maximum of ten hectares per household.

It may be provided by statute that in hilly and mountainous regions, the area of arable agricultural land owned by farmers may exceed ten hectares per household.

It shall be specified by statute within what limits and under what conditions farmers may own other land, and within what limits and under what conditions other citizens may own agricultural and other kinds of land.

Conditions and limits within which the right to own forests and woodland may be acquired shall be spelled out by statute.

Article 81. There may be no ownership right to land in cities and localities of an urban character, nor in other areas envisaged for housing and other complex construction, proclaimed as such by the Commune concerned in conformity with the conditions and pursuant to a procedure laid down by statute.

The conditions for and the mode and time of termination of the right of ownership of land over which an ownership right existed before the decision of the Commune, and compensation for such land, shall be spelled out by statute. The mode of and conditions for the utilization of such land shall be determined by the Commune in conformity with statute.

Article 82. Real property subject to the right of ownership may be expropriated against equitable compensation, or this right may be restricted if so required by the general interest determined in conformity with statute.

The fundamentals and scales for determining equitable compensation shall be regulated by statute. Such fundamentals and scales may not be determined in a way which would, through their application, result in a serious deterioration of the living and working conditions which the owner of expropriated real property had before on account of the use of this real property.

Equitable compensation shall not include any increase in the value of real property resulting directly or indirectly from investment of social resources.

Article 83. The right of ownership by citizens and civil legal entities shall be realized in conformity with the nature and purpose of real property and/or movables in their ownership, and in conformity with the social interest, as spelled out by statute.

Conditions for the sale of land and other kinds of real property subject to the right of ownership shall be regulated by statute.

Article 84. The right of ownership of objects of special cultural value may be restricted on the basis of statute, if so required by the general interest.

10. Goods of General Interest

Article 85. Land, forests, waters, watercourses, the sea and seashore, ores and other natural resources, goods in public use, also real property and other objects of special cultural and historic significance shall, as goods of general interest, enjoy special protection and shall be used under conditions and in the way specified by statute.

Article 86. All land, forests, waters and watercourses, the sea and seashore, ores and other natural resources must be used in conformity with statutorily-defined general conditions which ensure their rational utilization and other general interests.

The mode of management of forests, woodland, and ore deposits, and the mode of exploitation of forests, woodland, and ores shall be laid down by statute.

11. Conservation and Improvement of the Human Environment

Article 87. Working people and citizens, organizations of associated labor, socio-political communities, local communities, and other self-managing organizations and communities shall have the right and duty to assure conditions for the conservation and improvement of the natural and man-made values of the human environment, and to prevent or eliminate harmful consequences of air, soil, water, sea, waterways, or noise pollution, or other kinds of pollution which endanger such values and imperil the health and lives of people.

Chapter II. The Foundations of the Socio-Political System

1. Status of Working People in the Socio-Political System

Article 88. Power shall be exercised and other social affairs managed by the working class and all working people.

The working class and all working people shall exercise power and manage other social affairs, organized in organizations of associated labor, other self-managing organizations and communities, and in class and other socio-political and social organizations.

Article 89. Working people shall exercise power and mange other social affairs through decision-making at assemblies, through referenda and other forms of personal expression of views in basic organizations of associated labor and local communities, self-managing communities of interest, and other self-managing organizations and communities, through delegates in the managing organs of such organizations and communities, through self-management agreements and social compacts, through delegations and delegates to the assemblies of socio-political communities, and by guiding and supervising the work of organs responsible to the assemblies.

Article 90. Working people shall organize themselves on a self-management basis in organizations of associated labor, local communities, self-managing communities of interest, and other self-managing organizations and communities, and shall specify which common interests, rights, and duties they shall realize in them.

The common interests and functions of power and management of other social affairs which the working people, nations and nationalities will realize in socio-political communities, shall be spelled out by the constitution and statute.

Article 91. The organization and management of organizations of associated labor, local communities, self-managing communities of interest, and other self-managing organizations and communities must be regulated so as to enable working people in each part of the process of labor and in each part of their organizations or communities to decide on questions concerning their labor and other interests, to realize their self-management rights and common interests, and to exercise supervision over the execution of decisions and over the work of all organs and services of such organizations and communities.

Article 92. The functions of power and management of other social affairs in socio-political communities shall be discharged by their assemblies and by organs responsible to them.

Judicial functions shall be performed by regular courts of law as organs of state power, and by self-management courts.

Protection of constitutionality shall be vested in constitutional courts.

Article 93. The assemblies of socio-political communities and organs responsible to them shall discharge their functions on the basis and within the framework of the constitution, by-laws, and statutes.

In respect of organizations of associated labor, and other self-managing organizations and communities, state organs shall only exercise those rights with which they are vested on the basis of the constitution.

Article 94. No one shall exercise self-management, public, or other functions or public authority unless he has, in conformity with the constitution, statute, and by-laws, been vested with these by working people or the assembly of the competent socio-political community.

Article 95. All organs and organizations and other holders of self-management, public, or other social functions shall perform their functions on the basis and within the framework of the constitution, statute, and by-laws, and on the basis of powers vested in them, and shall be responsible for the performance of such functions.

All holders of self-management, public, or other social functions shall in the performance of their functions be subject to social control.

Every elected or appointed holder of self-management, public, or other social functions shall be personally responsible for their exercise and may be recalled or relieved of office. He shall have the right to resign and to give a statement of reasons.

The kinds of and conditions for responsibility of the holders of self-management, public, or other social functions, and the procedure for the realization of responsibility of the holders of such functions shall be laid down by statute and self-management enactments.

Article 96. A worker elected or appointed to a self-management, public, or other social function, the exercise of which makes it necessary for him temporarily to give up work in his organization of associated labor or work community, shall have the right, upon the termination of his function, to return to the same organization of associated labor and work community respectively, and to take up his earlier job or another job which corresponds to his abilities and qualifications.

Article 97. The work of state organs and of managing bodies of organizations of associated labor, and other self-managing organizations and communities, and of the organs of socio-political organizations and associations shall be public.

The mode of ensuring the public character of work shall be regulated by statute and self-management enactments.

Affairs and data which are considered to be secret and may not be made public shall be specified by statute and self-management enactments.

The principle of publicity may not be contrary to the security and defense interests of the country or to other social interests specified by statute.

2. Self-Management in Organizations of Associated Labor

Article 98. A worker in a basic or other organization of associated labor shall realize self-management, on terms of equality and mutual responsibility with other workers in the organization, through decision-making at workers' assemblies, through referenda and other forms of personal expression of views, through delegates in the workers' council elected and recalled by him together with other workers in the organization, and through supervision of the execution of decisions and the performance of work of the organs and services of this organization.

Workers shall have the right, for the purposes of realizing their self-management rights, to be regularly kept informed of the business, economic, and financial operations of their organizations, the realization and distribution of income and the use of resources in them, and of other questions of interest for decision-making and supervision in the organizations.

Article 99. Basic and other organizations of associated labor shall set up workers' councils to take charge of the management of the work and business of these organizations, or managing organs which in status and function correspond to a worker's council.

Basic organizations of associated labor with a small number of workers shall not set up workers' councils.

Specific executive functions in basic and other organizations of associated labor may be entrusted to the executive organs of the workers' councils.

Organizations of associated labor which in pooling labor and resources have not organized a separate organization may set up a joint organ for the conduct of affairs of common interest.

Article 100. In exercising the functions of management of work and business of its organization of associated labor, the workers' council shall draw up draft by-laws and pass other enactments, formulate business policy, enact working and development plans and programs, take measures for the implementation of business policy and working and development plans and programs, elect, appoint, and relieve of office the executive and business-managing organs or their members, ensure that the workers are kept informed, and shall conduct other affairs as specified by self-management agreements, by-laws, and other self-management enactments of its organization.

Decisions of the workers' council of a work organization or a composite organization of associated labor concerning the achievement of the inalienable rights of the workers in the basic organizations of associated labor, shall be made in agreement with each of these organizations in the way specified by the self-management agreement on association.

Article 101. The workers' council of an organization of associated labor shall consist of delegates of workers in all parts of the labor process in the basic organization.

The composition of the workers' council of a basic organization of associated labor must correspond to the social composition of the work community of the basic organization of associated labor.

The workers' council of a work organization or a composite organization of associated labor shall be made up of delegates of the workers in the basic organizations of associated labor elected directly in the way and by a procedure specified by the self-management agreement on association. Each basic organization of associated labor of a work organization must be represented in the workers' council of the work organization.

Delegates shall work in accordance with guidelines issued by workers or the workers' council of the basic organization of associated labor which has elected them, and shall be responsible to them for their work.

The rights and obligations of delegates, and their responsibility to the workers or managing organs of basic and other organizations of associated labor, shall be laid down by the by-laws of these organizations and the self-management agreements on association.

Article 102. The mode of electing, and the conditions for and the mode of recalling or relieving of office members of the workers' council and the executive organ in an organization of associated labor shall be specified by the self-management agreement on association, or the by-laws of the organization, and by statute.

Members of a workers' council or executive organ may not be elected for a term of more than two years.

No one may be elected to the same workers' council or executive organ for more than two consecutive terms.

A worker who as a sole business manager or member of the managing board is responsible to the workers' council may not be elected to it, nor may a worker who independently performs other managerial functions specified by the by-laws and statute.

Article 103. In every organization of associated labor there shall be a business-managing organ in charge of the business of the organization of associated labor, the organization and adjustment of the labor process, and the execution of decisions of the workers' council and its executive organ.

Every organization of associated labor shall be represented by its sole business manager or by the chairman of the managing board, unless otherwise specified by the by-laws or other enactments of this organization.

The business-managing organ shall be independent in its work and shall be responsible to the workers and the workers' council of its organization of associated labor.

The sole business manager or the chairman of the managing board shall also be responsible to the social community for the legality of work and the fulfillment of the statutorily-established obligations of their organization of associated labor. The sole business manager or the chairman of the managing board shall have the right and duty to stay, in conformity with statute, the execution of enactments of the workers' council and other organs of their organization of associated labor if he or it considers that such enactments are contrary to the law, and to inform thereof the competent organ of the socio-political community.

Article 104. The sole business manager or members of the managing board in an organization of associated labor shall be appointed and relieved of office by the workers' council.

A sole business manager shall be appointed on the basis of public competititon, on the proposal of a competition commission. In basic organizations of associated labor specified by statute and in other organizations of associated labor, a competition commission shall be composed of a statutorily-specified number of representatives of the organizations of associated labor and the trade union organizations concerned, and of representatives of the social community appointed or elected in conformity with statute.

Conditions for and the mode of formation of a business-managing organ, and conditions for and the mode of appointment of members of such an organ may be regulated by statute.

The tenure of a sole business manager and of members of a managing board shall not last longer than four years. After the expiration of their tenure, they may be reappointed to the same function by the same procedure.

It shall be specified by statute under what conditions a business-managing organ may be relieved of office before the expiration of the term for which it has been appointed. A proposal for relieving of office a business-managing organ may also be made by the assembly of the competent Commune or another socio-political community, and by the relevant trade union organization.

Special conditions for and the mode of appointment and relief of office, and the special rights and duties of business-managing organs in organizations of associated labor in charge of activities or affairs of special social concern, may be laid down by statute.

Article 105. Self-management agreements on association in work organizations or composite organizations of associated labor shall contain provisions on: joint affairs, coordination of the labor process, adjustment of working and development plans and programs, pooling of resources and their purpose; composition, election, and province of work of joint organs of management and their executive organs, business-managing organs of work organizations or composite organizations and their responsibilities; rights, obligations, and responsibilities of work communities in charge of affairs of common interest for associated organizations; mutual relations among basic and other organizations of associated labor and their rights, obligations and responsibilities in legal matters; conditions for the separation of individual basic organizations from a work organization, or of basic and work organizations from a composite organization. Such self-management agreements shall also contain other provisions concerning the joint work and business of composite organizations and the realization of workers' self-management rights in them.

A self-management agreement on association in a work organization or a composite organization of associated labor shall be concluded in agreement with the majority of all workers in each basic organization.

Article 106. All organizations of associated labor shall have by-laws.

The by-laws of a basic organization of associated labor shall be passed, on the proposal of the workers' council, by a majority vote of all workers in the basic organization.

The by-laws of a work organization or a composite organization of associated labor shall be passed, on the proposal of its workers' council, by workers in the associated basic organizations by a majority vote of all workers in each of these organizations.

The by-laws and other self-management enactments of organizations of associated labor may not be contrary to the self-management agreements on association.

Article 107. To achieve and safeguard their self-management rights, workers in basic and other organizations of associated labor shall have the right and duty to exercise self-management workers' supervision directly, through their organizations' managing organs, and through special organs of self-management workers' supervision.

Organs of self-management workers' supervision shall exercise supervision regarding: implementation of the by-laws and other self-management enactments of their organizations, and of self-management agreements and social compacts, execution of decisions of the workers, managing and executive organs and business-managing organs of the organizations, and compliance of such enactments and decisions with workers' self-management rights, duties, and interests; performance of work and self-management duties by the workers, organs, and services of the organizations; responsible and socially and economically opportune utilization of social resources and disposition thereof; application of the principle of distribution according to work performed in the distribution of income and allocation of resources for personal incomes; realization and safeguard of workers' rights in mutual labor relationships; keeping workers informed on questions of concern for decision-making and supervision in their organizations, and regarding the realization of other self-management rights, duties, and interests of the workers.

Organs of self-management workers' supervision shall have the right and duty to report occurrences noted in their organizations, together with their opinion thereon, to workers, organs, and services in the organizations in which such occurrences have been noted, and to organs of these organizations responsible for their elimination, and also to cooperate with social supervisory and controlling organs.

The composition, election, and recall of organs of self-management workers' supervision, and their rights, duties, and responsibilities shall be specified by the by-laws and other self-management enactments of the organizations concerned in conformity with statute.

Article 108. Every worker shall be personally responsible for the conscientious exercise of his self-management functions.

Members of the workers' council of an organization of associated labor shall be personally and materially responsible for decisions which, despite a warning by the competent organ, they have taken outside the framework of their powers. Delegates in the workers' council of a work organization or a composite organization of associated labor shall be responsible to the workers and the workers' council of the basic organization which have elected them as delegates.

Members of a collective executive body, the sole business manager, and members of the managing board shall be responsible for their work to the workers' council which has elected or nominated them, and to the workers of the organization of associated labor in which they perform their functions. They shall be personally responsible for their decisions and for the execution of decisions of the workers' council and of the workers, and also for keeping the workers' council and workers truthfully, timely, and fully informed. They shall also bear material responsibility for any harm caused by the execution of decisions taken on the basis of their proposals, if in making such proposals they concealed facts or consciously gave untruthful information to the workers' council or the workers.

Business-managing organs shall, within the framework of their rights and duties, also be responsible for the business results of their organizations and for the organization and adjustment of the labor process in their organizations.

The responsibility of members of managing boards, sole business managers, and members of managing boards shall be determined according to their influence on the making and implementation of decisions.

Material and other kinds of responsibility and conditions for responsibility shall be regulated by statute and by self-management enactments of the organizations of associated labor concerned.

Article 109. Provisions on the realization of self-management in organizations of associated labor shall also apply to workers in work communities set up for the conduct of affairs of common concern to several organizations of associated labor in line with the nature of such affairs and the common interests of the workers for whose sake such work communities have been formed.

3. Self-Management in Self-Managing Communities of Interest

Article 110. A self-management agreement on the formation of a self-managing community of interest and its by-laws shall regulate affairs of common concern to the members of the community, the mode of decision-making regarding such affairs, the province of work, the powers and responsibilities of the assembly and other bodies of the community of interest, and other questions of common concern to the working people and self-managing organizations and communities organized in the community of interest.

The by-laws of a self-managing community of interest shall be adopted in conformity with the self-management agreement on its formation.

It may be provided by statute that the founding self-management agreement and the by-laws of a self-managing community of interest in charge of affairs of special social concern must be confirmed by the competent organ of the socio-political community concerned.

Article 111. Affairs of a self-managing community of interest shall be managed by its assembly. The assembly shall be made up of delegates elected and recalled by the working people and organizations of associated labor and other self-managing organizations and communities, members of this community of interest.

Delegates to the assembly shall work in accordance with guidelines issued by the members of the self-managing community of interest who have elected them and to whom they shall be responsible for their work.

In a self-managing community of interest formed by working people and their organizations and communities with a view to satisfying their needs and interests, and by workers in organizations of associated labor that perform activities in the field for which the community of interest is being organized, the assembly shall be organized so as to enable these working people and their organizations and communities to decide, on an equal footing, on their mutual rights, obligations, and responsibilities.

The assembly may entrust specific functions to its executive organs, which shall be responsible to it for their work.

Article 112. A self-management agreement on the formation of a self-managing community of interest and other enactments of the community shall define direct responsibility to the members of the community of the managing organs of the community of interest and of delegates in such organs, the mode of exercise of supervision by the members of the community of interest over the work of the managing organs and the professional services, and the mode of keeping members of the community of interest informed of the work of such organs and services and of questions considered and dealt with in the community of interest.

Article 113. When, under the provisions of the constitution or the by-laws of a socio-political community, working people take part through the assemblies of the communities of interest in decision-making concerning questions falling within the competence of the assemblies of the socio-political communities, these working people shall organize themselves within the framework of the communities of interest, or shall integrate their communities of interest so that they can take part in decision-making on such questions in the assemblies of the socio-political communities.

4. Self-Management in Local Communities

Article 114. It shall be the right and duty of working people in a neighborhood, part of a neighborhood, or several interconnected neighborhoods to organize themselves into a local community with a view to realizing specific common interests and needs.

Working people and citizens in a local community shall decide on the realization of their common interests and on the satisfaction, on the basis of solidarity, of their common needs in the fields of: physical improvement of their neighborhood, housing, communal activities, child care and social security, education, culture, physical culture, consumer protection, conservation and improvement of the human environment, national defense, social self-protection, and in other spheres of life and work.

To realize their common interests and needs, working people and citizens, organized in a local community, shall through self-management agreements and in other ways establish links with organizations of associated labor, self-managing communities of interest, and other self-managing organizations and communities, within or outside the territory of their local community, which have an interest in and the duty to take part in the satisfaction of such interests and needs.

Working people and citizens in a local community shall take part in the conduct of social affairs and in decision-making on questions of common interest in the Commune and the broader socio-political communities.

The mode of and procedure for forming a local community shall be laid down by the by-laws of the Commune concerned.

The principles governing the procedure for forming local communities may be determined by statute.

Article 115. The by-laws of a local community shall be passed by working people and citizens in the local community.

The rights and duties of a local community, its organization, its organs, its relations with organizations of associated labor and other self-managing organizations and communities, and other questions of concern for the work of the local community and the life of working people in it, shall be laid down by the by-laws of the local community.

Local communities shall have the status of a legal entity.

5. The Commune

Article 116. A Commune is a self-managing community and the basic socio-political community based on the power of and self-management by the working class and all working people.

In Communes, working people and citizens shall create and ensure conditions for their life and work, direct social development, realize and adjust their interests, satisfy their common needs, exercise power, and manage other social affairs.

The functions of power and management of other social affairs, with the exception of those which under the constitution are exercised in the broader socio-political communities, shall be exercised in Communes.

In realizing their common interests, rights, and duties in Communes, working people and citizens shall make decisions organized in basic organizations of associated labor, local communities, self-managing communities of interest, other basic self-managing organizations and communities, other forms of self-management integration, and in socio-political organizations, through self-management agreements and social compacts and through their delegations and delegates to the Commune assemblies and other organs of self-management.

Article 117. The rights and duties of a Commune shall be laid down by the constitution and the Commune by-laws.

Citizens in a Commune shall in particular: create and develop material and other conditions of life and work, and conditions for the self-management satisfaction of the economic, welfare, cultural, and other common needs of working people and citizens; direct and adjust economic and social development and regulate relations of direct concern to working people and citizens in the Commune; organize the conduct of affairs of common and general social interest and set up organs of self-management and organs of power for the conduct of such affairs; ensure direct enforcement of statutes, unless their enforcement has under statute been placed within the competence of organs of the broader socio-political communities; ensure the realization and safeguard of the freedoms, rights, and duties of man and the citizen; ensure the realization of equality of the nations and nationalities; ensure the rule of law and safety of life and property; regulate the use of land and of goods in public use; regulate and organize national defense; regulate relations in the field of housing and communal activities; regulate and assure conservation and improvement of the human environment; organize

Yugoslavia

and ensure social self-protection and organize and ensure social control.

Article 118. In order to satisfy common needs in their Commune, workers in basic organizations of associated labor and other working people and citizens in local communities, self-managing communities of interest, and other self-managing organizations and communities, and in the Commune as a whole, shall by referenda and other forms of personal expression of views, and by self-management agreements and social compacts, decide on the pooling of resources and their utilization.

Within the framework of the statutorily-established system of sources and kinds of taxes, fiscal stamps and other dues, working people in Communes shall independently decide on the volume and mode of financing general social needs in the Communes.

Article 119. Communes may cooperate with one another voluntarily and on principles of solidarity; they may pool resources and form joint organs, organizations, and services for the conduct of affairs of common interest and the satisfaction of common needs, and may associate in urban and regional communities.

The constitution may make it obligatory for the Communes to associate in urban or regional communities, as special socio-political communities to which specific affairs falling within the competence of the Republics, Autonomous Provinces, or Communes shall be transferred.

Communes in towns shall associate, in conformity with the constitution, in urban communities as special socio-political communities to which the Communes may, in their common interest, entrust specific rights and duties. Specific affairs falling within the competence of the Republics and/or Autonomous Provinces may be transferred to such communities.

6. Self-Management Agreements and Social Compacts

Article 120. By means of self-management agreements and social compacts, workers and other working people shall, on a self-management basis, regulate their mutual relationships, adjust interests, and regulate relations of broader social significance.

Article 121. By means of self-management agreements, workers in basic and other organizations of associated labor and working people in local communities, self-managing communities of interest, and other self-managing organizations and communities shall, within the framework of their self-management rights: adjust their interests concerning the social division of labor and social reproduction, pool labor and resources and regulate mutual relations in conjunction with the pooling of labor and resources; form work and other organizations of associated labor, banks, business and other communities; lay down the fundamentals of and scales for the distribution of income and the allocation of resources for personal incomes; spell out mutual rights, obligations, and responsibilities and measures for their realization, and regulate other relations of common concern.

Self-management agreements shall, on behalf of the parties thereto, be concluded by their authorized bodies.

A self-management agreement relating to the realization of the inalienable rights of workers shall be considered accepted by a basic organization of associated labor or another self-managing organization or community, if it has been approved by the majority of the workers or working people of this organization or community.

Article 122. Trade unions shall have the right to initiate and propose the conclusion of self-management agreements, and may institute proceedings for the revision of a self-management agreement already concluded, if they consider that it infringes the self-management rights of workers and socio-economic relations laid down by the constitution.

The trade union organization designated by the trade union by-laws shall also take part in proceedings for the conclusion of a self-management agreement whose purpose is to regulate mutual relations among workers in labor or to lay down the fundamentals of and scales for the distribution of income and the allocation of resources for personal income, and shall also sign such an agreement. If the trade union organization refuses to sign such a self-management agreement, the organization of associated labor shall be authorized to apply this self-managing agreement and the trade union organization may institute proceedings before a court of associated labor.

Article 123. A basic organization of associated labor and any other self-managing organization or community which considers that its rights or interests based on statute have been infringed by a self-management agreement entered into by other organizations of associated labor or by other self-managing organizations and communities, may institute proceedings for the reconsideration of that particular self-management agreement.

Article 124. Organizations of associated labor, chambers and other general associations, self-managing communities of interest, other self-managing organizations and communities, organs of socio-political communities, trade unions, and other socio-political organizations and social organizations shall, by means of social compacts, ensure and adjust self-management regulation of socio-economic and other relations of broader common concern to the parties to the compacts, or of general social concern.

Social compacts shall, on behalf of the parties thereto, be concluded by their authorized bodies.

Article 125. The assemblies of socio-political communities shall stimulate the conclusion of self-management agreements and social compacts, and may make it obligatory for specified self-managing organizations and communities to conduct proceedings for the conclusion of self-management agreements or social compacts.

Article 126. Self-management agreements and social compacts shall be binding on the parties that have concluded or acceeded to them.

Article 127. Self-management agreements and social compacts shall lay down measures for their implementation, determine the material and social responsibility of the parties thereto, and specify the mode of and conditions for their revision.

Self-management agreements and social compacts may provide for arbitration or other means of settlement of disputes that may arise in the course of implementation of the agreements and/or compacts.

Article 128. Parties to self-management agreements and social compacts shall be equal in their conclusion.

Proceedings for the conclusion of self-management agreements and social compacts shall be public.

7. Social Protection of Self-Management Rights and of Social Property

Article 129. The self-management rights of working people and social property shall enjoy special social protection.

Social protection of the self-management rights of working people shall be ensured by the assemblies of socio-political communities and organs responsible to them, by courts of law, constitutional courts, public prosecutors, and social attorneys of self-management.

The forms and mode of realization of social protection of the self-management rights of working people and of social property shall be regulated by the constitution and statute.

Article 130. If in an organization of associated labor or another self-managing organization or community, self-management relations have been essentially disrupted, or if serious harm has been caused to social interests, or if an organization or community does not fulfill its statutorily-established obligations, the assembly of the socio-political community concerned shall have the right, under conditions and by a procedure specified by statute, to dissolve the workers' council or another corresponding managing organ of the organization of associated labor, and to call new elections for the members of this organ; to dissolve in this organization of associated labor, self-managing organization, or community its executive organs and to recall the business-managing organ and workers holding executive posts; to appoint provisional organs having statutorily-defined rights and duties; temporarily to restrict the realization of certain self-management rights of working people and managing organs; and to take other measures as spelled out by statute.

The assembly of the socio-political community may, in conformity with statute, stay the execution of decisions, other enactments, and acts which violate the self-management rights of the working people or cause damage to social property. If the assembly stays the execution of such enactments or acts, it must institute proceedings before the competent court.

Article 131. Social attorneys of self-management, as independent agents of the social community, shall take measures and use legal means and exercise other statutorily-defined rights and duties to ensure social protection of the self-management rights of working people and of social property.

Social attorneys of self-management shall institute proceedings before the assemblies of socio-political communities, the constitutional courts, or regular courts for the protection of the self-management rights of working people and of social property, or proceedings for the repeal or annulment of decisions and other acts which violate self-management and social property.

Social attorneys of self-management shall institute proceedings for the protection of the self-management rights of working people and of social property on their own initiative or on the initiative of workers, organizations of associated labor and other self-managing organizations and communities, trade unions and other sociopolitical organizations, state organs, and citizens.

State organs and organs of self-managing organizations and communities shall be bound, on the request of the social attorney of self-management, to supply him with data and information of concern for the performance of his function.

8. The Assembly System

Article 132. An assembly is an organ of social self-management and the supreme organ of power within the framework of the rights and duties of its socio-political community.

The formation, organization, and competence of the assemblies of socio-political communities and of organs responsible to them shall be regulated by the constitution, by-laws, and statute on the basis of uniform principles laid down by the present Constitution.

The composition, organization, and competence of the Assembly of the Socialist Federal Republic of Yugoslavia and of organs responsible to it at the federal level shall be laid down by the present Constitution.

Article 133. Working people in basic self-managing organizations and communities, and in socio-political organizations shall form delegations for the purposes of direct exercise of their rights, duties, and responsibilities and of organized participation in the performance of functions of the assemblies of socio-political communities.

Delegations in self-managing organizations and communities shall be formed by:

(1) working people in basic organizations of associated labor and in work communities in charge of affairs of common concern to several basic organizations of associated labor;

(2) working people who work in agriculture, crafts, and similar activities with means of labor subject to the right of ownership, together with workers with whom they have pooled their labor and means of labor and who are organized in communities and other statutorily-defined forms of association;

(3) working people in the work communities of state organs, socio-political organizations, and in other work communities which are not constituted as organizations of associated labor, and active military personnel and civil persons serving in the Armed Forces of

the Socialist Federal Republic of Yugoslavia, in the way specified by the constitution and statute;

(4) working people and citizens in local communities.

Students and pupils shall take part in the formation of delegations in organizations of associated labor under conditions and in the way specified by statute.

Delegations shall also be formed by working people who permanently work in a unit of a basic organization of associated labor which does not operate on the territory of the Commune in which this organization has its head office.

In basic organizations of associated labor or work communities with a small number of working people, all working people shall perform the functions of a delegation.

In socio-political organizations, the function of delegations shall be performed by their elected bodies specified by their by-laws or other decisions.

Article 134. Members of delegations shall be elected by working people in basic self-managing organizations and communities from among members of these organizations and communities by direct and secret ballot.

Basic self-managing organizations and communities shall in their by-laws, in conformity with statute, specify the number of members and the composition of their delegations, and the mode of election and recall of the delegations.

The composition of delegations must be such as to ensure adequate representation of workers in all parts of the labor process and to correspond to the social composition of the basic self-managing organization or community concerned.

Members of delegations shall be elected for a term of four years.

Workers who, according to the present Constitution, may not be members of a workers' council or of another corresponding managing organ may not be elected to the delegation in their basic organization of associated labor.

No one may be elected member of a delegation in the same self-managing organization or community for more than two consecutive terms.

Article 135. Candidates for members of delegations in basic self-managing organizations and communities shall be proposed and determined by the working people in such organizations and communities through organizations of the Socialist Alliance of Working People and trade union organizations respectively.

Procedure for the nomination of candidates shall be conducted by organizations of the Socialist Alliance of Working People and trade unions respectively.

Organizations of the Socialist Alliance of the Working People and trade unions shall have the right and duty, in cooperation with other socio-political organizations, to ensure such a democratic procedure for the nomination of candidates as will enable working people freely to express their will in the proposition and determination of candidates.

Procedure for the nomination of the delegations of military personnel and civil persons serving in the Armed Forces of the Socialist Federal Republic of Yugoslavia shall be conducted by organs specified by a federal statute. Other questions relating to the election and work of such delegations may also be regulated by such federal statute, in conformity with the principles laid down by the present Constitution and with the nature of the activities and organization of the Armed Forces.

Article 136. If during the term of the assembly of a socio-political community a new basic self-managing organization or community has been formed, the mode of inclusion of its delegation into the performance of functions of the assembly of the socio-political community shall be regulated by statute.

Article 137. In keeping with the interests and guidelines of basic self-managing organizations and communities, and taking into account the interests of other self-managing organizations and communities and general social interests and needs, delegations shall formulate basic stands for the delegates to follow in the work of the assemblies and in their participation in decision-making.

Delegations shall be bound to keep basic self-managing organizations or communities informed of their own work and the work of the delegates in the assemblies, and shall be responsible to these organizations or communities for their work.

Delegations shall cooperate with delegations from other self-managing organizations and communities in seeking, by mutual agreement, common solutions to questions falling within the competence of the assemblies, and in finding solutions, by mutual agreement, to other questions of common concern.

Article 138. One or more delegations from self-managing organizations and communities, linked by work or other joint interests or by interests in a socio-political community, or delegates from these organizations and communities to the Commune assemblies shall send delegates elected from among members of their delegations to the appropriate chambers of the assemblies of socio-political communities in the way specified by the constitution, by-laws, and statute.

The number of delegates from self-managing organizations or communities shall be determined proportionally to the number of the working people in these organizations or communities. This principle can be deviated from and other criteria applied in order to ensure adequate representation of specific spheres of social labor and/or territorial regions.

Article 139. Delegates to the assemblies of socio-political communities shall be delegated by workers and other working people and citizens organized in socio-political organizations, associated in the Socialist Alliance of the Working People, or as members of the organizations of the Socialist Alliance of the Working People.

Within the framework of the Socialist Alliance of the Working People, socio-political organizations shall by mutual agreement draw up a list of candidates for delegates to the assemblies of socio-political communities from among members of their delegations.

Working people and citizens shall elect such delegates to Commune assemblies by direct, universal, and secret vote on the basis of a list of candidates.

Delegates to the assemblies of the broader socio-political communities shall be elected by the councils of delegates from socio-political organizations in Commune assemblies by secret ballot from a list of candidates.

Article 140. No one who has been elected delegate for a term of four years may for more than two consecutive terms be delegated to the same assembly.

The function of a delegate to an assembly shall be incompatible with other statutorily-defined functions in the organs of the same socio-political community.

Article 141. In taking stands on questions being decided in their assembly, delegates shall act in conformity with the guidelines received from their self-managing organizations and communities, and with the basic stands of the delegations or of socio-political organizations which have delegated them, and in conformity with the common and general social interests and needs; they shall be independent in their options and voting.

Delegates shall be bound to keep the delegations and basic self-managing organizations and communities or socio-political organizations which have elected them informed of the work of the assemblies and of their own work, and shall be responsible to them for their work.

Article 142. Delegations and each of their members, and individual delegates to assemblies may be recalled.

The recall of delegations or delegates shall, in principle, be carried out in the way and by the procedure applicable to the election of delegations and delegates.

Delegations and each of their members and individual delegates to assemblies shall have the right to resign.

Article 143. An assembly shall, within the scope of the rights and duties of its socio-political community: formulate policy and decide on the basic questions of significance for political, economic, welfare, and cultural life and social development; pass social plans, budgets, regulations, and other enactments; consider questions of common concern to organizations of associated labor and other self-managing organizations and communities, and adjust their relations and interests; initiate and take part in the conclusion of social compacts; discuss questions concerning national defense, security, and social self-protection; consider the state of and general problems concerning constitutionality, legality, and the judiciary, and organize and exercise social control; lay down basic principles concerning the organization and competence of the organs of socio-political communities; set up administrative agencies; elect, nominate, and relieve of office specified officials of these agencies and judges; ensure the execution of established policy, regulations, and other enactments; formulate the policy of implementation of regulations and other enactments, and determine the obligations of organs and organizations in connection with the execution of such regulations and enactments; exercise political control over the work of executive organs, administrative agencies, and holders of self-managing, public, and other social functions responsible to the assembly, and direct the work of such organs with its guidelines.

Article 144. Every assembly shall form a chamber of associated labor, as the chamber of delegates of working people in organizations of associated labor and other self-managing organizations and communities of labor; a chamber of local communities, as the chamber of delegates of the working people and citizens in the local communities, or a chamber of Communes, as the chamber of delegates of the working people and citizens in the Communes; and a socio-political chamber, as the chamber of delegates of the working people and citizens organized in socio-political organizations.

Article 145. The province of work and the mode of decision-making of the assemblies of socio-political communities shall be specified by the constitution and by-laws.

The province of work of the chambers shall be regulated so as to enable the chamber of associated labor to decide questions of concern to workers and other working people in social labor, and the chamber of local communities or the chamber of Communes to decide questions of concern to the working people and citizens in the local communities or the Communes, and to enable the socio-political chamber to decide on questions concerning the realization, development, and safeguard of the socialist system of self-management established by the constitution.

Assembly chambers shall decide on questions falling within the competence of their assemblies independently, on an equal footing, or at joint sessions of all assembly chambers.

Assemblies of self-managing communities of interest concerned with education, science, culture, and health and social welfare shall decide, on an equal footing, together with the competent chambers of socio-political community, on questions in these spheres which fall within the competence of the assembly of the appropriate socio-political community. These or other specific decision-making rights in the assemblies of socio-political communities may, by the constitution and the by-laws of socio-political communities, also be vested in the assemblies of other self-managing communities of interest.

No decision calling for the allocation of part of income for common and general social needs, or concerning the purpose and volume of resources earmarked for such needs, may be taken if it has not been approved by the relevant chamber of associated labor.

Article 146. The assembly of a socio-political community may call a referendum to enable working people to express their views in advance on individual questions falling within the assembly's competence, or to endorse statutes, regulations, and other enactments. Decisions taken through referenda shall be binding.

Article 147. Each Republic and Autonomous Province shall form a presidency of the Republic and Autonomous Province respectively, which shall represent the Republic or Autonomous Province and exercise other rights and duties, as spelled out by the constitution.

Article 148. Every socio-political community shall form an executive council as the executive organ of the assembly.

An executive council shall be responsible to its assembly for the situation in its socio-political community, the implementation of policy, the enforcement of the regulations and other enactments of the assembly, and the direction and adjustment of the work of administrative agencies.

Article 149. Assemblies of socio-political communities shall set up administrative agencies.

Administrative agencies shall implement established policy and enforce laws, regulations, and other enactments of their assemblies and executive councils, carry into effect guidelines of the assemblies, be responsible for the situation in the fields for which they have been formed, follow the state of affairs in specific fields and take initiative for the solution of questions in these fields, decide on administrative matters, exercise administrative supervision and conduct other administrative affairs, prepare regulations and other enactments, and perform other professional work on behalf of the assemblies of their socio-political communities and their executive councils.

Administrative agencies shall be independent within the framework of their powers, and shall be responsible for their work to their assemblies and executive councils.

Administrative agencies shall through their work ensure efficient realization of the rights and interests of working people and citizens, organizations of associated labor, and other self-managing organizations and communities.

Administrative agencies shall cooperate with one another, with administrative agencies of other socio-political communities, and with organizations of associated labor and other self-managing organizations and communities in matters of concern to these organizations and communities, and shall keep themselves mutually informed.

Article 150. Relations among administrative agencies of individual socio-political communities shall be based on the rights and duties laid down by the constitution, the by-laws of the socio-political communities, and statute.

The rights and duties of republican and provincial administrative agencies regarding the enforcement of statutes and other regulations and enactments, and supervision of their enforcement, and their rights and duties *vis-à-vis* Commune administrative agencies in the enforcement of statutes, other regulations, and enactments, shall be laid down by the constitution and statute.

Article 151. Elected and appointed officials shall be elected or appointed for a term of four years.

Members of the presidencies of socio-political communities, and presidents of executive councils may not be elected for more than two consecutive terms.

Members of executive councils, officials in charge of administrative agencies, and other officials and holders of self-management, public, and other social functions, as specified by the constitution and statute, may be elected or appointed for two consecutive terms, and exceptionally, by a special procedure laid down by the constitution, for one more term.

Article 152. Organizations of associated labor, and other self-managing organizations* and communities, social organizations, citizens' associations, and other organizations may be vested by statute or a decision of the commune assembly based on statutory authority with the right to regulate by their acts in the sphere of their activity specified relations of broader concern, in individual matters to rule on specific rights and obligations, and to exercise other public powers.

The way public authority vested in individual organizations and communities can be exercised, and the rights of the assemblies and other organs of socio-political communities regarding the issuance of guidelines to these organizations and communities, and the exercise of supervision in connection with the performance of public powers, may be specified by statute or a decision of the communal assembly based on statutory authority.

Chapter III. The Freedoms, Rights, and Duties of Man and the Citizen

Article 153. The freedom and rights of man and the citizen, spelled out by the present Constitution, shall be realized through solidarity among people and through the fulfillment of duties and responsibilities of everyone towards all and of all towards everyone.

The freedoms of man and the citizen shall only be restricted by the equal freedoms and rights of others, and by the constitutionally-specified interests of the socialist community.

Each shall be bound to respect the freedoms and rights of others and shall be responsible therefor.

Article 154. Citizens shall be equal in their rights and duties regardless of nationality, race, sex, language, religion, education, or social status.
All shall be equal before the law.

Article 155. Working people and citizens shall have the inalienable right to self-management which enables each individual to decide on his personal and common interests in an organization of associated labor, local community, self-managing community of interest or other self-managing organization or community and socio-political community, and in all other forms of their self-management integration and mutual association.
Each individual shall be responsible for self-management decision-making and the implementation of decisions.

Article 156. All citizens who have reached the age of eighteen years shall have the right to elect and be elected members of delegations in basic self-managing organizations and communities, and to elect and be elected delegates to the assemblies of socio-political communities.
Workers in organizations of associated labor, and working people in all forms of pooling of labor, resources, and interests, regardless of age, shall have the right to elect and be elected to delegations to the assemblies of socio-political communities and to elect delegates to the assemblies of such communities.
Workers in organizations of associated labor and working people in all forms of pooling of labor, resources, and interests shall, regardless of age, have the right to elect and be elected members of or delegates in managing organs of such organizations.

Article 157. Citizens shall have the right to submit petitions and proposals to bodies and organs of socio-political communities and other competent organs and organizations, to receive an answer thereto, and to take political and other kinds of initiative of general concern.

Article 158. Everyone shall be bound conscientiously and in the interest of socialist society based on self-management to exercise self-management, public, and other social functions vested in him.

Article 159. The right to work shall be guaranteed.

Rights acquired on account of labor shall be inalienable.

All those who manage or dispose of social resources, and sociopolitical communities shall be bound to create increasingly favorable conditions for the realization of the right to work.

The social community shall create conditions for the vocational rehabilitation of citizens who are not fully able to work, and also conditions for their adequate employment.

The right to relief during temporary unemployment shall be guaranteed, subject to conditions spelled out by statute.

A worker may be dismissed from his job against his will only under conditions and in the way specified by statute.

Whoever will not work, although he is fit for work, shall not enjoy the rights and protection due to him on account of labor.

Article 160. Freedom to work shall be guaranteed.

Everyone shall be free to choose his occupation and job.

Every citizen shall have access, on equal terms, to every job and every function in society.

Forced labor shall be prohibited.

Article 161. Working people shall have the right to such working conditions as ensure their physical and moral integrity and security.

Article 162. Workers shall be entitled to limited working hours.

Workers shall not work more than 42 hours a week. In certain activities and in certain cases, it may be provided by statute that the working time may, for a limited period, exceed 42 hours a week, if so required by the nature of work or exceptional circumstances.

Conditions for still shorter working hours may be laid down by statute.

Workers shall be entitled to daily and weekly rest and to an annual holiday with pay of not less than eighteen working days.

Workers shall have the right to health and other kinds of care and personal safety at work.

Young people, women and disabled persons shall enjoy special protection at work.

Article 163. The right of workers to social security shall be ensured through obligatory insurance, based on the principles of reciprocity and solidarity and past labor, in self-managing communities of interest, on the basis of contributions collected from workers' personal incomes and contributions collected from income of organizations of

Yugoslavia

associated labor, or contributions collected on resources of other organizations or communities in which they work. On the basis of such insurance, workers shall have, in conformity with statute, the right to health care and other benefits in the case of illness, childbirth benefits, benefits in the case of diminution or loss of working capacity, unemployment, and old age, and other social security benefits, and for their dependents—the right to health care, survivors' pensions, and other social security benefits.

Social security benefits for working people and citizens who are not covered by the compulsory social insurance scheme shall be regulated by statute on the principles of reciprocity and solidarity.

Article 164. Citizens shall be guaranteed the right to acquire a tenancy title to a dwelling in social ownership, which ensures them permanent occupancy, under conditions specified by statute, of a socially-owned dwelling for the satisfaction of their personal and family housing needs.

The right of citizens to a dwelling subject to the right of ownership shall be regulated by statute.

Article 165. Primary education lasting at least eight years shall be obligatory.

Economic and other conditions for the opening and operation of schools and other institutions for the education of citizens and the promotion of their activities shall be ensured through self-managing communities of interest, on the principles of reciprocity and solidarity among working people, organizations of associated labor, and other self-managing organizations and communities and socio-political communities, in conformity with statute.

Citizens shall be entitled, under equal conditions specified by statute, to acquire knowledge and vocational training at all levels of education, in all kinds of schools and other institutions of education.

Article 166. Freedom of thought and determination shall be guaranteed.

Article 167. Freedom of the press and other media of information and public expression, freedom of association, freedom of speech and public expression, freedom of gathering and public assembly, shall be guaranteed.

Citizens shall have the right to express and publish their opinions through the media of information.

Citizens, organizations, and citizens' associations may, under conditions specified by statute, publish newspapers and other publications and disseminate information through other media of information.

Article 168. Citizens shall be guaranteed the right to be kept informed of developments in the country and in the world which are of concern for their life and work, and of questions of concern to the community.

The press, radio, and television, and other media of information shall be bound to inform the public truthfully and objectively, and to make public the opinions and information of organs, organizations, and citizens which are of concern to the public.

The right shall be guaranteed to cause correction of published information that has violated the rights and interests of an individual, organization, or body.

Article 169. Scientific, scholarly, and artistic creation shall be free.

Authors of scientific, scholarly, and artistic works, and of scientific discoveries and technical inventions shall have moral and material rights to their achievements. The rights of creators to their works may not be used in a way contrary to society's interest in applying new scientific achievements and technical inventions.

The volume, duration, restriction, termination, and protection of the rights of creators to their works, and the rights of the organizations of associated labor in which such works were created as a result of the pooling of labor and resources, shall be laid down by statute.

Article 170. Citizens shall be guaranteed the right to opt for a nation or nationality and to express their national culture, and also the right to the free use of their language and alphabet.

No citizen shall be obliged to state to which nation or nationality he belongs, nor to opt for any one of the nations or nationalities.

Propagating or practicing national inequality, and any incitement of national, racial, or religious hatred and intolerance shall be unconstitutional and punishable.

Article 171. Members of nationalities shall, in conformity with the constitution and statute, have the right to use their language and alphabet in the exercise of their rights and duties, and in proceedings before state organs and organizations exercising public powers.

Members of the nations and nationalities of Yugoslavia shall, on the territory of each Republic and/or Autonomous Province, have the right to instruction in their own language in conformity with statute.

Article 172. The defense of the country shall be the inviolable and inalienable right and the supreme duty and honor of every citizen.

Article 173. Citizens shall have the right and duty to take part in social self-protection.

Article 174. Profession of religion shall be free and shall be an individual's private affair.

Religious communities shall be separate from the state and shall be free to conduct their religious affairs and religious services.

Religious communities may found religious schools for the training of the clergy only.

Abuse of religion and religious activities for political purposes shall be unconstitutional.

The social community may provide financial help to religious communities.

Religious communities may have the right to own real property within the limits determined by statute.

Article 175. A man's life shall be inviolable.

Exceptionally, capital punishment may be provided for by federal statute for the most serious forms of grave criminal offense.

Article 176. Inviolability of the integrity of the human personality, personal and family life, and of other human rights shall be guaranteed.

Any extortion of a confession or statement shall be forbidden and punishable.

Article 177. Man's freedom shall be inviolable.

No one may be deprived of liberty except in cases and by the procedure specified by statute.

Deprivation of liberty may last only as long as there are statutory grounds for it.

Any unlawful deprivation of liberty shall be punishable.

Article 178. A person reasonably suspected of having committed a criminal offense may be detained and held in detention only when this is indispensable for the conduct of criminal proceedings or for reasons of public safety. Detention shall be ordered by a court of law; only exceptionally, under conditions spelled out by statute, may detention be ordered by another statutorily-empowered authority— for no longer than three days.

A written order with a statement of reasons must be served on a person detained at the moment of detention or not later than 24 hours thereafter. A person detained may lodge an appeal against such order, which must be decided by the court within 48 hours.

The duration of detention shall be kept within the shortest necessary period of time.

Detention ordered by a court of first instance may not last more than three months. Exceptionally, the Supreme Court may extend this time-limit for another three months. If upon the expiry of these time-limits no charge sheet has been filed, the prisoner shall be released.

Article 179. Respect for the human personality and human dignity shall be guaranteed in criminal proceedings and in any other proceedings in the case of deprivation or restriction of liberty, and during the enforcement of a penalty.

Article 180. Every person shall be entitled to equal protection of his rights in proceedings before courts of law, state organs, and other organs and organizations which decide on his rights, obligations, and interests.

Everyone shall be guaranteed the right to appeal or another legal remedy against decisions of courts of law, state organs, and other organs and organizations which decide on his rights or interests founded on statute.

Legal aid shall be provided through the Bar, as an independent social service, and through other forms of legal assistance.

Article 181. No one shall be punished for any act which before its commission was not defined as a punishable offense by statute or a legal provision based on statute, or for which no penalty was threatened.

Criminal offenses and criminal-law sanctions may only be established by statute.

Sanctions for criminal offenses shall be imposed by the competent court in proceedings regulated by statute.

No one may be considered guilty of a criminal offense until so proven by a final judgment of a court of law.

Any person who has been unjustifiably convicted of a criminal offense or who has been deprived of liberty without cause shall be entitled to rehabilitation and compensation for damage by society, and to other statutorily-established rights.

Article 182. The right to defend oneself against charges shall be guaranteed.

No one accessible to the court or another organ authorized to conduct proceedings may be sentenced without prior examination in the form specified by statute, or without being afforded an opportunity to defend himself.

In criminal proceedings, the accused shall be entitled to retain a defense counsel who shall be enabled, in conformity with statute, to defend and protect the rights and interests of the accused. Statutory provisions shall regulate when the accused must have a defense counsel.

Article 183. Citizens shall be guaranteed freedom of movement and abode.

Restriction of freedom of movement or abode may be provided for by law, but only in order to ensure the conduct of criminal proceedings, to prevent the spread of contagious diseases or protect public order, or when so required by the defense interests of the country.

Article 184. Homes shall be inviolable.

No one may enter, without a warrant, any dwelling or other premises of others or search them against the will of their tenant.

The person whose dwelling or other premises are being searched, or a member of his family or his representative, shall have the right to be present during the search.

A search may only be carried out in the presence of two witnesses.

Subject to conditions spelled out by statute, a person in an official capacity may enter a dwelling or premises of others without a warrant from a competent organ and carry out a search in the absence of witnesses, if this is indispensable for the immediate arrest of the perpetrator of a criminal offense, to protect the safety of life and property, or if it appears obvious that evidence in criminal proceedings could not be secured otherwise.

Any illegal entry into and search of a dwelling or premises of others shall be prohibited and punishable.

Article 185. Secrecy of mail and of other means of communication shall be inviolable.

Provisions to depart from the principle of inviolability of secrecy of mail and of other means of communication, pursuant to an order by a competent organ, may only be made by statute if this is indispensable for the conduct of criminal proceedings or for the security of the country.

Article 186. Everyone shall be entitled to health care.

Cases in which uninsured citizens are entitled to health care from social resources shall be spelled out by statute.

Article 187. Veterans, disabled veterans, and survivors of veterans killed in war shall be guaranteed rights which ensure their social security and special rights as spelled out by statute.

Disabled veterans shall be entitled to vocational rehabilitation, disability benefits, and other forms of care.

Article 188. Mothers and children shall enjoy special social care.

Minors deprived of parental care, and other persons unable to take care of themselves and to take care of their rights and interests shall enjoy special social care.

Article 189. Citizens who are not able to work and have no necessary means of support, shall be entitled to assistance by the social community.

Article 190. The family shall enjoy social protection. Marriage and marital and family legal relations shall be regulated by statute.

A marriage shall be validly contracted before a competent organ by free consent of the prospective spouses.

Parents shall have the right and duty to raise and educate their children. Children shall be bound to care for their parents in need of assistance.

Children born out of wedlock shall have the same rights and duties as children born in wedlock.

Article 191. Every individual shall have the right freely to decide on the number and spacing of children.

This right may only be restricted for reasons of health.

Article 192. Man shall have the right to a healthy environment.

Conditions for the realization of this right shall be ensured by the social community.

Article 193. Anyone who utilizes land, water, or other natural resources shall be bound to do so in a way which ensures conditions for man's work and life in a healthy environment.

Everyone shall be bound to preserve nature and its goods, natural landmarks and rarities, and cultural monuments.

Article 194. The right of inheritance shall be guaranteed.

Inheritance shall be regulated by statute.

No one may retain ownership of real property and means of labor on grounds of inheritance in excess of the limits laid down by the constitution or statute.

Inheritance of the property of a person who enjoyed social or other kinds of assistance from the social community may be restricted by statute.

Article 195. Everyone shall be bound to contribute, under equal conditions and proportionately to his economic possibilities, to the satisfaction of general social needs.

Article 196. Everyone shall be bound to help other persons in danger and, on the basis of solidarity, to participate with others in combating any general danger.

Article 197. Everyone shall be bound to abide by the constitution and statute.

Conditions under which failure to discharge duties established by the constitution and statute is punishable shall be spelled out by statute.

Article 198. Any arbitrary act which violates or restricts human rights shall be unconstitutional and punishable, regardless of who has committed the act.

No one shall use coercion or restrict the right of another, except in cases and in proceedings regulated by statute.

Article 199. Everyone shall be entitled to damages for any loss caused to him in connection with the performance of an office or other activity of state organs and/or organizations in charge of affairs of public concern, through any illegal or wrongful activity by an individual or organ in charge of such an office or activity.

Damages shall be paid by the socio-political community or organization in which this office or activity is performed. The party wronged shall also be entitled, in conformity with statute, to claim damages directly from the tort-feasor for the loss he has caused.

Article 200. Every citizen of the Socialist Federal Republic of Yugoslavia when abroad shall enjoy the protection of the Socialist Federal Republic of Yugoslavia.

No citizens of the Socialist Federal Republic of Yugoslavia may be deprived of citizenship, banished, or extradited.

A citizen of the Socialist Federal Republic of Yugoslavia who is absent from the country and who also has another citizenship, may exceptionally, upon authority of federal statute, be deprived of the citizenship of the Socialist Federal Republic of Yugoslavia, only if by his activities he causes harm to the international and other interests of Yugoslavia, or if he refuses to perform his civic duties.

Article 201. Aliens in Yugoslavia shall enjoy the freedoms and rights of man spelled out by the present Constitution, and shall have other rights and duties specified by statute and international treaties.

Article 202. Foreign citizens and stateless persons who are persecuted for supporting democratic views and movements, social and national emancipation, the freedoms and rights of the human personality, or the freedom of scientific and artistic creative endeavor, shall be guaranteed the right of asylum.

Article 203. The freedoms and rights guaranteed by the present Constitution may not be denied or restricted.

No one may use the freedoms and rights established by the present Constitution in order to disrupt the foundations of the socialist self-management democratic order established by the present Constitution, to endanger the independence of the country, violate the freedoms and rights of man and the citizen guaranteed by the present Constitution, endanger peace and equality in international cooperation, stir up national, racial, or religious hatred or intolerance or abet commission of criminal offenses, nor may these freedoms be used in a way which offends public morals. It shall be specified by statute in what cases and under what conditions the use of these freedoms, in a way contrary to the present Constitution, will entail a restriction or a ban on their use.

These freedoms and rights shall be realized and duties performed pursuant to the present Constitution. The mode of realization of individual freedoms and rights may only be regulated by statute, and this only when so provided by the present Constitution, or when this is indispensable for their realization.

The freedoms and rights guaranteed by the present Constitution shall enjoy judicial protection.

Chapter IV. Constitutionality and Legality

Article 204. Protection of constitutionality and legality shall be ensured in order to realize the socio-economic and political relations laid down by the constitution and statute, and to protect the freedoms of man and the citizen, self-management, social property, the self-management and other rights of organizations of associated labor and other self-managing organizations and communities and socio-political communities.

Article 205. Protection of constitutionality and legality shall be the responsibility of the courts of law, organs of socio-political communities, organizations of associated labor and other self-managing organizations and communities, and of those exercising self-management, public, and other social functions.

Constitutional courts shall ensure constitutionality and legality in accordance with the constitution.

Working people and citizens shall have the right and duty to initiate proceedings for the protection of constitutionality and legality.

Article 206. Republican constitutions and provincial constitutions may not be contrary to the SFRY Constitution.

All statutes and other regulations and enactments passed by organs and organizations of socio-political communities, and self-management enactments of organizations of associated labor and other self-managing organizations and communities, must be in conformity with the SFRY Constitution.

Article 207. All regulations and other enactments passed by federal organs must be in conformity with federal statute.

Republican and provincial statutes, and other regulations and enactments passed by organs of socio-political communities, and self-management enactments may not be contrary to federal statute.

If a republican or provincial statute is contrary to a federal statute, it will be temporarily applied pending a decision by the constitutional court, and if federal organs are responsible for its enforcement, the federal statute concerned shall apply.

If an organ, which has jurisdiction over individual cases, deems that a statute, other regulation, or enactment, or self-management enactment is not in accord with federal statute, or that it is contrary to federal statute, it shall be bound to institute proceedings before the constitutional court.

Article 208. Statutes and other regulations and enactments shall be promulgated before coming into force.

Self-management enactments may not be applied before they have been promulgated in an appropriate way.

Article 209. Federal statutes and other federal regulations and enactments shall enter into force not earlier than eight days from the date of promulgation.

Only for especially justified reasons may it be regulated that a federal statute, regulation, or other enactment shall enter into force within a period shorter than eight days from the date of promulgation, or on the date of promulgation.

Article 210. International treaties shall be applied as of the date they enter into force, unless otherwise specified by the instrument of ratification or by an agreement concluded on the authority of the competent organ.

International treaties which have been promulgated shall be directly applied by the courts of law.

Article 211. No statute, other regulation, or enactment passed by organs of socio-political communities may be applied retroactively.

Retroactive application of any provision of a statute may only be provided by this particular statute, if this is required by the general interest.

Punishable acts shall be determined and penalties for them imposed according to the statute or other regulation which was in force at the time of their commission, unless the new statute or regulation is more favorable to the perpetrator.

Article 212. All individual acts and measures of administrative and other state organs in charge of executive and administrative affairs, and individual acts of organizations of associated labor and other self-managing organizations and communities adopted in the exercise of public functions, must be based on statute or other lawfully adopted regulation.

Article 213. State organs, organizations of associated labor, and other self-managing organizations and communities which exercise public powers may in individual cases rule on rights and obligations or, in conformity with statute, apply coercive or restrictive measures only in proceedings regulated by statute in which all the parties concerned have the opportunity to defend their rights and interests, and file an appeal against decisions rendered, or have recourse to some other avenue of relief provided by statute.

Administrative agencies may issue binding orders to individual self-managing organizations and communities regarding their work only when expressly authorized by statute so to do, and only in accordance with a procedure specified by statute.

Article 214. Ignorance of the language in which proceedings are conducted shall not be an obstacle to the defense and realization of the rights and justified interests of citizens and organizations.

Every person shall have the right to use his own language in proceedings before a court of law or before other state organs, organizations of associated labor, and other self-managing organizations and communities which, in exercising public powers, decide on a citizen's rights and obligations, and to be informed in his own language of the facts in the course of the proceedings.

Article 215. An appeal may be filed with the competent organ against decisions and other acts of law courts, administrative and other state organs, and against such acts of self-managing organizations and communities vested with public powers, rendered in first instance proceedings.

Exceptionally, the right of appeal may in certain cases be ruled out by statute if protection of rights and the rule of law are ensured in some other way.

Article 216. The legality of final individual acts by which state organs or self-managing organizations and communities, vested with public powers, rule on rights and obligations shall be decided on by courts of law through administrative litigation if no other avenue of judicial relief is provided for by statute.

Only exceptionally may administrative litigation be ruled out by statute in specific kinds of administrative disputes.

Chapter V. Courts and Office of the Public Prosecutor

Article 217. Justice shall be administered within a uniform system of power of and self-management by the working class and all working people by regular courts as organs of state power, and by self-management courts.

Article 218. Courts shall protect the freedoms and rights of citizens and the self-management status of working people and self-managing organizations and communities, and shall ensure constitutionality and legality.

Article 219. Courts shall be independent in the performance of their judicial functions, and shall administer justice in accordance with the constitution, statute, and self-management enactments.

Article 220. Regular courts shall be established by statute.

The jurisdiction, composition, and organization of regular courts and proceedings before such courts shall be laid down by statute.

Article 221. Regular courts shall decide disputes involving: basic personal relations, the rights and obligations of citizens, and the rights and obligations of socio-political communities; impose punishments and other measures on perpetrators of criminal offenses and other punishable acts specified by statute; decide on the legality of individual acts of state organs and organizations in charge of public powers; decide disputes concerning property and labor relations, if the settlement of such disputes has not been vested in self-management courts, and shall decide on other relations when so provided by statute.

Criminal offenses committed by military personnel and certain criminal offenses committed by other persons relating to national defense and the security of the country, and other legal matters relating to disputes in connection with service in the Yugoslav People's Army, shall be decided upon by military courts.

Article 222. Regular courts shall monitor and study social relationships and occurrencies of concern for the discharge of their functions, and shall submit to the assemblies of the appropriate socio-political communities, and other state organs and self-managing organizations and communities, proposals for the prevention of socially-dangerous and harmful practices and for the strengthening of legality, social responsibility, and socialist morals.

Within the ambit of their jurisdiction, regular courts shall have the right and duty to keep the assemblies of the appropriate socio-political community informed of matters concerning the application of laws and of the work of the courts, and military courts—the SFRY Presidency or the President of the Republic in his capacity of Commander-in-Chief.

Article 223. Self-management courts shall be established by a self-management act or by the agreement of the parties, in conformity with the constitution and statute. For certain kinds of disputes, self-management courts may also be established by statute.

The jurisdiction, composition, and organization of self-management courts, and proceedings before such courts shall be regulated by statute or the founding acts of the courts in conformity with statute.

Article 224. Self-management courts shall decide specific kinds of disputes, as laid down by the constitution and statute, arising out of socio-economic and other self-management relations, and also disputes entrusted to them by working people in organizations of associated labor, self-managing communities of interest, and other self-managing organizations and communities, which disputes arise out of mutual relations which they independently regulate, or which stem from rights of which they freely dispose, unless it is specified by statute that certain kinds of disputes must be decided by regular courts.

Citizens may, by mutual agreement, entrust the settlement of individual disputes concerning the rights they may freely dispose of to conciliation councils or to arbitration tribunals or to other self-management courts, unless otherwise specified by statute.

Article 225. Self-management courts shall be established as courts of associated labor, arbitration tribunals, conciliation councils, chosen arbitration courts, and other kinds of self-management courts.

Article 226. Courts of associated labor shall decide on: the existence of conditions for forming basic organizations of associated labor and work communities; requests for the protection of the right to work with social resources and of other self-management rights, and for the protection of social property; disputes concerning the formation and separation of basic organizations of associated labor, and fusions, mergers, and division of organizations of associated labor; conclusion and implementation of self-management agreements on association and mutual relations in associated labor; and other kinds of dispute arising out of socio-economic and other self-management relations, as specified by statute.

The principles concerning the formation, jurisdiction, and composition of courts of associated labor and proceedings before such courts shall be laid down by federal statute.

Article 227. Court hearings shall be open.

Cases in which the public may be barred from judicial hearings in order to safeguard secrets or protect public morals, the interests of minors, or other special interests of the social community, shall be spelled out by statute.

Article 228. Courts shall sit in panels.

It may be provided by statute that certain kinds of cases shall be considered by a single judge.

Article 229. Justice shall be administered by judges and by working people and citizens acting as judges, lay-assessors, or jurors, in the way determined by statute or by the founding act of the court concerned.

It may be provided by statute that in certain courts judges alone shall administer justice in specific matters.

Article 230. Judges and citizens who take part in the administration of justice in regular courts shall be elected and relieved of office by the assembly of the competent socio-political community.

Judges of regular courts shall be elected and relieved of office in a way, under conditions, and by a procedure which shall ensure professional expertise and moral-political capabilities for the exercise of judicial functions, and assure judicial independence in the administration of justice.

Judges and citizens who take part in the administration of justice in regular courts shall be elected for a specific period of time and may be reelected.

Judges, citizens, and working people who take part in the administration of justice in self-management courts shall be elected, appointed, and relieved of office in the way regulated by statute.

Article 231. No one who takes part in the administration of justice may be called to account for an opinion given in the process of judicial decision-making, nor may he be detained in the proceedings instituted because of a criminal offense he has committed in the performance of his judicial duties, without the approval of the assembly of the competent socio-political community.

Article 232. A judge may not hold an office or carry out an activity incompatible with the judicial function.

Article 233. Appeals or other legal remedies against court decisions may only be decided by competent courts.

When and under what conditions a legal remedy will be allowed against decisions of a self-management court shall be specified by statute or the founding act of the court.

Conditions under which decisions of a self-management court may be contested before a regular court, and the enforcement of such decisions shall be regulated by statute.

Article 234. Court decisions shall be valid and enforceable throughout the entire territory of the Socialist Federal Republic of Yugoslavia.

Article 235. The Office of the Public Prosecutor is an independent state organ which shall be in charge of the prosecution of criminal and other statutorily-defined punishable acts and which, in addition, shall take specific statutory measures for the protection of interests of the social community, and use avenues of legal relief with a view to protecting constitutionality and legality.

The Office of the Public Prosecutor shall discharge its functions on the basis of the constitution and law, in conformity with the policy formulated by enactments of the assemblies of socio-political communities.

The Office of the Public Prosecutor shall have the right and duty to keep the assemblies of the appropriate socio-political communities informed of the application of laws, and on its work.

Article 236. The Office of the Military Prosecutor shall prosecute criminal offenses which fall within the jurisdiction of military courts, take specific measures for the protection of interests of the social community, and use avenues of legal relief with a view to protecting constitutionality and legality in the way specified by federal statute.

Chapter VI. National Defense

Article 237. It shall be the inviolable and inalienable right and duty of the nations and nationalities of Yugoslavia, working people, and citizens to protect and defend the independence, sovereignty, territorial integrity, and the social system of the Socialist Federal Republic of Yugoslavia established by the SFRY Constitution.

Article 238. No one shall have the right to acknowledge or sign an act of capitulation, nor to accept or recognize the occupation of the Federal Socialist Republic of Yugoslavia or of any of its individual parts. No one shall have the right to prevent citizens of the Socialist Federal Republic of Yugoslavia from fighting against an enemy who has attacked the country. Such acts shall be unconstitutional and punishable as high treason.

High treason is the gravest crime against the people and shall be punished as a serious criminal offense.

Article 239. The rights and duties of the Federation and its organs in national defense are regulated by the present Constitution.

It shall be the right and duty of the Communes, Autonomous Provinces, and the Republics and other socio-political communities, in line with the system of national defense, each on its own territory, to regulate and organize national defense and to direct territorial defense, civil defense, and other preparations for the defense of the country, and, in the event of an attack upon the country, to organize and direct total national resistance.

Organizations of associated labor and other self-managing organizations and communities shall exercise their right and duty to defend the country in conformity with statute and the plans and decisions of socio-political communities, ensure resources for national defense, and carry out other duties concerning national defense. Such organizations and communities shall be responsible for the execution of these duties.

Article 240. The Armed Forces of the Socialist Federal Republic of Yugoslavia shall protect the independence, sovereignty, territorial integrity, and the social system of the Socialist Federal Republic of Yugoslavia established by the present Constitution.

The Armed Forces of the Socialist Federal Republic of Yugoslavia shall make a unified whole and shall consist of the Yugoslav People's Army, as the common armed force of all the nations and nationalities and of all working people and citizens, and of territorial defense, as the broadest form of organized total national armed resistance.

Any citizen who with arms or in some other way takes part in resistance against an aggressor shall be a member of the Armed Forces of the Socialist Federal Republic of Yugoslavia.

Article 241. Military service shall be the duty of all citizens.

Article 242. As regards the composition of the officer corps and promotion to senior commanding and directing posts in the Yugoslav People's Army, the principle of the most proportional representation of the Republics and Autonomous Provinces shall be applied.

Article 243. The equality of the languages and alphabets of the nations and nationalities of Yugoslavia shall be ensured in the Armed Forces of the Socialist Federal Republic of Yugoslavia, in conformity with the SFRY Constitution.

In matters of command and military training in the Yugoslav People's Army, one of the languages of the nations of Yugoslavia may be used, and in parts of the country—the languages of the nations and nationalities, in conformity with federal statute.

PART III. RELATIONS IN THE FEDERATION AND THE RIGHTS AND DUTIES OF THE FEDERATION

Chapter I. Relations in the Federation

Article 244. In the Socialist Federal Republic of Yugoslavia, the nations, nationalities, working people, and citizens shall realize and ensure sovereignty, equality, national freedom, independence, territorial integrity, security, social self-protection, the defense of the country, the international position of the country and its relations with other states and international organizations, the system of socialist socio-economic relations based on self-management, the unity of the political system, the basic democratic freedoms and rights of man and the citizen, the solidarity and social security of the working people and citizens, and the unity of the Yugoslav market, and shall coordinate common economic and social development and their other common interests.

These common interests shall be realized through:

— federal organs, through equal participation and responsibility of the Republics and Autonomous Provinces in these organs in the formulation and execution of federal policy;

— federal organs and organizations on the basis of decisions of or agreement by the Republics and Autonomous Provinces;

— direct cooperation and agreement among the Republics, Autonomous Provinces, Communes, and other socio-political communities;

— self-management agreements, social compacts, and association of organizations of associated labor and other self-managing organizations and communities;

— the activity of socio-political and other social organizations and associations of citizens;
— free and all-round activities of citizens.

The SFRY Constitution lays down which rights and duties concerning the realization of common interests shall be exercised by the Federation through federal organs and which by the republican and provincial assemblies through their delegations to the SFRY Assembly and by direct decision-making, in the way specified by the present Constitution.

Article 245. The nations and nationalities of the Socialist Federal Republic of Yugoslavia shall have equal rights.

Article 246. The languages of the nations and nationalities and their alphabets shall be equal throughout the territory of Yugoslavia. In the Socialist Federal Republic of Yugoslavia, the languages of the nations shall be officially used, and the languages of the nationalities shall be used in conformity with the present Constitution and federal statute.

The realization of the equality of languages and alphabets of the nations and nationalities regarding their official use in areas populated by individual nationalities shall be ensured and the way of and conditions for its realization regulated by statute, the by-laws of socio-political communities, and by self-management enactments of organizations of associated labor and other self-managing organizations and communities.

Article 247. In order to ensure that its right to express its nationality and culture shall be realized, each nationality shall be guaranteed the right freely to use its language and alphabet, to develop its culture, and for this purpose to set up organizations and enjoy other constitutionally-established rights.

Article 248. In addition to the constitutional rights which they enjoy in other socio-political communities, the nationalities shall also realize their sovereign rights in the Communes as the basic self-managing and socio-political communities.

Article 249. Yugoslav citizens shall have a single citizenship—that of the Socialist Federal Republic of Yugoslavia.

Every citizen of a Republic shall simultaneously be a citizen of the Socialist Federal Republic of Yugoslavia.

Citizens of a Republic shall on the territory of another Republic have the same rights and duties as the citizens of that Republic.

Article 250. Decisions, documents, and individual acts issued by state organs and authorized organizations in one Republic or Autonomous Province shall be equally valid in other Republics and Autonomous Provinces.

Article 251. The working people, nations, and nationalities of Yugoslavia shall realize their economic interests within a unified Yugoslav market.

Working people and organizations of associated labor shall on the unified Yugoslav market enjoy equal rights in the performance of activities and income earning, on the basis of the action of market laws and social guidance of economic and social development and the adjustment of market relations.

Socio-political communities shall be responsible for securing the unity of the Yugoslav market.

Proceeding from the open character of the Yugoslav market, organizations of associated labor and socio-political communities shall, in order to realize common interests based on equal economic relations, enter into and develop economic cooperation with other countries in line with established policy and existing regulations.

Any act or conduct which disrupts the unity of the Yugoslav market shall be unconstitutional.

Article 252. The unity of the Yugoslav market shall be based on:
— free movement and pooling of labor and the means of reproduction, and free exchange of goods and services, scientific achievements, and technical know-how throughout the entire territory of the Socialist Federal Republic of Yugoslavia;
— uniform currency, uniform monetary and foreign exchange system, and uniform foundations of the credit system, a common monetary and foreign exchange policy, and common principles of credit policy;
— uniform system of and common policy concerning economic relations with other countries, uniform tariff system, and common tariff policy;
— free formation and association of organizations of associated labor and their freedom to operate throughout the entire territory of the Socialist Federal Republic of Yugoslavia;
— free operation on the market and conclusion of self-management

agreements and social compacts regarding the promotion of production and trade and the integration of social labor;
— guidance of economic and social development and adjustment of market relations through social planning based on self-management foundations.

Conditions under which goods and services shall be exchanged in internal trade may be laid down by statute.

The sale of goods and services which are in traffic on the entire territory of the Socialist Federal Republic of Yugoslavia may only be restricted by federal statute.

Conditions for the exchange of goods and services and conditions for business operations by organizations of associated labor in relations with other countries shall be regulated by federal statute.

Article 253. Citizens shall enjoy freedom of employment throughout the entire territory of the Socialist Federal Republic of Yugoslavia under the same conditions as obtain in the place of employment.

Rights stemming from labor which affect the realization of social security benefits and other similar rights shall be recognized throughout the entire territory of the Socialist Federal Republic of Yugoslavia, regardless of the socio-political communities in which they are acquired.

Conditions under which citizens may go abroad for the purpose of employment and performance of economic and other activities may be spelled out by federal statute.

The rights, duties, and obligations of citizens who perform an activity abroad or are employed abroad shall be regulated by statute.

Article 254. Organizations of associated labor and their communities and associations shall operate freely and on terms of equality throughout the entire territory of the Socialist Federal Republic of Yugoslavia, in conformity with regulations in force in their place of operation.

Any regulation or other act or conduct by which organizations of associated labor or working people from the territories of other Republics or Autonomous Provinces, and thereby also other Republics and Autonomous Provinces, are placed in an unequal position, shall be unconstitutional.

Article 255. Any combining of organizations of associated labor and any other activity or conduct by organizations or state organs aimed at preventing free movement and pooling of labor and resources and free exchange of goods and services, or at establishing monopolistic positions on the unified Yugoslav market through which material and other advantages that are not based on labor are acquired and unequal relations in business created, or which disrupt other economic and social relations determined by the constitution, shall be prohibited.

Article 256. If through an act pertaining to the formulation or implementation of common economic policy a federal organ has disrupted the equality of organizations of associated labor in income earning and in the use of the results of labor, or it has disrupted the equality of the Republics and Autonomous Provinces on the unified Yugoslav market, the federal organ involved shall simultaneously with the formulation of common economic policy and/or the enactment of measures for its implementation, fix and ensure compensation as a component part of measures of common economic policy for the planning period concerned.

Article 257. Social plans of Yugoslavia shall be based on agreements reached by working people, organizations of associated labor, self-managing communities of interest, and other self-managing organizations and communities, and on agreements reached among the Republics and Autonomous Provinces on economic policy of common concern.

On the basis of the working and development plans and joint assessment of the development possibilities and conditions of organizations of associated labor and other self-managing organizations and communities, and on the basis of the development plans and development possibilities and conditions of the Republics and Autonomous Provinces and the development of the social community as a whole, and taking into account international economic relations and international commitments of the Socialist Federal Republic of Yugoslavia, and common interests adjusted on this basis, social plans of Yugoslavia shall lay down a common economic policy and, in conformity with it, direct social reproduction on the basis of socialist socio-economic relations grounded in self-management.

Social plans of Yugoslavia shall also lay down guidelines and frameworks for measures of economic policy and other measures whose enactment, in conformity with the rights and duties spelled out by the present Constitution, falls within the competence of federal organs and/or organs of the Republics and Autonomous Provinces in order to ensure conditions for the realization of adjusted mutual interests of associated labor and of the common interests of the Republics and Autonomous Provinces within the unified Yugoslav market.

Article 258. A special federal Fund for Crediting Faster Development in Economically Underdeveloped Republics and Autonomous Provinces shall be set up.

Economically underdeveloped Republics and Autonomous Provinces shall be determined, and permanent sources for financing the Fund, special conditions for extending credits from its assets, and the mode of the Fund's operation, regulated by federal statute.

Compulsory loans may be floated by federal organs for the needs of the Federal Fund for Crediting Faster Development in Economically Underdeveloped Republics and Autonomous Provinces.

The Republics and Autonomous Provinces which are not able with their own resources to finance social and other services in the Republic or Autonomous Province, shall be ensured the necessary resources by the Federation under conditions spelled out by federal statute.

Article 259. The monetary system and the foundations of the credit system shall be uniform.

Money transfers shall be made according to uniform principles.

All those who use social resources shall make money transfers, conduct other affairs associated with money transfers, and shall deposit money in the way specified by federal statute.

Article 260. The National Bank of Yugoslavia, the National Banks of the Republics, and the National Banks of the Autonomous Provinces are institutions of the uniform monetary system responsible for the execution of common money supply policy, as laid down by the SFRY Assembly.

The National Bank of Yugoslavia shall issue bank-notes and coins. In conformity with common money supply policy, the National Bank of Yugoslavia shall control the amount of money in circulation and, together with the National Banks of the Republics and the National Banks of the Autonomous Provinces, take measures for the implementation of this policy.

The National Banks of the Republics and the National Banks of the Autonomous Provinces shall, within the framework of common money supply policy, also take other measures necessary for the implementation of the credit policy of the Republics and Autonomous Provinces respectively.

No one shall be placed in an unequal position in respect of the performance of activities and income earning as a result of measures for the implementation of joint money supply policy.

Article 261. The National Bank of Yugoslavia, the National Banks of the Republics, and the National Banks of the Autonomous Provinces shall, within the framework of their rights and duties, be responsible for the stability of the currency, general payment liquidity in Yugoslavia and abroad, and for the implementation of jointly formulated monetary-credit policy.

The National Bank of Yugoslavia, the National Banks of the Republics, and the National Banks of the Autonomous Provinces shall independently apply measures for the realization of the targets and tasks of monetary-credit and foreign exchange policy, as laid down by federal statute. Commercial banks and other financial organizations shall be bound to abide by the decisions of the National Bank of Yugoslavia, the National Banks of the Republics, and the National Banks of the Autonomous Provinces with a view to ensuring the realization of this policy.

Article 262. The National Bank of Yugoslavia, the National Banks of the Republics, and the National Banks of the Autonomous Provinces shall operate deposit accounts of socio-political communities and shall be authorized, on behalf of socio-political communities and on their account, to perform other banking affairs, if so specified by the constitution.

The National Bank of Yugoslavia shall act as a depositary of federal resources, conduct credit and other banking business for the needs of the Yugoslav People's Army and for the needs of national defense, as laid down by federal statute, and shall carry out other statutorily specified credit and banking operations on account of the Federation.

The National Bank of Yugoslavia, the National Banks of the Republics, and the National Banks of the Autonomous Provinces shall not engage in other activities of commercial banks.

Article 263. The status of the National Bank of Yugoslavia and uniform monetary operations of the National Banks of the Republics and Autonomous Provinces shall be regulated by federal statute.

The operations of the National Bank of Yugoslavia concerning the execution of common money supply, monetary-credit, and foreign exchange policy shall be managed by the Board of Governors. In managing such operations, the Board of Governors shall make decisions and take measures, and shall be responsible for their implementation.

The Board of Governors shall be composed of the Governor of the National Bank of Yugoslavia, the governors of the National Banks of the Republics, and the governors of the National Banks of the Autonomous Provinces.

Article 264. The system, sources, and kinds of taxes, revenue stamps, and other dues shall be regulated by statute.

All kinds of revenues realized through the taxation of the sale of goods and services which are in traffic throughout the entire territory of the Socialist Federal Republic of Yugoslavia, and the mode and rate of this taxation shall be defined by federal statute, except for goods and services whose mode and rate of taxation are on the authority of federal statute fixed by other socio-political communities.

An exemption from the payment of taxes and other dues on the resources, facilities, and installations serving exclusively for national defense and state security purposes may be provided for by federal statute.

Article 265. The Republics and Autonomous Provinces shall cooperate in the pursuance of tax policy and shall through compacts adjust the fundamentals of tax policy and the tax system if so required to ensure the unity and stability of the Yugoslav market.

In order to prevent and eliminate disruptions on the market, federal organs shall have the right and duty to propose to the Republics and Autonomous Provinces, in conformity with mutual compacts, to decrease or increase taxes and contributions fixed by socio-political communities, temporarily to postpone the spending of part of the revenue of socio-political communities, and to lay down common fundamentals of the tax policy of the Republics and/or Autonomous Provinces. Non-existence of compacts shall not prevent the Republics and Autonomous Provinces from passing regulations and other enactments in the sphere of tax policy and the tax system within the framework of their rights and obligations.

Article 266. Taxes and contributions payable on the income of basic organizations of associated labor shall be paid according to the regulations of, and in favor of, the socio-political communities on whose territory the basic organizations regularly perform their activities, or according to the decisions of, and in favor of, the self-managing communities of interest which satisfy the needs and interests of, or render services to, the basic organizations of associated labor for which contributions are paid to these self-managing communities of interest.

Resources which, as part of a bank's income, are distributed among basic organizations of associated labor and other social legal entities shall be taxed as income of such entities in accordance with the regulations of, and in favor of, the socio-political communities to which the tax on the income of such entities is paid.

Taxes and contributions levied on the personal incomes and revenues of workers and citizens, with the exception of taxes on property and revenue from property, shall be paid, in conformity with federal statute, according to the regulations of, and in favor of, the socio-political communities on whose territory the workers or citizens concerned live, or according to the decisions of, and in favor of, the self-managing communities of interest which satisfy the needs and interests of, or render services to, the workers and citizens and members of their families.

Article 267. When this is indispensable in order to prevent or eliminate any major disruption in the economy, or when this is required by the interests of national defense or other extraordinary needs of the country, federal statutes may:
— lay down the limits within which socio-political communities may fix their revenue deriving from the income of organizations of associated labor and from the sale of goods and services;
— make it obligatory for organizations of associated labor, self-managing communities of interest and other self-managing organizations and communities, and socio-political communities to form reserve social resources;
— impose a temporary ban on the use of part of the social means of consumption and of part of social resources earmarked for financing expanded reproduction by organizations of associated labor, self-managing communities of interest and other self-managing organizations and communities, and socio-political communities;
— regulate the mode of use of the budgetary surpluses of socio-political communities, and of the surplus revenue of self-managing communities of interest deriving from statutory obligations.

Article 268. In exercising the rights and duties laid down by the present Constitution, federal organs shall formulate policy and pass federal statutes and other regulations and enactments.

In the spheres regulated by federal statutes, the Republics and

Autonomous Provinces may pass statutes within the framework of their rights and duties.

If in areas to be regulated by Federal statute no such statute has been passed, the Republics and/or Autonomous Provinces may pass their own statutes if this is in the interests of the realization of their rights and duties.

Article 269. Federal statutes and other regulations and enactments shall be promulgated in the Official Gazette of the Socialist Federal Republic of Yugoslavia in authentic texts in the languages of the nations of Yugoslavia specified by the republican constitutions.

Federal statutes and other regulations and enactments shall be promulgated in the Official Gazette of the Socialist Federal Republic of Yugoslavia as authentic texts in the languages of the Albanian and Hungarian nationalities also.

Article 270. Federal statutes and other regulations and enactments shall be binding throughout the entire territory of the Socialist Federal Republic of Yugoslavia, unless their application is restricted by such statutes, regulations, or enactments to a narrower territory.

Article 271. International treaties which entail the enactment of new or amendments to existing republican and/or provincial statutes, or which entail special obligations for one or more Republics and/or Autonomous Provinces, shall be concluded in agreement with the competent republican and/or provincial organs. The procedure for the conclusion of such international treaties shall be regulated by federal statute, in agreement with the republican and provincial assemblies.

In cooperating with organs and organizations of other states and with international agencies and organizations, the Republics and Autonomous Provinces shall keep within the established foreign policy of the Socialist Federal Republic of Yugoslavia and international treaties.

In cooperating with appropriate foreign organs and organizations, international organizations, and territorial units of foreign states, Communes, organizations of associated labor, and other organizations and communities shall keep within the established foreign policy of the Socialist Federal Republic of Yugoslavia and international treaties.

The principle of the equality of languages of the nations of Yugoslavia, and analogously the principle of the equality of languages of the nations and nationalities, shall be applied in international communication.

When international treaties are drawn up in the languages of signatory countries, the languages of the nations of Yugoslavia shall be equally used.

Article 272. In exercising the rights and duties of the Federation, federal organs shall within their province of work be responsible for the situation in the relevant spheres of social life, for the initiation of policy and federal statutes, other regulations, and enactments, for the enforcement of federal statutes and other regulations and enactments, and for monitoring the implementation of policy and the enforcement of such regulations and enactments.

Article 273. Federal statutes and other regulations and enactments shall be enforced by republican and provincial organs, which shall be responsible for their enforcement, unless it is provided by the present Constitution that such statutes and other regulations and enactments shall be directly enforced by federal organs and that they shall be responsible for their enforcement.

Republican and provincial organs shall pass regulations concerning the enforcement of those federal statutes and other regulations and enactments for whose enforcement they are responsible. In these spheres, federal organs may, if explicitly authorized by a federal statute and within the limits specified by such statute, pass regulations concerning technical measures and record-keeping, and other regulations concerning the enforcement of federal statutes which ensure, in the interests of the country as a whole, uniform enforcement of such statutes.

In line with the responsibility of republican and provincial organs for the enforcement of federal statutes and other regulations and enactments, relations between federal organs and republican and provincial organs in the enforcement of such statutes, other regulations, and enactments shall be based on mutual cooperation, transmission of information, consultation, and agreement.

If republican and provincial organs do not enforce federal statutes and other regulations and enactments for whose enforcement they are responsible, the Federal Executive Council shall warn the Republican and/or Provincial Executive Councils thereof, and shall request them to take appropriate measures to ensure the enforcement of federal statutes, other regulations, and enactments.

Article 274. Federal organs shall be responsible for the enforcement of federal statutes and other regulations and enactments in the spheres in which, under the provisions of the present Constitution, the Federation ensures through federal organs the enforcement of federal statutes and other regulations and enactments.

Such federal statutes and other regulations and enactments shall be directly enforced by federal organs; they shall be enforced by republican and provincial organs when so specified by federal statute.

Where federal organs directly enforce federal statutes and other regulations and enactments, they may be empowered by federal statute to set up regional organs and organizational units to conduct specific administrative affairs falling within the competence of federal organs in the spheres of international relations, national defense, tariffs, foreign exchange and market inspection, supervision of the export and import of goods and services, supervision of weights and measures and precious metals, civil aviation safety, and radio communications.

Within the scope of the powers laid down by the present Constitution, federal organs shall pass regulations concerning the enforcement of federal statutes and other regulations and enactments for whose enforcement they are responsible. In such spheres, republican and provincial organs may pass regulations concerning the enforcement of federal statutes and other regulations and enactments, provided they are especially authorized to do so by federal statute.

When, under the provisions of the present Constitution, federal organs regulate matters concerning national defense, state security, and international relations, federal organs shall pass regulations concerning the enforcement of federal statutes, unless it is specified by federal statute that such regulations shall be passed by republican and/or provincial organs.

Article 275. Where administrative agencies in the Republics and Autonomous Provinces directly enforce federal statutes, regulations, and other enactments and international treaties for whose enforcement federal administrative agencies are responsible, the federal administrative agencies may be empowered by federal statute:
— to issue to competent republican and provincial administrative agencies binding instructions for the conduct of affairs for which they are authorized by federal statutes, other regulations, and enactments;

— to carry out supervisory work in line with the powers specified by federal statute;
— if a republican or provincial administrative agency has failed to perform a specific administrative act, and the non-execution of such act may cause serious harmful consequences, to perform such act and to notify thereof the Federal Executive Council. The Federal Executive Council shall inform thereof the Republican and/or Provincial Assembly concerned for the purposes of eliminating the cause for which it was necessary for the federal agency to perform this particular administrative act.

Republican and provincial administrative agencies shall be bound, in conformity with federal statute, to keep federal administrative agencies informed of the enforcement of federal statutes and other regulations and enactments and international treaties for the enforcement of which federal administrative agencies are responsible.

Article 276. The Executive Councils of the Republics and Autonomous Provinces may raise before the Federal Executive Council the question of enforcement of a federal statute, regulation, or other enactment passed by the Chamber of Republics and Provinces of the SFRY Assembly, if they consider that federal administrative agencies are not enforcing this statute, regulation, or enactment, or are not doing so in conformity with established policy.

Article 277. If a dispute arises between federal administrative agencies and republican and/or provincial administrative agencies regarding the fulfillment of the obligation of administrative agencies in the Republics and/or Autonomous Provinces to enforce a federal statute, other regulation, or enactment, the Federal Executive Council or the Executive Council of the Republic and/or Autonomous Province concerned shall inform thereof the SFRY Assembly.

The SFRY Assembly shall decide the controversial issue and rule on the obligation to enforce the federal statute, regulation, or other enactment involved.

Article 278. Federal administrative agencies shall communicate with administrative agencies in Communes through appropriate republican and/or provincial administrative agencies.

In affairs concerning national service and military mobilization of people and material resources, and in affairs concerning the protection of the rights and interests of Yugoslav citizens abroad, federal administrative agencies may, in conformity with federal statute, also directly communicate with administrative agencies in Communes.

Article 279. All revenues and expenditures of the Federation shall be determined by the Federal Budget.

Federal revenues shall include tariffs and other original revenues fixed by federal statute, and contributions by the Republics and Autonomous Provinces fixed in conformity with the principle of equality and mutual responsibility of the Republics and Autonomous Provinces for financing federal functions. It may be provided by federal statute that revenues from tariffs be not entered into the Federal Budget but should be used for the needs of the economy.

The total volume of expenditure in the Federal Budget shall be fixed in agreement with the Assemblies of the Republics and Autonomous Provinces, in line with the common economic policy for the year for which the Budget is being passed. Within the framework of total expenditure, resources shall be assured in the Federal Budget for financing the functions and obligations of the Federation spelled out by federal statutes and other enactments, and resources for the necessary federal reserves. Resources for financing national defense shall be ensured in the Federal Budget according to the medium-term plan for the development, buildup, and outfitting of the Yugoslav People's Army drawn up in line with the Social Plan of Yugoslavia.

The statutes, other regulations, and enactments of the SFRY Assembly and of other federal organs which create obligations for the Federal Budget may not be passed until the Assembly Chamber competent for the adoption of the Budget has established that resources for the fulfillment of such obligations have been secured.

The Federation may set up funds or raise credits and undertake other obligations beyond the limits of the total expenditure provided for by the Federal Budget only when so authorized by the present Constitution, or when the formation of funds or the undertaking of obligations has been agreed upon by the Republics and Autonomous Provinces.

For the needs of national defense and state security arising out of exceptional circumstances, the SFRY Assembly may, on the proposal of the SFRY Presidency, independently determine sources of finance or raise credits or undertake other obligations to meet such needs, if such needs cannot be met from the Federal Budget or federal budgetary reserves.

Chapter II. The Rights and Duties of the Federation

Article 280. The Socialist Federal Republic of Yugoslavia shall be represented by federal organs as specified by the present Constitution.

Article 281. The Federation shall through its organs:
(1) ensure the independence and territorial integrity of the Socialist Federal Republic of Yugoslavia and protect its sovereignty in international relations; decide on war and peace;
(2) ensure the system of socialist self-management socio-economic relations and uniform foundations of the political system;
(3) regulate those basic rights of workers in associated labor which ensure their status, as laid down by the present Constitution, in self-management and socio-economic relations, and the basic rights and obligations of organizations of associated labor, self-managing communities of interest, other self-managing organizations and communities, and socio-political communities regarding socially-owned resources; regulate the basic rights of working people concerning their social security and solidarity; lay down principles concerning the status, rights, and duties of the Social Attorney of Self-Management;
(4) regulate the fundamentals of the law of obligations (general provisions) and contractual relations, and other relations governed by the law of obligations in the field of the sale of goods and services; basic relations in the sphere of the law of property; basic relations which ensure the unity of the Yugoslav market; basic law of property relations and other substantive law relations in the fields of maritime shipping, inland and air navigation; copyright;
(5) regulate the fundamentals of the system of social planning and adopt social plans of Yugoslavia; lay down fundamentals for the preparation of the economy and public services for functioning in wartime; regulate the monetary system; determine legal means of payments, formulate money supply policy and ensure its implementation; regulate internal and external money transfers, formation of money and foreign exchange reserves, and their use when this is of concern to the country as a whole; regulate the fundamentals of the credit and banking system, and credit and other forms of investment by Yugoslav persons abroad and by foreign persons in Yugoslavia, and enact rules pertaining to the enforcement of federal statutes in this field, when in the interests of the country as a whole it is so specified by federal statute; regulate the fundamentals of the system of life and property insurance; regulate and ensure a system of

measures aimed at preventing the disruption of the unity of the Yugoslav market; regulate the system of social price control and ensure direct price control for goods and services of concern to the country as a whole; regulate and ensure federal commodity reserves to meet the country's needs in the event of war and other kinds of emergency, and to secure the stability of the market in the event of major disruptions on the market; regulate and ensure measures of protection against monopolies and unfair competition; regulate and implement measures for the restriction of the market and of the free sale of goods and services of concern to the country as a whole in the event of natural catastrophes or shortages of goods indispensable for the needs of the economy and the life of citizens, and when this is required by national defense interests; regulate the system of external trade and foreign exchange and other economic operations with other countries and ensure the enforcement of federal statutes in these spheres; regulate the customs system, customs tariffs, and measures of non-tariff protection, and ensure their implementation; regulate conditions for the opening and operation of duty-free zones; regulate and ensure the crediting of faster development in economically underdeveloped Republics and Autonomous Provinces; determine and ensure revenues accruing to the Federation under the present Constitution; regulate the fundamentals of the social system of information and the status of, and the fundamentals of, the functioning of the Social Accountancy Service; regulate the fundamentals of the legal status and operation of organizations of associated labor and of organizations of business associations in the unified economic area of Yugoslavia; regulate the integration of organizations of associated labor and their association in the Chamber of Economy for the territory of the Socialist Federal Republic of Yugoslavia; regulate obligatory association of organizations of associated labor in communities when so required by the technological unity of the system in individual spheres and when this is in the interests of the country as a whole; regulate conditions under which citizens may go abroad to perform economic and other activities or for the purposes of employment, and ensure the protection of citizens of the Socialist Federal Republic of Yugoslavia working abroad.

(6) regulate the fundamentals of the system of national defense and ensure their implementation; regulate the basic rights and duties of working people and citizens, organizations of associated labor and other self-managing organizations and communities, socio-political, and other social organizations in the sphere of national defense; regulate the basic rights and duties of socio-

political communities in the realization of the system of national defense; regulate special rights and obligations of organizations of associated labor and other self-managing organizations and communities regarding priority production and rendering of services for the needs of national defense and manufacture of arms and military equipment; regulate adjustment of regional and town plans and construction of capital projects to the defense needs of the country; lay down the fundamentals of plans and preparatory measures for the defense of the country; proclaim mobilization; regulate the administration and command of the Armed Forces of the Socialist Federal Republic of Yugoslavia and exercise supreme command over the Armed Forces; regulate and organize the Yugoslav People's Army, administer it, and exercise command over it; regulate the management and use of social resources utilized by the Yugoslav People's Army and for its needs; regulate citzens' national service and care for the families of persons doing national service; regulate matters concerning the status and other problems of persons serving in the Yugoslav People's Army and of military personnel; regulate the special rights and duties of military personnel in connection with their service in the Armed Forces; regulate and ensure military education and scientific research for the needs of the Armed Forces; regulate and organize military courts and the office of the military prosecutor; regulate and ensure social security and care for military personnel and military insurees and their dependents; regulate and ensure the basic rights of veterans, disabled veterans, and survivors of veterans killed in the war;

(7) formulate the foreign policy of the Socialist Federal Republic of Yugoslavia and ensure its implementation; maintain political, economic, and other relations with other states and international organizations; promote and stimulate cooperation with the developing countries and ensure resources for the development of economic cooperation with such countries and for the realization of solidarity with liberation movements; conclude, ratify, and ensure the enforcement of international treaties; ensure fulfillment of the international commitments of the Socialist Federal Republic of Yugoslavia; protect citizens of the Socialist Federal Republic of Yugoslavia and their interests, and the interests of domestic legal entities abroad; regulate matters concerning the realization of international relations; and regulate the organization and work of federal foreign affairs services;

(8) regulate the fundamentals of the system of protection of the order established by the present Constitution (state security); ensure the activity of the state security service indispensable for the realiza-

tion of responsibilities of federal organs, as specified by the present Constitution, and adjust the work of organs in charge of state security;

(9) regulate the citizenship of the Socialist Federal Republic of Yugoslavia; determine the basic data for registers of births, marriages, and deaths, and identity cards; determine public holidays and decorations of the Socialist Federal Republic of Yugoslavia; determine the anthem of the Socialist Federal Republic of Yugoslavia; regulate the use of the seal, coat-of-arms, and flag of the Socialist Federal Republic of Yugoslavia;

(10) regulate the supervision of exports and imports of goods and services and their crossing the state border; the status, stay, and protection of aliens in Yugoslavia; protection of life and health of people from contagious diseases endangering the country as a whole; marketing of medicinal drugs; protection of animals from contagious diseases and protection of plants from diseases and pests endangering the country as a whole; marketing of animal and plant protection preparations and supervison of transfer of animals and plants across the state border; imports and distribution of foreign printed matter and other public media of information and communication and enforcement of relevant federal statutes when, in the interests of the country as a whole, it is so specified by federal statute; regulate the regime of the territorial sea when it concerns international relations of the Socialist Federal Republic of Yugoslavia, the defense and security of the country and the unity of the Yugoslav market, and the mode of exercise of Yugoslavia's rights within the continental shelf and on the open seas; regulate supervision of passenger traffic across the state border; regulate the legal status of foreign legal entities in Yugoslavia; regulate the status of representatives of foreign states and foreign and international organizations; regulate representation of and agency for foreign economic and other organizations; regulate conservation and improvement of the human environment of concern to the country as a whole and to the international community; regulate the sale and transport of explosives and radioactive and other dangerous substances and transport of inflammable liquids and gasses, when this is in the interests of the country as a whole; regulate the sale of poisons and manufacture and sale of narcotics; regulate the fundamentals of the system of water management of concern to two or more Republics or Autonomous Provinces; regulate the status of foreign information agencies and representatives of foreign media of information; impose restrictions or bans on the freedom of use of printed matter and other media of information and communication

which are directed against the fundamentals of the socialist democratic order established by the present Constitution, or which endanger the independence of the country, peace, or international cooperation on terms of equality; determine elements of cartographic data of significance for the defense and security of the country and for general use in cartographic publications; regulate the status and powers of the Yugoslav Red Cross and other organizations which perform public functions on the basis of federal statutes and international treaties; regulate the marking and tending of the cemeteries and graves of members of the Allied armies and other foreign armies on the territory of the Socialist Federal Republic of Yugoslavia;

(11) regulate and ensure air navigation safety; regulate the fundamentals of safety in other fields of traffic; regulate matters relating to navigable waterways subject to the international or inter-state navigation regime and ensure the enforcement of federal regulations in this sphere when, in the interest of the country as a whole, it is so specified by federal statute; regulate matters concerning the system of communications of significance for the security of the country and the technological unity of the system of communications; regulate international communications and radio communications, and ensure the enforcement of federal regulations pertaining to international communications and radio communications, when, in the interest of the country as a whole, so specified by federal statute;

(12) regulate general conditions and principles concerning the imposition of sanctions for criminal offenses and economic violations, the system of sanctions, conditions for the extinguishment and expungement of sanctions, and general rules on the application of educational and punitive measures applicable to minors (the General Part of the Criminal Code and the Economic Violations Code); define criminal offenses against the foundations of the socialist self-management social order of Yugoslavia and the security of the country, against humanity and international law, against the reputation of the Socialist Federal Republic of Yugoslavia, its organs and representatives, against the reputation of foreign states and agencies and against the reputation of their heads and representatives respectively, against the official duty of official persons in federal organs, against the Armed Forces, and also criminal offenses and economic violations which disrupt the unity of the Yugoslav market or violate federal regulations; define responsibility and sanctions for administrative violations which infringe federal regulations; regulate administrative violations proceedings conducted by federal organs; regulate the general administrative procedure; regulate the code of

criminal procedure and other court procedures, with the exception of special procedures in the fields in which social relations are regulated by the Republics and/or Autonomous Provinces with their own rules; regulate amnesty and pardon for criminal offenses defined by federal statute;

(13) regulate the system of weights and measures and ensure supervision of weights and measures and of precious metals; regulate protection of inventions, technical innovations, trademarks, quality marks, marks of the origin of products, samples and models, and standards, technical norms, and quality standards for products and services, and ensure enforcement of relevant federal regulations when this is, in the interests of the country as a whole, so specified by federal statute;

(14) regulate and organize the collection, recording, and processing of statistical and other data on the situation in individual sectors of social life, demographic data, data on economic and other developments, and other data of concern to the country as a whole;

(15) regulate matters concerning settlement of conflicts of law between republican and/or provincial laws (conflict rules), and jurisdictional disputes between republican and/or provincial organs of different Republics; regulate matters concerning conflicts between domestic laws and legal rules of other countries;

(16) regulate and ensure: the organization, competence, and the mode of work of federal organs, and material and other relations among federal organs; elections for federal organs; the rights and duties of federal organs with regard to socially-owned resources used by them; the status, organization, and mode of work of institutions and schools founded by the Federation for the conduct of affairs of concern for the realization of the functions of the Federation and relations between federal organs and such institutions and schools; the rights, duties, and responsibilities of workers stemming from such work in federal organs and institutions and schools founded by the Federation;

(17) protect constitutionality as established by the present Constitution and legality in conformity with the present Constitution;

(18) exercise other rights and duties as laid down by the present Constitution.

When so specified by the present Constitution, federal organs shall exercise these rights and duties on the basis of decisions of and/or in agreement with republican and provincial organs in the way specified by the present Constitution.

PART IV. ORGANIZATION OF THE FEDERATION

Chapter I. The Assembly of the Socialist Federal Republic of Yugoslavia

1. Status and Competence

Article 282. The Assembly of the Socialist Federal Republic of Yugoslavia is a body of social self-management and the supreme organ of power within the framework of federal rights and duties.

The SFRY Assembly shall exercise its powers and duties on the basis and within the framework of the present Constitution and federal statutes.

Article 283. The SFRY Assembly shall:
 (1) decide on amendments to the SFRY Constitution;
 (2) discuss and lay down the fundamentals of the internal and foreign policy of the SFRY; pass federal statutes and other regulations and enactments;
 (3) adopt the Social Plan of Yugoslavia, the Federal Budget, and the Federal Annual Balance Sheet;
 (4) decide on alterations of the boundaries of the Socialist Federal Republic of Yugoslavia;
 (5) decide on war and peace; ratify international treaties pertaining to political and military cooperation, and international treaties entailing the passage of new statutes or amendments to existing ones.
 (6) formulate the policy of enforcement of federal statutes, other regulations and enactments, and lay down obligations of federal organs in conjunction with the enforcement of such regulations and enactments;
 (7) elect the President of the Republic, and proclaim the election of the SFRY Presidency;
 (8) elect and relieve of office the President and members of the Federal Executive Council;
 (9) elect and relieve of office the President and judges of the Constitutional Court of Yugoslavia and of the Federal Court; appoint and relieve of office the Federal Social Attorney of Self-Management; appoint and relieve of office federal secretaries, the Federal Public Prosecutor, and other officials of federal organs and members of collective bodies specified by the present Constitution and federal statute;

(10) exercise political supervision over the work of the Federal Executive Council and federal administrative agencies; exercise social control;

(11) conduct other affairs specified by the present Constitution.

2. The Chambers and Their Province of Work

Article 284. The rights and duties of the SFRY Assembly shall be exercised by the Federal Chamber and the Chamber of Republics and Provinces in accordance with the provisions of the present Constitution.

The Federal Chamber shall be composed of delegates from self-managing organizations and communities and socio-political organizations in the Republics and Autonomous Provinces.

The Chamber of Republics and Provinces shall be composed of delegations from the Assemblies of the Republics and the Assemblies of the Autonomous Provinces.

Article 285. The Federal Chamber shall:

(1) decide on amendments to the SFRY Constitution;

(2) lay down the fundamentals of the internal and foreign policy of the Socialist Federal Republic of Yugoslavia;

(3) pass federal statutes, with the exception of federal statutes which are passed by the Chamber of Republics and Provinces; issue authentic interpretations of federal statutes passed by it;

(4) formulate the policy of enforcement of federal statutes and other regulations and enactments passed by it, and lay down obligations of federal organs in conjunction with the enforcement of such regulations and enactments;

(5) adopt the Federal Budget and the Federal Annual Balance Sheet;

(6) decide on alterations of the boundaries of the Socialist Federal Republic of Yugoslavia;

(7) decide on war and peace;

(8) ratify international treaties pertaining to political and military cooperation and international treaties entailing the passage of new statutes or amendments to existing ones passed by it;

(9) lay down the fundamentals of the organization of federal organs and their competence;

(10) discuss, within the framework of its province of work, reports of the Federal Executive Council and federal administrative agencies, exercise political supervision over the work of these agencies, and issue guidelines for their work;

(11) discuss opinions and proposals of the Constitutional Court of Yugoslavia concerning the protection of constitutionality and legality by this court;

(12) discuss reports of the Federal Court and of the Federal Public Prosecutor on the application of federal statutes, on general judicial problems, and on the work of the Federal Court and the Federal Public Prosecutor;

(13) consider reports, opinions, and proposals of the Federal Social Attorney of Self-Management;

(14) grant amnesty for criminal offenses defined by federal statute;

(15) verify the credentials of and decide on credentials-immunity questions concerning delegates to the Chamber;

(16) adopt Rules of Procedure concerning its own work;

(17) conduct other affairs falling within the competence of the SFRY Assembly which do not come within the province of work of the Chamber of Republics and Provinces, or which it does not conduct together and on an equal footing with that Chamber.

Article 286. The Chamber of Republics and Provinces shall ensure the adjustment of stands of the Assemblies of the Republics and the Assemblies of the Autonomous Provinces in the spheres in which it passes federal statutes and other enactments on the basis of agreement with these Assemblies.

Acting in agreement with the Assemblies of the Republics and the Assemblies of the Autonomous Provinces, the Chamber of Republics and Provinces shall:

(1) adopt the Social Plan of Yugoslavia;

(2) formulate policy and pass federal statutes regulating relations pertaining to: monetary system and money issue, foreign exchange system, foreign trade, credit, and other economic relations with other countries; formation of money and foreign exchange reserves and their use, when this is of concern to the country as a whole; tariff and non-tariff protection; social price control for products and services; crediting faster development in economically underdeveloped Republics and Autonomous Provinces; determination of the revenues of socio-political communities accruing to them from the taxation of the sale of goods and services; system and sources of funds for financing the Federation; determination of measures of restriction of the market and the freedom of sale of goods and services, and measures providing a basis for compensation and the mode and form of compensation; association of organizations of associated labor performing economic activities and

of their association in the Chamber of Economy for the entire territory of the Socialist Federal Republic of Yugoslavia, and obligatory association of organizations of associated labor in communities; issue of authentic interpretations of federal statutes passed by it;

(3) determine the total volume of expenditure of the Federal Budget for every year;

(4) decide on the formation of funds of and the undertaking of obligations by the Federation, except in cases when under the provisions of the present Constitution federal organs are authorized independently to form funds and undertake obligations on behalf of the Federation;

(5) ratify international treaties entailing the passage of new statutes or amendments to existing ones passed by it;

(6) pass Rules of Procedure concerning its own work.

The Chamber of Republics and Provinces shall independently:

(1) pass laws on temporary measures when so provided by the present Constitution;

(2) determine, on the proposal of the SFRY Presidency, the sources and volume of finance, and decide on the raising of credits and undertaking of other obligations for the needs of national defense and state security arising out of extraordinary circumstances.

(3) discuss, within the scope of its province of work, reports by the Federal Executive Council and federal administrative agencies, exercise political supervision over the work of such agencies, and through provision of guidelines direct their work;

(4) formulate the policy of enforcement of federal statutes, other regulations, and enactments passed by it, and lay down obligations for federal organs concerning the enforcement of such regulations and enactments;

(5) carry out verification of credentials of and decide on credentials-immunity questions concerning delegates to the Chamber.

Article 287. The Federal Chamber and the Chamber of Republics and Provinces may take decisions, pass declarations and resolutions, and issue recommendations on questions falling within their province of work.

Article 288. Acting on terms of equality, the Federal Chamber and the Chamber of Republics and Provinces shall:

(1) elect and relieve of office the President and Vice-President or Vice-Presidents of the SFRY Assembly;

(2) elect and relieve of office the President and members of the Federal Executive Council; appoint and relieve of office federal secretaries and other officials and members of collective bodies in federal organs, as specified by the present Constitution and federal statute;

(3) elect and relieve of office the President and judges of the Constitutional Court of Yugoslavia and the Federal Court; appoint and relieve of office the Federal Social Attorney of Self-Management; appoint and relieve of office the Federal Public Prosecutor;

(4) elect and relieve of office members of the Council of the Federation;

(5) ratify international treaties entailing the passage of new republican and provincial statutes or amendments to existing ones;

(6) decide on the extension of the mandate of delegates to the SFRY Assembly;

(7) pass Rules of Procedure pertaining to the joint work of the Chambers of the SFRY Assembly and to their joint working bodies, and regulate the organization and work of the services of the SFRY Assembly.

Article 289. A proposal for the election, appointment, or relief of office of federal officials shall be adopted if it has been passed by both Chambers. If a proposal has not been adopted by one of the Chambers, the authorized proposer shall introduce a new motion.

Article 290. Bills on the ratification of international treaties, decisions on the extension of the mandate of delegates, the Rules of Procedure pertaining to the joint work of the Chambers of the SFRY Assembly, and decisions concerning the organization and work of the services of the SFRY Assembly shall be adopted if they have been passed in an identical text by both Chambers. If a bill on ratification, a decision, or the Rules of Procedure have not been passed in an identical text by both Chambers, the controversial act shall be taken off the agenda of the Chambers and may be again placed on it at two more consecutive sessions of the Chambers.

If even after that the controversial act has not been adopted by both Chambers, it shall be considered that the decision on the extension of the mandate of delegates has not been taken, the passage of the bill on the ratification of the international treaty concerned shall be adjourned for three months, and pending the adoption of the Rules of Procedure pertaining to the joint work of the Chambers of the SFRY Assembly, the Rules of Procedure adopted in the text passed by the Federal Chamber shall be applied.

3. The Composition and Mode of Election of the Chambers

Article 291. The Federal Chamber shall be composed of thirty delegates from self-managing organizations and communities and socio-political organizations from each Republic, and of twenty delegates from each Autonomous Province.

The nominating procedure shall be carried out by the Socialist Alliance of the Working People.

Candidates for delegates to the Federal Chamber shall be proposed by delegations from basic self-managing organizations and communities from among members of the delegations from these organizations and communities, and also by socio-political communities, within the framework of the Socialist Alliance of the Working People, from among members of their delegations.

The list of candidates for delegates to the Federal Chamber shall be drawn up by the nominating conference of the Socialist Alliance of the Working People of the Republics and Autonomous Provinces.

Delegates to the Federal Chamber shall be elected, on the basis of a list of candidates, by the Commune Assemblies on the territories of the Republics and the Autonomous Provinces by secret ballot.

The election and recall of delegates of the Federal Chamber shall be regulated by federal statute.

The nominating procedure for the election of delegates to the Federal Chamber to the posts of delegates, whose tenure has ended before the expiry of their terms, shall be regulated by federal statute.

Article 292. The Chamber of Republics and Provinces shall be composed of twelve delegates from each Republican Assembly and eight delegates from each Provincial Assembly.

Delegations to the Chamber of Republics and Provinces shall be elected and recalled by secret ballot by all Chambers of the Assemblies of the respective Republics and of the Assemblies of the respective Autonomous Provinces sitting in joint session.

Delegates elected to the Chamber of Republics and Provinces shall retain their tenure in the assemblies to which they have been elected.

4. The Mode of Work and Decision-Making in the Chambers

Article 293. Every delegate and working body in the Federal Chamber shall have the right to introduce federal bills and drafts of other regulations and enactments falling within the province of work of the Chamber.

Article 294. The Federal Chamber shall decide by a majority vote at sessions attended by a majority of delegates, unless a special majority is required by the present Constitution.

If a bill, draft regulation or draft enactment, or any other issue concerning the general interests of a Republic or Autonomous Province, or the equality of the nations and nationalities, is on the agenda of the Federal Chamber, and if so requested by the majority of delegates from one Republic or Autonomous Province, resort shall be made to a special procedure to consider and adopt such a bill, draft enactment, or issue, as laid down by the Federal Chamber Rules of Procedure.

Article 295. The Chamber of Republics and Provinces shall decide at sessions at which all delegations from the Assemblies of the Republics and the Assemblies of the Autonomous Provinces are represented, and which are attended by the majority of delegates to the Chamber.

Questions which must be decided in agreement with the Assemblies of the Republics and the Assemblies of the Autonomous Provinces shall be decided by individual delegations. A decision shall be considered as taken if it has received the vote from all delegations to the Chamber.

The Chamber shall pass laws on temporary measures by a two-thirds majority vote of all delegates to the Chamber.

On other issues falling within its province of work, and on questions which it decides upon together and on equal terms with the Federal Chamber, the Chamber of Republics and Provinces shall decide by a majority vote of all delegates present in the Chamber.

Article 296. In taking stands and expressing views on questions which are decided upon by the Chamber of Republics and Provinces, delegations from the Assemblies of the Republics and the Assemblies of the Autonomous Provinces shall represent the stands of their respective Assemblies.

Delegations from the Assemblies of the Republics and the Assemblies of the Autonomous Provinces shall keep their respective Assemblies informed of the work of the Chamber of Republics and Provinces respectively, of their own work relating to the questions being considered by this Chamber and of the stands of other delegations on such questions, and shall take part in the formulation of stands of the Assemblies of the Republics and the Assemblies of the Autonomous Provinces.

Article 297. The Federal Chamber shall set up working bodies to prepare and consider bills, draft regulations and other draft enactments, review the execution of policy and enforcement of statutes, other regulations and enactments passed by it, and study and discuss other questions falling within the province of work of the Chamber.

The Chamber of Republics and Provinces shall set up working bodies for the adjustment of stands in the preparation of statutes, other regulations and enactments, and for the consideration of other questions falling within the province of work of the Chamber. The working bodies shall be formed from among delegates to the Chamber in conformity with the principle of equal representation of the Republics and corresponding representation of the Autonomous Provinces. Representatives of the Federal Executive Council shall also take part in the work of the working bodies set up for the purpose of adjustment of stands concerning the preparation of statutes and other enactments.

The Chambers of the SFRY Assembly shall set up a joint commission for elections and appointments, and may also set up other joint bodies to consider questions of common concern.

The Rules of Procedure of the Chambers and the Rules of Procedure pertaining to the joint work of the Chambers of the SFRY Assembly may authorize the working bodies of the Chambers and the joint working bodies of the SFRY Assembly to conduct surveys and to demand from state organs and self-managing organizations and communities the necessary information, data, and documents, and vest them with other powers they may need to perform their work. Such working bodies may not have any investigative or other judicial functions.

5. Adoption of Enactments in the Chamber of Republics and Provinces in Agreement with the Assemblies of the Republics and Autonomous Provinces

Article 298. The right to introduce bills and other draft enactments which fall within the province of work of the Chamber of Republics and Provinces, and which must be adopted in agreement with the Assemblies of the Republics and the Assemblies of the Autonomous Provinces, shall be vested in every delegation to and working body of the Chamber, the Assemblies of the Republics and the Assemblies of the Autonomous Provinces, and the Federal Executive Council.

Article 299. On the basis of agreement given by the Assemblies of the Republics and the Assemblies of the Autonomous Provinces, and

Yugoslavia 545

on the basis of agreed views expressed in the Chamber regarding their motions and observations on the preliminary draft of a law or other enactment, the Chamber of Republics and Provinces shall adopt the final draft of the law or enactment concerned.

Article 300. When the Federal Chamber of Republics and Provinces has adopted the final draft of a law or other enactment, it shall refer it to the Assemblies of the Republics and the Assemblies of the Autonomous Provinces to decide on giving agreement to the adoption of the final draft as a whole.

The Assemblies of the Republics and the Assemblies of the Autonomous Provinces may, in discussing the preliminary draft of a law or other enactment, authorize their delegations to the Chamber of Republics and Provinces to give on behalf of their Assemblies agreement to the final draft of the law or enactment as a whole.

Article 301. If no agreement has been reached with the Assemblies of the Republics and the Assemblies of the Autonomous Provinces on the final draft of a law or other enactment, which the Chamber of Republics and Provinces must adopt in agreement with these Assemblies, the Federal Executive Council shall propose to the SFRY Presidency to pass a law on temporary measures, if it considers that the solution of specific questions on which no agreement with the Assemblies of the Republics and the Assemblies of the Autonomous Provinces has been reached is indispensable to prevent or eliminate major disruptions on the market, or that the non-settlement of such questions might result in serious harm for the social community, might endanger national defense interests, or might result in unequal economic relations between the Republics and Autonomous Provinces, or if it considers that this would render impossible the fulfillment of obligations towards underdeveloped Republics and the Autonomous Provinces, or the fulfillment of commitments of the Socialist Federal Republic of Yugoslavia towards other countries and international organizations.

If the SFRY Presidency finds that the temporary measures proposed by the Federal Executive Council are indispensable, the Federal Executive Council shall draw up a final draft of the law on temporary measures and refer it to the SFRY Assembly.

Article 302. If the final draft of the law on temporary measures has not been passed in the Chamber of Republics and Provinces by a two-thirds majority vote of all delegates to the Chamber, the SFRY Presidency may proclaim that the draft be applied in the text adopted by the majority of all delegates to the Chamber, pending the final passage of the law in accordance with the provisions of the present Constitution.

Article 303. The law on temporary measures shall remain in force until the law involved has been finally passed in the Chamber of Republics and Provinces in agreement with the Assemblies of the Republics and the Assemblies of the Autonomous Provinces, but not later than one year after its passage.

If, before the expiry of the law on temporary measures, the Chamber of the Republics and Provinces has not passed the law in agreement with the Assemblies of the Republics and the Assemblies of the Autonomous Provinces, the procedure for the adoption of the law on temporary measures shall be repeated.

Article 304. If, by the day the Federal Budget must be adopted, no agreement has been reached with the Assemblies of the Republics and the Assemblies of the Autonomous Provinces in respect of the total volume of resources for financing the Federation, the needs of the Federation shall be temporarily financed on the basis of the preceding year's Budget.

6. The Rights and Duties of the Delegates and Delegations

Article 305. Every delegate to the Chambers of the SFRY Assembly and every delegation to the Chamber of Republics and Provinces shall have the right, within the province of work of the Chambers, to initiate issues, put questions to the Federal Executive Council and officials heading federal administrative agencies, demand information, propose to the Chambers to request reports on the work of these agencies, demand professional assistance, and obtain information necessary for the performance of his functions.

At least ten delegates to the Federal Chamber and each delegation to the Chamber of Republics and Provinces may introduce an interpellation in their Chambers for the discussion of specific political questions in connection with the work of the Federal Executive Council.

Article 306. Delegates to the SFRY Assembly shall enjoy immunity.

No delegate may be called to account criminally, be detained, or punished for an opinion expressed or a vote cast in the Chamber of which he is a member, or in the SFRY Assembly.

No delegate may be detained without approval thereof by the Chamber of which he is a member, nor may criminal proceedings be instituted against him if he invokes parliamentary immunity.

A delegate may be detained without approval of the Chamber of which he is a member only if he has been caught in the act of committing a criminal offense which carries a penalty of more than five years of strict imprisonment. In such an event, the state organ which has detained the delegate shall be bound to notify thereof the President of the Chamber, who shall refer the matter to the Chamber to decide whether the proceedings should be continued and the arrest warrant remain in force.

The Chamber may decide to apply immunity to a delegate who has not invoked it, if this is necessary for the performance of his functions.

If the Chamber is not in session, approval of detention or for the continuation of criminal proceedings shall be given and the question of application of the immunity of the delegate decided by the Credentials-Immunity Commission of the Chamber, pending subsequent confirmation by the Chamber.

Article 307. The tenure of delegates to the Chambers of the SFRY Assembly shall last four years.

Elections for delegates to the Chambers of the SFRY Assembly must be held not later than fifteen days before the expiry of the election period of the delegates whose term is expiring.

Elections for delegates shall be called by the President of the SFRY Assembly.

From the day of the call for elections to the day of the election of delegates to the Chambers of the SFRY Assembly, not less than one month and not more than two months may expire.

The function of the delegates whose tenure expires shall be terminated on the date of the verification of the credentials of the new delegates.

Article 308. The Chambers of the SFRY Assembly may, under extraordinary circumstances, decide to extend the tenure of delegates to the SFRY Assembly for the time such situation lasts. The election of new delegates shall be held immediately after the circumstances because of which the tenure of the delegates has been extended have ceased to exist.

In the event of a state of war, the tenure of delegates to the SFRY Assembly shall be extended for the period such state lasts.

7. The Election and Powers of Officials of the SFRY Assembly

Article 309. The SFRY Assembly shall have a President and one or more Vice-Presidents, who shall be elected from among delegates to the SFRY Assembly.

The President shall represent the SFRY Assembly, convene joint sessions of the Chambers of the SFRY Assembly, preside over them, and sign *ukases* on the promulgation of statutes and decisions and other enactments adopted on terms of equality at joint sessions of the Chambers of the SFRY Assembly.

The President of the SFRY Assembly, together with the Vice-Presidents of the SFRY Assembly and the Presidents of the Chambers, shall consider questions concerning the adjustment and programming of the work of the Chambers and of the working bodies in the SFRY Assembly, and questions concerning Assembly procedures, and shall promote cooperation between the SFRY Assembly and other agencies and organizations in the Federation, Republics, and the Autonomous Provinces, and the Parliaments of foreign countries.

Article 310. Each Chamber of the SFRY Assembly shall have a President and a Vice-President. The President of a Chamber shall convene sessions of the Chamber, preside over them, and sign decisions and other enactments adopted by the Chamber.

Article 311. The President of the SFRY Assembly and the Presidents of the Chambers shall convene sessions of the SFRY Assembly and of the Chambers, respectively, on their own initiative or on the request of the President of the Republic, the SFRY Presidency, or the Federal Executive Council. The President of the Chamber of Republics and Provinces shall also convene sessions of the Chamber on the request of a delegation to the Chamber, and the President of the Federal Chamber—on the request of a specific number of delegates determined by the Federal Chamber Rules of Procedure.

Article 312. The President and Vice-Presidents of the SFRY Assembly and the President of the Chambers shall be elected for a term of four years.

The Presidents and Vice-Presidents of the SFRY Assembly and the Presidents of the Chambers may not be elected to the same office for more than two consecutive times.

Chapter II. The Presidency of the Socialist Federal Republic of Yugoslavia

Article 313. The SFRY Presidency shall represent the Socialist Federal Republic of Yugoslavia at home and abroad, and shall have other rights and duties as laid down by the present Constitution.

Within the framework of its rights and duties, and in order to realize the equality of the nations and nationalities, the SFRY Presidency shall look after adjustment of the common interests of the Republics and Autonomous Provinces in conformity with their responsibility concerning the realization of federal rights and duties.

The SFRY Presidency is the supreme body in charge of the administration and command of the Armed Forces of the Socialist Federal Republic of Yugoslavia in war and peace.

The SFRY Presidency shall consider the situation in the spheres of foreign policy and protection of the order established by the present Constitution (state security), and shall take stands with a view to initiating adoption of measures and adjusting the activities of competent organs in the execution of established policy in these spheres.

Article 314. The SFRY Presidency shall have the right to propose to the SFRY Assembly adoption of internal and foreign policy, and the passage of laws and other enactments.

Article 315. Within the framework of its rights and duties, the SFRY Presidency shall:

(1) propose to the SFRY Assembly a candidate for the President of the Federal Executive Council;

(2) announce the decision of the SFRY Assembly on the election of the Federal Executive Council;

(3) promulgate federal statutes by *ukases*;

(4) propose the election of the President and judges of the Constitutional Court of Yugoslavia;

(5) appoint and recall by *ukases* ambassadors and envoys of the Socialist Federal Republic of Yugoslavia, receive letters of credence and letters of recall from foreign diplomatic representatives accredited to it, and issue instruments of ratification of international treaties;

(6) appoint, promote, and relieve of duty generals and admirals and other army officers, as specified by federal statute; appoint and relieve of office the presidents, judges, and lay-assessors of military courts, and military public prosecutors;

(7) propose the election and relief of office of members of the Council of the Federation;

(8) confer decorations of the Socialist Federal Republic of Yugoslavia;

(9) grant pardon, in accordance with federal statute, for criminal offenses defined by federal statutes;

(10) adopt Rules of Procedure concerning its work.

Article 316. In matters concerning total national defense, the SFRY Presidency shall lay down the fundamentals of plans and preparatory measures for the defense of the country, issue guidelines for taking measures for alerting and mobilizing the country's potential and forces for defense purposes and for the adjustment of plans and measures of the socio-political communities, organizations of associated labor, and other self-managing organizations and communities, determine the existence of an immediate danger of war, order general or partial mobilization and, if the SFRY Assembly is not in a position to meet, proclaim a state of war.

The SFRY Presidency shall draw up a plan for the use of the Armed Forces of the Socialist Federal Republic of Yugoslavia in the event of war, and shall order the use of Armed Forces in peace-time.

The SFRY Presidency may transfer specific affairs concerning the administration and command of the Armed Forces of the Socialist Federal Republic of Yugoslavia to the federal secretary of national defense. The federal secretary of national defense shall be responsible to the SFRY Presidency for the conduct of affairs transferred to him.

For the purposes of reviewing the implementation of established policy concerning the administration and command of the Armed Forces of the Socialist Federal Republic of Yugoslavia, the SFRY Presidency may give instructions to delegates to the Federal Secretariat of National Defense and to other higher commands of the SFRY Armed Forces.

Article 317. During a state of war or in the event of an immediate danger of war, the SFRY Presidency may, on its own initiative or at the instance of the Federal Executive Council, pass decrees with the force of law on questions falling within the competence of the SFRY Assembly. The SFRY Presidency shall submit such decrees to the SFRY Assembly for approval as soon as this is in a position to meet.

Individual provisions of the present Constitution relating to the adoption of statutes, other regulations and enactments, and the taking of measures by federal organs in agreement with the competent organs of the Republics and Autonomous Provinces, and to individual freedoms, rights, and duties of man and the citizen, and the rights of self-managing organizations and communities, or to the composition and powers of executive organs and administrative agencies, may during a state of war exceptionally be suspended by a decree with the force of law for the duration of such state and if so required by the country's defense interests.

Article 318. The SFRY Presidency shall keep the SFRY Assembly informed of the state and problems of internal and foreign policy, and may propose to the SFRY Assembly to discuss individual questions and take decisions.

The SFRY Assembly may request the SFRY Presidency to present its views on individual questions falling within the competence of the Presidency which are of concern for the work of the SFRY Assembly.

Article 319. If the competent Chamber of the SFRY Assembly fails to endorse a proposal of the SFRY Presidency regarding the formulation of internal and foreign policy, or a motion for the passage of a bill, draft regulation, or other draft enactment whose adoption the SFRY Presidency deems to be indispensable, or if it fails to endorse a motion of the SFRY Presidency to adjourn debate on the passage of a bill or other draft enactment, the competent Chamber of the SFRY Assembly and the SFRY Presidency shall, by mutual agreement, determine a procedure for the consideration of the controversial issue and shall fix a time-limit for the reconciliation of views thereon. This time-limit may not exceed six months.

If even after the time-limit fixed no agreement has been reached regarding the formulation of internal and foreign policy, or regarding the motion for the passage or adjournment of passage of the bill or draft enactment in question, the controversial item shall be taken off the agenda of the Competent Chamber of the SFRY Assembly and shall be again placed on the agenda if so requested by the SFRY Presidency, or, if the competent Chamber of the SFRY Assembly so decides, on its own initiative.

If even after a fresh debate no agreement is reached within a period of three months, the competent Chamber of the SFRY Assembly shall be dissolved and the tenure of the SFRY Presidency shall be terminated.

Elections for the competent Chamber of the SFRY Assembly shall be called within fifteen days from the date of its dissolution, and the election of a new SFRY Presidency shall be held within fifteen days from the date of the constitution of the newly-elected Chamber of the SFRY Assembly.

The outgoing SFRY Presidency shall remain in office until the election of a new SFRY Presidency.

Article 320. The SFRY Presidency shall have the right to take stands on the implementation of policy and the enforcement of statutes and other enactments of the SFRY Assembly, and to request the Federal Executive Council to take measures conducive to the implementation of policy and the enforcement of statutes and other enactments of the Assembly.

The SFRY Presidency may call a sitting of the Federal Executive Council and place specific items on the agenda of this sitting.

The SFRY Presidency shall have the right to stay, before their promulgation, the enforcement of regulations of general political significance passed by the Federal Executive Council.

If the SFRY Presidency stays the enforcement of a regulation of the Federal Executive Council, it shall refer the controversial issue to the competent Chamber of the SFRY Assembly for decision.

In exercising its rights and duties, the SFRY Presidency may introduce in the SFRY Assembly a motion of no confidence in the Federal Executive Council.

Article 321. The SFRY Presidency shall be composed of a member from each Republic and Autonomous Province, elected by secret ballot by the Assemblies of the Republics and the Assemblies of the Autonomous Provinces, respectively, at a joint session of all Chambers of the Assemblies, and of the President of the League of Communists of Yugoslavia by virtue of his office.

Article 322. Sitting in joint session of both Chambers, the SFRY Assembly shall announce the result of the election and make known the composition of the SFRY Presidency.

Each member of the SFRY Presidency shall make a formal declaration at a joint session of both Chambers of the SFRY Assembly.

After making the formal declaration, the SFRY Presidency shall be constituted and shall assume its duties.

Article 323. Members of the SFRY Presidency shall enjoy immunity. Provisions pertaining to the immunity of delegates to the SFRY Assembly shall analogously apply to the immunity of the members of the SFRY Presidency.

Matters concerning the immunity of its members shall be decided upon by the SFRY Presidency.

Article 324. Members of the SFRY Presidency shall be elected for a term of five years.

No one may be elected member of the SFRY Presidency for more than two consecutive terms.

Members of the SFRY Presidency shall be elected thirty days before the expiry of the term of the outgoing members of the Presidency.

If a member of the SFRY Presidency is prevented for a prolonged period from performing his functions, he shall in his work be deputized for by the President of the Presidency of his Republic, or the President of the Presidency of his Autonomous Province.

If the tenure of a member of the SFRY Presidency has been terminated before the expiry of the term for which he was elected, the tenure of the newly-elected member of the SFRY Presidency shall last until the expiry of the tenure of the member of the Presidency whose term has been terminated.

If the tenure of a member of the SFRY Presidency has been terminated before the term for which he was elected, his function shall be terminated on the date he is relieved of office in the Assembly of his Republic or the Assembly of his Autonomous Province, and his function as member of the SFRY Presidency shall, until the announcement in the SFRY Assembly of the election of a new member, be discharged by the President of the Presidency of his Republic or the President of the Presidency of his Autonomous Province. The newly-elected member of the SFRY Presidency shall assume his duty on the date of the announcement of his election in the SFRY Assembly.

Article 325. In the event of an immediate danger of war or a state of war, the term of the members of the SFRY Presidency shall be extended until conditions have been created for the election of new members of the SFRY Presidency.

Article 326. A member of the SFRY Presidency may not concurrently hold any other self-management, public, or other social function, except functions in socio-political organizations, nor may he carry out any professional activity.

Article 327. The Presidency of the SFRY shall elect a President and a Vice-President from among its members for a term of one year, according to a schedule laid down by the Presidency Rules of Procedure.

The SFRY Presidency shall announce and make public the election of the President and Vice-President of the SFRY Presidency.

During a state of war, the SFRY Presidency may decide to extend the term of the President of the SFRY Presidency or to elect, before the expiry of his term, another Presidency member to be President of the SFRY Presidency.

Article 328. The President of the SFRY Presidency shall, on behalf of the SFRY Presidency, represent the Socialist Federal Republic of Yugoslavia, represent the SFRY Presidency, convene and preside over the meetings of the SFRY Presidency, sign acts adopted by the SFRY Presidency, ensure the implementation of acts and conclusions of the SFRY Presidency, issue instruments of ratification of international treaties, and receive letters of credence from foreign diplomatic representatives accredited to the SFRY Presidency.

The President of the SFRY Presidency shall, on behalf of the SFRY Presidency, be in charge of the command of the Armed Forces of the Socialist Federal Republic of Yugoslavia, in conformity with the present Constitution and federal statute.

The President of the SFRY Presidency shall be Chairman of the Council of National Defense.

During a state of war, in the event of an immediate danger of war, and in other similar kinds of emergency when the SFRY Presidency is not able to meet, the President of the SFRY Presidency shall, on behalf of the SFRY Presidency, exercise specific rights and duties if so authorized by the SFRY Presidency.

During his absence or prolonged inability to perform his office, the President of the SFRY Presidency shall be deputized for by the Vice-President, who may represent him in the conduct of affairs entrusted to him by the President.

With the termination of the office of President of the Republic, the SFRY Presidency shall exercise all rights and duties vested in it under the present Constitution, and the Vice-President of the SFRY Presidency shall become President of the SFRY Presidency until the expiry of the term for which he was elected Vice-President.

Article 329. The SFRY Presidency shall exercise its rights and duties on the basis of and within the framework of the present Constitution and federal statutes, and shall be responsible therefor.

Article 330. The SFRY Presidency shall work on the basis of adjustment of views of its members.

The SFRY Presidency shall make decisions in the way determined by the Rules of Procedure of the SFRY Presidency.

Article 331. The SFRY Presidency shall have a Council for National Defense.

The SFRY Presidency may also set up other councils or other working bodies required for its work.

The composition, organization, and province of work of the Council for National Defense, and the composition and province of work of other working bodies of the SFRY Presidency vested with the independent conduct of specific affairs within the framework of the rights and duties of the Presidency, shall be spelled out by federal statute.

Article 332. The SFRY Presidency may convene the Council of the Federation to consider issues of general policy.

The SFRY Presidency may entrust individual members of the Council of the Federation with the execution of specific tasks.

Members of the Council of the Federation shall be elected, on the proposal of the SFRY Presidency, from among socio-political workers and other public figures.

Chapter III. The President of the Republic

Article 333. In view of the historic role of Josip Broz Tito in the National Liberation War and the Socialist Revolution, in the creation and development of the Socialist Federal Republic of Yugoslavia, the development of Yugoslav socialist self-management society, the achievement of the brotherhood and unity of the nations and nationalities of Yugoslavia, the consolidation of the independence of the country and of its position in international relations and in the struggle for peace in the world, and in line with the expressed will of the working people and citizens, nations and nationalities of Yugoslavia,

— the SFRY Assembly may, on the proposal of the Assemblies of the Republics and the Assemblies of the Autonomous Provinces, elect Josip Broz Tito President of the Republic for an unlimited term of office.

Article 334. The President of the Republic shall be elected at a joint session of the Chambers of the SFRY Assembly by a majority vote of the delegates present, by secret ballot.

After the election, the President of the Republic shall make a formal declaration before a joint session of the Chambers of the SFRY Assembly.

Article 335. The President of the Republic shall represent the Socialist Federal Republic of Yugoslavia at home and abroad.

The President of the Republic shall be President of the SFRY Presidency.

The President of the Republic shall be Commander-in-Chief of the Armed Forces of the Socialist Federal Republic of Yugoslavia.

The President of the Republic shall preside over the Council for National Defense.

Article 336. The President of the Republic shall exercise his rights and duties on the basis and within the framework of the present Constitution and federal statutes.

Article 337. The President of the Republic shall:

(1) promulgate federal statutes by *ukases*;

(2) promulgate the decision of the SFRY Assembly on the election of the Federal Executive Council;

(3) appoint and recall by *ukases* ambassadors and envoys of the Socialist Federal Republic of Yugoslavia, receive letters of credence and letters of recall from foreign diplomatic representatives accredited to him, issue instruments of ratification of international treaties;

(4) confer decorations of the Socialist Federal Republic of Yugoslavia;

(5) determine the existence of an immediate danger of war, order general or partial mobilization, and proclaim a state of war if the SFRY Assembly and the SFRY Presidency are not in a position to meet;

(6) set up appropriate services to conduct affairs falling within his province of work.

Article 338. During a state of war or in the event of an immediate danger of war, if the SFRY Presidency is not in a position to meet, the President of the Republic shall pass decrees with the force of law on questions falling within the competence of the SFRY Assembly. The President of the Republic shall submit such decrees to the SFRY Assembly for approval as soon as it is in a position to meet.

Article 339. The President of the Republic shall keep the SFRY Assembly informed of the state of and problems in internal and foreign policy, and may propose to the SFRY Assembly discussion of individual questions and decisions to be taken.

Article 340. The President of the Republic may call a meeting of the Federal Executive Council and place specific items on the agenda of the Council. The President of the Republic shall preside over the meetings of the Council which he attends.

Article 341. The President of the Republic may convene the Council of the Federation to consider issues of general policy.

The President of the Republic may vest individual members of the Council of the Federation with authority to carry out specific tasks.

Article 342. As Commander-in-Chief of the Armed Forces of the Socialist Federal Republic of Yugoslavia, the President of the Republic shall:

(1) direct and command the Armed Forces of the Socialist Federal Republic of Yugoslavia and determine the fundamentals of plans and preparatory measures for the defense of the country;

(2) determine a plan for the use of the Armed Forces of the Socialist Federal Republic of Yugoslavia in the event of war, and order the use of Armed Forces in peace-time;

(3) appoint, promote, and relieve of duty generals and admirals and other officers, as specified by federal statute.

(4) appoint and relieve of office the presidents, judges, and lay-assessors of military courts, and military public prosecutors.

Article 343. The President of the Republic may transfer specific affairs concerning the direction and command of the Armed Forces of the Socialist Federal Republic of Yugoslavia to the federal secretary of national defense. The federal secretary of national defense shall be responsible to the President of the Republic for affairs transferred to him.

Article 344. The President of the Republic may convene joint sessions of the SFRY Presidency and the Federal Executive Council and shall preside over such sessions.

Article 345. The President of the Republic may vest the Vice-President of the SFRY Presidency with authority to conduct specific affairs falling within the President's province of work.

Chapter IV. The Federal Executive Council

1. Status and Competence

Article 346. The Federal Executive Council shall be the executive body of the SFRY Assembly.

The Federal Executive Council shall, within the framework of the rights and duties of the Federation, be responsible to the SFRY Assembly for the situation in all spheres of social life, for the execution of policy and enforcement of federal statutes and other regulations and enactments of the SFRY Assembly, and for the guidance and adjustment of the work of federal administrative agencies.

The Federal Executive Council shall exercise its rights and duties on the basis and within the framework of the present Constitution and federal statutes.

Article 347. The Federal Executive Council shall:

(1) monitor the state and realization of the policy of the SFRY Assembly and propose to the Assembly formulation of internal and foreign policy;

(2) introduce federal bills, draft regulations, and other draft enactments, and have the right to express its opinion on bills, draft regulations, and other draft enactments introduced in the SFRY Assembly by other authorized proposers;

(3) determine draft social plans of Yugoslavia;

(4) introduce proposals for determining the total volume of expenditure of the Federal Budget, determine the drafts of the Federal Budget and of the Federation's Annual Balance Sheet;

(5) pass decrees, make decisions, and adopt other regulations regarding the enforcement of federal statutes, other regulations, and enactments of the SFRY Assembly;

(6) ensure the execution of policy and the enforcement of statutes, other regulations, and enactments of the SFRY Assembly;

(7) ensure the execution of the country's defense policy and the implementation of preparations for defense within the framework of the rights and duties spelled out by the present Constitution and federal statutes;

(8) ratify international treaties whose ratification does not fall within the competence of the SFRY Assembly;

(9) coordinate and direct the work of federal administrative agencies with a view to ensuring the execution of policy and enforcement of statutes, other regulations, and enactments of the

SFRY Assembly; supervise the work of federal administrative agencies and repeal regulations of federal administrative agencies which are contrary to a federal statute, other regulation, or enactment of the SFRY Assembly, or to a regulation passed by the Council for the implementation of a federal statute, other regulation, or enactment, and may, under conditions specified by federal statute, annul regulations passed by such agencies;

(10) lay down general principles concerning the internal organization of federal administrative agencies; open diplomatic and consular missions of the Socialist Federal Republic of Yugoslavia abroad; set up professional and other services for its own needs and joint services for the needs of federal administrative agencies; appoint and relieve of duty officials as specified by federal statute;

(11) adopt Rules of Procedure concerning its own work;

(12) conduct other affairs specified by the present Constitution.

2. Compostion and Election

Article 348. The Federal Executive Council shall consist of a President, Council members elected in conformity with the principle of equal representation of the Republics and corresponding representation of the Autonomous Provinces, federal secretaries and other officials in charge of federal administrative agencies, and federal organizations specified by federal statute.

The President of the Federal Executive Council shall be elected by the Chambers of the SFRY Assembly on the proposal of the SFRY Presidency, and members of the Council—on the proposal of the candidate for the President of the Council, on the basis of the opinion of the Elections and Appointments Commission of the SFRY Assembly.

A new Federal Executive Council shall be elected each time after the constitution of the newly-elected Chambers of the SFRY Assembly.

In appointing federal secretaries and other officials who are in charge of federal administrative agencies and federal organizations, and who are members of the Federal Executive Council, due regard shall be given to their national composition.

The President and members of the Federal Executive Council elected from among delegates to the SFRY Assembly shall cease to be members of the SFRY Assembly.

The Federal Executive Council shall have one or more Vice-Presidents, who shall be elected from among Council members.

Article 349. The President and members of the Federal Executive Council shall be elected for a term of four years.

No one may be elected to the office of President of the Federal Executive Council for more than two consecutive terms.

Members of the Federal Executive Council may be elected for two consecutive terms and, exceptionally, by a special procedure laid down by federal statute, for one more term.

The President of the Federal Executive Council shall have the right to propose to the SFRY Assembly to relieve of office individual members of the Council, and to elect new members.

The resignation by, or relief of office of, the President of the Federal Council shall entail the resignation or dissolution of the entire Council.

Article 350. Members of the Federal Executive Council shall enjoy the same immunity as delegates to the SFRY Assembly.

Matters concerning the immunity of members of the Federal Executive Council shall be decided by the Council.

Article 351. Every member of the Federal Executive Council shall have the right to propose discussion of individual questions falling within the competence of the Council, to initiate preparation of statutes, other regulations, and enactments whose proposition falls within the competence of the Council, and of other regulations and acts which the Council is authorized to adopt, and also to propose to the Council to adopt stands of principle and to issue guidelines concerning the work of federal administrative agencies.

Members of the Federal Executive Council shall have the right and duty, in conformity with the Council's stands, to represent the Council in the SFRY Assembly.

Members of the Federal Executive Council may resign.

3. The Mode of Work and Adoption of Enactments in the Federal Executive Council

Article 352. The President of the Federal Executive Council shall call meetings of the Council on his own initiative or on the request of the President of the Republic, the SFRY Presidency, or on the request of at least five Council Members.

The President of the Federal Executive Council shall represent the Council, call Council meetings and preside over them, sign regulations and other enactments adopted by the Council and ensure their implementation, ensure the application of the Council's Rules of

Yugoslavia 561

Procedure, and the realization of cooperation between the Council and other agencies and organizations.

Article 353. The Federal Executive Council shall deal with and decide on questions falling within its competence.

The Federal Executive Council shall decide by a majority vote of Council members present at its meetings.

Article 354. In introducing bills and other draft enactments in the competent Chamber of the SFRY Assembly which must be adopted in agreement with the competent republican and provincial organs, the Federal Executive Council shall cooperate with the Executive Councils of the Republics and Autonomous Provinces.

Article 355. The Federal Executive Council shall, in agreement with the competent republican and provincial organs, adopt regulations concerning the enforcement of statutes and other enactments whose passage falls within the competence of the Chamber of Republics and Provinces, if such statutes and enactments provide for adjustment of views.

It shall be deemed that the competent republican and provincial organs have given their agreement if they have expressed their approval of the draft regulation concerning the enforcement of a particular statute, or other enactment of the SFRY Assembly, or if they have not opposed its adoption.

Article 356. If the Federal Executive Council has not reached agreement with the competent republican and provincial organs regarding a draft regulation concerning the enforcement of a statute or another enactment whose adoption falls within its competence, the Council shall propose to the SFRY Presidency to pass an ordinance on temporary measures, if it considers that the solution of the specific questions on which no agreement has been reached is indispensable to prevent or eliminate major disruptions on the market, or that the failure to solve such questions might cause serious harm to the social community, or that national defense interests might be jeopardized, or that unequal economic relations among the Republics and the Autonomous Provinces might be created, or if it considers that commitments towards underdeveloped Republics and Autonomous Provinces or commitments of the Socialist Federal Republic of Yugoslavia towards other countries and international organizations could not be fulfilled.

If the SFRY Presidency agrees with the need to pass an ordinance on temporary measures and with the reasons for its passage, the Federal Executive Council shall pass such ordinance.

The Federal Executive Council shall pass an ordinance on temporary measures falling within its competence by a majority vote of all Council members.

An ordinance on temporary measures shall remain in force until, on the basis of views adjusted with the competent republican and provincial organs, the question regulated by this ordinance has been settled, but for not longer than one year from the date of passage of the ordinance on temporary measures.

Article 357. In order to ensure participation of the competent republican and provincial organs in the adoption of regulations concerning the enforcement of statutes and other enactments of the SFRY Assembly which must be adopted in agreement with these organs, the Federal Executive Council and the competent republican and provincial organs shall by mutual agreement set up interrepublican committees for individual spheres.

Inter-republican committees shall be set up according to the principle of equal representation of the Republics and corresponding representation of the Autonomous Provinces. Members of inter-republican committees shall be delegated by the competent republican and provincial organs.

Chairmen of inter-republican committees shall be appointed by the Federal Executive Council from among its own members.

4. Relations between the Federal Executive Council and the SFRY Assembly, and the Responsibility of the Council

Article 358. The Federal Executive Council shall be bound to keep the Chambers of the SFRY Assembly informed of its work.

The Federal Executive Council may propose to the SFRY Assembly that debate on a bill, draft regulation, or draft enactment of the SFRY Assembly be adjourned or that a joint commission made up of members of the competent Chamber of the SFRY Assembly and of members of the Federal Executive Council be formed to debate a specific question, or that a meeting of the competent Chamber of the Assembly be called so that the Council can state its stand.

Article 359. The Federal Executive Council shall be responsible for its work to both Chambers of the SFRY Assembly in those spheres which fall within the respective provinces of work of the Chambers.

The Federal Executive Council may hand in a collective resignation to the Chambers of the SFRY Assembly.

If it considers that it is not able to ensure the execution of established policy and the enforcement of a statute, other regulation, or enactment of the SFRY Assembly whose passage is being proposed, or the implementation of the stands of, or measures proposed by, the SFRY Presidency, or that it cannot assume responsibility for the discharge of its function unless the federal statute, other regulation, or enactment whose passage is being proposed is passed, the Federal Executive Council may ask for a vote of confidence.

If the Federal Executive Council hands in a collective resignation or the SFRY Assembly passes a vote of no confidence in it, and in other cases when the function of the Council has been terminated, the Council shall remain in office until the election of a new Council.

Article 360. The Federal Chamber may, on the proposal of at least ten delegates to the Chamber, and the Chamber of Republics and Provinces on the proposal of a delegation to this Chamber, introduce a motion of no confidence in the Federal Executive Council.

A motion of no confidence in the Federal Executive Council shall be debated upon in the Chambers of the SFRY Assembly.

Article 361. The competent Chamber of the SFRY Assembly may set aside or annul any regulation of the Federal Executive Council which is contrary to the present Constitution, a federal statute, or another regulation or enactment adopted by the Chamber.

If the SFRY Presidency stays the enforcement of a regulation of the Federal Executive Council of general political significance, the controversial issue shall be decided upon by the competent Chamber of the SFRY Assembly.

Article 362. Members of the Federal Executive Council and officials in federal administrative agencies and federal organizations shall be responsible for the execution of policy and enforcement of statutes, other regulations, and enactments exclusively to federal organs and in the performance of their function may not receive directives or orders from organs and officials of other socio-political communities, nor may they follow such directives and/or orders.

Chapter V. Federal Administrative Agencies

Article 363. Federal secretariats shall be set up to conduct administrative affairs in specific spheres, within the framework of the rights and duties of the Federation.

Federal secretariats shall be set up and their province of work determined by federal statute.

Other federal administrative agencies and federal organizations in charge of specific administrative, professional, and other affairs falling within the framework of the rights and duties of the Federation, and schools, scientific, and other institutions in charge of affairs important for the realization of federal functions, may also be set up.

The status, rights, and duties of federal organizations in charge of specific administrative, professional, and other affairs falling within the framework of the rights and duties of the Federation, and their responsibility to the SFRY Assembly and the Federal Executive Council, shall be regulated by federal statute.

Professional and other services may be established for the needs of federal organs.

Article 364. Federal administrative agencies and federal organizations shall independently conduct affairs falling within their competence on the basis of, and within the limits set up by, the present Constitution and federal statutes.

In conducting affairs falling within their competence, federal administrative agencies and federal organizations shall abide by federal statutes and other regulations and enactments, guidelines of the SFRY Assembly, and stands of principle and guidelines of the Federal Executive Council.

Federal administrative agencies and federal organizations shall be bound to ensure enforcement of federal statutes and other federal regulations and enactments for whose enforcement they are responsible.

In enforcing federal statutes and other regulations and enactments, federal administrative agencies and federal organizations shall have the right to exercise supervision in conformity with the powers vested in them by federal statute.

Article 365. Officials in charge of federal administrative agencies and federal organizations may adopt internal rules, issue orders and directives concerning the enforcement of federal statute, other regulations, and enactments of the SFRY Assembly, and regulations passed by the Federal Executive Council, if so authorized by such regulations and/or enactments.

Article 366. Officials in charge of federal administrative agencies and federal organizations, and other officials appointed by the SFRY Assembly shall be appointed for a term of four years.

Officials in charge of federal administrative agencies and federal organizations, and other officials who are appointed by the SFRY Assembly may be appointed for two consecutive terms and, exceptionally, by a procedure laid down by federal statute, for one more term.

Article 367. Officials in charge of federal administrative agencies and federal organizations who are appointed by the SFRY Assembly shall be responsible to the SFRY Assembly and the Federal Executive Council for their own work, for the work of the agencies or organizations headed by them, and for the situation in the respective spheres of life falling within the province of work of the agencies and organizations headed by them.

Officials in federal administrative agencies and federal organizations who are appointed by the SFRY Assembly shall be responsible for their work to the SFRY Assembly and the Federal Executive Council.

Article 368. Officials in charge of federal administrative agencies and federal organizations shall be bound to keep the SFRY Assembly and the Federal Executive Council informed of the situation in their respective spheres of administration, and of the work of the agencies and organizations headed by them.

Such officials shall be bound to provide the Chambers of the SFRY Assembly and the Federal Executive Council, on their request, with information and explanations concerning questions falling within the province of work of the respective agencies and organizations headed by them. They shall also be obliged to give answers to questions put by delegates and delegations to the Chambers of the SFRY Assembly.

Chapter VI. The Federal Court, the Office of the Federal Public Prosecutor, and the Office of the Social Attorney of Self-Management

Article 369. The Federal Court shall:

(1) decide, under conditions and in the way laid down by federal statute, in last instance or in connection with extraordinary legal remedies, disputes arising out of unconstitutional or unlawful individual acts and deeds by which organizations of associated labor or

working people on the territory of other Republics or Autonomous Provinces, and thereby also other Republics and Autonomous Provinces, are placed in an unequal position on the unified Yugoslav market, including also damages disputes for losses caused thereby;

(2) decide property disputes between Republics and/or Autonomous Provinces, and between the Federation and a Republic or Autonomous Province;

(3) decide on the legality of finally-binding administrative acts of federal organs, unless otherwise specified by federal statute;

(4) decide on extraordinary legal remedies, if so specified by federal statute;

(5) review in last instance sentences passed by courts of law in the Republics and Autonomous Provinces, and sentences passed by military courts, if a death penalty for a criminal offense defined by federal statute has been passed;

(6) rule on jurisdictional conflicts between courts from the territories of two or more Republics and Autonomous Provinces, and between military and other courts;

(7) conduct other affairs placed within its jurisdiction by federal statute, within the framework of the rights and duties of the Federation.

Article 370. The President and judges of the Federal Court shall be elected and relieved of office by the SFRY Assembly.

The composition and number of judges of the Federal Court shall be determined according to the principle of parity representation of all Republics and corresponding representation of the Autonomous Provinces, according to the principles in force for other federal organs.

Article 371. The Federal Court, the Republican Supreme Courts, the Provincial Supreme Courts, and the corresponding military courts shall, through their delegates, jointly take stands of principle on questions of concern for the application of federal statutes, as provided for by federal statute.

Article 372. The function of the Office of the Public Prosecutor shall be discharged by the Federal Public Prosecutor, within the framework of the rights and duties of the Federation.

The Federal Public Prosecutor shall be appointed and relieved of office by the SFRY Assembly.

Article 373. The Federal Public Prosecutor shall take recourse to legal remedies for which he is authorized in matters falling within the jurisdiction of the Federal Court, and shall conduct other affairs specified by federal statute.

The Federal Public Prosecutor may issue binding instructions to the republican and provincial public prosecutors, and may take charge of criminal prosecution in cases falling within the competence of the republican or provincial prosecutors if criminal offenses defined by federal statute are involved. The Federal Public Prosecutor may issue binding instructions to the republican and provincial public prosecutors, and may take charge of prosecution in matters relating to economic violations defined by federal statutes, the enforcement of which is the responsibility of federal organs.

Article 374. The function of the Social Attorney of Self-Management shall, within the framework of federal rights and duties, be carried out by the Federal Social Attorney of Self-Management.

The Federal Social Attorney of Self-Management shall be appointed and relieved of office by the SFRY Assembly.

Chapter VII. The Constitutional Court of Yugoslavia

Article 375. The Constitutional Court of Yugoslavia shall:

(1) decide on the conformity of statutes to the SFRY Constitution;

(2) decide whether or not a republican or provincial statute is contrary to a federal statute;

(3) decide on the conformity of the regulations and other enactments of federal organs with the SFRY Constitution and federal statute;

(4) decide whether individual regulations or other enactments of the organs of socio-political communities and self-management enactments are in accord with the SFRY Constitution or contrary to federal statutes whose enforcement falls within the competence of federal organs;

(5) decide disputes involving rights and duties between the Federation and Republics and/or Autonomous Provinces, between Republics, between Republics and Autonomous Provinces, and between other socio-political communities from the territories of different Republics, if no jurisdiction of another court is provided for by statute for the settlement of such disputes;

(6) decide jurisdictional disputes between Republican or Provincial Constitutional Courts, between courts and federal organs, between federal organs and republican and/or provincial organs, be-

tween courts and other state organs from the territories of two or more Republics, or from the territories of the Republics and Autonomous Provinces.

The Constitutional Court of Yugoslavia may assess the constitutionality of statutes and the constitutionality and legality of regulations and enactments of the organs of socio-political communities, and of self-management enactments which have ceased to be valid, if not more than one year has expired between the cessation of their validity and the institution of proceedings.

Article 376. The Constitutional Court of Yugoslavia shall monitor developments of interest for the realization of constitutionality and legality, keep the SFRY Assembly informed of the state and problems of the realization of constitutionality and legality, and shall submit to the SFRY Assembly its opinions and proposals regarding the enactment of amendments to statutes and the taking of other measures aimed at ensuring constitutionality and legality, and the protection of self-management rights and other freedoms and rights of citizens and self-managing organizations and communities.

Article 377. If the Constitutional Court of Yugoslavia finds that a competent organ has not passed a regulation concerning enforcement of the provisions of the SFRY Constitution, federal statutes, or other federal regulations and enactments, and it should have passed such a regulation, the Court shall inform thereof the SFRY Assembly.

Article 378. The Constitutional Court of Yugoslavia shall inform the SFRY Assembly of its opinion as to whether or not the constitution of a Republic or the constitution of an Autonomous Province is contrary to the SFRY Constitution.

Article 379. The Constitutional Court of Yugoslavia may in the course of proceedings, before rendering a final ruling, stay the execution of an individual act or deed undertaken on the basis of statute, another regulation, or enactment of an organ of a socio-political community, or of a self-management enactment whose constitutionality or legality it is in the process of assessing, if their execution could result in irreparably harmful consequences.

Article 380. The work of the Constitutional Court of Yugoslavia shall be public.

Yugoslavia

Article 381. The Constitutional Court of Yugoslavia shall consist of a President and thirteen judges elected by the SFRY Assembly. Members of the Constitutional Court of Yugoslavia shall be elected according to the following formula: two from each Republic, and one from each Autonomous Province.

The President and judges of the Constitutional Court of Yugoslavia shall be elected for a term of eight years and may not be reelected to the office of President or judges of the Constitutional Court of Yugoslavia.

The President and judges of the Constitutional Court may not concurrently perform functions in state organs or self-managing bodies.

The President and judges of the Constitutional Court of Yugoslavia shall enjoy the same immunity as delegates to the SFRY Assembly.

Article 382. The President and judges of the Constitutional Court of Yugoslavia may be relieved of office before the expiry of their term only on their own request; also if they have been convicted of a criminal offense and sentenced to a term of imprisonment, or have become permanently unable to perform their functions.

The reasons for relieving of office the President and/or judges of the Constitutional Court of Yugoslavia before the expiry of their term shall be determined by the Constitutional Court, which shall inform the SFRY Assembly thereof.

If the President or a judge of the Constitutional Court of Yugoslavia requests to be relieved of office and the SFRY Assembly has not decided this request within a period of three months from the day of submission of the request, the Constitutional Court shall, on the request of the President or judge of the Court, note that his office in the Constitutional Court has been terminated and shall inform the SFRY Assembly thereof.

The Constitutional Court of Yugoslavia may decide that the President or a judge of the Court against whom criminal proceedings have been instituted may not perform his functions in the Constitutional Court as long as the proceedings are in course.

Article 383. Before assuming office, the President and judges of the Constitutional Court of Yugoslavia shall make a formal declaration before the SFRY Presidency.

Article 384. If the Constitutional Court of Yugoslavia finds that a federal, republican, or provincial statute is not in conformity with the SFRY Constitution, or that a republican or provincial statute is contrary to a federal statute, it shall render a ruling thereon and submit it to the competent assembly.

The competent assembly shall be obliged, within six months of service of the ruling of the Constitutional Court of Yugoslavia, to bring such statute into accord with the SFRY Constitution or to remove what is contradictory between the republican or provincial statute and the federal statute.

On the request of the competent assembly, the Constitutional Court of Yugoslavia may extend the time-limit for bringing a statute into accord for a maximum of six months.

If the competent assembly fails within the specified time-limit to bring a statute into accord with the SFRY Constitution or to remove what is contradictory between a republican or provincial statute and a federal statute, the provisions of the statute which are not in conformity with the SFRY Constitution, or the provisions of the republican or provincial statute which are contrary to the federal statute, shall cease to be valid, which the Constitutional Court of Yugoslavia shall announce by a ruling.

Article 385. If the Constitutional Court of Yugoslavia finds that a regulation other than statute, or an enactment of an organ of a socio-political community, or a self-management enactment, does not conform to the SFRY Constitution or that it is contrary to a federal statute, or that a regulation or other enactment of a federal organ is not in accord with a federal statute, it shall annul or set aside this regulation or enactment, or those of their provisions which are not in conformity with the SFRY Constitution or the federal statute, or which are contrary to the federal statute.

Article 386. Statutes which have been ruled to be no longer valid, and other regulations and enactments of organs of socio-political communities which have been annulled or set aside, shall not be applied to relations which came into being before the promulgation of the ruling of the Constitutional Court of Yugoslavia, unless they had been settled by then by a finally-binding decision.

Regulations and other enactments adopted for the purposes of enforcing regulations or self-management enactments which may no longer be applied, shall not be applied as of the date of announcement of the ruling of the Constitutional Court of Yugoslavia, if according to such ruling these regulations and enactments are contrary to the SFRY Constitution and federal statute.

Enforcement of finally-binding individual acts passed on the basis of regulations which may no longer be applied may not be allowed or carried into effect, and if their enforcement has already started, it shall be stayed.

Article 387. Anyone may initiate institution of proceedings for the assessment of constitutionality and legality.

Proceedings before the Constitutional Court of Yugoslavia may be instituted by:

(1) the SFRY Assembly, the Republican Assemblies, the Provincial Assemblies, and the assemblies of other socio-political communities;

(2) the SFRY Presidency, the Presidencies of the Republics, and the Presidencies of the Autonomous Provinces;

(3) the Federal Executive Council, the Republican Executive Councils or the Provincial Executive Councils, except for assessing the constitutionality and legality of regulations adopted by the respective socio-political communities;

(4) the Republican Constitutional Courts and the Provincial Constitutional Courts;

(5) a court of law, if a question of constitutionality or legality comes up in proceedings before this court;

(6) the federal, republican, or provincial public prosecutors or corresponding military prosecutors, if the question of constitutionality and legality comes up in the course of the work of the public prosecutor concerned;

(7) social attorneys of self-management;

(8) organizations of associated labor, local communities, self-managing communities of interest, or any other self-managing organization or community, if their rights established by the SFRY Constitution or federal statute have been violated;

(9) federal, republican, or provincial secretaries or other officials in charge of federal, republican, or provincial administrative agencies, or federal, republican, or provincial organs each within its province of work, except in matters concerning the assessment of the constitutionality of statutes, discord between republican or provincial statutes and federal statutes, and concerning the assessment of the constitutionality and legality of regulations of the executive councils of socio-political communities whose organs they are;

(10) any organ which is under the constitution and statute authorized to stay the execution of regulations or other enactments of organs of socio-political communities and self-management enactments which are not in accord with the SFRY Constitution;

(11) the Social Accountancy Service operating at federal, republican, and provincial level.

The Constitutional Court of Yugoslavia may also, on its own initiative, institute proceedings for assessing constitutionality and legality.

Article 388. Anyone whose right has been violated by a final or finally-binding individual act adopted on the basis of statute, other regulation, or enactment of an organ of a socio-political community, or by a self-management enactment, which pursuant to a ruling of the Constitutional Court of Yugoslavia is not in accord with the SFRY Constitution or federal statute, or is contrary to federal statute, shall have the right to request the competent organ to revise such individual act.

A proposal for the revision of a final or a finally-binding individual act adopted on the basis of statute, other regulation, enactment of an organ of a socio-political community, or a self-management enactment which, pursuant to a ruling of the Constitutional Court of Yugoslavia, is not in accord with the SFRY Constitution, or which is contrary to federal statute, may be submitted within six months from the date of announcement of the ruling in the Official Gazette of the Socialist Federal Republic of Yugoslavia, provided not more than one year has passed from the date of service of the individual act or the rendering of the ruling of the Court.

If a court rejects by a finally-binding ruling to apply a regulation or an enactment of an organ of a socio-political community or a self-management enactment owing to its not being in accord with the SFRY Constitution or federal statute, or owing to its being contrary to federal statute, and the Constitutional Court of Yugoslavia rules that such discord or contradiction does not exist, anyone whose right has been infringed thereby may demand that the finally-binding ruling of the court be revised within a time-limit of one year from the date of announcement of the ruling of the Constitutional Court of Yugoslavia.

If it has been established that, by revising an individual act, the consequences of the application of a regulation or other enactment which is not in accord with the SFRY Constitution or federal statute, or which is contrary to federal statute, may not be redressed, the Constitutional Court of Yugoslavia may rule that such consequences be redressed through the restitution of the previous condition, settlement of damages, or in some other way.

Article 389. If proceedings have been instituted for the assessment of the constitutionality and legality of a regulation or other enactment of an organ of a socio-political community or of a self-management enactment, which is claimed to be simultaneously contrary to the SFRY Constitution or federal statute and republican constitution, or to a provincial constitution, or republican or provincial statute, its constitutionality and legality shall be reviewed by the republican and provincial constitutional courts, respectively, which shall only assess the conformity of this regulation or enactment to the republican constitution or the provincial constitution, or to the republican, provincial, or federal statute whose enforcement falls within the competence of organs in the Republics and Autonomous Provinces.

If a republican or provincial constitutional court rules that a regulation or enactment conforms to the republican constitution and the provincial constitution, respectively, or to the federal statute whose enforcement falls within the competence of organs in the Republics and Autonomous Provinces, it shall refer the case to the Constitutional Court of Yugoslavia to assess the conformity of the regulation or enactment with the SFRY Constitution, or to assess whether or not the regulation or enactment is contrary to the federal statute whose enforcement falls within the competence of federal organs.

Article 390. State organs, organizations of associated labor, and other self-managing organizations and communities, and holders of self-management, public, and other social functions, shall be bound to supply the Constitutional Court of Yugoslavia, on its request, with data and information needed in the work of the Constitutional Court, and, on the order of the Constitutional Court, to perform acts of concern for the conduct of proceedings.

Article 391. The Constitutional Court of Yugoslavia shall render decisions and rulings by a majority vote of all members of the Constitutional Court.

Members of the Constitutional Court of Yugoslavia who have expressed a dissenting opinion shall have the right to submit such opinion to the Court in writing with a statement of reasons.

Article 392. As a rule, the Constitutional Court of Yugoslavia shall decide cases at open hearings.

Article 393. When in the course of proceedings a statute, other regulation, or enactment of an organ of a socio-political community or a self-management enactment has been brought into accord with the SFRY Constitution or federal statute, but the consequences of the unconstitutionality or illegality have not been eliminated, the Constitutional Court of Yugoslavia may rule that the statute, other regulation, or enactment concerned was not in conformity with the SFRY Constitution or federal statute, or that it was contrary to federal statute. Such a ruling of the Constitutional Court of Yugoslavia shall have the same legal effect as a ruling establishing that a statute has ceased to be valid or another regulation or enactment has been set aside or annulled.

Article 394. Decisions of the Constitutional Court of Yugoslavia shall be binding and enforceable.

If necessary, the enforcement of rulings of the Constitutional Court of Yugoslavia shall be ensured by the Federal Executive Council.

The Constitutional Court of Yugoslavia may request that measures by taken against the responsible person for non-execution of a ruling of the Constitutional Court of Yugoslavia.

Article 395. Rulings of the Constitutional Court of Yugoslavia shall be published in the Official Gazette of the Socialist Federal Republic of Yugoslavia, and in the Official Gazette which has published the statute, other regulation, or enactment of an organ of a socio-political community on which the Constitutional Court of Yugoslavia has ruled, or in the way in which the self-management enactment on which the court has ruled was published.

Article 396. Proceedings before the Constitutional Court of Yugoslavia and the organization of the Constitutional Court shall be regulated by the Constitutional Court of Yugoslavia.

Chapter VIII. The Formal Declaration

Article 397. On assuming office, the President of the Republic, the President and members of the SFRY Presidency, and the President and members of the Constitutional Court of Yugoslavia shall make a formal declaration.

The text of the declaration shall read:

> "I hereby declare that I will fight for the protection of the sovereignty, independence, and integrity of the country and the achievement of power by the working class and all working people, that I will strive for the achievement of brotherhood and unity and for the equality of the nations and nationalities, for the development of socialist self-management society and for the realization of the

common interests of the working people and citizens of the Socialist Federal Republic of Yugoslavia, and that I will abide by the SFRY Constitution and federal statutes, and will perform my duty conscientiously and in a responsible way."

The President and Vice-Presidents of the SFRY Assembly and the Presidents of the Chambers of the SFRY Assembly, the President and members of the Federal Executive Council, the President and judges of the Federal Court, federal secretaries, and other federal officials who are elected or appointed by the SFRY Assembly, shall, on assuming office, make a formal declaration as laid down by the SFRY Assembly.

PART V. AMENDING THE CONSTITUTION OF THE SOCIALIST FEDERAL REPUBLIC OF YUGOSLAVIA

Article 398. Amendments to the SFRY Constitution shall be decided upon by the Federal Chamber of the SFRY Assembly, in agreement with the Assemblies of all Republics and Autonomous Provinces; if an amendment to the SFRY Constitution only concerns the status of the Republics and mutual relations between the Federation and the Republics, it shall be decided upon by the Federal Chamber of the SFRY Assembly in agreement with the Assemblies of all Republics.

Article 399. A motion to initiate proceedings for amending the SFRY Constitution may be introduced by at least thirty delegates to the Federal Chamber, the SFRY Presidency, the Assembly of a Republic, the Assembly of an Autonomous Province, and the Federal Executive Council.

Article 400. A motion to initiate proceedings for amending the SFRY Constitution shall be decided upon by the Federal Chamber of the SFRY Assembly.

The Federal Chamber may decide to initiate proceedings for amending the SFRY Constitution if the motion for the initiation of amendment proceedings has been agreed upon by the Assemblies of all Republics and Autonomous Provinces or the Assemblies of all Republics.

Article 401. Draft amendments to the SFRY Constitution shall be drawn up by the Federal Chamber of the SFRY Assembly, which shall refer them to the Assemblies of all Republics and Autonomous Provinces for opinion, and shall submit them to public discussion.

Draft amendments to the SFRY Constitution shall be debated upon by the Assemblies of all Republics and Autonomous Provinces, which shall give their opinions thereon.

When the opinions of the Assemblies of all Republics and Autonomous Provinces have been obtained and public discussion conducted, the Federal Chamber shall draw up a motion for the amendment of the SFRY Constitution and take a vote thereon.

An amendment to the SFRY Constitution shall be deemed passed in the Federal Chamber if it has received a two-thirds majority vote from all delegates to the Chamber.

If an amendment to the SFRY Constitution has not been adopted in the Federal Chamber, a motion for the same amendment to the SFRY Constitution may not be introduced again before the expiry of one year from the date the motion was rejected.

Article 402. An amendment to the SFRY Constitution shall be deemed passed when the text adopted by the Federal Chamber of the SFRY Assembly has been agreed to by the Assemblies of all Republics and Autonomous Provinces or the Assemblies of all Republics.

If the Assembly of one or more Republics or the Assembly of either of the Autonomous Provinces has not agreed to the text of the motion for the amendment of the SFRY Constitution passed by the Federal Chamber, the motion for the amendment of the SFRY Constitution on which no agreement has been reached may not be placed on the agenda before the expiry of one year from the date the Federal Chamber ruled that no agreement had been reached.

Article 403. Once adopted, amendments to the SFRY Constitution shall be promulgated by the Federal Chamber of the SFRY Assembly.

PART VI. TRANSITIONAL AND CONCLUDING PROVISIONS

Article 404. The term "constitution" used in the present Constitution shall be understood to mean the provisions of the SFRY Constitution, the republican constitutions, and the provincial constitutions.

In the present Constitution, the term "self-management enactment" shall be understood to mean social compacts, self-management agreements which regulate in a general way self-management relations, and other enactments of organizations of associated labor and other self-managing organizations and communities.

Article 405. A special constitutional law shall be passed for the implementation of the present Constitution and to ensure transition to its application.

The constitutional law pertaining to the implementation of the SFRY Constitution shall be passed, on the proposal of the Chamber of Nationalities, by all Chambers of the Federal Assembly. The draft of the constitutional law shall be adopted by a two-thirds majority vote in each Chamber according to the provisions of paragraph 5, sections 4 to 8 of Constitutional Amendment XII.

The draft constitutional law pertaining to the implementation of the SFRY Constitution shall be promulgated and shall come into force simultaneously with the SFRY Constitution.

Article 406. The present Constitution shall come into force on the date of its promulgation.

APPENDIX: CZECHOSLOVAKIA

CONSTITUTIONAL LAW ON THE CZECHOSLOVAK FEDERATION OF 27 OCTOBER 1968 (AS AMENDED)

Preamble	582
Basic Provisions	583
Division of Jurisdiction between the Federation and the Republics	585
The Federal Assembly	594
The President of the Czechoslovak Socialist Republic	603
The Government of the Czechoslovak Socialist Republic	605
The Constitutional Court of the Czechoslovak Socialist Republic	609
The State Organs of the Czech Socialist Republic and the Slovak Socialist Republic	613
General, Transitional, and Concluding Provisions	621

CONSTITUTIONAL LAW ON THE CZECHOSLOVAK FEDERATION*

Sbírka zákonů. Československá socialistická republika 1968 No. 143, as amended 1970 No. 125; 1971 No. 43; 1975 No. 50.

The National Assembly of the Czechoslovak Socialist Republic has decided to establish the following Constitutional Law:

We, the Czech and the Slovak nations, advancing from the ascertainment that our contemporary history is leavened by the bilateral will to live in a common state,

appreciating the fact that fifty years of our life in a common state has deepened and strengthened our centuries-old bonds of friendship, enabled the development of our nations and the realization of their progressive, democratic, and socialist ideals, and trustworthily evidenced their existential interest to live in a common state but at the same time has shown that it is necessary to build our common relationship on new and more righteous foundations,

acknowledging the indefeasibleness of the right of self-determination as far as separation, and respecting the sovereignty of each nation and its right freely to create for itself the way and form of its national and state life,

convinced that a voluntary federative state connection is an adequate assertion of the right of self-determination and equality before the law, but likewise that it is the best warranty for our full internal, national development and for the protection of our national identity and sovereignty,

resolved to create, in the strain of the humanist ideals of socialism and proletarian internationalism, in the common federative state the conditions for an all-round development and prosperity of all citizens, and to guarantee to them equal, democratic rights and freedoms regardless of their nationality,

represented by their delegates in the Czech National Council and in the Slovak National Council, we have agreed on the creation of the Czechoslovak federation.

*Translated by Th.J. Vondracek.

Chapter I. Basic Provisions

Article 1. (1) The Czechoslovak Socialist Republic is a federative state of two coequal fraternal nations: the Czechs and the Slovaks.

(2) The Czechoslovak Socialist Republic is founded on the voluntary bond of the equal, national states of the Czech and the Slovak nations, based on the right of each of them to self-determination.

(3) The Czechoslovak Federation is an expression of the will of two individual sovereign nations, the Czechs and the Slovaks, to live in a common federative state.

(4) The Czechoslovak Socialist Republic consists of the Czech Socialist Republic and the Slovak Socialist Republic. Both Republics have an equal position within the Czechoslovak Socialist Republic.

(5) Both Republics mutually respect their sovereignty, as well as the sovereignty of the Czechoslovak Socialist Republic; the Czechoslovak Socialist Republic likewise respects the sovereignty of the two national states.

Article 2. (1) The Czechoslovak Socialist Republic, as well as the Czech Socialist Republic and the Slovak Socialist Republic are built on the principles of socialist democracy. Their political system is the same in essential matters.

(2) State power is exercised by the working people through their representative bodies which are: the Federal Assembly, the Czech National Council, the Slovak National Council, and National Committees.

(3) The political rights of individuals and the guarantees of their assertion are the same throughout the Czechoslovak Socialist Republic.

Article 3. (1) The territory of the Czechoslovak Socialist Republic consists of the territory of the Czech Socialist Republic and the territory of the Slovak Socialist Republic.

(2) The borders of the Czechoslovak Socialist Republic and the borders of the Czech Socialist Republic and the Slovak Socialist Republic may be changed only by a Constitutional Law of the Federal Assembly.

(3) The borders of either of the two national Republics may be changed only with the approval of the respective National Council. The National Council grants such approval by a Constitutional Law of its own.

Article 4. (1) The economy of the Czechoslovak Socialist Republic is unitary and develops on the basis of the socialist economic system.

(2) The Czech and the Slovak nations unite, within the Czechoslovak Federation, their endeavors in the interest of the intensive development of the socialist economy. The Czechoslovak Socialist Republic, the Czech Socialist Republic, and the Slovak Socialist Republic administer the social product they create in accordance with the economic development plans of the Czechoslovak Socialist Republic. The economy in the Czechoslovak Socialist Republic develops in cooperation and with the assistance of both nations and of all nationalities in the Czechoslovak Socialist Republic.

(3) In the unitary planned economy of the Czechoslovak Socialist Republic, a uniform system of socialist social ownership, one currency, a uniform economic policy, a uniform system of direction, and a uniform policy of employment and distribution of labor forces are pursued.

(4) The organs of the Czechoslovak Socialist Republic safeguard the common needs and interests of the Czech and the Slovak nations and of all nationalities; they direct the organs and organizations in all the branches administered within the jurisdiction of the Czechoslovak Socialist Republic. The organs of the Czechoslovak Socialist Republic exercise jurisdiction in matters relating to the administration of national property in the branches they administer. The task of the organs of the Czechoslovak Socialist Republic is first and foremost to ensure in a planned manner the optimum trends of economic development, to develop economic relations with foreign countries, and to create uniform conditions for the operation of the system of planned direction; for this purpose, they influence the relations which arise in the distribution of the social product and the national income, and support progressive forms of integration of socialist organizations. A significant task of the Czechoslovak Socialist Republic is to level the economic and social differences which exist between the Czech Socialist Republic and the Slovak Socialist Republic, in particular by shaping equal conditions and opportunities for the creation and use of the national income.

(5) The organs of the Czech Socialist Republic and of the Slovak Socialist Republic direct the organs and organizations operating in the branches administered within the jurisdiction of these Republics; insofar as the activity of such organs and organizations affects the other Republic, they do so in coordination with the organs of this Republic. The organs of the Czech Socialist Republic and the Slovak Socialist Republic exercise jurisdiction in matters of administration of the national property in the branches directed by them.

Appendix: Czechoslovakia 585

Article 5. (1) Czechoslovak state citizenship is unitary.

(2) Every Czechoslovak citizen enjoys the same rights and has the same duties throughout the Czechoslovak Socialist Republic.

(3) Every Czechoslovak citizen is simultaneously a citizen of the Czech Socialist Republic or of the Slovak Socialist Republic.

(4) The acquisition and the loss of Czechoslovak state citizenship is regulated by a Law of the Federal Assembly.

Article 6. (1) The Czech and the Slovak languages are used on equal legal footing in the promulgation of laws and other generally binding legal regulations.

(2) Both languages are used on equal legal footing in the dealings of all state organs of the Czechoslovak Socialist Republic and of both Republics, in proceedings held before them, and in all other contacts with citizens.

Chapter II. Division of Jurisdiction between the Federation and the Republics

Article 7. (1) To the Czechoslovak Socialist Republic belongs the exclusive jurisdiction over:

a) foreign policy, conclusion of international agreements, representing the Czechoslovak Socialist Republic in international relations, and deciding in matters of war and peace;

b) the defense of the Czechoslovak Socialist Republic;

c) the currency;

d) federal material reserves;

e) federal legislation and administration within the scope of the federal jurisdiction and control of the federal organs;

f) protection of federal constitutionality.

(2) Within the areas specified in paragraph 1, the legislative and executive organs of state power, the organs of state administration, and the judicial organs of the Czechoslovak Socialist Republic have exclusive jurisdiction.

Article 8. (1) To the Czechoslovak Socialist Republic and the two Republics belongs joint jurisdiction over:

a) planning;
b) finance;
c) banking;
d) prices;
e) economic relations with foreign countries;

f) industry;
g) agriculture and food-supply;
h) transport;
i) post and telecommunications;
j) development of science and technology and investment activity;
k) labor, wages, and social policy;
l) social economic information;
m) legal regulation of socialist enterprises and economic arbitration;
n) standardization, matters relating to measures and weights, industrial rights, and the state testing system;
o) internal order and security of the state;
p) matters regarding the press and other means of information;
q) control.

(2) In the areas specified in paragraph 1, organs of the Czechoslovak Socialist Republic have jurisdiction in the exhaustively enumerated matters, and in other matters jurisdiction belongs to the organs of the Czech Socialist Republic and the Slovak Socialist Republic.

Article 9. Matters which have not been specifically entrusted to the jurisdiction of the Czechoslovak Socialist Republic are under the exclusive jurisdiction of the Czech Socialist Republic and the Slovak Socialist Republic.

Article 10. (1) The Czechoslovak economy is, in accordance with the socialist economic system, a planned economy.

(2) The principles of national economic planning as the uniformly organized process of establishing and securing national economic plans and controlling their implementation, as well as the determination of their system, functions, and relations, are regulated by Laws of the Federal Assembly; Laws of the Federal Assembly also regulate the relationships of organs and organizations in this activity and sanctions in the case of nonfulfillment of their duties.

(3) The state plan for the development of the national economy and other economic plans serve as a binding basis for management and economic activities.

(4) The state plans for the development of the national economy are:
a) the State Plan for the Development of the National Economy of the Czechoslovak Socialist Republic;

b) the State Plans for the Development of the National Economies of the Czech Socialist Republic and the Slovak Socialist Republic.

(5) Medium-term state plans for the development of the national economy are promulgated by a Law. The Law on the State Plan for the Development of the National Economy of the Czechoslovak Socialist Republic is adopted by the Federal Assembly; in accordance herewith, the Laws on the State Plans for the Development of the National Economies of the Czech Socialist Republic and of the Slovak Socialist Republic are adopted by the respective National Council.

(6) Draft bills of the State Plan for the Development of the National Economy of the Czechoslovak Socialist Republic and of the State Plans for the Development of the National Economies of the Czech Socialist Republic and of the Slovak Socialist Republic are drawn up on a concurrent and cooperative basis by the Federal planning organs and the planning organs of the Republics according to the directives issued by the respective Governments.

Article 11. (1) Financial operations of the Czechoslovak Socialist Republic are governed by the Federal State Budget. Financial operations of each Republic are governed by its own State Budget. The Federal State Budget is approved by the Federal Assembly, and the State Budgets of the Republics are approved by the National Councils by their own Laws, each time for a period of one year.

(2) The State Budget of each Republic covers financial relations in all sectors of the economy and state administration, with the exception of activities financed out of the Federal State Budget. Each Republic includes in its State Budget financial relations with the budgets of the National Committees.

(3) The revenue of the Federal Budget consists of exhaustively listed taxes and levies, portions of these, and other receipts mentioned by a Law of the Federal Assembly, as well as receipts from the activities of federal agencies and their subordinate organizations.

(4) The Federal State Budget is aimed at financing:

a) expenditures for the defense of the Czechoslovak Socialist Republic, the activities of federal organs, the creation of federal material reserves, and allocations to federal organizations;

b) allocations and subsidies for selected actions, insofar as their extent and importance for the entire Federation so require, as well as allocations and subsidies for leveling the economic differences between the Czech Socialist Republic and the Slovak Socialist Republic;

c) allocations and subsidies to the State Budgets of both Republics for the further development of the national economies;

d) other expenditures determined by the Budgetary Law of the Federal Assembly.

(5) The manner of securing the revenue of the Federal State Budget, the relations between the Federal State Budget and the two State Budgets of the Republics, as well as the principles of financial operations are established by a Law of the Federal Assembly.

(6) The Czechoslovak Socialist Republic and each constituent Republic may create their own funds for special purposes tied to their State Budgets; these funds are established by a Law.

(7) The Czechoslovak Socialist Republic determines the general principles of allocation and amortization policy.

Article 12. (1) Taxes and duties may be levied only by virtue of a Law.

(2) Laws of the Federal Assembly regulate enterprise taxes and levies, the turnover tax, the pension tax, the agricultural tax, the tax on wages, the tax on artistic and literary activities, the motor vehicle tax (the road tax), the tax on the income of the population, and the taxation (levies) of banking institutions and insurance companies. Laws of the Federal Assembly also regulate charges which by their nature have an exclusive or predominant relationship to foreign countries or are related to the exercise of the jurisdiction of federal organs.

(3) Other taxes and duties are established by Laws of the National Councils.

(4) The administration, collection, and control of all types of taxes (levies) and duties (fines) appertain to the central organs of the Republics and, under their authorization, to National Committees or other organs, with the exception of cases where the exclusive jurisdiction of the Czechoslovak Socialist Republic provides for the collection of duties (fines) by federal organs. Federal organs may control payments made into the Federal State Budget. A Law of the Federal Assembly may entrust the decision-making regarding exemptions and relief to organs of the Federation in the case of the taxes and duties mentioned in paragraph 2, paid by organizations directly managed by federal organs, or in the case of the duties mentioned in paragraph 2, collected by federal organs.

Article 13. (1) The territory of the Czechoslovak Socialist Republic constitutes a unitary customs territory.

(2) To the jurisdiction of the Czechoslovak Socialist Republic

belong the customs system, customs policy, and the issuing of customs tariffs.

Article 14. (1) To the jurisdiction of the Czechoslovak Socialist Republic belong, in the banking-sector:

a) the establishment of the concept for a foreign-exchange and credit policy, and the determination of the instruments for their implementation;

b) the determination of the extent of foreign-exchange reserves and the establishment of the method of their administration.

(2) The position, duties, and responsibility of the Czechoslovak State Bank, as well as the method of its administration and its relationship to the organs of the Republics are established by a Law of the Federal Assembly. A Law of the Federal Assembly also establishes the position and legal relationships of the other banks.

Article 15. A uniform system of prices is in force in the Czechoslovak Socialist Republic. To the jurisdiction of the Czechoslovak Socialist Republic belong, in the area of price policy:

a) the establishment of the principles governing price policy and price regulation;

b) the determination of the prices of raw materials, products, and services, this to the extent established by a Law of the Federal Assembly.

Article 16. To the jurisdiction of the Czechoslovak Socialist Republic belong, in the area of foreign economic relations:

a) the establishment of the principles governing foreign trade policy and the direction of its execution;

b) the legislation on the regulation of the relations arising from the conduct of foreign trade;

c) the coordination of economic cooperation with foreign countries, in the first place with the socialist states;

d) the organization and direction of foreign trade activity;

e) the arrangement of the basic economic instruments.

Article 17. To the jurisdiction of the Czechoslovak Socialist Republic belong, in the area of industry:

a) the establishment of the principles governing industrial policy;

b) the creation of conditions to link the industry directed by the Federation and the Republics to international industrial cooperation, specialization, and research;

c) the coordination of tasks resulting from the needs of the defense capability of the country;

d) the establishment and direction of organizations administering fuels, energy, metallurgy, and engine-building, and organizations engaged in the extraction and processing of ores, magnesite, and radioactive raw materials, and the exercise of state administration in these areas to the extent established by Laws of the Federal Assembly.

Article 18. To the jurisdiction of the Czechoslovak Socialist Republic belong, in the area of agriculture and food-supply:

a) the establishment of the principles governing agricultural policy and food-supply policy;

b) the coordination of state involvement in agriculture and food-supply;

c) a uniform legal regulation of matters of veterinary and phytopathological care, the protection of the agricultural soil fund, the system of agricultural cooperatives, the purchase and quality of agricultural products and food, which require a uniform approach in the Czechoslovak Socialist Republic, as well as a uniform legal regulation of the principles governing the organization of the direction of agriculture.

Article 19. To the jurisdiction of the Czechoslovak Socialist Republic belong, in the area of transport:

a) a uniform legal regulation of matters regarding transport and roads;

b) the establishment of state standards of the technical state of the means of transport, transport installations, and transportation routes;

c) the determination of the principles governing transport policy and elaboration of the concept for the development of the transport system;

d) the establishment and direction of organizations operating in the areas of railroad transport and civil aviation, organizations for the administration of motorways, organizations or maritime transport and, insofar as they are engaged in international transport, also of organizations of river transport;

e) the exercise of state administration in matters of railroad transport, civil aviation, maritime and river navigation, and motorways.

Article 20. To the jurisdiction of the Czechoslovak Socialist Republic belong, in the area of post and telecommunications:
  a) the legislation in postal and telecommunications matters;
  b) the organization and direction of a uniform system of postal services and telecommunications.

Article 21. (1) In the Czechoslovak Socialist Republic, a uniform scientific, technological, and investment policy is carried out in basic questions.
  (2) To the jurisdiction of the Czechoslovak Socialist Republic belong, in the area of scientific, technological, and investment policy:
  a) the elaboration of the concept and plans for the development of science and technology, and the establishment of the method of the direction of science and technological development;
  b) the development of international cooperation, including the licensing policy;
  c) the establishment of a uniform state investment policy and the principles governing state housing policy;
  d) the uniform legal regulation of matters of research and development;
  e) the resolution of matters regarding investments of federal significance and the securing of the realization of investments in branches directed by the Federation.

Article 22. To the jurisdiction of the Czechoslovak Socialist Republic belongs, in the area of labor, wages, and social policy, the establishment of uniform principles governing:
  a) labor law relations;
  b) wage policy and regulation of wages;
  c) pension and health insurance;
  d) social policy.

Article 23. To the jurisdiction of the Czechoslovak Socialist Republic belong, in the area of social-economic information:
  a) the establishment of the method of acquiring social-economic information necessary for the assessment of the development of the Federation and for fulfilling the duties arising from international commitments and the organization of the overall process of shaping and providing such information;
  b) the determination of the extent of information needed for the following up of the development of the economy, the standard of living, and the development of society;

c) the establishment of the method and time-periods for providing social-economic information, as well as of the principles governing the verification of their correctness, and the gathering of statistical data in accordance with the special needs of federal organs;

d) the provision of social-economic information to international organizations.

Article 24. (1) Socialist enterprises conduct their economic activity in the Czechoslovak Socialist Republic on the territory of both Republics under the conditions which are valid therein.

(2) To the jurisdiction of the Czechoslovak Socialist Republic belong:

a) the uniform regulation of socialist social ownership, the administration of national property, as well as the regulation of the establishment, the legal relations, and the methods of the direction of economic organizations;

b) the adoption of principles governing the regulation of cooperative and small-scale enterprises;

c) the regulation of economic relations between socialist organizations;

d) the regulation of the protection of production and trade, as well as the protection of the interests of the consumers, in particular the regulation of industrial rights, standardization, state testing system and state inspection, the weights and measures service, and the exercise of state administration in the aforementioned sectors established by a Law of the Federal Assembly;

e) the adoption of principles governing the protection and utilization of mineral resources;

f) the regulation of the organization and competence of the organs of economic arbitration, the regulation of proceedings held before those organs and, to the extent established by a Law of the Federal Assembly, the settlement of disputes by the organs of economic arbitration.

Article 25. Organs of the Czechoslovak Socialist Republic, to which the President of the Czechoslovak Socialist Republic has conveyed the powers to negotiate some international agreements, proceed, when negotiating such agreements regulating international cooperation in the area of joint jurisdiction, in cooperation with organs of both Republics; they also cooperate with them when representing the Czechoslovak Socialist Republic in international organizations which operate in the aforementioned areas.

Article 26. To the jurisdiction of the Czechoslovak Socialist Republic belongs the uniform legal regulation of the civil registry, identity cards, travel documents, registration of the population, and residence permits for foreigners.

Article 27. To the jurisdiction of the Czechoslovak Socialist Republic belongs the regulation of the position, competence, and other relations of the armed security corps.

(2) The division of jurisdiction among the Czechoslovak Socialist Republic and the two Republics in matters of internal order and security is regulated by a Law of the Federal Assembly.

Article 28. The division of jurisdiction among the Czechoslovak Socialist Republic and the two Republics in matters of the press and the other means of information is established by a Law of the Federal Assembly.

Article 28a. (1) To the Czechoslovak Socialist Republic belongs the control of all branches and activities of state and economic administration falling under its jurisdiction.

(2) To the Czechoslovak Socialist Republic furthermore belong, to the extent established by a Law of the Federal Assembly:

a) the control, in cooperation with the competent organs of the Republics, of the execution by organs of the Republics directed by organs and organizations of the Republic of measures adopted by federal organs;

b) having advised the competent organs of the Republics, the organization of joint control actions by organs of the Federation and the Republics, and the authorization of control organs to control those branches and activities which otherwise fall under the jurisdiction of the Federation.

(3) To the Czechoslovak Socialist Republic furthermore belong:

a) the methodical guidance of the activity of the organs which operate in the field of control;

b) the establishment of the plans of control activity to the extent and under the conditions as established by a Law of the Federal Assembly;

c) the determination of uniform principles of organization and performance of control activity.

Chapter III. The Federal Assembly

Article 29. (1) The Federal Assembly is the supreme organ of state power and the sole legislative body of the Czechoslovak Socialist Republic.

(2) The Federal Assembly consists of two Houses: the House of the People and the House of Nations. Both Houses are equal.

(3) A valid decision of the Federal Assembly requires the concurrent decision of both Houses, unless the present Constitutional Law provides otherwise or unless an internal matter of only one of the Houses is involved.

Article 30. (1) The House of the People consists of two hundred deputies who are elected by direct vote throughout the Czechoslovak Socialist Republic.

(2) A deputy of the House of the People may not be at the same time a deputy of the House of Nations.

(3) The House of the People is elected for a term of five years.

(4) The conditions under which the right to elect and to be elected to the House of the People is exercised and the manner in which the election and recall of its deputies are performed are determined by a Law of the Federal Assembly.

Article 31. (1) The House of Nations represents the equal constitutional position of both Republics.

(2) The House of Nations consists of one hundred and fifty deputies, seventy-five of whom are elected by direct vote in the Czech Socialist Republic and seventy-five by direct vote in the Slovak Socialist Republic.

(3) The electoral term of the House of Nations terminates with the electoral term of the House of the People.

Article 32. (1) The Federal Assembly is in session at least twice a year (a spring session and a fall session).

(2) The Federal Assembly is convened and the end of its sessions is declared by the President of the Czechoslovak Socialist Republic.

(3) If the President of the Czechoslovak Socialist Republic does not convene the spring session by the end of April or the fall session by the end of October, the session is convened by the Presidium of the Federal Assembly. In such a case, the session of the Federal Assembly is proclaimed by the Presidium of the Federal Assembly.

Article 33. (1) The President of the Czechoslovak Socialist Republic must convene the Federal Assembly at the request of at least one-third of the deputies of either House.

(2) If the President of the Czechoslovak Socialist Republic does not convene the Federal Assembly within fourteen days or within another term mentioned in such a request, the Assembly is convened by its Presidium. In such a case, the end of the session of the Federal Assembly is declared by the Presidium.

Article 34. (1) Each House meets in session by virtue of the decision of the Presidium of the respective House.

(2) The two Houses meet in joint session if they are to elect the President of the Czechoslovak Socialist Republic or the Chairman and Deputy Chairman of the Federal Assembly, if they are to debate on a declaration of policy of the Government of the Czechoslovak Socialist Republic, and in other cases where the Houses so decide.

Article 35. (1) The meetings of both Houses are, as a general rule, public.

(2) Closed meetings may be held only in cases established by the Rules of Order of the Federal Assembly.

Article 36. (1) To the Federal Assembly belongs in particular the jurisdiction to:

a) decide on the enactment of the Constitution of the Czechoslovak Socialist Republic and Constitutional and other Laws of the Federal Assembly and ascertain how they are executed;

b) deal with basic questions of foreign policy;

c) deal with basic questions of internal policy;

d) approve medium-term state plans for the development of the national economy of the Federation and the Federal State Budget, verify their fulfillment, and approve the final account of the Federation's State Budget;

e) elect the President of the Czechoslovak Socialist Republic and deal with his reports;

f) deal with declarations of policy of the Government and control its activities and those of its members, as well as deal with the question of confidence in the Government;

g) elect and recall members of the Constitutional Court of the Czechoslovak Socialist Republic;

h) establish by Constitutional Law federal ministries and establish by Law other federal organs of state administration;

i) establish by Law the control organ of the Federal Assembly.

(2) The Federal Assembly decides on a declaration of war, if it is

necessary to meet obligations arising from international agreements concerning joint defense against an attack.

(3) International political treaties and international economic agreements of a general nature, as well as international agreements whose implementation requires a Law of the Federal Assembly, require the approval of the Federal Assembly prior to their ratification.

(4) The Federal Assembly may repeal a decree or a decision of the Government or a generally binding legal regulation of a federal ministry or another federal central organ of state administration if they violate the Constitution or another Law of the Federal Assembly.

Article 37. (1) The Federal Assembly exercises legislative power in matters:

a) entrusted by the present Constitutional Law to the exclusive jurisdiction of the Czechoslovak Socialist Republic (Article 7);

b) under joint jurisdiction (Article 8 and Articles 10 to 28a) in that part which is entrusted to the Czechoslovak Socialist Republic.

(2) The Federal Assembly furthermore adopts Laws whose implementation—with exceptions established by Constitutional Laws—belongs to the full extent to the organs of the Republics, namely the Family Law, the Civil Code, the Code of Civil Procedure, the Law on Private International Law and Procedure, the Criminal Code, the Code of Criminal Procedure, the Law on the Execution of the Punishment Consisting of Deprivation of Liberty and on the Imposition of Custody, the Law on General Procedure Before Administrative Organs, the Law on University-level Schools, the Weapons and Munitions Law, and the Geodesic and Cartographic Law. The performance of acts under the Code of Criminal Procedure by the Corps of National Security regarding offenses against the security of the state belongs to the competence of federal organs.

(3) Insofar as the uniformity of the legal order so requires, the Federal Assembly realizes fundamental legislation in matters of public health care, housing and creation of life environment, the system of elementary, secondary general, and vocational schools, association and assembly, nationalities, copyright, the position of churches and religious societies, and in matters of forestry and water conservation, settlement of complaints and initiatives of workers, as well as in matters of savings banks and insurance companies.

Article 38. (1) A Law of the Federal Assembly may entrust the

Appendix: Czechoslovakia 597

regulation of the questions specified in Article 37, para. 1(b), and Article 37, para. 2, to legislation by the Republics.

(2) Insofar as federal legislation does not regulate to the full extent the matters specified in Article 37, para. 1(b), and Article 37, para. 2, they may be regulated by legislation of the National Councils.

(3) Insofar as the Federal Assembly does not issue basic legislation on the matters specified in Article 37, para. 3, the full legislative regulation appertains to the National Councils.

Article 39. The executive power over the matters specified in Article 37, para. 1(b), is divided between federal organs and organs of the Republics according to the respective provisions of the present Constitutional Law (Articles 10 to 28a).

Article 40. (1) The House of the People is capable of taking decisions if a simple majority of its deputies is present.

(2) The House of Nations is capable of taking decisions if a simple majority of its deputies elected in the Czech Socialist Republic and a simple majority of its deputies elected in the Slovak Socialist Republic are present.

(3) A valid decision requires the approval of a simple majority of deputies present in each House, unless the present Constitutional Law provides otherwise (Articles 41 to 43).

Article 41. The adoption of the Federal Constitution, a Constitutional Law of the Federal Assembly, their amendment, the election of the President of the Czechoslovak Socialist Republic, and decisions on the declaration of war require a three-fifths majority of all the deputies of the House of the People, as well as a three-fifths majority of all deputies in the House of Nations elected in the Czech Socialist Republic and a three-fifths majority of all the deputies of the House of Nations elected in the Slovak Socialist Republic.

Article 42. (1) In cases where under the present Constitutional Law outvoting is prohibited, the deputies elected in the Czech Socialist Republic and the deputies elected in the Slovak Socialist Republic vote separately in the House of Nations. A decision is adopted if a majority of all the deputies elected in the Czech Socialist Republic and a majority of all the deputies elected in the Slovak Socialist Republic have voted in favor of it, unless the present Constitutional Law requires a qualified majority (Article 41).

(2) The prohibition of outvoting applies to the approval of:

a) the draft bill on the acquisition and loss of Czechoslovak state citizenship;

b) medium-term state plans for the development of the national economy of the Czechoslovak Socialist Republic;

c) draft bills on questions specified in Article 10, para. 2;

d) draft bills establishing the method for securing the revenue of the Federal State Budget, relations between the Federal State Budget and the State Budgets of the Republics, as well as the principles of budgetary administration;

e) Federal State Budgets and the final budgetary accounts of the Federation;

f) draft bills setting up funds for special purposes tied to the Federal State Budget;

g) draft bills on the questions specified in Article 11, para. 7;

h) draft bills establishing taxes, levies, and duties under Article 12, para. 2;

i) drafts of legal regulations relating to the questions specified in Article 13, para. 2;

j) draft bills regulating the Czechoslovak currency and the Laws specified in Article 14, para. 2;

k) drafts of legal regulations relating to the questions specified in Article 15;

l) draft bills relating to foreign economic relations;

m) draft bills in matters specified in Article 21, para. 2, and Article 22;

n) draft bills regulating the establishment, the legal position, and the method of direction of economic organizations;

o) draft bills issued under Article 27, para. 2, Article 28, as well as under Article 28a;

p) draft bills establishing federal organs of state administration, with the exception of ministries.

(3) The prohibition of outvoting also applies to the approval of declarations of policy of the Government of the Czechoslovak Socialist Republic and to votes of confidence in the Government.

Article 43. (1) The Government of the Czechoslovak Socialist Republic may ask any House for a vote of confidence. A motion of no confidence in the Government of the Czechoslovak Socialist Republic may be introduced by at least one-fifth of the deputies of either House.

(2) A vote of no confidence in the Government of the Czechoslovak Socialist Republic requires the approval of a simple majority of the deputies present of the House of the People or the

Appendix: Czechoslovakia

approval of a simple majority of all the deputies of the House of Nations elected in the Czech Socialist Republic or the approval of a simple majority of all the deputies of the House of Nations elected in the Slovak Socialist Republic. The voting in the House of Nations is performed by roll call.

(3) The provisions of paragraphs 2 and 3 also apply to a vote of no confidence in an individual member of the Government of the Czechoslovak Socialist Republic.

Article 44. (1) Each House must decide on a proposal adopted by the other House within three months. If it does not so decide within this term, the proposal is adopted.

(2) If the two Houses do not reach a concurrent decision, they may decide to initiate proceedings to agree on a common text. In such a case, each House elects ten representatives from among its deputies to a conference committee for the aforementioned proceedings, unless they agree on a different number of representatives.

(3) If the two Houses do not adopt a concurrent decision on a draft bill even on the recommendation of this committee or otherwise within five months of the first vote, the same draft bill may be introduced at the earliest after the lapse of one year following its rejection.

(4) If the two Houses do not reach a concurrent decision on the Federal State Budget, the proceedings to agree on a common text under paragraph 2 is obligatory. If no agreement is reached on the Federal State Budget before the beginning of the budgetary year, the legal provisions on provisional budgeting are applicable.

(5) If those proceedings do not produce a concurrent decision of both Houses, the Federal Assembly may be dissolved. New elections are called by the Presidium of the Federal Assembly within sixty days.

Article 45. (1) Draft bills of the Federal Assembly may be introduced by deputies of the Federal Assembly, the committees of both Houses, the President of the Czechoslovak Socialist Republic, the Government of the Czechoslovak Socialist Republic, the Czech National Council, and the Slovak National Council.

(2) Laws of the Federal Assembly are signed by the President of the Czechoslovak Socialist Republic, the Chairman of the Federal Assembly, and the Chairman of the Government of the Czechoslovak Socialist Republic.

(3) A Law of the Federal Assembly comes into force only if it is promulgated in the manner established by a Law of the Federal

Assembly. Laws of the Federal Assembly are promulgated by the Presidium of the Federal Assembly within fourteen days of their adoption.

Article 46. The rules governing the proceedings of the Federal Assembly and the mutual relations of the two Houses, as well as relations with the Government and with other institutions, are regulated by the Law on the Rules of Order of the Federal Assembly. Each House regulates its internal relations by its own decision.

Article 47. The validity of the election of deputies of the Federal Assembly is verified by the respective House. It does so on the proposal of the Mandates and Immunities Committee.

Article 48. (1) A deputy of the Federal Assembly makes the following vow at the first meeting of his House, which he attends:

> "I promise upon my honor and conscience to be faithful to the Czechoslovak Socialist Republic and to the cause of socialism. I shall respect the will and the interests of the people, observe the Constitution and other laws, and work for their implementation."

(2) A refusal to make the vow, or a vow made with a reservation, results in the loss of mandate.

Article 49. (1) The House of the People and the House of Nations, as well as their individual deputies have the right to interpellate the Government of the Czechoslovak Socialist Republic and its members, and to put questions to them on matters within their jurisdiction. The Government and its members are bound to answer such interpellations and questions.

(2) The Chairman and the other members of the Government have the right to attend meetings of both Houses of the Federal Assembly, and of their committees, as well as meetings of the Presidium of the Federal Assembly. They are given the floor whenever they so request.

(3) If either House, its committee, or the Presidium of the Federal Assembly so request, a member of the Government is bound to attend a meeting of the House, its committee, or the Presidium of the Federal Assembly.

Article 50. A deputy of the Federal Assembly may not be subjected to criminal or disciplinary prosecution or be taken into custody without the approval of the House of which he is a member. If the

Appendix: Czechoslovakia 601

House refuses to give such approval, the prosecution is excluded for good.

Article 51. A deputy of the Federal Assembly may never be prosecuted for his voting in a House, its organs, or in the Presidium of the Federal Assembly. A deputy is subjected only to the disciplinary jurisdiction of his House for statements made in the exercise of his functions in either House, its organs, or in the Presidium of the Federal Assembly.

Article 52. If a deputy of the Federal Assembly is caught and arrested in the act of committing a criminal offense, the competent organ immediately notifies the Presidium of the Federal Assembly. If the Presidium does not grant approval, the deputy must be released immediately.

Article 53. A deputy of the Federal Assembly may refuse to testify on matters which he has come to know in the exercise of his function, even after he has ceased to be a deputy.

Article 54. Each House elects its Presidium which consists of three to six deputies.

Article 55. Each House sets up committees as its initiatory and control organs, and elects their chairman and other members.

Article 56. (1) Both Houses of the Federal Assembly elect the Presidium of the Federal Assembly from among the deputies.

(2) The Presidium of the Federal Assembly has forty members, twenty of whom are elected by the House of the People and twenty by the House of Nations. The House of Nations elects ten members from among its deputies elected in the Czech Socialist Republic and ten members from among its deputies elected in the Slovak Socialist Republic.

(3) The Presidium of the Federal Assembly maintains its functions after the expiration of the electoral term until the newly-elected Federal Assembly elects its own Presidium.

(4) Members of the Presidium of the Federal Assembly are accountable to that House of the Federal Assembly which elected them. The House may recall them at any time.

(5) The Chairman and the Deputy Chairman of the Federal Assembly are elected by the House of the People and the House of Nations from among the members of the Presidium of the Federal

Assembly. If a deputy who is a citizen of the Czech Socialist Republic is elected Chairman, a deputy who is a citizen of the Slovak Socialist Republic is elected First Deputy Chairman, or *vice versa*.

Article 57. (1) The Presidium of the Federal Assembly decides by a simple majority of all its members.

(2) The provisions of Article 42, regarding the prohibition of outvoting, also applies to the taking of decisions of the Presidium of the Federal Assembly.

Article 58. (1) At the time when the Federal Assembly is not in session either because it has been terminated or because its electoral term has expired, the jurisdiction of the Federal Assembly is exercised by the Presidium of the Assembly. The Presidium is, however, not empowered to elect the President of the Czechoslovak Socialist Republic, adopt or amend Constitutional Laws, decide on the Federal State Budget, declare war, or to pass a vote of no confidence in the Government of the Czechoslovak Socialist Republic or in its members.

(2) At the time when the Federal Assembly is not in session due to extraordinary causes, the Presidium of the Federal Assembly exercises the full jurisdiction of the Assembly except for the right to amend the Constitution of the Czechoslovak Socialist Republic and to elect its President.

(3) Urgent measures requiring the enactment of a Law are taken by the Presidium of the Federal Assembly in the form of Legal Measures signed by the President of the Czechoslovak Socialist Republic, the Chairman of the Federal Assembly, and the Chairman of the Government of the Czechoslovak Socialist Republic. Legal Measures are promulgated in the same manner as Laws.

(4) Measures taken by the Presidium of the Federal Assembly under paragraphs 1 to 3 must be approved at the next session of the Federal Assembly; otherwise, they cease to have effect.

(5) The Presidium of the Federal Assembly may make a decision on a declaration of war only if a session of the Federal Assembly is made impossible by extraordinary causes. Such a decision takes effect only if approved by three-fifths of all the members of the Presidium of the Federal Assembly who are citizens of the Czech Socialist Republic, and by three-fifths of all the members of the Presidium of the Federal Assembly who are citizens of the Slovak Socialist Republic.

(6) At the time when the Government of the Czechoslovak Social-

Appendix: Czechoslovakia 603

ist Republic is exercising the function of the President of the Czechoslovak Socialist Republic, the Presidium of the Federal Assembly is competent to appoint and recall the Government of the Czechoslovak Socialist Republic and its members and to entrust them with the direction of ministries and other federal organs.

Article 59. The Presidium of the Federal Assembly calls elections to the Federal Assembly.

Chapter IV. The President of the Czechoslovak Socialist Republic

Article 60. (1) At the head of the Czechoslovak Socialist Republic is the President. He is elected by the Federal Assembly.

(2) The President of the Czechoslovak Socialist Republic is accountable to the Federal Assembly for the discharge of his functions.

Article 61. (1) The President of the Czechoslovak Socialist Republic:

a) represents the Czechoslovak Socialist Republic in foreign relations, negotiates and ratifies international agreements; he may delegate the negotiation of international agreements which do not require approval by the Federal Assembly to the Government of the Czechoslovak Socialist Republic or, with the latter's approval, to its individual members;

b) receives and accredits envoys;

c) convenes sessions of the Federal Assembly, and proclaims these sessions to be terminated;

d) may dissolve the Federal Assembly in the case specified in Article 44, para. 5;

e) signs the Laws of the Federal Assembly and the Legal Measures of its Presidium;

f) is entitled to submit to the Federal Assembly reports on the state of affairs of the Czechoslovak Socialist Republic and on significant political questions, to propose necessary measures, and to be present at meetings of the Houses of the Federal Assembly;

g) appoints and recalls the Chairman and the other members of the Government of the Czechoslovak Socialist Republic and entrusts them with the direction of federal ministries and other federal central organs;

h) is entitled to attend and to preside over meetings of the Government of the Czechoslovak Socialist Republic, to request reports from the Government and from its individual members, and to discuss with the Government or its members questions necessary to be resolved;

i) appoints higher state functionaries of the Czechoslovak Socialist Republic in cases established by law; appoints and promotes generals; appoints on the proposal of the competent organs of the Czech Socialist Republic and the Slovak Socialist Republic professors and rectors of university-level institutions;

j) awards decorations, unless he empowers another organ to do so;

k) has the right to grant amnesty, to pardon and to mitigate punishments imposed by criminal courts, and to order the noncommencement or discontinuation of criminal proceedings and the expunction of sentences;

l) is the commander-in-chief of the armed forces;

m) proclaims a state of war on the proposal of the Government of the Czechoslovak Socialist Republic and declares war on the strength of a decision taken by the Federal Assembly if the Czechoslovak Socialist Republic is attacked or if it is necessary to fulfill obligations arising from international agreements on joint defense against an attack.

(2) The President of the Czechoslovak Socialist Republic also exercises powers which are not explicitly specified in the present Constitutional Law, if a Law of the Federal Assembly so provides.

Article 62. (1) Any citizen who is eligible to be a deputy in the Federal Assembly may be elected President of the Czechoslovak Socialist Republic.

(2) The President is elected for a term of office of five years. He takes office by making the vow.

(3) The election of the President of the Czechoslovak Socialist Republic is held within the last fourteen days of the Presidential term of office. If the office of the President becomes vacant prior to the expiration of the term of office, the election is held not later than within fourteen days.

(4) The President of the Czechoslovak Socialist Republic may not simultaneously be a deputy of any representative body, a member of the Government or the Constitutional Court, or a judge.

(5) If a deputy of a representative body, a member of the Government or the Constitutional Court, or a judge is elected President of the Czechoslovak Socialist Republic, he ceases to exercise his previous function from the day of his election. His mandate or membership in the Government or the Constitutional Court, or his judicial office, ceases on the day on which he makes the vow.

Appendix: Czechoslovakia

Article 63. The President of the Czechoslovak Socialist Republic makes the following vow before the Federal Assembly:

> "I promise upon my honor and conscience to be faithful to the Czechoslovak Socialist Republic and to the cause of socialism. I shall fulfill my obligations in accordance with the will of the people and in the interests of the people. I shall cherish the welfare of the Czechoslovak Socialist Republic and observe the Constitution and the other laws of the socialist state."

Article 64. If the office of the President of the Czechoslovak Socialist Republic becomes vacant and a new President has not yet been elected and has not made the vow, or if the President is unable to exercise his office for serious reasons, the exercise of his functions appertains to the Government of the Czechoslovak Socialist Republic. In such a case, the Government may entrust its Chairman with some of the powers of the President of the Czechoslovak Socialist Republic; the supreme command of the armed forces passes during this time to the Chairman of the Government.

(2) If the President of the Czechoslovak Socialist Republic is unable to exercise his office (paragraph 1) during a period longer than one year, the Federal Assembly may elect a new President of the Czechoslovak Socialist Republic for a new term of office.

Article 65. The President of the Czechoslovak Socialist Republic may not be subjected to judicial prosecution for actions connected with the exercise of his office.

Chapter V. The Government of the Czechoslovak Socialist Republic

Article 66. The Government of the Czechoslovak Socialist Republic is the highest executive organ of state power in the Czechoslovak Socialist Republic.

Article 67. (1) The Government of the Czechoslovak Socialist Republic consists of the Chairman, Deputy Chairman, and ministers.

(2) The function of a member of the Government of the Czechoslovak Socialist Republic is incompatible with the function of a member of the Presidium of the Federal Assembly or with the function of a member of the Constitutional Court.

Article 68. Members of the Government of the Czechoslovak Socialist Republic make the following vow before the President of the Czechoslovak Socialist Republic:

> "I promise upon my honor and conscience to be faithful to the Czechoslovak Socialist Republic and to the cause of socialism. I shall fulfill my obligations in accordance with the will of the people and in the interests of the people. I shall observe the Constitution and the other laws and work for their implementation."

Article 69. The Government of the Czechoslovak Socialist Republic, after its appointment, is obliged to submit to the Federal Assembly at its next earliest session, its declaration of policy and to ask for a vote of confidence.

Article 70. (1) The Government of the Czechoslovak Socialist Republic is accountable for the exercise of its functions to the Federal Assembly; either of the two Houses of the Assembly may pass a vote of no confidence in the Government.

(2) The Government of the Czechoslovak Socialist Republic may ask the Federal Assembly for a vote of confidence at any time.

Article 71. (1) The Government of the Czechoslovak Socialist Republic may submit its resignation to the President of the Czechoslovak Socialist Republic.

(2) If a House of the Federal Assembly passes a vote of no confidence in the Government of the Czechoslovak Socialist Republic or if it refuses to express its confidence, the President of the Czechoslovak Socialist Republic recalls the Government.

(3) The Government of the Czechoslovak Socialist Republic always submits its resignation after the first meeting of a newly-elected Federal Assembly.

Article 72. If the President of the Czechoslovak Socialist Republic accepts the resignation of the Government of the Czechoslovak Socialist Republic, he entrusts the Government with the exercise of its functions temporarily until a new Government is appointed.

Article 73. (1) A member of the Government of the Czechoslovak Socialist Republic may submit his resignation to the President of the Czechoslovak Socialist Republic.

(2) The House of the People or the House of Nations of the Federal Assembly may also express their lack of confidence in an individual member of the Government of the Czechoslovak Socialist Republic. In such a case, the President of the Czechoslovak Socialist Republic recalls that member of the Government.

Appendix: Czechoslovakia

Article 74. If the President of the Czechoslovak Socialist Republic accepts the resignation of a member of the Government of the Czechoslovak Socialist Republic, he may determine who of the members of the Government may temporarily take charge of the matters previously administered by the member of the Government whose resignation he accepted.

Article 75. A decision of the Government of the Czechoslovak Socialist Republic takes effect if it is approved by a simple majority of all the members of the Government.

Article 76. (1) The Government of the Czechoslovak Socialist Republic secures the fulfillment of the tasks of the Federation in the areas of defense of the Czechoslovak Socialist Republic, strengthening of the security of the country, development of a peaceful foreign policy, economic construction, and other areas within the jurisdiction of the Federation. For this purpose, it ensures the implementation of the Laws of the Federal Assembly, and unifies, directs, and controls the activity of the federal ministries and the other federal organs.

(2) In securing the fulfillment of the tasks of the Federation, the Government of the Czechoslovak Socialist Republic also considers questions of principle and concept significant to the whole society in the areas which belong to the jurisdiction of the Republics and coordinates the solution of questions resulting from the need of a uniform conduct of state policy of the Federation throughout the whole territory of the Czechoslovak Socialist Republic; in agreement with the Governments of the Czech Socialist Republic and the Slovak Socialist Republic, it may establish for this purpose the necessary coordinating organs of the Government of the Czechoslovak Socialist Republic.

Article 77. (1) The Government of the Czechoslovak Socialist Republic as a body decides in particular on:
 a) draft bills of the Federal Assembly;
 b) Government decrees;
 c) the implementation of its declaration of policy;
 d) basic questions of internal and foreign policy;
 e) drafts of state plans for the development of the national economy, the [Federal] Budget, and the final [budgetary] account of the Federation;
 f) basic economic measures for securing the economic policy;

g) the appointment of functionaries in cases established by a Law of the Federal Assembly;

h) motions asking the Federal Assembly for a vote of confidence;

i) other questions, if a Law of the Federal Assembly so provides.

(2) For the purpose of exercising its current decision-making activity, the Government of the Czechoslovak Socialist Republic may set up as its own organ the Presidium of the Government of the Czechoslovak Socialist Republic, and determine its competence and establish the principles governing its activity.

Article 78. The Government of the Czechoslovak Socialist Republic cooperates with the Governments of the two Republics when negotiating international agreements whose implementation belongs to the jurisdiction of the Republics; it also cooperates when representing the Czechoslovak Socialist Republic in international organizations operating in areas which are within the jurisdiction of the Republics.

Article 79. The Government of the Czechoslovak Socialist Republic may issue decrees for the purpose of implementing a Law of the Federal Assembly and within the limits of such a Law, if the Law regulates questions which fall within the jurisdiction of the Federation.

Article 80. Federal ministries and the other central organs of the Federation may issue generally binding legal regulations on the basis and within the limits of Laws enacted by the Federal Assembly, if they are authorized by a Law to do so.

Article 81. (1) Federal ministries operate in the area of exclusive jurisdiction of the Federation and in the area of joint jurisdiction.

(2) Federal ministries are established by a Constitutional Law of the Federal Assembly.

Article 82. (Repealed by Constitutional Law No. 125, *Sbírka zakonů ČSSR* 1970.)

Article 83. In addition to federal ministries, other federal organs of state administration operate in areas under Federal jurisdiction. These organs are established by Laws of the Federal Assembly.

Article 84. State organs of the Republics implement Laws of the Federal Assembly on the territory of the Republics, insofar as their

Appendix: Czechoslovakia

implementation has not been entrusted to the competent federal organs.

Article 85. Insofar as the administrative organs of the Republic exercise competence in matters falling under the jurisdiction of the Federation, they are obliged to observe directives of organs of federal administration.

Article 85a. The Government of the Czechoslovak Socialist Republic is authorized to suspend the implementation of a measure taken by the Government of a Republic, or to repeal it if it is contrary to measures taken by the Government of the Czechoslovak Socialist Republic issued within the scope of the jurisdiction of the Federation.

Chapter VI. The Constitutional Court of the Czechoslovak Socialist Republic

Article 86. (1) The Constitutional Court of the Czechoslovak Socialist Republic is a judicial organ for the protection of constitutionality.

(2) Members of the Constitutional Court are independent in their decision-making and make decisions only on the strength of the Constitution of the Czechoslovak Socialist Republic and Laws of the Federal Assembly.

Article 87. The Constitutional Court of the Czechoslovak Socialist Republic decides on:

a) the concurrence of Laws of the Federal Assembly and Legal Measures of its Presidium with the Constitution of the Czechoslovak Socialist Republic;

b) the concurrence of Constitutional Acts of the Czech National Council and the Slovak National Council with the Constitution of the Czechoslovak Socialist Republic, and the concurrence of Laws enacted by the National Councils with the Constitution of the Czechoslovak Socialist Republic;

c) the concurrence of decrees of the Government of the Czechoslovak Socialist Republic and generally binding legal regulations of federal ministries and other central organs of state administration, as well as decrees issued by the Governments of the Republics and generally binding legal regulations of ministries and the other central organs of state administration of the Republics with the Constitution of the Czechoslovak Socialist Republic and Laws of the Federal Assembly.

Article 88. The Constitutional Court of the Czechoslovak Socialist Republic settles conflicts of competence between:

a) organs of the Czechoslovak Socialist Republic and organs of one or both Republics;

b) organs of both Republics.

Article 89. The Constitutional Court of the Czechoslovak Socialist Republic may initiate improvements of legislation of the Czechoslovak Socialist Republic, as well as of legislation of the Republics.

Article 90. (1) If the Constitutional Court of the Czechoslovak Socialist Republic establishes a contradiction between legal regulations in the sense of Article 87, it rules that the relevant regulations, a part thereof, or some provisions become inapplicable; the competent organs are obliged to amend the relevant regulations within six months of the publication of the finding of the Constitutional Court of the Czechoslovak Socialist Republic so as to bring them into agreement with the Constitution of the Czechoslovak Socialist Republic or other Laws of the Federal Assembly. If they fail to do so, the relevant regulations, a part thereof, or some provisions cease to have legal effect six months after the publication of the finding.

(2) A finding of the Constitutional Court is published in the Official Gazette used for the promulgation of Laws of the Federal Assembly.

Article 91. The Constitutional Court of the Czechoslovak Socialist Republic decides on complaints against failure to certify the mandate of a deputy of the Federal Assembly and against a verdict recalling a deputy of the Assembly, as well as against a decision refusing to register a candidate deputy.

Article 92. The Constitutional Court of the Czechoslovak Socialist Republic decides on the protection of the rights and freedoms guaranteed by the Constitution where they have been infringed upon by a decision or another intervention of a federal organ, unless the law grants other judicial protection.

Article 93. (1) The Constitutional Court always initiates proceedings if a motion has been introduced by:

a) a House of the Federal Assembly, the Presidium of the Federal

Appendix: Czechoslovakia

Assembly, the Government of the Czechoslovak Socialist Republic, or another federal organ;

b) the Czech National Council, its Presidium, the Slovak National Council, its Presidium, or the Government of a Republic;

c) a court;

d) the Procurator General;

e) an individual citizen in the cases specified in Article 91.

(2) The Constitutional Court of the Czechoslovak Socialist Republic may initiate proceedings on the basis of its own decision.

(3) The Constitutional Court of the Czechoslovak Socialist Republic may also initiate proceedings on the motion of citizens and organizations.

Article 94. (1) The Constitutional Court of the Czechoslovak Socialist Republic consists of twelve members, of whom eight are judges and four substitutes. The Constitutional Court decides by a panel.

(2) Any citizen who is eligible for the Federal Assembly, who has reached the age of thirty-five years, is a graduate of a university law school, and has been active in the legal profession for at least ten years may be elected member of the Constitutional Court of the Czechoslovak Socialist Republic.

(3) Members of the Constitutional Court of the Czechoslovak Socialist Republic are elected by the Federal Assembly for a term of seven years. A judge of the Constitutional Court may not be elected for more than two consecutive terms.

(4) Four judges and two substitutes are elected from among the citizens of the Czech Socialist Republic and four judges and two substitutes are elected from among the citizens of the Slovak Socialist Republic.

Article 95. (1) The Chairman and Deputy Chairman of the Constitutional Court of the Czechoslovak Socialist Republic are elected by the Federal Assembly from among the members of the Constitutional Court.

(2) If the Chairman of the Constitutional Court of the Czechoslovak Socialist Republic is a citizen of the Czech Socialist Republic, a citizen of the Slovak Socialist Republic is elected Deputy Chairman, or *vice versa*.

Article 96. (1) The Chairman of the Constitutional Court of the Czechoslovak Socialist Republic calls a substitute to serve as judge if a judge falls sick, if his seat becomes vacant, or if he has lost his office.

(2) If a judge of the Constitutional Court of the Czechoslovak Socialist Republic has lost his office, the substitute becomes a judge on a permanent basis up to the expiration of the electoral term of the Constitutional Court.

Article 97. (1) Members of the Constitutional Court of the Czechoslovak Socialist Republic enjoy the same immunity as deputies of the Federal Assembly.

(2) Permission to proceed with criminal or disciplinary prosecution of a member of the Constitutional Court or to take him into custody is granted by the Constitutional Court.

Article 98. (1) The function of the Constitutional Court of the Czechoslovak Socialist Republic is incompatible with the function of deputy of the Federal Assembly, the Czech National Council, the Slovak National Council, and member of the Government of the Czechoslovak Socialist Republic or the Governments of the Republics, or with a function in the administrative or economic apparatus.

(2) A Law of the Federal Assembly may establish the incompatibility of the function of member of the Constitutional Court of the Czechoslovak Socialist Republic with further functions.

Article 99. A member of the Constitutional Court of the Czechoslovak Socialist Republic may resign from his function. The Federal Assembly may recall him following disciplinary proceedings or on the basis of a sentence in a criminal case. The Federal Assembly may also recall a judge in the case that he has not attended the sessions of the Court for more than a year, provided this fact has been ascertained by the plenum of the Constitutional Court of the Czechoslovak Socialist Republic.

Article 100. The details of the jurisdiction and organization of the Constitutional Court of the Czechoslovak Socialist Republic and its rules of procedure are regulated by a Law of the Federal Assembly.

Article 101. There are Constitutional Courts in the Czech Socialist Republic and the Slovak Socialist Republic. Their jurisdiction and principles of organization are established by Constitutional Laws of the National Councils.

Chapter VII. The State Organs of the Czech Socialist Republic and the Slovak Socialist Republic

Part I. The Czech National Council and the Slovak National Council

Article 102. (1) The Czech National Council is the representative of the national sovereignty and identity of the Czech nation and the highest organ of state power in the Czech Socialist Republic.

(2) The Slovak National Council is the representative of the national sovereignty and identity of the Slovak nation and the highest organ of state power in the Slovak Socialist Republic.

(3) The National Council is the highest representative body of the Republic and its only legislative organ.

Article 103. (1) The Czech National Council consists of two hundred deputies. The Slovak National Council consists of one hundred and fifty deputies.

(2) The National Council is elected for a term of five years.

(3) The conditions under which the right to elect and be elected to the National Council is exercised and the manner in which the election and recall of its deputies are performed, are established by a Law of the National Council.

Article 104. (1) The National Council is in session at least twice within a year (a spring session and a fall session).

(2) The National Council is convened and its sessions are declared to be terminated by its Presidium.

(3) The National Council must be convened by its Presidium at the request of at least one-third of its deputies. The Presidium of the National Council convenes the session within fourteen days or within another term specified in the request.

Article 105. Individual meetings of the National Council are convened by its Chairman.

Article 106. (1) Meetings of the National Council are, as a general rule, public.

(2) Closed meetings may be held only in cases established by the procedural rules of the National Council.

Article 107. (1) To the jurisdiction of the National Council belong in particular:

a) deciding on Constitutional and other Laws of the Republic and observing how they are executed by the organs of the Republic;

b) the granting of approval to international agreements whose implementation requires a Law of the National Council;

c) dealing with basic questions of internal policy;

d) approving medium-term state plans for the development of the national economy and the State Budget of the Republic, controlling their fulfillment, and approving the final state budgetary account of the Republic;

e) electing and recalling the Chairman of the National Council and the other members of the Presidium of the National Council;

f) dealing with the declaration of policy of the Government of the Republic and controlling its activity and the activity of its members, as well as dealing with the question of confidence in the Government;

g) setting up by a Law ministries and other central organs of state administration of the Republic;

h) electing and recalling members of the Constitutional Court of the Republic.

(2) The National Council may repeal a decree or decision of the Government of the Republic or a generally binding legal regulation of a ministry or another central organ of state administration, if they contradict the Constitution or another Law of the National Council.

Article 108. As the highest representative organ of the Republic, the National Council considers initiatives of the National Committees, deals with their activities, and decides on measures regarding their extension.

Article 109. The National Council is capable of taking decisions if a simple majority of all the deputies is present.

(2) A valid decision requires the approval of a simple majority of the deputies present.

(3) The adoption of a Constitutional Law requires the approval of a three-fifths majority of all the deputies of the National Council.

Article 110. (1) The Government of the Republic may ask the National Council for a vote of confidence. A motion of no confidence in the Government may be submitted by at least one-fifth of the deputies of the National Council.

(2) The provisions of paragraph 1 also apply to a vote of no confidence in an individual member of the Government of the Republic.

Article 111. (1) Draft bills may be submitted by deputies of the National Council, committees of the National Council, and by the Government of the Republic.

(2) Laws of the National Council are signed by the Chairman of the National Council and the Chairman of the Government of the Republic.

(3) A Law of the National Council takes effect if promulgated in the manner established by a Law of the National Council. Laws of the National Council are promulgated by the Presidium of the National Council within fourteen days after their approval.

Article 112. The rules governing the proceedings of the National Council, and its relations with the Government and with other institutions are regulated by the Law on the Rules of Order of the National Council.

Article 113. The validity of the election of deputies is verified by the National Council. The Council does so on the proposal of its Mandates and Immunities Committee.

Article 114. (1) A deputy makes a vow at the first meeting of the National Council he attends.

(2) A deputy of the Czech National Council makes the following vow:

"I promise on my honor and conscience to be faithful to the Czechoslovak Socialist Republic, the Czech Socialist Republic, and to the cause of socialism. I shall respect the will and the interests of the people, be guided by the Constitution and the other Laws of the Czechoslovak Socialist Republic and the Czech Socialist Republic, and shall work for their implementation."

(3) A deputy of the Slovak National Council makes the following vow:

"I promise on my honor and conscience to be faithful to the Czechoslovak Socialist Republic, the Slovak Socialist Republic, the cause of socialism, and to the heritage of the Slovak National Uprising. I shall respect the will and the interests of the people, observe the Constitution and the other Laws of the Czechoslovak Socialist Republic and the Slovak Socialist Republic, and shall work for their implementation."

(4) A refusal to make the vow, or a vow made with a reservation, results in the loss of the mandate.

Article 115. (1) The National Council, as well as individual deputies have the right to interpellate the Government of the Republic and its members, and to put questions to them on matters within their jurisdiction. The Government and its members are bound to answer such interpellations and questions.

(2) The Chairman and the other members of the Government of the Republic have the right to attend meetings of the National Council, its Presidium, and committees. They are given the floor whenever they so request.

(3) If the National Council, its Presidium, or committee so requests, a member of the Government is bound to attend a meeting of the National Council, its Presidium, or committee.

Article 116. (1) A deputy may not be subjected to criminal or disciplinary prosecution or be taken into custody without the approval of the National Council. If the National Council refuses to give such approval, the prosecution is excluded for good.

(2) A deputy of the National Council may never be prosecuted for his voting in the National Council or its organs. A deputy is subject only to the disciplinary jurisdiction of the National Council for statements made in the exercise of his function in the National Council or its organ.

(3) If a deputy has been caught and arrested in the act of committing a criminal offense, the competent organ immediately notifies the Presidium of the National Council. If the Presidium does not grant approval, the deputy must be released immediately.

Article 117. A deputy of the National Council may refuse to testify on matters of which he has come to know in the exercise of his function, even after he has ceased to be a deputy.

Article 118. The National Council sets up committees as its initiatory and control organs, and elects their chairmen and other members.

Article 119. (1) The National Council elects the Presidium of the National Council from among its deputies.

(2) The Presidium of the National Council consists of the Chairman, Deputy Chairman, and other members. The number of members of the Presidium is established by the National Council.

(3) The Presidium of the National Council maintains its functions after the expiration of the electoral term until the newly-elected National Council elects its own Presidium.

(4) The Presidium of the National Council and its members are

accountable to the National Council. The National Council may recall them at any time.

Article 120. The Presidium of the National Council decides by a simple majority of all its members.

Article 121. (1) At the time when the National Council is not in session because it has been terminated or because its electoral term has expired, the jurisdiction of the National Council is exercised by the Presidium of the National Council. The Presidium is, however, not empowered to adopt or amend Constitutional Laws, or to decide on the State Budget of the Republic.

(2) At the time when the National Council is not in session due to extraordinary causes, the Presidium of the National Council exercises the full jurisdiction of the Council except for the right to adopt or amend Constitutional Laws.

(3) Urgent measures requiring the enactment of a Law are taken by the Presidium of the National Council in the form of Legal Measures signed by the Chairman of the National Council and the Chairman of the Government of the Republic. Legal Measures are promulgated in the same manner as Laws.

(4) Measures taken by the Presidium of the National Council under paragraphs 1 to 3 must be approved at the next session of the National Council; otherwise, they shall become null and void.

Article 122. (1) To the competence of the Presidium of the National Council furthermore belong:

a) the appointment and recall of the Chairman and other members of the Government of the Republic and entrusting them with the direction of ministries and other central organs;

b) the appointment of state functionaries, in cases where such appointment has been entrusted to the Presidium by a Law;

c) the granting of prizes and the awarding of decorations according to the Laws of the Republic.

(2) The Presidium of the National Council calls elections to the National Council and general elections to National Committees.

Article 123. The Chairman of the National Council:
a) represents the National Council;
b) signs Laws of the National Council and Legal Measures of its Presidium;
c) administers the vow of the members of the Government of the Republic;

d) convenes and presides over the meetings of the National Council.

Part II. The Government of the Czech Socialist Republic and the Government of the Slovak Socialist Republic.

Article 124. The Government of the Republic is the highest executive organ of state power of the Republic.

Article 125. (1) The Government of the Republic consists of the Chairman, Deputy Chairman, and ministers.

(2) The function of a member of the Government is incompatible with the function of a member of the Presidium of the National Council or with the function of a member of the Constitutional Court.

Article 126. (1) The members of the Government of the Czech Socialist Republic make the following vow before the Chairman of the Czech National Council:

> "I promise on my honor and conscience to be faithful to the Czechoslovak Socialist Republic, the Czech Socialist Republic, and to the cause of socialism. I shall fulfill my obligations in accordance with the will of the people and in the interests of the people. I shall observe the Constitution and the other Laws of the Czechoslovak Socialist Republic and the Czech Socialist Republic, and work for their implementation."

(2) The members of the Government of the Slovak Socialist Republic make the following vow before the Chairman of the Slovak National Council:

> "I promise on my honor and conscience to be faithful to the Czechoslovak Socialist Republic, the Slovak Socialist Republic, the cause of socialism, and to the heritage of the Slovak National Uprising. I shall perform my obligations in accordance with the will of the people and in the interests of the people. I shall observe the Constitution and the other Laws of the Czechoslovak Socialist Republic and the Slovak Socialist Republic, and work for their implementation."

Article 127. The Government of the Republic, after its appointment, is obliged to submit to the National Council at its next earliest session its declaration of policy and to ask for a vote of confidence.

Article 128. (1) The Government of the Republic is accountable for the exercise of its functions to the National Council which may express its lack of confidence in it.

(2) The Government of the Republic may ask the National Council for a vote of confidence at any time.

Article 129. (1) The Government of the Republic may submit its resignation to the Presidium of the National Council.

(2) If the National Council passes a vote of no confidence in the Government of the Republic or if it denies it a vote of confidence, the Presidium of the National Council recalls the Government.

(3) The Government of the Republic always submits its resignation after the first meeting of a newly-elected National Council.

Article 130. If the Presidium of the National Council accepts the resignation of the Government, it entrusts the Government with the exercise of its functions temporarily until a new Government is appointed.

Article 131. (1) A member of the Government of the Republic may submit his resignation to the Presidium of the National Council.

(2) The National Council may express its lack of confidence in individual members of the Government of the Republic. In such a case, the Presidium of the National Council recalls the member of the Government.

Article 132. If the Presidium of the National Council accepts the resignation of a member of the Government of the Republic, it may determine who of the members of the Government will temporarily take charge of matters previously administered by the member of the Government whose resignation it accepted.

Article 133. The Government of the Republic decides in a body, which is capable of taking decisions if a simple majority of its members is present. The validity of a decision requires the approval of a simple majority of all the present members of the Government.

Article 134. The Government of the Republic organizes and secures the fulfillment of tasks in the area of the economic, cultural, and social construction of the Republic, as well as in further areas which fall, by the present Constitutional Law, under the jurisdiction of the Republic. For this purpose, the Government of the Republic ensures the implementation of Laws, unifies, directs, and controls the activity of the ministries and other organs of state administration of the Republic, and follows and secures the fulfillment of its decrees and decisions.

Article 135. (1) All governmental and executive powers ensuing from the legislative competence of the National Council belong to the Government of the Republic.

(2) To the competence of the Government of the Republic furthermore belong matters which are regulated according to the present Constitutional Law by Laws of the Federal Assembly, if their implementation belongs to the Governments of the Republics (Article 37, para. 2).

(3) To the competence of the Government of the Republic also belong matters designated to the Governments of the Republics within the scope of joint jurisdiction according to Article 8 and Articles 10 to 28 of the present Constitutional Law.

Article 136. The Government of the Republic directs and controls the activity of the National Committees.

Article 137. (1) The Government of the Republic as a body decides in particular on:

a) draft bills;
b) Government decrees;
c) the implementation of its declaration of policy;
d) the approval of international agreements whose execution belongs to the jurisdiction of the Republic;
e) drafts of state plans for the development of the national economy, the [State] Budget, and the final [budgetary] account of the Republic;
f) basic economic measures for securing the economic policy;
g) the appointment of functionaries in cases established by a Law;
h) motions asking the National Council for a vote of confidence;
i) other questions, if a Law of the National Council so provides.

(2) The Government of the Czech Socialist Republic and the Government of the Slovak Socialist Republic may, with the aim of exercising their current decision-making activity, set up a Presidium of the Government as their organ, and determine its competence and establish the principles governing its activity.

Article 138. The Government of the Republic may issue decrees for the purpose of implementing a Law of the National Council and within the limits of such a Law. It may likewise issue decrees for the implementation of a Law of the Federal Assembly, if it is empowered to do so.

Article 139. The ministries and the other central organs of state administration of the Republic may issue generally binding legal regulations on the basis and within the limits of Laws of the Federal Assembly and Laws of a National Council, if they are authorized by a Law to do so.

Chapter VIII. General, Transitional, and Concluding Provisions

Article 140. (1) The territory of the Czech Socialist Republic consists of the current territory of the Czech provinces.

(2) The territory of the Slovak Socialist Republic consists of the current territory of Slovakia.

(3) The territorial division of the Republics is established by Laws of the National Councils.

Article 141. (1) The capital of the Czechoslovak Socialist Republic and the regular seat of its organs is Prague. The position of Prague as capital of the Czechoslovak Socialist Republic is regulated by a Law of the Federal Assembly.

(2) The capital of the Czech Socialist Republic and the regular seat of its organs is Prague.

(3) The capital of the Slovak Socialist Republic and the regular seat of its organs is Bratislava.

Article 142. (1) The Constitution of the Czechoslovak Socialist Republic may be only amended by a Constitutional Law of the Federal Assembly.

(2) Both Republics approve their own Constitutions, together with the approval of the Constitution of the Czechoslovak Socialist Republic. Until the Constitution of the Czech Socialist Republic and the Constitution of the Slovak Socialist Republic are approved, the constitutional relations of these Republics are governed by the present Constitutional Law and the other constitutional regulations.

(3) Laws of the Federal Assembly, Laws of the National Councils, and other legal regulations of the federal organs and the organs of the Republics may not contradict the Constitution and the Constitutional Laws of the Czechoslovak Socialist Republic. The interpretation and application of all legal regulations must be in conformity with the Constitution and the Constitutional Laws of the Federation.

(4) Laws of the National Councils and other legal regulations of the Republics may not contradict the Constitutional Laws of the

National Councils. The interpretation and application of all legal regulations of a Republic must be in conformity with the Constitutional Laws of the respective National Councils.

Article 143. (1) The provisions of Article 1, para. 2, and Article 12, of Chapters III, IV, V, and VI (Articles 39 to 85), as well as of Articles 107 to 109, and Article 111 of the Constitution (Constitutional Law 1960 No. 100) are repealed.

(2) Wherever the provisions of the Constitution and other Laws mention the Czechoslovak Socialist Republic, this term is understood according to the nature of the matter to mean also the Czech Socialist Republic and the Slovak Socialist Republic.

(3) The President of the Republic elected according to the provisions of Article 63 of the Constitution remains in office as the President of the Czechoslovak Socialist Republic according to the present Constitutional Law; his electoral term of office is computed as of the day of his election.

(4) The Presidium of the National Assembly remains in office until the election of the Presidium of the Federal Assembly.

(5) The Government of the Czechoslovak Socialist Republic exercises the function of the Government of the Czechoslovak Socialist Republic until the appointment of the Government of the Czechoslovak Socialist Republic according to the present Constitutional Law.

Article 144. (1) All Laws and other legal regulations in force on the day when the present Constitutional Law comes into effect continue to be in force. Insofar as they regulate matters which do not belong to the jurisdiction of the Federation according to the present Constitutional Law, they may be amended by Laws of the Czech National Council or the Slovak National Council, or by other legal regulations of the Republics.

(2) Insofar as the existing Laws and other legal regulations enumerate the jurisdiction of the National Assembly, the Government, the Slovak National Council, or of other central state organs, such jurisdiction is exercised in matters reserved by the present Constitutional Law to the Czechoslovak Socialist Republic by the Federal Assembly, the Government of the Czechoslovak Socialist Republic, or by other central federal organs; in other matters, such jurisdiction is exercised by the Czech National Council, the Slovak National Council, the Government of the Czech Socialist Republic, the Government of the Slovak Socialist Republic, or other central organs of both Republics.

(3) A Law of the Federal Assembly may determine to which organs (organizations) and to what extent the jurisdiction passes of the present organs (organizations)—with the exception of ministries or other central organs of state administration headed by a minister—which have been entrusted by the present Laws with nationwide jurisdiction in matters which according to the present Constitutional Law belong to the joint jurisdiction of the Czechoslovak Socialist Republic and to the two Republics. Such a Law may also regulate the necessary transfer of rights and obligations of the present organs (organizations).

Article 145. The organization of courts and the Procuracy in the Czechoslovak Socialist Republic is regulated by a Constitutional Law of the Federal Assembly. Until the day such Constitutional Law comes into effect, the Federal Assembly is competent to:

a) elect and recall judges of the Supreme Court and professional judges of military courts;

b) propose to the President of the Czechoslovak Socialist Republic to recall the Procurator General;

c) discuss reports of the Supreme Court and the Procurator General on the state of socialist legality.

Article 146. (1) As long as the Czech National Council and the Slovak National Council are not elected on the basis of the present Constitutional Law,

a) the Czech National Council formed according to the Constitutional Law 1968 No. 77, exercises the jurisdiction of the Czech National Council according to the present Constitutional Law;

b) the Slovak National Council extended according to Article 6 of the Constitutional Law 1968 No. 77, exercises the jurisdiction of the Slovak National Council according to the present Constitutional Law.

(2) The Czech National Council extends the number of its members by election so as to have two hundred members.

(3) The Slovak National Council extends the number of its members by election so as to have one hundred and fifty members.

(4) The members of both National Councils have the rights and obligations of deputies according to the present Constitutional Law.

Article 147. As long as the Federal Assembly is not elected in the sense of Article 30, para. 1, and Article 31, para. 2:

a) the National Assembly becomes in its present composition the House of the People of the Federal Assembly, and

b) the deputies of the House of Nations are elected by the Czech National Council and the Slovak National Council, extended on the basis of Article 146, from among their members who are not deputies of the National Assembly.

Article 148. (Repealed by Constitutional Law No. 117, *Sbírka zakonů ČSSR* 1969.)

Article 149. (Repealed by Constitutional Law No. 57, *Sbírka zakonů ČSSR* 1969.)

Article 150. (1) The National Assembly, the Czech National Council, and the Slovak National Council may take measures necessary for the implementation of the present Constitutional Law prior to the day when it comes into effect.

(2) If the National Assembly deals with some of the draft bills specified in Article 42, para. 2, prior to the day specified in paragraph 1, their adoption requires the approval of a majority of all the deputies of the National Assembly elected in the Czech provinces and a majority of all the deputies of the National Assembly elected in Slovakia. The adoption of a Constitutional Law requires the approval of at least three-fifths of all the deputies of the National Assembly elected in the Czech provinces and at least three-fifths of all the deputies of the National Assembly elected in Slovakia.

(3) The draft bills according to paragraph 2 are voted on separately by the deputies elected in the Czech provinces and the deputies elected in Slovakia.

Article 151. (1) The present Constitutional Law comes into effect on 1 January 1969.

(2) The provisions of Article 146, paragraphs 1 and 3, and Articles 149 and 150 come into effect immediately.

SYSTEMATIC INDEX

EDITOR'S NOTE

The index to this volume is arranged systematically to provide easy comparative reference to the constitutions of the communist world. To give the reader an overview of the system used, which is loosely based on the chapters of the 1977 USSR Constitution, the systematic headings of the index are presented on the facing page. Within any systematic heading, the subheadings are arranged in alphabetical order. The numbers given in the systematic index refer to articles of the constitution of a particular country, not to page numbers; the "P" denotes a constitutional preamble. Under the column for Czechoslovakia, the italicized "*P*" and numbers are references to the 1968 Constitutional Law on the Federation which is found in the Appendix to this book.

The abbreviations used in this index are as follows:

USSR (Soviet Union), *Al* (Albania), *B* (Bulgaria), *PRC* (People's Republic of China), *Cu* (Cuba), *Cz* (Czechoslovakia), *GDR* (German Democratic Republic), *H* (Hungary), *Kam* (Kampuchea), *DPRK* (Democratic People's Republic of Korea), *Mon* (Mongolia), *PL* (Poland), *R* (Romania), *V-N* (Viet-Nam), and *YU* (Yugoslavia).

SYSTEMATIC HEADINGS

Political System	628
Economic System	629
Social Development and Culture	631
Foreign Affairs	632
National Defense	633
Citizenship. Equality	633
Citizens' Rights/Freedoms	634
Citizens' Obligations	636
Administrative/Territorial Structure/Subdivisions	637
Elected Representative Bodies	637
Electoral System	637
Elected Representatives	637
Organs of State Power and Administration: Supreme	638
Organs of State Power and Administration: Regional/Local Levels	641
Courts/Arbitration	642
Procuracy	644
Miscellaneous Provisions	644
Constitution (Amendment/Legal Force)	644

Systematic Index

	USSR	Al	B	PRC	Cu	Cz	GDR	H	Kam	DPRK	Mon	PL	R	V-N	YU
Political System	1-9	1-15	1-12	1-19	1-27	1-6, 1-3	1-8	1-16	1	1-17	1-7	1-10	1-16	1-8	P, 1-9
Civil servants,		9		15-16											
Communist Party,	P, 6, 100	P, 2, 3, 10, 67, 88-89	P, 1	P, 2, 19, 22, 56	P, 5, 6	P, 46	1	3		4	P, 82	3	3, 25--27, 52	P	P, 321
Constitution/laws, observance of,	4, 73	12, 67, 72	8, 85	16, 36 43	88	88		77		17, 136, 144	7	8		6, 77	197
Democratic centralism,	3	11	5	3	66	11, 18	47			9	5			4	
Dictatorship of the proletariat,	P	P, 2		P, 1, 19						10					
Ideology,	P, 6, 28	P, 1, 4, 15, 33, 37	45	P, 2, 11 14, 16	P, 5-6, 38, 54	16, 18, 24	1			2, 4, 11-13, 16, 27, 44	P, 94			9	P
Labor collectives/ unions,	7-8, 10, 23, 48, 100--101, 149		22-23, 80, 120		7, 86, 99	5, 11	29, 44--45, 65	4			19, 82	84-85	27, 80	10	P, 29-31, 47, 68, 104, 122, 124, 131, 135
National front parties,			P, 11, 80			6	3, 56	4				3	25	P	P, 135, 139
People, source of power	2	5	2	2-3	4	2, 2	2	2		2, 7	2	1	2, 4	4	P, 1, 3-4, 88-91
People's control,	92, 126		4			8, 28a						34-36	27		
Referenda,	5, 108, 115, 137	67, 77, 93	78, 93, 117		P, 73, 88, 134, 141		53	30			34, 81			53	89, 98, 118, 146

Systematic Index

	USSR	Al	B	PRC	Cu	Cz	GDR	H	Kam	DPRK	Mon	PL	R	V-N	YU
Self-management,															88–152
Socialist democracy,	P, 9	P	4–5, 13	17	66	P, 2	17					6	73		P
Socialist federalism,	70–75														
Socialist legality,	4	12, 96, 101	5, 125		9, 105, 123, 130	17, 106a, 145	19, 70, 81, 90, 97						13, 86		
Socialist society, developed,	P	P, 1, 4				P	P, 2, 70								
State, definition of,	1	1–2	1	1	1	1	1	1–2	1	1, 3	1–2	1	1	2	1–3
goals of,								P, 5		5–6		4–5, 7	13		P
Working masses/social organizations (participation in/control of public life/management),	P, 7–9, 23, 48, 94, 113	7, 10, 13, 92	3, 10–11, 24, 120	17	66, 108	P, 2, 5, 11, 18, 28, 87–89, 92, 95, 106	3, 9, 21, 42, 46, 56, 78, 81, 83	2, 4, 42, 68		62	5, 49, 55, 60, 81	5, 9, 45, 80, 84, 86	27, 86	10	P, 88–91
Economic System	10–18	16–31	13–33	4–12	1–27	P, 7–14, 4, 10, 11–28a	9–16	6–14	2	18–34	8–17	11–19	5–12	9–21	P, 10–87, 251–267, 279
Centralized economy/plan,	16, 73, 92, 102, 108, 131, 137, 143, 146	25–26, 67, 81, 93	22, 77–78, 95, 103, 114	8, 11, 22, 32, 36	8, 16–17, 73, 96, 104, 116	7, 13, 90, 96, 10, 36, 42, 48, 76–77, 107, 137	9, 12, 24, 44, 49, 76	7, 19, 35, 43, 55		24, 30–32, 76, 109, 118, 130	15–16, 20, 41, 55	11, 24, 34, 41, 49, 60	5, 13, 43, 64, 77, 87, 95	10, 16–17, 30, 50, 74, 82, 94	69–77, 257, 279

	USSR	Al	B	PRC	Cu	Cz	GDR	H	Kam	DPRK	Mon	PL	R	V-N	YU
Cooperative/collective, property,	12	21–22, 24	19–20	5, 7–8	20, 23–24	8	10, 13	10		20, 21, 70, 136, 144	9, 11–12	16	9–10	11, 13	19, 79, 83, 174
Cooperatives, agricultural,	12, 164	22–23, 96	23, 30		20	8, 11	13, 46	2, 7, 10, 38		26, 125	1, 9, 11–12, 55	15	9–11	14	P, 29, 62–63, 65
Environmental protection,	18, 67, 73, 131	20	31	11	27	15, 39	15	57				12, 71			87, 114, 117, 192–193
Expropriation,		24	28	6	15, 25		16						12	20	25, 28, 81–82
Incentives,	14, 16	30	22	10											28
Labor/work,	14, 21, 40, 60	29–30, 44	32, 40–41, 59	10, 48	44, 48, 54	P, 7, 18–19, 21, 22	24, 34, 44	14, 55	4, 12, 14	25, 27–29, 56, 69	15, 17, 77, 79, 89	5, 19, 68, 70, 78	5, 18, 68	21, 30	P, 11, 16–17, 159–162
agricultural,	17, 22, 41	P	30		20		46			26		14–15	10–11	14	P, 61–63
discipline,	8, 60		125	57	63	17		14		28	14, 89	19		39	
individual,	17		21, 25	5	22	9	14	12						15	31, 61, 64–68
productivity,	15, 23, 40		32			14, 21	2, 24			69		14–15, 19, 90			P, 32
Personal property,	13	23–24, 50	21, 27	9	20–22, 24	10	11	11, 13	2	22	13	17–18	9, 11, 36–37	11, 14–19	P, 19–20, 22, 78, 80, 83, 194
Self-management,															P, 10, 14 18, 88–152

Systematic Index 631

	USSR	Al	B	PRC	Cu	Cz	GDR	H	Kam	DPRK	Mon	PL	R	V-N	YU
Socialist economy/ ownership,	P, 10	P, 16–17, 20	13, 125	6, 8	13, 14–15, 17, 52	7–8, 89, 4, 24	2, 9–10, 24, 81	6, 43	2	18, 32, 144	8, 41	11	5–6	11, 40	P, 10
State enterprises,	8, 73, 77, 83, 131, 135, 146–148, 164	85–86, 93, 96, 104	31,		17, 85, 116	11, 89, 8, 24, 42	41–44, 78	38, 44		19, 125, 136, 144	55	13, 47	77, 83, 87, 95		
State property,	11, 16, 73, 77, 83, 92, 103, 105, 131, 135, 146–148, 163–164	26	18		17, 116	8, 11	9, 12, 41–42, 44, 78, 81	7, 9, 38		17, 19, 125, 136, 144	10, 55	13	77, 83, 87, 95	16, 82	
Subsidiary households,	13		21	7	20					22	11, 13		9		80
Taxation,	14, 73	31	64, 78			11–12, 42	9			33				41, 50	33, 118, 264–266
Trade,	73, 131	27–28	29		18, 96	16, 24	9			34, 109	41	11	8	74	27, 43–44, 61, 252
Social Development and Culture	19–27	32–37			1–27	15–18	17–18, 25		3	35–48					
Communist upbringing,	P, 25, 66	32, 49	11, 38–39, 45	13	6, 37–99	97	25			99	89				P
Culture,	P, 27, 68	P, 35	33	13	38	16	18, 25	18, 25, 35	3	35–38, 46–47		5	13		P, 85

Systematic Index

	USSR	Al	B	PRC	Cu	Cz	GDR	H	Kam	DPRK	Mon	PL	R	V–N	YU
Education,	25, 45	P, 32–-33, 52	39, 45	13, 51	38, 42, 50	16, 24, 37	17, 24–-26	16, 18, 59		39–43, 59	80	5, 72, 74, 80	13, 21, 24	33	P, 165
Individual development, P, 20		32, 36			38	15, 19, 28	2, 4, 9, 18–19, 25								P
Public funds,	23	30	32								17				195
Religion,	34, 52	P, 37, 55	53	46	54	32	39	61, 63	20	52, 54	76, 86	3, 81–-82	30	23, 26	174
Science/technology,	P, 96, 73, 131	P, 34	33	12–13	38	8, 21	17, 25	18, 35		25, 44		5	13	9	P
Social services,	22, 24			50	8	22	45	17, 35		48		5			114, 117
Youth/minors,	25, 35, 42, 45–-46	32, 36, 46	39, 47	51	29, 31, 36–38	24, 26	20, 25, 38	16		29, 39–-43, 58, 62	84	5, 78–-80	18, 24	24, 35	P, 133, 188
Foreign Affairs	P, 6, 28–-30, 73, 80, 121, 131	P, 15, 67, 77, 81	P, 3, 73, 78, 93, 94, 103	P, 25–26	P, 10–-12, 73, 79, 88, 91, 96	P, 14, P, 7–8, 12, 16, 21, 23, 25, 36, 42, 61, 76–-78, 107, 137	6, 51–-52, 66, 71, 76–77	5, 19, 30, 35	19, 21	16, 76, 96–97, 103, 109	P, 20, 34, 41	P, 6, 30, 41, 43	13–14, 43, 64, 71, 73, 75, 77	P, 53, 61, 63, 74	P, 271, 281, 313–314
Socialist inter-nationalism/proletarianism,	30, 36	15	5, 12	P	P, 12		6, 25			16	P, 89	14			P

632

Systematic Index

	USSR	Al	B	PRC	Cu	Cz	GDR	H	Kam	DPRK	Mon	PL	R	V-N	YU
National Defense	P, 31–32, 62, 73, 121, 146	41, 67, 78, 81, 87–92	61–63, 93, 94, 114	19, 22, 25, 58	54, 64, 73, 88, 96, 105	P, 37, 89, 7, 11, 17, 36, 41, 58, 61, 76	7, 23, 49–50, 52, 73	7, 19, 31, 70	P, 3, 14	14, 31, 47, 71–72, 76, 93, 103	14, 20, 34, 41, 89	10–11, 33, 41, 48, 92	13, 41, 43, 64, 75	8, 42, 50, 63, 74, 94	P, 114, 117, 172, 237–243, 262, 279, 281, 316–317, 328, 342, 347
Armed forces,	P, 31–32, 63, 73, 100–101, 121, 131, 152	88–89	78, 93–94, 103	19, 21	42, 91, 96, 137	37, 27, 61, 64	7–8	30	P, 19	14, 52, 61, 72, 93, 109, 135		10, 41, 76, 93, 98	13, 73, 74, 77	8, 23, 65, 74	P, 30, 54, 133, 135, 240, 262, 279, 281, 313, 316, 337, 342
Military service,	31, 63, 131	63	62	58	64	37	23	70	14	72	41, 89	41, 92	40, 77	42	241
Citizenship, Equality															
Asylum,	38, 121	65	65, 93	59	13, 96	33	23	67		66	83	88	38, 75	37	202
Citizens, foreign,	37			54		26							75		201
nationals abroad,		64	57				33			15, 65		89		36	200, 278, 281
Citizenship,	33–38, 121	38, 77	34, 93		28–33	5, 42	19	61	13		34		16, 75		200, 249, 281
Equality, of citizens,	34, 156	40	35	4	40–43	20, P	20	61		51	76	67, 81	17	22	154, 180
of nationalities,	34, 96, 64	40, 42	35, 45		41	20, P, 6	20, 40	61			76, 83	67, 81	17, 22	3, 23, 82, 102	P, 1, 3, 117, 154, 170–171, 243, 246–248, 271

634   Systematic Index

	USSR	Al	B	PRC	Cu	Cz	GDR	H	Kam	DPRK	Mon	PL	R	V-N	YU
of races,	34, 36, 64	40	35		41	20	20	61-62	13	52	76	67, 81	17	23	154
of sexes,	34-35	P, 40-41	35-38	53	41, 43	20, 27	20, 38	54-70	12-14	52, 62	76, 84	67, 78, 97	17, 23	23-24	154
Citizens' Rights/ Freedoms,	39-69	38-65	34-65	44-59	44-65	19-38	19-40	54-70	12-14	49-72	76-89	67-93	17-41	22-42	P, 153-203
Conscience,	52	37	53	46	54	32	20, 39	63	20	54	86	82	30	26	174
Creation (intellectual, scientific, technical, artistic)	47	51	26, 46	52	38, 51	18	34	60		60		73-75, 77		34	P, 169
Cultural achievements,	46		46									73			
Deprivation of,	96	43		18, 44	135		30-31, 99	72		52		87, 99	25	23	
Education,	45	52	45	51	38, 42, 50	24	25-26	59		59	80	72, 74, 80	21, 24	33	165
Eligibility to run for office,	48, 96	43	6		136-137	3, 30, 62, 94	22	73		52	68, 81	96-99	25	23	156
Exercise of rights/freedoms not to harm others/the state	13, 39, 65	23, 39	9, 21, 26, 52-53		38, 54, 61	32, 38	11, 17	54			13	84	29	17, 38	P, 169, 203
Family/marriage, protection of,	53-54	48-49	38	53	34-37	26	38	15		63		5, 79	23	24	188, 190--191

Systematic Index

	USSR	Al	B	PRC	Cu	Cz	GDR	H	Kam	DPRK	Mon	PL	R	V-N	YU
Governmental tort liability,	58	59	56		26		104			58			35, 103	29	181, 199
Health care,	42	47	47	50	42, 48–49	23	35	57		58	79	70	20	32	163, 186
Home, inviolability of,	55	57	48	47	55	31	37	66		64	88	88	32	28	184
Housing,	44						37					79			164
Improvement of rights/freedoms,	39	39				19	19		12	50					
Movement,					31	32								28	183
Person, inviolability of,	54	56	48	47	57	30	30	66		64	88	87	31	27	175–179
Political fundamental freedoms,	50	53	54	45	52–53	28	27–28, 33, 43	64		53	87	83	28–29	25	166–168
Privacy,	56	58	51		56	31	31	66		64	88	88	33		185
Proposals/petitions to state organs/officials,	48–49	59	55	55	52, 63, 82	29	21, 56, 103	68		55	85	9, 86	34	29	157
Protection of,	4, 57–58, 131, 146	56, 81	3, 50, 103, 114, 125, 133	32, 36	96, 105, 123	19, 81, 89, 97, 2, 92	19, 41, 81	4, 5, 35, 50–51	9	6, 109, 130, 136, 144	41, 55	41, 48, 58, 64	13, 34, 77, 86, 102, 112	74, 82	P, 117, 180, 198, 203
Rights/duties, linkage of,	P, 59	39						54							
Social organizations, uniting in,	51	54–55	52–53		7		29	65			82	84–85	27, 29		P

	USSR	Al	B	PRC	Cu	Cz	GDR	H	Kam	DPRK	Mon	PL	R	V-N	YU
Social security,	43	46	43–44	50	46–47	23	36	58		58	79	70	20	32	163, 187, 189
Work/profession (as a right)	40	44	40–41	48	44, 48	18, 21	24, 34	55	12	56	77	68	18	30	159–162
Citizens' Obligations															
Constitution/laws, observance of,	59	60	8, 58	43, 56	65, 123	34		77		17, 67, 136, 144	89	8, 90	39	39	197
Cultural treasures, protection of,	27, 68														193
Duties/rights, linkage of,	P, 59	39						54							
Environmental protection,	18, 67	20	31		27		15					71			192–193
International peace/ friendship, promotion of,	69		63				23	65		71	89	81			
Military service,	31, 63	63	62	58	64	37	23	70	14	72	89	92	40	42	241
State/socialist property, protection/ strengthening of,	61–62	61	60	57	63	35	10	69		70	89	91		40	
Treason,	62	62, 90	61	18	32, 64			70	10	72		93	41	7	238

Systematic Index

	USSR	Al	B	PRC	Cu	Cz	GDR	H	Kam	DPRK	Mon	PL	R	V-N	YU
Administrative/ Territorial Structure Subdivisions	70–88, 108, 122, 137–144	67, 77	93, 109	4, 22, 32–33, 38–40	73, 100			41		103	36, 46		15, 43	3, 50, 74, 78, 92–96	1–4, 147, 150, 244–281
Elected Representative Bodies	89–94	5–8	6–7	3, 21, 34, 38	67, 101, 139	2	5	19, 42		8, 73, 115	4	2	4	4–6	
Citizenry, reliance upon/contact with,	94	7	120	15	66, 82, 103	2–3, 87–89, 92	5, 56	42			5	9	86	6	
Electoral System	90, 95–102	8		21, 35	66, 134–140	2, 47		71–73	6			94–102	25, 43	5	134–135, 291
Elections,	90, 121	8, 67–77	6, 69, 70, 74, 93	21, 25, 38	69, 71, 88, 134, 139	86, *113*	62–63, 72	30	6	8, 74–75, 87, 116	4, 21, 23, 34, 47	2, 21, 30, 94	4, 44, 46, 63	5, 53, 81	291–292
Nomination of candidates,	100						22					100, 102	25		P, 135, 291
Right to vote,	48, 96	43	6	44	135, 137	3, 30	22	72		52	4, 81	95	25	23	156
Elected Representatives	103–107	7, 8, 72, 96	7, 86–89, 111, 121	21, 28–29, 35–36	66, 69, 80–85, 112–113	3, 86, 88, 48, *91*	54–60	20–21, 42	6	8, 74, 84, 116	6, 31–32, 62	2, 21, 27, 101–102	25, 44, 58–61, 92	5, 59–60	305–308
Accountability,	94, 107	72, 96	7, 121	29	66, 82, 113	3, 86, 88	56–57	20, 42		8	6	2, 101	60, 92	80	

638   Systematic Index

	USSR	Al	B	PRC	Cu	Cz	GDR	H	Kam	DPRK	Mon	PL	R	V-N	YU
Immunity,	106, 118	73, 96	88–89		81	50–53, 97, 116–117	60	20		84	32, 62	21	61	60	306
Recall,	107	8	7	29, 35–36	66, 83, 112	3, 86, 90	57	20, 42, 71, 73			6	2, 102	25	5	134, 142, 291–292
Right of inquiry,	105, 117	72, 96	87	28, 36	84	49, 115	59	21, 27			31	27	58–59	59	305
Organs of State Power and Administration: Supreme															
Central People's Committe,										76, 80, 91, 100–107, 113, 142, 144, 146					
Council of Ministers,	77, 117, 121–122, 128–136	79–86	78, 87, 93, 98–108, 124, 143	30–32	73, 84, 86, 88, 91, 93–99	36, 43, 45, 49, 58, 61–62, 64, 66–85a, 87, 93, 143–144	49, 59, 76–80	19, 25, 27, 29, 33–40, 43	8	92, 103, 107–114, 144	94, 37–45	35, 37–42	53, 75, 77–85, 95, 99	53, 59, 66, 71–77, 91, 105	346–363
accountability,	130	78, 82	91, 93, 102	30, 43	97		76	39	8	113	38	38	64, 82	53, 71	358–362
chairman,	122, 129, 132	83	94, 99, 101			45, 49, 58, 64, 67	79–80	37		92	42	35–37, 40	64, 75	50, 63, 67, 72, 75	348–349
composition,	129	80	99	31	94, 99		79	33		108	42	39	79	72	348

Systematic Index

	USSR	Al	B	PRC	Cu	Cz	GDR	H	Kam	DPRK	Mon	PL	R	V-N	YU
ministries/state committees,	122, 131, 134–136, 142, 164	67, 81, 84–86, 104	76, 78, 93, 99, 100, 103, 105–108, 124	28, 32	91, 95–96, 98	104, 36, 42, 76, 80–81, 83, 87	34, 40, 78	19, 33–35, 37	8	108, 109, 114	20, 34, 41, 43–45, 61, 72	41–42	43, 63–64, 75, 77, 81, 83–85	50, 74, 76	363–368
powers,	113, 122, 131, 133–134	74, 77, 81–82, 105	80, 103–104	32	96		65, 76–78	25, 33, 35–36	8	80, 109, 113	19, 39–41	25, 36, 40–41	77, 81	46, 73–74	352–357
presidium,	132	83		9		77	80			110–111		39–40			
selection/appointment,	122, 129	67, 78, 80	94–95, 101	22	73, 88, 91	61	50, 79	19, 33	8	76, 103	20	37	43, 64, 78	50, 53, 63	288, 348–349
Council of State,			71, 78, 80, 84, 88, 90–97, 102, 106, 132, 134, 143	22, 23, 25, 28, 30–32, 43	30, 32, 71–73, 79, 81, 84, 86–92, 131, 141	101, 105–106a, 29–59, 87, 143, 147	49–50, 52, 60, 65–75, 79, 93, 98		11			21–22, 25, 28–33, 35–38, 60–61, 65	43, 44, 52, 54, 61–70, 75, 82, 115		
Parliament,	77, 108–127	66–79, 105	66–89, 94–95, 132, 134	20–30, 32, 42–43	67–92, 131, 141	48–66, 76–78, 89–93, 98	19–32, 39, 48, 52	5–9, 11	7–8, 73–88, 98, 106, 113, 142, 146	18–36, 38, 66	2, 20–33, 35, 38, 41	4, 42–65, 70, 72–73, 75–76, 82, 115	4, 43–60, 63, 67, 71, 104, 108	132, 282–312
bicameral/unicameral,	109, 110	68	69	21	68	29–31	54		5		21	21	44		284, 291–292
chairman,	111	69	72–73		71, 79	45, 56		21		79	26, 30	23, 29	50–51		288, 309–312
commissions,	91, 110–115, 121, 125	71	74, 76, 80	27	73, 79, 80, 86	44–45, 47, 49, 55	61, 65	21, 25		81, 83, 87	19, 27–28	23, 26	52–53	56–58	144–145, 297

	USSR	Al	B	PRC	Cu	Cz	GDR	H	Kam	DPRK	Mon	PL	R	V-N	YU
election,	110, 121	68, 77	70, 74, 93	21, 25	69, 88	30-31, 47, 91, 147	54, 64, 72	20, 30, 73	6	74-75, 87	21, 23, 34	2, 21, 30, 94	44-47, 63	45, 53	291-292
laws adoption,	108, 114	74, 77	79, 83	22	74	45	63, 65	26		82	20, 30	25	56	48	294-295, 298-304
promulgation,	116	74	73, 84, 93		75, 79, 91	45, 61	65, 89	26			30	25	57	49	269
legislative initiative,	113	74	80, 93, 103		86, 88, 96	45	44, 65	25, 30		80	19	25		74	272, 293, 298, 313, 347
powers,	108, 118, 126, 129--131, 153, 165, 174	66, 80, 101, 106	67, 74, 78, 85, 92, 101, 102, 132, 134, 143	22-24	71, 73	3, 10--12, 14--15, 17, 24, 29a, 30, 36--39, 41, 43, 50--51, 58, 64, 69--71, 73, 77, 93--95, 98--100, 144	49-52, 67, 79, 80, 89	19, 30, 33, 48, 52	7-9	76, 84, 90	15, 19, 20, 35--36, 42, 66, 73	20, 24, 31, 33, 36-37, 106	43, 48--49, 52, 56, 65, 72, 78, 106, 114, 119	50, 60, 62, 74, 97, 112	283, 285--290
presidium,	77, 112--114, 116, 118--125, 130-131, 135, 152, 165, 171	67, 74, 79, 82, 89, 105--106		24-27, 32, 39, 42-43		32-33, 45, 49, 51-52, 54, 56--59, 67, 87, 93	55, 62	19, 22, 25, 27--33, 48--49		75-77, 80, 84--88, 134, 144	19-20, 23-25, 29-30, 32-36, 38, 48, 66, 73		50, 54, 59	46-47, 51-55, 57-58, 60, 63, 67, 71, 74, 86, 94, 104, 108	

Systematic Index

	USSR	Al	B	PRC	Cu	Cz	GDR	H	Kam	DPRK	Mon	PL	R	V-N	YU
sessions,	112, 121	70, 77	70–73, 81–82, 93	21, 25	70–72, 76–79, 88	32–35, 46, 61	62–63	22–24		77–78, 87	24–25, 34	22–23, 30	51, 54–55	46, 53	295, 311
term,	90	68	6, 69	21	70	30–31	54	20	6	75	22	28	45	45	307–308
President/Presidency,					79	105, 25, 32–33, 36, 41, 58, 60–65, 71–74, 143		21		76, 80, 89–99, 101, 107, 113, 142, 144, 146			43, 57, 66, 69, 71–76	50, 61–70	222, 283, 313–345
Organs of State Power and Administration: Regional/Local Levels	83, 86, 88, 113, 137–150	79, 92–100	78, 93–94, 103, 107, 109–124	25, 33–40	69, 73, 88, 96, 100–120	86–97, 104, 38–39, 76, 78, 84–85a, 87, 93, 102–139, 146	58, 70, 81–85, 89	30, 35, 41–44		7–8, 103, 115–132, 142	34, 46–62	2, 32, 43–55, 64	4, 43, 86–100	4, 53, 74, 78–96, 104–105	116–119, 132–152
Commissions,	91		118		105, 109–110	95, 113, 115, 118	83	44		103	60	50, 53	89, 100		144–145
Election,	95–102	77, 79, 92	93, 111	35, 38	106, 111	86, 103, 113, 122	72	30, 42, 71, 73		87, 116, 125	47–48	2, 80, 94	63, 88	81	
Executive organs,	91, 139–142, 144, 149–150, 164	79, 81, 82, 86, 93, 95, 97–100	93, 94, 103, 107, 118–119, 124	37–38	88, 105–106, 109, 114–120	95, 107, 110–112, 115, 121–139, 144	83	44		118–119, 122–132	41, 49, 51–55, 57–59, 61–62	51–52	52, 77, 87, 90, 94–100	84–85, 87–90	148

	USSR	Al	B	PRC	Cu	Cz	GDR	H	Kam	DPRK	Mon	PL	R	V-N	YU
powers competence,	113, 137–144, 146–148	93, 95	112–115, 122–124	36, 38––39	102–105	3, 10–12, 107–108, 126–128, 144	81–85	118		125, 130, 134	55–58, 67–68	44–49, 54–55	87, 93	82–83, 85–86, 94–96	92, 129, 131, 217–234, 369––371
presidium,	138, 144					104, 111, 116, 119––122, 125, 129–132				118–119, 122–127		50			
sessions,		94	116	35	107–108, 116, 120	104, 106, 115				119–120, 122, 125	49	50	90–91		
term,	90	92	6	35		86		42		117	47	43	88	81	
Courts/Arbitration	151–163	101–104	78, 125––132	28, 36, 41–42	88, 121–129	98–104, 24, 86––101, 145	86–96	45–50	9–10	103, 133–142	63–71	56–63	101–111	97–104	92, 129, 131, 217–234, 369––371
Accountability,	152	67, 78	132	25, 42	73, 128		74, 93, 95			142	66		43, 106	53, 104	231
Bar,	161														180
Courts, associated labor,															122, 226
constitutional,						36, 62, 67, 86––101, 107, 125									92, 129, 131, 205, 208, 282, 285, 288, 315, 375–396

Systematic Index

	USSR	Al	B	PRC	Cu	Cz	GDR	H	Kam	DPRK	Mon	PL	R	V-N	YU
military,	151		126			98–99, 101, 106a, 145	92						101, 107	97, 103	221–222, 296, 315, 342, 371
self-management,															92, 217, 221, 223–225
special,							101	45		133, 135	63	56, 59		97, 103	
supreme,	113, 153	67, 78, 101	16, 80, 195, 132	22, 23, 25, 28, 42	73, 86, 124, 131	99, 101, 145	93	19, 27, 47–48		76, 87, 134–135, 141–142	19, 63, 65–66	56, 61, 64	43, 53, 58, 64, 75, 104–106	50, 52, 98, 103–104	283, 285, 371
Defense, right to	158	102	138	41	58	103	102	49		138	70	63	31	101	182
Election/selection,	152–153	67, 78, 101	78, 95, 128, 131	22, 23, 25, 36	73, 105, 121	98, 101, 106a, 36, 94–96, 107, 145	50, 94–95	19, 30, 48	9	76, 87, 118, 134–135	66–68	59–60	43, 75, 87, 106, 108	50, 84, 98	230, 283, 371
Independence,	155	103	129		122, 125	98, 102	96	50		140	71	62	111	100	219
Judgments,	160	103	129		60, 126	103				133, 136		56–57, 59			
Lay representation/ participation,	162						90								
Nature/function,	151	101	125	41	121, 123	98	90–91	45	9	133	63	56	101	97	217–218, 220–221, 369
People's assessors,	152–155	102	127	41	127	100	95–96	46		118, 134–135, 137	64	59	87, 107–108	99	229
Proceedings,	159	102	137	41		100, 103				139–140	69		107, 109	99, 102	214, 228

	USSR	Al	B	PRC	Cu	Cz	GDR	H	Kam	DPRK	Mon	PL	R	V-N	YU
Sessions (open/closed),	157	102	137	41	103	103		49		138	70	63	110	101	227
Procuracy	113, 164–168	104–106	78, 80, 133–135	28, 36, 43	86, 88, 130–133	104–106a, 98, *145*	49–50, 97–98	27, 51–53		103, 143–146	19, 72–*75*	64–66	43, 52, 58, 64, 112–115	105–108	129, 131, 235–236, 285, 288, 372–374
Accountability,	165	67, 78	94, 134	25, 43	73, 131, 133	105–106	74, 98	52		146	75	65–66	43, 64, 115	53, 108	
Independence,	168		135		131	106						66			235
Recall,			134	23, 36	132	105	50, 98			76		65			
Selection,	165–166	67, 78, 106	78, 95, 134	22, 23, 25, 36	73, 132	105, *145*	50, 98	19, 52–53		76, 145	73	65	43, 75, 87, 114	50, 53	283, 372, 374
Social attorneys of self-management,															129, 131, 281, 283, 285, 288, 374
Miscellaneous Provisions	169–172	107–109	139–142	60	2–3	110, *140–151*	1	74–76	15–18	147–149	90–92	103–105	116–119	109–111	6–9, 397, 403–406
Constitution															
Amendment,	108, 137, 143, 174	67, 78, 111	78, 143	22	73, 141	41, 58, *142*	63, 106	24, 30		76, 82	20, 93	106	43, 56, 64	50, 112	398–403
Legal force,	173	110, 112				112, *150–151*	105	77			94		120–121		405–406

Colophon

letter: Baskerville 10/12, 8/10
setter: The European Printing Corp.
printer: Samson Sijthoff Grafische Bedrijven
binder: Callenbach
cover-design: W. Bottenheft

DATE DUE

DEMCO 38-297

DE PAUL UNIVERSITY LIBRARY

30511000079478

342.02C758S C001
LPX THE CONSTITUTIONS OF THE COMMUNIST